"VILLASEÑOR IS A BORN STORYTELLER . . . an inspirational epic full of wild adventure, bootlegging, young love, miracles, tragedies, murder and triumph over cultural barriers."—*Publishers Weekly*

"*AN ABSORBING AND TIMELESS STORY.*"★

Critical acclaim for

RAIN OF GOLD
by VICTOR VILLASEÑOR

"SWEEPING SCOPE . . . HARD-EDGED REALITY . . . transcending race and culture, it contains rare insights on the universal themes of love, hate, family, and forgiveness."

—*Hispanic* magazine★

"A WORK OF HEROISM AND MYTH played out in the lives of two ordinary yet remarkable Mexican-American families."

—*St. Louis Post-Dispatch*

"As literature, this is an important book, but as a literary reflection of the experience of countless Mexican immigrants to the United States, it is A REMARKABLE COLLECTIVE MEMOIR OF A PEOPLE AND A TIME."

—*Beaumont Enterprise* (Texas)

"*RAIN OF GOLD* HAS IT ALL: mystery, passion, beauty, hatred, lust, birth, blood, death, miracles. All the elements for a blockbuster of a novel. Plus, something extra: truth."

—*San Antonio Light*

Please turn the page for more reviews . . .

Rain
of
Gold

Victor Villaseñor

Delta
Trade Paperbacks

A DELTA BOOK
Published by
Dell Publishing
a division of
Random House, Inc.
1540 Broadway
New York, New York 10036

ISBN: 0-385-31177-X
Cover painting by Alfonso Corpus
Cover design by Phil Rose

Reprinted by arrangement with Arte Publico Press

Printed in the United States of America

Published simultaneously in Canada

October 1992

20   19   18   17

This book is dedicated to my father and mother and my grandmothers, two *gran mujeres*, who inspired me to put into words their life story, the ongoing history of women and men.

ACKNOWLEDGMENTS

This volume is made possible by a grant from the
National Endowment for the Arts, a federal agency, and
the Texas Commission on the Arts.

FOREWORD

It all started in the barrio of Carlsbad, California, when I used to walk to my grandmother's home behind my parents' poolhall. My grandmother on my mother's side, Doña Guadalupe, would sit me on her lap and give me sweetbread and yerba buena tea and tell me stories of the past, of Mexico, of the Revolution, and of how my mother, Lupe, had been just a little girl when the troops of Francisco Villa and Carranza had come fighting into their box canyon in the mountains of Chihuahua.

My father, Juan Salvador, also a great storyteller, would tell me of his own family and how he and his mother and sisters had escaped from Los Altos de Jalisco during the Revolution and how they'd come north to the Texas border. He told me of the horrible times that they'd endured on each side of the border, and how these horrible times had actually—in some strange way—become good, because they'd taught them so much about love and life and united them closer and stronger as a family. Often during these talks, my father, a big strong man, would cry and cry and hold me in his arms and tell me how much he still loved his poor old dead mother and how there wasn't a night that passed that he didn't dream of her, the greatest woman who had ever lived.

Reaching my teens, the stories of my parents' past grew distant and less important as I became more and more Anglicized. And in my twenties, I reached the point where, regrettably, I didn't want to hear about our past because I couldn't really believe in my parents' stories anymore.

Then, turning thirty and finding the woman that I wished to marry and have my children with, I suddenly realized how empty I'd feel if I couldn't tell my own children about our ancestral roots.

The year was 1975 when I began to interview my father and mother in earnest. I bought a Sony tape recorder and looked up my aunts and uncles and godparents. I accumulated well over two hundred hours of taped conversations over the next three years.

But, still, some of the things that my parents and relatives told me were just too foreign, too fantastic, for my modern mind to accept. For instance, the gold mine where my mother was born had been purchased by a man who'd skinned out a steer—because the hide was more valuable than the meat—and he'd run the naked animal up the mountainside to pay the Indians off. My God, I couldn't write that down with conviction. First, it was too barbaric and, secondly, I didn't think it was possible. But my relatives kept insisting that it was absolutely true. I grew to doubt all their stories and began to think that they only spoke in metaphors, at best.

Then with the birth of our first child, I decided to make the big leap. I went down into Mexico with the exclusive mission of researching my parents' past—of questioning everything that I'd been told—and see if once and for all it was possible for me to believe enough in my ancestral past so I could write about it.

I went by plane, by bus, by truck, by burro, by foot. It took me two days to climb the mountains of La Barranca del Cobre where my mother was born. One morning, I saw Indians so shy that when I waved hello to them they froze like deer, then ran away from me with the agility and speed of young antelope. I saw swarms of butterflies so vast that they filled the entire sky like a dancing tapestry. I saw skies so clear and full of stars that I felt close to God. I spoke with a local rancher who butchered cattle for a living and I asked him if it was possible to skin out a steer alive and run him up a mountain. He said, "Sure. You knock the animal out with a sledge and four good men could have him skinned before he came to. Then, believe me, he'd run like hell for a couple of miles before he died."

I took a big breath and, little by little, I began to see that maybe one person's reality was, indeed, another's fantasy—especially if their childhood perceptions of the world were so different. I came to understand why my father had always told me that it was easy to call another's religion superstitious.

For the next five years, I wrote and rewrote, first in Spanish in my head, then in English on paper. I wrote my father's story in the first person, just as it came from his mouth. I wrote my mother's story in the third person because more of her relatives were alive and I could verify situations from different points of view.

But then as I kept writing and rewriting, another problem presented itself. Both of my parents used the words "miracle," "greatness," "devil" and "God" so often that when I translated these words into English, the whole story just didn't sound right or believable. And, also—to add to my problems—my parents and relatives kept telling me how they'd grown up feeling so close to the Almighty that they'd spoken to Him on a daily basis as one would speak to a friend and how, now and then, God had actually spoken back to them in the form of miracles. I was stumped. I thought if I wrote this down, I'd look totally foolish.

But as the years passed and I recorded their stories and listened more and more to my parents and relatives, I began to see that, yes indeed, they had lived in a world engulfed by God's spirit.

Or, as my grandmother Doña Margarita once told my father, "Do you really think God stopped talking to us, His people, with the Jews and the Bible. Oh, no, *mi hijito*, God lives and He still loves to talk, I tell you. All you have to do is look around and open your eyes and you'll see His greatness everywhere—the miracles of life, *la vida*."

And so I kept going—feeling inspired—and got up most mornings at 4:30 AM and worked until late at night, writing and rewriting and checking with my parents and relatives to make sure that I had it right.

This, then, isn't fiction. This is a history of a people—a tribal heritage, if you will—of my Indian-European culture as handed down to me by my parents, aunts, uncles and godparents. The people in this story are real. The places are true. And the incidents did actually happen. Thank you.

Con gusto,

VICTOR VILLASEÑOR
Rancho Villaseñor
Oceanside, CA
Spring, 1990

ONE

RAIN OF GOLD

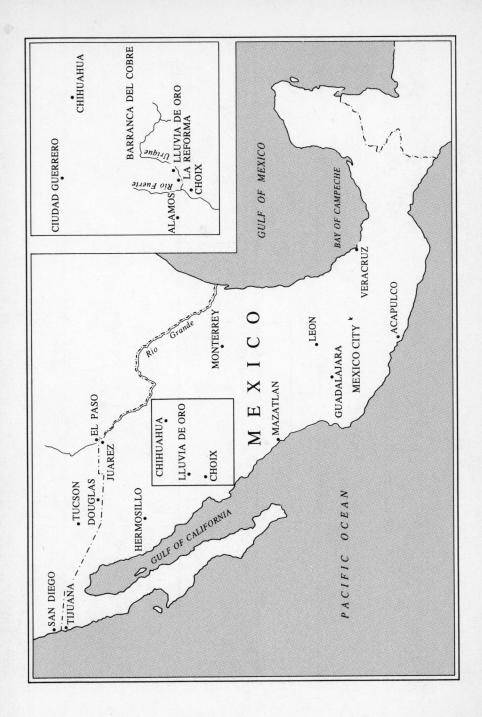

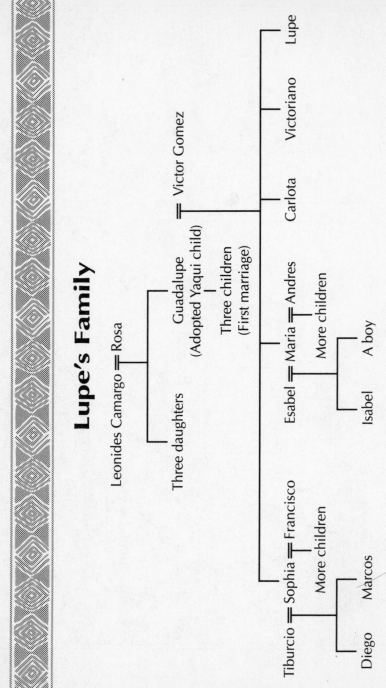

Lupe's Family

Leonides Camargo ═ Rosa

Three daughters

Guadalupe
(Adopted Yaqui child)

Three children
(First marriage) ═ Victor Gomez

Carlota   Victoriano   Lupe

Tiburcio ═ Sophia ═ Francisco

More children

Diego   Marcos

Esabel ═ Maria ═ Andres

More children

Isabel   A boy

Juan Salvador's Family

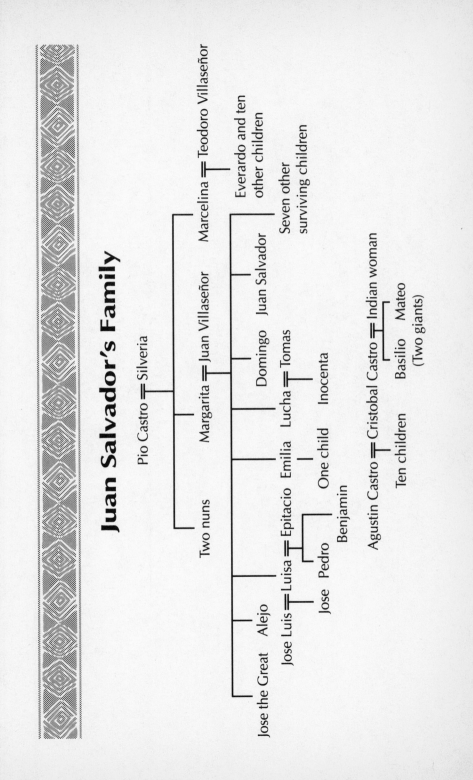

High in the mountains in northwest Mexico, an Indian named Espirito followed a doe and her fawn in search of water. The spring in the box canyon where Espirito and his tribe lived had dried up.

Following the deer through the brush and boulders, Espirito found a hidden spring on the other side of the box canyon at the base of a small cliff. Water dripped down the face of the cliff and the whole cliff glistened like a jewel in the bright mid-morning sunlight.

Once the deer were done drinking, Espirito approached the spring and drank, too. It was the sweetest water he'd ever tasted. Filling his gourd with water, Espirito pulled down a couple of loose rocks from the cliff and put them in his deerskin pouch. He knelt down, giving thanks to the Almighty Creator. He and his people weren't going to suffer the long, dry season, after all.

Then that winter came a torrent of rain and it got so cold that the raindrops froze and the mountaintops turned white. Espirito and his tribe grew cold and hungry. Desperately, Espirito went down to the lowlands to see if he could sell some of the sweet water that he'd found.

Walking into a small settlement alongside the great father river, El Rio Urique, Espirito told the store owner, Don Carlos Barrios, that he had the sweetest water in all the world to trade for food and clothing.

Laughing, Don Carlos said, "I'm sorry, but I can't trade for water, living here alongside a river. Do you have anything else to trade?"

"No," said Espirito, turning his purse inside out. "All I have are these little stones and this gourd of water."

Don Carlos's fat, grey eyebrows shot up. The stones were gold nuggets. Picking one up, Don Carlos put it to his teeth, marking it. "For these I can trade you all the food and clothing you want!" he screamed.

But Espirito was already going for the door. He'd never seen a man try to eat a stone before. It took all of Don Carlos's power to calm Espirito down and get him to come back into the store to trade.

Then, having traded, Espirito loaded the food and clothing into a sack, and he left the settlement as quickly as he could. He didn't want the crazy store owner to go back on their deal.

The winter passed and Espirito made a dozen trips down the mountain to trade stones for food and clothing. Don Carlos made so much money from the gold nuggets that he quit attending to his store and began having great feasts every evening. He begged Espirito to sell him the place where he got the nuggets. He offered to send his fat son up the mountain with his two burros loaded with merchandise every week so Espirito wouldn't have to come down the mountain anymore.

"I can't do that," said Espirito. "I don't own the stones or the spring any more than I own the clouds or the birds in the sky. The stones belong to my people who use the spring."

"Well, then, talk to them," said Don Carlos excitedly. "And offer them my deal!"

"All right," said Espirito. He went back up into the mountains and he talked it over with his people. They agreed to Don Carlos's deal, but only on the condition that he'd never dig into the cliff itself and ruin the spring which held the sweetest water in all the world.

Coming down from the box canyon after delivering the first two burro-loads of merchandise, Don Carlos's fat son was beside himself with joy. "Papa," he said, "it's not just a pocket of gold. No, it's a whole cliff of gold raining down the mountainside!"

"How big a cliff?" asked Don Carlos, his eyes dancing with gold fever.

"As tall as twenty men standing on each other and twice as wide as our house."

Don Carlos bit his knuckles with anticipation. He began to send his fat son back up the mountain for more gold as soon as he'd come down.

Don Carlos's son lost all his soft flesh and grew as strong and slender as a deer. Espirito and his people came to like the boy and named him Ojos Puros because of his light blue eyes.

Years passed and all was going well in this enchanted box canyon of raining gold, until one day Ojos Puros came down the mountain and told his father that there wasn't any more gold.

"What do you mean no more gold?" demanded Don Carlos, who now wore fine clothes from Mexico City and boots from Spain.

"All the loose nuggets are gone," said Ojos Puros. "To get more gold, we'd need to dig at the cliff, and that would ruin their spring."

"So do it!" ordered Don Carlos.

"No," said Ojos Puros. "We gave our word not to ruin their spring, Papa."

The rage, the anger, that came to Don Carlos's face would have cowed Ojos Puros a few years before. But it didn't now. So Don Carlos slapped his son until his hand was covered with blood, but still his son never gave in nor did he hit him back. That night Don Carlos drank and ate with such rage that he came down with a terrible stomachache. He slept badly. He had nightmares. And in his sleep he saw an angel of God coming to kill him for having tried to go back on his word.

Three days later, Don Carlos awoke with a fever and he apologized to his son and wife for all the bad he'd done. Then he sold the mine to a local rancher who didn't know the meaning of the word "fear." This rancher's name was Bernardo Garcia. The next day Bernardo had a steer knocked down that Don Carlos still owed to the Indians and he had the animal skinned alive so he could keep the valuable hide. Then he forced the naked animal to run up the mountain to Espirito's encampment.

Seeing the naked animal come into their canyon, Espirito and his people were terrified. Bernardo himself cut the steer's throat in front of them, told the Indians that he'd bought the gold mine from Don Carlos, and he put a dozen men to work digging at the cliff. He ruined the spring and, when the Indians complained, he shot them and ran them out of their box canyon, even over Ojos Puros's protests.

In less than five years, Bernardo became a man so rich and powerful that he bought a home in Mexico City among the wealthiest of the world. He became a close friend of the great President Porfirio Diaz himself, and he took a second wife of European breeding, as Don Porfirio had done. Then, in 1903 he sold the mine to an American company from San Francisco, California, for unheard-of millions on Don Porfirio's advice for modernizing Mexico.

The American mining company came in with large equipment and dammed up the Urique River, put in a power plant, and built a road from the coast. The mine came to be officially known as La Lluvia de Oro, "The Rain of Gold," and thousands of poor Mexican people came to the box canyon hoping to get work.

Every six months the Americans loaded thirty-five mules with two sixty-pound bars of gold each and drove the mules out of the canyon and down the mountain to the railhead in El Fuerte. There, the Americans loaded the gold bars on trains and shipped them north to the United States.

The years passed, and the people who lived in the bottom of the box canyon made houses out of stone and lean-tos out of sticks and mud.

The American company prospered, grew, and built permanent buildings inside an enfenced area for their American engineers.

But then, in 1910, a huge meteorite came shooting out of the sky, exploding against the towering walls of the box canyon. The people who lived in the canyon thought it was the end of the world. They prayed and made love, asking God to spare them. And in the morning, when they saw the miracle of the new day, they knew God had, indeed, spared them. They thanked Him, refusing to go to work inside the darkness of the mine anymore.

The Americans became angry, but no matter how much they beat the people, they still could not get them to go back down into the darkness of the devil's domain. Finally, the Americans brought back Bernardo Garcia from Mexico City, and he threatened the people with God and the devil and got them back to work.

That same year, President Porfirio Diaz used La Lluvia de Oro as one of his examples to show to foreign dignitaries—whom he'd invited to celebrate his eightieth birthday—of how foreign investors could make a profit in helping him modernize Mexico.

The celebration for Don Porfirio's birthday lasted one month, costing the Mexican people more than twenty million dollars in gold. Bernardo Garcia stood alongside Don Porfirio in gold-plated *charro* dress, welcoming the different foreign dignitaries with a present made of pure gold.

Both Don Porfirio and Bernardo wore white powder on their dark Indian faces so that they'd look white-European. No Indians were allowed in Mexico City during the celebration. No mestizos or poor, dark-skinned people. So for thirty days the foreign dignitaries were driven in gold-studded carriages up and down the boulevard of La Reforma in Mexico City, which had been specially built by Don Porfirio to be an exact replica of the main boulevard in Paris, and the foreign visitors only saw beautiful homes, prosperous factories, well-cared-for haciendas and well-to-do European-looking people.

This, then, was the last straw that broke the burro's back. And the poor, hungry people of Mexico rose up in arms by the tens of thousands, breaking Don Porfirio's thirty-year reign, and the Revolution of 1910 began.

Broken-hearted, Espirito and his people watched from the top of the towering cliffs as their beloved box canyon—in which they'd lived peacefully for hundreds of years—turned first into a settlement of electric fences, grey stone buildings and terrible noises, and now into a bloodbath for the soldiers of the Revolution.

Then, one cold, clear morning, Ojos Puros and his Indian wife—he'd married Espirito's youngest daughter—found the legendary Espirito dead up on the towering cliffs. It was said that Espirito had died of grief because he'd misled his people and brought them to ruin.

Ojos Puros and his wife buried Espirito where he'd died so that his soul could look down into their beloved box canyon for all eternity.

1

*And so she, a child of the meteorite, found her truelove
among the shooting and killing and raping and fire.*

Dreaming, Lupe reached across the bed. Dreaming
as she lay there, facedown on the lumpy-hard straw mattress, she reached
under warm-smelling cotton covers, searching for her mother, but she didn't
find her.

Opening her eyes, Lupe yawned and stretched, her long thick hair falling
about her neck and shoulders in dark, rich curls. Her mother was sitting at
the end of the bed, surrounded by long spears of silvery moonlight coming
in through the cracks of their lean-to. A cock crowed in the distance, a coyote
howled, and the dogs in the village began to bark.

Smiling, Lupe rubbed her sleep-swollen eyes and crawled across to her
mother. Coming up behind her, Lupe put her arms around her mother, and
snuggled in close to her soft, plump body. Her mother, Doña Guadalupe,
stopped braiding her long grey hair and turned about, taking her youngest
child into her arms. Lupe was six years old, and she'd been sleeping with her
mother ever since her father, Don Victor, had left them to look for work in
the lowlands.

Feeling her mother's arm around her, Lupe closed her eyes and drifted
back into dream, feeling the cool morning breeze coming in through their
open doorway and hearing her mother's heartbeat against her left ear as she
held there, dreaming, feeling, drifting, allowing the miracle of the new day
to come to her gently, softly, slowly. Her mother held her in her arms,
humming, "*Coo-coo rrroo-coo cooo paloma,*" and Lupe breathed deeply,
feeling her mother's great, wonderfully-warm breasts against her face and
neck and chest.

Then Lupe's three older sisters began to stir, too. Carlota, Lupe's eleven-
year-old sister, was the first to come and get in bed with Lupe and their
mother.

"Move over," said Carlota, snuggling in between Lupe and their mother.
"You get to sleep all night long with Mama!"

"Quiet," said Doña Guadalupe calmly, "there's enough of me for all of you."

She hugged her two youngest daughters close to her heart, and then came Maria, who was thirteen, and Sophia, who was fifteen, and they, too, got into the little straw bed.

Outside, the cock crowed again, and the coyote continued howling in the distance. Lupe's brother Victoriano came inside the lean-to with his dog. He was ten and the only one allowed to sleep outside under the stars, because he was a boy.

"*Buenos días,*" he said, not coming near the bed. Victoriano had been trying very hard to act like the man of the house ever since Don Victor had left them.

"*Buenos días,*" said his mother and sisters.

And so the first miracle of the new day had been completed; Lupe and her family were awake and the world was still alive.

"All right," said Doña Guadalupe, "now we must all get to work."

And saying this, she pushed away from her children like a mother dog disentangling herself from her litter of pups, and she stood up. She finished brushing out her long grey hair and wrapped it into a tight bundle at the nape of her neck. With her teeth, she opened the wooden fork that her son had made for her out of an oak branch and used it to fasten her hair.

Watching her mother in the starry light, Lupe felt so warm and good that she could still feel the touch of her mother all over her as she slipped on her *huaraches* and went out of the lean-to to do her chores.

Walking around the huge, dark boulder to which their lean-to was anchored, Lupe looked up at the stars and moon and pulled up her dress and squatted down on her heels on the steep hillside, facing downhill with her feet apart, and relieved herself in the privacy of her coarse white cotton dress, which was made from the sack that the flour came in.

Wiping herself with a corn husk that she'd softened by chewing the night before, Lupe stood and looked over the huge boulder to the main part of the village below them, which was just beginning to stir. The American enfencement at the gold mine across the box canyon was still asleep.

Having cleansed herself, Lupe now knelt, as she did each morning, feeling the greatness of the stars and the moon and she gave her personal thanks to God, completing the second miracle of the day. Then she continued around to the steep side of the boulder, gripping the huge rock, to get up to the gate of the goats' pen.

Seeing Lupe in the pale moonlight, the two big milk goats and their two young ones called to her in tight, forceful voices.

"Good morning," said Lupe, gathering up the armful of grass that she'd picked the evening before. "I hope you all slept well and had good dreams of green meadows."

The two big milk goats answered her, and she petted them and fed them. The two baby goats in the next pen called out for attention, too. All four of these animals were fine goats, and they were the pride of Lupe's family. They made cheese from the milk of the two big goats and served the cheese in their kitchen.

"I hope the coyotes didn't bother you too much last night," she said to them. "After all, remember, last night was a full moon, and you know that every full moon the coyotes call to the heavens for the wheel of cheese that the she-fox stole from them and hid at the bottom of the river."

The two big milk goats loved Lupe and her gentle voice and ate contentedly. "Good morning to you, too," said Lupe to the babies in the next pen. "I'll be with you right after I do the milking."

Picking up her two clay pots and the little stool her father had made for her, Lupe walked around to the left side of the first goat and sat down on the stool. She petted the big goat on her rump in long, slow strokes. Then she swept back her own long, dark hair, tied it behind her head, and rested her forehead on the goat's hard belly. Taking one large rosy tit in each hand, she closed off the top of the tit with her thumb and index finger and rolled down with the rest of her hand, forcing the milk out in a hard-sounding hiss as it hit the empty pot. Humming as she milked, Lupe worked hard and steadily, feeling goose bumps as she now performed the third miracle of the day— work—using the hands and body which God had so wisely given her for making her way in the world.

Spitting on her hands and rubbing her palms together, Lupe now picked up the rhythm of her milking as she listened to the noises of the night beginning to fade and the sounds of her family beginning to take on life. Her brother chopped wood in front of their lean-to, and her sisters laughed and talked as they helped their mother in the kitchen under the *ramada*. The stars and night were going and her whole world was coming to life.

When Lupe was done with the first goat, she went to the second animal, and her two cats and dog came up and she sprayed them in their faces with the milk, laughing happily.

Finishing up with both animals, Lupe poured out a little milk on a hollow spot on top of the big boulder for the pets, then she walked over to feed the two baby goats.

The little goats called to her as if she were their mother. Lupe lowered the pot to the ground and dipped her right hand into the sticky warm milk so that the little goats could nurse off her fingertips. They were still too young to drink the milk without having her fingers to suck.

Finishing, Lupe wiped the goats' milk from her right hand with her left, remembering her mother's words that any girl who ever rubbed fresh goat's milk into her hands every morning would never have wrinkled hands as an old lady.

Going inside the *ramada*, Lupe put the milk on the counter and hurried over to the stove to get one of the hot tortillas. Her three sisters were at the long pinewood counter, rolling out the tortillas as their mother cooked them.

With great relish, Lupe took a hot tortilla off the stove, rolled it, and sat down on the well-swept hard-packed dirt floor alongside the stove that her father had made for them. She ate happily. The freshly-made corn tortilla smelled wonderful, but she could also still smell the goat's milk on her hands. And the smell of the goat's milk was strong; it smelled of grass and brush and the earth itself.

"So, yes, that's right," Carlota was saying. "We found Lydia practicing her English. She plans to steal Scott, the American engineer, from Carmen!"

"But Scott is already engaged to Carmen!" said Maria angrily. Carmen was Maria's best friend and Maria knew how much her friend loved the tall handsome engineer.

"Oh, I know," said Carlota, her big green eyes dancing with mischief as she rolled out her tortilla. "That's why Lydia is doing it!"

Lydia was Don Manuel's daughter. Don Manuel was their town mayor, but he also took care of the payroll for the Americans at the mine, so he was the most powerful and wealthy Mexican in their village.

"Oh, that's dirty!" said Maria. "I think I'll thrash Lydia next time I get her alone!"

And Maria could do it. She was tall and strong with a wide, handsome Indian face and huge dark eyes and a big full-lipped mouth. She was one of the most powerful girls in the village.

"Calm down," said Sophia, who was older than Maria but shorter and more delicately made. "She won't get him, Maria. What's wrong with you? Love is more powerful than English or fine dresses."

"Oh, I know that!" said Maria. "But still, it makes me so mad! Why does Lydia even bother to tempt him?"

Sophia giggled. "Because he's the only American who doesn't follow Her Majesty around the plaza like a dog, and it drives Lydia crazy like a tick up a dog's tail."

Lupe and her sisters laughed so hard that the *ramada* echoed with sound.

"All right," said their mother, smiling. "No more. I don't want the miners arriving and hearing my fine daughters talking like cutthroat thieves in the night."

Still laughing, Lupe glanced from her mother to her sisters. Oh, how she loved them and their little house and their animals and the smell of their life together. She could smell the *chorizo* that her mother was cooking, she could smell the smoke from the hard-wood fire in the stove, and she could smell the strong, sweet, herb-like scent of the goat's milk on her hands. She felt rich with the good, full promise of life.

Finishing her tortilla, Lupe got up and kissed her mother and hurried outside to finish her chores before the men arrived. Ever since their father had left them, she and her family had been making their living by feeding the miners. She had to help Victoriano sweep the ground and water it down. Their mother was a very proud woman; she kept one of the cleanest homes in all of the village.

Meeting her brother out front, Lupe quickly took the broom made from a bush with small yellow flowers called the Mexican-Broom, and she swept the hard-packed ground as her brother sprinkled it with water. They didn't have much time. He, the sun, was already making the eastern sky pale, and the Americans who lived up high on the barren slope across the canyon didn't tolerate anyone being late.

Lupe and her brother were just finishing when the first two miners arrived. One was tall and thin and his name was Flaco. The other was short and wide and his name was Manos because of his huge, thick hands. Flaco and Manos were both in their late twenties; they were two of the oldest men that the Americans still employed at the mine.

"*Buenos días*, Victoriano. And look at you, Lupe," said Flaco, touching her hair, "every day I swear that you grow more beautiful!"

Lupe blushed, saying nothing. And Victoriano stepped aside so the two miners could go inside.

"*Buenos días*," said Manos as he passed by Lupe and her brother.

Lupe nodded to Manos. She liked Manos better than she like Flaco. Manos never touched her or embarrassed her by saying how beautiful she was. Ever since Lupe could remember, men—perfect strangers—had been stopping her and touching her hair and telling her how beautiful she was. It angered her. She was no dog to stop and pet.

"*Buenos días*," said Lupe quietly to Manos.

Then, just as Lupe was going to follow the two miners inside to help serve them breakfast, there came the sun, *la cobija de los pobres*, the blanket of the poor.

The two miners stopped and took off their hats and gave witness to the right eye of God, Himself, the sun, the greatest miracle of the day. Lupe and Victoriano quit their labor and joined the two men, bowing their heads in greeting. And Doña Guadalupe and her other daughters came out from under the *ramada* and joined them.

And here came the sun, reaching up, filling the box canyon with brilliance, and suddenly the whole canyon was alive—every rock and tree and blade of grass. And the birds and people and livestock came to life, too. One moment the canyon had been silent, and the next it was noisy, the birds chirping and the dogs and cats running around looking for something to eat, and the children shouting in the village below, and the goats and cattle pawing at the ground and the burros and mules braying, filling the canyon with a symphony of sounds.

Flaco and Manos put their hats back on and sat down at the first table under the *ramada* so they could look through the vines of the bougainvillea and keep watch on the sun's progress. Lupe now went in to help her sister Carlota do the serving. Carlota and Lupe were the youngest, so Doña Guadalupe had them do the serving while she kept her older daughters in the kitchen. Maria and Sophia were just too ripe for the touching of men's quick hands.

Bringing Flaco and Manos their hot cinnamon coffee, Carlota joked with the two men. But Lupe didn't. She was too shy. For as long as Lupe could remember, her sisters and brother had made fun of her because she kept by her mother's skirts, refusing to talk to anyone.

"Lupita," her sisters would say, "some day you're going to have to talk to people and let go of our mother's skirts, you know."

"No, I'm not," she'd always say. "I'm going to stay by Mama's side all my life!"

"Well, then, what will you do when you marry?" they'd tease her.

"My husband will come and stay with Mama and me or he can get out!"

For Lupe, her mother was everything. She was the perfect gift given to her by God.

Lupe and Carlota were feeding the last of the miners when Old Man Benito arrived. Old Man Benito was the only miner who didn't work at the American-owned gold mine. He was a strange old man with brown blotches running up and down the sides of his face. He'd never married and he'd searched for gold all his life. Once, long ago, he'd had a gold mine of his own, until the Americans had taken it from him.

Seeing Old Man Benito coming down the steep trail to the *ramada*, Lupe quickly poured a full cup of coffee and took it out to him so he wouldn't have to come inside with the younger miners. He was fifty years old, the oldest man in the village, and many of the young miners had no respect for him. They would tease him and call him a fool.

"You are an angel," he said, putting the earthen cup to his lips, blowing on it and drinking in a big air-sucking swallow. "And I swear to it, *mi hijita*, that as soon as I find gold again, I'm going to give you and your family half, so we'll all be rich!"

Lupe's eyes filled with mischief. She loved the way he called her *mi hijita*, my dear little one. Don Benito had been like a part of their family for as long as she could remember, and this was a little game that they played each morning. "Rich is the cream of the fat cow's milk," she said. "Rich is the love of God that we receive each new day! Rich isn't gold! Gold is only for people that are poor of heart!"

Don Benito laughed. "Yes, of course, you're absolutely right, *mi hijita*," he said. "But also, believe me, rich is being able to sleep in late if you wish, or not work all day if you're tired."

"That's not rich," she said again, eyes dancing happily. "That's lazy, Don Benito!"

He laughed, too. "Well, then lazy is richness for these old bones!"

And saying this, they both began to laugh again, but the huge generators from the American enfencement started up and the box canyon was suddenly filled with a low rumbling sound. The lights came on inside the six stone buildings up on the opposite side of the box canyon and Lupe shivered, feeling cold all over.

"Well, Don Benito," said Lupe, "excuse me, but I must hurry back inside and finish my work before they blow the horn."

"Pass your day with God, *mi hijita*," said the old man.

"Thank you, and you do the same, Don Benito."

"Of course," he laughed. "Who else but God is crazy enough to follow me up to the cliffs where I work?"

Lupe was just going to go inside when the bellowing horn exploded. Lupe gripped her ears. Quickly, all the miners were up and out of the *ramada* as fast as they could move.

Passing by, one of the young miners saw Lupe holding her ears and the old man cringing. "Hey, Benito!" he said with his mouth full of food. "Have you struck gold yet?" He was a boy in his early teens.

"Almost," said Don Benito. "Just another shovel of rock, and I'll be rich again."

"Rich, hell!" said the young miner, winking at the other miners. "You had it once, old man, and you lost it to drink and women! Lady Luck is never going to give you another chance! Eh, Lupita?"

Lupe said nothing.

"All right," said Manos, coming up behind the young miners, "you heard the bull's roar! Move your tail!"

The young man laughed, and he and the other miners started up the rocky pathway.

Manos shrugged to Lupe and Don Benito. "They're just young," he said. "They don't know that in less than three years, Lady Luck will abandon them. Their lungs will be gone and their hands will be crushed."

Don Benito nodded sadly. "Yes, I know about luck," he said. "She can be cruel."

Lupe glanced from Don Benito to Manos, wondering why it was that men always put misfortune into the dress of a fine woman. But, before she could say anything, the horn blew again and Manos was off.

"Well," said Don Benito once they were alone again, "thank you for passing the sunrise with me."

"The pleasure was mine," she said.

"Oh, no, the pleasure was all mine, *mi hijita*," he insisted, reaching into his pocket. "Here, I almost forgot, I brought you a little present, Lupita."

And opening his twisted, torn right hand, Lupe saw the most beautiful feather she'd ever seen in all her life. It was green and bright blue with a touch of red and yellow near the tip. It was a feather from one of the huge flocks of parrots that came to roost in the towering mighty cathedral-like cliffs where the old man worked, and where only the eagles soared above the wild white pine trees.

"Oh, Don Benito," Lupe said excitedly, "it's absolutely beautiful!"

"Yes," he said, "and when I found it yesterday while I was working at the base of the cathedral rocks, I thought of you—the most beautiful child God's ever created."

And saying this, he smiled, and his whole face lit up. Lupe smiled, too, not taking offense at his compliment.

The sun was only two fists off the horizon when Lupe and her family finally sat down to eat their own breakfast. Outside, the dog barked and started growling. Victoriano got up and went out and glanced around. He could see nothing. But his little brown dog continued growling and looking up toward the cliff rocks on the western side of the box canyon.

"What is it, boy?" asked Victoriano, petting his little brown dog. "Do you still smell the coyotes from last night?"

But then, suddenly, Victoriano felt it, too; here it was under his bare feet, the trembling of the earth. He could feel it before he heard it. His eyes went huge with fear, racing back inside the *ramada*.

"Mama, soldiers!" he screamed.

But his mother and sisters were already up and running, before the first sounds of the thundering horsemen even came echoing into their box canyon. Lupe felt her little heart wanting to burst. Ever since she could remember, her family had been running and hiding when soldiers came racing into their canyon.

Quickly, she grabbed all the food off her plate with her tortilla and fell chest-down to the earth along with her mother and sisters as the shooting began. Bullets were singing over their boulder as Lupe shoved the food into her mouth—chewing, swallowing, realizing that it would be a long time before she got to eat again. Then Lupe and her family were crawling, hearts pounding against the earth, going under the chairs and tables as fast as they could so that they could get to the safety of the big boulder at the back of their lean-to.

Spitting out what she hadn't eaten, Lupe kept close to her mother, gripping the sun-warmed ground with her hands and pushing with her knees. The Revolution had started coming into their box canyon three months before Lupe was born. Bullets and death were a way of life for Lupe, but, still, she dreaded them as much as her goats dreaded the coyote's fangs.

Quickly, Lupe and her mother got behind the big boulder below the goat pens. Victoriano and Maria were already digging into the pile of manure behind the boulder.

"Hurry!" said their mother. "You're going to have to hide, too, Carlota!"

"No, I'm still little!" said Carlota.

"Carlota! Do as I say! Even Lupe could be in danger!"

Wet, soggy, smelly manure was flying all around Lupe's face as her brother and sisters burrowed into the pile of chicken and goat waste. The last time soldiers had come through, even small girls not yet in their teens had been raped and beaten and taken away.

Suddenly, the screaming horsemen were in the canyon itself, circling above them on the main road. That meant that theirs would be one of the first homes to be struck, unless, of course, the soldiers took over the gold mine first.

"Faster!" screamed their mother, digging herself, making room for Sophia, Maria and Carlota. Lupe couldn't help it; she began to puke. Egg and tortilla and *salsa* got all over her hands and face. Her mother's fear frightened her more than even the thundering sounds of the horsemen and the screaming shouts of men with their exploding rifles.

Down below in the main part of the village, the people were running in terror, hiding as quickly as they could while the monstrous sounds of the galloping horsemen shook the very earth.

Lupe and her family now had the pile of manure pulled out. Sophia and Maria crawled inside the crevice behind the boulder.

"Get in there, Carlota!" said Doña Guadalupe.

"But, Mama," said Carlota, her face expressing pure repulsion, "that *caca* is all wet."

Having no more patience, Doña Guadalupe slapped Carlota, pushing her face-first down into the crevice. Maria and Sophia gripped their sister by the hair, pulling her in with them under the boulder.

Quickly, Lupe and Victoriano first tossed the straw over their sisters and then the wet, fresh manure. But Carlota kept shouting, trying to get out of the crevice until she got a wet piece of chicken shit in her mouth. She gasped and choked. Everyone, in spite of themselves, began to laugh.

Then, here came the horsemen, a hundred of them, leaping off the main road as they flew over the rock walls and lean-tos, racing down into the main part of the village. For the first time, Lupe couldn't hear the Americans' generators, the horsemen were screaming and shooting so loudly.

And now with her older sisters hidden, Lupe got down with her mother and brother behind the big boulder, hugg . the earth, heart-to-heart against each other in horrible fear. Up above them, some ten feet away, the two big milk goats were going crazy in their pen, leaping at the fence, trying to get to their young ones, but they couldn't make it over the sharp cedar-picket fence.

Hearing a terrible cry, Lupe looked up and saw the two big mother goats jumping at the fence and their babies crying in terror in the other pen. Lupe started to get to her feet so she could open the gate for her goats when two bullets came hissing over her head, splattering against the top of the big boulder.

Doña Guadalupe screamed, grabbing her youngest daughter and throwing her down on the ground.

Crying with fear, Lupe closed her eyes and crouched down between her mother and brother. She began to pray. But then she heard a terrible cry from her goats and she opened her eyes and saw that one mother goat had leaped on the fence with her big awkward body and her huge udder had caught on a picket post and ripped open like a paper bag.

Red blood and white milk and a piece of inner tissue splattered against the cedar fence as the mother goat kicked and screeched. But still she did not die. No, instead, she continued to live and suffer her entire predicament.

Lupe lay there screaming and crying until she could cry no more. She lay there, held down by her mother and brother as the horsemen turned the *ramada* inside out, knocking over their sheet-metal stove, setting the place on fire.

Then the horsemen passed on, sweeping down into the main part of the village. Lupe and her mother and brother got to their feet and saw that the big goat had kicked her last.

They hurried inside to get blankets and water to put out the fire as quickly as they could. And, as Lupe fought the fire and helped throw the flaming chairs and table outside, what she saw that hurt her most of all was that the hard-packed earth, that she and her family had swept and watered for so many years to get it to look like polished tile, had now been turned to rubble by the horses' hooves. She screamed, feeling invaded, trampled, raped, but no sounds came out.

It was noon. The shooting had ceased and the people were coming out of hiding. Victoriano and Old Man Benito were skinning out the dead mother goat.

"Lupe," said Doña Guadalupe, "I think it's safe now for you to go get fresh water."

"Yes," said Lupe.

Cautiously, she made her way down the steep hillside through the still-smoldering huts to get water at the creek at the bottom of the canyon. Getting to the tall foliage alongside the bubbling brook, Lupe glanced all around before bending over to fill her clay pot. She felt nervous, tense, exhausted.

The main part of the village lay burning behind her, and across the creek, up the slope a few hundred feet, she could see the piles of yellow chalk-like waste from the mine, and she could hear some of the soldiers further up the slope at the American enfencement laughing and joking, truly enjoying themselves.

Señor Jones, who ran the American mine, had prepared a feast for them. This was how the Americans always dealt with the soldiers who came shooting into their canyon. They fed the soldiers, made them welcome, and then calmed them down by promising them weapons from the United States.

Lupe was bent over between two huge ferns, concentrating on filling her pot, when suddenly she felt a dark shadow fall over her.

Instantly, Lupe knew it was a soldier and he was going to grab her. She sprang to her feet as quickly as a deer and was halfway across the creek before she turned and saw the man mounted on his horse.

But then, she didn't know why, she stopped and stared at him. There he sat on a sorrel orange-red stallion, smiling down at her with the whitest teeth she'd ever seen.

"Hello," he called gently.

"Hello," she said cautiously, looking at him in the sunlight coming down through the tree branches, surrounding him and his horse in a halo of golden-pale light.

Her heart went out of her and she didn't run across the creek; no, she just stood there, facing him, and she felt such wonder. The stranger was in uniform. He wasn't wearing a big straw hat and the coarse white clothes like the others. And his uniform had shiny buttons and was well-kept and clean and beautiful, even in the midst of battle. Lupe swallowed, not moving, and saw that his blue eyes were kind and gentle. He was, indeed, the most beautiful man she had ever seen.

The soldier smiled down at her as she stood there in the middle of the creek, balanced on two stones, and she just knew that something was happening inside her heart that would be with her for all the days of her life. He was so tall and handsome. And his big moustache reminded her of her father.

Her heart stopped and the world held still and, suddenly, she just knew why she'd always been so shy and unable to speak to anyone except her mother. No one had ever come into her world before that truly mattered. No one had ever come up inside her and touched her very soul.

"*Buenos días*," he said in a rich, strong voice, still smiling.

"*Buenos días*," she said back to him, smiling too.

"Do you live around here?" he asked.

"No," she shook her head. "I live way up there near the top of the village."

"Good," he said, "because I'm looking for a home away from the center of town for my wife."

Lupe's heart leaped. He was married. She felt her knees go weak. The stone under her right foot moved and she began to fall. But in a lightning-blur of motion, he was off his horse and had her in his arms.

He carried her to the riverbank, putting her down on the tall green ferns. Taking off his cap, he placed it under her head and then brought out his handkerchief of white silk, wet it in the clear cool water, and soothed her forehead.

"There," he said, "better?"

She nodded yes, not once taking her eyes off him. He saw and laughed and combed back her dark, curly hair with his fingertips. She looked at him, surrounded by golden-pale light, and she just knew that this man was her shining prince that her sisters were always reading about in books. He was her perfect love, made for her in heaven by God, Himself. Nothing bad could ever again happen to her as long as she was in this man's arms.

Lupe closed her eyes, dreaming, praying, hoping never to awake from this magical moment.

"Well, *querida*," he said, "if you are better, let's go. I need to find a home for my wife so I can attend to my duties."

Lupe finally opened her eyes. She saw the man before her in his grey uniform with shining buttons; she saw the great trees overhead, and she realized that she wasn't asleep and dreaming.

"Are you sure that you're all right, *querida*?" he asked again.

"Yes," she said.

"Good," he said. "Then, let me put you on my horse and I can carry your pot for you so we can go up to your home."

She said nothing, feeling a great warmth go all through her body as he picked her up in his arms.

"Can you ride?" he asked.

She nodded.

"Good," he said, and he lifted her high into the sunlight and put her gently in the saddle of his great orange-red stallion. Then he took the animal's reins with his left hand and picked up her pot in his right, starting through the ferns and trees. Never had Lupe been on such a tall, magnificent animal. Even the great green ferns below her seemed small from way up there.

Coming into the little plaza, Lupe could see over the soldiers' heads. The soldiers were lining everyone up against a stone wall. She could smell the smoke of the homes that had been set on fire, and she could see the terrible fear in the people's eyes as they were lined up.

Then she saw Lydia and her family. Lupe didn't mean to, but she giggled. The mayor Don Manuel and his family looked so out of place in their fine clothes along with all the other townspeople.

But then Lupe stopped giggling. Her mother's best friend, Doña Manza, and her two sons and two daughters were up against the wall, too.

"Doña Manza!" cried out Lupe.

"Lupe!" cried out the old lady.

"Your mother?" asked Lupe's handsome prince.

"No, she's my mother's best friend," said Lupe anxiously. "And she makes the best sweetbreads in all the village!"

Her prince laughed. "Well, that's good to know," he said, handing the pot to a passing foot-soldier dressed in coarse white cotton. "Lieutenant!" he said in the loud, booming voice to the soldier in charge. "Have that woman, Doña Manza, and her family released immediately so they can get back to their task of making fresh bread for all of us!"

"Yes, *mi coronel*!" said the well-dressed lieutenant, rolling a heavy "R" sound into the word, "colonel." He had a pistol in one hand and a sword in the other.

"And the others?" asked Lupe. "What will happen to them?"

"They'll be questioned, *querida*," said her Colonel, "so we can find out who's who and what they do."

"Then you're not going to harm them?"

"No, of course not."

And saying this, her Colonel put his left foot in the stirrup and swung up into the saddle, lifting Lupe forward with his right hand so he could fit in behind her. Then he took the reins in hand, motioning the soldier to follow with the pot. Lupe and her prince snuggled in close as his great orange-red stallion pranced up the cobblestones out of the plaza and up the steep hillside.

The homes got smaller and poorer as they climbed up the twisting pathway. Finally the homes were nothing more than lean-tos made of sticks and mud, anchored to a tree or a boulder. Approaching her home, Lupe turned to her Colonel.

"Excuse me," she said, "but I'll have to go inside by myself."

"But why?" he asked.

"Because," she said, feeling her heart wanting to hide, "my mother doesn't allow soldiers in our home, so I'll have to speak to her alone first."

"I'm glad to hear that, my angel," he said. "If I had a home, I wouldn't want soldiers in it either." And saying this, he kissed her on the cheek and then swung her down from his horse, putting her gently on the ground.

She stood there, looking up at him.

"Well, *querida*," he said in his strong but gentle voice, "I'll wait here for you."

"But, excuse me," she said, "I don't even know your name."

"Can you read?" he asked, getting off his horse.

She shook her head. "I don't start school until next season."

"Well, then, you'll be reading soon," he smiled, "so here's my card." And saying this, he handed her a card made of stiff white paper. "Colonel Manuel Maytorena at your service!" he said, tipping his cap and snapping his tall black boots together.

Lupe blushed; she'd never seen such a card before, nor a man tip his hat and snap his heels together. She picked up the hem of her dress and curtsied.

Looking at her white homemade dress and her fine manners, he smiled grandly. "Oh, child," he said, "since the first moment I saw you, you captured my heart. I only pray to God that some day I have a daughter half as beautiful as you! For truly, you are an angel!"

For once, Lupe didn't blush. Instead, she looked at him, thinking that maybe it was true, after all: she was beautiful. She turned and ran up the hillside like a deer, flying over the rocks to their *ramada*. She was in love with her truelove. And he loved her, too.

Coming under the *ramada*, Lupe found her mother and brother still cleaning up the mess the soldiers had made. Her three sisters were nowhere in sight.

"Mama! Mama!" yelled Lupe, "I found him and he wants to keep his wife here at our home!"

"Who?" asked Doña Guadalupe. "I don't permit soldiers in my home! Tell him to stay down by the plaza!"

"But, Mama," said Lupe, her heart wanting to burst, "he's my prince! And he's strong! Why, even the soldiers obeyed him when he told them to let Doña Manza and her family go."

Hearing this, Doña Guadalupe quit her labor. "He what?" she asked.

"At the plaza, the soldiers were lining up everybody and they had Doña Manza and her family, but when I told him that she made the best sweet-bread in the village, he said for them to let her go so she could go back to her work."

"And they released her?"

"Immediately," said Lupe.

"I see," said Doña Guadalupe, sitting down and smoothing out the apron on her lap. "And this prince of yours, where is he now?"

Lupe pointed. "Right down the path waiting for your answer. I told him that you didn't allow soldiers in our home. And he said good, he wouldn't either, if he had a home."

"I see," said the old grey-haired lady, quickly thinking over the situation. No, she didn't want a soldier in her house. But, if he was married and he did have the power to command soldiers, then maybe he'd be a good ally for her to have so she could bring her daughters out of hiding. "Very well, *mi hijita*," said Doña Guadalupe, once more smoothing out the apron on her lap, "bring in this soldier and I shall speak to him. But I promise nothing."

"Oh, thank you, Mama!" shouted Lupe. "I love you with all my heart!" She leaped forward, kissing her mother, then flew out of the *ramada* and down the rocky path, shouting as she went, shouting with such gusto that her little voice echoed off the mighty cathedral-like cliffs. "My mother will talk to you!" she yelled. "My mother has agreed to let you speak!"

Hearing her words, Colonel Manuel Maytorena laughed, knowing that he'd chosen the right home for his young wife. This child's mother was the power of her home.

It was late that afternoon when the Colonel brought his wife. Her name was Socorro, and she was every bit as lovely as her name. She had large, dark, almond-shaped eyes, long auburn hair and tawny-colored skin that was as smooth as porcelain. She was big with child and exhausted. Gratefully Socorro followed Doña Guadalupe inside the lean-to to rest on her bed.

It was sundown when Lupe and her sisters came in, and they sat down on their mother's bed and listened to Socorro tell them of the world outside of their canyon. She was shy and soft-spoken as she told them of her village and how it had been destroyed. She'd left and gone to Mazatlan along the coast, where she'd met the Colonel and began following him from battle to battle.

"Was it love at first sight?" asked Maria.

"Oh, it was!" said Socorro. "I was working at the hospital when the Colonel came to check on some of his men. He was so considerate and thoughtful."

"And handsome!" said Carlota.

They all burst out laughing, except Lupe. Her perfect love wasn't just married; his wife loved him, too.

Then the sun, the right eye of God, was going down behind the towering cliffs. Lupe and her family gathered to give their thanks to the Almighty. It had been another good day. No one in their family had been harmed, and the mother goat that had died would now be their evening meal.

Watching the sky turn pink and rose and lavender, Lupe put her hands together and prayed for God to please help her not to hate Socorro, but instead to allow her to just love her truelove. And God, in His infinite wisdom, granted her the wish. For that evening, when the miners came to eat dinner under the *ramada*, Lupe could see that they, too, loved her Colonel. They were all so boisterously happy.

"Doña Guadalupe," said Manos, taking off his hat as he sat down under the *ramada* along with Flaco to eat, "I swear, this Colonel is a wonderful man! If he were a woman, I think I'd love him! He's increased our wages, lessened our hours, and he's made good on many of our complaints about safety."

"But best of all," added Flaco, "the Colonel is a Carrancista under the command of General Obregon and he told the Americans in front of us all that from now on they can't blow their horn at us!"

" 'We're not dogs,' he told Señor Jones right to his face," continued Flaco, tearing his tortilla in two as he took up a piece of barbecued goat that Lupe had brought them. "So they have no right to use the horn on us like cattle!"

This evening the miners under the *ramada* were so happy that they didn't even tease Don Benito when he sat down to eat with them. Lupe served the men as quickly as she could, along with the help of her sister Carlota. She was filled with the excitement of all the men's happiness. Her Colonel was, indeed, wonderful.

Then, once the miners were finished eating and gone, Lupe's truelove walked into their *ramada*.

"Well, I hope you saved something for me to eat," he said, smiling at Lupe and her family as he hugged his wife. "Señor Jones had a big feast prepared for my officers and me, but I declined. No food on earth compares to the taste of the true Mexican kitchen!"

He sat down and patted his knee, calling to Lupe. "Come, my angel, and sit on my lap."

Lupe didn't have to be asked twice. She flew to him. And when he took her in his great arms—as he'd done by the river—she felt her whole body melt and then grow warm with that same good feeling.

"I was glad to see the miners happy as I came down the path," he said. "Wars aren't won by soldiers. They're won by you women here in the kitchens who feed the fighting men and by the miners and farmers who keep the nation going. This is the genius of my great General Obregon. He gives the common worker his due credit."

He continued talking and bouncing Lupe on his knees. And Lupe felt safe and wonderful. When it was time to eat, Doña Guadalupe asked her children to leave the room so the Colonel and his wife could eat alone.

"Oh, no, Señora," said the tall handsome man, "please join us. This is my pleasure, to be part of your family. And you, young Victoriano," he said to Lupe's brother, "come and sit beside me so we can speak man-to-man."

Victoriano looked at the Colonel. "No, thank you," he said, "I'm not hungry." And he went out of the *ramada*.

Doña Guadalupe looked after her son. But she decided to say nothing of his rudeness and speak to him later.

When it was time to go to bed, Lupe and her mother went outside to sleep with Victoriano and the girls so that the Colonel and his wife could have the privacy of their lean-to.

"I don't like it," whispered Sophia to her mother as she lay down on her own straw mat. "He should get his own bedding from Don Manuel's store."

"Shhhh!" snapped their mother quickly. "Give our thanks to God that the Colonel has agreed to give his personal protection to our home. And you, *mi hijita*," she said to Lupe, drawing her close, "you and I need to pluck a chicken."

"But why?" asked Lupe, feeling herself wanting to hide. "I've done nothing wrong." To pluck a chicken meant that you were going to get your own feathers pulled with a scolding. Lupe was suddenly very anxious.

"No, you haven't really done anything wrong yet, *mi hijita*," said her mother, stroking her, "but I know you like this man very much, and so you're going to have to be careful and give him time alone with his wife or they'll grow to dislike you."

"But why, Mama?" asked Lupe. "I'm not doing anything bad. He loves me and I love him, too."

Doña Guadalupe took a big breath, smoothing out the blanket across herself and her daughter. Her youngest child had been very young when Don Victor had left, so she could well understand her daughter's hunger for the love that this tall, handsome man was giving her. It had been a special evening for all of them, having a man at their dinner table.

"*Mi hijita*," said Doña Guadalupe, "for you to like this man is fine; nothing wrong with that. But, you must also understand that when a man and a woman are married, they need special time alone so their world can grow together. You're a child, *mi hijita*; you're not a woman yet. You must accept what I say, or they are going to come to consider you an intruder, and they'll leave our home because of you."

In the star-bright light coming in between the burnt vines of the *ramada*, Lupe's eyes filled with tears. "But, Mama, he called me! He's the one who asked me to sit on his lap tonight! I wasn't being an intruder."

Taking pity on her, Doña Guadalupe drew her smallest daughter closer. "*Mi hijita*," she said, "you are absolutely right: the Colonel did call you. But believe me, I know, if you keep going to him every time he calls, he and his wife will grow to resent you. A man is like an ill-mannered billy goat, *mi hijita*, he wants much more than his stomach can hold, so he must be ignored half of the time. Do you understand?"

Lupe's eyes were overflowing with tears. "No," she said, "I don't understand! He's my prince, Mama!"

"Oh, *mi hijita*," said Doña Guadalupe, "you're just listening to your heart too much. Open your eyes and see: he's already married, and you're a child."

Lupe felt her whole body tremble. This was just awful. How could her mother say such a terrible thing to her? Of course he was married. But she was no child when it came to love. Hadn't she been giving love to her mother and to her family and to God, Himself, all her life?

The moon came up and the stars filled the heavens and the night began. The sun, the greatest miracle of all, had gone to rest and now was the time that all good people turned into angels in their sleep.

*And so Saint Peter opened the flood gates of heaven
and the rainy season began, washing the earth of its
dust and all the people of their sins.*

Twice her truelove came home with wounded men who'd been shot by the Villistas as they forged their way through the jungle. But her Colonel was never shot, so Lupe took heart, figuring that God was on their side.

On the evenings when he came home, they'd warm water for him and he'd bathe inside the room that they'd added to the lean-to. Sometimes his wife would join him, and he'd pull down the Indian blanket which covered their doorway.

On these occasions, Lupe and her family would take a walk, and Maria and Carlota would giggle, and Sophia would reprimand them. It seemed that everyone was thinking of love. It was said that even their sister Maria had been making eyes at a boy lately.

Then the rainy season began with a mighty roar from the heavens, and a sudden, terrifying explosion of water came down, filling the canyon with a crashing sound. It rained for three days and three nights. The two main waterfalls of their canyon gushed forth with the roar of water, crashing over the rim of the towering wall of mighty rock. The canyon echoed with the water's thunderous sound, and it continued raining steadily, every afternoon for fourteen days. Finally, neither beast nor human could leave its shelter, the water was gushing down so powerfully between the three cathedral peaks. The force of the two main waterfalls grew to such magnitude that it deafened the ears and numbed the brain.

The boulder behind Lupe's home divided the waters that came down the steep slope, keeping it away from their lean-to, and sent it down the rock-laid pathways toward the plaza. There it formed small rivers, shooting through the village toward the creek below, which had swollen and overflowed into a mighty torrent of white water as it roared out of the box canyon, all the way to the Rio Urique six miles below.

The Colonel's young soldiers got restless, not being able to work on the new road through the jungle, and so two of them, who were from the lowlands and didn't know the way of the mountains, got on their horses and tried to cross the creek. They were young, spirited men, and they thought that no little creek could stop them and their great horses of the Revolution. They whipped their frightened mounts into the creek, yelling defiantly, and the gushing waters took them off the embankment of great ferns like toy soldiers and sent them cascading with their horses down through the boulders and roaring white water.

One horse managed to climb up on the side of the creek farther downstream, but the other poor animal went kicking and whinnying with his rider over the series of short waterfalls below the town, and then off the mighty three-hundred-foot waterfall at the end of the box canyon. Neither the bodies of the two young men were ever found, nor the body of the horse.

The rainy season abated, raining only two or three hours every afternoon, and the canyon filled with new green growth. Then it was time for school to start. Lupe became very apprehensive. The schoolhouse was inside the American enfencement and Lupe had never been away from home before, much less inside the American compound. That evening, Colonel Maytorena noticed that Lupe was very quiet, so he called her to his lap after they'd eaten.

"What is it, *querida*?" he said to Lupe, bouncing her on his knee. "You have nothing to worry about. I won't be going out for several days."

"It's not that," said Lupe. "It's that school is about to begin . . . and, well, when my sisters went they used to go together, and I'll be going all alone."

He laughed. "But, my love, the schoolhouse is just across the canyon."

Lupe tensed, realizing that he didn't understand. Across the canyon was as far away as the moon to her. Why, she'd never been away from her mother or sisters before. This was, indeed, one of the most frightening moments of her entire life.

"Listen, *querida*, I'll tell you a story," said the great man, and he held Lupe to his chest, and he told her of having grown up in a large white house on a hill, surrounded by patios and tall palm trees and sisters and brothers and many servants.

Lupe closed her eyes, listening in rapture as she felt the buttons of his shirt press against her ear and felt his chest go up and down.

"And I remember well the first day I had to go to school and my mother had the coachman take me in our great carriage drawn by two grey horses and how I wanted to cry when he left me there. Oh, I was so frightened, looking at the nuns dressed in black, that I broke from the classroom, climbed over the fence and ran home so fast that I beat our coachman to the gates."

"Really? You did that?" asked Lupe, sitting up attentively.

"Oh, yes," he said, laughing, "and when my mother took me back there, I ran home again. It wasn't until my mother threatened to tell my father that I finally stayed at school. So you see, *querida*, going to school isn't just a frightening experience for you. It's going to be the same for most of the new children, too."

"But I've never been inside the American place before, and the noise from the crushing plant sounds like the devil himself."

"Look, *querida*," said her Colonel, "do you still have the card I gave you?"

"Yes," she said.

"Good," he said. "Because I'm going to ask you to be very brave and do a very big favor for me. Will you do it?"

"Yes, of course," she said, her heart pounding with anticipation.

"Well, I'll be going out again in a few days and, while I'm gone, I want you to be very brave. Very brave. And on your first day of school I want you to take my card to your teacher and ask her to teach you how to read it. Please, this is important. For if you are brave and true, then the other new children will take heart from you and all will go well. Will you do this?"

Lupe could feel her little heart pounding. She was so frightened. But finally, she nodded yes.

The morning that school was to begin, Lupe was as frightened as a hen who'd just found the scent of the coyote near her nest. Her Colonel was gone, and she really didn't want to go to school, but she'd promised her truelove that she would, so she had to do it.

Milking the goats and doing her chores, Lupe quickly helped feed the miners, and then she brushed her hair again and again, trying to look her very best.

The sun was a full three fists off the distant horizon when Doña Guadalupe walked her youngest daughter out to the front of the *ramada* to go to school. Lupe was wearing her new flour-sack dress that Sophia had embroidered with red and pink flowers around the collar and over her heart.

"Here," said Doña Guadalupe, handing her daughter a little basket full of flowers that she'd picked from her potted plants, "take these to your teacher, Señora Muñoz, and remember, *mi hijita*, wherever you go in life, flowers aren't just beautiful; they also have thorns to protect themselves. So always be proud, my love, and strong like a well-thorned flower."

"Oh, Mama," said Lupe, beginning to cry.

"None of that; Doña Manza's daughters are waiting for you. Now go with God, *mi hijita*."

They kissed and Lupe turned and started down the pathway, stopping to turn and wave to her mother several times before she disappeared.

Arriving at Doña Manza's house, Lupe saw that Cuca and Uva were ready and their older sister Manuelita was telling their mother goodbye. Lupe could see that all three girls wore dresses made from material that had been purchased at the store.

Walking down to the plaza, Lupe and the three girls were met by Don

Manuel's youngest daughter, Rose-Mary, and a half a dozen other children. Lupe couldn't imagine why, but she thought that Don Manuel's finely dressed daughter gave her a nasty look. But then Lupe quickly forgot about it as they all went out of the plaza, on the path down to the creek, and they started jumping from rock to rock alongside the rapidly running water. The children laughed, and Lupe joined their laughter, truly enjoying herself so much that she forgot all about her shyness.

But then, getting to the steep path which twisted up through boulders alongside the chalk-like molds of waste from the mine, all the children had formed a single file when Rose-Mary bumped Lupe, almost knocking her into the molten waste. Now Lupe fully realized that Don Manuel's daughter was, indeed, angry with her, but she had no idea why. Continuing up the pathway, Lupe was careful to stay away from Rose-Mary.

Then, high up on the slope, Lupe glanced down the steep hillside and her heart stopped. Below them the whole village was bathed in bright golden sunlight. It looked so toy-like that Lupe didn't recognize it. And the part of the village where she lived looked almost nonexistent, as it lay hidden among the big boulders and huge oak trees. In fact, she couldn't even see her home; it was so well hidden by the wild peach tree that grew beside their boulder.

"Hurry," said Manuelita. "We have to walk through the gates all together and go straight to the schoolhouse. The Americans don't want us being around the gates."

Quickly, Lupe followed the older girl and her sisters. And once inside, Lupe could see why the Americans didn't want them staying by the gates; wagons and mules were going every which way. The whole place was a beehive of activity. Up ahead, Cuca took Lupe's hand as they walked behind Manuelita and Uva across a huge barren field. It was also Cuca's first day of school, so she, too, was frightened.

Going across the open granite compound, Lupe saw the six American buildings. They looked long and dark and huge. She also noticed that they had no trees or flowers around them. And armed men walked back and forth on their terraces.

Straight ahead was the crushing plant, making a terrible rumble, and from the plant Lupe could see the cables that carried the iron boxes down from the mouth of the dark mine high above them. Two men and a team of mules came rushing by them in a hurry. One of the men was shouting orders in a hard, sharp-sounding language that Lupe had never before heard.

Staying close to Manuelita and the other girls, Lupe passed by many tall Americans. Some were almost as tall as her Colonel. Lupe recognized one American. He was the young, handsome engineer named Señor Scott who was engaged to Maria's best friend, Carmen. Many of the girls from La Lluvia had married Americans over the years. But it didn't always turn out well. Most of the Americans gave children to these girls but then they didn't take their Mexican families back home with them when they left the country. There were many brokenhearted, abandoned young women with fair-haired children in La Lluvia because of this. Lupe and her sisters were always told to keep away from the Americans; they were as bad as the *Gachupines*, meaning the Spaniards.

Up ahead, Lupe could see that they were approaching a little white building with a soft yellow palm roof that sat all alone on the edge of a little knoll. There was an open field in front of the little building where children were playing ball. Some of the children were pure Tarahumara Indians, possibly descendants of the great legendary Espirito. Lupe had never imagined that there was so much open ground up here inside the American enfencement. Why, it was a whole city in itself with fields and corrals for their livestock.

Approaching the little building, Lupe saw a tall American woman and her lovely daughter. They both had long golden hair and they were speaking to a pretty, dark, slender Mexican woman.

"That's our teacher, Señora Muñoz," said Manuelita, excitedly to Lupe. "And that's Señora Jones, the wife of the man who runs the mine. And that's her daughter, Katie, who also goes to our school part of the year." Manuelita was very proud, telling them what she knew. "Come and I'll introduce you! Señora Jones likes me! She's always lending me books in both English and Spanish!"

Hearing that she was going to be introduced to this American woman, Lupe became frightened. She'd never met an American before. Quickly, she closed her eyes, asking God to please help her not get impregnated. But then remembering her Colonel's card, she opened her eyes, trying to be brave.

"Excuse me, Señora Jones and Señora Muñoz," said Manuelita, "but my sister Uva and I would like you and Katie to meet our sister Cuca and our friend Lupe."

The two women turned to look at Manuelita and the three younger girls. And Lupe was just going to hand them the flowers that her mother had sent and show them her Colonel's card when Rose-Mary rushed in, pushing Lupe aside.

"Look at my new dress," said Rose-Mary. "My mother had it made especially for me!"

The two women looked at Rose-Mary's dress and watched her whirl around for them. Then the bell rang for school to start. Rose-Mary took Katie's hand and they were off together. Lupe hid the Colonel's card behind the flowers. She felt too embarrassed to try to give it to her teacher now.

"Well, excuse me," said Señora Muñoz, turning back to the American woman, "but I have to go inside."

"It was nice visiting with you, Esperanza," said Señora Jones in Spanish. "And I'll send down those new supplies I told you about as soon as they arrive."

"Thank you," said Señora Muñoz, also in Spanish, "that will be wonderful."

Then the bell rang again and all the children stopped playing and hurried inside the little palm-roof building.

Following Manuelita and her sisters inside, Lupe saw that the schoolhouse was a large, long room with long, child-size tables and benches. A large desk with two chairs was up at the front of the room. Lupe wondered if her father had helped build the furniture; after all, he was a finish carpenter.

She glanced around and saw that the walls of the room were made of sticks and mud and were painted white. They weren't weathered and brown like the walls of her home. There was a huge earthen water pot in the back corner resting in the fork of a big oak tree branch for water. Lupe loved the clay pot; it looked so peaceful.

Gently, Manuelita ushered Lupe and Cuca toward the front of the room. Lupe noticed that most of the boys, who were all young like herself, remained near the rear. They reminded her of rebellious male calves refusing to follow their mother on a path around the mountain.

Lupe knew one of the boys. His name was Jimmy. His father was one of the American engineers who'd married a local girl and then abandoned them. Lupe nodded to Jimmy as she went down the aisle. Jimmy smiled at her. He had large blue eyes, dark hair, and was extremely good-looking. He lived up the *barranca* from them and his home was even smaller and poorer than theirs.

"Lupe, you sit here with Cuca," said Manuelita. "And you help them, Uva. I have to sit up there, in front, with Señora Muñoz to help her with the lessons."

Lupe pursed her lips together, shuffling her feet, but she said nothing. She sat down, doing as she'd been told, but she didn't like it. She gripped Cuca's hand under the table. Cuca gripped her back. She, too, was scared. Katie and Rose-Mary came down the center aisle, laughing happily, and sat down directly in front of Lupe and Cuca. They were by far the two best-dressed girls in the school. Lupe was glad that she had worn her new dress.

Then Señora Muñoz came to the front of the classroom and got behind her desk made of fine, white pine. She said good morning to Manuelita, who stood alongside her, then she turned to the class.

"My name is Señora Muñoz," she said, smiling kindly. "I'm your teacher and we'll be working together." As she spoke, she waved her hands about so elegantly, like birds in flight. Lupe was enthralled; all her fears went out of her. Señora Muñoz was like her Colonel: a person who'd come into her life and touched her.

And so everything was going very well until each student had to stand up and introduce himself. Suddenly, Lupe's heart wanted to hide.

"And we'll start with the first row," said Señora Muñoz. "So, please, don't be shy and, if you're new and get a little bit nervous, please don't worry about it. Someone who knows you will be glad to assist you."

Lupe could have died. She was in the second row. And so, there it came, and Katie got up first and she was tall and confident and poised.

"My name is Katie Jones," she said. "I live with my father and mother in the last building up the hill. My father is Mr. Jones and he manages the gold mine. My mother's name is Katherine and she was a school teacher in San Francisco, California, where we have our permanent home on Nob Hill, overlooking the Bay. I'm ten years old, and this is my second year here in La Lluvia de Oro. But I'll only be here for part of the year. My mother and I have to return to San Francisco for the Christmas holidays. Thank you very much. I'm sure we'll have another fine school year together."

Everyone applauded, saying hello to Katie. She sat down and Rose-Mary stood up. Rose-Mary looked confident, too, but there was something different about her.

"My name is Rose-Mary Chavez," said Don Manuel's youngest daughter, glancing around with a smile, "and my father is the accountant at the mine. He makes the payroll and sees to it that all your fathers, who are lucky enough to work at the American mine, are paid. I live in the largest house down in the main plaza next to the market, which, of course, you all know, my father also owns. We have the only home in all the village that has tile in every room of our house. I, too, will not be here for the entire school year; I'll be going with Katie to do the Christmas holidays in San Francisco, where I stayed with Katie and her family last summer to learn English, which, I might add, I speak without accent, just as my two older sisters do. Thank you."

And saying this, she sat down, too, and everyone applauded again. Then it was Uva's turn and next it would be Cuca's, then it would be Lupe's and she was so scared that she wasn't even able to hear what Uva or Cuca said about themselves. Then it was Lupe's turn, but she couldn't even move, much less say anything.

"It's all right," said Señora Muñoz, seeing the young girl's difficulty, "just take your time. Everything is fine."

Lupe sat there staring at the floor, beginning to tremble, she was so frightened.

"Well, then," said Señora Muñoz, "would anyone like to help her?"

"Yes," said Rose-Mary, quickly getting to her feet, "I'll do it! Her name is Lupe Gomez. She's Carlota Gomez's sister, and they live so high up on the hill that they don't have a real home. They live in a shack and they make their living by feeding miners and taking in their laundry, because they have no father and they're so poor."

The shock, the rage, the anger that came bursting into Lupe's heart when she heard these awful lies brought her to her feet before she realized that she'd even moved. "No!" she screamed. "That's not true!" She was trembling with fear, but she didn't care. "I do have a father! And we do have a real home!" Her heart was going wild. "Rose-Mary is wrong," she said, tears coming to her eyes. "My name is Guadalupe Gomez Camargo, and my father's name is Don Victor, and he's a fine carpenter. In fact, he probably built these tables and benches that we're sitting on. But when the American buildings were finished, there was no more work for him, so he went down to the lowlands looking for work. And yes, we are poor and we do feed the miners and take in their laundry, but our home was built by my father for us with his own two hands, and we have a roof that's good to keep the rain out and walls that block the wind.

"My mother is a fine cook and everyone respects her and she keeps potted flowers in front of our *ramada* and . . . and . . . she leads us in prayer three times a day, and that's what makes a home!" And saying this, Lupe burst into tears, got out over her bench, and took off running down the aisle between the long tables and benches.

Jimmy clapped and whistled. "There, Rose-Mary," he shouted, "start trouble, and you get the goat's horn!"

"Jimmy," said Señora Muñoz, "you stop that! And Rose-Mary, I'm ashamed of you. You'll stay after school!"

"But, why? I only told the truth. That's what my father told us!"

"That's quite enough, Rose-Mary," said their teacher.

"But I did nothing wrong," she pleaded. "I'll tell my father," she added angrily.

"Fine," said the teacher patiently, "but you'll still stay. Now, no more."

Outside, Manuelita caught Lupe before she ran out of the main gates.

"Lupe," said Manuelita, "you did wonderfully! I'm so proud of you. You put that nasty, jealous Rose-Mary in her place and yet you behaved like a perfect lady."

"Jealous," said Lupe. "Rose-Mary? Of me?"

"Of course," said Manuelita. "Ever since the Colonel has been living with your family, the mayor and his family have been green with envy!"

"I'll be," said Lupe. "I didn't know."

Lupe dried her eyes and Manuelita took her in her arms. And there it began; a friendship, a new kind of love. So Lupe relaxed, let herself go, and she cried on the older girl's shoulder until she felt good and clean inside.

The rainy season was almost over. Colonel Maytorena had completed his road through the jungle, and they were now ready to take out the first shipment of gold. The whole pueblo hissed with excitement. And Lupe asked to stay home from school that day so she could watch her truelove go out of the canyon.

"*Mi hijita*," said her Colonel early that morning, "I'd like to speak to you privately and ask you for another favor."

"Yes, my Colonel," said Lupe. And she was so excited. Maybe he was going to ask her to go with him and tell her that he would marry her when she grew up.

"*Mi hijita*," he said, kneeling down on one knee before her. "I'll be gone two weeks this time, if I'm lucky. But if I have to accompany the shipment to the Arizona border, then I'll be gone maybe a month. So I want to ask a special favor of you."

Her heart swelled, and her large dark eyes danced. "Anything," she said.

"Good," he said, "because what I'm going to ask you is very close to my heart."

"Ask me," she said.

"Well, what I want is for you to take care of Socorro. She's going to have our child any day now, and she'll need a close friend."

Lupe felt her heart explode. Why, she loved this man, and this was all he'd wished to ask of her?

"Well, will you?" he asked again.

She nodded, saying yes, not knowing what else to do.

"Good," he said, smiling, showing his fine, white teeth. He kissed her on the forehead and drew her near. Quickly, she cuddled into him with all her body, clinging to him, wishing he didn't have to go, that he'd stay and hold her like this forever and ever.

"All right, *querida*," said her Colonel, "I must go now, and I want you to know how proud I am of you for doing so well in school. For, without education, a person can't go very far in life. This is what the whole war is about: the uplifting of our people. I love you and hope my children are even half as beautiful as you, my angel."

Then he kissed her again, and he was gone. A soldier was holding his orange-red stallion for him up the pathway by the wild peach tree. Lupe watched him mount. He wore a long sword on one hip and a pistol on the other. Then he turned and looked over her shoulder. Suddenly Lupe realized that they weren't alone. His wife had come rushing out of the lean-to and there came her mother and sisters, too.

Quickly, Socorro rushed up to him. "But how could you leave without telling me goodbye?"

"I didn't want to wake you, my love."

"My love?" repeated Lupe.

"Come," said Doña Guadalupe to Lupe, "we have things to do."

"But, Mama, I can't go right now!"

"Lupe," said her mother, coming up as quickly as a snake and gripping her daughter by the left ear, "I said now." And she twisted Lupe's ear and took her away before anyone noticed what had happened.

The sun was two fists off the horizon when the first little mule came out of the American enfencement. The Colonel followed behind the frisky little mule on his glistening orange-red stallion. Then came the next little mule, and the next; they all looked ready to go, having rested the long rainy season.

Lupe and her family stood in front of their *ramada* along with Socorro, their necks straining as they looked up the steep canyon wall, watching the mules, one by one, come out of the big wire gates.

Lupe's Colonel was now in the lead with two of his officers, climbing up the twisting steep trail over the northern wall of the canyon which he had built. Each mule had a sixty-pound bar of pure gold strapped on each side of its pack, and the gold bars reflected like glistening jewels in the early morning sunlight.

Maria and Carlota counted the mules; there were thirty-five in all. But still, it was said that not all the gold had been taken out. So as soon as the Colonel delivered this shipment, he'd be right back with his men to take out another shipment. The Americans had so much gold stored in their concrete hole that it made them very nervous with the Revolution going on and Francisco Villa still at large.

The little dark mules came out of the gates, zigzagging up the trail like a long, dark centipede. The mule train cut back and forth up the steep wall of the canyon, going through the trees and boulders with the bars of gold shining bright white on their backs. It took a full hour for the centipede of mules to spiral up to the white pines near the rim of the canyon.

Lupe's family and the entire village watched until the backs of their necks hurt; then they went back to work. But Lupe and Socorro never moved, standing there, rooted to the ground as they watched the man they both loved going up the canyon wall at the head of the long pack train, his horse glistening orange-red like the rising sun.

"Lupita, please," said Socorro after an hour, "could you bring me a chair? This baby is just too heavy."

Lupe didn't want to leave her post. She wanted to stay and watch after her truelove. But then she remembered the promise she'd made, so she ran into the *ramada* and brought Socorro a chair and helped her to sit down.

Her Colonel was now up into the white pines where only the eagles flew, and any moment he'd disappear over the rim of the canyon. Lupe felt like her little heart would burst. Socorro had tears in her eyes. The man that they both loved was now no more than a tiny dot on the horizon as the mule train made its way out of the canyon, zigzagging back and forth with the bars of flickering gold. The mules were making their way over the break to the right of the cathedral rocks, the very same break where the meteorite had hit the earth the night Lupe's parents had made desperate love, thinking it was the end of the world, and she'd been conceived. The mule train was now drawing close to the second waterfall. Lupe just knew that the mules were getting wet and shiny.

Not once did Lupe or Socorro stop watching as the line of little mules went over the break. Then the Colonel was gone. And the rest of the long centipede followed him, the mules so far away that each looked like no more than a tiny dark dot as they went over the canyon rim.

Then they were all gone. Lupe and Socorro gripped their breasts, ready to burst out crying when, suddenly, they saw a dazzling beam of orange-red light come racing back over the rim and instantly they both knew that this was their Colonel! And there he was, mounted on his great sorrel stallion, waving down at them with his light-catching sword, just to the right of the roaring waterfall.

Lupe screamed; she couldn't help it.

Socorro did, too. And they both waved back at him, but there was no way for him to see them.

"Lupe!" cried Socorro. "Quickly! Run in and get my big, new white bedspread so we can wave it!"

Running in, Lupe picked up the bedspread and hurried back out. Together they waved the big, handwoven cloth, and he saw them. He reared up his stallion, waving at them again, and then he was off, going over the rim of the box canyon, through the break made by a falling star.

Every day was a lifetime for Lupe with her truelove gone. By the fourth day, she was at her world's end. Coming home from school one afternoon, Socorro saw Lupe's long face and she took pity on her.

"Lupe," she said, "please come in here." She patted the bed next to her. "I have something to show you."

Lupe came into her room and sat down on the bed. Socorro brought out a small box made of dark wood and shiny metal. She opened it. It was full of beautiful pictures of her husband and herself and of their days in Mazatlan when they'd first met.

"Oh, my God!" said Lupe, taking a picture and looking at her Colonel standing with his wife by the seashore. "This is wonderful!"

Socorro saw the young girl's joy and her heart was moved. They spent the afternoon like schoolgirls, looking at the pictures and talking together.

That night, Lupe slept well for the first time since her truelove had left. And in the morning when she awoke, she decided that some day she, too, would have a little secret box of her own so she could keep all her treasures, including her Colonel's card. Oh, how she just loved running her fingertips over her Colonel's name, letter by letter, feeling so close to him.

It had been two weeks since her Colonel had left. Lupe asked her mother if she could go up to the high country above their canyon.

"I think my Colonel might be coming back today. I'd like to meet him," she said.

Doña Guadalupe saw her daughter's eyes and felt sorry for her. "All right," she said, "but you better take Victoriano's dog with you and be careful. A jaguar was seen up there several days ago."

"I will," said Lupe.

Lupe packed some peaches and a tortilla with fresh goat's cheese and started up the pathway from the house with her brother's little brown dog. Mounting the main road above their home, Lupe followed the road around the canyon above the village toward the American enfencement. Then she turned left off the road and took the new zigzagging trail that her Colonel had built. She climbed fast and steady through the oaks and boulders, and her legs never cramped. Like all the children of the village, walking and climbing were such a large part of her life that she could carry a large load of laundry or wood up and down steep trails without tiring.

Within an hour, Lupe came to the short new pines that had grown after the white pine forest had been burnt by the meteorite. The sound of the waterfalls was devastating. Carefully, Lupe continued through the young white pines and went out through the loose rock break on the north rim of the canyon. Her legs were so strong and her heart was so full of love that she'd climbed out of the canyon as fast as a quick-footed little mule.

Suddenly, passing through the break, the whole world opened up. She was above the mountain peaks and flat mesas piled up for hundreds of miles in every direction. There was beauty to the left, beauty to the right. Beauty surrounded Lupe. This was the high country of northwest Mexico, unmapped and uncharted. Some fingers of the canyon of La Barranca del Cobre ran deeper than the Grand Canyon of Arizona.

Following one of the little waterways, Lupe crossed the meadows of tightly woven wildflowers of blue and yellow and red and pink. It was quiet up here without the waterfall's terrible roar. Her brother's little dog flushed out deer and mountain quail as they went along.

Crossing a tiny creek, Lupe saw the fresh tracks in the cold mud of the terrible jaguar. The little dog's hair came up on his back. Lupe petted him, looking around carefully, but saw nothing. Jaguars, after all, were fairly common, and so people were more respectful than afraid of them, just as they were of any other natural force.

Up ahead, by a scattering of yellow and pink wildflowers, Lupe found a small formation of rock piled up like a stack of tortillas with a twisted little pine tree on top of it. The little high country pine tree was no more than eight feet tall, fully grown, and Lupe could see where its roots had split the rock, looking for soil. These high country pines were entirely different from the big, tall, handsome white-pine trees that grew on the uppermost sides of their protected canyon.

Climbing the formation of the tortilla rocks, Lupe took hold of a strong lower branch of the twisted little pine and pulled herself into the sturdy little tree. From up here, she could look to the west and see the shorter mountains stepping down into the jungles of the lowlands and then, way over there in the distance, a flat shiny mist which she had been told was the Sea of Cortez. Oh, she'd hoped so much to see her truelove riding across the high country, leading his men, mounted on his great stallion of glistening orange-red fire. But no matter how much she searched, she saw no one.

She leaned back against the trunk of the little tree. She saw an eagle circling in the distance, sweeping down across the wind-worn smooth rock and clearings of dazzling bright wildflowers. She brought out the card that her Colonel had given her and read it aloud, "Colonel Manuel Maytorena," as she ran her fingertips over the large dark letters. Tears came to her eyes.

She listened to the wind, the father of the high country, whistling, singing, talking to the rocks and flowers and little scattered trees.

Wiping the tears from her eyes, Lupe brought out her lunch and began to eat. She breathed deeply. "Dear God," she said in a soft, gentle voice, "I need Your help. My truelove, Colonel Maytorena, is in danger. I just know it. So I want You to please take care of him and bring him back to me safely.

"I ask You in the name of the Virgin Mary and Our Lady of Guadalupe. After all, dear God, remember that it was You who made my perfect love for me up in heaven, so please protect him for me." Saying this, Lupe looked out on the beautiful country, feeling so close to the Almighty.

Going down, Lupe's heart felt heavy and her body tired quickly. The hope of seeing her truelove had propelled her up the steep mountain with power. But coming back down, she felt so sad of heart that she tripped and fell several times.

Lupe and the little dog were just entering the new white pines when the dog stopped. Lupe turned and saw that the little brown dog was looking nervously toward the waterfall. Here, the water was falling through space in silent sheets of glistening white spray before it crashed with thundering sound into the rock pool far below. She quickly remembered the jaguar's tracks that she'd seen earlier.

"What is it?" she asked, petting the little dog. He turned and looked at her and then took off, cutting across the rock, through the pine trees, toward the falling water.

Lupe didn't know what to do, but she decided that it was best to stay near her brother's dog in case the jaguar was, indeed, nearby. Running through the rock and pines, Lupe caught glimpses of the little dog racing off in front of her as he dodged through the trees and rocks. But then he disappeared and Lupe stopped and glanced around, suddenly feeling that she was in grave danger. She began to hiccup, moving cautiously toward the place where she'd last seen the dog.

The roar of the waterfall was tremendous. It was just a few hundred feet beyond her, crashing into the pool below.

Reaching the first oak tree, Lupe put her hand on the tree trunk as she came around it, little by little, holding onto the oak's rough bark. Suddenly, she gasped, gripping her chest, because there below her, in a deep break to the left of the waterfall, she saw Old Man Benito and her brother Victoriano. They were helping her mother over a boulder, pointing to something not far from the pool below the falling water. Swallowing her hiccups, Lupe wondered what her mother was doing up here. But then, suddenly, she knew everything. Her brother and Don Benito had found gold; that was what they'd been whispering about with her mother for several months now.

Then the little brown dog came out above them, and Lupe barely had time to get back behind the oak tree before her brother glanced up the hillside. Closing her eyes, Lupe hugged the oak tree's huge trunk. Then, quickly, carefully, she started to back around the tree so they wouldn't see her.

Suddenly she felt a dark presence behind her. She turned and there was Don Benito's huge black dog on a rock, growling as he crouched to leap on her. She screamed. The black dog had a terrible reputation. His teeth were bared and his eyes were bloodshot with hate. But then a stick came whirling down on the dog. "No, Lobo!" yelled Victoriano, leaping from behind a tree. "Damn it, Lupe! What are you doing here?" he shouted above the waterfall's roar.

Lupe had never heard her brother curse at her before.

"You are alone?" he snapped.

"Yes," she nodded.

"All right, then, come on," he said, putting down his machete and giving her his hand.

Lupe took his hand and quickly followed him. And what Lupe saw next, she could never have imagined even in her wildest dreams. Why, there was her mother and Don Benito, just this side of the crashing water, standing in a pocket of gold the size of a room, glistening bright-wet in the soft sunlight coming in through the misty spray from the thundering water.

"But when did you find this?" shouted Lupe above the noisy waterfall. "You never told me!"

"So you could tell your Colonel and have him steal it from us?" yelled Victoriano.

"*Cálmate,*" said their mother loudly. "Lupe's no child! She can understand our situation!"

The waterfall was no more than two hundred feet away, and they were getting soaked in a fine, cool mist.

"But, Mama, you've seen how she is when he's around!" continued Victoriano. Lupe had never seen her brother so upset with her. "She'll never be able to keep anything from her thieving Colonel!"

"But, Victoriano," said Lupe, "why are you talking like this? My Colonel isn't a thief!"

"You're right," said Old Man Benito, getting close to Lupe so he wouldn't have to shout. "He's a fine man, *querida*. But understand this: he needs guns to continue his useless war against Villa, so he'll take our gold away from us in the name of the Revolution if he finds out about it!"

Lupe looked from Don Benito to her brother and her mother, and she felt her heart wanting to break. Why, they all hated her Colonel, and he was the finest man God had ever created. Her eyes filled with tears.

Doña Guadalupe motioned both men away so she could be alone with her daughter. The two men climbed out of the pocket.

"Come here," said Doña Guadalupe, taking her daughter in her arms as they sat down on a wall of gold.

"Oh, Mama," said Lupe, "they just hate my Colonel and he's been so good to everyone."

"No, they don't hate him, *mi hijita*," said her mother. "It's just that your brother and Don Benito have been searching for gold for so long that they're very frightened. Look around, *mi hijita*, and understand that they've found a fortune and so they have every right to be nervous, especially after Don Benito lost his last mine to the *americanos*."

She stroked her daughter's long, rich hair. It was shiny-wet from the spray. "What Don Benito said is true, *mi hijita*, your Colonel can't be trusted. He's a fine man, but as sure as God lives in the heavens, he'll take our gold away from us and give it to the Americans for guns and supplies if he finds out about it." She took a big breath; she could feel her daughter's little heart pounding wildly.

Lupe didn't know what to think. She just didn't want to believe that what her mother was saying was true.

"Oh, no, Mama, you're wrong!" she said. "Over and over my Colonel has told me that he's fighting this Revolution for us, the people of Mexico, and so he'd never steal our mine away from us and give it to the *americanos*, Mama."

"Lupe," said Doña Guadalupe, "listen to me. I know how you love this man and you think the heavens revolve around him. And I don't blame you, because your father left when you were very little. But, *mi hijita*, you're six, so it's time for you to see this short dream we live here on earth as a woman. And a woman, above all else," she said, "must keep both of her eyes open when it comes to matters of the heart or she will come to ruin. No man, no matter how wonderful, is to be put before a woman's first loyalty, which is her family."

She gripped Lupe, holding her at arm's length. "Do you understand?" she asked.

Lupe shook her head. "No, Mama. I'd always thought that true love came first."

"Oh, *mi hijita*," said her mother, "you've just been listening to too many stories of princes from your sisters. True love might be blessed by heaven but, believe me, it's not made there. And besides, this Colonel isn't part of our family. He'll be gone as soon as his job is done here. So understand, you're not a child, and you must see that your first loyalty is to your brother and sisters and me—*la familia*."

Lupe nodded, eyes brimming with tears. "Yes, I understand. But when I marry, won't my husband be a part of our family and then my loyalty will be for him?" she asked, feeling so confused.

"I hope so," said the old woman, taking a deep breath. "But unfortunately, as a woman with both eyes open, you can't depend on that either."

Hearing this, Lupe's whole world was shattered. All her life, she'd heard her sisters reading books of love and romance. She'd always assumed that one's family revolved around the man you married and that each marriage had been blessed by God, Himself, in heaven.

Lupe squeezed her mother close, burying her face into her warm, good body. She cried and cried. Her brother and Old Man Benito came back and saw her sorrow. Victoriano picked up a stick and broke it with his hands. Oh, how he'd hated the day the Colonel had come to live with them. Who did he think he was, anyway, talking to them so wonderfully each night? He wasn't their father.

Don Benito saw Victoriano's anger, but he said nothing. Bringing out his paper and tobacco, he rolled a cigarette and sat back, lighting it up. He smoked and stroked his dog's thick mane with his callused bare feet. Don Benito was half Tarahumara Indian. The big toe of each foot was huge, powerful and separated from the rest of his toes like the thumb from the fingers. His big toes had become so big from going barefoot through the rock so that they could grip the earth like the split hoof of a deer.

"All right, *mi hijita,*" said Doña Guadalupe, "no more. You've cried and I've held you; now you must put away the things of a child. You're almost seven, a responsible human being, and so I know that you can keep our secret.

"Now come, Don Benito and Victoriano," she added, "and let us all pray together for guidance, giving thanks for this miracle of gold that God has given to us."

They all knelt down on the smooth rock at the bottom of the pocket of gold and began to pray. The sunlight played in and out of the treetops, giving colors of red and orange and yellow to the stone all around them.

Selecting a few gold nuggets, Doña Guadalupe put them in her leather pouch and started down the steep slope with Lupe. Don Benito and Victoriano stayed behind to cut down trees and hide their find.

3

*And so Saint Peter closed the flood gates of heaven and
the rainy season ended and everywhere the birds and
the bees and the wildflowers began to make the
courtship of love.*

For the next two days Don Benito and Victoriano
hammered the rich ore that they'd brought out, then they gave it to Doña
Guadalupe for her and her daughters to grind in their dark stone *metates*
until it was as fine as sand. They didn't want anyone to see the raw ore. They
wanted the gold to look like they'd found it in one of the streams below the
town.

"Well," said Doña Guadalupe after the miners had eaten and gone to
work, "I think it looks good. What do you think?" she asked Don Benito.

Inspecting their little pile of ground-up gold, Don Benito nodded. "It
looks as fine as if we'd just panned it from a stream," he said, smiling
grandly. "So let's go sell it!"

And so he and Victoriano took the gold down to Don Manuel's store in a
soft deerskin pouch.

"So you found a little color," said Don Manuel, putting the pile on the
scale.

"Yes," said Don Benito, "we got a little lucky. You know how it is after
the rains."

"Oh, yes," said the mayor, "all the Indians get rich in the area for a few
months. I hope your luck lasts a little longer."

"I think it will," said the old man, winking at Victoriano.

The mayor paid them for the gold, asking no questions, and Don Benito
and Victoriano rushed back up the hill with the money. Victoriano could
hardly keep from shouting to the heavens. It was over a hundred pesos, and
half was for their family.

Lupe had never seen her brother filled with such pride as when Don
Benito handed their mother the money.

"*Dios mío*," said their mother, "why this is more money than we could
save in five years with our little restaurant."

Tears came to her eyes, she was so happy. The whole family joined her, crying, too. But they had to keep their voices down so Socorro, who was asleep in the next room, wouldn't overhear them.

"And this is for you, *mi hijito*," said their mother, handing Victoriano some money.

"But it's five pesos!" shouted Victoriano, forgetting himself and talking too loudly.

"Shhhhh!" said Doña Guadalupe, pointing toward the next room with her chin. "Go on, it's for you. Buy a new hat or whatever you want," she whispered.

"Really?" said Victoriano. He'd never had any money before in all his life. And five pesos was a fortune. It was more than Flaco or Manos, who were big shots at the mine, made in a whole week.

"But, Mama," Victoriano said, "I don't need this much."

"Of course you don't," she said, "but take it anyway."

His eyes shone like stars, he was so excited. "All right," he said, "I'll do it! And I'll get myself my first professional haircut!" Saying this, he kissed his old mother and then took off, catching up with Don Benito who'd already started down the hill to go to town to get a scented bath.

That evening when Victoriano and Don Benito came under the *ramada* to eat, Lupe didn't recognize them at first. They'd both gotten their hair cut short and they were wearing big new hats, brightly colored shirts, and new white pants. Why, they looked like men on their way to a great celebration.

"So you two struck gold, eh?" said one of the young miners, grinning sarcastically at them.

Don Benito only shook his head, sitting down to eat. "No, not really," he said. "But we did find a little color in the creek below the town."

"How much?" asked another young miner.

"Hell, it couldn't be very much," said a third young miner, "or else he'd be down at the plaza buying music and drinks for everyone like he did last time. Eh, old man, you kept the music going for six months, I've been told."

"Almost a year," said Don Benito. "But I'll tell you this, if I ever strike it big again, I won't be buying music for fools like you this time." A hissing rumble went through the *ramada*. "No, this time I'll just be right here like I am right now, eating under the *ramada* of this fine family that has never lost faith in me and has fed me free of charge for over a year.

"This family is my partner and one day soon, I swear it, I'll strike it big while you boys can only hope to keep digging gold you don't even own."

Manos roared with laughter. "Well, look who got the horn for a change," he said, as he dug into his food. "You young ones play with old bulls long enough and you'll get the horn every time!"

"You're damned right," said Flaco, glancing around and then sneaking a drink from the tequila bottle that he kept hidden under the table. "Here," he said, passing the bottle to Don Benito, "take a belt!" shaking an upright fist.

"By all means," said Don Benito, accepting the bottle. But he, too, glanced around before pushing back his hat and drinking. Doña Guadalupe didn't allow any alcohol in her home. That was one of the first rules that she had laid down right after her husband had left.

Then, after dinner, when all the young miners were gone, Manos and Flaco approached Don Benito and Victoriano. The old man and the boy were done eating. They were leisurely drinking a delicious cup of *atole* together, which was made with warm goat's milk, raw brown sugar and cornmeal.

"Congratulations," said Manos.

"Thank you," said Don Benito.

Victoriano tried to keep his pride intact, but it was difficult.

Leaning in close to the old man and the boy, Manos whispered, "If you two ever need any powder or tools, just tell us and we'll get them for you."

Don Benito nodded. "Thank you," he said. "But like I said, we just found a little color in the river, so we have no need of powder or tools."

Manos only grinned. "Keep saying that. But Flaco and I know that it's too early after the rains to get any gold yet."

"Old man," said Flaco, "what Manos is telling you is that the Americans are hungry now that they're getting their gold out once again, so be careful. And don't spend your money so wildly."

Don Benito put his cup of *atole* down. Victoriano could see that he was shaken. "Look," said Don Benito, "I appreciate your concern, but I assure you that my partner and I have found nothing."

"Good," said Manos, "keep saying that. But just in case you ever need a powder man, just say so. I'm getting tired of working for the gringos."

"How much do you charge?" asked Victoriano, before he could stop himself.

Manos grinned. "So it's that big, eh?" said Manos.

Don Benito said nothing. He just stared at the heavy cup in his hand: it was a pinched-together clay cup with places for the fingers to grip, instead of a handle.

Manos reached out, plucking a loose thread off Benito's new shirt. "Don't worry," he said, "it's safe with us." And saying this, he and Flaco left.

"I'm sorry," said Victoriano, once they were alone.

"It's okay," said the old man.

"I just wasn't thinking."

"I said it's okay," said Don Benito. "I only hope that your little sister can keep quiet when her Colonel returns."

Victoriano said nothing more, and Old Man Benito brought out a cigar. "The first time I found gold I couldn't keep still about it, either. Gold, I swear, robs men of their minds. Believe me, I know. There's just nothing like it to make the blood boil and the mind go crazy."

He blew out, catching his breath, then he picked up his hat. "Come on, partner, let's go take a little stroll down to the plaza, buy another cigar, and look around."

Quickly, Victoriano picked up his new hat. "Just let me run in and tell my mother that I'm going," he said.

"Of course," said Don Benito.

Inside, Victoriano found his mother with his sisters and Socorro going over the material that they'd bought to make dresses.

"Mama," he said, "can I go back down to the plaza with Don Benito?"

"Twice in one day?" said Doña Guadalupe, smiling happily. "Sure, go with God, *mi hijito.*"

Victoriano kissed his mother, then he was off. Lupe watched after her brother, feeling so glad that he wasn't angry with her anymore.

The sun was going down toward the towering cliffs when Victoriano and Don Benito came out of Don Manuel's store. Don Benito had bought another cigar and a stick of hard candy for Victoriano. Walking side by side, they crossed the plaza and said good evening to the soldiers that the Colonel had left behind. The old man smoked his cigar and the young boy sucked his stick of candy. They bought two big beautiful handwoven handkerchiefs from an Indian woman and tied them about their necks. They were men of leisure, strolling peacefully. They decided to go down by the springs below the town.

The rainy season had ended. The creek was subsiding rapidly and the foliage was growing back in profusion along the banks. The flocks of parrots had returned to the box canyon by the thousands and were nesting in the tall trees. The wildflowers were blooming in abundance, filling the canyon with fragrance. This was the time of year that the deer had their young, the birds mated, and the canyon filled with insects and butterflies by the millions. It was the season of life.

"Smell the air," said Don Benito as they went along. "I swear that the world has grown more beautiful and I've gotten twenty years younger since we struck gold. That first time I found gold I was too young to appreciate anything. I was only going on twenty and went crazy with gold fever. I couldn't stop talking. I had to tell everyone! And every night I sang to the heavens—I couldn't even sleep—I was making so many plans of buying land! *Haciendas!* Whole villages!

"Oh, I was a king, I tell you! Nothing was beyond my grasp! I was immortal!" He laughed, putting his arm around his young partner. They were now down by the small ponds below the plaza and there were hundreds of tiny frogs along the edge of the water. Victoriano watched the little frogs jumping about.

Don Benito puffed on his cigar and they continued down the pathway through the tall, thick, new foliage. It was getting late and the sun was painting the sky with colors of pink and rose and lavender above the towering walls.

Coming around a large boulder surrounded by great ferns, Don Benito suddenly saw Lydia, Don Manuel's oldest daughter. She was dressed in white lace, running down an open meadow just beyond the creek, and her long, chestnut hair was flying in the wind. She was with two other girls and they were laughing, turning, whirling, as they came down the meadow carpeted with wildflowers, chasing after an enormous swarm of butterflies, flashing orange and silver in the going sunlight.

Don Benito stood there, rooted to the ground, when the lightning bolt of God's miracle of love came down from the heavens, hitting him between the eyes.

And there she was, his queen, his truelove, whom he'd been dreaming of for as long as he could remember. And she was laughing, dancing over the meadows of flowers as she came into the cloud of butterflies with her long hair flowing, golden in the bright sunlight.

Gasping, mouth open, Don Benito watched Lydia go whirling, flying into the tapestry of butterflies, and he saw the delicate white flesh of the underside of his queen's arms.

Lunging from out of the ferns, Don Benito grasped Lydia in his arms. Startled, she looked at him, not recognizing the old man at first. But then, when she did, she yelled, struggling to get away, but he held her fast in his powerful arms, powerful from having moved rock all his life.

"He's crazy, Lydia!" screamed the girls. "Get away from the fool!"

"Crazy in love, yes!" he shouted. "But I'm no fool! I'm rich, Lydia! Marry me and I'll have slippers made of gold for you so your feet will never touch the dirt of the world again!"

"Rich?" she asked.

"Yes," he said, still holding her close, "ask your father, he'll tell you! This is our fate, and you are my queen! And we will have a house in Mexico City, another in Paris and a third one here in La Lluvia de Oro, if you wish."

Victoriano came running up, and seeing Don Benito with the mayor's oldest daughter, he dropped his candy. It was that time of year when the butterflies robbed mortal men of their senses.

"Don Benito," said Lydia, using the word "Don" as she'd never used it toward him before, "if you're lying and causing me embarrassment, I swear I'll have my father shoot you! But, if what you say is true, and you are rich, then you must present yourself to my father like a king!" And she said "king" with such authority that it echoed out over the clearing filled with butterflies and dazzling wildflowers, all the way to the towering mighty cliffs.

Victoriano turned, and ran as fast as he could.

Doña Guadalupe and her daughters had just finished the dishes and were laying out the material when Victoriano came running under the *ramada*. They could see in Victoriano's eyes that something terrible had happened.

"What is it?" asked his mother.

"Don Benito just told Lydia about our gold."

"So what?" said Carlota.

"So what?" repeated Victoriano angrily. "Don't you see? The whole town will know by tomorrow, and the Americans will come and take our gold from us!"

"Oh, Mama, Mama!" screeched Carlota. "Don't let them do it! I still need new shoes!"

Everyone burst out laughing.

"All right, *mi hijita*," said Doña Guadalupe, "I won't let the Americans take the gold before you get your shoes." Then she turned to her son. "Now go on, tell me everything, but keep your voice down. Socorro is in the next room sleeping, and I don't want us disturbing her."

The sun had just gone down behind the towering walls when Don Benito came whistling up the hill.

"Don Benito," said Victoriano, standing in one of the long dull shadows of the dimming light, "my mother wishes to speak to you."

"Why, of course," said the old man cheerfully. He was so much in love, his feet had not touched the ground.

"All right," said Doña Guadalupe when she saw her son come up with the old man, "leave us alone, Victoriano. Don Benito and I have some business to discuss alone."

Victoriano didn't like it, but he did as he was told. Going into the *ramada*, he passed by his sisters who were working on their dresses.

"What did Mama tell him?" asked Carlota.

"They're just getting started," he said, going out the backside of the lean-to.

Lupe and her sisters stopped their work and glanced at each other, then Sophia giggled with mischief and went out the back of the lean-to, following her brother. Lupe and Carlota quickly followed. Maria was the last one to quit her work and go. She was seeing a boy and she wanted to finish her dress so she could wear it on their next walk together. But her curiosity was even greater.

Outside, Lupe tried to climb up on the backside of the boulder after her two sisters, but she was too small. With one hand, Maria came up behind her and lifted Lupe up on the boulder. Quickly, Lupe crowded in close to Sophia and Carlota. Victoriano was already perched on the high point of the rounded boulder like an eagle, looking down at their mother and Don Benito. The big mother goat came to the edge of her pen, looking down on the young people on top of the rock below her.

"I tell you," Old Man Benito was saying, "your son came to me just in time. That's all I needed, a little extra muscle. And now, we're rich!"

"Please, keep your voice down," said Doña Guadalupe, smoothing the apron out on her lap.

"Oh, I'm sorry," he said.

Looking at him, Doña Guadalupe felt such an anger rising up inside her that she knew she would scream if she didn't calm herself.

"Don Benito, was it not our agreement that we would tell no one of our find?"

He stared at her. "So Victoriano told you, eh?"

"He's my son; it was his duty."

Quickly, the old man got to his feet. "Look," he said, "I'm a man, and I know what I do!"

She took a big breath. "No one said you aren't," said Doña Guadalupe. "But we are partners, and we do have a deal."

Quickly, Don Benito picked up his hat to go. "I will listen to this no more," he said. "You're a woman, after all, Doña Guadalupe. And so you just don't know the ways of this world. Don't you see? I couldn't wait. I need to dig up the gold right now so I can present myself to Lydia's father like a king!"

Lupe and her brother and sisters had to cover their mouths so they wouldn't giggle aloud.

"All right," said Doña Guadalupe, seeing how insane he was. "So you love her and you couldn't wait. But tell me, just how do you expect to present yourself like a king once you get the gold?"

Don Benito rolled his eyes to the heavens. "Woman," he said sarcastically, "why, I'll buy myself a suit and shirt and tie. I'll get boots, instead of these huaraches, and I'll dress myself like a gentleman." He smiled, glowing, trembling, feeling on fire he was so proud and sure and confident. He absolutely could not understand how anyone could even doubt him. He was rich, after all.

Doña Guadalupe took pity on him. She'd been in this canyon long enough to see what the migration of butterflies did to people every season. She smoothed out her apron once again. She'd have to go easy so she wouldn't offend the gold-crazy, love-crazy old man.

"All right," she said, trying to keep calm, "that's all very good indeed, Don Benito. But now, you tell me, how exactly do you expect to get this suit and tie with our gold? No one up here in this whole region sells a suit or tie."

Don Benito stared at her. "You're right, Doña Guadalupe," he said, his lower lip beginning to tremble. "I guess I'll have to go to Mexico City. And then, while I'm there, I'll have them make slippers of gold for her feet, too."

"And so who will attend to the mine while you're gone?" she asked.

The rage that flashed into the old man's eyes took Doña Guadalupe by surprise. Why, it looked like he was going to strike her.

"Doña Guadalupe, you've gone too far!" he said. "You're my partner, yes, but you've forgotten your place as a woman! Good night!"

But she was on her feet. "Wait!" she said. "I fed you! I've seen you through sickness! We can't afford to lose what we've found!"

He stopped, his whole body trembling. "Doña Guadalupe," he said, "you've provoked me beyond all reason! I will listen to you no longer! Tomorrow I shall blow out that hole we covered and take out enough gold to prove myself, and that's that!"

"And the Americans," she asked, "wouldn't they hear the explosion and come running to see what's happened?"

His eyes twisted, but he held his ground. "All right," he said, "so I won't use powder then. But I will dig it out by hand."

"Oh, please," she said, "wait a few weeks and, I tell you what, if you cooperate with me, then my daughters and I will help you, and we'll make the clothes for you."

His eyes widened. "You'll help me, then, to present myself like a king?" he asked.

She nodded. "Yes," she said.

"Oh, Doña Guadalupe, you are a hard woman," he said. "But, yes, I'll agree to this, but only for a few weeks. Then I'll be out of money, and I'll need more gold."

The grey-haired old woman glanced up toward the towering walls of rock, thanking God.

And up on the boulder, Lupe and her brother and sisters could see it was over, so they quietly slid off the backside of the boulder. They didn't want their mother to know that they'd been listening. They rushed back inside to continue working on their dresses. But then, when their mother came in, the first thing she said was, "And, children, the next time you decide to hide on top of the boulder to listen to one of my conversations, lock up the goat first. She was right behind you the whole time, showing me where you were."

Lupe and her sisters and brother all burst out laughing. Doña Guadalupe joined them, and the little lean-to was filled with their happy sounds.

4

And so the box canyon filled with the fragrance of
wildflowers and the sound of newborn parrots. Love
was in the air, choking the very atmosphere.

The moon was full and the coyotes were howling and
the dogs of the village were barking. Doña Guadalupe decided that she
couldn't deliver Socorro's baby alone. The full moon was the most powerful
time of the month, and strange things happened to women in labor during
this time. Doña Guadalupe sent Lupe and Victoriano for the midwife while
she and her three daughters heated water and prepared for the birth. Lupe
and her brother ran up the pathway to the main road and then out the mouth
of the canyon into the bright moonlight.

The midwife's name was Angelina. She and her husband lived just outside
of the canyon on a little *ranchería*. They had their home in a small hole nested
up against the mountain.

Scrambling down into the hole, Victoriano called loudly so the ranch
dogs wouldn't attack them. Angelina heard them calling and came out to
quiet the dogs. At this time of the month, the midwife was very busy. More
babies were born during the full moon than at any other time.

The midwife was a full-blooded Tarahumara Indian and she was married
to the town drunk, El Borracho, who was the finest guitarist in all the region.
There wasn't a family in all of La Lluvia de Oro who hadn't been serenaded
by El Borracho at their wedding or helped in childbirth by his wife Angelina.

"Who's in need?" asked Angelina. Her two front teeth were missing and
her smile looked like a dark hole in the moonlight.

"The Colonel's wife," said Victoriano.

"Oh, she's big," laughed the midwife. "I saw her the other day when I
brought your sister Maria a love note." Angelina was also the local match-
maker who delivered messages back and forth between prospective lovers.
"Well, let's go," she said, and she took off at a run.

Going back up into the canyon, neither Lupe nor Victoriano was able to
keep up with the old midwife. Once, long ago, when the first Americans had
come in to work the mine from California, Angelina had run a foot race
against six young engineers who'd said they were great athletes. The distance

had been twenty-five miles. She'd been five months pregnant, but still she arrived an hour ahead of them.

Arriving at their *ramada*, the old midwife was hardly out of breath. Quickly, she examined Socorro. Then she gave her the heart of a dried cactus to chew. It was the same kind of cactus that the great Tarahumara runners used when they ran a race worthy of a man, meaning a hundred or more miles. She told everyone to leave the lean-to except for the women who were going to assist her.

"All right, out, *mi hijita*," said Doña Guadalupe to Lupe, ushering her out the door along with Victoriano and Don Benito.

"But no, Mama," said Lupe, "I want to stay."

"Let her stay," said the midwife, rubbing an oily liniment on Socorro's legs and feet. "No girl is ever too young to learn the ways of a woman. Believe me, I know, it's the ones who never see who end up having the most difficulties."

"Please, Mama," said Lupe, not once taking her eyes off the midwife and the shiny herbal oil she was rubbing onto Socorro's limbs. The oily substance smelled good and strong and brush-like. "I want to help. I promised my Colonel."

Doña Guadalupe didn't like it, but she was too busy to argue. Socorro was crying out in pain and the coyotes were answering her from the distance. The whole night was full of eerie sounds.

"Oh, all right," said Doña Guadalupe, "but you leave the moment you can't stand it, you understand?"

"Yes, Mama," said Lupe, and she came close to help her sisters.

They had a lot of work to do. They had to get the big rope tied to the stout center post of their lean-to, keep the water hot, and help the midwife give comfort to Socorro. A mother in labor, after all, had to be kept relaxed so the child would come happily into the world.

Lupe could feel the nervous anticipation inside the dimly lit lean-to as the women went to work. This was a place where no men were allowed; it was only for women. All her life, Lupe had been told that men simply couldn't endure the pain a woman could.

Outside of the *ramada*, Victoriano sat with Don Benito, looking up at the stars and listening to Socorro's cries of pain.

"I love Lydia," said Don Benito, "but those screams scare me more than bullets."

Two days before, Don Manuel had taken two shots at the old man when he'd come to serenade his daughter, Lydia, under her bedroom window. The whole pueblo was hissing with gossip about Don Benito's courtship of the mayor's daughter, whom the mayor had specially groomed to marry an American.

"I'll never do this to my Lydia," said Don Benito. "It's just awful what women have to suffer to bring life into the world."

Inside, the midwife was trying to get Socorro to open her mouth wide

and let the pain come out. "Open your mouth," said Angelina, massaging
Socorro's neck and shoulders, "and let out what you feel. Don't keep it in,
querida; let it out."

Socorro cried softly at first, but little by little she loosened up and she
began to let out long, ear-piercing screams.

"Good," said the midwife, "now breathe deeply, deeply, and then cry
out again, letting all the pain go out of your body."

Socorro did as she was told, letting out another cry. Lupe, to her own
surprise, wasn't getting upset by them. No, she felt relieved. The cries just
seemed so natural. But Lupe could see that the cries were making her sister,
Carlota, very nervous.

"Good, *mi hijita*, good," said the midwife, "that last one truly came up
from here, in your stomach. Now roll softly side to side, yes, that's it, and
roll out long, soft guttural grunts like a pig. No, don't laugh," she smiled,
"the pig is a very good mother, *mi hijita*, and she's also very strong and
brave.

"Now, grunt, that's right, grunt strong and deep, and with each sound
imagine your body opening up, opening up, larger and larger like a rose, like
a flower opening up to the sunlight, like you're going to make love to an
enormous watermelon."

Doña Guadalupe didn't like it. Sophia and Maria blushed. Carlota
screeched with embarrassment. Lupe didn't understand. But even Socorro,
in the midst of her pain, had to smile. The thought of making love to a
watermelon sounded simply awful.

"Oh, you think that's funny?" said Angelina, turning to Carlota who
couldn't shut up. "Well, you young girls just remember what you're seeing
here the next time a boy makes eyes at you. For the man, it's only joy, but
for a woman, she has to carry the responsibility of that joy and confirm it
before God in PAIN!" She yelled out the word "pain," deliberately scaring
the young girls.

Doña Guadalupe went to attend to the water on the wood-burning stove
across the room. She'd never liked this midwife and her famous tongue. But
she was the best midwife in the area, and she'd known Socorro was going to
have a difficult time.

The cries of pain continued, and Doña Guadalupe and Maria and Sophia
helped the midwife massage and comfort Socorro as Lupe and her mother
kept the boiling water coming so the lean-to would keep warm and moist.
But Carlota wouldn't help. She just stood there, holding her ears, not able to
bear Socorro's screams anymore.

And then Lupe smelled something that she had never smelled before.
And the smell got stronger as the cries and groans of pain continued.

Suddenly, the cries stopped. A steady rhythm of rolling, guttural sounds
began, slowly at first, then faster and stronger. And outside, Lupe could hear
the coyotes in the distance and the dogs and the goats and cattle in the town.

It was a symphony of sound, rolling and growing and echoing off the mighty cliffs.

"Drink, *mi hijita*," said the midwife to Socorro, "you're losing your water."

"No," said Socorro. She was full of pain and wanted to be left alone. But her water had broken, so the midwife insisted.

"Open your mouth," she said, "and do as I say. Drink, drink, yes, that's right, all of it." It was a specially prepared potion of wild herbs and roots that women took in this region of Mexico while in labor.

Reluctantly, Socorro drank it. The hours passed and the moon moved across the heavens. The pains of childbirth continued as Socorro's body opened up, bones and flesh moving, opening up like a rose, a flower welcoming the birth of new life. And all the women in the lean-to knew that God, the Father, was here on earth with them, giving them power through the spirit of the Virgin Mary and helping them in their time of need.

And then it was time, and Angelina reached up inside Socorro with her hand, checking the movement of the bones spreading.

"You're ready," said the old midwife. "Your bones have moved, and the baby's in place." The old woman had beads of sweat running down her face. "You're doing good, *mi hijita*," she added. "Very good. The spirit of Our Lady is with us tonight. But virgin, she never was." She laughed. "Hell, giving birth to God must have moved more bone than a mountain, I tell you," she said, in her coarse, happy voice. "Now come, Sophia and Maria, you two help me lift her and put her to the rope so you'll both know how to do this when your time comes."

Sophia and Maria came forward and lifted Socorro by the armpits, helping her to the thick rope which hung at the center of the lean-to.

"Get hold of the rope," said Angelina.

Lupe could see that it took all of Socorro's power to obey the midwife and grip the rope.

"Now squat," said Angelina, "like you're going to take an enormous *caca*."

Maria and Sophia laughed.

"Stop that," said the midwife, "and hold her strong so she can squat Indian-style on her haunches. This is the best way for childbearing, and I don't care what the priests or doctors say!"

The old woman now knelt down close to Socorro and massaged her great stomach and buttocks as she told her to push and grunt in rhythm. The young pregnant woman gripped the stout rope and pulled and grunted as she forced down with all her power. Lupe watched her, squatting there, face straining like she was constipated, forcing down with more power than she'd ever thought a woman had in her.

"Good, *mi hijita*," said the midwife, "push down and pull on the rope and stare straight ahead and keep in mind only what I'm telling you. Don't fight; your body and your baby know everything. Good, catch your breath, and we'll do it again.''

Lupe and her mother brought over another pot of hot water. The lean-to smelled warm and moist. Lupe could hear Socorro's quick, little breaths, catching her strength between pushes, and then here it came again, another long roll of forceful grunts as she pushed and pulled.

"Good," said the midwife in her ear, talking so softly that it almost sounded like Socorro's own brain was talking to her.

Then it came again, a series of terrible cries, and a small, hairy wet spot poked out between Socorro's muscular legs as the midwife talked faster and faster, massaging Socorro's huge stomach with one hand and helping her between her legs with the other.

Lupe froze, staring in disbelief as she watched and heard and felt the power of this miracle of miracles. Her eyes filled with tears.

The head of the baby was now beginning to come out, to appear in the yellow glow of light from the hanging lantern, and Lupe stood there, wide-eyed with excitement.

Upon seeing the baby's head, Carlota ran out of the lean-to. "I'll never have children as long as I live!" she screamed.

The midwife had Socorro lean back on the mattress they'd brought up and rest with her legs wide apart. Lupe couldn't take her eyes away. She'd never seen a woman in this position before; all hairy and open and wet with the top of the infant's head coming out of her.

Then, having given her blood-gorged legs a rest, the midwife had Socorro squat down once more and grip the stout rope. Pushing and pulling and forcing down with all the power of her young, strong, supple body, Socorro pulled on the rope with her strong, young hands and she pushed again and again, long and hard and steady, sweating profusely. The midwife wiped the sweat from her face, and Maria and Sophia supported her under the armpits while Doña Guadalupe helped the midwife with the baby.

Suddenly, the whole head of the baby popped out, long and lopsided, wet and shiny as a big-headed rabbit, covered with a transparent, silvery, slippery mess of non-smelling film. And Socorro now did everything by herself, screaming, pulling, pushing, as if she'd been doing it for ten million years. And the cries were good, coming from her gut, and her pushes were good, too, coming down with all the power of her young, strong body. Even the baby was helping. He was moving inside the transparent film, fighting for his life. And Socorro cried out so loud that her sounds went up to the mighty cliffs, hitting them, and then they came back down, echoing in a symphony of sound. And the baby came sliding, slipping out between her taut legs like a huge *caca*.

The coyotes went silent, and the dogs quit barking. The goats and mules went silent, too, listening to Socorro's great cries, now echoing off the mighty cliffs.

Then it was done, just like that, and Lupe was amazed at the odorless smell that filled the room. With all the blood and flesh and slimy liquid that had come out of Socorro, Lupe had expected a much stronger odor. But then she remembered that women up here in the mountains always drank a lot of herbs during their pregnancy.

Holding the newborn up high in the dim light, the midwife now stretched the long cord from the baby's belly to the placenta and gently took it in her hand.

"Look," she said to the three young girls helping her, "you can see life passing through the cord if you look closely."

Drawing close, Lupe saw it was true. She could actually see the cord pulsating with life between Socorro and the child. But then, like magic, the flow of life quit between the mother and child. Lupe watched the midwife clip the cord with her mother's sewing scissors. Quickly, she tied the cord with a string next to the baby's stomach, then put the baby to his mother's warm, soft flesh. The child hugged in close, instinctively trying to find a nest as warm and moist as the one he'd just left.

Maria and Sophia helped the midwife lay Socorro down on their mother's straw mattress. Doña Guadalupe began to wash the child off with warm, clean water as he hugged in close, smelling and getting to know his mother, his first full contact in the world.

Doña Guadalupe put the baby's little feet in a bowl of warm water, and the child continued clinging to his mother. He never cried, listening to her heartbeat, the same music that he'd heard from inside the womb. No, he was quiet, content, doing what nature had taught him to do since prehistoric times: to keep quiet so the coyotes and other predators wouldn't find him.

Looking at Socorro with her child, Lupe had never seen a more exhausted and yet happy-looking woman in all her life.

"Come," said the midwife, "let's leave them alone."

Lupe followed her mother and sisters and the midwife out of the lean-to. Outside, the old woman stretched her tired limbs and caught her breath. Lupe and her mother and sisters joined her, stretching and looking up at the stars and the full moon.

"This one, your youngest," said the midwife, turning to Doña Guadalupe as she stretched and worked the small of her back, "is going to be a fine woman. Why, Lupe was sniffing the air, she so much wanted to get into the birth.

"Now, please give this old woman a drink, Doña Guadalupe," continued the midwife, "and let's take a little rest, because in a few moments, the next baby will be coming."

"Another?" said Sophia and Maria at the same time.

"Yes," said the old woman, "another."

Quickly, Doña Guadalupe went and got the bottle of tequila she kept hidden in the kitchen. She had a drink along with the midwife. Lupe was shocked. She'd never seen her mother drink alcohol before.

Then, they were just catching their breath when there came a new series of cries from Socorro again.

They all hurried back inside.

The light of the full moon was dancing off the towering mighty cliffs when Lupe came out of the lean-to holding one child and Maria holding the second one. Victoriano came rushing up with Don Benito and Carlota. They saw the two little infants in Lupe's and Maria's arms. They were overwhelmed by the miracle of life.

The newborns were moving, squirming, reaching out for life. It was truly a sign from God. Up in her pen, the mother goat smelled the excitement and called out. The dogs began to bark once more, and the coyotes answered them. Then the cattle and mules came in, too, and the canyon filled with a symphony of sounds. Carlota forgot her fears and came to Maria, and took the child. Lupe gave the other to her brother.

Lupe and her mother, sisters and brother stayed up the rest of the night with the midwife, talking and drinking and warming their feet on a shovel full of hot coals in front of the *ramada*. The stars and the moon kept them company and the hard-packed earth in front of the *ramada* felt good under their bare feet.

Lupe sat there with her mother and sisters, as Socorro and her two little boys slept in the lean-to, and she listened to the talk and laughter of the women. The midwife poured tequila in her herbal tea and told story after story of the different children she'd delivered who were now adults in the community. Lupe felt good being introduced by these women into the mystery of life. She felt more complete inside her deepest self than she'd ever felt before.

Then the eastern sky began to pale. It was the coming of a new day. They all got up to stretch so they could go to work. But instead of feeling tired, Lupe felt refreshed and strong.

"Let us pray," said Doña Guadalupe, and they all knelt down. And as they prayed and Lupe saw the eastern sky growing yellow and rose and pink, she felt herself fill with such power, with such a strength and well-being, that she just knew in her bones that life was eternal.

Her eyes filled with tears, she felt so close to these women. The whole world sang and danced before her very eyes as the cycle of life continued and the new day came forth in all its wondrous beauty—a gift from God.

5

And so she dreamed of her truelove coming to get her on his orange-red stallion to take her to his home on the top of a small white cloud.

Early one morning the half dozen soldiers that the Colonel had left behind disappeared without a word. Rumor had it that General Obregon was in a major battle with the Villistas down in the foothills, so the Colonel's men had rushed out to reinforce him.

Lupe prayed that day as she'd never prayed before, asking God to protect her truelove, if, indeed, he was in the battle, and to bring him safely back to her. The following afternoon Lupe was coming up with her sisters from the springs below the town with their baskets of laundry when she saw two Tarahumara Indians come into the plaza, dropping from exhaustion. Lupe and her sisters put down their baskets and quickly rushed up. They heard the Indians tell the townspeople that a terrible battle was going on down below near the Rio Fuerte.

Lupe's heart leaped. That was the direction in which her Colonel had cut his new road.

"Who's winning?" asked the mayor. "The Villistas or the Carranzistas?"

"Who knows?" shrugged one of the Indians. "But it's terrible. Dead bodies lying everywhere. The creeks run red with blood."

"Vultures circle by the thousands," said the other Indian, waving his arms like a great bird.

Lupe covered her ears, not wanting to hear any more. She picked up her basket and started back up the rocky path out of the plaza. Her sisters quickly followed, climbing up the steep hillside with their baskets on their heads, their necks straight and their heads held high, with the small of their backs arched and their chests upward so their hips could come under their torsos, riding directly over their legs.

Getting home, Lupe put her basket down and rushed to her mother. Oh, she just didn't want to believe what her heart was telling her.

That night Socorro held her twins in deadly fear as they lit candles and said a rosary together. They prayed that their beloved Colonel was away from the battle and still at the border, delivering the gold.

The next morning, Lupe watched her brother take off early with Don Benito. The love-struck old man couldn't wait anymore. He figured that this was a perfect time for him to take out the gold he needed, since everyone was preoccupied with the outcome of the battle.

Then on the third day, word came that the battle was over, but still no one knew who had won.

That night, Victoriano came to his mother, saying that Don Benito had decided to use dynamite to uncover their find.

"But why?" asked his mother.

"Because, well, when we covered the pocket up," said Victoriano, "we felled a couple of good-sized trees, and a lot more rock got into the hole than we'd expected."

"But wouldn't the powder destroy the gold?" asked his mother anxiously.

Victoriano shook his head. "No, not if we use just a little."

Quickly, Doña Guadalupe thought over the situation. She didn't like it one bit, but she also realized that she couldn't very well keep holding back the old man. He was crazy. Now he was even bragging about the shots that Don Manuel had taken at him, saying that it proved that his love for Lydia was true since he was willing to die.

"All right," said Doña Guadalupe, "go ahead. But talk to Manos and Flaco about it first. I don't want any accidents. My God, this gold is our chance of getting out of this canyon and going across the border to the United States until this awful war is over."

"There won't be any accidents," said Victoriano. "We'll be careful and by tomorrow we'll be rich. You'll never have to work again, Mama."

The old woman saw her son's joy and it gladdened her heart. She drew him close, hugging him.

Then that evening, Victoriano and Don Benito took Manos aside after dinner and the old man asked Manos if he could get them some powder.

Manos grinned. "So then you did hit a vein?" he said, rocking back and forth on the balls of his feet.

"Well, yes, a little one," said Don Benito.

"A burro's cock, you old fox!" said Manos, laughing happily. "No wonder you're in love! You found a big one!"

In Mexico, a burro's cock was much admired, being the biggest sex organ on any animal, pound for pound. The old man smiled. "Well, maybe, but not quite as big as a burro's cock," he said.

Manos laughed all the more, slapping the old man on the back. "No wonder you're after Lydia. With that much gold up your ass, you're probably bigger than any burro's!"

Victoriano turned as red as chili. Sex wasn't a thing that was normally mentioned in front of young people like himself. But he also knew that the men were talking like this in front of him because they finally considered him to be one of them.

"All right," said Manos. "I'll get you the powder tomorrow afternoon."

"No," said Don Benito. "I need it first thing in the morning."

"Why?"

"Because we've got to get the gold out and then cover it back up before the victors of the battle arrive."

"I see," said Manos. "Well, I'll see what I can do. I have some old powder lying around my home, I think."

"Oh, thank you," said the old man. "That's all I need. Just a little, and then I'll be able to . . . Oh, *Dios mío*! It's been so many years!"

Manos saw the joy, the longing, in the old man's eyes, and he took him in his arms, hugging him in a big *abrazo*, heart-to-heart between men. Then he reached out with his huge, thick hand and he brought in Victoriano, too. And Victoriano hugged into the two of them. It felt so good to be included.

The first light of the new day was just making the eastern sky pale when Lupe came around the lean-to from the goats' pen. She saw Manos and Flaco coming down the pathway, carrying a sack. Her brother and Don Benito were waiting for them outside the *ramada*. No other miners had arrived yet. Manos handed Don Benito the sack. The old man quickly took it around to the side of the *ramada* and hid it by the wild peach tree. Lupe decided to pretend as if she hadn't seen the whole thing. After all, she was a woman and, like Lady Luck, she didn't want to be blamed for anything that might go wrong.

Lupe and Carlota were serving Manos and Flaco, who were sitting with their brother and Don Benito, when the other miners arrived. This morning none of the young miners teased Don Benito. No, they seemed to smell something brewing in the air.

Then the right eye of God came over the jagged horizon of purple mountain peaks beyond the mouth of the box canyon. Lupe and her mother and sisters came out to give witness to God's miracle. Victoriano joined them and they all knelt down to give thanks to the Almighty. The men under the *ramada* took off their hats and joined them, too, and they all gave greeting to God's greatest miracle, the sun. Lupe closed her eyes and gave an extra little prayer for her truelove. The battle was over, but still, they hadn't received word of who had won or if, indeed, her Colonel had even been in it.

Then the miners were gone. It was time for Don Benito and Victoriano to climb the *barranca*, up to where only the eagles flew.

"Go with God, *mi hijito*," said Doña Guadalupe to her son.

"I will, thank you, Mama," he said, hugging his mother with all his might. Victoriano was only ten, but already he was as tall as his mother. "After today, we'll never be poor again," he added.

"And I'll get my red shoes!" said Carlota.

"Red?" said Maria. "Where have you ever seen red shoes?"

"I haven't," said Carlota. "But rich people are supposed to have what poor people have never seen before!"

They all laughed. Don Benito got the sack of dynamite.

"*Vayan con Dios*," said Doña Guadalupe.

"Don't worry," said Don Benito. "Lady Luck is riding with us. And she's a fine lady when she's with you."

Then Victoriano kissed Lupe and his sisters goodbye and went up the pathway, carrying an extra shovel.

Victoriano and Don Benito had hired a boy named Ramon to help them for the day. Ramon was fourteen years old. He was a big, strong boy, but he was mentally slow, so he couldn't get work at the American mine along with his older brother, Esabel.

Lupe stood by her mother's side as she watched her brother and the old man disappear into the trees above their home. She was very nervous. Oh, how she just wanted to pull her hair out of her head by the roots, she was so worried about her truelove.

The sun was five fists off the jagged horizon when Don Benito and the two boys got to the hole that they'd covered with trees, then dirt and rock. Victoriano and Ramon just couldn't stop joking and laughing, they were so excited.

"All right, settle down," said the old man. "We can't afford to make any mistakes when we're using powder!"

The two boys tried to settle down, but it was difficult. Ever since Don Benito had proposed to the mayor's daughter, the whole pueblo had been humming with excitement. It seemed as if what the old man had done was so outrageous that now everyone else wanted to be crazy, too, so that they might find riches and love.

Putting down their tools, the old man and the boys took a drink from the gourd they'd brought. Overhead came a flock of parrots, swooping into the treetops above them. The two boys had to strain their heads back to watch the birds. All around them the land went straight up into the wall of towering cliffs.

"All right, let's go to work," said Don Benito, "for today is the beginning of a whole new life!" Saying this, he spat into the palms of his hands, rubbing them with vigor. He picked up his shovel and quickly went to work. The two boys joined him, grabbing rock and pulling branches. When they'd felled the trees above the pocket, a whole chunk of earth had come down with the trees.

The sun grew hot and they began to sweat. Ramon outworked them both with ease. Not many people hired him, so he wanted to prove his worth to two new bosses.

It was almost noon when they'd cleaned away the first layer of debris so that they could now set the charge.

"Well," said Don Benito, glancing things over, "why don't we rest a little and eat lunch before we use the explosives. A tired man is a careless man."

They went to the shade to eat, but they found that they'd forgotten their lunches.

"I'll go get them," said Ramon.

"No, you stay and finish that hole under those roots," said Don Benito. "And you go get our lunches, Victoriano."

"All right," said Victoriano, fully realizing that Ramon was bigger and stronger and could cut through the upright roots with his machete faster than he could.

"Whatever you say, boss," said Ramon, petting Don Benito's dog and getting his machete.

Victoriano started down through the trees, running alongside the waterfall that had become much smaller in the last few weeks. In another three months, it would be nothing but a trickle of water.

Lupe was just coming home from school for lunch when Victoriano rushed into their *ramada*.

"Is something the matter?" asked their mother.

"No, nothing," said Victoriano. "We just forgot our lunches, so I came down to get them." He picked a tortilla off the stove, and rolled it. "We're almost down to the gold!" he said. "Ramon was really a big help. My God, he's strong."

"Wonderful," said Doña Guadalupe. "And the explosives, is Don Benito being careful with them?"

"Oh, yes," said Victoriano. "At first I thought that he might try to get to the gold in one blast. But no, he's going about it quite calmly. We're going to do three separate charges."

"Good," said their mother. "Here, sit down and eat with your sister and let her tell us about her schooling, then you can go."

They were sitting in the kitchen, talking, laughing, truly enjoying themselves when suddenly they heard an explosion.

At first they didn't know where it had come from. But then they felt the ground shake under their feet and the lean-to jerk from side to side. The crucifix fell off the wall. Victoriano was out the door, running as fast as he could. Lupe and their mother were right behind him.

Instinctively, Victoriano repeated all the prayers he knew as he ran. He prayed to God that he was wrong and that the explosion had come from the American mine.

But then he heard a deep rumbling. He stopped and heard a second explosion and saw a huge piece of the mighty cliffs go up, hold in space ever so slightly, and then come crashing down with a terrifying roar into the treetops.

Lupe came running up. She saw her brother standing in white-faced terror. Looking up toward the cliffs, she saw a cloud of dust boiling up out of the treetops.

"Oh, my God, no!" screamed Victoriano, and he was off like a shot.

Quickly, Lupe followed him.

When Doña Guadalupe got to the main road above the village, several neighbors and a dozen men from the mine were there.

"Who's up there?" asked Manos.

"Ramon and Don Benito!" she screamed.

"Oh, my God!" said Esabel, Ramon's older brother.

Esabel took off up the steep hillside like a young stallion, leaping over rock and fallen trees. The seventeen-year-old was stripped to the waist, and his arms and back rippled with muscle. Esabel had been taking care of Ramon ever since their father was killed in the mine six years before.

Manos and Flaco raced right behind him, carrying picks and shovels. Landslides were a common part of life in the canyon, and so men were always struggling to help each other.

Running up alongside the waterfall, Esabel was the first one to get to Victoriano and Lupe.

"Where?" screamed Esabel, looking up at the new cut that the landslide had made, bringing down trees and rocks with the huge explosion.

"Up there," said Victoriano, pointing, "that's where we set the charge. But I found Don Benito's hat on that side."

"By that uprooted tree?"

"Yes," said Victoriano, showing him the man's hat.

"Then, maybe, they could still be alive," said Esabel, and he went to work with power, pulling and digging and chopping, calling his brother's name. "Ramon! Ramon! I'm coming!"

Rushing up, Manos and Flaco joined Esabel. The amount of earth that they moved in minutes was incredible.

Then the rest of the miners arrived and Victoriano joined them. They all went to work, grabbing, pulling, grunting, using their hands and picks and shovels with all their power. Several women arrived. They had *frijoles* and tortillas. They made a fire of dry bark and heated the food for the men. Señora Muñoz showed up with the children from the school. She had them build a little altar of stone and light a piece of pine-pitch so they could pray.

When Lupe's sisters arrived—they'd been below the town doing laundry—they had Angelina with them. The old midwife had her herbs and healing remedies with her. As soon as she arrived, Angelina gave Maria and Sophia the heart of a special dried cactus to distribute among the working men. The cactus heart was greyish-brown and looked like a dried fig. It tasted bitter, but it relaxed the body, took away the pain of exhaustion and allowed men to work all day and night.

Maria went up to Esabel and handed him a cactus heart. "Here," she said. "*La curandera* wants you to take this."

Taking the dried cactus heart, Esabel looked into Maria's large dark eyes. Esabel was the young man that Maria had been making eyes at for several

months now. He was one of the tallest and handsomest young men in all of
La Lluvia.

"*Gracias*," he said, popping the heart into his mouth.

"I'm happy to help," said Maria, putting her hands on her hips. "I know
how much you love your brother."

"Maria!" shouted Doña Guadalupe. "Get away from there and let him
work!"

"All right," said Maria, blushing, "I'm coming, Mama."

All afternoon the men worked below the towering cliffs. They looked like
tiny dark ants alongside the waterfall and cathedral rocks, which climbed for
well over five hundred feet above them into the sky.

It wasn't until late afternoon that they came to Ramon's hat. Then,
digging a little further, they came to a hand, then a leg, and then they found
both bodies.

And the way in which they found the bodies told a heart-moving story.
The brave, simple boy must have seen the slide coming, so he'd thrown
himself over Don Benito, trying to protect him.

Esabel screamed to the heavens. Victoriano fell into his mother's arms,
crying desperately.

Señora Muñoz led the children in a chant and the box canyon filled with
sound, echoing off the towering walls down into the village below.

Several young miners kept asking Victoriano where the gold was, and
they kept digging further into the debris.

"Keep digging, you fools," said Manos, "and we'll be pulling out your
dead bodies, too! Don't you see that the big tree and boulders are ready to
come down any moment?"

Looking up the mountainside, the young miners saw the hanging tree
with half of its roots exposed and the rocks behind it. They quit their labor.

The sun was going down behind the mighty cathedral rocks when Esabel
carried his brother down the hillside into the plaza at the center of town.
They laid out both bodies, placing torches of pine-pitch all around them.

Ramon's mother knelt down beside the broken body of her youngest son
and wailed to the heavens.

There was no priest in town, so Angelina was asked to prepare the dead.
She had Sophia and Lupe help her gather vines and flowers. Then she
dressed the two bodies with the greenery and flowers, adding healing herbs
so their bones would grow back together in the next world.

Lupe and the school children lit small pieces of pine-pitch and they held
them in their hands as they prayed in a circle around the two bodies.

The entire pueblo participated in the celebration of the dead. Angelina's
husband, El Borracho, brought out his guitar and sang long into the night.

Señor Jones sent down a case of tequila from the mine, fully realizing that
the people wouldn't be going back to work until they'd completed their
mourning, anyway. That night men got drunk and yelled to the heavens.

The coyotes were still yelping early the next morning when Lupe went out of the canyon with her family, joining the long procession of people on their way to the cemetery.

Señor Scott and several of his young American friends came down from the mine. One of them set up a camera to take pictures.

Don Manuel led the people in prayer, and it was said that even Lydia shed tears when Don Benito's body was lowered into the earth.

Later that day, Don Tiburcio, who owned the second largest store in town, slaughtered a steer and donated a sack of *frijoles*, and a celebration began. People heard of the mourners ten miles away and came to join the celebration. By late afternoon, the plaza was full of people and the steer was taken out of the ground, filling the air with a wonderful spicy barbecue smell.

Lupe and her family went to the plaza and got a piece of the *barbacoa* and took their plates up to eat on the terrace of Doña Manza's house overlooking the plaza. A funeral wasn't just a time to mourn the dead; no, it was also a time for friends and relatives to get together and rejoice with the living.

After eating, Carlota and Maria went back down to join the festivities along with Cuca and Uva. Sophia, Lupe and Manuelita remained on the terrace with their mother and Doña Manza.

Everywhere people were laughing and talking excitedly, visiting with people that they hadn't seen in months. Suddenly, two gunshots rang out in the plaza below. And there was Scott, the tall, handsome engineer, in the middle of the crowd with his pistol in hand.

"Carmen and I have decided to get married," he announced.

"When?" asked El Borracho, tequila bottle in hand. "Now? Or at sunset?"

"At sunset," said Scott, grinning wildly. His girlfriend, Carmen, screeched with joy, getting on her tiptoes, kissing him. Then she took Maria's hand and they ran off to her home to get ready for the wedding.

Lupe and Manuelita glanced at each other, giggling happily. Love was still in the air, and no one wanted to miss their chance of catching a part of this miracle of life before they made their eternal peace with God.

"Lupe," said Doña Guadalupe, "you and Sophia better go with Maria and see that she just helps her friend get ready for a wedding. I don't want any surprises, you understand me?"

"Oh, Guadalupe!" said Doña Manza. "You're just too suspicious! Let Maria have her time in the sun."

"It's not her time in the sun that I'm worried about," said her mother. "It's the coyote that's sniffing the hen coop that I'm suspicious of."

The two old ladies laughed. Lupe glanced around, seeing how happy everyone was, except her brother. Victoriano was sitting alone, carving on a piece of wood with his knife. He hadn't said a word since the funeral.

The sun was just sliding down the last piece of the tall flat sky when Lupe and her sisters came walking down the pathway from their home to the plaza. They were all wearing new dresses. Lupe's was a pale rose and she had matching wild orchids braided into her long, dark hair. Sophia's was also pale rose, but she had a pink ribbon and white flowers in her hair. Carlota and Maria, on the other hand, had chosen material of the brightest red for their dresses and wore matching red ribbons in a bow, tying their long hair back.

Doña Guadalupe came behind her daughters, feeling very proud of how they looked in their fine new dresses. But she was afraid that maybe this was all the wealth that they'd ever see from the gold that her son and the old man had found.

Arriving at the plaza, Lupe's sisters quickly ran off to where all the young girls had gathered by Carmen's side. They were talking so excitedly that they sounded like a thousand birds.

Lupe stayed by her mother's side, searching through the crowd for her friend, Manuelita. She felt so self-conscious in her new dress that she didn't want to leave her mother.

Then Don Manuel, who was going to officiate the wedding, came out of his house with Josefina, his tall, well-dressed wife, on his arm. Rose-Mary and Lydia were right behind them.

Finding Manuelita, Lupe took her hand. The ceremony was just about to begin.

"Look!" said Carlota, who was standing to one side of Lupe, right next to Cuca and Uva. "Don Tiburcio is making eyes at Sophia!"

Don Tiburcio was dressed in a beautiful grey *charro* outfit with silver adornments. He was in his early thirties but lived with his mother. He'd never been married.

"No," said Cuca, giggling. "Really?"

"Of course," said Carlota, bubbling with mischief. "Just look at him!"

Lupe got on her tiptoes to look, and it was true. Don Tiburcio was standing alongside Sophia, talking to her with rolling eyes and great charm. Lupe glanced behind herself to see if her mother was watching, and she saw that she was.

Then Don Manuel raised up his hands, silencing everyone. "All right," he said, "are we ready?"

"Well, not quite, Manuel," said Scott, with his heavily accented Spanish. "I was hoping that Jim would be coming." Jim was who the Americans called Señor Jones.

"All right, we can wait a few more minutes if you like," said Don Manuel, glancing at his watch, then up at the sun which was just dropping behind the cliffs.

But everyone in the plaza knew that the young engineer's wait would come to nothing. Señor Jones always refused to attend a wedding between his men and the local girls. But then, to everyone's surprise, there came Señor Jones and his wife and daughter, riding fine horses. Everyone moved aside, making room for the great man and his well-dressed family.

"Thank you, Jim," said Scott, holding the horse so Señor Jones could dismount.

"You can thank Katherine," said Señor Jones in a long, Texas drawl. "She's the one who convinced me that this one will be different, since you and Carmen have been engaged for over a year."

Two other men took hold of the horses for Katherine and Katie so that they could dismount. Then they led the horses away, and tied them under a tree.

"All right!" said El Borracho, strumming his guitar as everyone gathered for the ceremony. "Now quiet down! Don't you see that our mayor, Señor Proper-Tight Pants, has raised his arms to start the wedding!"

The people burst out laughing. El Borracho was as famous for his wit as his wife was for her sharp tongue.

The ceremony began. With great dignity, Carmen's father walked her across the rock-laid plaza. Scott stood there, tall and handsome, waiting for his bride.

Lupe glanced at Manuelita, and their eyes filled with tears. Oh, it was all so beautiful, everyone standing under the tall tree in the middle of the plaza—Carmen on her father's arm, and Scott standing alongside Señor Jones—with the sunlight coming down through the treetops, filling the entire plaza in soft, golden light.

Lupe and Manuelita held each other's hand, weeping through the entire ceremony.

Then, Scott's best man handed him the wedding ring, and he was just slipping it onto Carmen's finger when a shot rang out.

At first no one knew what was going on. People just thought it was somebody shooting in premature celebration. But then a dozen more bullets came ricocheting over the rooftops of the stone houses, and the people shrieked in terror, "Soldiers! Soldiers!"

Suddenly, everyone was running every which way. Lupe and Manuelita rushed up the steep steps with their mothers to Doña Manza's house. Maria and Sophia got lost in the crowd, along with Carlota and Cuca.

Señor Jones and the Americans never moved. No, they just stood there, as if they thought they were impenetrable to the bullets of the Revolution.

Hearts pounding against their little breasts, Lupe and Manuelita crouched down inside the stone house. Their mothers rushed back outside, shouting for their daughters who were still down in the plaza. Bullets were flying all around them, and horsemen came down between the homes, screaming like the devil.

Lupe could hear her mother's panicked voice calling for her sisters. Trembling with fear, Lupe got to her feet so that she could help her mother hide her sisters, as she always did.

"No, Lupita!" shouted Manuelita, gripping Lupe's leg. "Stay down until the shooting stops!"

"But I have to help my mother hide my sisters!" she cried.

"Not now!" screamed Manuelita, pulling Lupe back down.

The shooting continued and the horsemen came leaping over the stone walls. Lupe could hear people being trampled and dogs yelping as they ran for their lives. Finally, she couldn't stand it anymore; if she was to die, she wanted to die by her mother's side. So she broke free from her friend and scrambled as quickly as she could across the room.

Looking through the open doorway from under a table, Lupe could see her mother and Doña Manza in front, crouched down behind the low wall of the terrace. Her sisters, Maria and Sophia, were racing up from the plaza, bullets striking all around them. But Carlota and the others were nowhere in sight.

"Mama!" screamed Lupe, crawling as fast as she could under the chairs and tables.

But then, suddenly, she looked up and saw the two white front stockings of a horse in front of her. Her heart soared to the heavens. She could only see the legs and hindquarter of the horse, but she instantly recognized her Colonel's stallion with its underside of shiny, orange-red fire.

"*Dios mío!*" she screamed, getting to her feet, running, yelling, waiting to be taken into her Colonel's great, strong arms so that nothing bad could happen to her ever again. Lupe came racing across the little room, gaining more and more view of the horse and rider as she came, and her little heart wanted to burst.

But then, reaching the doorway and looking straight up no more than six feet away, she got a full view of the man on her Colonel's horse, and she saw a dark, wild-eyed black-haired stranger dressed in rags. One whole side of his face was twisted with long, red, terrible scars.

Lupe screamed, her arms still open. Hearing the scream, the many-scarred man turned, saw Lupe, and his face broke into a vicious grin. "Oh, I'd heard there were beauties up in these mountains," he bellowed, "but this little one is going to be an angel!"

He put his pistol into his holster and reached down to take Lupe into his arms. But out of nowhere came Doña Guadalupe, charging in like a wild she-boar willing to do battle with the devil himself. She hit the man on the great stallion with a broom, then rammed the broom's long bristles into the stallion's eye.

The horse reared back in shock, whirling, losing his footing as he tried to get away from this raging woman who was trying to blind him. The stallion bolted over the short stonewall, and the many-scarred man almost fell off as the great stallion went rearing and turning, as he went down through the steep rock garden, falling over the second stonewall into the courtyard below. Hitting the plaza, the great horse slipped, slid, reared in pain. His left front leg was broken, dangling at an ugly angle.

Up on the terrace, Lupe was still screaming. That man's face had looked like the devil himself. And, in her heart, Lupe suddenly knew that her beloved Colonel was, indeed, dead. And it had been this ugly savage who'd killed him.

"Arrest those people!" bellowed the many-scarred monster. "*Cabrones, chingaron* my horse!"

The magnificent stallion was limping on three legs, trying to keep his balance. The many-scarred man leaped off with a whirl of speed. He drew his pistol and shot the stallion through the head, blowing out his white, oatmeal-like brains. The great animal fell over backwards, hitting the grey-white cobblestones with a dull thud, red blood and white brains splattering across the courtyard.

Then the man turned, feet apart, roaring in a mad, vicious rage, "I want that old lady and her family lined up so I can personally shoot them! They killed the horse that Villa gave me!" He was livid with rage. His young, once darkly-handsome face was bursting with ugly vengeance. "You stupid old bitch! I wasn't going to harm your daughter, but now I'll kill you all! That horse, he was my special gift from Villa himself!"

Quickly his men dismounted and rushed up onto the terrace to arrest Lupe and her family. Victoriano saw the men coming, he grabbed the little knife that he'd been using to carve wood off the wall, and rushed to his mother. He planted himself firmly in front of his mother and sister, willing to die to protect them.

"No, *mi hijito*," said Doña Guadalupe, tears coming to her wrinkled-up old eyes, "there are too many. Give me the knife and run!"

But Victoriano refused and he stood there, eyes focused, feet set. And he looked so little and skinny and helpless against the on-rushing armed men.

The first ragged soldier saw the knife in Victoriano's hand. He was preparing to hit Victoriano in the face with his rifle butt when Maria grabbed his rifle and Sophia helped her sister push the man over the wall.

"No!" yelled their mother. "Run, both of you! And take your brother and Lupe with you! I'm the one who caused his horse to fall!"

But neither Maria nor Sophia obeyed their mother. It took four soldiers to subdue them. Then the armed men pushed Doña Guadalupe and her family down the steep pathway at gunpoint.

Carlota was across the plaza with Uva and Cuca, screaming at the top of her lungs, "Don't shoot them! Please, don't shoot them!" But she never came any closer.

Lupe and her family were put up against the tall stone retaining wall on the high side of the plaza. The many-scarred man, whom his men called La Liebre, raised up his pistol to shoot them. Lupe closed her eyes, burying her face into her mother's warm, plump body. She could hear Carlota's screams of terror across the plaza. Lupe tried to push the screams out of her mind so that she could make her peace with God, but her sister was wailing in such horror that Lupe just couldn't concentrate.

Lupe squeezed her eyes tighter, expecting the bullets to come any moment. She prayed as fast as she could for a quick, painless death. But the bullets didn't come, and they still didn't come. Then her sister stopped screaming. Lupe opened her eyes and saw that Carlota was on the ground, vomiting uncontrollably.

The man called La Liebre, meaning "the jack rabbit," wasn't aiming his pistol at them anymore. Now he had it rammed under Señor Scott's chin, who was trying to hand him the reins of Señor Jones's fine horse.

Lupe began hiccuping, not able to stand it anymore. Her whole body jerked in convulsions.

"No!" yelled one of the other young engineers, rushing in to help Señor Scott. "Don't! We're American citizens!"

In a blur of motion, La Liebre whirled about, leaping into the air just like a jack rabbit, hitting the second American across the face with his pistol. Blood and teeth burst from the American's face. And, still moving in one continuous motion, La Liebre leaped on Señor Jones's horse and gave him the spurs. The big, handsome bay bolted across the plaza. The many-scarred man rode past Don Manuel, still raging crazy with vengeance, until he saw Lydia. He reined in, looking at her with her fine dress and beautiful golden-brown hair. He put his pistol away.

"*Mira, mira*, what do I have here?" he said, taking off his *sombrero*. He grinned, turning the unscarred side of his face to Lydia. It was easy to see that he'd once been a very handsome, almost feminine-looking, young man, and he was still in his early twenties.

"Well," said Señor Jones, coming up and putting his arm about Don Manuel, "maybe we can handle this wild man yet."

Don Manuel said nothing, staring with hate at the man who was smiling at his daughter.

The midwife came to their lean-to that evening and saw to Maria's broken hand and Sophia's bruises. But no matter what she did, she couldn't get Carlota to stop crying. Carlota just knew that she'd failed her family in their hour of need, and now she wanted to die.

"Don't be ridiculous," said the midwife, "I've seen two husbands die so far and I didn't rush in to help them, either!"

"But this was my mother and family!" cried Carlota.

"Well, feel guilty if you must," said the midwife, and she left Carlota to her thoughts and attended to Victoriano's bruises.

That night Doña Guadalupe held Carlota long into the night. "It's all right, *mi hijita*," she kept saying over and over again. "If we'd been killed, someone had to go on living for us."

"But I'm no good, and you hate me," said Carlota, eyes swollen from crying so much.

"Does the mother deer hate her fawn that stays hidden in the rocks while the lion eats her? Oh, no, the mother deer rejoices in the act of giving her earthly body so her children can go on living."

But no matter how much their mother spoke, it was a long, terrible night for Carlota. Her shame was killing her more surely than all the guns that they'd faced earlier that day.

6

And so Lupe thought she would die, not being able to live another day. But then in her sorrow, she found a strange, wonderful kind of joy among the ashes of her truelove.

La Liebre and his men took up residence by the plaza, throwing people out of their homes. They terrorized the town, taking whatever they wanted. La Liebre took Lydia for his woman and threatened to hang the mayor if he tried to interfere.

Señor Jones tried to control the soldiers, as he had all the others. But they just laughed at him and took the gold that he had already and sent it over the mountains to Chihuahua. They said they'd keep it as ransom until he got weapons for them from the United States.

Lupe had a difficult time sleeping at night, and when she did finally fall to sleep, she could still see La Liebre in her mind's eye raising up his pistol to shoot them.

Socorro didn't invite Lupe into her room anymore. She'd spend her days attending to her twins. She played all day with them in the sunshine, acting as if she didn't have a worry in the world.

But then one morning, Socorro got up screaming and she threw out all of her husband's clothes.

"You fool!" she bellowed at the top of her lungs. "I never want to see your clothes again! Over and over I asked you not to fight! I asked you to take us to Europe, but you refused, thinking you were immortal and you'd save Mexico! Oh, I hate you, you fool! You had no right to leave me!" She continued to shout and throw out his belongings. She was a wild she-boar bursting with rage. And she wasn't done until she fell down with exhaustion, dry-mouthed and cleansed, and he was gone. He was truly gone from her.

Lupe took her Colonel's jacket with the shiny brass buttons from the pile of clothes that Socorro had thrown out. The neighbors came and took what they wanted, too.

That night, Lupe slept with her Colonel's jacket close to her heart. The following morning she packed it in an empty sack. She told her mother that she wished to go up to the high country for the day.

"But why, *mi hijita?*" asked her mother.

Lupe shrugged. "I don't know, exactly. But I must go, Mama."

"All right," said her mother, sensing her daughter's need, "but your brother will have to go with you."

"I know," said Lupe.

She didn't wish to go alone, either. No girl was safe anymore. La Liebre and his men were raping any girl that happened to walk by the plaza unescorted.

Leaving the village, Lupe and Victoriano walked around on the main road, then took the zigzagging trail that her Colonel had built up the steep canyon wall. Lupe tired often, and it took them a long time to just get to the white pines. Her heart felt empty. She had no more hopes of ever seeing her truelove again.

Going through the break where the meteorite had split the earth, Lupe felt none of the mystical joy that she'd felt the time before. And up on top, the high country was still stunningly beautiful, but it brought her very little pleasure. But then crossing the meadows, Lupe spotted the little twisted pine tree on the formation of flat tortilla rocks, and she suddenly knew why she'd come to the high country. Anxiously, she began to run.

"What is it?" asked her brother.

"That tree! That's where I'm going to bury my Colonel's coat!"

"But why? Are you crazy?" he yelled.

Victoriano watched his sister run across the meadow. The little waterways had all but dried up; the winter grass was green-blue, it was so thick and lush. Deer trails were everywhere, cutting through the knee-high grass. It was truly a land of plenty.

"Okay," he said, and he, too, took off running after his little sister.

Ever since the landslide, Victoriano had been torturing himself, thinking that if he hadn't gone down for their lunches, maybe Don Benito and Ramon would be alive today. He figured that maybe he could have gotten Don Benito to use only two sticks of dynamite and not all sixteen. If only he'd remained behind.

Victoriano came to the pile of flat, round rocks and climbed up after his sister. "But what's so special about this place?" he asked. "We could have buried his coat down in the canyon if that's what this is all about."

Lupe shook her head, glancing around. "Oh, no," she said, shivering with wonderful, good feelings. "This is my Colonel's place! Just look, it's so beautiful! Why, over there we can even see the silvery mist over the Sea of Cortez!"

Victoriano turned and looked. It was true. Mountain peaks and flat-topped mesas stretched out as far as the eye could see, and way over to the west they could see the coastline stretching out for miles with piled-up clouds. Lupe seemed so happy that he couldn't help but smile, too.

"So, how will we bury his coat?" he asked.

"We'll have to gather flowers and build an altar first," she said.

"Oh, Lupita, you are crazy."

"Will you help?"

"Of course," said Victoriano.

And so, saying this, Lupe put her Colonel's jacket down and they climbed off the rock pile, went down to the meadow and began to pick wildflowers. And as they worked together, Lupe began to hum to herself. She was so happy; she was finally making preparations to put her truelove to rest.

Victoriano watched his sister gathering the flowers of pink and blue and yellow, and little by little he began to feel better, too.

"Come," said Lupe, "we have more than enough flowers; let's go build an altar for him under the little pine."

They climbed back up the pile of tortilla rocks, brother and sister, happy to be working together. Work was the third miracle of each day; work, a deliberately chosen duty by the people; work, a job done with the hands, the greatest tools given to man by the Almighty, making man equal to God in the creation of His own world.

"Over there," said Lupe. "We can bury his coat in that crevice behind the roots of the little pine."

But then, when Lupe climbed around to the other side of the little twisted tree, Victoriano suddenly saw his sister freeze.

"What is it?" he asked, thinking she'd seen a snake or something equally dangerous.

But she only laughed. "Look," she said excitedly.

Victoriano came close and there, in the shallow little crevice, was a tiny spotted fawn with huge frightened eyes.

"Why, it's a miracle," said Lupe. "Just look at him; he has eyes just like my Colonel."

Victoriano laughed; he could see that his sister was right. She'd found her truelove once again.

In the months that followed, there wasn't a place that Lupe would go, except to school, without her pet deer. They became inseparable, and at night Lupe would even prefer to sleep with her fawn on a mat on the ground than with her mother in her soft straw bed.

Fed goat's milk by hand, the fawn grew quickly. And thinking that Lupe was his mother, he'd call out to her in his little, forceful high-pitched deer voice whenever he'd see her coming up the trail from school. The Indian kids at school began to call Lupe "the deer girl." They'd race with her and her pet deer over the slopes above the town, shouting to the heavens.

Katie Jones left the school and went out of the canyon with her mother on the pretense that they had to spend the holidays in San Francisco, California. But everyone knew that Señor Jones had sent his family to the United States permanently. La Liebre was smoking Señor Jones's cigars and eating dinner with him, but still the Americans had very little control over the man of lightning-quick reflexes.

Then one afternoon, Señora Muñoz asked Lupe if she could please stay after school so that they could talk. Lupe became apprehensive, thinking that she'd done something wrong.

"Lupe," said Señora Muñoz once they were alone, "I wish to compliment you on how well you've done this year. Already you're at a third grade level in your reading and in your second year in arithmetic."

Nervously, Lupe watched her teacher rub her hands together. She felt that she was going to get it now. Many times her mother gave her compliments before she hit her between the eyes.

"Lupe," said Señora Muñoz, "I don't know just how much longer I'm going to be able to be here. So I want you to know that you have a great future in your studies. I hope that you will never forsake them, as so many young girls do."

Lupe's eyes filled with tears. She just couldn't listen anymore. She loved her teacher almost as much as she'd loved her Colonel. How could she possibly be leaving her, too? "Oh, please," she said, interrupting her teacher, "you can't go! We need you! I'd never have learned to read and write if it hadn't been for you."

"Oh, *querida*," said Señora Muñoz, "please don't make this any harder for me than it is. I love you, too."

They took each other in their arms, student and teacher, holding and hugging and feeling so close.

"All right, now," said Señora Muñoz, bringing out her handkerchief for them, "no more of this. I'm not leaving immediately and so, well, I'd like to ask a favor of you."

"Anything," said Lupe, drying her eyes.

"Well, I've always heard so much about your mother's kitchen," she said, "so I was wondering if you couldn't please, maybe, bring me some of your mother's famous goat cheese and a few tortillas, too."

"Why, of course," said Lupe. "I'd love to!"

"Good, and if you'd give it to me privately in the mornings, I'd appreciate that," she added.

"By all means," said Lupe. "I'll bring you some tomorrow."

In the next two weeks, Lupe brought her teacher a little goat cheese almost every morning. And a couple of times Lupe thought that she saw her teacher almost salivate, she was so hungry. Then one day Lupe noticed that Manuelita was also bringing Señora Muñoz sweetbreads in the mornings. Lupe began to get suspicious, especially after she and Manuelita talked things over one afternoon on their way home from school.

Then it happened. One morning Doña Guadalupe found Lupe putting a piece of cheese into her school bag just as she was about to leave.

"Are you still hungry?" asked her mother.

"No, I mean yes," said Lupe quickly.

"But you ate such a good breakfast, *mi hijita*," she said, coming closer.

She saw Lupe's eyes dart about like a frightened mouse. "What is it?" she asked.

"Nothing, Mama," said Lupe. "I just have to go. Bye now!"

"Just wait, young lady, what's going on?"

Lupe stopped. "Please, Mama," she said, "don't ask me."

"Lupe," said her mother, "talk to me. I'm your mother."

"Oh, Mama," said Lupe, feeling like a traitor, "the cheese isn't for me. It's for my teacher."

"Señora Muñoz? But why didn't you just tell me, *mi hijita?*" said Doña Guadalupe. "There's nothing wrong in taking your teacher a little present now and then. As it is, they pay her very little and she's always needed help."

"But she asked me to keep it just between us," said Lupe.

"Why?" asked her mother.

Lupe shrugged. "I don't know. The only thing I know is that Manuelita is also taking her sweetbread."

"My God!" said Doña Guadalupe.

"Oh, please don't be angry with her, Mama," said Lupe.

"I'm not angry with your teacher, child!" said Doña Guadalupe. "I bet that Don Manuel has stopped paying her since Señora Jones left. And that poor woman has been starving!"

Doña Guadalupe went to the narrow work counter and cut a larger piece of cheese. "Take this to her," she said, "but don't say anything. She's a good, proud woman, and we don't want to cause her any more embarrassment!"

That afternoon when Lupe got home from school, her mother took her by the hand and they quickly walked down the hill to Doña Manza's house. Several other parents and their children were already there. When Don Manuel came home from the mine that evening, they were waiting for him. Lupe had never seen so many mothers ready to do battle.

"But how could you have stopped her wages without telling us?" said Doña Manza.

"I don't work for you!" said Don Manuel. "And furthermore, it wasn't me who stopped her wages, it was Señor Jones. He's under no written obligation to supply a school for the village." And Don Manuel would have closed his door on their faces if Don Tiburcio hadn't put his foot in the way. He was only a couple of inches taller than their short mayor, but he was so wide of shoulder that he dwarfed the proper little man.

"But you are our town mayor," said the man who owned the second largest store in the village, "so I do believe that it was your obligation to inform us of Señor Jones's decision, so at least we would not have let the poor woman starve." Saying this, Don Tiburcio held the door open to the mayor's large stone house. Don Manuel knew that he'd just lost all the respect that had taken him years to develop with townspeople. His chief rival had just stepped forward and made him out to look like a weak, disgusting turncoat.

"I have nothing to say!" said Don Manuel. "I was told what to do by the office, so I did it. Good night," he added, closing the heavy door made of iron and thick oak.

That night, Lupe sat alongside Manuelita and she heard her mother and the other mothers talking. Finally, it was decided that they'd all take turns inviting Señora Muñoz to their homes for dinner and they'd also contribute a couple of pennies each week so that they could make up, in part, for the fifty cents that she'd been getting paid per day.

But when Señora Muñoz found out what was going on, she was overwhelmed with such emotion that she refused the people's offer. "Oh, you shouldn't!" she said. "I know how much trouble you're all having already."

"But we need you, this is only right," said Doña Manza. "The joy that you've brought us with the knowledge that you've given to our children, we can never repay, no matter how much we try."

"Besides," said Doña Guadalupe, "what's one more mouth to feed when we all have a houseful of children?"

With tears in her eyes, Señora Muñoz hugged Doña Manza and Doña Guadalupe and accepted the people's offer.

But the situation with the school didn't stop there. Now that his wife and daughter were gone, Señor Jones acted as if he hated the people of the canyon and he was out to destroy them. Two days later he bolted the door of the school, closing it down. But the people simply assembled again and moved Señora Muñoz down into town. They had her teach school behind Doña Manza's bakery shop so that Manuelita could keep all the books and supplies in her room for their teacher.

The townspeople were proud of themselves. They saw that they could get things done if they united.

One evening, just as the sun was disappearing behind the towering walls, Don Tiburcio rode up to Lupe's home on his little, quick-footed white mule. In these mountains no one owned horses except for the Americans and the passing soldiers. Anyone who'd lived up here any length of time knew that a small-hoofed mule was much safer and faster in this steep, treacherous country.

"Good evening," said Don Tiburcio, coming under the *ramada*. He was all dressed up and had flowers and a burlap sack in his hand.

"And a very good evening to you, too," said Doña Guadalupe. She had been feeling very proud of this quiet little man ever since he had spoken up to their town mayor.

Taking off his hat, Don Tiburcio glanced about, blushing when his eyes met Sophia's. He'd never been to their home before, but it was quite obvious why he'd come.

"Please, bring up a chair for Don Tiburcio," said Doña Guadalupe to

Victoriano, "and move over, girls, make room for our guest to join us by the warmth of the coals."

Lupe and her sisters and Socorro pulled their chairs back, making room for the well-dressed man.

"Oh, thank you," he said, sitting down nervously. "It's been quite a day. I just got back from the lowlands with a mule train of merchandise. Every day it's becoming more difficult to depend on the muleskinners.

"But what can I do? I got to have fresh supplies if I'm to compete with Don Manuel's store."

"And you do," said Doña Guadalupe. "In fact, you always have fresher and better fruit and vegetables than Don Manuel, and you don't have the help of the Americans every time they return with the empty mules after delivering the gold."

Don Tiburcio laughed. "That's true, and I doubt if Don Manuel will be getting any more help from the *americanos,* either," he said. "It is said that Villa kept the mules that La Liebre's men used to take the gold!" He stole a quick glance at Sophia. "Well, when I was down in the lowlands, *señora,*" he said, looking back at their mother again, "I took the liberty of buying a box of sweets for you and your family."

He had to continually tug at his collar, he was having so much trouble getting his words out.

"Here," he said, pulling the present out of the burlap sack and handing it to their mother. "A box of chocolates."

Carlota screeched with anticipation. None of them had ever seen such a beautifully wrapped present.

"Oh, Don Tiburcio," exclaimed their mother, "but you didn't need to do this!"

He only blushed the more, then stood up and reached across the shovelful of hot coals to hand the flowers to Sophia.

"*Gracias,*" said Sophia, accepting the flowers with a flutter of her long eyelashes. "They're beautiful."

He sat back down, still blushing.

"Well," said their mother, feeling the nervous anticipation in the room, "why don't you open the chocolates, Sophia?"

Sophia shook her head. "Oh, no, you do it, Mama," she said, smiling behind the flowers.

Chocolates were a great luxury up here in the mountains. In fact, Lupe and her family had never had a chocolate candy. They'd had hot cocoa to drink—which came in crude, round spicy cakes—and they'd had candied fruit that Doña Manza was famous for making in her bakery at Christmas time, but they'd never before seen, much less eaten, an individually wrapped piece of creamy-filled hard, brown chocolate candy.

"All right," said their mother, turning the beautiful box of blue paper and red ribbon in her hands, "I'll open it."

She untied the wide, red ribbon carefully, wrapped it about her open hand into a neat fold and put it aside to use later. Then she undid the ends of the box, being very careful not to ruin the fine blue paper. She was just going to slip out the box when Carlota squealed with delight, jumped from her chair and pranced about the *ramada* like a pony.

"Oh, hurry, Mama! Hurry! Chocolates are the candy of love, and I just know that they're my favorite!"

Maria and Sophia blushed, having been thinking the very same thing about this legendary sweet.

Don Tiburcio looked like he'd die. Facing bands of bandits when he went up and down the mountain didn't frighten him nearly as much as this did now. He was thirty years old and he'd been watching Sophia grow up ever since she was a child. In his estimation, she was by far the most beautiful and lady-like girl in the region. Oh, the day that La Liebre had made his move on Lydia, he'd been grateful that the man hadn't set his eyes on Sophia or he would have killed him.

"Mind your manners," said their mother to Carlota.

Doña Guadalupe brought the box out of the wrapping, folded the blue paper and put it away, too. Then she opened the box, revealing a beautiful assortment of individually wrapped candies. Each candy was wrapped in different colored foil—gold, silver, metallic red, green and blue—that made them glow like jewels in a treasure chest.

"Oh, give me one!" yelled Carlota, reaching to grab one with her hand.

"No," said her mother, slapping her hand away. "Our guest, Don Tiburcio, goes first."

"Oh, no," said Don Tiburcio, "please, you ladies go first."

"Well, if you insist," said Doña Guadalupe, handing the box to Sophia. Carlota snatched up a silver one with the speed of a lizard and took off. "Where are your manners?" said her mother. "You won't be getting another one if you behave like that!"

Going over the assortment carefully, Sophia took a green one and passed the box to Maria. Licking her lips excitedly, Lupe watched Sophia unwrap the fantastic jewel. She wondered why Sophia had taken green; she, herself, was going to take a blue one. Maria took a golden one. Victoriano handed the box to Socorro before taking one for himself. Socorro chose a red one. Victoriano took a red one, too.

Then it was Lupe's turn but she just couldn't make up her mind. They all looked so wonderful. But she finally took the blue one that she'd wanted originally and passed the box to her mother, who also took a blue one.

When Lupe unwrapped the candy and bit into the hard chocolate with the cream filling, she thought that she'd died and gone to heaven, she was so mystified with all the incredible tastes that filled her mouth. And the smell! The fragrance! She took tiny nibbles with her two front teeth, savoring each morsel before swallowing.

The *ramada* was filled with quiet moans of ecstasy as they all ate their carefully chosen chocolates. Each of them had two pieces the first night before their mother put her foot down. "No more," she said. "And I'll be sleeping with the box by my pillow, so I don't want to hear any little footsteps in the night searching about."

They laughed; the thought had crossed their minds.

Don Tiburcio said good night and left, but then, miracle of miracles, he was back the very next evening with more flowers and another box of sweets. This box was wrapped in white paper and white ribbon as fine as a wedding dress.

It wasn't just Carlota who squealed in delight this night when it took her mother too long to undo the present. Maria and Sophia and Lupe were also beside themselves with anticipation. They'd tasted the legendary candy of love and they couldn't say "no" any more than Adam had said "no" to the forbidden fruit.

This night Lupe selected green. And she knew that she would take a silver one next, if she had the chance.

"Well," said Don Tiburcio after they all had their piece of chocolate, "I fully realize that I'm not the most handsome man in the world, but, well, I've known your family all my life, *señora*, and I greatly respect how you've raised your family." He blew out, trying to calm down, he was so nervous. "So what I'm saying, *señora*, is that I've spoken to my mother, who is a great woman, and I have her permission to ask for your daughter Sophia's hand in marriage," he said, squeezing his hands together.

Smoothing out the apron on her lap, Doña Guadalupe glanced down at the hardwood coals in the shovel, giving herself time to gather her thoughts. "And you'd take Sophia to live under your mother's roof, no doubt."

He was taken aback. He hadn't expected this. "Well, yes," he said. "I hadn't thought that far ahead, but I guess I would," he admitted.

"Well," said their mother, glancing at Sophia, "my daughter and I greatly appreciate the respect that you've shown to our house, but," she added, "we will have to speak privately and consider the matter most carefully before we give you our answers."

"By all means," he said, picking up his hat and getting to his feet. "But I might add that with the situation being what it is with these soldiers we have in town, we just don't have the luxury of time that we once had, *señora*." And he bowed, saying good night. "I'll be back in a few days for your answer," he added.

For the next two days, Lupe heard her mother and Sophia talking the situation over and over, but they just couldn't seem to come up with an answer. Sophia liked Don Tiburcio very much, but she didn't know if she loved him.

"Your love for the man is the least of our problems," said their mother. "For a woman can always learn to love the man she marries if he's good to her and he is a good provider. But," she added, "the problem we have here is that Don Tiburcio has never been a man to show much interest in women or drink or cards, and he's been living with his mother all these years without ever marrying, so I'm just suspicious that he might be looking for a servant instead of a wife, now that his mother is getting up in years."

"Oh, Mama," said Sophia, "you don't have to worry about that. He does love me!"

Lupe watched their mother turn and look at her older sister. "Oh, and how do you happen to know this?"

Sophia blushed. "A woman can tell about such things," she giggled. "Why, every time he comes near me, I swear I think he's going to die."

Everyone under the *ramada* burst out giggling. Lupe saw Sophia turn a dozen shades of red.

"Well, this being the case, then maybe we should consider his offer, Sophia," said her mother. "But you're so skinny, *mi hijita*. I think we should postpone this for a few months and put a few pounds on you, so you'll be able to go to your marriage bed without fear."

Lupe looked straight down at the floor, thinking of the cattle and burros and goats she'd seen mate. She was shocked that her mother had made such a direct reference to what a man and woman did in the privacy of their bed.

7

*And so the descendants of the great Espirito looked
down into their beloved canyon, watching the people
leave by the hundreds. And step by step, the basin
returned quickly, quietly, to the jungle.*

Señor Jones blew out the main part of the mine and
laid off a hundred workmen, telling them that he would be closing down the
whole mine in a few more months. Two days later, the family who lived
directly below Lupe's house packed their belongings and told everyone
goodbye. The family's name was Espinoza. They'd come up to La Lluvia the
very same year that Doña Guadalupe and her husband had come. Señor
Espinoza had been a close friend of Don Victor and worked side by side with
him.

"We have relatives in Los Angeles, California," said the proud, hard-
working man to Doña Guadalupe, "and we're going to join them while we
can. This situation is only going to grow like the steer's tail, down toward the
ground until it reaches hell!"

He had a huge moustache and dark, blazing Indian eyes. He'd had a very
well paying job at the crushing plant for over ten years, working his way up
the ladder from a laborer by putting in long hours with all his power.

The same day that the Espinoza family left, Lupe saw some Tarahumara
Indians come down the pathway and tear out the picket fence behind the
Espinozas' lean-to; they carted it off to build pens for their herds of goats.

In the following weeks Lupe and her family watched more than thirty
other families leave the canyon, going where, they didn't know, but thinking
that it could only be better than this canyon, which was falling to ruin. It
seemed to everyone that Señor Jones and La Liebre were set on destroying
the town.

Within a month, Lupe's family lost half the number of men coming in to
eat under their *ramada*. Their mother wasn't making enough money to pay
for the groceries that she'd taken on credit from Don Tiburcio's store. And
now that Don Tiburcio was courting her daughter, Doña Guadalupe couldn't
very well ask for an extension on her credit and put her daughter's relationship in jeopardy. Especially not after Sophia and her mother had told Don

Tiburcio that Sophia was still too small and they'd have to put a few pounds on her before she would be prepared to marry.

That night, Lupe heard her mother crying in the quiet of the night. Lupe was sleeping with her pet deer on a straw mat alongside her mother's bed. At first Lupe thought she was only dreaming; her mother couldn't possibly be crying. But then she remembered that her mother had cried often when their father had first left.

"Mama, what is it?" she asked, crawling into bed with her mother.

"Nothing, just go back to sleep," said Doña Guadalupe, quickly drying her eyes.

"Mama," said Lupe, "please talk to me. Is it about the food we give to Señora Muñoz?"

"Oh, no, *mi hijita*, that only comes to a few mouthfuls," she said. "It's the miners. We don't have enough of them coming anymore for me to pay the bills."

Lupe had never realized that they had bills to pay. But she could now see that she'd been naïve, for every day their mother went down the hillside to get groceries from Don Tiburcio's and Don Manuel's stores.

"Mama, I'll help," said Lupe. "I'm fat, so I won't eat so much anymore."

Her mother laughed. "You skinny mouse, how can you call yourself fat, *mi hijita*? I can feel all your bones. My God, you're big. Why, soon you'll be taller than me."

"I'm almost as tall as Carlota now," said Lupe.

"Yes, I know. You and your brother have your father's long bones."

"That's it," said Lupe excitedly. "We could write to Papa and get him to come back to help us."

"You must be reading my mind," said her mother, lying in the silver spears of light coming in through the cracks of the lean-to.

In the morning when Lupe went out to do her chores, Victoriano stopped her, quickly taking her aside. "Mama was crying last night, wasn't she?" he asked.

Lupe could see that her brother was very upset. "Yes," she said.

"I thought so," he said, taking a big breath. "And it's about money, isn't it?" Lupe nodded.

"Damn it," he said, "I should have taken out more gold while I had the chance." Saying this, he turned and ran down the hillside with a basket before he'd even eaten breakfast.

The sun was high overhead and Victoriano was several hundred feet below the crushing plant of the mine. He was going through the mountain of waste that the Americans had dumped down the *barranca*. He was bent over, going through the rock, stone by stone, looking like a tiny ant among the huge pile of waste that had accumulated over the last decade. He was working, sweating fast, looking for the richest rock he could find so they'd have something worthwhile when he took it home to break it down with his hammer.

Suddenly, Señor Jones appeared above him. La Liebre and two of his gunmen were at his side, smoking cigars, looking well-fed.

"Hey, you down there! What are you doing?" shouted Señor Jones.

Victoriano glanced up and saw all four men. His heart took off. "Nothing," he said, "just looking through the rock you threw away, hoping to find a little color!"

"Get his basket and bring it to me," said Señor Jones to one of the men.

A gunman quickly went down the hillside through the broken sharp rock. La Liebre raised his bullwhip, signaling the other gunman to go down, too. Victoriano didn't know what to do. A part of him felt like running. But another part of him knew that he had done nothing wrong. People had been searching among the waste ever since he could remember.

"Bring him up!" yelled La Liebre to his men. "I think I've seen this one before."

The chubby redheaded soldier grabbed Victoriano and shoved him up the hillside through the broken rock. This was the same redheaded soldier who'd abused a twelve-year-old girl the week before. He was second in command, after his captain, La Liebre.

"Well, well," said Señor Jones, looking through Victoriano's basket as the two soldiers stood by him. "What do we have here? This is pretty good ore. Tell me, boy," he said with his Texas drawl, "you got some deal with someone in the mine to throw you out first class rock?"

"No, of course not," said Victoriano.

But then, glancing about and seeing their faces, Victoriano saw it coming. Nothing he could say would stop these vicious men. Why, they were sneering at him like huge, hungry cats ready to pounce on a mouse.

"But it's true!" cried out Victoriano. "I worked hard to find these rocks. Please, come down and I'll show you!" But he saw Señor Jones nod to them and he knew it was no use. They'd made up their minds before they'd ever come down to get him. Suddenly, smiling happily, La Liebre stepped in, hitting him in the stomach with the hard handle of his whip.

"All right," he said to Señor Jones as Victoriano doubled over in pain, "we'll take it from here."

Catching his breath, Victoriano turned and ran, leaping over the broken rock to go down the steep hillside. But he'd gone only three strides when La Liebre leisurely caught him by the ankles with the crack of his bullwhip. Victoriano went face first into the rock, cutting up his face and hands, the red blood beginning to run down his face and white cotton shirt.

"Get him to his feet!" ordered La Liebre, grinning.

The two armed men ran down and jerked Victoriano to his feet, pinning his arms behind his back.

Smoking lazily, La Liebre came up and looked into Victoriano's young, handsome face. "We're going to make an example of you, boy," he said.

"Brand you and then hang you." And saying this, he took the big cigar out of his mouth and rammed it into the boy's face.

Screaming, Victoriano tried to jerk his face away, but the two armed men held him fast.

"And now to hang you, *muchacho*," laughed La Liebre, realizing that he'd been just about this boy's age when they killed his mother and sisters and disfigured him. "We got to show the people what happens to a thief!"

They took Victoriano down through the waste and dragged him across the creek to the plaza. Señor Jones went back to the crushing plant and took the main road around the canyon so he could watch without seeming to be involved.

Lupe was in the back of Doña Manza's bakery, doing her studies with the rest of the children when she heard the bell tower down in the plaza. The ringing of the bell was normally a sign of celebration. So Lupe and the other children hurried around the stone building with their teacher to see what was going on, when she suddenly saw some men throwing a rope into the tree above her brother's head, preparing to hang him.

Lupe let out a scream, putting her hands over her face in horror.

"Run!" said Señora Muñoz to Lupe, recognizing Victoriano, too. "Get your mother! Doña Manza and I will see what we can do!"

Lupe was off like a shot, racing past Señor Jones, who was lighting a fresh cigar in the shade of a tree as she went flying up the pathway to her home.

"Mama! Mama!" screamed Lupe, rushing into the kitchen. "They're hanging Victoriano in the plaza!"

Doña Guadalupe was at the stove. She'd been putting together what little bits and pieces she had, trying to assemble a meal for the miners tonight. "Who? What are you talking about?" said her mother, seeing Lupe's terror-filled face.

"Victoriano!" wailed Lupe in terror. "La Liebre is going to hang him!"

Doña Guadalupe dropped the huge kettle, staring at her daughter in disbelief. Then she was moving, doing, not asking another question. And she rushed into the lean-to, all her blood pounding through her body and exploding in her head.

"Quick," she said, ravaging through her wooden chest, "run down to the plaza and get Don Manuel to stall them; tell him that I'm coming to give my son his final blessing!"

"Yes!" yelled Lupe, running back out of the lean-to, through the *ramada*, and flying down the steep hillside in great leaps.

Finding her father's gun at the bottom of the chest, Doña Guadalupe took a deep breath. The man who'd raised her and whom she'd called "father" for over thirty years had been the greatest, bravest man that she'd ever known. She'd never forget, as long as she lived, the morning that their destinies had crossed. She'd been nothing but a child, just starting to talk, and at daybreak the soldiers had hit their encampment, setting fire to their homes and shooting her people, who were Yaqui Indians, as they'd come screaming out of their huts.

Her parents were shot and left to bleed to death. Their home was leaping in flames. Her hair had caught fire and she'd come out of hiding behind her mother's dead body. She'd run out of the door, straight toward her enemy with open arms.

The-Man-God-Had-Sent-To-Her turned and saw her. He was just going to lower his rifle but, instead, he whirled about and shot the soldier right next to him who had taken aim at her. Then The-Man-God-Sent-to-Her got a blanket and smothered the fire in her hair and, while the slaughter continued, he mounted a horse and took off with her. They rode night and day and when one horse dropped, he stole another. Getting to his house, he packed up his wife and children and they fled into the night. They set up residence in a new town high in the foothills. He named the child Guadalupe and raised her as his own.

Remembering all this in exploding flashes inside her mind's eye, Doña Guadalupe now checked her father's pistol to make sure that it was loaded. Then she calmly got her black shawl, placed the pistol underneath it, up inside the armpit of her dress. She took a big breath, picked up her Bible and rosary, and got a small knife from the kitchen, which she put under her Bible before leaving the lean-to.

People had already begun to gather outside the *ramada* to give her their condolences, but she didn't see them as she passed by. She was of one heart, one mind; she was a mother, a woman, concentrated down to the marrow of her bones on doing one thing, and nothing—absolutely nothing—could distract her, not even death itself.

And there she came, short and plump, walking quickly down the rocky trail that zigzagged between the houses, and the village people saw her coming and they moved aside.

In the plaza, Doña Guadalupe saw that they had her skinny little son under the tree with a noose about his neck. She could also see that they'd abused him, he had so much blood running from his face and the front of his shirt. It took all her power to not cry out in pain and rush up to her baby boy. But remembering her father, Doña Guadalupe held herself strong and continued with all the dignity she could, going down the steep steps into the plaza itself.

Her daughters were being held back by a dozen soldiers, and Don Manuel was arguing with the monstrous-faced man as she came through the crowd.

Soldiers were everywhere. Señor Jones was over to the side, smoking a cigar. This was going to be much more difficult than she'd expected.

"Here she comes now, for God's sake!" shouted Don Manuel, seeing Victoriano's mother coming through the crowd.

"All right," said La Liebre. "She can give him her last blessing, but then no more! He hangs, and that's final!"

Seeing her mother, Lupe got down on all fours to crawl under the soldiers' legs who were holding her and her sisters back with the crowd. But one of the soldiers saw her and grabbed her by her hair, jerking her back so viciously that Lupe felt the skin pull away from her eyes.

"Don't you do that again!" said Sophia, grabbing Lupe in her arms. "All we can do now is pray for a miracle, *mi hijita.*"

"Mama will save him!" screamed Carlota. "I know she will!"

Maria was holding Carlota in her arms. Esabel was standing behind Maria, giving her comfort.

Don Manuel was still arguing, trying to prove to the people that he was a just man and that he wasn't a pawn of the American company.

And all this time, Señor Jones stood over to the side, joined by a couple of his young engineers. One was eagerly setting up his camera to take pictures.

And then out came El Borracho, getting up from behind the huge tree in which they were going to hang Victoriano. He'd been asleep in a drunken stupor the whole time. Glancing about, he couldn't figure out what was going on.

Doña Guadalupe rushed forward. She was just about to hug her son when the man called The Jack Rabbit stepped in front of her. "Wait!" he said. "What do you got there with that Bible?"

"My rosary," she said.

"Let me see," he said.

"No, let her be!" yelled Don Manuel. "Haven't you done enough?"

"You better shut up, old man," said La Liebre, turning on the mayor. "We caught him with the gold!"

As they spoke, Doña Guadalupe rushed to her son and hugged him, covering him with her shawl and whispering in his ear. But Victoriano was so far gone that he didn't recognize her, much less understand what she was saying.

Doña Guadalupe cried out in grief, pretending to lose control.

La Liebre could see that the crowd was getting louder and his men were having a hard time holding them back. People were coming out from everywhere—from rooftops, from over walls—and they outnumbered his men sixty to one.

"All right," said La Liebre, "to show I'm a fair man, she can give her son her blessing, but then no more!" He drew his revolver. "The law must be respected! He's a thief and he must hang!"

Hearing this, El Borracho laughed and turned his ass toward the many-scarred leader, lifted his right leg and let out a tremendous fart.

"This is what I think of you and your law!" said El Borracho, cranking his ass around and around, farting all the while. "You don't do shit unless Señor Jones pulls your rope. You ugly abortion of the devil!"

Everyone in the plaza heard his words, and they were just going to laugh when La Liebre brought up his pistol, firing once, twice, three times, sending El Borracho's body jerking forward with each shot.

Blood and foam boiled out of El Borracho's mouth as he came to rest in a sitting position, eyes still staring in shock.

Silence fell over the plaza. No one so much as breathed. But then people started screaming, bellowing, raising their fists in anger. El Borracho was one of their most beloved people. He and his wife had brought their children into the world and sang and danced at their weddings.

And at this moment, Doña Guadalupe took her knife from under her shawl and tried to cut the rope between her son's two fists. But Victoriano's hands were tied so close together that she couldn't get the blade between them.

"Turn your wrist," she said, "quick, we don't have much time!"

But Victoriano didn't move his wrists and so, out of desperation, Doña Guadalupe took his ear between her teeth, biting and twisting it with all her might. He opened his eyes wide with pain. Suddenly, he saw his mother and realized what was going on. His mother told him what to do again, and this time, Victoriano understood her words and his mind came reeling to the present. He turned his wrists. He could feel her cutting. But they'd tied him up with a twisted rawhide rope and it was tough cutting.

Then Victoriano saw La Liebre coming toward them, reloading his pistol.

"All right," said La Liebre, grabbing Doña Guadalupe by the shoulder. "That's enough! Get away from there!"

The people screamed, yelling for La Liebre to let her finish her blessing. Their roar was so great that the many-scarred man lifted his arms, gesturing that it was all right.

"*Mi hijito*," Doña Guadalupe whispered, "I have a gun under my shawl. And as soon as you're free, I'll give it to you, then I'll leap back, screaming. And you run to the creek." She was cutting the final strand. "Understand, *mi hijito*, I'm not cutting you free so you can be brave and get killed. I want you running so you can live. You run, you hear me? You run for the creek when I jump back."

His hands were suddenly free.

"Don't move yet," she said. "Work your hands. Get circulation into them. Do it now!"

He did as told. And she could see that his eyes looked alert now. She felt he was ready. "Here's the gun, take it. I love you, *mi hijito*. I love you with all my heart. Run! When I leap back!"

And she leapt back with her arms stretched up toward the sky, giving him cover as she screamed to the heavens, "God be with you, my son!"

But it was all for no good. The man called The Jack Rabbit had been through many battles. So, when he saw the old woman leap back with arms stretched up toward the heavens, he drew his gun, knowing it was an escape, and rushed in, knocking her out of the way.

In that split moment, just as he was turning to run, Victoriano saw the man of lightning reflexes come racing behind his mother. He stopped. He crouched, spinning about, fully realizing that he could never get away from this man who was so fast. He fired over his mother's shoulder just as La Liebre's ugly face suddenly appeared before him.

The man's face exploded with red blood and pieces of white bone, and then Victoriano was running, shooting into the air as he ran, drawing the soldiers away from his beloved mother.

People scattered—soldiers and villagers alike. Lupe and her sisters broke from the crowd and rushed to their mother as half of the armed men chased after their brother.

But Victoriano was gone, racing through the thick foliage below the plaza, jumping over the rocks that he'd known all his life. Then he leapt into the water, going over the series of short waterfalls where the roaring white waters went down to a steady, blue flow.

The soldiers fired a few quick shots at his turning, twisting, swimming body, but then quit the chase and went back to the plaza.

When they got back, they found the courtyard full of people. The chubby redheaded man was in charge now that La Liebre was dead. He'd arrested the old woman and the mayor.

"But I didn't know she had a gun!" shouted Don Manuel, as they dragged him and Doña Guadalupe across the cobblestones.

Under the big tree, the soldiers put a rope around the necks of the mayor and Doña Guadalupe. But the people had had enough; they were willing to die so they could live. They came pouring through the armed men like rain through an open hand, mobbing the walkways, climbing over rooftops and stone fences by the hundreds.

Señora Muñoz brought all her children under the tree where they were preparing to hang Doña Guadalupe and Don Manuel. She sat down with them on the cobblestones and they began to sing. Lupe and her family joined them and so did Doña Manza's family. The rest of the people understood what was happening, and Lupe and her sisters watched them carpet the plaza with their bodies packed so tightly together that the soldiers couldn't move, much less throw the rope up into the branches to do the hanging.

The singing filled the canyon, traveling up to the mighty cathedral rocks and coming back down in an echoing symphony of sound.

Lupe gripped her mother's hand with her right hand and Manuelita's with her left. The singing continued and grew in strength until it was of such naked, raw magnitude that Lupe just knew to the marrow of her bones that they were united with God. They were with God Almighty and He was giving them His power.

Señor Jones was the first one to realize what was happening, and he threw his cigar down and left quickly.

Then the redheaded leader glanced about, trying to figure out how he could get out of the plaza before they ripped his weapons away from him and beat him to death. He took the rope off Doña Guadalupe's neck and fled. The other soldiers followed him.

People saw the fear in the soldiers' eyes as they fled, fear that they'd been feeling themselves all their lives. It gave them heart; they raised their voices all the more. Tears came to Lupe's eyes. They'd done it, they really had. And she continued to sing.

Well over five hundred men, women, and children were singing. Their united voices drowned out even the great thundering noises of the American gold mine company. The miners quit their labor and stood up to listen. Then they dropped their tools to go see what was going on with their families down in the town.

Lupe and her sisters hugged their mother, weeping with joy. A great flock of parrots came sweeping down from the towering cliffs, squawking loudly.

"Angels," said Lupe, and everyone turned and saw that it was true. The parrots were, indeed, angels.

All that night, the Americans slept with guns at their sides for the first time since the Revolution had begun. Soldiers, they'd always been able to handle in one way or another, but this was something entirely different.

The moon came out and the coyotes howled, and the people of the canyon remained united in God's wondrous spirit far into the night.

TWO

THE HAND
OF GOD

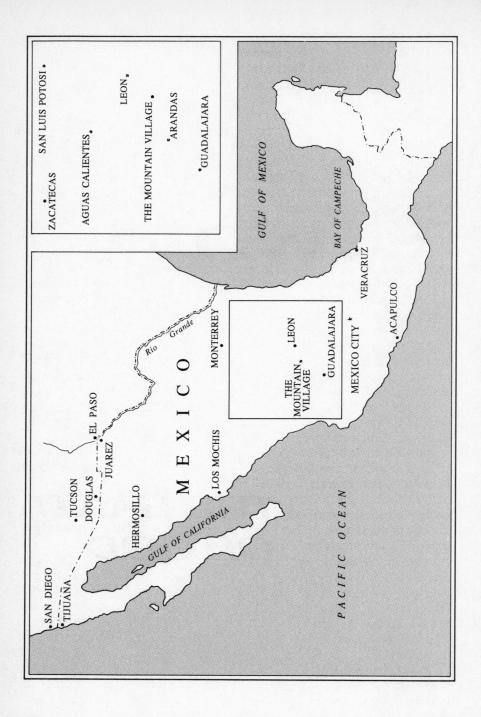

ZACATECAS
SAN LUIS POTOSI
AGUAS CALIENTES
LEON
THE MOUNTAIN VILLAGE
ARANDAS
GUADALAJARA

GULF OF MEXICO

BAY OF CAMPECHE

VERACRUZ

ACAPULCO

M E X I C O

Rio Grande

MONTERREY

THE MOUNTAIN VILLAGE
LEON
GUADALAJARA
MEXICO CITY

EL PASO
JUAREZ
LOS MOCHIS

TUCSON
DOUGLAS
HERMOSILLO

GULF OF CALIFORNIA

SAN DIEGO
TIJUANA

PACIFIC OCEAN

The year was 1869 and his name was Don Pio Castro. He was short, dark, strong, heavy-bearded, and he was riding north from Mexico City along with his two older brothers, Cristobal and Agustin, looking for raw, unused land.

Don Pio was one of the greatest horsemen in all the republic, and he'd fought alongside the great Don Benito Juarez against the French. He'd risen to the rank of Colonel and, after they'd defeated the French, he'd laid down his arms, leaving the army of his own free will, thinking that it was now time to put together the nation that had been torn apart by war.

Riding north from Mexico City on fine horses and leading two good mules, Don Pio and his two older brothers passed through the pastoral valley of Guanajuato and saw the rich haciendas and the well-watered fields and the well-fed livestock. But they found nothing they could use. All the good lands had long ago been taken by the Church or the rich and powerful.

On the twenty-first day of their journey north, Don Pio and his brothers came to the mountains on the west side of the Guanajuato Valley and they climbed up into the high country called Los Altos de Jalisco.

That night Don Pio and his brothers camped on a knoll high above the valley floor and they looked down into the rich valley controlled by the rich *hacendados*. Don Pio's heart grew heavy.

He was married, he had three daughters, and he'd been fighting for the welfare of his beloved country for well over twenty years. First, he'd fought as a boy down in the lower part of the boot of Mexico against the *hacendados*, who'd kept him and his parents in servitude for generations.

Then he'd taken up arms along with Benito Juarez and Porfirio Diaz. They'd fought the well-armed, well-trained French soldiers with nothing but their bare hands and the hope to see a better day for their children. The people died by the thousands. Don Pio alone lost six brothers, five sisters, both of his parents, and all of his uncles and cousins. But for what? Even after they had won, the rich still controlled the good lands like the valley before him.

Don Pio sat there, looking down into the darkness, feeling perplexed and tired. But he couldn't sleep. It seemed to him that maybe it was never going to change. He'd seen good men from humble origins get a little power and change overnight into ruthless monsters against the poor.

Cristobal and Agustin said good night to Don Pio and went to sleep rolled up in their blankets. Don Pio put some more wood on the fire and stayed up, looking at the stars and heavens. He and his brothers had been looking for undeveloped land for over a year and they didn't have much time. Of the thousand who'd followed Don Pio out of the army, he only had about a hundred good men left. The others had lost faith in him and had gone back to work under the same yoke of the *hacendados*—whom they had fought so hard to escape—or they'd turned into bandits.

Don Pio sat there on the grassy knoll, small and wiry. He looked more Spanish-Moor than full-blooded Indian. He stared down into the darkness. He knew he couldn't afford to fail his few remaining men, and he knew he couldn't afford to pass up the offer that he'd recently received from a rich man named La Farga. La Farga had offered to back Don Pio and his men with enough money so they could build up a ranch and they could all make a good profit.

He sat there, thinking, figuring, looking up at the stars and heavens and then down into the darkness of the valley.

A coyote called in the distance and the moon went behind some clouds. Don Pio brought out his rosary and began to finger the crude, round beads made of stone, rolling them between his thumb and index finger as he asked God for guidance.

He sat there on the knoll, listening to their horses and mules grazing alongside him in the quiet of the night and he prayed long and hard, truly needing God's help as he'd never needed it before.

Suddenly, across the valley, he saw a small pale light and he knew it was God coming to speak to him. He could feel it in his heart. The coyote called again. Don Pio sat on the knoll, looking at the small, pale light across the valley of darkness and he felt no fear. God was with him. God, the Creator of all things, was here with him. Don Pio gave himself over to God, without question, and a great peace came over him.

The light exploded, bursting through the rosy-white clouds in beautiful colors of yellow and pink. Don Pio sat up, captivated by the magic of it all. Then he realized that this was, indeed, the miracle of a whole new day.

His eyes filled with tears and he sat there in rapture, giving witness to the new day that Almighty God was giving him and he suddenly realized what a new day really was; it was a fresh start in *la vida* for mankind. Each morning was a whole new beginning.

He smiled, tears of joy coming to his eyes, and he watched the light of the new day come across the darkness of the valley, reaching out to him on God's rosy-light fingers over the distant mountains, across the valley of Guanajuato some two hundred miles away. He fingered the stone rosary in his dark, small, well-made, callus-hard hands, and instantly, in one bursting, flashing moment, he knew everything.

"Wake up!" he yelled, leaping to his feet and shouting to his brothers. "We've found it! This is the place!"

His two brothers awoke. Cristobal, big and strong, growled like a bear for having been awakened. But Agustin, of medium height and build, simply sat up, rubbing his eyes.

"This is the place we've been searching for!" repeated Don Pio excitedly.

Looking around, his two brothers scrutinized the knoll on which they'd camped and they saw nothing but dark rocks and cliffs, groves of wild oaks and steep gullies.

"Don Pio," said Cristobal, "you've lost your mind, go back to sleep—nothing will grow here!"

But Don Pio refused to be silenced, standing up tall and proud—all five foot, two inches of him. "That's it exactly! It will be hard to get anything to grow here! That's why nobody wants this land! They only think it's fit for goats and snakes! That's why we can build our homes here and raise our children in peace for generations to come!"

"And they'll be strong, hard-working children because every man will have to do his own labor! And at no time will our children or our children's children get so rich that they'll be able to enslave their neighbor!"

"You're damned right, they won't!" bellowed Cristobal, tossing his blanket to the side and leaping to his feet in raging anger. "Because they'll starve!"

"No, not starve," said Don Pio, "but stay strong! And be able to live in peace for generations because the rich and powerful won't ever want these lands! Believe me, dear brother, this is the place we've been searching for all of our lives!"

Towering over Don Pio, Cristobal glanced around at the cliffs and rocks and trees and he spat on the ground. "If you choose this place," he said, "then I'm out, Don Pio! I fought too long and too hard to end up in these God-forsaken mountains like *un indio sin razón!*"

But Don Pio wasn't about to lose his oldest brother; he was the most loyal and greatest of all fighters. "Please," he said, "calm down, *hermanito*. This morning I had a vision. God spoke to me, and showed me that each new day is a miracle. Each new day is a whole new beginning. That's why I see everything so clearly right now and I can say to you, without a shadow of a doubt, that this, my dear brothers, is the place that we've been looking for. Not that rich valley down below where powerful men can enslave the poor, no matter how many battles we fight and win. This is the place where we can reach up to the heavens every morning of our lives and touch the hand of God with an honest heart!"

Don Pio reached up to the heavens with both hands, arms rippling with muscle. Cristobal saw his brother's large, dark eyes, and he knew that he was insane with joy.

Screaming with rage, Cristobal continued to argue. But Agustin, the middle brother, the calmer brother who was married and had six sons and five daughters, simply rolled out of his blanket and put some wood on the fire, heated a bunch of tortillas, cut some hard, cured cheese, and handed each brother a *burrito*.

Cristobal ate and shouted at Don Pio until the food hit his stomach. Then he quit and they saddled up their horses, rode over the top of the knoll, through the oak forest and to the high lakes covered with wild lilies.

Their horses and mules drank and they rode down into the deep canyons where the wild orchids grew. They saw deer and quail, forest and grassland, cliffs of rock and flat-topped mesas. They shot a fat deer and ate to their fill. They grazed their horses and two mules, then returned to Mexico City.

Six months later they came back with fifty men and their families. They worked like free men from sun to sun, building roads, houses, and a small settlement on the knoll on which they'd camped that first night.

The following year Don Pio brought his wife, Silveria, a woman of Indian and European breeding, and his three teenaged daughters. He built his home on the highest point on the knoll. He faced the front door of their *casa* to the east so he and his family could give witness to the miracle of each new day.

The years passed by and Don Pio was fast at work on a schoolhouse for his children when word came that his great friend, Benito Juarez, had died.

Don Pio mourned Don Benito's death as if his own father had died. The great Benito Juarez had been Don Pio's inspiration of what a man could be: strong, serious, respectful, and yet gentle, good and loyal.

Years later Don Pio was made the marshal of the whole region by the new *Presidente*, Don Porfirio. It saddened Don Pio's heart when he and his Rurales had to hunt down good men, ex-soldiers, who'd refused to settle down into the hard task of earning their daily bread. In the years that followed, Don Pio and his Rurales became so feared that bandit groups would rather ride a hundred miles around them than come through their mountainous area of Los Altos de Jalisco.

Don Pio's daughters grew, matured, married, and had children. He tried to find time to finish the schoolhouse for his grandchildren, but he just didn't seem to find time. And yet, the years were kind to Don Pio and his beautiful wife, Silveria. They grew old together and every morning took their first cup of hot, spicy chocolate with the rising sun on the terrace of their home so they could watch their grandchildren on their way to work in the fields.

But then, just before the turn of the century, Don Pio was asked to do something by his old friend Don Porfirio that he didn't think was just: to become a guard for the rich *hacendados* down in the valley. Don Pio refused and was relieved of his duties as a marshal.

New lawmen were brought into the area by Don Porfirio's people. These lawmen didn't work the land with their hands. They weren't married. They were from other regions and knew nothing of the local people. They wore beautiful uniforms, rode great horses, and would shoot a boy for just taking a few corn cobs from a field to eat.

Then came word that Don Porfirio had proclaimed himself the permanent

President General of Mexico. He wasn't going to allow any serious contenders to run against him anymore. Don Pio thought his old friend had gone too far, but still he said nothing.

The years passed, the injustices grew, and finally a grandson of one of Don Pio's ex-soldiers was shot for cutting a little alfalfa in a field for his horse. So Don Pio saddled up to go to see this man, *El Presidente,* with whom he'd fought, shoulder-to-shoulder, for over two decades.

The day that Don Pio and a dozen of his old *compadres*-in-arms rode down the mountain with their sons and grandsons, the whole settlement came out to watch them go. And his oldest daughter, Margarita, who had married Juan Villaseñor, brought out her two youngest boys, Juan and Domingo, to say goodbye to their beloved grandfather.

Domingo was eleven years old and Juan was six. Don Pio kissed each boy, holding him to his heart. Little Juan got the full smell of his grandfather and felt his hard, white beard against his cheek. Then Juan watched his *abuelito* ride off on his stallion with the four white stockings.

It had been more than thirty years since Don Pio had been to the Capitol. Arriving at the outskirts of the city, Don Pio and his men were stopped by a hundred well-fed, well-equipped soldiers in beautiful uniforms who said that no dirty Indians were allowed into the Capitol during Don Porfirio's great celebration.

Foreign dignitaries from all over the world were in town celebrating Don Porfirio's eightieth birthday, and so *El Presidente* had given word that absolutely no one was to interrupt his celebration.

With all the dignity he could muster, Don Pio refused to take the insult and informed the officer in charge that he was Colonel Pio Castro, also ex-marshal of Los Altos de Jalisco, and that he was a close friend of Don Porfirio and had an urgent message for him.

The handsome young officer, Lieutenant Manuel Maytorena, only smiled and said, "That's fine, my Colonel, and now you, too, can camp here alongside the river with your men along with the thousands of other Colonels who've come to see his majesty."

Two of Don Pio's old soldiers went for their guns. No one had ever spoken abusively to Don Pio and lived. But Don Pio told his old *amigos* to hold their weapons and simply repeated his message to the well-dressed officer.

Then Don Pio and his men went down to the river to camp. And it was true; camped alongside the river were thousands of ex-soldiers and among them were, indeed, dozens of great, old Colonels who'd fought alongside Don Porfirio and Benito Juarez shoulder-to-shoulder.

Don Pio and his men waited for ten days, camped outside the Capitol for which he'd fought for two decades. Finally, two of Don Pio's grandsons and four of their young friends couldn't stand the abuse that the great Don Pio had received. They rode into the city in the cover of night, unarmed, carrying a white flag, only to be shot down.

The well-fed, well-armed soldiers hit Don Pio's camp at dawn, killing five of his old *compadres*-in-arms and ten of their sons and grandsons. Don Pio cried that day as he'd never cried before.

The French, whom he'd beaten in battle time and again with sometimes nothing but his bare hands and rocks, had won, after all. Don Porfirio, his old friend, had become white, rich, and French.

8

*He was the baby of the family, the nineteenth child,
having come to his mother on her fiftieth birthday—a
gift from God, he was told.*

His name was Juan Salvador Villaseñor Castro, Don
Pio's thirty-seventh grandson. He was eleven years old and full of the devil as
he came running down the dirt road as quickly as his short legs could carry
him. He was barefoot, lifting dust as he came, and his little pot-belly swung
side to side. There was a rich corn field to the left of him and a huge, walled-
in *hacienda* in the distance. Coming to a small rise, Juan Salvador gripped his
little straw hat so it wouldn't blow off and upped his pace, screaming
frantically as he came down the other side of the hill.

"Soldiers!" he yelled. "Villistas!"

Up ahead he could see his old, grey-haired mother, his two sisters and his
little niece and baby nephew get to their tired feet in a hurry so that they
could get off the road, not wanting to be trampled by the approaching
soldiers.

Seeing the fear that he'd caused, Juan Salvador laughed, loving it, and
screamed all the more. He could see the rest of the people, who'd been
resting in the shade of the big mesquite tree, get to their tired feet to escape
the approaching soldiers, too. And further down the road, a good quarter of
a mile beyond where his mother and sisters were, Juan also saw the foreman
from the big *hacienda* turn his white horse and look at him.

Jerking his hat off his head, Juan waved it, screaming as loud as he could,
"Villistas! Villistas!"

Hearing the sharp cries, the foreman whirled his bony old horse around.
He shouted a warning to the workers he was overseeing and took off for the
safety of the *hacienda* as fast as he could go. His workers, mostly women,
children and old men, were on foot and they didn't follow him. Instead, they
ran through the corn field and jumped into a ditch.

Seeing the ruckus he'd caused, Juan tried hard not to laugh as he now
watched the foreman, Cara de Nopal, screaming, "Soldiers! Soldiers!" as he
ran through the gates of the big *hacienda* with his poor animal's tail whirling
about from being over-spurred.

Stopping, Juan caught his breath, then put his straw hat back on and continued down the white, hot, soft dirt road at a leisurely trot toward his family who was hiding behind their little cart and a tired old burro so that they wouldn't be trampled by the approaching soldiers.

Juan and his family had been on the road for weeks. They were on their way north, hoping to cross the Rio Grande at El Paso, Texas, into the safety of the United States. Their settlement up in Los Altos de Jalisco, that Don Pio had built to last for ten generations, had been destroyed.

"Oh, Mama," said Juan, coming up to his tired old mother, Doña Margarita, "come out of hiding. I lied! No soldiers are coming!"

"Oh, I'm going to kill you!" yelled Luisa, who at eighteen years old was Juan's oldest living sister.

"No, not now!" laughed Juan. "Quick, we've got to get the cart back on the road and pick all the corn we can and get out of here before Cara de Nopal comes back out with his rifle!"

The pock-faced foreman's reputation for shooting defenseless women and children was known up and down the valley. But also it was known that he was a coward when it came to armed men.

"Oh, *mi hijito*," said Doña Margarita, "may God forgive you, because I'm not going to. You scared me to death!"

"Don't worry, Mama," said Juan, grinning, "don't you see? God has already forgiven me; it worked, and we're alive!"

His mother laughed. Her youngest child was only eleven years old, but he'd been fighting and twisting between the lines of the war for so many years that he was very experienced at the art of holding onto life and not dropping down death's dark canyon.

He took his mother's hand, helping her out of the ditch that ran alongside the road. The ditch was full of brush and thorny cactus, and there was a stone wall behind it.

Luisa already had hold of the burro's reins, pulling at the little animal to get the cart back on the road. Juan's other sister, Emilia, was sixteen and she was pushing at the back of the cart. Emilia was tall and slender and big with child. She had been raped by soldiers several months before and the humiliation had caused her to go blind.

"Come on, Emilia, and you, too, Inocenta, push, while I pull!" yelled Luisa.

Luisa was Juan's oldest sister. She was wide and strong and redheaded like their father, Juan Villaseñor.

Inocenta, small and dark with big beautiful eyes, was five years old. She got behind the cart and pushed along with Emilia. She was the daughter of their sister, Lucha, who'd abandoned them a few weeks before when they'd been attacked by soldiers.

Getting his tired old mother on the road, Juan went back down into the ditch to help his sisters and niece push the cart up on the road. Luisa's three-month-old baby, Joselito, was in the cart, sleeping peacefully.

"All right, Mama," said Juan, "you and Emilia start the burro up the road while Luisa and Inocenta help me pick the corn! We don't have much time, unless we want to get our asses shot!"

And he laughed, running across the road with Luisa and Inocenta into the corn field. They began picking the corn as fast as they could, not bothering to even knock off the big red stinging ants that crawled on their hands and arms.

The other people saw what was going on, and some of them ran across the road to pick some corn, too. But most of them didn't dare. Two days before, Cara de Nopal had shot a boy for stealing corn. His body still hung in the tree outside the gates of the *hacienda*.

Anxiously, Doña Margarita kept glancing toward the big stone walls of the *hacienda* as she held the reins of the little burro. Oh, she just didn't want to lose any more children; she only had these three left of all nineteen that she'd brought into the world.

Seeing that Juan was coming with another armful of corn, Doña Margarita turned to her blind daughter. "Get in the wagon, Emilia," she said. "We're going to have to run as soon as they finish."

"Oh, no, Mama," said Emilia. She also had reddish-auburn hair like their father, but she wasn't wide and strong like Luisa. She was delicately beautiful. "I may not see, but I can still run, Mama. You get in the wagon and hold the baby while I run behind, holding onto the wagon."

"Emilia," said Doña Margarita, glancing toward the gates once more, "it's rocky up ahead and you might trip. Remember, you're not just half blind, you're big with child, too!"

Just then, Juan came running with a third armful of corn, tossing it into the wagon.

"Get in, both of you!" he yelled. "Quick! Before Cara de Nopal comes out! And cover up the corn with your shawls and dresses!"

"But, *mi hijito*," said Doña Margarita, "the burro's too old to pull us both."

"Not half as old as you, Mama," said Juan, shoving his mother into the back of the wagon.

"Oh, you are spoiled!" said his mother, settling herself in the wagon and covering the corn with her dress and shawl. "May the dog of the moon bite your silver tongue tonight!"

"Only if he can catch me, Mama," said Juan, kicking the burro in the ass. "Let's go, *burrito*! *Vámonos!*"

And there came Luisa with her arms full of corn. Inocenta was right behind her.

"You, too, Emilia, get in!" said Luisa. "And cover up the corn with your dress like Juan said."

Emilia quickly obeyed her husky, strong-willed sister and got in the cart with no more argument.

Pulling and jerking, Juan could hear the hollow, gurgling noise of their little burro's belly as they hurried down the road. The little burro's face was all white from age, but still he farted and pulled, doing the best he could. Juan hated to push the tired old animal, but they had to get past the *hacienda* before Cara de Nopal come out again. Juan loved this little burro. This was the animal that he'd learned how to ride on up and down the *barrancas* of his grandfather's settlement.

Juan was wide like his sister Luisa, but he wasn't light-skinned like her. He was dark like his mother's side of the family, and his eyes were surrounded with beautiful, long, thick eyelashes.

Then they were just coming up by the tall, solid planked gates of the *hacienda* when Juan glanced up and saw the body of the boy who'd been shot, hanging upside down in the tree with his swollen, dry tongue sticking out. Flies were buzzing all around his head. Juan gasped, realizing he never should have looked. At that moment, the huge gates opened, and there was Cara de Nopal, mounted on his bony, old white horse with a rifle in his hand.

"Why are you running?" he shouted, pointing his rifle at them. He was in his late twenties, and from up close looked even uglier than his reputation.

"The soldiers!" said Juan.

The foreman glanced down the road. "I see no soldiers," he said, pointing his rifle at Juan. "Let me see what you and your family have in your wagon, *muchacho*."

Juan swallowed. He didn't know what to say. He was only a good liar when he could plan out his lie ahead of time. But then his sister Luisa, hot-tempered and quick-witted, screamed. "Oh, my God! Here they come! Villistas! And they told us that they're going to kill you because you helped the Carranzistas yesterday!"

"But I didn't!" cried Cara de Nopal, jerking his horse back inside between the tall gates. "They forced me! You tell them that for me!" He whirled his horse around. The two old men closed the solid wood gates behind him.

Luisa and Juan glanced at each other, laughing, then started down the road with the cart as quickly as they could go. They had to put as much distance as they could between themselves and this big *hacienda* before nightfall.

The sun was going down behind the mountains in the distance when Juan and his family stopped to make camp alongside a small river outside San Francisco del Rincon with two dozen other people fleeing from their homes. They could hear the cannons and see the flashes of the shooting ahead in the flat distance of the wide valley. The word was that Francisco Villa was in a battle with General Obregon just outside of Leon, the capitol of the state of Guanajuato.

Juan unharnessed the burro and watered him, then massaged his back and shoulders and hobbled him for the night so that the little tired animal could graze freely. While his mother and sisters began building a shelter for the night, Juan and his niece, Inocenta, went into the flat little breaks to gather dry cow pies for the evening fire. Dried-out cow manure made a much better fire than wood. It burned longer, hotter and caused less smoke.

Gathering an armful of big, round, grey-brown cow droppings, Juan headed back to the camp in the soft, rosy-colored light of the ending day. They had chosen a good place to make camp. There was lots of brush and rock for them to build a shelter to protect them from the wind and cold.

Back in camp, Juan quickly started a fire with leaves and twigs and then Inocenta helped him build a little tepee of up-ended cow pies over the top of the small fire. Once the fire was going well, the family gathered around and roasted the ears of corn that they'd soaked in chile water with plenty of salt. It was wonderful, sitting around the smokeless fire and smelling the corn cook.

Up the line, someone began to strum a guitar and sing as the last of the daylight disappeared back up on the mountains to the east, the very same country in which Don Pio had camped on a knoll some fifty years ago, searching for an answer for living in peace.

Smiling, Juan took his corn cob off the fire and began to eat it while it was still so hot that it burned his fingertips and hurt his lips. It was delicious, spicy-hot and salty. He ate with relish, licking his fingers.

"Oh, I wish we hadn't come so far," he said, "so I could sneak back in the morning and steal more corn!"

"You ever yell 'soldiers' like that again—without telling us first—and I'll kill you!" said Luisa.

"Only if you can catch me," said Juan.

They all laughed and continued eating, truly enjoying themselves. It had been another good day; they'd gotten food to fill their bellies and they were still alive.

Finishing his third ear of corn, Juan began to feel sleepy, so he lay back on his mother's lap, watching the last of their fire. His mother stroked him softly, gently.

"All right," said their mother, pushing Juan away, "we better clear the ground and check for scorpions so we can go to sleep. Tomorrow we're going to have to get an early start so we can get past Leon and wait out the heat of the day in the shade."

Juan burped, got to his feet and helped his family sweep the ground around the shelter they'd built. And as Juan worked, he saw his blind sister's leg and he just couldn't help himself. He dragged the burro's rope across her naked calf, yelling, "Snake!" Emilia jumped up, screaming in fear.

Juan burst out laughing. Luisa was on him in a flash, gripping him by the ears. "You monster!" she yelled, hitting him across the skull.

"No!" shouted their mother. "Stop that, Luisa! His ears are too big already!"

"But he's getting wilder every day we go!" said Luisa, hitting him again as Juan dodged and jerked.

"*Mi hijita*," said their mother, "he was only playing. And, Emilia, I don't care how blind you are, you can still tell the difference between a rope and a snake. Now come, all of you, let us kneel so we can do our evening prayers."

They all knelt down inside the little shelter that they'd built on the well-swept earth and their mother led them in their evening prayers as the cannons continued to shout in the distance.

"Thank you, dear God," she said, "we are far from home and the land we know but still You provided us with corn, the staff of life. We are Your humble servants and appreciate how You always give us Your helping hand in our hour of darkness. I have lost my husband and most of my children and we don't know our way. We can hear the explosions of death in the distance, but with Your guidance, we have no fear, for You are our Shepherd, dear merciful God."

And so she prayed, not saying the usual memorized prayers that people learned in church. But, instead, she made up her own words for the Almighty, and she spoke each word, each syllable, as if it had never been spoken before.

She was Don Pio's daughter, after all. And so like him, she was stout-hearted in her absolute belief that all things were possible in life, if only one was open and true to God.

Doña Margarita knelt there, and her family repeated each word she spoke, clearly, distinctly and with all their hearts. And as they prayed, Juan looked up into the heavens, fully expecting to see God come riding across the sky on His great stallion with four white stockings. God was the horseman of the universe, after all, who rode herd on all the stars and planets, keeping them in order. God was the force that gave men and women heart in their hour of darkness. And, at any moment, Juan expected to see God coming across the heavens, mounted on a great stallion with a star-studded sombrero and a lariat in His hand.

O nly once during the night did Juan awaken. And he almost cried out in fear, thinking they were back home and their house was on fire and screaming horsemen were stealing their livestock. But then he saw his mother lying beside him on the rock-hard ground, and he saw the stars overhead and he heard the river running gently nearby. He knew he wasn't home and all was safe.

The coyotes were calling on the other side of the river. The coyotes were working and teaching their young how to hunt together like a family, and so everything was fine.

Juan turned over and saw his mother's large, dark eyes shining there in the night, and he drew himself closer to her. She took him in her arms and he was her little lost, scared child once again. The night was a very different time for Juan than the day. At night Juan would forget that he was eleven years old and big and strong. At night Juan was his mother's little baby, a gift from God, he'd been told.

Juan went back to sleep, listening to his mother's heartbeat, knowing that the world was good when he was in her arms.

In the morning when Juan awoke, he was so hungry that he couldn't think of anything else. So he quickly got up, relieved himself, and hurried to the warm ashes of the cow dung and poked through them with a stick, searching for the corn nuts that they'd shredded off the cobs the night before to roast. Finding some, his face lit up with joy as he took them in his hand, blew off the ashes and popped them into his mouth.

"*¡Qué bueno!*" he said, chewing noisily and rubbing his stomach like a little bear. "Hurry, Mama! The nuts are delicious! Oh, I'm so glad that ugly, no-good Cara de Nopal is so ruthless. He saved more corn for us to steal from him."

"*Mi hijito,*" said Doña Margarita, rubbing her tired, sleep-swollen old eyes, "I've told you a thousand times, if you speak badly of people, God will punish you and make you just like them."

Juan laughed, eating vigorously, "Good," he said, "because I speak badly of the rich all the time, so when is God going to punish me and make me rich, too?"

His mother laughed. "You are the devil, aren't you, *mi hijito,*" she said, "twisting your mother's words like that." And she knew that she'd spoiled this last child of hers, but she didn't mind. He was always so happy and full of life that it gave her heart reason to live. He was like the baby chick that broke the shell; he didn't ask any questions or bother looking right and left. No, all he did was stare straight ahead and start pecking the ground, filling his little starving belly.

She was so glad that her father, the great Don Pio, had lived long enough for little Juan to get to know him. Juan was turning out to be, in many ways, a lot like her legendary father: quick-witted, resourceful and, yet full of happy mischief.

"All right, *mi hijito,*" said Doña Margarita, getting the twigs and leaves out of her hair, "don't eat so much. Save a little for the others."

"Don't worry," said Juan, "we'll have plenty to eat from now on. All I have to do is fool a foreman every day and get more corn for us."

"Oh, no you won't," said Doña Margarita. "You were lucky yesterday that you didn't get us all shot. I don't want you doing that ever again, *mi hijito.*"

"Oh, Mama," laughed Juan, his mouth full of dung-roasted corn, "don't be ridiculous! You're too old and worthless for anyone to waste their good bullets on you!"

But before his mother could laugh, Luisa came out of her blanket as angry as a tiger.

"I swear it, Juan!" she yelled. "You insult Mama once more and I'll brain you!" she said, picking up a stick to hit him.

But Juan dodged and ran, then he got a stick, too. Luisa was almost eight years older than Juan and all her life she'd been as hot-tempered as their father, but Juan wasn't afraid of her.

"Luisa!" shouted their mother. "Put that stick down!"

"No!" yelled Luisa, swinging at Juan again. "He needs to be hit, Mama! We have months of traveling to do and he gets worse every day!"

"Luisa!" said their mother, getting between them. "Stop that! I don't think it's your brother that you're angry at. You're just mad because your new husband deserted us!"

"Mama!" she screamed, raising the stick in the air, she was so mad. "I've told you a thousand times that Epitacio didn't desert us! He just went ahead to find the best route for us to take! I swear it, if you let Juan get away with talking like this, it's not fair! When I was small, Papa would have slapped us!"

"But, *mi hijita*," said the old woman, reaching for the stick her daughter held in her raised hand, "when you were small we had a home and a family. Now your father is gone and we have nothing, so what else do I have to give your brother? Eh, you tell me. We were already growing down like the steer's tail to the ground when Juanito came to me. He never got to see any of the riches that you saw in the settlement your grandfather built on the mountain, *mi hijita*."

Luisa still didn't like it, but she finally let go of the stick, giving it to her old mother. She went to get her little baby, who had started to cry. Lifting up Joselito, Luisa pulled up her blouse and gave her milk-gorged breast to the infant.

"All right, Mama," she said, "I can see that everything is different; but still, I'm mad at Juan. Not at Epitacio," she said, tears coming to her eyes as the baby continued to suck, gripping her large breast with his fine little hands.

It was mid-morning and the sun was bright white when they came to the flat, open country at the outskirts of Leon, Guanajuato. Up ahead they could see that the city was in flames and that people were fleeing from the city on foot. Then, in the confusion, Juan and his family saw some horsemen chasing after some men on foot, shooting at them.

Crouching down, Juan and his family watched. They saw an unarmed man on foot—who'd obviously been hiding—get up behind the horsemen and start running across the broken terrain, directly toward them, less than a quarter of a mile away. The man was short and had sandy hair. He was waving at Juan and his family as he came.

Two of the horsemen saw him and turned about, shooting at him too, as they gave chase. The bullets ricocheted by Juan and his family.

"In the ditch!" yelled Juan, getting the burro and cart off the road as fast as he could.

The shooting continued, and the shouts of the man running toward them grew louder. Juan peered over the rim of the ditch between two rocks. He saw that the two horsemen were gaining on the man who was racing desperately just in front of them like a rabbit, dodging through the brush and cactus. Juan thought that there was something familiar about the man as he got closer. Then Luisa screamed.

"Epitacio!" she yelled, passing her baby to Emilia and getting to her feet. "Oh, he better pray they kill him before I get my hands on him!"

Juan watched in disbelief as his sister leaped from the safety of the ditch, screaming murder as she charged across the broken terrain after the man whom she thought had done her wrong. Bullets sang past her ears, but she paid no attention to them.

"I'm going to kill you, Epitacio!" she yelled.

The two horsemen saw the woman running toward them. They quit shooting and reined in their horses. And Luisa, bellowing like a cow who'd lost her calf, went racing across the rocky ground, screaming vengeance at this man who'd serenaded her with his guitar after the death of her first husband.

The sandy-haired man saw Luisa racing toward him and he turned, saw the armed horsemen behind him, and he took off in a third direction, looking even more scared of Luisa than he'd been of the horsemen.

But Luisa was strong and fast. Having been raised on the ranch, she knew all about catching wild farm stock. Quickly, she picked up a stick and threw it sideways, down low, over the ground. It whirled in a circular motion, catching Epitacio by the ankles and knocking him to the earth. Then she was on him before he could get to his feet.

"You left me, you *cabrón* son-of-a-bitch!" she bellowed, hitting him and biting him, then picking up a rock to pound his skull as he fought for his life.

"But I didn't leave you, my love!" he shouted at her. "Truly, I just went ahead to find us a safe passage!"

"You lie with all your God-forsaken soul!" she screamed, yanking at his hair and biting him in the face, drawing blood. "You only came back because they were after you to force you to join the army!"

"Oh, no, my turtle dove! I came back because I love you! You are my life!"

"You played with my heart!" she screamed, pressing down on him with her larger, stronger bulk. "And I'm going to cut your *tanates* off!" She continued screaming, biting, hitting and gouging and yanking at him until she was so exhausted that she couldn't do it anymore.

The horsemen lowered their weapons.

"Well, I guess he really is married," said one of them. They laughed and turned their horses about, going back toward the burning buildings in the distance.

Juan stood up. Now Luisa was crying and acting hurt. And Epitacio, who was a bloody, torn mess, was kissing her gently and trying to make up.

"I believed in you, Epitacio," cried Luisa softly, gently, "when you said you loved me and I was your life."

"Oh, you are, you are," he said, sitting up and kissing her, wiping the tears from her eyes, "you are the heart of my life."

"Then why did you leave in the night without a word?"

"I didn't want to disturb your beauty sleep, my angel."

"My beauty sleep?" she said. "Then you really do think I'm beautiful?"

"Oh, yes, my dear. You are the earthworm of my heart."

"Earthworm?" she yelled.

"I mean, the earth, the ah, ah" he quickly added, "the earth soil of my life. You are the rich harvest of my dreams!"

"All right, don't say anything more," she said, jerking him close and kissing him hard. Then she started laughing and laughing, and he did, too. "Earthworm? What a mouth you have!"

It was late in the afternoon when they got into the burning, smoldering city of Leon. Luisa hadn't hurt Epitacio's legs when she'd beaten him, so he was able to walk alongside Juan and help him pull the wagon while Luisa and her child rode in the back along with Doña Margarita. Emilia and Inocenta came behind the wagon, holding hands as they walked over the debris caused by the cannons.

Coming down the narrow street, Juan and his family saw the remains of the battle. The bloated carcasses of dead horses lay in the harnesses of their overturned wagons. The air was pierced by the anguished voices of people begging for help, for water, for comfort. But Juan and his family had nothing to give the hundreds of outstretched hands.

"Just don't look at them," said Epitacio. "We've got to get to the train. It's our only chance of getting north."

"I'm not closing my eyes," said Doña Margarita. "We don't have much, but at least we can draw water from the well and give these people a cup of water in the name of our Savior, Jesus Christ." She got down from the wagon, making the sign of the cross over herself, and proceeded to a well in the middle of the square.

Juan could see that as much as Epitacio didn't like it, he was also not prepared to argue with his mother. Once Doña Margarita had made up her mind, she wasn't a woman to be taken lightly.

"All right," begged Epitacio, "but please, let's hurry, Doña Margarita. They have empty trains going to the north right now."

"God will provide," she said confidently.

Epitacio glanced up at the heavens. Sometimes he wished he'd never even met this family. But a man without a family was forced into the army, so there wasn't much he could do.

Juan was with his mother giving water to a wounded man when a dozen armed horsemen came galloping up the street, pulling a cannon. Seeing the burro and the little wagon, they reined in.

"Take the burro and wagon!" shouted the man in charge.

"Oh, I knew we shouldn't have stopped," said Epitacio, getting out of the way so the armed men wouldn't do him any harm.

But Juan wasn't about to be pushed aside. "No!" he yelled. "That's our wagon! We need it to get to the train!"

"Out of my way, *muchacho*," said the man in charge. He was a big, tall, handsome man with a huge *sombrero*. He was in his twenties and he had a thick, furious-looking moustache.

"But our burro is old," said Juan, taking up ground. "If you misuse him, you'll have nothing!" He could feel himself getting angrier and angrier. He loved their little burro.

"My little brother is right," said Luisa, coming up, too. "We've come a long way, and we wouldn't even be here now if we hadn't stopped to help your wounded men."

"That's enough!" said the big moustached man, and he spurred his big sweat-lathered horse, leaping him forward to grab the *burrito* by the reins.

But Juan didn't shy away. Neither did Luisa. They knew horses, so they held their ground, waving their arms and shouting loudly as they stared up at the horseman standing between him and their little cart and burro.

The horse of the big moustached man reared up, pawing the air with power. He was used to battle. He foamed at the bit, wanting to trample these people who stood in his master's way.

Doña Margarita came up, holding Luisa's child in her arms.

"If you're going to trample them," she said, "you might as well trample me and this child, too, for we won't want to live."

"Damn it!" yelled the man, his eyes raging with anger. "Where in hell are you people from?"

"Los Altos!" said Juan and Luisa, together, not once taking their eyes off him.

"I thought so!" yelled the man. "Only from up there, where people were raised free, do we get people who won't bow!" His horse was snorting, wild-eyed; he wanted to charge and bite and kick these people who opposed his master. "Did you know a man named Jose Villaseñor?" he asked.

Juan and Luisa glanced at each other. They didn't know what to say. Jose was their brother, the great protector of their beloved mountains, the man who'd managed to keep the Revolution out of their mountains, with just a couple of dozen young men for nearly four years.

Seeing her children's silence, Doña Margarita stood up. She wasn't about to lie or hide the truth from any mortal man. She was her father's daughter, after all.

"Yes, señor!" she said loudly, distinctly, fully prepared to meet death if this was God's wish. "I don't know why you ask this, or if you'll kill us because we know him, but yes—God as my witness—I have no earthly fear of you. So I say to you, Jose Villaseñor Castro was my son, and I'm proud of it!"

She stood up tall and straight, all five feet of her, prepared to meet her fate, however it came.

"Jose was your son?" roared the man, his horse leaping forward, wanting to trample Juan and Luisa. "Well, I'll be!" he said, jerking his horse back. He smiled, pushing back his hat, showing the line of white that ran across his forehead where his great *sombrero* blocked out the sunlight. "I rode with him! He was my friend! I salute you, *señora*! Your son was the greatest, smartest, most daring horseman the earth has ever produced!" He whirled his horse about. "How is he? I'd heard he'd gotten captured."

"He escaped that, thank God," said Doña Margarita, "then he was killed in the United States—God rest his soul."

"You have my deepest regrets, *señora*," he said, tipping his hat. "With ten men like him, I'd have an army! God keep you well! And keep your wagon!" he said. "Get to the train immediately! They're loading families to go north. And if anyone troubles you, you just use my name, General Felipe Kelly!"

He gave his horse the spurs, leaping off at a gallop with his horsemen pulling the cannon.

Up ahead were alleys full of dead human bodies, piled up two or three deep. Heads and arms and legs were twisted every which way, and rats were running over the gruesome mounds of the dead.

Juan thought he'd vomit. These corpses were infested with flies. Stomachs open and rotted, the smell was terrible. They must have come from the battle that had been fought the week before. The rumors had it that the fighting in Leon had been going on for nearly a month.

"Don't look," said Epitacio, covering his nose. "Quick, just keep going!"

"What is that awful smell?" asked Emilia, looking around blindly and gagging.

But no one answered her. She just held on to the side of the wagon and they pressed on, further into the smoldering city and the awful smells of death and destruction. Epitacio couldn't stop talking, he was so nervous.

"Remember, I speak English," he said to Juan, "so once we get across the Rio Grande, everything's going to be fine. I've worked all over the United States. I know places like Miami, Arizona, as well as I know the palm of my hand. I know El Paso, Texas, and Albuquerque, New Mexico as good as most Mexicans know Guadalajara, Torreon and Gomez Palacio. Oh, I tell you, all we have to do is get on the train, Juan, and get shipped up north, and then everything will be paradise."

Epitacio just couldn't stop talking, but Juan didn't pay any attention to him. He was too tired, exhausted, and gagging at the smell; all the years of seeing the Revolution up in their mountains hadn't prepared Juan for what he was seeing now. Up in their beloved mountains of Los Altos de Jalisco, he'd seen a few men shot and their homes burned and their animals stolen and slaughtered, but never had he seen so much death and blood and total destruction.

At the railhead, Juan and his family found people backed up by the thousands for more than a mile. They were all hungry, thirsty, lost, and crying in despair. Juan and his family now knew that it had been a mistake ever to have left their beloved mountains. Up there, at least, people had known who they were and they could always dig up wild roots to eat and trap quail to roast on a fire.

That night they made their home out in the open, next to their wagon, but they could find nothing to build a fire with. All the nearby trees and brush had already been taken by the masses of people. So Juan and Inocenta went out beyond the breaks to look for wood or cow pies, but they came up with nothing. Everything had been used up by the people waiting for the train.

The wind came up, and suddenly it began to grow cold as the sun went down. Shivering, Emilia asked why they didn't just go back home.

"She's right," said Juan. "Let's go back home."

"But we've been on the road two weeks," said Epitacio. "And believe me, once we get to the border our troubles are over. I've been there. The Rio Grande valley's all green and beautiful, and I can get a job with ease."

"Oh, no," said Emilia, "I just know that it's going to get worse."

"Shut up!" said Luisa. "For being blind, you sure claim to see everything. Especially the future!"

"All right," said their mother, "no more of this. We're all tired and hungry. This isn't the best time to make decisions. So now come, all of you, and let's kneel down and say our evening prayers. We're alive, so we've had another good day."

They all knelt down alongside the railhead with thousands of people all around them, and Doña Margarita led them in prayer.

"Oh, thank You, God," she said. "Yesterday You gave us food for our bodies, and today You gave us food for our souls. It gave my heart wings that the name of my son Jose caused a perfect stranger to show us not just mercy, but respect. You were so good to us, dear God, giving us Your hand in this miracle of human kindness.

"And, also, dear God, I must admit that, well, when You first delivered us into this sea of hunger, I was disturbed. But now, in Your infinite wisdom, I see that this, too, is but another test for us to prove our love to You. And so, yes, we are going to share our little burro with the multitudes as You so well showed us how to do through Your own beloved Son, Jesus Christ, our Savior, when He shared His fish and loaves of bread."

At first, Juan didn't fully comprehend what it was that his mother was saying. But then, when he did, and he realized that she meant for them to kill his little burro to feed the people, he stopped praying.

"But, Mama," he said, interrupting her, "we can't kill my little burro. I've had him since I was little! And he's old—he won't even taste good." Tears came to his eyes. "Why, don't you remember that even the coyotes refused to eat him when they stole the goats because he stinks with age?" Juan's face was running fast with tears. "Oh, please, Mama," he continued, "I love him!"

"*Mi hijito*," said his mother calmly, "but what do you think will happen to him once we get on the train? You tell me."

There was a long silence as Juan thought of his mother's statement.

"They'll work him to death," she said. "Then they'll eat him. This way we can at least know he will have a painless death among friends, *mi hijito*."

Kneeling on the ground, Juan looked at his little burro and all the people around them and his eyes cried freely, but a part of him knew his mother was right. He began to tremble, getting a sick feeling as they went on with their evening prayers.

"And so, dear God," said Doña Margarita, "I thank You a million times for this great opportunity that You've presented to us. For You are all merciful, dear God, and we thank You with all our hearts for giving us this opportunity to serve You. And, also, once again, I thank You for showing us the inspiration that the very name of my son, Jose, carries. He was a great, great son, rest his soul."

They finished their prayers, but Juan just couldn't believe it. If God was so big and powerful, then why did they need to show Him anything? Especially when it came to eating a good, loyal friend like his little burro. Tears ran down Juan's face, but still he made the sign of the cross over himself. He went over to his little burro and he petted him and hugged him, talking to him gently so he'd relax and not feel alone when he went into the next world.

The people were already gathering around with their clay pots and knives so they could get a good, fresh piece of meat. But they were basically God-loving, good country people, so they kept back at a respectful distance as Epitacio now walked up to Juan. Gently, Epitacio moved Juan aside, then he quickly pushed his sharp, thin blade into the little white-faced burro's throat, right under his jaw, cutting the jugular so fast that the little animal didn't really know what had happened. The little animal just felt a sharp pain like a horsefly biting him. He stomped his right hoof, turned and looked at Epitacio, then at his lifelong friend, Juan, who'd ridden him as a boy up and down the hillsides. His big, dark, liquid eyes moistened, blinked rapidly, and he whirled his tail around, farted, felt weak and went down to his knees. He was unconscious before his body hit the ground.

Quickly, Luisa rushed in and put a pot under his throat to catch the fresh warm blood for cooking. Some of the other people also stepped in to help skin him. But the little burro's body suddenly went into the reflexive kicks of death. The hungry people had to get back to avoid a blow. These kicks of death were so strong that they could cripple a person. But once the kicks subsided, the people rushed in again.

That night, not one single piece of the little animal was wasted. Not even his intestines or the long, furry ears. The people were starving; they hadn't eaten well in months, so they used every tiny piece of the fine, wonderful, loyal little animal.

But no matter how much Juan tried, he couldn't eat any of his little burro. And, when Juan went to sleep under the stars that night, he cried and cried until his mother drew him close.

"*Mi hijito*," she said, "cry if you must, because crying cleanses a troubled heart, but also realize the truth. The most anyone can hope for in life is to go out quickly like your burro just did, and be surrounded by those we love in our hour of death. I truly hope I'm as lucky as your burro when my time comes."

Hearing this, Juan turned and looked at his mother's large eyes, shining there in the darkness, and he started to cry all the more. "Oh, no, Mama, you can't ever die!" he said. "Please, I love you! I don't want to be left alone!"

"But who says I'm dying now?" she snapped. "I'll live to see you old and married, *mi hijito*!"

"Oh, yes! And I'll marry someone as wonderful and perfect as you!"

"Me, perfect? Oh, your father turns in his grave to hear those words. I'm not perfect, *mi hijito*, and far from wonderful. Believe me, I'm just a woman prepared to see her duty done!"

"Yes, just like the girl I'll marry—an angel!"

"Oh, you silver-tongued devil, I love you!"

She laughed and he did, too, and they held each other close—mother and son—alongside the railroad tracks with thousands of people all around them.

That night the coyotes howled in the distance, but Juan paid them no attention. After all, he was in the arms of his greatest love in all the world, so what could possibly go wrong? Nothing.

9

And so they could no longer see the mountain range on which Don Pio had touched the hand of God. But still, they were strong-hearted in their belief in the Almighty.

During the next few days, Juan met many boys his own age as they waited alongside the railroad tracks. There were boys from all over the Republic of Mexico, and they were on their way north to the United States with their families, too.

A few of the boys liked to gamble, so Juan set up foot races with them to see who was the fastest, and they threw rocks to see who was the strongest. And Juan, who'd always thought he was pretty strong and fast, lost most of the contests.

Many of these boys were really powerful, especially the full-blooded Tarascan Indians from the State of Michoacan. In fact, Juan figured that some of them were probably as good as his long-legged brother, Domingo, who'd been five years older than him, and one of the fastest and strongest boys in all their region.

Domingo and Juan had been closest in age and they'd been raised together. Juan missed Domingo dearly. He'd disappeared just two months before they'd left, but their mother thought that there was a good chance Domingo was still alive.

Juan and his newfound friends played up and down the tracks and through the burned-out buildings, pretending to be Villa and Zapata and other heroes of the Revolution. They were mostly nine, ten and eleven years old, and they couldn't wait for the day when they'd be big enough to take up arms.

Juan told the boys about the different incidents of war he'd seen up in his mountainous region, and how brave and courageous his brothers and uncles had been. Hearing Juan's stories, the other boys told their stories, too, and little by little Juan grew to understand that either these boys were huge liars or they'd truly had it much worse in other parts of Mexico than his family had it up in their desolate mountains. Not until the last year had the war really hit them up in Los Altos de Jalisco. Before that, Jose, Juan's oldest brother, and a handful of local boys had managed to keep their mountains free of war, just as Don Pio and his Rurales had managed to keep them free of bandits years before.

"*¡Mira!*" yelled Juan, hitting his legs with a stick. "I'm my brother's famous, white-stockings stallion! And here come five hundred horsemen after me, but I jump across to another cliff, and they all fall to their death!"

"Me, too!" said another boy, named Eduardo. "I'm the great Villa! And here I come to help you, Juan, with my Dorados del Norte, the finest horsemen on earth!"

"Oh, no, they're not!" said a third boy, named Cucho. "General Obregon's cavalry led by Colonel Castro are the finest!"

"Hey, that's my cousin!" said Juan excitedly. "On my mother's side! My Great Uncle Agustin's fifth son!"

"But I thought you were for Villa!" said Eduardo. He was almost twelve and the strongest of them all.

"I am!" said Juan. "But I'm also for my cousin! How can I not be, eh?"

The boys played and challenged each other, throwing stones and racing. Then it was the day for Juan and his family to go north. They got on the train along with the thousands of other people. The family climbed into one of the tall, empty cattle cars. But the floor of the car was so full of cow manure that they had to get back out and shovel all the manure out by hand before they could find a place to sit down for the long ride north.

They had no more than settled in when the train started to move, and Juan got up and sneaked out of the boxcar along with five of his new friends. The day before, Juan, Eduardo, Cucho and three other boys had made a bet among themselves to see who was the bravest of them all. The bet was to see who would stay alongside the tracks as the train took off and be the last one to run and jump on the train. *Toreando*, or bullfighting with the train, they called it, and all six boys realized that this was a very risky game because if they didn't catch the train and got separated from their families, it could be death for them.

Juan's heart was pounding with fear as he now stood alongside the tracks and watched the huge iron wheels of the train turning slowly in front of him, carrying the long row of cars down the tracks. He watched the train weighted down with people, stuffed full in the boxcars, piled high in the flatbeds with more people and their bags and boxes. His heart went wild, but still he held and watched people hold on to anything they could so that they would get to the safety of the north.

Juan was full of the devil; he just knew this was one event he was sure to win. After all, he was a Villaseñor with Castro blood, and all week long these boys had been outdoing him in throwing rocks and running foot races, but now he'd show them in one great swift challenge what he was truly made of. For Juan was the boy who'd gotten a man's reputation up in his mountainous region at the age of six years old when he'd proved himself to be so brave it was said his blood ran backwards from his heart.

Oh, he'd never forget that night. It had been a full moon and the local witch had put a curse on his family and so it was up to the youngest, who was purest of heart, to redeem the family, and he'd done it.

Licking his lips, Juan glanced at his friends as the train started to move a little faster. He felt like a fighting cock. He had the blood of his grandfather, Don Pio, running through his veins.

"Getting scared, eh?" said Eduardo to Juan as the train slipped past them. He was the oldest and strongest of them all and the second fastest runner.

"Not me," said Juan.

"Nor I," said Cucho.

The big iron wheels were turning faster, crying metal to metal as the long line of boxcars and flatbeds went by. Five thousand people were going out that day, and there wouldn't be another empty train traveling north for weeks.

Juan's heart began to pound. Oh, how he wished these boys would just get scared and run for the train so he, too, could run after his family.

The huge iron wheels turned faster and faster. A part of Juan's mind started telling him to stop this ridiculous game and jump forward and get on the train to join his mother while he still had the chance. But he wouldn't move. No, he just held there, alongside the other boys, refusing to be the first one to give in.

The sounds of the big, turning, sliding, moving iron wheels on the shiny-smooth steel rails were getting louder and louder. The huge long train—well over fifty units and two locomotives—was picking up speed. Finally, one of the younger boys couldn't stand it anymore and screamed out, "I'm going!" He leaped forward and caught one of the passing boxcars and swung on.

"He wants his mama!" laughed the boys.

Juan and the other boys laughed at him, saying that he was a cowardly little tit-sucking baby. Why, the end of the train hadn't even slid by them yet. But still, down deep inside their souls they all knew that he'd done the right thing and they all wanted to be with their mamas, too.

Then there came the end of the train, passing by them at a good pace, but still not going so fast that a good runner couldn't catch it. Juan grinned, feeling good. Now it truly took balls, *tanates*, not to cry out and run. So there went the end of the train, cranking iron to iron, past Juan's face. It left him and all the other boys behind, going up the long, desolate valley. A second boy now cried out in fear.

"This is stupid!" he screamed. "We could lose our families forever!" He took off running after the end of the train and swung on. Once more Juan and the boys who'd remained behind laughed, calling this other boy a coward, too.

"Well, I guess this only leaves us, the real men!" said Juan, watching the train beginning to pick up speed as it went up the long, flat valley.

"Yeah, I guess so," said Cucho, "but at least I'm the fastest runner so I can afford to wait. I don't know what you other slowpokes are doing here. It's four days by horseback to the next town." And saying this, he suddenly took off running up the track, he, Cucho, the fastest boy among them. Juan wanted to scream out in fear, but he didn't. He held strong. He had to. He was from Los Altos de Jalisco, after all.

"Damn Cucho," said Eduardo, who'd been left behind with Juan and another boy, "trying to scare us. Hell, a good man can always out walk any train. All you need is water."

"Right," said Juan, trying to act like he, too, wasn't scared. But inside he was ready to pee in his pants, he was so terrified. "With water, a good man can always survive," he added.

Juan held himself alongside the two tall, lanky Indian boys, but it was hard. Juan was beginning to lose the power inside himself. He wasn't one of the fastest runners, and the train was getting farther down the tracks.

Then one of the other boys took off. He was tall and fast, but still he was having an awful time catching the train. He held on to his hat, running as fast as he could, arms swinging, bare feet lifting, and got up close to the end of the departing train, but he just couldn't get a hold.

Juan glanced at Eduardo next to him.

"Hey," he said, "we even out-waited Cucho, the fastest of all, so I think we've shown our worth!"

"Yeah, let's go!"

"Yeah!" said Juan. "We've both won!"

So they both took off down the tracks and, in the distance, the last boy finally got hold of the train. He tried to swing up but he lost his footing and his legs almost went under the steel wheels.

Seeing this, Juan screamed out in terror and ran with all his might—arms pumping, feet climbing, having run up and down mountains all his life. He ran and ran, gaining on the train, but the pace was killing him.

But then the front end of the long train hit a small downward grade. Suddenly, the whole train jerked forward, picking up speed. Eduardo gave it all he had, pulling ahead of Juan.

Juan saw the train going and he thought of his mother and his sisters and Inocenta. He could imagine the grief and terror in his mother's old face when she discovered that he wasn't on the train and she'd lost yet another child. Tears came to his eyes and he became more scared than he'd ever been in all his life.

"Mama! Mama!" he cried out in anguish.

He raced on with all his heart and soul. The people on top of the boxcars looked back and saw the two boys running after them, but they thought they were only local boys playing, so they just waved.

Gripped with the sudden understanding that he'd lost his mother forever, Juan lost all hope and he tripped, falling face first into the sharp rocks between the railroad ties, ripping open his mouth.

He lay there spitting blood and choking; his eyes flowed with tears. Eduardo, the tall, lanky Indian, who'd gotten a good fifteen yards ahead of him, came walking back slowly.

The long train was gone now. It was a good quarter of a mile down the tracks, whistling and picking up more and more speed as it went north from the city of Leon toward Aguascalientes, Zacatecas and Gomez Palacio, where it was to stop over for the night and refuel before going on to Chihuahua and the Ciudad Juarez, across the Rio Grande from El Paso, Texas, in the United States.

Coming back, Eduardo saw that Juan was all bloody and he offered him his hand.

"Well," said Juan, getting to his feet and wiping the blood from his face, "let's go! We've got to catch that train!"

"Don't be crazy, *mano*," said the tall, lanky boy in a relaxed manner. "Not even a horse could catch it now."

"But we got to," said Juan desperately. "Our families are on that train!"

"Yes," said the tall boy, casually, "that's true, but I also have an uncle and aunt back here in Leon, so I can always catch the next train."

"You mean you still have family back here?" screamed Juan, suddenly getting so raging mad that all fear was gone.

"Well, yes," said the boy, not knowing why Juan was getting so upset.

"Well, then, you lied!" screamed Juan. "You tricked me! You didn't make your bet with your whole family on the train!"

The boy only laughed. "Well, no, of course not, *mano*," he said. "Only a fool would bet everything."

"You son-of-a-bitch!" said Juan.

"Eh, don't swear at me or I'll beat you, Juan. I'm the strongest boy among us, remember? You wouldn't have a chance."

"I spit on your strength!" said Juan to the bigger, older boy. "I'll fight you to the death right now, *cabrón*! Come on, let's do it the way the devil painted it!"

Seeing Juan's insane rage, the larger boy backed off. "Eh, *mano*, I'm sorry," he said. "Look, you can come and stay with me and my family until we go."

"Stick your family up your ass!" said Juan. "I'm catching that train!" He picked up his hat and turned, taking off down the tracks.

The train was so far away now that it looked like nothing more than a small, dark line, smoking in the distance as it headed for the far end of the long, flat valley. Way ahead of the train, Juan could see a bunch of little red-rock hills no bigger than fresh cow-pies, but he didn't lessen his pace. His most perfect love in all the world was on that train. So he'd run to the end of the earth if he had to.

The sun was high and Juan talked to God as he went, stepping quickly from tie to tie. He didn't want to wear out the bottoms of his worn-out *huaraches* on the crushed sharp rocks between the wooden ties.

"Oh, dear God," said Juan, watching the tar-painted ties slide under his feet as he went, "I know I've sinned many times in the past but I swear to You that I'll never sin again if You help me this time. Give me the wings of an angel so I can fly across this land and catch the train. For remember, You're all-powerful and can do whatever You please and, besides, it's not just me who'll suffer if I die, dear God. It will be my beloved mother who loves You more than life itself!"

And saying this, Juan smiled as he ran on. He liked how he'd added his mother there at the end and he hoped it would make God feel guilty and force Him to come through and give him the wings of an angel. But the wings didn't come, so he kept running, eating up the miles. And to his surprise, instead of getting weaker and weaker, he got stronger.

The morning passed by and Juan noticed that the railroad men had cheated and started putting the ties farther apart. He began to miss the wooden ties as he ran, hitting the sharp rocks instead. Juan's *huaraches* came apart and twice he had to stop to fix them with a piece of his shirt. He began to get thirsty and thick-tongued, but there were no signs of water anywhere.

"Oh, Mama," he said, glancing up at the great white sun, "what have I done to us? Without water, even a good man from Los Altos can't survive."

"Oh, dear God," he said, "Lord and Master of all the heavens, forgive me, for I'm a fool. And I know that I played around and gambled when I should have been serious, but . . . well, if You help me this time, dear God, and give me the wings . . . look, if it's bothering You to make me an angel because I've never been that good, then how about the wings of an eagle and I swear to You that I will never gamble or play around again when I should be serious."

So Juan talked to God, his old companion, who'd helped him all his life. The miles went by and the sun grew hotter and hotter, but not once did he slow down.

He was strong; he'd been raised in the mountains at nearly six thousand feet and, ever since he could remember, he'd been running from sun to sun with his brother Domingo and their giant cousins, Basilio and Mateo, chasing the wolves and coyotes away from their herds of goats.

But it was hotter down here in the valley. Juan was sweating more than he was used to. The powerful sun grew larger and larger and the high desert insects began to screech. Once, way ahead in the distance, Juan thought he saw a group of green trees. He thought it was a water hole.

"Oh, thank You, God," he said, and his mouth began to water, feeling better as he approached the trees.

But then, getting there, he saw that the water hole had long ago dried up. Why, even in the shade of trees, the earth was nothing but dead-cracked skin.

"Oh, God!" he screamed. "Why do You tease me?"

And he thought he'd die, he was so thirsty. But then he remembered his mother and how she'd lost child after child in the Revolution and he stopped his rage. He had to be strong for her. He glanced around. He saw the little red hills. They were much bigger now. He looked back. The city of Leon was nothing but a wrinkle in the distance.

"I can make it," he said, taking courage. "I know I can."

He rested a few moments in the shade of the trees along with a few lizards and a fat, reddish rattlesnake, then he took off once again, but this time at an easy-going dog trot.

The sun, the blanket of the poor, continued its journey across the tall, flat sky and the day grew so hot that the black tar on the railroad ties melted and came off on his *huaraches*. Heat waves danced in the distance and mirages of huge blue lakes glistened all around.

Juan became so thirsty that his mouth turned to cotton and his vision blurred. Finally, he began to walk. He started talking to himself so he wouldn't go crazy. He remembered the stories that his mother had told him of his grandfather, the great Don Pio, and of his two brothers, Cristobal and Agustin.

Time passed and the insects grew louder and the sun grew hotter, and Juan concentrated way back to those wonderful days up in Los Altos de Jalisco before the Revolution had come to them. He smiled, feeling good, remembering how cool and green the meadows of his youth had been. He began to trot and thought back to those days of his youth when he and his brother Domingo had played with Basilio and Mateo, the two bastard sons of their great Uncle Cristobal.

Oh, those were the days! Playing with those huge, dark Indian-looking men who'd even towered over their father, who was a very big man. Juan ran on. Why, they'd had heavy-boned Indian faces and small, yellowish teeth, and they'd been well into the age of wisdom when Juan had first started playing with them. But still, they'd been as simple as children, refusing to live indoors and, instead, they had slept under the oak leaves when the weather got cold.

They wouldn't come inside when it rained; instead, they loved to race and dance and shout to the heavens every time it stormed. They had no sense of money or personal property and would give away anything that anyone asked them for. They never rode a horse or a burro, but would challenge any horseman to a race across that meadow, over that ridge and to that distant rise. And they almost always won, even against the fastest horses, because they knew the mountains like the fingers of their hands. And even though many people called them simple, everyone knew that they were not fools.

Oh, he was feeling good now, running up the tracks at a good dog trot, thinking of his two giant cousins. And no, he would never forget the day that he'd seen his two great cousins follow an armadillo into a cave where they'd found a chest of gold so big that a burro couldn't carry it. Oh, that had been such a wonderful day, taking the mountain of gold home to Don Pio and his Uncle Cristobal.

The bottoms of Juan's *huaraches* were gone. The rocks were poking up between them and getting caught in the leather straps. Sitting down on the iron rail, Juan took off his *huaraches* and decided he'd probably be better off barefoot. But walking on the ties, his feet stuck to the boiling hot, half-melted tar. He found he was better off going on the sharp stones between the ties.

"Oh, Basilio," he said aloud as he limped along, "If only you and Mateo were here right now to put me on your shoulders and run with me like you used to do when I was a boy." His eyes filled with tears. "But don't worry," he said. "I'm not giving up. Your blood is my blood!"

And saying this, he started loping once again, flying over the stones with his bare feet. He could almost feel his giant cousins here beside him. He could feel their love, he could feel that they'd always be here inside him, giving him strength, giving wings to his feet as long as he remembered them. He raced on.

The sun inched its way across the towering flat blue sky and the little redrock hills continued dancing between the heat waves in the distance. Juan Salvador remembered the day that his brother, Domingo, had finally become so big that he thought he could beat Basilio and Mateo in a foot race. Boys from all over the mountains came to see. The race was set up in the green meadow by the three lakes.

"But wait," said Basilio. "I don't race for free no more. Every month some new boys wants to challenge me and my brother. We got to get paid."

"How much?" said Domingo. He was hot. He really wanted to beat them.

"Well, I don't know," said Basilio, his eyes dancing with merriment, "but my brother and I were talking and, well, we figure that we never had enough peanuts to fill our bellies, so we'd like a sack of peanuts."

"Jesus Christ!" screamed Domingo. "That would cost a fortune!"

Basilio and Mateo roared. But Domingo wanted to race, and so he stole one of their father's goats, trading it to some passing mule skinners for a twenty-kilo sack of peanuts.

The marks were set, Domingo and the two giants got in place, and then the call was made and they were off. And Domingo, blue-eyed and redheaded like his father, took off like lightning, barefoot and stripped to the waist. The muscles on his back rippled as his legs and arms worked so fast they became a blur of motion. He was flying, sailing over the short green meadow grass, but he never had a chance. For he'd gone no more than ten rods when the two giants went racing past him, each carrying a young calf on their backs like they always did when they raced against human beings and not against horses. They leaped over the short rock fence at the end of the meadow and began to dance with the glee of children.

Oh, those were the days! Domingo had gotten so mad that his face had become as red as the setting sun. Everyone laughed at him, but he'd had to admit that he was still a long way from ever beating the giants in a race.

Basilio and Mateo had shared their twenty-kilo sack of peanuts with all of them. They'd have other races with the younger boys and then they'd eat the peanuts—shells and all—so they could fill their starving furnaces of youth.

Juan ran on, feeling tired, drained, exhausted, but he never once lessened his pace. He had his grandfather, Don Pio, in his soul. He had his cousins, Basilio and Mateo, in his legs. And his brothers, Domingo and Jose, were in his heart. And his mother—the greatest woman in all the world—was waiting for him up ahead; he ran on.

The sun was blasting hot and the valley was flat and wide and filled with nothing but dead, dry brush. He licked his lips, but he found that he had no saliva, so he stopped and picked up a small stone and wiped it off. He put it in his mouth to suck on. Oh, he'd never forget the day of the race when they'd also bought a basket of oranges and he'd tasted his first orange. They had cut one into quarters and he'd seen the luscious slices, juice dripping down, golden and wet and as sweet as honey. He ate three big oranges that day and he felt strong.

Running up the valley, still tasting the sweet wetness of that golden orange, he now saw that the sun was beginning to slide down the tall, flat sky. Why, he'd run all day without realizing it. God's eye was going down and the long, dark shadows of the coming night engulfed him as he came up to the first little hills. He'd made it across the valley with the help of his family, powerful men and women whose belief in God was so strong that life was indestructible.

He stopped. His feet were swollen and bloody. He wondered if he could find some water here in these little hills and stay for the night before going on.

Looking back, he saw that he must have been climbing for the last hour. The long, flat valley now lay way down below him. There were no traces of Leon, not even of the smoking, burned-out buildings.

He turned, went on, and the farther he went, he saw that the hills became taller and the vegetation thicker. Now there were long-shadowed cactus trees and tight, twisted, low-creeping, thorny plants. Juan stopped to look for some cactus to suck on. But he was from the mountains, so he didn't know which plant to choose. He sat down to rest. His mouth felt so dry, he was choking. But then he saw his mother in his mind's eye, searching for him with her eyes swollen with tears. He struggled to his feet to go on. But his feet hurt so much, he couldn't stand to touch the ground.

"Oh, Mama," he cried, "please, help me!"

And he continued stumbling up the tracks, with his feet on fire.

Then, coming around a long uphill bend in the tracks, he saw something move ahead of him in the dim light of the going day. Quickly, he grabbed a rock. He figured it was a deer and so, if he got the chance, he would hit it on the head and then break its neck, so he could suck its blood and eat its meat.

But when he got closer to the rocks where he'd first seen movement, he saw nothing. He glanced all around; still, he saw nothing but long, dark shadows and the last little, thin yellow veins of the evening light.

He was just beginning to believe that it had all been a mistake and he'd seen nothing when suddenly, there, right before his eyes—no more than twenty feet away between two small, low rocks—he saw the large, round eyes of a jaguar, his spots visible in the dim light.

Juan froze.

"Oh, Mama, Mama," he said to himself, losing all courage as he stared at the big cat's eyes. And he wanted to turn and run, but the big cat's tail was now up and moving side to side like an upright snake, hypnotizing him.

The big cat shifted his feet, crouched down, getting ready to leap, and Juan knew this was his last chance to do something, but he was just too scared to move. Then, Juan heard his mother's voice inside himself and she said, "Attack, *mi hijito*! Don't run! Attack! Or he'll kill you!"

"Yes, Mama," he found himself saying. And he let out a howling roar with all his power and attacked the tiger of the desert.

The spotted tiger heard Juan's mighty roar and saw him coming at him in leaping bounds. The big animal leaped up, too, roaring out a terrible scream, but then he turned and ran.

Juan Salvador stopped dead in his tracks, turned tail, too, and took off up the side of the tracks as fast as his little legs could go. The big desert cat never looked back; he just kept racing in the other direction.

Juan's feet didn't hurt anymore and he ran up the tracks without once slowing down until the sun was long gone and the moon had come out. He went all night—walking and running—until he came out of the other side of the small red-rock hills and the morning stars were his companions.

He ran, not stopping, not caring how much his bloody, swollen feet hurt or his throbbing head pained until, way up there in the distance in the darkish daybreak, he thought he saw the little flickering lights of a hundred campfires.

He slowed down, catching his breath, and he could hear people talking. He listened carefully as he came and then, up ahead in the middle of the flat, he saw the train, the train he'd been after all this time. He began to sob. He'd made it; he'd caught the train. He was going to be able to find his mother and family and not be lost forever and ever.

But then, getting near the campfires, he felt a strange anger come into him, so he circled around the camp, cautious as a coyote, wary as a young deer, making sure that they weren't bandits but were, indeed, his people.

One of the boys who'd raced with him saw him coming.

"*¡Dios mío!*" said the startled boy. "You came the whole way on foot, Juan?"

But Juan couldn't hear the boy, much less see him. Juan was gone. He was as white as a ghost. His whole face, neck and shoulders were white from where the salty sweat had dried on his skin. He was falling, stumbling, gasping, crying as he came toward their fires, white-lipped and wild-eyed.

"Your mother," said the boy, "she said you'd catch us. She told my father last night that you'd . . ."

But Juan paid no attention to the boy. He just walked on, staring at the fires ahead of him. He was hypnotized by the little leaping flames. He was dead on his feet. He'd been running half-conscious since he'd raced away in terror from the spotted desert tiger.

A man turned and saw Juan and leaped up, grabbing him under the armpits just before Juan pitched face first into the fire.

But, still, Juan's feet kept climbing. He couldn't stop. He had to get past those little dancing hills of flaming fire so he could reach his mother, the love of his life, the only living thing that gave meaning to his entire existence.

For three days, Doña Margarita massaged her son with herbs and had him suck bitterroots. She prayed to God and thanked Him for this miracle. Luisa, Emilia and Inocenta joined her in her prayers. And, miracle of miracles, Juan's feet, which were bloody stumps filled with cactus thorns and deep gashes, began to heal. And his mouth, which was ripped open, began to mend.

On the fourth night, Juan awoke and he was fully conscious for the first time. He came to understand that they were now outside Torreon, near Gomez Palacio, and they'd been put off the train once more.

Francisco Villa, the commander-in-chief of the northern division, had to get thirty thousand of his men south in time to reinforce his most famous of all fighters, Fierro, the executioner, who'd taken four thousand of Villa's cavalry and made a lightning attack, fighting his way back through Leon, Silao, Irapuato, Salamanca, Celaya, Queretaro, San Juan del Rio and Tula, where he'd destroyed Obregon and was now ready for Villa to come and reinforce him so that, together, they could recapture Mexico City.

Juan awoke and he could feel the excitement. Everyone was talking about the terrible Fierro—the man of iron, the cruel right hand of Villa—who'd just recaptured all the territory that Villa had lost since Celaya.

But Juan didn't care; he was now here by his mother's side, safe at last in her arms. So he hugged his old mother close, kissing her, becoming her tired little baby, and he promised to never do anything so foolish again as long as he lived.

Emilia and Inocenta watched, both having prayed day and night for the recovery of their little Juan, the last surviving masculine child of their once great, proud family.

Juan noticed that Luisa and Epitacio weren't with them. He wondered if Luisa had deserted them, just like his other sister Lucha. But then to his relief, Luisa and Epitacio came out of the dark. They had a pot of water and they put it on the fire to boil the two rats that their mother had caught.

"It's bad," said Epitacio, "with this new battle going on, there aren't going to be any empty trains going north for a long time."

That night they ate well, sucking clean the bones of the two fat rats. But most of the people all around them refused to eat the rodents, preferring to boil their old *huaraches* for nourishment instead.

That night Luisa and Epitacio had a big fight and she blamed him for all their misery.

"Please," said Doña Margarita, "if we start blaming each other for everything, we will destroy ourselves. Think and take heart, *mi hijita*. In the last few days, Epitacio has shown himself to be a fine man."

"But, Mama, how can you side with him?" said Luisa angrily. "I'm your blood, not him!"

"*Mi hijita*, that was the wisdom of Don Pío," she said. "Blood is blood, but justice is justice. And Don Pío never let blood blind his eyes to justice."

"Thank you, *señora*," said Epitacio. "I appreciate your wisdom."

"Not at all," said Doña Margarita. "Now let us pray, we're alive and so we've had another good day."

Juan could see that his sister didn't like it, but still, Luisa lowered her head to pray. They prayed, giving thanks to God. In the morning, they felt better.

"I had a vision last night," said their mother, "and I can now see that Juan has shown us the way. With God's help we can walk all the way to the United States if we need to."

"But, señora," said Epitacio, "the border is well over a thousand miles away!"

"So, how far do you think I've walked in my life, from the stove to the bedroom, to the cow's corral, to the church?" she asked. "At least a hundred times that distance, I'm sure."

Epitacio nodded, not being able to think of anything else to say, and they picked up their belongings and started out that morning, going north alongside the tracks with thousands of other homeless people. They couldn't afford to wait for the trains anymore; they had to get north, even on foot if they had to, before they became too weak from hunger to walk.

Juan walked alongside his mother, his feet wrapped in wet herb-soaked cloth. He held onto her leather-tough, wrinkled old hand. Inocenta walked on the other side of his mother, holding hands with Emilia. Inocenta and Emilia had grown very close since they'd been on the road. Inocenta had become Emilia's eyes and Emilia had become the little girl's mother. Lucha, who'd abandoned them, was becoming forgotten.

Luisa walked in front with Epitacio. Epitacio carried Joselito along with all their blankets and cooking utensils in a huge bundle on his back.

They were a ragged mass of dark ants, lifting dust as they walked along the railroad tracks by the thousands, going up the long, wide valley. There was brush and rock and scattered chaparral all around, and high overhead was the bright blue sky and the great powerful sun.

Juan felt pain in his legs and feet, but he was young and strong, so he kept quiet about his pain and forced his body on. He'd caused enough trouble to his family as it was.

The morning passed. The sun grew hot. The ground began to sear their feet. Twice they had to stop and Doña Margarita changed the rags on Juan's feet.

It was midday before they decided they could go no further in the heat. They took up residence along with the rattlesnakes in the shade to wait out the heat.

Juan had never seen country like this. The rivers that they'd seen south of Leon had all been replaced by white, dry riverbeds. And the tall cactus of the red-rock hills where the desert tiger had scared him were gone, too. Here, there was nothing in all directions as far as the eye could see, except sand and rock and granite and the dancing heat waves. It seemed to Juan that the farther north they went, the more desolate the landscape became. Why, the green meadows of their homeland were now nothing but a dream. And the cool, high lakes of their beloved mountains seemed so unreal that he was beginning to believe that they'd never existed.

"Mama," he said, "you know, it's like I'm almost not able to remember our wild orchids anymore."

His old mother smiled sadly, sitting in the shade. "I know what you mean, *mi hijito*," she said. "At times like this, it truly tries my patience with God."

"Then you're losing hope, too, Mama?" he asked.

"Hope? Oh, no, *mi hijito*, not hope nor faith, but patience, yes," she said, laughing lightly.

Juan lay back on the hard, rocky ground, breathing easy. He tried to figure out what it was that his mother had said. He tried to understand the difference between "faith" and "hope" and "patience." Ever since he could remember, he loved talking with his mother. She always made life seem so important and grand and full of mystery. He thought about the deep, cool canyons that they'd had back home where the wild orchids grew. He thought of the shallow lakes covered with white lilies during the rainy season. Oh, how he'd loved to watch the goats nibble the water lilies and eat the orchids, sucking down their milky-white, bittersweet liquid.

He must have fallen asleep, for when he awoke the sun was going down in the tall, flat sky. It was time for him and his family to start walking once again.

That night they camped alongside a foul-smelling water hole just north of Torreon. And even though they had Villista money and they were in Villa's territory, no one would accept the money of Francisco Villa in the town of Torreon.

Two weeks later, still camped alongside the water hole, Juan and his family began to starve. And being too weak to walk any further, they didn't know what to do.

But then, early one morning down in the stockyards where Villa loaded his horses into the train to go south, Juan saw a flock of black birds going through the horse manure. Instantly, he got an idea and ran the birds off and searched through the wet, round horse manure and found good, undigested seed.

Racing to their shelter made of brush, he yelled, "Mama, everyone, come quick! I found grain for us! Hurry!"

"But where, *mi hijito*?" asked his mother. She didn't want him stealing anymore.

"Down at the corral! But we have to hurry before other people get to it!"

They all got to their feet and followed Juan down to the corral.

"In there," he said, "I found lots of seed in the horse manure! But the cattle's *caca* isn't so good, I found out."

The laughter, the cries of joy that came from his old mother's lungs, filled the corral with sound.

"Oh, you are wonderful, *mi hijito*! No matter how life twists you, you always manage to come up with a rain of gold!"

"Yes, let's get all the seed we can and cook up a feast that even a no-good rich man will envy!"

"*Mi hijito*, I've told you a thousand times . . ."

"But I like talking bad about the rich, Mama! It's fun and maybe God will punish me and make me rich someday, too!"

She laughed and they went to work searching through the manure and they quickly came to realize that horse manure was best. Cattle digested their food too well.

The days passed, and the other people began to go through the horse manure, too. Juan now had to keep watch every time Villa's men brought in new horses so he and his family could be the first ones there.

"Mama," said Juan early one morning when the sun was barely coming up on the far horizon, "get up. They just brought in new horses."

Quickly, the old woman got up and they all went to the stockyards to go through the new piles of horse manure. Emilia, with her blind eyes, had become the quickest one to find the seeds. Her fingertips were her eyes as she sifted through big round manure, finding the wet, warm undigested seeds. These horses were well fed, so there was a lot of seed.

"Oh, are we going to eat good today!" said Juan.

And so they took all the seed they'd found and washed it clean in the foul-smelling water hole, and then they boiled water and added cactus and two lizards that Epitacio had caught.

Juan and his family ate the soup with relish and felt better than they'd felt in days. Epitacio took heart and began to teach them English again so they'd be prepared when they got across the Rio Grande.

"And so remember," said Epitacio, "when you speak English, you have to keep your upper lip tight and you don't move your tongue very much like you do in Spanish."

Juan and Inocenta laughed, feeling good to have their little bellies full of hot soup, and they practiced keeping their upper lips tight as they spoke English.

The sea of escaping people remained outside Torreon until they'd stripped every blade of grass, cactus and piece of manure for miles in every direction. They were starving once again, they were crying, they were beginning to die from hunger.

Then late one night, Epitacio came running up. "Hurry," he said, whispering to them all as quickly as he could. "Drop everything! There are four empty boxcars going north to Ciudad Juarez right this moment to get ammunition for Villa. But don't say a thing. Let's just go before everyone runs ahead of us and beats us to the train."

They grabbed their things and disappeared into the night, going down a dry riverbed, following Epitacio through the heavy brush. The mosquitoes were out in droves, but they had to be careful not to slap them away so they wouldn't make any noise.

"Hurry," said Epitacio. "If we miss this train, I don't know when we'll get another!"

There were campfires burning all around them, and they trotted along as quickly and quietly as they could.

"Damn it!" said Epitacio, getting ahead of them once again. "Hurry!"

"We're hurrying," said Doña Margarita, helping her blind daughter through the brush.

But then up ahead Emilia fell, and when Doña Margarita went to help her up, Emilia waved her mother away. "No, Mama," she said. "Go on without me. I'll only hold you up."

In the distance they could now hear the soft, hard, rumbling sounds of the locomotives warming up.

"I'll stay with you, *mi hijita*," said Doña Margarita. She turned to Luisa. "Luisa, you go on ahead with your family and take Juan and Inocenta with you. I'm staying with your sister."

"No!" said Luisa. "Come on, Mama!"

"But it's no use, *mi hijita*," said their mother. "This is the time for you and your husband to go on with Juan and Inocenta. Emilia and I, we talked this over a few nights ago, and we decided that if this situation ever came up, it would be best for you strong ones to go on without us. It's God's will."

"No, Mama," said Juan, his eyes filling with tears. "You are our life, Mama!"

"Juanito's right," said Luisa. "So no more of this! We're not going without you, Mama, and that's that!"

"But, *querida*," said Epitacio, "maybe your mother is right and this is God's will."

"You bastard!" screamed Luisa, leaping at him with clawed hands. "You stand up like a man right now, or I'll castrate you on the spot! You had a mother once, too, you *cabrón!*"

Such stark-naked fear came into Epitacio's eyes, it was almost comical. But no one laughed. The man just stared wild-eyed with fear at Luisa as if she were some great demon with the power of life and death over his very soul.

"All right," he said, "we won't leave them, *querida.*" His eyes were darting about like a trapped rabbit. "But maybe I should just run ahead and get us a place on the train."

"Epitacio!" roared Luisa. "Don't you dare!"

"*Querida,*" he begged, "believe me, it's our only hope. Here, Juan can even go with me, then I'll send him back so he'll show you the way while I stay there and hold our places!"

Epitacio looked so desperate that Doña Margarita spoke up in his behalf. "*Mi hijita,*" she said to Luisa, "you must trust the man you love or you will never have a home. Believe me, trust is the foundation of the *casa.*"

"Oh, all right, Mama," said Luisa, not liking it. "Go on, Epitacio, but don't leave us. Please, I love you, and we're depending on you."

"I won't!" he said, and he took off running and Juan was right behind him.

Up ahead, Juan and Epitacio left the main riverbed and went up a small, twisting *arroyo* and Juan tried to watch how they went up the many-fingered gully so he'd know how to get back to his family, but it was impossible. And as they went, they could hear the low, rumbling sounds of the big locomotives warming up to go.

"Epitacio," Juan finally said, "let's climb out of the *arroyo* and run up on top so I can see where we are, or I don't know if I'll be able to find my way back to our family."

"Don't be stupid, Juan!" said Epitacio. "People will see us then, and they'll rush ahead of us and fill the train!"

"But . . ."

"No buts; come on!" said Epitacio harshly.

Juan said no more and they ran on. They got to the train and Epitacio took up a place for all of them in one of the boxcars.

"Hurry, Juan!" he said. "Go back and get the others and I'll wait here!"

Juan took off like a deer. His feet were healed and he was strong once more.

But, when Juan tried to retrace his steps in the dark to find his family, he saw it was impossible. He began to think that it had been Epitacio's plan all along. And when he finally did find his family, he could hear the locomotives building up power in the distance.

They never had a chance. The train was long gone, blowing a tall column of fire in the night, when Juan and his family came running up. They all realized then that Epitacio had betrayed them. Numbed with despair, they huddled in the moonlight. But then, to their surprise, Epitacio came out from behind a cactus.

"Epitacio!" said Luisa, handing baby Joselito to Juan. And she took off running with open arms. "You do love me! You didn't leave us!"

She threw her arms around his neck, hugging him, kissing him. But Luisa never saw the armed men on the other side of the big cactus who'd taken Epitacio off the train because he was a single man.

No, she just threw Epitacio to the ground, kissing him, fondling him, caressing him, and then she picked up her dress, swinging a white, naked leg over him, straddling him like a wild mare in heat.

"Come," said Doña Margarita, seeing her daughter's lust. She and Emilia and Inocenta turned to go back down into the *arroyo* to give the two people privacy, but Juan couldn't move.

He stood transfixed by the sight of his sister, silhouetted against the dark moonlit sky, as she now threw back her head, hair flying, and she howled with joy, riding her man on the hard granite ground, bucking and howling and gaining power as she repeated the words *mi amor* again and again.

It was another month before they found a train to take them north to Chihuahua and then to Ciudad Juarez.

They were a very different family now. They were tired, quiet, and little Juan didn't have a pot belly anymore. He was as skinny as a rabbit. Not only had they starved for days on end, losing much of their strength, but they'd seen more blood and death and destruction in the last few months than in the last five years of this terrible Revolution.

But still that night as they traveled north on the train, Epitacio couldn't stop talking. He was so positive that everything would be fine once they got to the border.

He was nineteen years old, six months older than Luisa, and he'd done very well two years ago when he'd gone to the United States with his two older brothers.

"Oh, I tell you, Luisa," he said, hugging her close, "as soon as we get to Ciudad Juarez, I'll get us across the Rio Grande into the United States and get a job at the smelter plant where I used to work, and everything is going to be fine, *querida*.

"Me and my two older brothers—God rest their souls—found work easily the last time we came. The United States is a wonderful land, I tell you! It's at peace, and it's a land of infinite opportunity!"

Epitacio's eyes sparkled every time he spoke of the United States. This country across the border was heaven to him. "Why, even the dogs of the rich wear gold chains around their necks, I swear it," he said, "and they're fed three times a day!"

"Three times a day?" said Juan jokingly. "Oh, come on, Epitacio! The gold chain I can understand, because I've seen horses with fine silver bridles, but to eat three times a day . . . oh, Epitacio, even a man would blow up!"

"But, Juanito, it's true," insisted Epitacio. "In the United States, people have no wrinkles on their faces, they're so well fed. And they keep a toilet inside their homes so they can use them constantly . . . they're so full of shit!" he laughed.

"Oh, no, Epitacio," cut in Luisa, laughing loudly. "You've gone too far! How could they possibly keep a smelly toilet inside their homes?"

"Easy," said Epitacio, "they run it with water and perfume!"

At this, Luisa screeched. "Oh, *querido*!" she screamed, hugging him. "Even I, who love you, can't believe this one!"

Their excitement grew that night as the train sped north, singing on the rails. Luisa finally lay down to sleep. Epitacio and Juan stayed up together, looking out into the star-filled night.

Juan practiced his English with Epitacio, keeping his upper lip tight and sticking his tongue way out, saying the words, "Hello, mister! Where's the alligator?" as they traveled north.

Epitacio had explained to Juan that in the middle of El Paso there was a big pond full of huge lizards the size of dragons with big rows of sharp teeth, and every night these monstrous alligators were turned loose into the Rio Grande to eat Mexicans who tried to get across the border illegally.

"So, Juan," Epitacio said, "you have to practice these words carefully and be able to say, 'Hello, mister, where's the alligator?' so you'll know where to cross the river safely!"

Juan laughed excitedly and practiced his English so he'd be able to cross the river without getting eaten alive. He dreamed of a place across the river with tall, magnificent buildings and rich green fields and high country meadows and a great forest of mighty trees as far as the eye could see. He put together everything good that he'd seen back in their beloved mountains and all the stories he'd heard his mother tell of her days when she'd lived in Mexico City. He dreamed of all the good and wonderful possibilities in the world and then put them all together, across the Rio Grande in the United States.

But that morning, as they came around the last, short hill into the El Paso basin, Juan couldn't believe what his eyes saw.

The sun was just coming up over the jagged horizon of solid rock mountains and, where Juan had expected to see the Rio Grande and a luscious green valley, he saw nothing but dry earth. Not even one blade of grass for as far as the eye could see.

Juan turned, looking in all directions as the train came into the basin, still expecting to see the river and trees and grass, and tall, well-constructed buildings like he'd seen back in Leon; but he could see nothing other than orange rock, grey granite and white sand.

He didn't even see cactus trees or brush in the low places, or chaparral on the surrounding mountains.

"Epitacio," he said, feeling his chest constrict with fear, "but where's the Rio Grande and the rich valley you told us about?"

Epitacio's eyes were looking like a trapped mouse. "I don't know," he said. "But the river was big and wide the last time I came with my brothers. Honestly. I swear it before the Holy Virgin! There was a rich valley, too, all the way down from Las Cruces, Nuevo Mexico, to here in El Paso."

Juan said nothing more and decided that it was good that his mother and sisters were still sleeping. They'd be shocked enough once they awoke. Nothing could live here except lizards and snakes. Why, this was the end of the world.

Then, as the train entered the town, it got even worse. Everywhere, Juan saw that there were poor, ragged, starving people. And not just two or three thousands, as they'd seen back in Torreon, but ten or twenty times that number of people.

"Oh, *Dios mío*," said Epitacio, making the sign of the cross over himself, "it wasn't like this two years ago. I swear it, Juan!"

Juan said nothing. He just turned to his mother. "Wake up, Mama," he said.

"Are we there?" she asked, rubbing the layers of sagging old brown skin about her eyes. She was the only one who hadn't lost any weight. She had none to lose.

"Yes," said Juan. "But it's not what we expected, Mama."

Leisurely, the old woman stretched and then got to her feet and glanced around at the dried-out country and the mob of desperate-looking people. "Why, it's a beautiful day, *mi hijito*," she said. "See those vultures in the sky over there? They're telling us there's so much to eat here that even the vultures get their share."

Juan began to laugh. He just couldn't help it. No matter what life dealt them, their mother always came up smiling.

Leaving the train, Juan and his family shouldered their belongings and tried to find some shade. It was only an hour after daybreak, but already the sun was so hot that the air felt like a furnace blast. But they were not able to find any shade. Every tree, every bush, every rock was already taken by ten or twelve people.

Luisa and Epitacio got into another argument.

"Stop it!" said Luisa's mother. "No more blaming each other! We're here, and so God must have His reason. Now open your eyes and let's look around and see what it is that He has for us!" she ordered.

"Look!" shouted Juan, dashing ahead. "A pair of *huaraches* that someone threw away!"

He'd had nothing to wear on his feet other than rags since his long walk.

"You see?" said Doña Margarita. "Already, God is giving us riches!"

Putting the *huaraches* on his burning feet, Juan strutted about. "They fit perfect," he said.

His mother smiled. "Of course," she said. "God's gifts always fit us perfectly, if only we have eyes to see."

They continued walking until they came to the little hills at the outskirts of the town. A family took pity on them and let them set up house under the brush alongside their fence. This way, at least, they could keep out of the sun and maybe even the wind, too.

It was late afternoon before Juan and Epitacio located the Rio Grande way across on the other side of town. The land was jammed with people for so many miles that even Epitacio hadn't realized where the big muddy river was at first.

Looking across the slow moving water, Juan could see the well-kept buildings of the *americanos*, untouched by war. There were tall, well-fed, uniformed American soldiers patrolling the river, keeping the Mexican people from crossing into the United States. Asking around, Epitacio found out that Mexicans couldn't cross the river freely into the United States anymore to look for work. It cost ten cents for each adult and five cents for children to cross, an unheard of fortune.

Going back to their home in the brush that evening, Epitacio told Luisa what he'd found out, and they had another fight. Luisa pulled his hair and bit him in frustration, but the next thing Juan knew, they started kissing and hurried off in the dark.

Later that same night, Emilia went into labor. Doña Margarita and Luisa boiled water and washed their hands and arms all the way to their armpits. They helped Emilia to relax, to push with all her strength, and, in the moonlight, the child came screaming into the world, being born right there, under the brush, alongside the fence.

The newborn was undernourished and Emilia didn't have enough milk. Mother and child cried long into the night.

The next morning the wind picked up and the sun drained them of their strength. They weren't even hungry anymore, their stomachs felt so bloated.

But then that evening, Inocenta screamed and they found a rattlesnake under the blankets where she slept. Emilia thought it was a sign from the devil and they were all going to be sent to hell. But their mother calmed Emilia down while Juan and Epitacio killed the snake and skinned it out.

It was a big, fat old snake, and although they knew it was a sin before God to eat it because snakes were of the devil's domain, they decided that God would forgive them this one time. They cut the snake into pieces and fried it in its own grease. The owners of the house, whose fence they lived by, gave them some tortillas, and they had one of the most wonderful meals they'd had in months.

Feeling stronger, they got together that night and talked about the future. But they could come to nothing, since all Luisa wanted to do was kill Epitacio for having talked them into leaving their mountains.

"All right," said Doña Margarita, "no more! We must keep strong of mind and open our eyes so we can see the good in our predicament or, believe me, we have nothing! Now, let us pray. Right now! On our knees!" she commanded.

And so they all knelt down on the hard white granite and they prayed, repeating their mother's words.

"Look," said Epitacio when they were going to bed down for the night, "Luisa is right; I am responsible for us being here at the border. So, well, I think that it's only right that I break across the Rio Grande *a la brava* and get a job so we can eat."

"But the alligators!" said Luisa, suddenly looking fearful for him.

"To hell with the alligators!" he said. "The river's down and I'm as fast as a rabbit when I'm scared."

They all laughed. And that night they could hear Luisa and Epitacio making love again and again. Then in the morning, he ate all the rattlesnake soup he could eat, rolled up two tortillas and put them in his pockets, and he left.

Luisa cried the whole first day that he was gone, saying how much she loved him and that she wished she'd never been so mean to him.

"You were right, Mama, he's a good man," she said. "He's stayed by us through everything."

Three days later, Epitacio returned and he had a treasure of food. He had canned fruit, American bread, tomatoes and cheese, and even a big piece of meat. They all ate well that night, sitting around the fire like fat cats after a kill, switching their tails and farting happily.

"Mama," said Luisa the next morning as she stroked her husband's back, "Epitacio and I have talked it over, and he thinks that I should go across the border with him." Her eyes filled with tears. "We'll come back for you as soon as we have money. But, oh, Mama!" she cried, coming to her mother's arms, "I love you so much, I just don't want to leave you!"

"*Mi hijita*," said the old lady calmly, "don't worry. You are a fine, courageous daughter, and we believe in you. So go, do what you must, and with God willing, *querida*, we'll be here when you return."

"Of course you'll be here," snapped Epitacio quickly. "Look at the food I brought you!" He glanced at Juan, eyes darting. "You must understand, *hermanito*, that I had to argue with my *gringo* boss to get him to advance me the money for this food and passage. And now I have to get Luisa and me back across the border as quickly as I can so I don't lose my job."

Juan was wondering why Epitacio was bothering to explain all this to him. No one had questioned his words. But Epitacio just couldn't seem to stop talking.

"So we'll be back, Juan, as soon as I find an older man to sponsor you," he continued. "You see, I have to find a man who has a job and yet is old enough to say that he's married to your mother." He laughed, showing his beautiful white teeth. "But don't worry, I'll pay some old fart a few pesos and everything will be fine, Juan, I swear it!"

And he took Luisa's hand. "Come, *querida*," he said. "We must hurry!"

"Oh, my God," said Luisa. Her eyes overflowed with tears as she hugged and kissed each one of them. Then she and her husband were gone, taking Joselito with them.

With Luisa gone, the family felt much smaller that night when they said their evening prayers. Luisa had always brought such strength and vitality to all of them. That night Juan dreamed of alligators chasing Luisa and Joselito across the Rio Grande, and he became so frightened for them that he hugged close to his mother, trembling like a leaf.

Doña Margarita held her little son close to her bony old chest, lying there on the hard granite ground alongside the fence of upright sticks and cactus, and she hummed to him and rocked him in her arms.

"God is with us, *mi hijito*," she said. "Look at the stars and the moon; God is here. God is everywhere. Our life here on earth is good, if only we keep our faith and our hearts and souls open."

Hearing his mother's calm voice, Juan went back to sleep. In the morning when he awoke, he found ants crawling underneath his legs. He sat up and watched the ants working their way alongside the fence, and he started counting them. They numbered in the thousands and they looked so strong as they came out of their ant hole, going to work for the day. Oh, how he wished he were an ant and he could just live in the ground.

The sun climbed into the sky, hotter and brighter than usual. The insects sang and the flies buzzed around, but they didn't act quite normal. Then, when the sun was only three fists off the horizon, Juan noticed that the ants began to go back into their hole. After that, he noticed that the flies had also disappeared. All the insects had gone quiet.

Juan looked off into the distance and he saw a black storm coming their way.

"Mama!" he said. "Look, rain!"

But, as the storm came into the basin, they could see that it wasn't rain. No, it was the devil's wind, blowing from hell. The ants and insects must have known what was coming.

The sandstorm hit Juan and his family with such force, each grain of sand stinging like a bullet, that they had to get under their blankets so they wouldn't be skinned alive.

All day long the wind howled across the basin of El Paso, whistling in a torrent of sound and fury, tearing at them with such force that it felt like they'd be blown off the face of the earth if they didn't keep down tight.

The blasting, hot sand was so fine, it shot through the blankets and got into their noses and mouths, between their teeth, and into their eyes, burning them.

Never in his life had Juan ever felt a wind like this. It dried the skin all the way to the bone. It blasted so much sand into their eyes that it hurt to blink.

For three days and nights the wind blew, and Juan hugged close to his mother under their blanket; Emilia and Inocenta hugged close together under theirs. By the third day, they were so dried out that they couldn't even cry. And Doña Margarita's old eyes were so inflamed, she couldn't see.

Juan began to pray as he'd never prayed before. Here, they weren't just going to starve to death; no, they were getting cooked alive by the devil's wind.

By the fourth day, the wind was still howling and Juan remembered how the ants had gone underground. He came out from under their blanket and decided to dig a hole. Now his mother was coughing and choking, too. So much sand had gotten down her throat that she could hardly breathe.

Crawling around in the sandstorm, Juan found some rocks. He started to build a shelter for his family, but being half blind himself and working alone, he couldn't do much. Emilia and Inocenta moaned and whined and the baby lay in a dead stupor. The wind continued for days on end.

Then, one morning the wind suddenly quit—just like that—and all was calm. The ants came out and the flies began buzzing about. Juan stood up and glanced around, thinking all was well. But then to his absolute horror he saw that his mother's eyes were swollen shut and oozing with infection.

"Mama, you're blind!" he yelled.

"Oh, no!" screamed Emilia, holding her infant to her breast, "it's the end of us! God has forsaken us and we're going to die!"

"Emilia, stop it!" said her mother, staring with red-swollen, infested eyes. Flies were buzzing about her face. "I can't see, but that doesn't mean I'm blind to the powers of the Almighty!" She grabbed her daughter. "We're not going to die! Do you hear me? We are going to live!"

"Just hear these flies buzzing around us, full of vitality, and look at those ants over there. They hid during the wind, but they didn't die! Look at these bushes; they swayed in the wind, but they didn't break!"

"But, Mama, you're blind!" said Juan. "So how do you know about the ants and the bushes?"

Opening her mouth wide, the old woman tried to laugh, but started coughing instead. "*Mi hijito*," she said between coughs, "I've seen dozens of winds sent by the devil before. I know how life goes on."

A terrible coughing fit gripped her body and she doubled over in pain.

Juan glanced at Inocenta and Emilia and her newborn. Oh, he just couldn't understand how God could allow all this to happen to them. Their mother coughed uncontrollably until the woman came out of the little shack nearby and gave them a cup of water.

Juan and Inocenta decided to go across town to the river and get a pot of water while the winds were still calm.

Getting to the Rio Grande's bank, they found the air was cool and moist.

People were gathered there by the thousands, having come to refresh themselves.

Stepping into the shallow, muddy water, Juan and Inocenta bent over and washed their faces and worked their toes into the itchy-good sandy soil. Oh, it felt so wonderful to get the sand and dirt out of their eyes and soak in the cool wetness of the water. They were as happy as little ducks, splashing about and laughing along with all the other people who'd come out of hiding after the winds.

Across the river, on the American side of the bridge, armed soldiers were patrolling the river, making sure that no Mexicans crossed except on the bridge where they could be properly checked.

Juan watched the tall Americans. He saw how clean and well-dressed they were. He wished with all his heart he could get his mother across the river before she coughed herself to death or became permanently blind like Emilia.

He wondered if Luisa was ever going to come back for them, now that she was across the river in safety. And suddenly, he had a mad urge to just race across the river and find his sister. But then he remembered the alligators.

Quickly, he glanced around, but he saw no big-toothed monsters, so he took heart. "Hello!" he yelled across the river to one of the soldiers. He'd never spoken English to a real American before, and his heart was pounding. "Where's alligator?" he said, smiling a big smile.

The American soldier turned around and looked at him with real interest. "What'd you say, kid?" yelled the soldier. "I didn't hear ya!"

"Hello!" repeated Juan as loudly and distinctly as he could. "Where's alligator?"

"Alligator?" the tall boy in uniform shouted back. "What the hell are you talking about?" He spat out a long, wet wad of brown tobacco juice.

"What did he say?" asked Inocenta, running through the calf-deep water to hear her Uncle Juan speak English.

"Quiet!" said Juan sternly. "Don't you see I'm busy?"

The other people in the river now turned to watch, too. So Juan once more smiled his best smile and yelled out to the soldier the next words Epitacio had taught him.

"All right! Where's shit house, mister boss?" And he pronounced the words so perfectly, so distinctly, just like Epitacio had shown him, that the young soldier understood him and doubled over with laughter.

"Hell, I don't know," said the young man. "I guess you can crap right over there in those bushes next to you," he said, pointing at the brush alongside Juan and Inocenta.

But seeing where the soldier pointed, Juan thought he was telling him of the alligators, and he screamed in fear. "*Caimán! Caimán!* Alligator! Alligator!"

And he grabbed his niece and the pot full of water and took off running from the river. Half the people in the river took off, too, thinking he'd seen a huge alligator.

The soldier watched all these desperate-looking Mexicans running in fear, and he couldn't understand what had happened, so he brought his rifle up to ready and continued patrolling down the Rio Grande.

For three more days the wind didn't come up but, still, there was no sign of Luisa or Epitacio. Juan began to think hard about their situation. He decided it was possible that Luisa and Epitacio would never come back. Luisa was gone, just like Lucha and Domingo. Once they'd gotten across the border, Juan figured that Epitacio had been able to convince Luisa that she didn't have any responsibilities to her family anymore.

"Well, God," said Juan quietly, "I guess it's up to me. I'm the last man." He got up and washed his face and drank down plenty of water. "Mama," he said, "I'm going to go out into the hills and look for firewood to sell so we can eat and be strong to travel when Luisa returns," he lied, deciding that it was best not to tell his mother that he'd figured out that Luisa was never going to come back for them.

"Are you all right?" asked his mother suspiciously, looking at him with her swollen, blind eyes.

"Yes," he said, "I'm strong, Mama."

"Good," she said, smiling up at him with her wrinkled, old face, "for, remember, even God needs help to make miracles." And saying this, she made the sign of the cross over herself and then she opened up her old skinny arms for Juan to come to her. And they hugged and kissed, heart-to-heart.

"Oh, I love you so much, Mama," he said. "I'm never going to leave you as long as I live! I swear it!"

She laughed. "Not even when you marry, *mi hijito*?"

"No, not even then!" he said. "I'll always stay by you!"

"Well, then, you'll have to find a very special wife," she smiled, "who's willing to come and live here with us under this brush."

"I will," he said. "She's going to be an angel, just like you, Mama."

The howl of laughter that came up from the old lady's body was so huge that it caused the people nearby to turn and look at them. "Oh, you poor child," she said, "if only your father could hear you call me an angel! Half of the time he accused me of being the devil."

She continued laughing and it was wonderful. Laughter not only gladdened the heart, but it loosened all the muscles of the face and gave sunlight to the soul.

And so Juan took off to search for firewood. He climbed the steep hill behind them, searching every gully and *arroyo*, but he couldn't find any. The masses of waiting people had stripped the surrounding countryside bare.

The sun was painting the sky pink and yellow and lavender when Juan decided to head for home. He was trudging through the sand when he suddenly heard gunfire just beyond the ridge. Quickly, he ran to the rocks ahead of him. And there, across a sandy hill, he saw that six horsemen were being ambushed by more than a dozen wild men.

They all disappeared into a gully, shooting and screaming. Carefully, Juan got up and crept closer. The men who'd come out of the rocks were on foot and they leaped onto the men on horseback, pulling them off their mounts, hacking them with their machetes, and shooting their horses out from under them if they tried to get away. Like a pack of wolves, the men on foot made short work of the half a dozen horsemen.

Laughing, they stripped off the dead men's shoes and clothes, fighting amongst themselves for the best ones. Then they took the four horses that they hadn't killed and headed toward town.

Glancing around and not seeing anyone left, Juan inched his way down into the gully and saw the six dead men and the two dead horses. The men's naked bodies looked ghostly white in the dimming light.

Approaching the first dead horse, Juan saw the moist, red flesh where the bullets had made big holes, and he licked his lips with hunger.

Quickly, he looked around for something that he could use for a knife. He scrambled around in the rock looking for a sharp stone. Finding a broken rock, he ran back down to the dead horse and began to hack at its exposed flesh. But the rock was too dull.

"Damn it!" he said. "I need claws! What's wrong with You, God, we eat meat but we didn't get fangs or claws!"

Two vultures came swooping down, red-necked and bald-headed.

"Get away!" Juan screamed at them. "They're mine! I found them first!"

But the vultures just landed leisurely in the rocks above to wait him out.

Juan took a big breath, looking at the dead horses and men. He didn't like what went through his mind. He was a Christian, after all, he wasn't a cannibal; but he was sure he could cut through the men's limbs easier than he could the horses' hairy hides.

"Oh, God," he said, tears coming to his eyes, "help me. My family's hungry, and I'm going crazy!"

He looked at the horse once more, and he saw flies swarming about the open wounds. Then the ants came, too, by the thousands. He saw how well-equipped they were to do what they had to do to survive. He went crazy with rage.

Screaming and yelling, he threw himself at the dead horse, knocking the ants and flies away and biting at the bloody, hairy hide with his teeth. The flies rose in clouds above his head as he bit and pulled, but he just didn't have big enough teeth, nor enough saliva to get at the piece of dirty, dry meat, and he began to choke.

Rolling over on his back, face smeared with blood and flesh, he suddenly knew why dogs had such long, wet tongues. Humans just don't have enough spit in their mouths to yank and tear at dry flesh and hide.

Lying there, Juan saw movement out of the corner of his eye and he turned and saw four hungry-looking coyotes come over the ridge. They'd smelled the blood and were coming his way. Juan realized that he could be in danger. He got up, throwing a rock at the skinny, grey-brown animals, but they only dodged and came closer.

Step by step, he watched the four animals circling, closing in on him and the dead bodies.

"All right, you win this time," he said. "But I'll be back!"

He turned and was just scrambling over the top of the gully, when he heard a scream. He turned around and couldn't believe his eyes. One of the men was still alive and was screaming as he tried to crawl away from the coyotes. But they had him, ripping, biting, like cats on a rat.

Juan felt his whole body shiver. Why, he'd been thinking of doing the very same thing to that poor man.

That night, Juan barely had the strength to make it back to their home alongside the fence. Once more they had nothing to eat. Juan went to sleep, trembling. He had terrible dreams of boys with faces of wolves trying to eat him.

In the morning, he was delirious. Doña Margarita, still blind, groped to make a fire and put water to boil. Then she woke Inocenta and had her help make *yerba buena* tea along with some of the other dry healing herbs she always carried.

"We must break his fever," said the old woman. "The devil is wrestling with God for his soul!"

Inocenta helped her grandmother as best she could, and together they made Juan drink down the tea. Then they massaged the soles of his feet, the mirrors of the entire body. Juan began to calm and his breathing changed. But still, he made no sense when he talked.

"Oh, Mama," he kept saying, "don't let them eat me."

"Who?" said his mother.

"The coyote boys!" he screamed.

"No one's going to eat you, *mi hijito*. I'm here and God is with us, and all is well."

"Oh, Mama, how can you say that? All isn't well! We got nothing!"

"Nothing," she said. "And my love for you, is that nothing?"

"Well, no, not your love. But . . . but . . ."

"But what?"

He looked straight into his mother's red, swollen, infected eyes. "I'm crazy with hunger! And love can't feed us, Mama!" he yelled.

"Oh, is that so?" she said.

He nodded. "Yes, that's so!" he said angrily.

"Give me your hand," she said, reaching out and taking his hand, "and feel my pulse, feel my power, and I will give you the food of my love for you to eat."

"Oh, Mama," he said, trying to jerk his hand away from her. "I need real food!"

"Oh," she said, "and your father who had pigs and goats—real food as you said—all around him to eat, what did he die of? Eh, you tell me. He starved to death of a broken heart.

"*Mi hijito*, we are human beings, made in God's own image, and so above all else we live because of love. Now, relax, feel my hand and open your heart and soul to God's power of pure love and you will be fed."

And it was true; as his mother held his hand, Juan felt a warmth—a pulsating strength—come pouring into him and, yet he didn't want it. He wanted meat; he wanted tortillas; he wanted food.

"Oh, Mama," he said, "please, this is no good."

"If you're fighting it, no. But if you're willing and open, yes. You tell me, who was the strongest of all the animals up in our mountains?"

"Well, the bull, of course," he said.

"And when sick," she asked, "how does the bull become?"

"A coward," he said.

"Exactly, the great, powerful bull becomes a coward; but the horse, he doesn't. The horse remains brave, even in the face of sickness and tragedy, and is willing to travel over yet another mountain for his master, whom he loves." She took a deep breath, filling herself with power and confidence. "And we, *mi hijito*, are worlds and worlds ahead of that horse.

"Do you really think I could have endured these last few years without love? It's love here, inside my heart, for my family, that has kept me alive and going. Love is our greatest nourishment."

"But, Mama," he said, going crazy with frustration, "I need to eat food, too!"

"And so do I, so hold my hand and you feel my love, and together we'll go on and find our earthly food, too."

Juan relaxed and held his mother's hand and he felt the warmth grow and grow. A hot, good power came into him, little by little, with such force that he just knew he was, indeed, connected to the cord of life. His mother's spirit was overwhelming him with strength.

"Oh, Mama," he cried, feeling the ghosts of the night slipping away, "don't ever leave me. Please, swear it! Swear it! You are my life!"

"All right," she said, "you keep your faith, *mi hijito*, and I, in turn, promise you with all my heart and soul, that I will not break or die or leave you alone until you, my last child, are grown and safely married.

"We're going to live," she continued, "I can feel it here in my bones. We are going to live and you're going to grow to be a fine man and marry and have children, and have a great house on a hill where all hearts open, just as your grandfather Don Pio had. For you are the miracle child of my old age, *mi hijito*. You came to me when I was years beyond giving any more life.

"Now squeeze my hand and promise me that you'll never let the devil of doubt rob you of your faith in God again."

He looked at her, feeling her power come pulsating into his body like a newborn still connected to his mother by the umbilical cord. "I promise you, Mama," he said, tears coming to his eyes.

"Good," she said, "and so now you can depend on me not to die or leave you as surely as you depend on the sun to rise and the stars to shine in the heavens, for I will live and see my responsibilities done!"

And hearing this, Juan let himself go and went off to sleep, dreaming, feeling peace at last.

It was early the next morning when Juan awoke and he could see that Emilia and his mother were arguing. Emilia was in tears, she was so frightened.

"Emilia," said Doña Margarita, "get hold of yourself. I'm not leaving you. I'm only going to town to get a job so we can get something to eat."

"But, Mama," cried Emilia, "you're blind just like me and the town is full of starving people! You'll get lost, or worse, killed!"

"Are you going to town, Mama?" asked Juan, sitting up. "I'll go with you." But when he tried to move, he fell back down.

"No, *mi hijito*," said his mother, "you stay here and get your strength."

"But, Mama," said Emilia, "at least take Inocenta with you."

The old woman shook her head. "No, I'm going alone," she said. "And I'm not blind. All night I put herbs on my eyes and I can see pretty good." She stood up. "And besides," she added, "I'm not going to town alone, I'm going with God. And He will be my eyes."

Saying this, Doña Margarita kissed each of them and she covered her head with her black shawl, got a stick from the broken fence, and started across the granite-hard white sand toward town.

All afternoon Juan watched Emilia cry like a frightened child, but he didn't. He had all the faith in the world that his mother would return. They were human beings, after all, made in God's own image. They weren't like the bull at all. No, they were like the horse.

But that evening, when the sun was going down and their mother still hadn't returned, even Juan began to get frightened.

"Let us kneel and pray," he said. "This is what Mama would tell us to do if she was here."

So they knelt down and they were just beginning to pray when Inocenta shouted, "Mamagrande! Mamagrande!" as she raced down the slope. And there she was, a short little figure, coming up the slope in the evening light, weaving between the open campfires, and they couldn't believe their eyes. It really was their mother, skinny and twisted with age, stumbling as she came.

Juan was on his feet, too, crying with joy. Here came their old mother. It was a miracle of miracles. Their mother hadn't just returned to them safe and sound, she'd returned with a bag full of eggs, milk, tortillas and beans, and even a big, juicy tomato and three long chiles.

It was a feast! They started a fire to cook the food, giving thanks to the

Almighty. They had so much food that Doña Margarita gave some to the fine, generous people inside the house who'd been giving them little bits and pieces.

"Oh, Mama," said Juan, eating with *gusto*, "I was beginning to get frightened when the sun went down and you still hadn't returned."

"Not me," lied Emilia, holding her child, "I was sure you'd return, Mama."

Juan and Inocenta laughed and they ate until they were full, laughing and joking, and feeling warm and good, especially when the sweet juice from the tomato and chile hit their stomachs.

The next day their mother went to town again, and once more she returned with food. When they asked her how she'd been able to get all the food again, she only laughed.

"Why, I went to church," she said, "and God showed me the way." Their mother said no more, and they rejoiced.

By the end of the week, Juan's fever was gone and he was strong and able to move around. And once again, Emilia's breasts had enough milk so her baby didn't cry in the night.

Then one day, Juan asked his mother if he could accompany her to town, but she said no. After she was gone, Juan decided to go into town by himself anyway. He felt strong, so he thought he'd look for a job, too, and help their family.

Juan walked around the center of town near the tall, thick-walled church, enjoying the sights of the Revolution. He suddenly saw a big powerful man yell, "Watch out! Here comes that filthy, old son-of-a-bitch woman again! Let's get across the street before she gets us!"

Four big men took off, running as fast as they could across the dirt road filled with ragged people and worn-out horses. Juan laughed. This was so ridiculous. Here they were, in the middle of war and hunger and death, and yet these grown men were running in fear from an old woman.

Still laughing, Juan went around the corner, wondering what this terrible old woman could possibly look like. When suddenly, before his very eyes, he saw a wrinkled-up old lady, all dressed in black, hands twisted. She was a pitiful sight as she grabbed at each passing person, no matter how poor they looked. She was such a disgusting, dirty old lady, whining and crying as she clawed at every person, that she was, indeed, the most repulsive thing Juan had ever seen.

Why, she wasn't just old, filthy, and sick-looking, begging in the street like the lowest beggar on earth, but she was . . . Then she turned in his direction and Juan recognized her, but he couldn't believe his eyes; this dirty old woman was his own beloved mother.

And in that moment of confusion, in that instant of gut-hurting recognition, Juan screamed, slapping his hand over his mouth so he wouldn't make a sound, and he turned, running in panic. He didn't want to shame his mother any more. He didn't want to add to her burden, this great woman, educated in Mexico City, the daughter of the great Don Pio Castro who'd fought alongside Benito Juarez himself.

Juan ran, screaming around the corner, away from the tall ornate church, the crowds of people and the shocking sight he'd just witnessed. He cried all the way back to the brush alongside the fence where they lived.

Out of breath, he reached out for his blind sister, holding on to her with all his strength.

"It's our mother, isn't it?" she said. "She was begging, wasn't she?"

Juan pulled back, wiping away his tears, and he stared at his sister's blind eyes. "But how did you know?" he asked.

Emilia stared straight at him with her blank, flat, piercing blue eyes. "Because I saw her, too, *hermanito*, here in my head. I've been seeing her for days, begging, and people running from her in disgust."

She began to cry, too, and she drew her little brother close, hugging him. Inocenta came to them and they all held together, crying, feeling terrible shame of what had come to pass, and knowing deep down inside that this was, indeed, the end of them, that they'd just died, having lost all honor, and they were a *gente sin nombre*, a people without a name.

10

*And so they were lost, far from home, and no one knew
their name. But then there, at the end of the world,
came the miracle of salvation.*

Juan was with his brother Domingo and they were
racing up a cool, moist canyon where the wild orchids grew. Juan was
running alongside his brother and their pet bull, Chivo, and the three of
them were leaping from rock to rock as they ran, herding the white and
brown goats up to where the green grass grew.

Juan and Domingo had raised Chivo from a little baby calf. The big black
bull loved them and followed them everywhere they went. The two boys
raced on, feeling cool and strong and happy. Sheets of golden light poured
down through the huge oak trees. Juan could hear the deep belly rumblings
of Chivo's stomach as he went flying over the rock, grunting, bellowing,
blowing air out through his big, black, round nostrils as he ran alongside the
goats, thinking that he was a goat, too, since he'd been raised with them.

Suddenly, Juan awoke, knocking ants off his face. Hot sunlight beat down
on him through the cracks of the fence. He glanced around, fully expecting
to see Domingo and Chivo, but neither one was there. Juan sat up. He was
sweating profusely. Suddenly, he remembered where he was and that his
mother had been begging. He screamed. He just couldn't believe it. His
mother, the greatest woman on earth, begging like the lowest beggar.

"What is it?" asked Emilia.

"Oh, Emilia! I was just back home!" said Juan, crying desperately. "I
was running with Domingo and Chivo up this deep canyon, herding the
goats, when I suddenly awoke and remembered that I saw Mama begging
and I . . . I couldn't believe it. It was so real being back home!"

"Oh, my poor *hermanito*," said Emilia, hugging him. "I do that all the
time. I'm back home sewing or cooking or helping with dinner, and the birds
are in cages, singing under our *ramada*, and then I wake up and remember
where we are, and I want to die!"

Tears burst from her blind blue eyes. "Truly, I just don't want to know
what's become of us!"

"Oh, no," he said, drying his eyes. "We have to know what's become of us, Emilia. Or we really will die."

"No," she answered, "we must hold on to what we had, Juan, or we'll be crushed!"

Hearing this, Juan stared at his sister, and for the first time he truly saw her for what she was. Why, his once beautiful sister was now nothing but a dirty, desperate, wind-burnt rag. He glanced at his niece and to his horror he saw how scrawny and sickly she was, too.

Suddenly, Juan felt even more repulsed by his blind sister and his little niece than by his mother. At least his mother hadn't given up. She'd faced up to the naked, awful truth of what they'd become, and she'd done what she had to do: beg in the streets.

His heart overflowed with love for his mother, and his eyes ran freely with tears. His mother, this great woman, hadn't lied to herself and pretended they were still a great family. No, she'd kept her eyes open like the newborn chick that breaks the shell, and she'd just started pecking, begging, before God's very own house.

Juan took a deep breath, wiping his eyes, and he stood up. "Emilia," he said, getting his hat, "I'm going. I'll be back by dark."

"But where are you going, Juanito?" she asked. "You can't go back to help Mama. It will only kill her with embarrassment."

"I know that," he said. "I'll go into the hills to look for firewood again."

"But you might be killed this time just like those horsemen," she said. "Please, don't go. Stay here with us until Mama returns. The we'll talk to her and figure out what to do."

"Emilia," said Juan, putting on his straw hat, "there can be no talking to our mother. Don't you see, we can't even let her know that we know she was begging. I must go now, while she's gone, and find a way for us to live."

"But, Juanito," she whined, "Mama told us to wait here for her and not go anywhere."

Suddenly, Juan knew why his beautiful sister had gone blind and why his father, the tall, handsome, redheaded man, had gone up into the mountains to die after their rancho had been destroyed. His father and Emilia were bulls of little faith. They just didn't have the power of the horse in their souls that the dark Indian side of his family had.

"Emilia," he said, "I'm going, and I'll be back by dark, so don't worry; everything is going to be fine."

"But how can you say that? You're only a child!" she snapped.

Losing all patience, he exploded. "I'm no child!" he yelled. "Damn it! None of us who've been through what we've been through is a child!"

"But you might be killed!" she screamed. "Please, don't leave me!" She reached for him, groping desperately.

"No," he said, staying out of her reach. "I'm going, Emilia, and I'm not going to die! Do you hear me? We're going to live!"

"No, Juan, please! For the love of God! Stay with me!" she yelled, grabbing his leg.

"No, Emilia, let go of me," he said, pushing her away. "I must go! It's our only chance! I'll be back, I promise!"

Hearing this and seeing her twisted, wretched face, he suddenly knew the secret to his mother's power. Why, there it lay inside every person, like a tiny seed just waiting to be spoken to, to be watered, so it could burst forth and grow into a mighty tree and it was called faith! Vision! Knowledge in the absolute power of God!

"But, Juan," she begged, wiping her eyes, "you're not God. You can't say that."

"Emilia," he said, "but we are God. That's the whole point. That's what Mama has always been telling us, we are a piece of the Almighty."

"Yes, but . . ."

"No, Emilia, there are no 'buts,' " he said confidently. "Like I said, I'll be back. You can depend on it."

And saying this, a power, a strength came shooting into Juan and he suddenly knew how his brother Jose had become the protector of their mountains while still only eighteen years old. And he also knew how his grandfather, Don Pio, had spoken to God that day on the knoll. And here it was inside him, the secret of life, the power of his mother, so clear, so perfect, and he knew that it all came down to faith and the strength of a man or woman saying it, committing it to words, inside, forever. Now he was good, complete, and at peace inside himself.

He was a child no more; he was a man, a man of his word, for he had no questions. And all of life was now set on course, as true as all the rivers from the mountains to the sea for all eternity.

An hour later, he was walking across the barren sands, headed for the distant hills south of town, and he was walking good and strong and confident.

Villa's army was fighting west of Ciudad Juarez in the canyons along the Rio Grande. Juan could see the cannons blasting fire and hear the roaring explosions, but he didn't care. He had his own battles.

Topping the first series of hills to the southeast of town, Juan still couldn't find anything to gather for firewood. The people had already stripped all the wood off these first hills. He continued, hill after hill, until the El Paso basin was nothing more than a tiny dot in the distance and the cannon fire sounded like firecrackers. Here, Juan finally did find some wood, but it wasn't enough. He had no axe to cut the wood, so he began to dig out the dead scrub brush by their roots.

And the digging was difficult. The ground had a rock-hard crust. He had to get a stone to pound the crust around the base of the root until it loosened. Then he dug by hand, scratching at the granite-like earth, pulling out handful after handful of the hard-packed soil.

His nails began to separate from the flesh, and the pain was so great that he cried out, "Oh, please, dear God, help me!" feeling so much pain that he couldn't stand it. "Give me the power You gave the ants!"

He continued digging, clawing, pulling until the pain was so terrible that his fingers went numb. Then miracle of miracles, Juan discovered that there was more wood to these bushes underground than on top of the earth.

"Oh, thank You, God!" he cried out, and he yanked up the hard, solid piece of underground root and began to dig with new vigor. His mother was never going to have to beg again! God had shown him the way!

So Juan continued to dig out bush after bush, shoving his fingers down deep into the cool, hard granite soil that surrounded the heavy roots. He pulled and pushed and dug, working with all his might, digging until his hands and arms were a bloody, torn, cut-up mess, but he never stopped. All he did was think of his mother, the great woman, seated there at the long, pinewood table to the right side of his grandfather, Don Pio, and Juan dug on, squeezing his eyes, holding back his tears, his pain, as he asked God for strength.

The shooting continued in the distance, but Juan paid no attention and just thought of his mother, of the centuries of history that ran through his veins—not of ants and flies, but of men and women like his mother, like his brothers, like the giants, like his grandfather. Not one of them would have ever allowed a member of their *familia* to be a beggar. He worked on, and he never once thought of his own pain or suffering; no, he only thought of his mother begging with her face twisted in agony.

He continued, raw and bloody, dripping with sweat, tongue turning to cotton, but he never slowed down. The sun set and the sky filled with rosy, long fingers of light and he could see the flashes of the cannons in the distance, but he had no fear.

Finally, he was done. He'd dug up a whole pile of dead scrub brush roots, and he was going to be able to sell it and make, maybe, as much as ten cents.

"Thank You, God," he said, lying down on the ground like a panting dog and looking up at the stars and sky and flashes of light from the cannons. "We're doing good, eh?" he said, wiping the sweat off his face with dry, blood-caked hands.

He must have fallen asleep, for the next thing he knew it was dark and he was cold. Quickly he got to his feet and glanced around and saw the pile of wood. He remembered where he was and what he was doing, so he took off the long rope he used for a belt and gathered the wood, tying it into a bundle as he'd done many times back home. But then, when he went to lift the wood to his back, he felt a hot, searing pain.

"Oh, my God!" he gasped, falling to the ground. He sat there, stunned, taking deep, gasping breaths. "God," he said, "this is no time to abandon me. Look, I worked hard. So now help me get this wood on my back." Saying this, the pain seemed to lessen. He got to his feet and took off his shirt to use it as a pad on his shoulders. But then, getting the wood ready and squatting to lift it again, the pain sent him down with another scream.

"God!" he cried in frustration. "Don't You see I need Your help? I've done my share, now I need one of those miracles You're always giving out. Make me strong!" But no matter what, he just couldn't swing the bundle of hard root onto his back as he'd always done. And it wasn't that big of a bundle, either. Back home he'd carried loads of wood that had towered over his head.

"Oh, God!" he cried, losing all patience. "What's wrong with You? I thought we had a deal!"

But God didn't answer or give him a sign.

"All right," said Juan, "have it Your way! With You or without You I'm going to carry this wood! Do You hear me? I'm not going to let my mother beg!" And saying this, Juan went crazy with rage, straddling the pile of dead, heavy ironwood, a type of dense wood that he knew nothing about, and he screamed at the heavens.

"No one on earth has ever gone to church to see You more than my dear mother!" he bellowed. "All through this war, she always made plenty of time for You! It's not right what You've allowed to happen to us! She was begging in the street, God! Begging! Don't You understand? There, in front of Your very own church, begging! AND I'M MAD AT YOU, GOD!"

Screaming these last words, Juan stopped dead, looking up toward the heavens, feeling sure that he was going to be struck down by lightning. He swallowed. He thought of his mother. He saw the cannons firing in the distance. But the skies didn't open and strike him dead and yet he could see very clearly that he truly did mean what he had said. He was, indeed, mad at God.

"God!" he shouted. "Look at that war going on, look at what we've been through! I can't wait for You anymore! You've had Your chance to help us again and again and You've failed! Do You hear me, You failed!" Saying this, Juan looked up at the moon and the stars again, feeling so scared and nervous and yet, wonderfully happy. He knew that what he was doing was wrong, was going against everything he'd ever been taught by the Holy Catholic Church, but he was being truthful, too.

A coyote called in the distance and the moon went behind a cloud. The night grew dark and cold.

"God," he said, continuing his talk with the Almighty, "my mother, she was Your closest friend, and You abandoned her and so . . ." He stopped. He swallowed. "I'm sorry to say this, but if I have to kill and steal . . . I will. My mother will never beg again!"

And there Juan Salvador held, staring up at the heavens full of stars and moonlight and exploding cannons in the distance, but no lightning came and the earth didn't part and swallow him, either. He wiped the sweat from his face and, strangely enough, instead of feeling abandoned by God, he felt closer to Him. He felt as if a great burden had just been taken off him; as if this was the first in a long time that he had truly spoken to God and told him what he really thought.

He took another deep breath and looked at the pile of wood he'd gathered. Then, he saw it so clearly; there it was, the problem. "Why, this bundle of wood is too big," he said. "These are heavy, hard roots. Not even a burro could carry this load."

He spat in his hands and went to work, taking off half the wood from the pile. This wood, he could now see, was a lot heavier than even the oak wood they had back home. He tied together only as much as he knew he could carry. And it wasn't very much wood, either.

Facing downhill, he put his back to the wood, squatted, and pulled the load to his back as he leaned forward with a grunt and rolled to his feet. "There, You see," he said to God, catching his balance with the pile of wood on his back, "You should have paid closer attention, God, and then I wouldn't have had to get so mad at You."

Below, in the distance, the cannons were firing once again on this side of the Rio Grande, and Ciudad Juarez was leaping in flames. But Juan didn't care; he'd done his part. He'd talked to God.

Step by step, he headed for town. His mother would never beg again . . . with or without God's help, he was going forth. Alone and strong and sure.

THREE

THE
CRYING
TREE

The year was 1872 and Leonides Camargo was twenty-one years old. He was having a good time, stumbling drunk along the beach just north of Mazatlan, Sinaloa.

He was singing as he went, howling at the heavens, when the local *federales* came out of the dark and arrested him. They beat him, tied his hands behind his back, took him to the Army garrison outside of town and forced him to join the Army to fight the Yaqui Indian wars.

Sobering up, Leonides didn't want to fight any war. So he tried to explain to the *federales* that he was married and had three daughters and a wife to take care of and he had no time to go and fight. But they paid no attention to him, pushed a rifle into his hands, and marched him north, along with two thousand other men.

For two years, Leonides Camargo and his fellow soldiers fought the terrible Yaquis, who were so fierce, it was told, that they ate human babies and sucked the blood of soldiers.

They ran the Yaquis out of their rich, green valleys; valleys that they'd been farming for hundreds of years before the Spaniards ever came. And they burned their homes and shot their women and children. After all, the Yaquis were savages, and so by killing their earthly bodies, the *federales* were saving the Yaquis's immortal souls, the priest told them.

But then one day, just at daybreak, when Leonides and five hundred well-armed soldiers hit a Yaqui camp, shooting the men and women and children alike as they came out of their burning huts, something happened to Leonides.

He saw a child, no more than fifteen months old, come running toward him. She was on fire, her arms open as she came begging for help.

And in the early morning light, standing there with his rifle to his shoulder, looking over the gunsights at this little girl, Leonides suddenly thought of his three little daughters back home. And he saw that this was no blood-thirsty savage racing toward him, as he'd been told. No, she was just a little girl. So he lowered his rifle to help the burning child when he saw one of his fellow soldiers taking aim at her.

Without thinking, without hesitation, Leonides whirled around and shot the man down. Then he grabbed the child, smothering the fire. He got on a horse with the little girl, and took off as fast as he could.

For six days and seven nights, Leonides was on the run, and he ran eight horses to death. When he got home, he explained to Rosa, his young eighteen-year-old wife, what he'd done, and she was filled with terror.

"Oh, Leonides, they're going to come and kill us all!"

"But what else could I have done?" he asked Rosa. "She's just an innocent child and she was on fire!"

Rosa looked at the little chubby-cheeked girl and it was true; she didn't look at all like the terrible savages she'd always assumed the Yaqui Indians were.

"Oh, I don't know, Leonides, but we better get out of here as quickly as we can."

And so that very night they packed their meager belongings, wrapped up their children, and left in the middle of the night. They headed north, thinking the authorities would expect them to go south, and they went up into the mountains to hide in the French-Basque settlement of Choix.

Leonides changed his name to Pablo and took up the trade of furniture maker. His young wife Rosa tried to love the little Yaqui Indian girl and treat her well, but it was difficult. Rosa had had to leave her home and parents and brothers and sisters because of this child.

But then one dark night, while Rosa wrestled with her conscience, an angel of God appeared to her, standing on top of a burning hut, and the angel said, "Rosa, it isn't your husband Leonides who saved the Indian child; it was the child who saved Leonides's immortal soul."

Waking up that morning, Rosa saw it all so clearly. Her husband had, indeed, been killing women and children for two years and so, if he'd been killed, his soul would have gone to hell. Yes, it was this little Indian girl who'd not only brought her husband safely home to his family, but she'd saved his immortal soul.

Rosa was suddenly overwhelmed with love for the little Indian girl. That same week, Rosa and Pablo went to the priest and they had the little Indian child baptized. They named her Guadalupe, in honor of Our Lady of Guadalupe, because it had been she who'd saved their home. Pablo and Rosa raised Guadalupe along with their own children and they loved her and cared for her as their own. They sent her to school and Guadalupe learned to read and write quickly.

The authorities never found them and Pablo and Rosa always knew in their hearts that Leonides had done the right thing the day he'd turned his rifle from the burning child to kill his fellow soldier.

After all, it was they, the soldiers, who'd been the savages and not the Yaqui Indians, whom they'd been exterminating like lice.

Guadalupe grew into a beautiful woman with a quick, agile mind and big, happy eyes. When she was fifteen, she married and had two wonderful children before her husband left her. A few months later, she met a tall, handsome man while she cooked in the house of a rich family. The tall man's name was Victor Gomez. He was a finish carpenter. He told Guadalupe stories about a fabulous gold mine high in the mountains called La Lluvia de Oro.

When Victor completed his work for the rich family, he packed his tools and took Guadalupe aside. "*Señora,*" he said, "I'm going up to La Lluvia de Oro. There'll be a lot of work for me up there. I know we don't know each other very well, but, still, would you please consider marrying me and going up to the gold mine with me?"

Sitting down, Guadalupe's eyes filled with tears of joy. After all, this was all that she'd been thinking since she'd first seen Victor. "Don Victor," she said, "I'm not going to be coy with you. I've been watching you for weeks. I see how hard you work and how patient you are. You're a good man. And so, yes, I'd be honored to be your wife and I'll be a good, fine, loving wife to you, but only on the condition that you treat my two daughters as your own and we always have room in our home for my parents when they grow too old to be alone."

"Why, of course," said Victor, smiling happily, "that's why I chose you, *querida*; you are the most loving woman I've ever met."

Victor brought Guadalupe a box of fine chocolates, the candy of love, and they were married with Rosa and Pablo at their side. Then they packed up their daughters and set out for La Lluvia de Oro. It took them two weeks of climbing treacherous trails to reach the canyon.

Immediately Victor got a wonderful job with the Americans, building structures inside their enfencement. The years passed and Victor and Guadalupe did very well and had seven more children.

But then in 1910, a huge meteorite hit the towering cliffs above the box canyon and the whole north rim of the canyon burst into flame. The people who lived down in the bottom of the canyon thought it was the end of the world. All night they prayed and looked up at the night sky full of stars and moon and great leaping flames. In the distance they could hear the howling of the coyote people, the last remaining descendants of the great legendary Espirito.

Holding her husband's hand, Doña Guadalupe remembered that terrible morning when her parents' home had been put to fire and her family had been shot as they'd come screaming out of their burning hut. All night Guadalupe led her family in prayer, listening to the distant howls of Espirito's descendants: people who'd been wronged, just like her own Yaquis.

In the twilight hours of the morning, Doña Guadalupe and her husband made desperate love, thinking they were all sure to die. But then in the morning when they awoke, they saw the miraculous light of a whole new day. The world had not ended; no, it was still here, full of God's love. Doña Guadalupe and her family went outside their little lean-to and they knelt down and gave thanks to the Almighty.

Then, on the third day, the fire on the rim of the box canyon subsided, and Doña Guadalupe and her family picked wildflowers and made a pilgrim-

age on their hands and knees with the other people of the village up to the
place where God's power had kissed the earth.

And there, up on top of the towering cathedral rocks, they found a new
little virgin spring where the meteorite had split the rock. In the distance,
they saw a group of ragged-looking people huddled together in a crevice.
Doña Guadalupe went up to them and invited them to come and pray with
them, but they only hid all the more. They were the last remaining Indians
of Espirito's original tribe.

An old man named Ojos Puros came out of the crevice, leading his wife
Teresa by the hand. Raising up his arms, he called all the rest of the people.
"Don't hide," he said. "Come! We must join them in prayer."

The descendants of the great legendary Espirito took heart and came
forward out of caves, from under crevices, down from trees, and they
gathered in force. By the time they reached Doña Guadalupe, they numbered
six children, four old women, two crippled old men, and Ojos Puros and
Teresa, who resembled her father so much that she looked like Espirito's
ghost.

For two days and nights, Ojos Puros and the few remaining descendants
of Espirito prayed with Doña Guadalupe and Don Victor and all the people
who lived at the bottom of the box canyon. They prayed and made peace
among themselves. They drank the water from the virgin spring and became
pure of heart.

When Doña Guadalupe and her family returned to the box canyon, Don
Victor and many of his fellow workmen refused to go back to work at the
American mine. They were fired and other men were hired. Don Victor
began to drink.

The months passed and word came up the mountain that Doña Guadalupe's father had died. Doña Guadalupe mourned her father's death as no
one else in all her family. He'd saved her, he'd loved her, he'd been the
greatest man in all the world. She asked her husband to go down the
mountain and get her beloved mother to come and live with them.

Nine months later to the day that the meteorite kissed the earth, a female
child was born to Doña Guadalupe and Don Victor. Rosa named the newborn
child Guadalupe, the miracle child, in honor of her beloved dead husband,
whose immortal soul had been saved by a burning child.

11

And so they were now a people so isolated from the world that they were becoming as shy as Indians.

A large, dark form entered the canyon. Slowly it came around on the main road. It was bent over like a huge bear and had a reddish tint on its back as it came, step by step, passing through the golden columns of the dimming light.

Watching, Lupe felt an icy chill slip down her spine like a cold, wet snake. She squatted down alongside her pet deer above the pile of waste just below the black mouth of the abandoned mine. It was late afternoon and the sun was dropping behind the towering cliffs. As she squatted, watching the large form enter their canyon, she realized that her family, down below in the deserted village, couldn't see it.

"Easy," said Lupe, petting her young buck deer, who was arcing his thick neck, shaking his forked horns. "It's a long way off. We have plenty of time to run down and give warning."

But still, the young buck didn't like it and the hair came up on his back as he stood alongside Lupe, the girl with whom he'd grown up.

Since the Americans had left over a year ago, no one had come to the canyon except the bands of renegade soldiers who came to abuse them. Lupe had no idea what this strange reddish creature could be. It didn't look human, much less like a group of bandits, so the only thing that she could think of was that maybe it was some evil spirit coming to take their souls in the form of a bear.

The people who'd remained in La Lluvia de Oro were so isolated that they'd reverted to Indian ways and were constantly talking about *brujas*, *espantos* and evil spirits.

"Come," said Lupe, stroking her pet deer. And standing up on her long, slender legs, Lupe was taller than the antlers of her deer. She was only ten, going on eleven, but she was no longer a child. She was all arms and legs and long, loose hair—a young lady only waiting to get the flesh of a woman on her bones.

"Let's go!" she said, leaping across the rock in a tremendous jump. Then she was racing down through the brush and vines that had grown back inside the abandoned American enfencement.

Sprinting in great bounds, the young buck was after her, flying over the brush and dodging through the vines. But he wasn't able to catch her until she was past the ruins of the last American building and they came to the foliage at the bottom of the creek.

Going up the opposite embankment, the young buck flew past Lupe as they entered the plaza which was also overgrown with vines and weeds and thick tree roots. Here, the young deer stopped and glanced about cautiously. The stores were all boarded up. Hardly anyone lived in the plaza anymore. But there were still some stray dogs about, so the deer was very wary.

"It's all right," said Lupe, coming up beside her deer. She was hardly out of breath. "The dogs won't hurt you. You have your horns now."

Once, a few months back when he hadn't had any antlers, two dogs had cornered Lupe's deer and almost killed him. But now with his forked horns, Lupe was sure that he could gut any dog in a minute.

Just then, Lupe saw Rose-Mary running down along the side of her house, holding up the ends of her long, beautiful dress. Her mother was right behind her, shouting.

"Rose-Mary, you come back here this instant and help me with the laundry!"

"No," said Rose-Mary. "I wasn't brought up to be a laundry woman!"

"Was I?" snapped the old woman. "You come back here and help me, or I'll tell your father!"

"So what? Tell him!" shouted Rose-Mary. "I don't care!"

Turning, she saw Lupe with her deer. "And what are you staring at?"

Rose-Mary was thirteen, a fully-developed woman, but Lupe stood half a head taller.

"Nothing," said Lupe. "I was just coming to give warning. A strange-looking red beast has come into our canyon on the main road."

"Does it walk like a man?" asked Rose-Mary, turning to her mother. Lupe nodded. "Oh, my God, Mama!" said Rose-Mary fearfully. "Lupe has seen the devil, and he's coming our way!"

"Good," said the old woman, lugging the basket of laundry. "I hope he grabs you by your fine hair and thrashes you until you learn respect!"

Rose-Mary laughed. "You didn't really see anything, did you?" she asked, smiling coyly at Lupe.

"Yes, I did," she said. "And here he comes!" she screamed, taking off across the plaza. Rose-Mary's eyes filled with terror. Smiling, Lupe continued up the steep steps to Doña Manza's house, three at a time. "Manuelita! Manuelita!" she shouted, coming to Doña Manza's house. "A bear-like thing has just entered the canyon up on the main road."

Manuelita and her sisters and brothers rushed out.

"But what is it?" asked Manuelita.

"I don't know," said Lupe, shrugging. "The sun's going down, so it was hard to tell. But from up above our home, maybe we'll be able to tell." She continued racing up the pathway through the deserted houses to their own lean-to.

"Mama! Mama!" she yelled, coming under the *ramada* of their lean-to. "Something has just entered our canyon!"

"Bandits?" asked Victoriano, grabbing his machete.

"No," said Lupe, "it looks more like a big bear walking on two legs."

Sophia laughed. "Or the devil coming in the form of a bear to steal our soul!" she said, enjoying herself.

"Don't make fun!" cried out Carlota. "Or *el diablo* really will come and snatch our souls away!"

Victoriano went out the back, climbing up on their boulder. "Come up here," he said. "I can see it! And it is big! But it's too dark to make out what it is!"

Lupe and her mother and sisters climbed up on the boulder with Victoriano and they could see the strange dark form in the distance, coming step by step down the main road that circled the canyon above the village, going around to the abandoned American compound. Whatever it was, it was huge, the size of an enormous bear. The whole family kept their eyes on the creature as it passed under the shadow of the great cliffs, slipping through the last few remaining slender columns of golden light.

By now every dog and all of *la gente* in the village were up on rocks, watching the large, dark, bent-over creature. It was coming down the road without any sign of fear or caution.

The dogs began to bark, and the people made the sign of the cross over themselves. Doña Guadalupe brought out her rosary and Lupe began to finger the small cross she wore about her neck.

Now the bear-like form was coming out from the shadow of the first peak of the cathedral rocks, entering a pool of light that shone down into the canyon between the first two peaks.

Lupe felt her heart pounding. This was going to be their first good chance to see what this creature really was.

"What is it?" asked Socorro, climbing up the side of the boulder. Her twins tried scrambling up the rock after their mother. Victoriano picked up one of the little boys, pushing up the other as he followed Socorro.

The large creature came into a pool of light, illuminating its dark form. Suddenly, without question, they could all see that it wasn't a bear at all. No, it was a human being, carrying a huge load on his back wrapped in a red Indian blanket.

Lupe's heart came out of hiding and she glanced up at the towering cathedral rocks, thanking God. Lately, all the talk of *brujas* and *espantos* had made it very difficult for Lupe to believe in anything good outside of their canyon.

"Whoever he is, he's a big man," said Victoriano.

"And strong," added Maria. "Look at the size of that load."

"Could he be one of the *americanos*," asked Socorro, "coming back to re-open the mine?"

Maria laughed. "When have you ever seen an *americano* carry anything when he has us to do it for him?"

They all laughed, except Victoriano. Protectively, he put his arm around Socorro's shoulder.

Seeing this, Carlota winked at Sophia, nudging her. But Sophia gave Carlota the mean eye, telling her to stop it and to not embarrass Victoriano, who in the last year had become very close to Socorro.

"Well, if it's not an *americano*," continued Socorro, "then I hope it's someone that my family has sent for me. I just can't go on being a burden to you people."

"But you're not a burden," said Victoriano. "You're part of our family, Socorro."

"Thank you, Victoriano," she said. "But, no, I have to make my own way in the world. I can't just expect your family to keep feeding me and my two sons forever."

She shook her head, feeling terrible. For nearly three years, she'd been sending letters down the mountain to her home every chance she had, asking for one of her brothers to please come and get her.

By the time the stranger got to the outer edge of their village, every man, woman and child was waiting anxiously. There were only six families left in the canyon, and none of these had any relatives who came to see them anymore.

At the first of the deserted houses, the stranger came off the main road, but he didn't take the good trail toward the center of town. He took a lesser trail, staying up close to the main road that circled the canyon, and it looked like he was coming straight to Lupe's family's home.

Lupe glanced at her mother with amazement. No one had come to their home since Flaco and Manos had left the canyon nearly a year before.

Coming down the trail, the stooped-over man was stepping quickly as though he knew the trail well. But, he also looked so drained and tired that he could hardly keep the huge load, which towered over his head.

Then, suddenly, for no apparent reason, Doña Guadalupe turned and hurried inside the *ramada*. Lupe turned to her brother.

"Do we know him?" she asked.

Victoriano shook his head. "No, I don't think so," he said. "He's probably just some poor man who thinks the mine is still open and he's come to sell us goods."

Saying this, Victoriano took up ground, preparing to tell the man to move on. But then, coughing, clearing his voice, Victoriano was just getting ready to speak when Carlota suddenly darted down the pathway, screaming, "Papa! Papa!"

Sophia and Maria were right behind her, running, too.

Lupe stared at her brother in complete shock. Then she suddenly understood why her mother had gone inside.

"I'm going inside with Mama," said Lupe to her brother.

Victoriano nodded. "And I'll stay out here." He now understood, too. Their mother had recognized their father long before any of them.

Inside the lean-to, Lupe found her mother at her bed, brushing out her long, silvery hair. In the soft, golden sunlight coming in through the cracks of the lean-to, Lupe could see that her mother had tears in her eyes.

"Mama," said Lupe, "it's Papa."

"Yes, I know," she said. "Please, go on out with the others and greet him. I want to be alone."

Lupe heard her mother's words and yet, she didn't obey her. "Mama," she said, "you don't have to see him if you don't want to."

Putting her brush down, Doña Guadalupe turned and looked at her youngest daughter. "Oh, *mi hijita*," she said, seeing her baby of the family standing there so strong and ready to defend her.

Doña Guadalupe burst into tears and Lupe went to her and held her in her arms, feeling her mother's large, soft breasts go up and down against her own lean, hard chest with each sobbing cry. Crying was good; it opened the heart and cleansed the soul.

Outside, the right eye of God was slipping down behind the mighty cliffs, and the canyon was getting dark and cold. Lupe's sisters were laughing and helping their father get the huge load off his back.

"Oh, Papa," said Sophia with tears of joy in her eyes, "I was so afraid that you were angry at us and weren't going to come for my wedding."

"But how could I be angry with my angels?" said the old man, hugging Carlota and talking to Sophia at the same time. "You are my loves. Look at all the presents I brought you for the wedding."

"For us?" screeched Carlota. "All that's for us?"

"Why, of course, *mi hijita*, it's all for you," he said.

"Oh, Papa! Papa!" screamed Carlota, kissing him on the cheeks, the mouth, the nose, the chin. Then she let go of him and ran to undo the bundle that he'd carried up from the lowlands.

Sophia took her father's hand in hers and she looked at him in the eyes for a long time. "I'm so glad you came," she said, wiping the tears from her eyes. She kissed him respectfully on the cheek, holding him close. Sophia was eighteen years old. She was a fully-grown, mature lady, and she'd remained short and delicately made like Carlota. "Come, Papa," she said, leading him up the pathway.

At the top of the pathway stood Maria and Victoriano, both tall and large-boned. Maria was grinning ear-to-ear with her large full-lipped mouth. But Victoriano wasn't grinning. He was as cautious as a young buck just before the rutting season.

Instantly, Maria flew into her father's arms, almost knocking him down.

"Maria," laughed her father, "please, not so strong, my God! Give your old father a few days rest before you decide to break his bones! Oh, you're strong!"

"I'm sorry, Papa," she said, "but I'm so happy to see you! We'd thought you'd abandoned us and didn't want to see us anymore."

"But how could you imagine such a sacrilege?" he said.

"Well, you never answered mother's letters, and she wrote to you three times, putting back Sophia's wedding twice because of you."

"Oh, I'm sorry to hear that," he said. "But you must realize that this Revolution has destroyed Mexico. And with the *americanos* gone, all communication with La Lluvia has died."

He kissed Maria again, then he looked up at Victoriano, who, because he was standing on the uphill side of the walkway, appeared even taller than his father.

"Look at this man!" said Don Victor. "This giant who towers over me! Why, could this be my little boy, Victoriano?"

Against his will, Victoriano blushed. His father came up to him, taking him in his arms and hugging him. Victoriano stood rigid. He and Lupe were the youngest. They didn't remember many good things about their father.

"Oh, *mi hijito*," said the grey-haired old man, tears coming to his eyes, "I've dreamed of this moment so many times." His breath quickened, eyes flooding with tears, he was so moved.

Victoriano felt his father's heart pounding against his chest and he truly wanted to say that he'd dreamed of this moment, too. But the words just wouldn't come. A part of him hated his father, resenting that he'd even returned. Besides, he was embarrassed of doing all this hugging in front of Socorro. He didn't want to be treated like a child in front of the woman he loved.

Lupe came out of the *ramada*. Don Victor saw the long-legged girl and his eyebrows knitted together.

"No," he said, "this young lady couldn't be my Lupita, could she?"

"Yes," said Carlota excitedly, "it's Lupe, Papa, and Mama's inside. I'll go get her."

"No," said Lupe quietly. "Mama wants to be alone."

"But Papa's here!" said Carlota.

Lupe held her ground. "She knows that, Carlota."

Carlota's face twisted with sudden, unexpected anger. "You lie," she yelled at Lupe. "I'm going to get Mama!"

Instantly, Sophia was on her. "No, Carlota!" she said, holding her by the arm. "You wait out here with the rest of us. Lupe doesn't lie, and if Mama says she wants to be alone, then she wants to be alone."

"But Papa's home," pleaded Carlota, trying to get away from her older sister.

"*Mi hijita*," said their father, stepping forward, "everything is going to be all right." He took Carlota tenderly in his arms, then turned to Lupe.

"And thank you, Lupita, for coming out and informing us of your mother's wishes." He reached for Lupe, too, but she didn't go to him.

"Lupe!" screamed Carlota. "He's our father! What's wrong with you?"

But Lupe said nothing. She just stood there, nervously holding her ground. She didn't even know this man, so how could she possibly go to him and allow him to hug her?

"*Cálmate*, Carlota," said Don Victor, his lower lip beginning to quiver. "She was very little when I left. She doesn't remember me. Isn't that right, *mi hijita*?" he asked.

Trying to keep calm, Lupe nodded yes. But inside, her heart was racing so fast that she felt she'd burst. All she'd done was come outside to say that their mother needed to be alone. She hadn't meant to start all this trouble.

It was dark down in the canyon when everyone in the village gathered to see what things Don Victor had brought. There were bright pieces of material for dresses, long pieces of delicate white lace for Sophia's wedding dress, four new pair of huaraches—which were about three sizes too small for the children. And there were bags of dry beans, dry meat, flour, raw sugar, salt, and several long rolls of bright, colorful ribbon, and two new Indian blankets. The whole front of the *ramada* looked like an open-air market with all the new wonderful things.

"Oh, the lace is so beautiful," said Sophia, holding the fine material in her hands.

"It came from Guadalajara," said Don Victor proudly.

Carlota and Maria were jumping up and down with joy, showing off all the different materials.

Victoriano brought out a chair and helped Socorro to sit down so she could nurse her twins. The two little boys were really too big for nursing but still, Socorro insisted on breast-feeding them. Victoriano tried hard not to look at her large, full breast when she opened her blouse and put her rosy nipple into the baby's mouth, but it was very difficult. Nervously, Victoriano went inside and got a couple of pieces of pine pitch. He lit them and was placing them around the front of the *ramada* when their mother came out of the lean-to.

"Good evening," said the short, plump, grey-haired old lady, standing at the entrance of the *ramada* in the dancing light of the pitch-pine torches.

Everyone turned to look at her, and they were shocked. She didn't look at all like their mother. Her hair was all tied up and she wasn't wearing her eternal apron. She had some of Socorro's red lipstick on her mouth and some rose-colored powder on her cheeks.

"Oh, Mama!" said Carlota. "What have you done to yourself? You look awful!"

Sophia stepped forward. "Just don't pay any attention to her, Mama," said Sophia. "You look perfectly wonderful, Mama. Doesn't she, Papa?"

"Why, of course," said Don Victor, smiling grandly. "She looks just like my angel on the first day I saw her."

He took off his hat and bowed to her with a flair and everyone gasped—he was so bald.

"*¿Cómo estás, querida?*" he said.

"*Muy bien, gracias,*" said their mother.

And Lupe saw an expression come into her mother's eyes that she'd never seen before. Her mother and father were flirting and yet being as cautious with each other as the coyote who'd just found another coyote in his territory.

"You must be very tired," added their mother.

"Oh, yes, I almost died, I tell you, coming up the last hill. But, well, seeing you, my love, I'm rejuvenated," he laughed.

"I see," she said, blushing.

The whole *ramada* became so quiet that the soft breeze sounded noisy in the tree branches behind their home.

"Are you hungry?" she asked.

"Oh, yes," he said, "for a kiss from your lips and the touch of your skin."

And saying this, he came toward her with his hands outstretched. For a moment, it looked like their mother wasn't going to allow him to touch her. But then she did, and they were in each other's arms.

High above, the towering cathedral rocks were on fire as the last of the sun turned into liquid flame, dissolving into the darkening night. He, the day, was going; and she, the night, was coming.

Then they all went inside—Doña Manza and her family and all the other people who'd come to hear the news of the outside world. Don Manuel and his family were the only ones who weren't present, and Don Tiburcio had sent word that he'd be up later.

Sitting down before her father, Carlota took off his boots and brought a pan of warm water to wash his swollen feet. Don Victor moaned and groaned with pleasure as he pushed back his hat, bringing out a bottle of tequila.

"It's a miracle that this bottle got here at all," he laughed. "I fell so many times that I was sure it had broken."

He drank down a big swallow, then passed the bottle to the other men, who numbered seven, including Ojos Puros.

"Well, tell us," said one man, "is it true that Francisco Villa was killed and the Revolution is over?"

"Oh, no," said Don Victor, "that rumor is two years old. Villa has fully recovered from his wounds, and he's up and strong as ever."

Everyone was shocked. They'd thought that the Revolution had finally come to an end.

Their father continued talking. Lupe sat across the shovelful of coals from him, watching her mother sit beside him, serving him tea and sweetbreads.

Once, Lupe saw her father put his hand on her mother's leg and her mother's eyes danced with merriment. Lupe got embarrassed and glanced at her sisters and brother to see if they'd noticed. But only Victoriano seemed to have noticed.

"So there I was, hiding in town," laughed Don Victor, "with dead people piled up all around me, when these armed men came riding into town. This blind old woman was out in the middle of the street, and I thought they'd run her over. But to my surprise, seeing the blind woman, their leader reined in his horse, reached in his saddlebags and brought out a gold coin, dropping it into her can. '*Gracias, mi general!*' said the old woman. 'But I thought you were blind,' he said to her, 'so how did you know I was a general?' The toothless old woman laughed. 'Easy; these days every other son-of-a-bitch is a general!' "

Don Victor laughed and everyone joined him. "The officer got so mad, I was sure he was going to shoot the old woman, so I took off down the alley as fast as I could go. Oh, to disappear, I tell you, is the only way to survive a war!"

And Don Victor continued drinking and telling story after story, and the *ramada* filled with laughter.

"And now for my final story," said Don Victor, "I'd like you all to see what I brought special for my girls. It's the newest thing in Europe and Mexico City!" He rolled out a bolt of shiny pink material, more delicate and fine than anyone had ever seen, and he shouted, "Underwear for my daughters!"

Doña Guadalupe gasped, spilling her tea. Carlota leaped up, prancing about the *ramada* like a pony. Sophia hugged Lupe close with terrible embarrassment. Hiding her face, Maria ran out of the *ramada*, colliding into Don Tiburcio.

"What's the commotion?" he asked. He was all dressed up with a coat and tie. He had flowers in one hand and a gift wrapped in beautiful white paper in the other.

"Oh, *Dios mío!*" screamed Maria, running back into the *ramada*. "Sophia! Sophia! He's here!" she yelled. "And I think he heard what Papa said!"

Turning crimson with embarrassment, Sophia saw her short, dark fiancé come inside. "Oh, no, Papa!" she begged. "Please don't say another word!"

Sophia was horrified. In their culture, no one ever spoke of a woman's undergarments, much less in front of her betrothed. But Don Victor wasn't to be stopped. He had the entire *ramada* howling with laughter, and he loved it.

Standing up, Don Victor met his future son-in-law at the entranceway. He hadn't seen Tiburcio in nearly eight years. Towering over him, Don Victor extended his hand. "Come right in," he said, "and take a look at this fine pink material I bought. Did you really think I was going to let my daughter marry you with old, worn-out underwear?"

Don Tiburcio stopped dead in his tracks, wringing the little bouquet with both hands.

"Well, speak up, Tiburcio," continued Don Victor. "Did you?"

Don Tiburcio was as red as three-day-old chili. "Well, I must confess, I never thought about it, Don Victor."

"But you should. Why, a woman's underwear is the most important part of her wedding dress!"

Finally, Doña Guadalupe couldn't stand it anymore. "All right," she said, getting up. "That's enough!"

"But why?" asked Don Victor, reaching for the box of candy and flowers that Don Tiburcio had brought Sophia. "Look what he brought me, *querida*!"

"Please," said Doña Guadalupe, taking the flowers and box from her husband, "make room for Don Tiburcio."

"Oh," said Don Victor, rocking on his feet as he grinned ear-to-ear. And suddenly it was obvious that he'd drunk too much. "So it's now 'Don' Tiburcio to you, eh? Why, I remember when you were nothing but a runny-nosed *muchacho* and your mother ran the store," he said.

The *ramada* went silent. No one knew what to say. But, before things could get worse, Doña Guadalupe spoke up.

"Don Victor," she said calmly but firmly, "ever since the *americanos* closed down the mine and abandoned us, it's been only Don Tiburcio who has kept us alive up here. He's been the one willing to go down to the lowlands—with the mountains full of bandits—and get us supplies. None of us would be alive if it wasn't for this man's great bravery."

"I see, I see," said Don Victor, reaching for the last of the tequila. "And money-tight-pants Manuel, doesn't he send his muleskinners down the mountain every month for merchandise anymore?"

Lupe lowered her head, clutching her chair. She was so embarrassed to realize how little her father knew about his family's situation.

"No," said Doña Guadalupe, handing the flowers and beautifully wrapped present to her daughter, "since the *americanos* left, Don Manuel has been . . . well, like in mourning."

"In mourning?" asked Don Victor, rocking on his feet.

"Yes," said Doña Guadalupe, "for the last few months no one has even seen Don Manuel."

"It's true, Don Victor," said Doña Manza, "the *americanos* were Don Manuel's entire life. He thought that he'd become one of them and that they were going to take him and his family to the United States with them when they left. But they didn't; they left him here instead, to watch over the abandoned mine."

"And," said one man, laughing, "the great *americanos* were gone no more than a couple of days when Ojos Puros, here, and his wild *indios* came and ripped down the gates," he said. He slapped Ojos Puros on the back. "Don Manuel went crazy, trying to protect the enfencement."

"Yes, that's true," laughed Ojos Puros. "We needed something to build fencing for our goats and, when we took down the gates, the mayor came out of his office with his pistol to run us off, but it misfired," he said, laughing all the more. He was drunk, too. "I think that's what killed him. He's been in his house ever since."

Lupe watched her father take a deep breath. "You know, I never liked that little proper man," he said. "But I'll tell you, when he first came here, the *americanos* accused him of stealing from the payroll and they hung him by his thumbs, but he never gave in. Then they found out that it was the big German bookkeeper who'd been stealing from them all those years. I gained respect for that little man. He might be a pretentious little *cabrón*, but he's got big *tanates*."

Taking another deep breath, Don Victor turned and looked at Don Tiburcio with new eyes. "So, well, you must also be a very brave man, Don Tiburcio," he said, "because, I'll tell you, I was so scared coming up through the *barrancas* with all those bandits, that my asshole was hanging out two fists!"

Saying this, Don Victor burst out laughing again and everyone joined him. They just couldn't help it. He was so outrageous.

Opening the box, Sophia saw that it was another assortment of fine chocolates. She passed them around for everyone to take one. The people did, treasuring each chocolate as if it was a jewel from heaven.

"Oh, Papa!" shouted Carlota, nibbling her candy, "you should see the chocolates we've been getting since Don Tiburcio became engaged to Sophia!"

"That's enough," said Doña Guadalupe sharply.

But Carlota wasn't to be silenced. "Mama told Don Tiburcio that Sophia was too small to marry him, so he's been bringing her boxes of candy to fatten her up for over a year now."

Don Victor roared with laughter, mouth open, showing all his broken teeth. "Shame on you, *querida*!" he said to his wife. "Why, this is the very same trick that this old woman used on me when we got married! She said she was too skinny so I'd have to bring her chocolates so she could put on weight before we married."

Doña Guadalupe turned red and everyone roared with laughter until the *ramada* echoed with happy sounds.

That night Lupe went to bed on a straw mat with her sisters and brother under the *ramada* while her father and mother slept inside the lean-to.

It was a full moon and Lupe must have been sound asleep, for the next thing she knew, she awoke with a start. She could hear coyotes howling in the distance and something turning and thrashing nearby. At first, she thought it was her deer fighting off some dogs, but then she heard the springs of her mother's bed making sounds like two cats fighting.

The two cats screeched and cried out in pain, going faster and faster.

Then Lupe heard her parents breathing like two burros going up a steep hillside.

Their little dog barked outside and Lupe glanced up to the sky. She saw two little white clouds passing, hand-in-hand, like silent lovers over the mighty peaks. Tears came to her eyes and she grew frightened. She thought of her Colonel and how he'd also made violent noises when he'd slept with Socorro.

She could now hear her parents moaning, groaning like two great trees bending in the wind. She turned and her eyes met Sophia's, and Sophia opened her arms. Quickly, Lupe went to her sister and they hugged each other close, holding there in the darkness. Lupe thought of all the animals that she'd seen mate and of her pet deer when he'd tried to get at their milk goat with his long, red shiny thing.

Her parents were now running up a steep hill like charging wild-pigs, and the two cats screamed in a quickening fight. Then, suddenly, her father cried out and her mother started to giggle.

Lupe trembled, holding Sophia close. She looked out between the vines of the bougainvillea and she saw that the two little white clouds had moved past the cathedral rocks and were now slipping by the full moon, so bright and round and wondrous.

In the morning, coming under the *ramada* after doing her chores, Lupe found Sophia and Maria singing happily together as they made breakfast. Lupe wondered if they hadn't heard all those terrible sounds the night before.

"Hurry!" said Sophia excitedly. "Help Carlota set the table. We're making a special surprise breakfast for Mama and Papa."

Lupe put the milk on the counter and went to help her sister finish setting the table, but she felt very confused. She couldn't figure out why her sisters were so happy.

Then, when they had everything ready, they called their parents to the table, and Lupe got the full smell of her parents as they entered the *ramada*. Suddenly she knew that yes, indeed, she had heard all those terrible sounds last night. She remembered how her Colonel and Socorro had smelled like this and been so happy, too, after they'd had a night of violent sounds. She said nothing and just watched her sisters and her parents.

"Why, look what we've got here!" said Don Victor, seeing the table set with flowers and food for him and his wife. "It's better than our honeymoon, *querida*!"

"What honeymoon?" said their mother, laughing. "You mean that awful trip we had coming up here to La Lluvia, trudging up trails?"

"Exactly, and those wonderful nights we spent under the stars," he said, kissing her.

"All right, stop it you two, and sit down," said Sophia, "before your *huevos rancheros* get cold."

"You know," said Doña Guadalupe, sitting down to eat, "in all these years I've never once had the pleasure of sitting under my *ramada* at this hour. Just look at that view; it's beautiful—a painting by the hand of God. No wonder Manos and Flaco always enjoyed sitting here."

"Whatever became of those two?" asked Don Victor, eating in large, hungry bites.

"They stayed on with a few other men for a couple of months after the *americanos* closed the mine down," said Doña Guadalupe. "But, well, Señor Jones had the new section dynamited before he left, so Manos and Flaco weren't able to get at it."

"It figures," said Don Victor. "Señor Jones has it figured out to come back after the Revolution. These tricky *gringos*, I swear, they got it all planned out for us for the next two hundred years!"

Doña Guadalupe and Don Victor ate and talked and the children waited on them hand and foot. Lupe came to realize that she'd never seen her mother sit down to eat through an entire meal before. No, she was always getting up to wait on everyone else.

Then, when their parents were done eating and their father rolled a cigarette, Doña Guadalupe called them together.

"*Mil gracias,*" said their mother, "that was a wonderful breakfast, and your father and I appreciated it very much. But, well, now I want all of you children to listen very carefully—and you, too, Socorro—because last night, Victor and I had a very important talk." She smoothed out her dress on her lap. "Tell them, *querido.*"

"Well," said Don Victor, "your mother and I have decided that we have two choices. And only two. One, we wait out the war here in this canyon, hoping that the bandits don't kill us; or two, we go to the United States and wait out the war there."

They were all shocked.

"Across the border?" asked Maria. "But when would we go?"

"As soon as possible," said their father.

Victoriano and Socorro looked at each other.

"But I'm getting married," said Sophia.

"Yes, we know," said their mother, "and we've considered that, too. But you tell me, how many more times do you think Don Tiburcio can go down the mountain to bring us our supplies and return unharmed, *mi hijita?*"

Sophia wrung her hands. "Yes," she said, "I've thought of that, too. But I know that he'd never leave without his mother. And she's not in good health."

"That's why we have to talk," said their mother, "and figure out our situation."

"Will we ever return?" asked Maria, no doubt thinking of Esabel and that she didn't want to leave him.

"With the help of God, yes," said their mother. "This is our home, after all. And when the war is over, I'm sure that someone will re-open the mine, and we can make our living here again."

"But I don't want to return!" said Carlota excitedly. "I want to see cities and big dances and have new shoes and dresses and never come back!"

Everyone looked at her and laughed.

"That's fine," said their mother. "I hope you can get your dresses and shoes, Carlota. But remember why we're leaving—not for pleasure, but so we can survive."

The *ramada* became quiet; each person thinking of what this big move meant to them. Lupe thought of her deer and her Colonel's grave and all the life that she knew here in this canyon.

"So when do you think we might leave?" asked Sophia.

Doña Guadalupe turned to her husband.

"It wouldn't be too soon," he said, "because, as I told your mother, the worst thing we could do is leave here with just the clothes on our backs. We need gold—lots of gold—so we can buy our passage north and, when we get to the border, we can buy contracts to do work on the American side.

"You must realize, *mis hijitos*, that for the past seven years people have been fleeing to the border every day by the thousands, and so you can't just get across the border anymore. The situation is grave. No matter how bad it's been up here, it's a thousand times worse down below."

"And," said their mother, "your father doesn't say this lightly. I've explained everything to him." She stopped, tears coming to her eyes. "I told him about La Liebre and how they . . . they were going to hang Victoriano, but . . . but . . ." She shook her head, unable to go on until their father reached out, taking her hand.

"I just don't have it anymore," she said, trembling. "A large part of me, here in my heart, died the day I saw Victoriano with that rope around his neck."

She gasped, trying to catch her breath. There wasn't a dry eye in the *ramada*. They all remembered that awful day their brother had been branded and almost hung.

"I'm finished," said their mother. "I have no more power."

She squeezed her husband's hand.

"But, Mama," said Carlota, "what does this mean . . . that you're going to die?"

"No, of course not, *mi hijita*," said their mother. "With your father's help, I'll mend. But I cannot continue to be the rock of *nuestra casa*. Your father must take the reins and lead us to *Los Estados Unidos*."

Saying this, the great lady turned to their father, tears streaming down her face. He soothed her hand gently, tenderly, quietly.

And it was true; for the first time in her life, Lupe could see that their great, powerful mother wasn't a rock anymore. She looked small, tired, fragile, all used up and very old.

Lupe's whole body shivered.

Sophia's wedding was pushed back for several days while all the people of the canyon went to work, preparing to make this wedding the biggest celebration that they'd had in years. The mine had closed, the village and American enfencement lay in ruins, the people were ragged and hungry, but this was no reason for them to lose their spirit. No, they'd make a big celebration in the wonderful tradition of their mountains.

On the morning of the wedding, Lupe awoke to what seemed like a dream. The sky was still full of stars, and she could hear music outside their *ramada* through the vines of the bougainvillea.

Lupe drew close to Sophia, and they lay together on their straw mats, enjoying the cool morning breeze and the soft, gentle music.

Don Tiburcio was keeping faithful to tradition. He'd brought musicians to serenade his wife-to-be so she'd know that no matter how desperate times became, there would always be song in the heart of their new home.

Maria and Carlota awoke and they listened, too. Don Tiburcio sang "Las Mañanitas" and then went off into the early morning mist as quietly as he'd come. Lupe had tears running down her face. Oh, she was so happy for her sister, and yet another part of her just knew that they were also saying goodbye to their canyon—*adiós* to their whole way of life.

The sun was three fists off the jagged horizon when Victoriano and Esabel were in the plaza helping Don Tiburcio wash his two little white mules. Down below by the creek, Lupe and Carlota and Doña Manza's daughters were picking baskets of wildflowers so they could decorate the bridles and saddles of the white mules and the little altar where the ceremony would be held.

It was noon when Lupe and the girls finished the decorations. The spotted little mules had flowers braided into their mane and bridles and long red ribbons into their tails. The two little animals loved the attention they were getting, and they stamped their feet, feeling proud.

All around the plaza were small groups of people. They'd been waiting for over an hour for Don Manuel to come out of his home to perform the ceremony.

The closest priest was more than three days away by mule, so Don Manuel—even though he was no longer considered the town's mayor—was still called upon to perform the services of birth, death and weddings.

Lupe and her girlfriends were across the plaza where the women had gathered by the stone wall at the foot of Doña Manza's house. They'd put a blanket up and Sophia was behind it so the groom wouldn't see her. Don Tiburcio was with the men across the plaza.

Lupe's sister Maria was dressed in her new pink dress. She looked so beautiful—tied in so small at her waist and yet showing off her wide shoulders and muscular arms. Lupe had never realized how beautiful Maria was. She'd always assumed that to be beautiful, a woman had to be small and delicate, like Sophia and Carlota.

Coming around the side of the blanket, Lupe saw Sophia sitting on a stool and their mother was braiding white orchids into her long, dark hair. Lupe was overwhelmed by Sophia's beauty. She had their father's fine, good looks and their mother's small body.

As Lupe listened to the talk of the women, Angelina, the midwife, arrived with a group of Tarahumara Indians. The men wore loose white pants and their faces were painted white with small reddish suns. The women were dressed in colorful blouses and skirts, their faces and hands painted white with half-moons of pink and yellow around their eyes and mouths.

"Well, well," said the old midwife, coming up close with two of the women, "I see that Sophia looks like an angel right now. But how will she be tonight when the coyotes howl and she has to lie in a pool of blood, proving her virginity!"

Doña Guadalupe was barely able to control her anger. "Angelina," she said, "you've been drinking. Now stop it! I'll have none of this superstitious Indian talk!"

The midwife only laughed. "But this isn't superstitious Indian talk, Doña Guadalupe," she said. "This happens to come with your own priests when they brought the Virgin Mary up to our mountains. And, I was only coming as a friend to offer you my services in showing your daughter how to bleed if she needed to."

The rage, the anger, with which Doña Guadalupe turned on the woman took Lupe by surprise. "Go," she yelled, fluffing up like a mad mother hen, "before I lose all patience!"

But Angelina only laughed again, showing her missing teeth. The midwife hadn't been taking care of herself since her husband, El Borracho, had been killed.

"Oh, Mama," said Sophia kindly, "it's all right, she's only trying to help. But don't worry, Angelina, I'll bleed just fine."

"I'm glad to hear that," said the midwife. Then she turned to Maria. "And you, Maria," she said, "will you bleed just as fine on your wedding night, *querida*?"

Maria almost dropped—she was so stunned.

"I've been watching you with Esabel," said the old midwife, enjoying Maria's shock. "And he's no boy, believe me. That one's so ripe that he can impregnate an innocent girl by just rubbing her dress!"

Maria's eyes filled with horror. "Mama," she said, "is that true?"

But Doña Guadalupe didn't answer her daughter. First she looked across the plaza and saw Esabel, who was standing alongside Victoriano. She saw his darkly handsome face, his full mouth of glistening white teeth, and his head of coal black bangs dancing about his eyes. She could see why her daughter was taken by him. He was one of the most handsome young men that she'd ever seen.

"No," said Doña Guadalupe, turning to Maria, "it's not true, *mi hijita*. But believe me, more than that, and you will be."

Maria glanced up at the heavens, mumbling a quick prayer.

The sun was starting down and the wedding couldn't be delayed any longer. Excusing himself, Don Tiburcio left the men and went across the plaza to Don Manuel's house, knocking on his door. No one else in all the plaza would have dared to do this. The proper little man hadn't just been their mayor, but also their most important citizen, other than the Americans.

Finally, the door opened and out came Don Manuel's wife, Josefina. She was dressed in green and had a big red flower in her hair.

"Yes?" she said.

"Well," said Don Tiburcio, pulling his watch from his vest, "is your husband ready? We've been waiting over two hours, *señora*."

She glanced around at everyone in the plaza. "He'll be right out," she said, closing the door.

Don Tiburcio put his watch back, not knowing what to do. He was just going to walk away when the door opened again and out came Don Manuel, supported by Lydia and Rose-Mary on each side.

As he came into the sunlight, everyone was shocked. Their ex-mayor was nothing but a shriveled-up little man with huge, sunken red eyes.

His two daughters towered above him, dressed in beautiful, many-layered dresses and their hair done up with ribbons and flowers as they helped him across the plaza to the small altar where the ceremony was to take place.

"Not one word," whispered Doña Guadalupe to her family. "Did you hear me, Carlota? Not one word."

"But why do you say that just to me, Mama?"

"I'm not saying this to just you, Carlota, but to everyone," said her mother.

"Exactly," said Doña Manza, making the sign of the cross over herself without even realizing it until it was too late. "Remember," she said, "to respect a fallen star takes much more dignity than to admire the rising sun."

None of the girls said a word, and the silence grew out over the plaza. Most of the people in the plaza didn't really like their ex-mayor but, still, the sight of him touched their hearts. They wanted to see him strong so they could feel good about hating him.

And the power, the arrogance with which his wife Doña Josefina walked beside her husband to the little decorated altar, moved the people's hearts.

"She's a good woman," said Doña Manza, wiping her eyes.

"Yes, she is," said Doña Guadalupe. "She's *el eje de su familia*."

Hearing this, Lupe was amazed. There could be no higher compliment for any woman. *El eje* was the center of the home; it was the hub from which all the spokes of power flowed out to the rest of the family, like the umbilical cord from a mother to her child.

"Well," said Don Manuel, having shuffled his way up to the little altar, "bring your bride up, Don Tiburcio, and let's get this service going."

He tried to smile, showing the people that he was still a man to be reckoned with, but his lower jaw quivered and he just wasn't able to bring it off.

Lupe and the girls cried all through the ceremony. Don Tiburcio and

Sophia stood side by side, looking so beautiful. And sometimes it looked like Don Manuel just didn't seem to know where he was, or what he was supposed to do next. At one of these awkward moments, Don Victor reached out, handing the ex-mayor a glass that looked like it was full of clear water.

"Excuse me," said the proper little man. With both hands trembling, he took the glass and sucked down half of its contents.

But it was straight tequila, and Don Manuel had never drunk alcohol in his life. It hit him like a lightning bolt, burning all the way down to his stomach. His eyes bulged and he gasped for air, letting out a blood-curdling cry.

Josefina rushed to his side, but the ex-mayor shoved her away, bellowing like a bull.

"*¡Ay Chihuahua!*" he roared. "That's fire! Give me another!"

"No!" begged his wife. "It will kill you, *querido*."

"Good," he said.

Don Victor poured him another glass over his wife's protests and, drinking this glass down, he bellowed again.

"Tequila! The blood of *los mejicanos*! *¡Ayyyy Chihuahua!*"

The people laughed, and the ex-mayor, who'd come out of his house smelling of death, now stood up straight, performing the rest of the wedding with *gusto*.

After the ceremony, the music started and the women gathered by the bride, and Doña Guadalupe hugged Sophia close. The men gathered around the groom, and they finished off the bottle of tequila.

It was getting late, so Sophia and Don Tiburcio said their goodbyes, mounted their two little mules, and they were off on the quick-footed animals, going out of the plaza and up to the main road. They were going over the mountain to Batopilas for their honeymoon.

"Be careful," shouted Doña Guadalupe. "Don't camp where you can get surprised by bandits!"

"Don't worry," shouted Don Tiburcio. "I'll take good care of Sophia, Doña Guadalupe."

"God be with you!" called her mother.

And Lupe watched after her sister and her husband, looking so beautiful on their little decorated white mules. They reminded her of the little clouds that she'd seen pass hand-in-hand, like silent lovers over the cathedral rocks.

The following day, Victoriano took his father up to the base of the cliffs to show him where he and Don Benito had found the pocket of gold. Then, that night, they all got together under the *ramada* and had a family meeting.

"As I see it," said Don Victor, "Victoriano is right. It's going to be too difficult to uncover that pocket, so we're going to have to work the waste below the mine. And in the meantime, I'll go down the mountain and find work so I can pay for our food; that way we can save all the gold we find."

"Can I go with you?" asked Carlota. "I'll cook and clean for you while you work."

"What do you think?" asked Don Victor, turning to their mother.

"Oh, Mama, please, say yes!" screamed Carlota.

Doña Guadalupe smiled, figuring that maybe this way her husband would be sure to return. "All right," she said.

Don Victor opened his arms. "Then you'll come," he said to Carlota, and she flew to his arms.

"How much gold will we need before we can go?" asked Maria.

"That will depend," said their father, "on how we decide to go—by ship up the Sea of Cortez, or by train up to Nogales. But anyway, the more gold we have, the easier it will be so we don't get stuck like so many thousands at the border."

"Remember," said their mother, "Doña Manza's sister is still at Nogales, with no means to get across."

"I figure," said their father, "that if we're lucky and work hard, it's going to take about a year."

"A year? But the bandits will come and steal whatever we got!" said Maria.

"No, they won't, I swear it!" said Victoriano. Ever since his encounter with death, he'd become braver instead of more cautious.

Don Victor looked at his son. "No, *mi hijito*, your mother and I don't want you being brave. We want you staying alive." He breathed. "Tell me," he said, "what do people do up here with the rats when they store their corn?"

"Well, you board the corn up the best you can, but you just figure that the rats will take so much," said Victoriano.

"Exactly," said their father. "And that's what we got to do here. We have to hide our gold so when the bandits come, they'll find just a little corn and go away without harming us."

"Will that work, just giving them a little corn?" asked Lupe.

These were the first words that she'd spoken. Everyone laughed.

"Oh, no, *mi hijita*," said her father, "by corn, I meant a little gold."

"Oh, I see," she said, blushing.

The following morning Lupe went down the hill and across the creek to the piles of waste below the mine with her father, Victoriano, Carlota, Maria and Esabel. They worked all day in the hot, bright sun, pulling and digging and searching for good ore. At the end of the day they had a couple of piles of rock, about the size of a cow's head, and they lugged it down the *barranca*, across the creek, and up the hillside through the deserted village to their home. There, behind the boulder, their father and Victoriano and Esabel pounded the rock with hammers until it was all down to the size of peanuts.

After dinner, Lupe and her mother and sisters went at the peanut-sized ore in their dark stone *metates*, grinding it with their fist-sized stones called *tejolotes* until it was down to coarse sand. That night, Lupe went to bed with raw knuckles and tired arms and legs. Working the ore from sun to sun was a lot harder than anyone had anticipated. They were trying to do by hand what the American mining company had done with a huge crushing plant and strong chemicals and thousands of hands.

The following morning, Lupe stayed behind and she helped her mother and sisters pound the ore with the big iron spikes that they'd found in the ruins of the American crushing plant. They worked under the *ramada* like a little factory of women while her brother and father and Esabel went down the hill to work the piles of waste again.

By noon, Lupe and her mother and sisters had the ore down to fine sand, and they now began the long, tedious process of washing it in flat pans by swishing it around and around with a little water and washing off the dirt and lighter elements.

By the time the men came lugging up the hill with more rock from the waste that afternoon, Lupe and her mother and sisters had a little color. It was as yellow and as shiny and fine as the gold taken from a stream that had taken nature millions upon millions of years to reduce from rock to fine sand.

"Well," said Don Victor, "you keep working like this every day, and I think we can do it. And when I leave, I'll take this little bit of color with me and buy some mercury to send back up with Don Tiburcio so you can clean the gold completely and form little nuggets. The nuggets will be easier to hide from the bandits, and also easier to take with us when we go north."

They looked at the tiny bit of gold that they'd accumulated. After two days work it was smaller than the size of a thumbnail. Lupe thought of the thirty mules with two bars of gold each that the Americans had taken out of the canyon three times a year, and she thought of the whole pocket of gold nuggets that Victoriano and Don Benito had found under the waterfall. She thought of the new tunnel of gold that Manos had said he'd seen with veins as big around as his arm, and she felt that they were so small—inadequate— and yet, very determined.

"Yeah, we can do it!" Lupe heard her father say once again. "And who knows, maybe as we dig down deeper into the waste, we'll find better ore."

The weeks passed and on some days Lupe would accompany her father and brother and Esabel to the waste. Lupe's deer would go with her and he'd stay by her all day long, nibbling off the vines and brush that had grown back over the entrance of the mine.

The people saw them working the waste, so they got baskets and hammers and joined them. Soon, every day, there were well over a dozen people working the huge pile of rock, looking like tiny dark ants against the towering *barrancas* of broken rock.

Late one afternoon, some dogs went after Lupe's deer. The young buck was fast, and he fended off the first two dogs. But the others would have gotten him if Lupe's father and brother hadn't thrown rocks at them. The people who owned the dogs got angry, and Don Victor told Lupe that she'd have to take her deer home.

"Lupe," said Don Victor that evening after dinner, "come, let's go outside so we can talk."

Lupe glanced at her mother, but then followed her father out of the *ramada*. She watched him bring out a little sack of tobacco and a booklet of cigarette papers. He loosened the strings of the little sack and tapped the tobacco out of its mouth. The leafy brown tobacco looked like a fat worm as it gathered on the thin white paper.

"You know," he said, rolling the cigarette and licking it with the tip of his tongue, "I once had a little deer, too." He put the sack of tobacco in his shirt pocket and he brought out a big wooden match.

"Was it a fawn?" she asked.

"Oh, yes, she was just a little fawn. I raised her with a bottle, so she grew up thinking I was her mother. She followed me everywhere and slept with me every night until she got too big to bring into the house."

"That's what I used to love to do with my deer, too," Lupe said excitedly. "And what happened to her, Papa?" suddenly realizing she'd never used the word "Papa" before.

Her father blew out a long cloud of blue-white smoke. "Unfortunately, she got too big and started to roam and some dogs attacked her, maiming her."

"Oh, no!" said Lupe.

"Yes, *mi hijita*," he said, "and this is what we have to talk about."

A cold chill gripped Lupe, taking the breath out of her.

"*Mi hijita*," repeated her father, "I had to take my deer up into the mountains and let her go."

Lupe could feel her heart pounding. She just knew where this conversation was going.

"It took me three weeks just to nurse my deer back to health," said her father. "And after that she had a limp and couldn't run fast anymore. So my older brother told me that I should turn her loose. But I didn't want to because I loved her. But my brother insisted and so did my mother, telling me that my deer had a better chance in the wild where there were other deer. So, I finally agreed.

"My brother and I took my deer and we traveled for two full days. We saw coyote signs and bear markings but still, we continued higher into the mountains. I really wondered if my little deer would be any safer here among these beasts than she would be among the dogs in town. But my brother told me to notice how strong she was getting and to watch her ears and see how she flicked them when we stopped. He assured me that she would get wild up here again and would be able to protect herself much better than in town where dogs and coyotes were so plentiful and she'd become too tame for her own good.

"That evening some deer came by our camp, and my little deer just ran off and joined them as if it were the most natural thing for her to do. Seeing that, it was hard, I tell you, but I loved her and I knew I'd done the right thing."

Don Victor stopped. He saw that Lupe had tears in her eyes.

"You're trying to say that I should turn my deer loose, too, aren't you?"

He nodded. "Yes. I saw what happened with those dogs. Today could've been—"

"But my deer is male!" she said. "He has horns and he can defend himself!"

"Yes," said her father, "but no deer is a match for a pack of dogs. And, also, these horns that he can defend himself with are the very reason he might hurt you some day."

"But he'd never hurt me! He loves me!" she said.

"*Mi hijita*," he said, "love can only go so far. He's a mature animal now and he's in season. He needs to find a mate or, believe me, he'll turn on you as surely as the sun comes up."

"You tricked me!" she yelled.

"But *querida*, I love you, and I know what a male deer can do when he's in season."

"No!" she yelled. "You left us! You have no right to tell me what to do!"

And she turned, running off to get her deer so her father couldn't take him away from her.

Don Victor sat there, stunned. Never in all his life had he ever seen so much hate in a little girl. And he knew that he should get up and run after her and thrash her with a belt for being disrespectful, but he was just too brokenhearted to move.

12

And so her heart was ready to break once again but then, to her surprise, each new peril only showed her a deeper mystery in this dream called life, la vida.

The right eye of God was just coming up over the jagged horizon when Carlota came out of their lean-to. She was wearing her new dress, and she'd put white powder on her face, neck, and hands and red coloring on her lips and cheeks. Seeing her, everyone burst out laughing.

"Don't you dare laugh at me!" commanded Carlota. "I'm going with Papa, and I want to look civilized!"

"But," said Victoriano, trying not to laugh, "you look like a Tarahumara Indian dressed for a funeral!"

"No, a clown!" laughed Maria.

"Enough," said their father, bringing up one of the little mules that he'd borrowed from his son-in-law.

Don Tiburcio was also going down the mountain with them. But he was still below, saying goodbye to his mother, who wasn't feeling well.

"You look fine, *mi hijita*," said Don Victor to Carlota. "But I think that you should maybe save your best clothes and your fine face-paints for when we get closer to town, *querida*. You see, we'll be walking through nothing but jungle for days and we'll only pass a few little *rancherías* here and there."

"Who cares?" said Carlota, eyes dancing with *gusto*. "I want to look my best when we go out of the canyon so Lydia and Rose-Mary will choke with envy!"

Don Victor burst out laughing. "All right, if that's what you want," he said. He turned to his wife, who was standing by the bougainvillea at the entrance of the *ramada*.

Lupe was at her mother's side. Seeing her father turn towards them, she hid behind her mother. Ever since her father had tried to take her deer away from her, Lupe had been avoiding him, thinking that he was, indeed, that evil, bear-like spirit she'd seen enter their canyon that first day.

"Well," said Don Victor to his wife, "I guess we're ready to go." He took a big breath. "It will take us at least five days to get down and then Don Tiburcio another week to get back with the supplies. He's a brave man."

He reached out to take his wife in his arms. Lupe moved away so he wouldn't touch her.

"Lupe," said her mother, "now come around here and hug your father goodbye, too."

But Lupe wouldn't move. Doña Guadalupe reached around and got hold of Lupe by her left ear, pulling her around to the front. Lupe cringed in pain.

"Oh, please," said Don Victor, "she doesn't have to hug me if she doesn't want to."

"But she wants to," said her mother, twisting Lupe's ear all the more. "She has to understand that you are right about her deer. Now hug your father goodbye," said Doña Guadalupe, pulling Lupe about.

"For the love of God!" said Don Victor. "Let go of her, woman!" He yanked his wife's hand away from Lupe, taking his youngest into his arms. "Oh, *mi hijita*," he said, "I love you so much. I'm sorry this happened."

Feeling her ear freed, Lupe hugged her father, crying desperately. Doña Guadalupe smiled, realizing that she'd gotten what she wanted.

Just then, Don Tiburcio came up the pathway with the other mule. "It's time to go," he said anxiously.

Quickly, he took Sophia aside and told her of his mother's condition and how to attend to her.

Don Victor told Maria and Esabel goodbye, then went over to Victoriano. They looked at each other at arm's length, as men do, and then hugged, heart-to-heart, in a big *abrazo*.

"We must hurry," said Don Tiburcio. "We have a lot of ground to cover before dark!"

Don Victor let go of his son, threw another kiss to his wife, and started up the path with Carlota at his side. Socorro got hold of her two boys and started up the pathway, too.

Suddenly, unexpectedly, Victoriano shouted, "Socorro!" and ran up the trail.

Lupe dried her eyes and watched her brother go up to the woman that he'd become so close to over the last year.

"I'll walk you to the rim," he said.

"I'd like that," she said, smiling.

Lupe watched her brother pick up one of the twins and take Socorro's hand as they went up the pathway behind the others.

Lupe and her family watched them go around on the main road, all the way to the mouth of the canyon. Then, at the canyon's end, Don Tiburcio and their father and Carlota stopped and waved back at them. Lupe and her family waved back, too.

Victoriano put the twin down and it looked like he and the beautiful widow were going to kiss; and then they did, holding each other in their arms, truly kissing.

"Oh, the poor boy," said Maria, wiping her eyes. "He loves her so much. But there's nothing that can be done. He's too young."

Tears came to Lupe's eyes, too, recalling how much she'd loved her Colonel.

Socorro pulled back from Victoriano, staring at him, and then she turned and hurried after the others.

Victoriano didn't move. He just stood there at the mouth of the canyon like a love-sick dog, looking into the jungle where she'd disappeared.

That night, they lit three candles and their mother led them in prayer. They prayed for their father and Carlota and Don Tiburcio to have a safe journey. They prayed for Socorro and asked God to help her find her family. Tears came to Victoriano's eyes and he asked to be excused. He was fourteen years old; he was a man, and his feelings for the widow weren't childish.

Then it was time to go to bed. Lupe knew that her mother's bed was free now that their father was gone, but she was still so angry at her mother that she just didn't want to be near her.

Getting her straw mat, Lupe laid it out under the *ramada* to sleep alongside Maria and Victoriano. Sophia wasn't sleeping with them any longer. She was staying at Don Tiburcio's home, looking after her sick mother-in-law.

But lying down, Lupe wasn't able to go to sleep, so she went out to see her pet deer. The sky was full of stars, and the young buck quickly came to her.

"Don't worry," she said, hugging her deer close. "You're my special gift from God and no one's going to take you away from me." She breathed deeply, thinking of her Colonel and of Socorro and the twins; they were all gone. "But you'll never leave me. We were meant to be together forever."

Suddenly, her mother's voice startled her. "Lupe," she called. Lupe turned and saw her mother standing behind her in the silvery light of the star-studded heavens.

"Yes," she said, drying her eyes.

"I want to talk to you."

Lupe felt her skin crawl. Oh, she just didn't want to have another talking-to. But, still, she obeyed her mother and went down the steep embankment.

"Sit down here beside me," said her mother, patting the stone beside her. Lupe did as she was told, and her mother didn't say anything for a long time. But then, finally, she took a big breath.

"Well, I guess that maybe I should have been the one to speak to you about your deer myself. But your father asked me if he could, since he has the reins of our family now."

"You mean you think I should get rid of my deer, too?" asked Lupe.

Her mother nodded. "Yes, and right now before the mating season is over."

"Oh, Mama!" cried Lupe, her eyes brimming with tears.

"Lupe," said her mother, "you're not a child anymore; you must realize how animals get during their season."

Lupe's mind went reeling, and she thought of her deer trying to mount their milk goats, and she thought about her own parents and how they'd sounded so awful that first night.

"Mama," said Lupe, "is Papa really going to stay?"

"Yes," said her mother.

"And you want him to?"

"Yes."

"Do you love him?"

Her mother swallowed. "Very much."

Hearing this, Lupe looked up at the heavens, not having expected to hear this. Her eyes filled with tears as she looked out at the millions upon millions of stars as far as the eye could see.

She thought of all the bad things that she'd heard about her father over the years—his gambling and drinking—and thought of how he'd left them; she felt so confused and troubled that her mother could love such a man. But what could she do? He was her father, and he was back to stay, and her mother did say that she loved him.

She turned and her mother took her into her plump, strong arms, holding her. And Lupe and her mother cried and cried, heart-to-heart, two women sitting under the star-filled heavens.

It was the longest night of Lupe's whole life. But the following morning, she got up and took her pet deer up over the north rim of the canyon. Victoriano and his little brown dog went with her. His was the only dog that the young buck allowed near him—since he'd known the little animal all his life.

Going out of the canyon through the break where the meteorite had split the rock, Lupe saw her twisted little pine tree in the distance, and her heart raced away. Quickly, she began to run. Coming up here, she always felt so free and close to God.

The young buck ran past Lupe in a burst of leaping bounds, also feeling good in the spacious meadows. But then, suddenly, he stopped, raising up his head and arching his thick, muscular neck. At the far edge of the meadow was a herd of deer.

"Leave him alone," said Victoriano, coming up behind his sister.

"But I don't want him to go before I hug him," she said.

The herd of deer had spotted him, too, and they looked very cautious. Lifting up his shiny, black nose, the young buck sniffed the air and the hair came up on his neck. He took off, not once looking back at Lupe.

"No!" yelled Lupe, starting to run after him, but her brother caught her by the arm.

"Lupe," he said, "he'll have enough trouble with our scent on him. Don't add to his problem."

Lupe could feel her heart wanting to burst; she'd never said goodbye to her Colonel, either. But then, just before her young buck got to the herd of deer, he stopped, turning to look at Lupe.

"He wants to come back!" she cried.

"Don't call him," said her brother. "Don't do it! Let him go, Lupe!"

Tears ran down Lupe's face but she bit her tongue, not calling out. And the young buck looked at her for a full twenty seconds before he shook his antlers and took off.

"Good girl," said Victoriano to his sister, "I'm proud of you."

But Lupe could say nothing. She just stood there, tears streaming down her face as she watched her fine young friend go off with the deer herd, racing across the meadow with big, graceful leaps.

The months passed and they worked the waste. Don Tiburcio came and went. Sophia was big with child, so Doña Guadalupe sent Lupe down the hill to stay with her. Sophia's mother-in-law was bedridden, and she needed help.

Late one afternoon, Lupe was going down the hill to spend the night with Sophia while her husband was gone, when she came around the side of a deserted house and heard familiar voices in the foliage just beyond the plaza.

Stopping, Lupe could hear that her sister Maria was whispering to someone in the heavy green foliage that grew along the creek.

"I swear it," Maria was saying, "if you don't come and steal me tonight, I'm coming to your house to get you!"

"But you can't," pleaded the man that Lupe recognized as Esabel, "my mother would—"

"I don't care about your mother!" snapped Maria angrily. "Two times you've promised to steal me, and you haven't!"

"Look, I'm sorry, *querida*," said Esabel in a smooth, caressing voice, "but if you'll come close and let me hold you, we won't have to run away to—"

"How dare you!" shouted Maria.

Suddenly, Lupe heard a tremendous slapping sound and she saw Esabel come flying through the brush, landing on his butt. And Esabel wasn't a small man, either; he was huge.

"Damn it, Maria!" he yelled. "I've told you a dozen times to not hit me!"

"Well then, make good your word and steal me!"

"All right, damn it, I'll do it tonight!"

"Promise?"

"Yes."

"Oh, good," she said as sweetly as honey. "Then come here, and I'll help you up."

Lupe saw her sister come into view and help Esabel up, taking him into her arms.

Quietly, Lupe turned around. She had to hurry home to warn their mother. No decent girl was supposed to act like this. But backing up, Lupe caught her heel in a vine and she tripped, falling with a yelp. Instantly Maria came bursting out of the brush.

"Lupe!" she yelled, seeing her sister going up the trail. "Don't you dare!" And she took off after her.

But Lupe was fast and she had a head start, so she raced hard up the steep hillside. But Maria wasn't just wide and powerful; she was also lean as a jaguar and she had wonderful, long legs like her father. Her bare feet grabbed the rock and granite, spraying the debris behind her, and she quickly overtook Lupe.

But Lupe was small and agile. she dodged into a deserted house.

"All right, now I got you," said Maria, gasping.

"I'm still going to tell Mama," said Lupe.

"How'd you like to get killed?" said Maria.

"I'll tell Sophia, too," said Lupe.

"She already knows," said Maria.

"No, you lie," said Lupe. "Or she'd stop you!"

Maria laughed. "Lupe, she's the one who told me that I had to get Esabel to steal me."

Lupe couldn't believe it. "No!" she yelled. "Sophia would never say such a thing. She's decent!"

Maria only laughed all the more. "Lupe," she said, "you have to stop thinking that Sophia's such an angel. She's not. She's as conniving as our mother!"

"Oh, Maria!" said Lupe, hearing this awful thing about their mother. She dropped to the ground, sliding under the broken wall of upright sticks.

"Ask Sophia! She'll tell you!" shouted Maria.

Racing to Sophia's house, Lupe asked her sister if it was true.

"Yes," said Sophia.

"But how could you?"

"Lupe," said her sister, "they're in love, and what are they to do? None of us have the means to give them a proper wedding anymore. And if he steals her, they'll have to get married, and so she's kept her honor."

Lupe shook her head. "But only the lowest of the girls beg for a boy to steal them."

"Oh," said Sophia, "and was Mama begging when she wrote to Papa to come back because she needs him? Is it begging for me to ask Don Tiburcio to not charge Mama for the staples he brings you people?" She took a big breath. "We're all doing the best we can, *querida.*"

Lupe puckered her lips. She just couldn't believe what was becoming of their family. Why, they were becoming as lost as Don Manuel's family.

"And now I suggest," continued Sophia, "that you go catch Maria before it's too late and tell her that I spoke to you and you'll keep her secret."

Lupe didn't want to, but she finally agreed.

"Good girl," said Sophia, "and then go home. I think that you'll be needed there tonight."

Lupe went back up the hill. She found Maria and told her that she'd keep her secret. Maria thanked Lupe a thousand times.

That night after dinner, Maria got a pan of hot water and she knelt down on the clean, well-packed earth in front of her mother. She massaged the soles of her mother's feet, lathering her palms with the rough, good-feeling heart of a tender, young cactus. Their mother moaned and groaned with pleasure. Victoriano glanced at Lupe, raising up his eyebrows. Lupe said nothing, just praying that her mother wouldn't find out about Maria.

"Well," said their mother, "I don't know why, but all my children are so well-behaved tonight that I feel like the saint the old couple cover with their *sarape* every time they make love."

Flushing red as fire, Maria dropped her mother's foot. "Mama, how can you say that? We're always well-behaved."

Doña Guadalupe only laughed. "Tell that to the beavers with no ears, *mi hijita*," she said. "Not to your mother who knows every cockroach that crawls across your little mind."

Blushing, Maria picked up her mother's foot again and went back to work.

By the time they went to bed, Lupe was exhausted—she'd been so tense all evening. But under the covers, Lupe watched her mother quickly drop off to sleep and she felt much better.

The moon came out and the coyotes howled. It was late at night when Lupe awoke, hearing the sound of quiet footsteps coming up the pathway to their home. She wondered if it was Esabel or a hungry coyote. But then Victoriano's little dog let out a yelp and someone screamed out in pain and took off running. Instantly, Maria was up and out the doorway.

"Don't," she yelled. "Come back here, Esabel! I have to get my things!"

"No! That little bastard bit me!"

"But I haven't got my things!" begged Maria.

Lupe didn't know whether to laugh or what. She started to get out of bed to help Maria so she wouldn't wake up their mother. But to her surprise, her mother gripped her.

"No," she whispered.

"What?"

"Shhhhhh, leave them alone," said her mother.

Lupe heard Maria come in and get her things and go out quietly.

"Well, at least kiss me," Maria whispered to Esabel.

"Not here," he said.

Through the crack of their lean-to, Lupe could see her sister and Esabel silhouetted against the sky.

"Just one kiss," she insisted.

And so they kissed and kissed again, then hurried up the pathway toward the main road.

Doña Guadalupe threw off her covers and sat up, laughing hysterically. Lupe stared at her mother in shock. Then to further confuse Lupe, Victoriano came into the lean-to and said, "They're gone, Mama."

"Yes, I heard them, *mi hijito*," she said, still laughing.

Lupe looked from one to the other. "You mean you both knew about this all along?" she asked.

"Of course," said her mother.

Lupe's mind went reeling. "Then you also know that Sophia told Maria to do it?"

She nodded. "I told her to, *mi hijita*."

"Oh, Mama, how could you?"

"Lupita," said her mother calmly, "it was going to come to this anyway. And I want my daughters protected before the bandits come again." She made the sign of the cross over herself. "We've been a very lucky family so far, *mi hijita*."

Hearing the words, "so far," Lupe felt a chill like a cold, wet snake crawling up her spine. She knew exactly what her mother was saying. Of all the families in La Lluvia de Oro, they'd been one of the lucky ones. They never had a girl raped or stolen.

"Mama," said Lupe, "does this mean that I'm going to be hiding under the manure now?

Her mother took a big breath. "*Desgraciadamente*, yes, *mi hijita*. You're only ten, but you're as tall as me."

"Oh, Mama!" cried Lupe, feeling the snake come lunging out of her stomach with such force that she thought she'd faint.

"This is also why we must get out of this canyon," continued her mother. "These aren't soldiers anymore. These are savages, abortions *del diablo*! They use the Revolution as an excuse to steal and plunder!"

"We'll take care of you," said her brother, his eyes filling with tears. "Truly, I'd die a thousand deaths before I'd let anything happen to you, Lupe."

All that night Lupe hugged her mother close, but she couldn't sleep. She now realized how her older sisters must have felt all these years when they'd had to run and hide under the manure. For the first time in all her life, Lupe wished that she'd never been born a woman.

Late one afternoon, when Lupe and Manuelita finished their work for the day, they decided to do their studies in the shade of the peach tree behind the lean-to. Two little Indian girls came down from the American enfencement and they squatted down at a respectful distance.

"These are the same girls that I told you of," Lupe whispered to Manuelita. "I've caught them watching me read several times, but they always run and hide when I call them."

"Well, then, let's just not say anything to them and keep reading and let them do as they like," said the other girl.

Lupe and Manuelita continued with their studies, and the little Indian girls watched them all afternoon. It was fun; it made Lupe and Manuelita feel like teachers, having the little, wide-faced girls watching them.

A couple of days later, when Lupe and Manuelita sat down to read again, the same two little girls came. This time they had bunches of beautiful feathers in their hands.

Lupe and Manuelita waved for them to come closer and, to their surprise, the little girls came forward, step-by-step as shyly as fawns. They placed the feathers before Lupe and Manuelita, then sat down, hiding their faces in their hands, giggling uncontrollably.

And so there it began—a little school all of their own. Lupe and Manuelita met with the two little girls, Paloma and Cruz, every other day after work. The girls were so quick to learn that within a few weeks they actually understood the miracle of the written word.

Books were alive; the words gave life to the written page as surely as God breathed life into the flowers and the trees of the land, and into the birds and the stars of the sky.

Then one afternoon, Lupe, Manuelita, Cuca and Uva were playing jump rope with Cruz and Paloma and singing:

> *Naranja dulce, limón partido,*
> *Dame un abrazo, por Dios te pido.*
> *Si fueran falsos tus juramentos,*
> *En algún tiempo se han de acabar.*
> *Toca la marcha, mi pecho llora,*
> *Si tus juramentos serán verdad*
> *Duran el tiempo que naranjas dulces.*

> Sweet orange, split lemon
> Give me a hug, for the love of God.
> If your promises are false
> Sometime they will end.
> The march sounds on, my heart cries out,
> If your promises are true
> They'll last as long as oranges are sweet.

And they were singing and jumping and truly enjoying themselves when Victoriano came rushing by and climbed up on the big boulder.

Instantly, Lupe quit jumping and her heart pounded with fear, realizing that if it was bandits, she'd have to run and hide.

"What is it?" asked their mother, coming out of the *ramada*.

"I don't know," said Victoriano, looking into the distance.

Cruz and Paloma took off, running down the path to the thick foliage.

Lupe felt like screaming. But she kept calm and ran around to the back of the boulder and started digging into the manure so she could hide, but there wasn't enough to cover her.

Then she heard her brother shout, "It's Don Tiburcio and Papa and Carlota!" Lupe began to cry—she was so relieved.

When Carlota and the two men reached their home, everyone in the canyon was waiting for them. It quickly became a time of wet eyes and big *abrazos*. Even Don Manuel and his family came up the hill.

Sophia hugged her husband and took him aside so he could feel her big stomach. Their child was due any day now. Maria hugged her father and explained to him that Esabel and she had gotten together and she, too, was with child.

Don Victor stood up erect, staring at Maria and Esabel. But then, instead of becoming enraged, he simply embraced Maria.

"Then you're not mad at me?" asked Maria, tears coming to her eyes.

"No, of course not," he said. "Times are difficult. We do the best we can." And he put out his hand for Esabel, but the young man was too embarrassed to take it. "Come now, Esabel," said Don Victor, "take my hand like the man you've chosen to be and promise that you'll be a responsible man."

Esabel took Don Victor's hand, but he couldn't meet his eyes—he was so embarrassed.

Lupe could see that their mother was relieved to see how well Don Victor had taken the news.

Carlota came up and took her mother in her arms. "Oh, Mama," she said, her eyes overflowing with tears, "I've missed you so much!" She turned to Lupe. "And you, too, you skinny rat!" She squeezed Lupe so hard that Lupe lost her breath.

Across the way, Victoriano and their father were regarding each other cautiously.

"I brought the new shovel you asked me for," said Don Victor.

"Oh, you remembered!" said Victoriano.

"Why, of course," said the older man.

"Good," said Victoriano," and, well, did . . ." He could hardly speak, he was so nervous. "Did Socorro find her family?" he asked finally.

Don Victor shrugged. "I don't know. She stayed in El Fuerte with us for a few weeks, but then she went with some people to the coast."

He reached out, squeezing his son's arm. "I'm sorry I don't know more but, well, it was very hard for us, too."

Quickly, suddenly, Victoriano took his father into his arms, crying desperately. His father held him, chest-to-chest, in a big *abrazo*.

A few days later, when Lupe was with her mother and Maria under the *ramada* grinding the ore into fine sand, Don Tiburcio came rushing up the hill.

"She's ready!" he said. "Hurry! Please!"

Carlota and their father had gone out the day before, taking Don Manuel and his family with them. Don Tiburcio had stayed behind so he could be with Sophia when she gave birth.

"Go and get the midwife while the girls and I attend to her," said their mother to the frightened-looking man.

But he couldn't move. His face had lost all color, and his legs buckled under him. He fell.

"All right, then lay down and rest," said Doña Guadalupe, laughing at him, "and you, Lupe, go for the midwife while Maria and I go down."

"Yes," said Lupe, and she was off like a shot.

By the time Lupe got to Sophia's house, her mother and Maria were there, and Sophia was crying out in pain.

Sophia's mother-in-law was in the next room. She hadn't been out of her bed for over a week. Poor Don Tiburcio was pacing about the house, feeling crazy; he felt so useless.

"Isn't there anything I can do?" he pleaded.

"Nothing," said Doña Guadalupe. "Now, please, just go outside and leave us alone."

"But I want to help her," she said.

Lupe felt sorry for him. He just didn't know what to do with himself.

"Look," said Doña Guadalupe, "I know you love Sophia and you want to help, but there are certain things that happen at childbirth that no man should see."

"Is she in danger?" he asked.

"No, she's fine, but it's not going to be an easy birth. The moon isn't full, so the great waters of the world aren't moving, and Sophia's water won't want to break. Please, now, leave before you witness something you shouldn't."

Doña Guadalupe ushered Don Tiburcio out of the door in a hurry. Lupe felt such tenderness for him. But he wasn't a woman, so he couldn't stay and help.

"Now come here, Maria and Lupe," said their mother. "If the midwife doesn't come soon, we'll have to get started ourselves."

Lupe obeyed her mother and helped her tie Sophia's long hair back, slip off her skirt, and then they prepared the rope and the water and the clean cloths.

But Sophia was angry; she didn't want anyone to come near her, and she hissed at them like a snake, belching out great burps of gas.

Lupe had never seen her sister behave like this before, and it frightened her. But her mother just ignored Sophia's demon-looking ways and massaged her limbs with warm oil and herbs.

"Get away from me!" yelled Sophia angrily. "I never knew it was going to be like this! It's awful! I hate this baby!" she screamed. "It's killing me!"

Lupe made the sign of the cross over herself. No wonder their mother had sent Don Tiburcio out. Why, her sister had turned into *el diablo*.

But her mother only winked at Lupe. "Just ignore her, *mi hijita*," said their mother reassuringly, "and do as I tell you, and everything will be fine."

"Oh, no, it won't!" snapped Sophia angrily. "I hurt! Get away from me!"

When the midwife arrived, she immediately took over. The old woman laughed and joked and told Sophia to scream all the blasphemies she wished.

"After all, God needs to be reminded that it's no joke what He puts us women through!"

The old woman cursed at the heavens herself, telling Sophia to curse, too. Sophia did so at the top of her lungs, chilling the canyon with such blasphemies that even the coyotes quit howling in the distance.

Outside, Victoriano and Don Tiburcio were shocked at the words they heard. They moved further away, trying to ignore her shouts. But it was difficult; Sophia sounded like a monster.

Don Tiburcio brought out some paper and tobacco. He tried to roll a cigarette, but his hands were shaking too much.

"Here," said Victoriano, "let me help you."

"I didn't know you smoked," said the older man.

Victoriano blushed. "Sometimes," he said.

Don Tiburcio handed him the makings. "Then go ahead. Roll us two."

"Two?"

"Sure."

Victoriano's eyes grew so big that their whites could be seen even in the dark of the night.

Don Tiburcio laughed, slapping the tall, thin boy on the back. "You've never smoked in front of your elders, eh?"

Victoriano shook his head. "No, of course not."

"You know," said the older man, "I was twenty-seven years old and owned two deaths before I dared to smoke in front of my mother.

"We're a strange people," he added. "So much respect, so many traditions, and yet we kill each other like dogs and we don't think nothing of that."

Finishing the two cigarettes, Victoriano handed one to Don Tiburcio and the older man brought out a match. He was just going to light them up, when a wailing scream was heard.

Inside the house, Sophia was screaming and pulling on the rope as she squatted down, pushing and straining. The midwife and their mother helped Sophia between her legs, and Lupe and Maria held her by the armpits.

A series of wailing screams followed as Sophia pushed, strained, until the baby emerged. Lupe held her sister with all her might and the baby was coming, coming, fighting with all his power, too.

Time stood still and the women worked together inside the house. Outside, the men stood about—holding in terror.

Then the baby came, wet and raw, slipping out into the world—another miracle of God's.

When Lupe came outside with the newborn infant, her brother and Don Tiburcio were pale.

"Is Sophia all right?" asked Don Tiburcio, trembling like a leaf.

"Yes," said Lupe. "She's fine. And look, you have a son."

Don Tiburcio took his son in his arms, crying with relief. He thanked the heavens that it was finally over. Oh, he'd never felt so helpless in all his life.

A few weeks later, Lupe and Manuelita were under the peach tree behind their home giving lessons to five Indian children when Ojos Puros came and sat down on a rock some fifteen feet away. He brought out a pair of wire-rimmed glasses that he'd found in the deserted American office and put them on.

"Go on," he said, "I'm just going to read the paper."

Lupe and Manuelita went on with their lesson, but it was very difficult. Because, when Ojos Puros took up his newspaper, it was upside down. And all the children tried hard not to laugh, for they could now see that Ojos Puros, the leader of their people, didn't read but, of course, he was too proud to admit it.

"Pay close attention," said Manuelita loud enough for the old man to hear, too. "See these letters and how they go?"

"Yes," said the children.

"Oh," said Ojos Puros to himself, uprighting his paper as he pretended to read.

Again the children tried hard not to laugh as Lupe and her friend continued with their lesson. Dark clouds started gathering overhead. The rainy season had begun a couple of weeks ago, and it was now raining a little every afternoon.

Ojos Puros folded his newspaper very carefully at each crease and put it under his poncho to keep it from getting wet. Lupe and all the children went inside the *ramada*.

Suddenly, the sky exploded with thunder and lightning, and the rain came down in white sheets, making a mighty roar.

Dripping wet from head to toe, Victoriano burst into the *ramada*. "Where's Mama?" he said. "I got some good ore!"

He had a basket of rock.

"She's down with Sophia," said Lupe.

"Oh, that's right," he said, taking off his wet hat and poncho.

Ever since Sophia's mother-in-law had passed away, their mother was spending a couple of hours every afternoon with her daughter at her house.

The wind came up and the water came down in white torrents of rain. The thunder echoed off the towering cliffs, filling the canyon with sound. The lightning flashed in great, zigzagging lines of fire, breaking the sky open.

Victoriano got a shovelful of hot coals and put them by the girls' feet to keep them warm, then put some water on the stove to boil for tea. He was tired. For nearly a year they'd been working the waste, sun to sun, seven days a week. Victoriano was still skinny, but his legs and arms were as strong as iron.

Lupe and the children watched the storm. It was pleasant, standing there by the glowing warm coals. The main part of the storm passed and a gentle rain came into the canyon. The sky opened up, exposing startling patches of blue sky.

"Look!" said Lupe, pointing to a cloud. "A deer!"

"Yes," said Cruz. "And over there, a chicken!"

"And look at that huge spider that's chasing the chicken!" said Paloma.

The girls all laughed, and Ojos Puros and Victoriano glanced at each other, smiling happily. The tea was ready and Victoriano served a cup for the old man and another for himself.

Then the storm passed and the clouds broke up, rolling, turning, doing somersaults in the sky like happy children.

"Look, a rainbow!" shouted Manuelita.

Everyone turned to see, including Victoriano and Ojos Puros. And there it was, a miracle of God's magic, holding beyond the mouth of the canyon in a spectacle of color—red, pink, yellow, green, blue and lavender.

Suddenly, Victoriano's little dog lifted up his head, but it was too late. There they were at the back door—two men with guns in their hands, grinning lecherously from under their big *sombreros*.

Seeing his dog, Victoriano whirled about, and without hesitation, threw the pot of boiling tea at them. The men leaped back, screaming, and Victoriano yelled, "Run, Lupe!" as he grabbed a rock from the basket full of ore, throwing it.

Lupe was out the door and running with Manuelita and the little Indian children. But then she looked back and saw that they had her brother cornered.

"Victoriano!" she yelled.

Ojos Puros was nowhere to be seen. He'd disappeared, even before the children.

"Go!" screamed her brother, kicking and fighting as they struck him with their rifles. "Warn the others!"

But when Lupe turned to run, there was a third man behind her. He lunged at her.

"Don't run, little one," he said, smiling. He had a red bandanna about his curly brown hair. She could see that he was young and handsome but, also, he had a gleam in his large dark eyes that told her that he was a no-good.

She moved to the left; he moved, too. But then she dodged under the *ramada*, scrambling on her hands and knees, and she leaped over the stone wall between her mother's potted plants like a deer.

"¡*Órale*, Chuy!" yelled one of the other men. "Don't tell us you're going to let that little virgin get away!"

The handsome one named Chuy was quick and he was after Lupe. But Victoriano, who was on the ground with his face covered in blood, whistled to his little spotted dog. In a flash, the little dog was after Chuy, grabbing him by the calf, biting and snarling.

"¡*Cabrón, perro!*" bellowed Chuy, trying to kick free from the little dog. But he couldn't, so he brought up his rifle, hitting him.

The brave little dog went down, but still Chuy shot him, blowing out the animal's lungs through his backside.

"You stupid fool!" yelled the older man who'd knocked down Victoriano. "Now you've warned everybody!" He turned to the man beside him. "Stop that girl!"

Now this second man and Chuy were both after Lupe, going through the wet foliage like two hungry-eyed hounds.

"You damn boy!" said the older man to Victoriano. "Look what you have done!"

He raised up his rifle to crush Victoriano's skull, when Ojos Puros materialized from a dark shadow behind the stove. He came swiftly, silently, like a ghost across the hard-packed earth on his callused bare feet, driving his thin, long, pig-killing knife through the bandit's throat, slashing out his jugular.

The man was dead on his feet, eyes staring in shock, never having known what struck him. Victoriano rolled out of the way as the bandit came down with a flood of blood, face-first into the earthen floor.

Down the steep hillside, Lupe was dodging through the rain-dripping underbrush like a frightened rabbit—slipping, sliding, wet and cold. The two young men chasing after her saw her here, then over there, and then she was gone once again as she went scurrying like a cottontail through the underbrush, her heart pounding with terror.

Lupe came to the roaring creek with the series of waterfalls. The two men thought that they had her now. The one named Chuy put down his gun and unbuckled his pants, grinning at his friend.

Looking down into the racing white water, Lupe was horrified. She didn't know how to swim. Only the boys learned how. But, still, she'd rather die than be soiled by this man. She turned to leap when suddenly Don Tiburcio—high above them on a boulder—aimed his rifle and fired. The man's head exploded, with brains and pieces of red bandanna, before Lupe heard the report of the rifle. The other man ran into the brush as Don Tiburcio continued shooting.

Lupe leaped for cover. And then, shooting broke out everywhere. Scrambling through the wet foliage, Lupe found a small hole in the rocks. But to her complete, horror, someone was already there. With relief, she realized that it was Cruz.

"Where's Manuelita and the others?" whispered Lupe.

Cruz shrugged. "I think they got them."

"Oh, my God," said Lupe, drawing close to the girl.

The shooting continued, and Lupe and Cruz held each other in the hole of the rock under the cold, wet foliage, listening to the screams, the shooting, and the men racing everywhere. Lupe and her little friend hid there, hearts pounding, until they were numb with cold and fear.

Suddenly, the shooting stopped. All was quiet. Not a sound was heard but the drip-dropping of the wet foliage all around them. And this silence grew and grew until finally, it was even more frightening than the shooting. Lupe's mind ran amuck, thinking that maybe everyone in the canyon had been killed and there was no one left in all the world except her and Cruz.

Lupe glanced around and she could smell the powder of the spent guns and the wet burning of the palm leaf roofs of their homes. Then at last, from far away, she thought she could hear the crying of a child. Someone had lived. There was still life. They held their breaths, straining to listen. But all they could hear was the breathing of the plants and the insects coming back to life.

Time passed. And more time passed. Then they heard men's angry voices and horses coming their way on the trail alongside the creek at a slow, deliberate walk.

Lupe and Cruz crouched down, and they saw the horses' hooves pass by, underneath the foliage no more than an arm's length away.

Lupe started to make the sign of the cross over herself, but Cruz shook her head no. Lupe stopped and suddenly remembered her father's words, that to disappear was the only way to survive in war.

Tears came to Lupe's eyes and she and her little friend stayed in hiding until the sun went down and the long shadows of the coming night covered the canyon like secret ghosts.

Finally, coming out of hiding, Lupe approached Sophia's house, going from shadow to shadow like a small nocturnal animal. She could hear weeping up ahead, but it wasn't the crying of a child. No, it was the soft, lost wailing of a broken heart.

Then, looking in through the open doorway, Lupe saw dead men lying everywhere. The whole house was a shambles. Then she saw Sophia in the middle of the destruction, holding Don Tiburcio in her arms at the head of a wide beam of late afternoon sunlight coming in through an open window. Lupe gasped. There were two great blood-gorged holes in Don Tiburcio's white shirt on his chest.

"I love you so much," Don Tiburcio was saying to Sophia. "*Júrame* that you'll never marry again."

"But, *querido*," said Sophia, brushing his hair out of his eyes, "how can

I promise you that? I'm with child, and we have our little boy, too. If I get through this, I'll have to marry again just to live."

"Sophia, I'm dying," he gasped, gurgling blood. "Please, this is no time to be difficult!"

"But I'm not being difficult, *querido*," she said, stroking his forehead lovingly.

"Look," he said, suddenly getting stronger, "I want you to clean the fireplace, then go north immediately."

"The fireplace?"

"Yes, do as I say!"

"All right, as soon as I can," she said.

"No, now, immediately, clean the fireplace and leave before the rains set in! And you won't have to marry again. Please, *¡júramelo!*"

"But, dear husband, how can I promise you that?" she said, getting annoyed. "You're dying and I must think of our children."

"Well, then," he said, twisting his eyes and gathering all the strength he could, "*júrame* that if you marry again, you won't love him, so you can join me in heaven!" he begged.

"Oh, dear Tiburcio," said Sophia, "stop all this nonsense and prepare your soul to meet God. Really, you tell me, how can I possibly remarry and not be in love again? I'm only nineteen years old, my love."

Hearing this, he gasped, eyes rolling, and his head fell back, orange foam gurgled up from his mouth and his eyes stared out at the beam of sunlight coming in their open window. He was dead.

"Oh, my God!" screamed Sophia. "Don't die! I wasn't trying to be difficult! Please, believe me, I love you, too!" And she fell over his body, weeping huge, wrenching cries.

Lupe sank down to her knees, crying, too. Don Tiburcio had saved her life. Next to her brother and her Colonel, he'd been the only man that she'd ever really loved.

13

*The plants and insects flourished where the human
blood washed the earth, and* la gente *grew so desperate
that they were ready to give up . . . even the Holy
Ghost.*

It took three days for Lupe and her family to scrape
away the last of the blood from Sophia's house. The three bandits that Don
Tiburcio killed had drenched the whole home with blood.

Lupe never realized how much blood the human body had. Why, one
body alone flooded the entire kitchen and, when it dried and thickened,
there was just no way to get it off the hard-packed dirt floors.

Finally, Lupe and her mother and sisters had to dig down several inches
into the dirt floor so they could get rid of the blood smell which was attracting
snakes and lizards and other animals.

Then one day, Lupe and Sophia were sitting together, listening to the
breeze—just being quiet—when, for no apparent reason, they both started to
cry. They'd worked so hard and suffered so much. And, not only had the
bandits killed Don Tiburcio, they'd taken their gold, raped Paloma and two
other little Indian girls, killing all of them. Oh, *la vida* was just too difficult
to bear at times. But then, after having a good cry, Lupe and her sister felt
better and they went inside to have a cup of tea.

The water just began boiling when a mouse ran out from under the stove
and Sophia's baby, Diego, let out a screech of joy and started crawling after
the mouse. But then came a snake, darting out of a dark corner after the
mouse. Sophia let out a scream, rushing to pick up her child.

The mouse ran into the fireplace and the snake followed. Sophia gave the
child to Lupe and got a broom, going after the snake.

"Get out of my house! Get out!" she screamed, taking out all of her
frustration on the reptile. "You are not permitted in this house, do you hear
me? My husband is gone and I will not have you sleeping in his home!"

The child screeched with delight in Lupe's arms as the snake slithered
past Sophia.

But this snake was no laughing matter for Sophia and she went to war,
kicking and swatting and screaming at the snake until the reptile finally

zigzagged out of the fireplace with his head up, tongue darting, testing the different scents in the air, and went out the door.

Sophia was left trembling. "We're going to have to clean out this fireplace," she said, "and get the mice out of there so the snakes won't come back."

"All right," said Lupe.

Lupe gave the child to Sophia and got down on her knees to clean the fireplace. She was moving the half-burned wood when she struck something hard under the ashes.

"There is something here," said Lupe.

"I'll be," said Sophia. "I remember Tiburcio telling me at his death to clean out the fireplace."

They quickly brushed the ashes aside, and there was a metal box about a foot long. Dragging it to the middle of the room, they opened the strongbox. It was full of gold!

Two days later, Sophia was ready to go out of the canyon along with another family that was leaving.

"But, *mi hijita*," said her mother, "you shouldn't go out now. Wait until after the rainy season."

"I gave my word that I'd go out the moment I could, and I'm going, Mama. Besides, it's not like we're parting. You'll be coming in a few months, and I'll be waiting for you across the border."

Doña Guadalupe's eyes swelled with tears. "Oh, I'm so frightened for you, *mi hijita*," she said, hugging her daughter, heart-to-heart.

"And I'm frightened for you staying here in the canyon," said Sophia.

"No, we're safe here now until after the rains," said her mother.

And so Lupe watched her mother and sister hold each other desperately.

"Will you be going by boat or train?" asked Maria.

"Oh, I don't know," said Sophia, turning and taking Maria, who was big with child, into her arms.

"I'll ask Papa what he thinks when I see him in El Fuerte."

"Good," said their mother. "God go with you, my love."

Lupe and Victoriano walked Sophia up the trail to the main road and around to the canyon's end. There, Lupe brought out a flower tied up with a piece of red ribbon and gave it to Sophia.

"Here," she said to Sophia. "It's for you."

"Oh, thank you, Lupita," she said. "Take care of Mama. She'll need you. You're the only woman at home now that Maria's with Esabel."

"I will," said Lupe, drying her eyes.

"*Adiós*, Victoriano," said Sophia, hugging her tall, thin brother. "You take care of Mama, too. I'll be waiting for all of you across the border. Oh, how I wish Mama would accept part of my treasure and you could all come with me now."

"No, Sophia," said Victoriano, "there are too many of us and Don
Tiburcio died so the money could be for you and your children. Besides,
who knows, maybe this rainy season will uncover another pocket of gold and
we, too, will be rich."

"I hope so," she said.

Sophia hugged her brother and sister once more and then she went down
the trail with the family that she was going with. She had one child in her
belly and another in her side cloth.

Lupe watched until her sister disappeared in the bend of the overgrown
trail. Wiping her eyes, Lupe glanced up at the sky and saw the wind in the
trees above her and the jungle out beyond. She took a deep breath and
wondered about this world that lay outside their world. Everyone was going—
Don Tiburcio, her Colonel and Paloma and the two other little girls. Her
eyes filled with tears. Everyone just seemed to be disappearing—some to
heaven and some to the outside world.

Victoriano put his arm around his little sister, holding her close, and they
both looked out at the sky and the land, stepping down into an infinity of
mountain peaks. Like in a dream, Sophia was now gone, too, vanishing into
the great vastness of sky and jungle and screeching insects.

The rainy season continued, but still, Lupe and her
family worked the waste every day; they weren't finding as much gold as
they'd hoped. They began to fear that they'd be trapped in the canyon for
yet another whole year. And then the bandits would be sure to come again.

Late one afternoon, Lupe was with her mother down at Doña Manza's
house, sitting on the terrace, when their mother spotted a shiny rock down
in the plaza. It had just stopped raining, and they were drinking tea and
eating wild roots to numb their hunger.

"Look," said Doña Guadalupe to Doña Manza, "see that rock in the
middle of the plaza? Now that the sun has come out, it shines."

"My children and I were commenting on that same stone the other day,"
said Doña Manza. "Now that the roots have turned up the cobblestones,
every time it rains, there seems to be a little color here and there, all over the
plaza."

"So what are we waiting for?" said Doña Guadalupe. "Maybe it's gold!"

"Oh, no," said Doña Manza, laughing lightheartedly, "it's just water
drying up. The Americans were wasteful, but not that wasteful," she added,
laughing again.

"Well, I don't know," said Doña Guadalupe. "This plaza was one of the
first places that the Americans built, and they had gold coming out of their
ears back in those days.

"Lupe," she called, "get your brother and go down to the plaza and dig
up that shiny rock for me."

"Yes," said Lupe, getting to her feet. She'd been reading a book with Manuelita.

"You go with her, too, Manuelita," said Doña Manza. "And take a shovel and a bar."

"Good," said Doña Guadalupe, "this way, if it is gold, we'll split it fifty-fifty."

Doña Manza laughed. "Oh, don't worry, *querida*. I'm only being courteous."

"Then you don't want half?" asked Doña Guadalupe, eyes full of mischief.

They both had a good laugh together as they watched their children go down to the plaza and start digging up the stone.

And then came a screaming shout.

"It's gold!" screamed Lupe. "Gold!"

The others were screaming, too, and the two old women were out of the chairs, racing down the steep steps to the plaza. And there it was, before their very eyes, shining up at them: a rock, the size of a burro's head, with a miracle of gold marbled into the side of the stone like a spider web—each strand of the web as big around as a child's finger.

In the next two days, they dug up the whole plaza, and they had so much gold that they couldn't process it fast enough.

Victoriano and Esabel did the pounding, and Maria, Lupe and their mother did the grinding; but there was just no way that they could clean the gold fast enough. The last two steps of cleaning the gold with water and then with mercury in a flat pan just couldn't be rushed or muscled. No, it took great patience and eye-and-hand coordination or the gold would go spilling over the side of the pan. Only the women seemed able to do it. The men were just too slow and awkward, and they got impatient.

"Damn it!" said Esabel, throwing a rock at a passing dog. "Now we have gold coming out of our asses, but we can't get it cleaned in time to get out of here after the rains, the way we're going!"

Esabel and Victoriano were sitting behind the big boulder next to a huge pile of gold ore that they'd pounded down with hammers. They had a year's worth of gold ore crushed and ready to grind, but there was no purpose to go any further since they wouldn't be able to clean it fast enough anyway.

That first stone that they'd uncovered at the plaza that afternoon had just been the beginning. After that, they'd found gold all over the plaza and up and down the walkways. Why, the whole town had been paved with gold in those early days.

"Well," said Victoriano, watching the two dogs fighting over a set of bull's horns, "if only we could build something to help the women clean the gold faster."

"What, a miracle?" said Esabel, throwing another rock at the growling dogs.

"Well, no, just something that we could use like a funnel to wash the ore and, yet, not spill it," said Victoriano.

"Sure, that would be great," said Esabel. "But since we're wishing for the impossible, then why don't we just wish that we could find one of those sixty-pound bars that the Americans took out? Hell, one bar and we'd have . . . but what are you doing?" he yelled after Victoriano.

Victoriano had jumped to his feet and was chasing after the two dogs. "I got it!" yelled Victoriano, grabbing the set of bull's horns away from them. "I got it!"

Victoriano raced under the *ramada* to his mother and sisters who were working side by side like a little factory. And it turned out to be true. Splitting the horn lengthwise, it, indeed, became a funnel and the rough, inside tissue of the horn held the gold back when they washed it with the water and, then, acted like a million tiny hands, slowing down the gold when they mixed it with the lightning-quick mercury.

Now Victoriano and Esabel were able to help the women clean the gold, too. They began to go twenty times faster than they'd ever been able to go before. Within a week they'd cleaned so much gold that it became necessary for Lupe and her mother and brother to stay up late at night to form the little gold balls, the final step of the entire process.

Staying up at night after everyone else had gone to bed, Lupe and her mother and brother cut up old dresses and other material into little square pieces. Then they took a pinch of the pure gold and placed it in the middle of each little square piece of cloth. They gathered up all four ends of the cloth and squeezed the gold with their fingertips, milking the water and mercury out of the gold until the little ball was round and firm. Then they twisted the ball around and around, holding fast the ends of the cloth, and tied a string around the top.

They began to do more than a dozen little balls like this each night, putting them into the glowing, hot coals of the stove before they lay down to sleep. Lupe loved to hear the hissing of the little cloth-wrapped balls of gold and watch the mercury burn off in quick blue flames.

In the morning, Lupe and Victoriano couldn't wait to get up and dig the little burnt balls of gold out of the ashes and wash them off. These were their final product: little gold balls about the size of a little finger nail, weighing about five grams each and having little fine lines running all over the ball—the imprint of the cloth that they'd wrapped around the gold.

The rainy season continued, and the box canyon filled with the deafening roar of the waterfalls. The creek at the bottom of the canyon swelled up into a torrent of rushing white waters, and each morning, Lupe and her mother and brother took the little balls of gold that they'd made the night before and hid them in the potted plants in front of their house. The bandits had found the gold that they'd hidden inside their home last time, so they had to be very careful and not lose this gold.

It rained every afternoon and Lupe and her family continued working day and night, but it was getting more difficult for them each day. They'd run out of food and had to spend a lot of time every day digging for roots so they could eat. Gold was no problem anymore. It was food that they now lacked.

A couple of families couldn't stand the hunger, so they left the canyon over the north rim, hoping to get out on the trail that Lupe's Colonel had forged through the jungle. Word came back a few weeks later that both families had drowned while crossing El Rio Fuerte, only a few miles away from safety, because they'd refused to let go of the gold they were carrying.

Digging up roots below the town one day, Lupe smelled meat cooking above her in the deserted village. Following the wonderful aroma, she saw a group of excited people at the edge of the abandoned plaza. They had a fire going inside the ruins of Don Manuel's store and were preparing a feast. Lupe felt her mouth water with the good smell of the *barbacoa*, until she turned the corner and she saw the deer hanging in the tree. The animal was half-skinned, but still Lupe could see that it was her pet deer.

She gasped, wanting to vomit, but seeing how anxious the people were to eat, she turned, going off to be sick by herself. It was one of the most difficult things Lupe had ever done.

That same afternoon, Lupe saw her father coming down the trail, returning from the lowlands. His clothes were torn and he looked wild.

"Papa," she said, "what happened? Where's Carlota?"

"Not now," he said, pushing by her like a madman. "Your mother, I must speak to her!"

He staggered into the plaza where *la gente* were still feasting on Lupe's pet. Doña Guadalupe saw her husband's face and she gripped her chest.

"It's Sophia, isn't it?" she said.

"Yes," said Don Victor. "Her ship went down in a storm."

"Oh, my God!" said Doña Guadalupe. "And Carlota?"

"I left her in El Fuerte so I could get here as quick as I could," said the old grey-haired man, trembling so hard that his whole body jerked in quick vibration. "I never slept. I came night and day, *querida*. She wanted to go by train but, no, I told her that she'd be safer at sea."

Saying this, Don Victor collapsed. He'd made the trip on foot in three days that normally, in good weather, took a man a week by mule. He was dead on his feet.

All night, Don Victor was unconscious, and he tossed and cried out in his sleep. He began to sweat and run a fever. The old midwife, Angelina, was called. She checked him carefully and boiled a pot of herbs.

Lupe and Maria helped their mother, and the midwife soaked their father's feet and chest with the hot, foul-smelling mixture and vigorously massaged the soles of his feet—the gateway to the soul.

Ojos Puros came down and he put a sacred rope of garlic around Don Victor's neck and slit the throats of three chickens, hanging them upside down at the foot of the bed.

The garlic gave off an aura of magical healing powers, and the three chickens communicated with the blessed Trinity of God. The Catholic Church and Ojos Puros's Indian beliefs were so interwoven inside the deep crevices of his mind that his knowledge of the Almighty was so complete that he had no questions.

"Doña Guadalupe," said Ojos Puros, "I'm sorry about Sophia's death. But I swear it, unless you and your family abandon the gold that you've mined, the same evil spirits that destroyed Sophia will never let you get out of this canyon alive. For no one can leave this sacred place of God with gold and expect to start a new life. See what happened to the two families who tried to go out over the north rim? See how the Colonel was tortured to death for trying to take gold? They all died terrible deaths, just like my own father!"

The dogs barked and the coyotes howled and *la gente* began to chant in eerie sounds outside of the *ramada*. "Gold is evil!" continued Ojos Puros. "You must abandon it. Or the same monster of the deep that crushed Sophia's ship will come out of the depth of your souls and destroy you, too!"

Watching her father lying there, Lupe began to think that maybe Ojos Puros was right. All night Lupe and her mother attended to Don Victor, but it was very difficult to keep heart with Ojos Puros shouting at them about their evil ways and the Indians chanting eerie sounds.

But how could they possibly do what Ojos Puros demanded, asked Lupe to herself. They'd worked so hard for the gold and they'd starve to death down in the lowlands without it.

The next morning, when Lupe awoke, her mother was gone. Quickly, Lupe and Victoriano set out to look for her. The sun was going down when Lupe came through a break between two large, white boulders and found her mother sitting at the base of a huge oak tree. Giving her thanks to God, Lupe came close, step by step, not wishing to startle her mother.

"Is that you, *mi hijita?*" said the old grey-haired lady, blinking her eyes into the dimming light.

"Yes," said Lupe. "Where have you been?"

"I've been here all day, *mi hijita*."

"But we've been so worried! You didn't say anything to anyone!"

The old woman took a big, long breath. "Yes, I know . . . sometimes a woman needs to just leave, *mi hijita*, without a word or she'll go crazy, I swear."

Lupe didn't know what to think.

"Come here," said the old woman, "and sit by me."

Lupe came close and sat down on the ground with her mother. Sheets of golden, pale light came down through the tree branches, surrounding them.

"You know, *mi hijita*," said her mother, "last night I got so confused and tired that I didn't know what to think. I was so worried about your father and brokenhearted over Sophia's death that I was beginning to believe that Ojos Puros was right and we'd have to abandon our gold.

"But then, coming up here this morning to my crying tree, I cried and cried, and now I feel much better, because I now know that Sophia isn't dead. No, she's alive."

"But what about her ship going down?" asked Lupe.

Her mother shrugged. "So what about the ship? All I know is that down deep in my heart, I'd know if Sophia was dead and I don't know that, so that means she's alive."

"Oh, Mama, you really think so?" asked Lupe excitedly.

"Yes," said her mother, "absolutely." She stroked Lupe's hair. "*Mi hijita*, I tell you, every day that I grow older I see that life is much bigger than we realize. For instance, what you did yesterday was so much bigger and braver than I thought was possible for a girl your age that I'm still astonished."

Lupe lowered her head, feeling her little heart beginning to pound.

"Lupe," continued her mother, "I saw you when you saw your deer."

"You did?"

"Yes. And I also saw that you saw how hungry all the people were and you turned and went away so they could enjoy themselves. That was very, very brave of you, *mi hijita*," said the old woman, tears coming to her eyes. "And no one had to tell you to do that. No, you just knew; you knew about your deer before you'd even seen him, and you knew about the people's hunger and how to handle it before you'd even really thought about it.

"Well, *mi hijita*, the more I live and see, I'm beginning to think that the most important things in life seem to come to us like, well, in a gift, a vision, a special knowledge so deep inside us that we actually know things before we even know them." She took a deep breath. "And I can tell you, now that I've rested here with my great friend, this mighty oak tree, that Sophia isn't dead. No, she's alive! And we're going to be re-united with her someday and we can keep our gold! Men do not tell me what to think or how to live anymore. I think and live as I, a woman, see the world around me, and that's that!

"Here, take a good look at my crying tree, and see her mighty limbs, her great trunk, and where her limbs have been broken by fire and lightning, but how she's mended herself. Imagine, *mi hijita*, all that this tree has been through. Look at her broken places and see the tender new growth that she's sprouted. Look at the great burn that reached the heart of her trunk and, yet, she withstood that great fire of the meteorite that burned down all the big pines. No, *mi hijita*, as sure as this tree lives, so does my heart tell me that Sophia lives! And yes, one day, I swear it before God, we'll find Sophia and the tree of our family will be mended, too!"

Lupe glanced up at the huge oak tree and she saw its big, broken limbs and how they'd grown new life. She looked at its mighty trunk and saw how the fire had half destroyed it and, yet, it lived. She felt a great peace sweep through her. Her mother was right; Sophia had to be alive. Or she, their mother, the trunk of their *familia*, would know it here inside her soul.

"This is my crying tree," said Doña Guadalupe, "and ever since we came to this canyon, I've been coming up here when I feel sad or lonely or just too tired to go on. This tree listens to me, giving me strength, breathing new hope and power into my . . . my very soul." She smiled, drying her eyes. "My daughter lives. She lives, and all is well, and yes, we'll keep our gold!"

Lupe glanced up at the tree again, and she felt the peace grow inside her. "But how will we ever find Sophia, Mama?" she asked.

Doña Guadalupe shrugged again. "I guess by just going on with our lives," she said, "and keeping our faith in God."

Lupe breathed and she felt so happy, so fortunate that she had found her mother here by this wonderful tree.

"You know, Mama," said Lupe, "I guess that I also have a crying tree, too. When I feel sad, I go up to the high country and I sit by the little pine tree where I buried my Colonel's coat and I talk to God until I feel all better inside."

Doña Guadalupe reached out, stroking her daughter's hair. "Good, wonderful, *mi hijita*, for no matter how young or old, every woman needs her own crying tree."

"And men?"

"Men? Who knows?" said her mother. "They drink, they gamble, they do so many other things," she said, laughing. "Remember, even God doesn't allow the great huge sun out in the night because he's a male."

Hearing this, Lupe laughed, too, remembering the saying that God didn't allow the sun out after dark because he was a male and scared of the unknown; he'd upset the harmony of the stars who were, of course, all females and at peace, even in darkness.

Walking home that night, holding hands, Lupe felt closer to her mother than she'd felt in years. But then, arriving, they found that the Indians were still chanting in front of the *ramada* and Ojos Puros was still shouting about Sophia's death and the evils of gold.

Instantly, without hesitation, Lupe saw her mother turn into a mighty she-boar willing to do battle to the devil himself, and she rushed forward, ripping down the three hanging chickens and yelling at the chanting Indians.

"Stop it! Stop it!" she shouted. "Sophia isn't dead! And we have no evil spirits in this home! Get out! Get out! We are good, God-loving people! We have done no wrong!"

"No, you must understand! Your daughter died because of the gold!" yelled Ojos Puros. "You must repent!"

"No! Sophia is alive! And we have nothing to repent! Nothing! Get out of my home! In the name of the Lord God, I will not permit you here!"

And Lupe couldn't believe it, before her very eyes she saw her dear old mother become so huge, so powerful that she pushed Ojos Puros and the Indians out of their home, shouting and yelling until her mighty voice echoed up to the towering cathedral rocks.

Four days later, Don Victor finally began to move about. Doña Guadalupe decided that they'd go out of the canyon while she was still strong. Doña Manza and her family decided to go out, too, but a few days earlier so they wouldn't be a big group and could get out of the mountains without being noticed.

The day Doña Manza was ready to leave, Don Victor explained to her and her two sons where the river was low and how to get across it.

Lupe gave Manuelita a big *abrazo*. "Oh, I only wish we could all go out together!"

"No, it's better this way," said Manuelita, drying her eyes. "If we all went together, we'd attract too much attention."

"True," said Lupe. "But what if we never see each other again?"

"We will," said Manuelita, hugging Lupe again. "With the help *de Dios*, we'll always be close, Lupe."

Lupe and Manuelita cried together, feeling so scared of being separated. Lupe walked her friend and her family to the canyon's end. There, Lupe watched her best friend disappear down the overgrown trail into the vastness of the jungle. Everyone was gone now. Only Lupe and her family and the Indians were left in the canyon.

The following day, Lupe climbed up over the north rim of the canyon with Cruz to tell her Colonel goodbye. Getting to the pile of flat rocks, Lupe's eyes filled with tears. She and Cruz rebuilt the little altar that the wind and rain had eroded. Then they gathered flowers and placed them on the altar and knelt down to pray.

An eagle flew overhead, letting out a screeching scream.

"That's the spirit of my great grandfather, Don Espirito," said Cruz. "His remains were also buried in this same pile of flat rocks."

"No, really?!" said Lupe excitedly. "Well, then, when you come up to visit your great grandfather, you can keep my Colonel's altar for me, too, until I return."

"Then you'll be coming back for sure?" said Cruz.

"Of course," said Lupe. "This is our home. And when I return, I want to see you reading well."

"I promise," said Cruz, feeling so important to be entrusted with the altar of Lupe's love.

But walking home that afternoon, Lupe wondered if, indeed, she'd ever return. A part of her felt as if they'd never come back.

Then it was the morning that they were to go out. They were all packed, but Lupe just couldn't figure out how to protect her Colonel's card and her other treasures for the long journey. Finally, she called her brother aside.

"Look," she said, "I know how much of a hurry we're in, but could you please help me build a box to put my special treasures in?"

Seeing how anxious his sister was, Victoriano pulled some boards off their home and built a little box no bigger than two fists.

Quickly, Lupe put her Colonel's card, the red ribbon for her wedding dress, and her rosary inside the box. Then she wrapped the box in the blanket that she'd carry her clothes in.

They were all ready to go when the old midwife came to get the milk goats that they'd given her. Ojos Puros and the Indians came to tell them goodbye and get whatever else there was left behind.

It became a time of wet eyes and big *abrazos*, then they were on their way—Maria, Esabel and their child, Lupe, Victoriano, and their parents. Don Victor was leading Don Tiburcio's little white mule up the rocky trail to the main road when, suddenly, Doña Guadalupe yelled.

"No!" she said. "I can't go!"

Lupe almost screamed with joy, not wanting to go, either.

"But what are you saying?" said Don Victor, taking off his straw hat and throwing it on the ground. "You're sending me to damnation, woman! It was you who said we had to go before we lost all hope!" He began jumping up and down on his hat, crushing it.

"Yes, I know," she said sadly. "But I just can't leave. I need to take something with me to keep our canyon in my heart."

"All right," he said, trying to keep calm. "I can understand that. But what is it you want, my dear?" he asked through his teeth.

"The smell, the feel . . . my lilies!" said his wife. "My white mountain lilies!" And she put down her load. "Help me, quick! We'll take my lilies! They smell of the canyon!"

"But we can't take them!" shouted Don Victor, losing all patience. "Each of us is already packed with more than he can carry!"

"I'll carry them for Mama," said Victoriano.

"Me, too," said Maria.

"I'll dig them up for you," said Lupe.

Don Victor shook his fist at the heavens. "Give me patience, dear God! And right now!"

The sun was five fists off the jagged horizon when they were ready to go once more. Don Victor was in the lead with the little white mule, and Esabel and Victoriano and Lupe were in the rear with their mother. Maria was in the middle and she had her child strapped to her back.

"Don't look back," said Don Victor as they came to the canyon's mouth. "Please, I'm warning all of you, don't, or you'll be crying for the whole first day!"

But no one could help themselves. And when Lupe looked back, she saw the luscious green growth at the bottom of the canyon and splashes of colorful wildflowers up on the *barrancas*. And in the distance, the towering, gigantic cathedral rocks, reaching for the sky. Then, there came a cloud of dancing color, flying into the canyons—tens of millions of butterflies, filling the canyon in a dancing tapestry of light, dazzling the early morning sunlight in flashing colors of red and orange and bright gold.

"Look!" yelled Lupe, making the sign of the cross over her heart.

"God is with us," said their mother. "He's come to tell us goodbye."

They all knelt down to pray, giving their thanks to the Almighty, then they got to their feet and started down the trail.

Tears streamed down Lupe's face as she walked on, her head down, forehead pushing against the shawl that was strapped to her basket. The silent tears continued to run down her cheeks as each step took her farther and farther from home—from the memories of her goats, her pet deer, her Colonel and the old midwife and El Borracho and the little Indian girls. She walked on, head bent down, stepping quickly, as they picked up the pace and took the first turn in the overgrown trail. And then it was all jungle, nothing but jungle. Birds and insects everywhere. Lupe walked on, passing snakes and lizards and wide trails of huge red ants.

It was late afternoon when they came to the cliffs called the Gateway Del Diablo on this side of the great father river of El Urique. The right eye of God was going down behind the cliffs and the fading light was tricky, holding between the long, dark shadows.

"Careful, very careful," said Don Victor to all of them. "When we go on these cliffs Del Diablo, I want you all to stay close. There's a lot of loose rock, and so pay attention so you don't fall."

Starting around the first bend, Lupe was truly amazed that Don Tiburcio and their father had made this trip so often without ever getting hurt. The trail was nothing but a crack in the rock, and the river was more than three thousand feet below them. At each bend, Don Victor told them to look out for this rock and that batch of loose gravel.

It was almost dark when the wind picked up. Lupe began to feel deep cramps in the middle of her stomach. Her head went dizzy and she struggled to keep up. But she was in such pain that she started falling behind. Coming around the last bend on the trail, a huge valley lay ahead. Lupe gasped, momentarily forgetting her pain. This was the first time in her life that she'd ever seen flat country.

"We made it," said Don Victor, pushing back his hat proudly. "There's a little *ranchería* up ahead by the river where we can sleep, and in the morning they'll help us across on a raft. But we have to hurry if we want to get there before dark," he added.

Doña Guadalupe got hold of the little white mule's tail, and they continued down the wider, soft dirt trail.

But Lupe just wasn't able to keep up, no matter how hard she tried. The terrible pain in her stomach now took her legs away. Still, she said nothing and tried her best to stay with her family. But the aching of her stomach just grew, making her want to vomit. Her head went dizzy, and the pain drove down into her body with a terrible force. Suddenly, Lupe felt herself break inside, and a thick wetness seeped down between her legs. She touched herself through her coarse cotton dress, looking in horror at her blood-soaked fingers. She cried out in fear, but no sounds came out; she fell to the soft, warm earth.

Victoriano was the first one to notice that his little sister was missing and he ran back. Maria came, too.

"I'm dying!" said Lupe, showing them the blood when they came up.

"Oh, no, Lupita," said her older sister, squatting down next to her. "You've just become a woman, you poor child."

Breathing hard, Doña Guadalupe and Don Victor came rushing up, too. Victoriano took off his shirt and went down to the river.

Maria and Doña Guadalupe helped Lupe to her feet and took her off the road to the privacy of the thick foliage. Birds, ants and insects were everywhere. Victoriano came back and handed his mother his wet shirt. Doña Guadalupe thanked him and told him to go and stay with his father and Esabel.

"Oh, *mi hijita*," said Doña Guadalupe, feeling terrible, "I just had no idea you'd grown so much. I should have prepared you like I did your other sisters but, well, I just didn't, I'm sorry to say."

The sun was going down beyond the short, little rolling hills in the flat distance. Maria and their mother helped Lupe take off her dress so they could wash it in the river before going on.

That night after eating, they all prayed alongside the river's edge. They could hear soft guitar music coming from the ranch house across the water. Lupe felt so tired and worn out that she could barely keep awake.

Putting her little straw mat on the soft earth by the riverbank, Lupe lay down by her mother's side, feeling so warm and good being with her mother. She looked out on the water and she saw that the moonlight and the stars were dancing on the flat surface of the river. She listened to the small waves slapping the banks of the great father river, and she absolutely knew for sure that she was now a woman, capable of having children.

Tears came to her eyes and she cuddled up close to her mother's warm plump body, listening to the river rushing past them, filled with stars and moonlight. She dreamed, thinking of her mother's crying tree and the great cathedral rocks and how the human heart never broke. No, it just regrew with life like the mighty oak and the wildflowers that came back each Spring. Lupe slept, dreaming, knowing that the truelove of her youth was gone, as was their beloved canyon, and a whole new life was about to begin—she continued dreaming, dreaming, dreaming of life, the dream.

FOUR

EVEN GOD NEEDS HELP

"**O**kay," said Epitacio as he and Juan came walking down the busy street of Douglas, Arizona, "I feel lucky! Let's have a drink and double our paychecks!"

Juan and Epitacio had been working at the Copper Queen Mining Company for over a month and they'd just been paid.

"All right, whatever you say," said Juan, feeling good about his brother-in-law who'd returned across the border to get them.

But Epitacio got drunk and lost both of their paychecks, then he refused to go home with Juan. The next day Epitacio didn't show up for work. Rumor had it that he'd taken off, gone back to Mexico.

Juan wasn't able to support his family by working only one shift at the Copper Queen, so he decided to change his name to Juan Cruz and get a second job on the night shift. After all, he was going on thirteen. He figured that he could hold down both shifts.

But, getting into line that night, one guy recognized Juan. His name was Tomas. He was seventeen years old and he had been in the poolhall the night Epitacio lost both of their paychecks.

Quickly, Juan winked at Tomas, signaling for him to keep still and not let on that he knew him. And it went easier than Juan had expected. Hell, the big, thick-necked *gringo* boss couldn't tell him apart from all the other Mexicans.

"Hey, Juan," said Tomas, once they were inside the smelter. Molten ore moved all about them in great kettles. "You want to make some extra money?"

"Sure," shouted Juan above the noise of the smelter. "Why the hell you think I'm working a second shift? Because I love the smell of wet armpits?"

"Well, then, meet me at midnight on our taco break," winked the handsome young man. "And I'll show you a fine trick."

"Sure thing!" yelled Juan. So they met at midnight and ate together and Tomas explained to Juan the plan. First, they'd put a sack of copper ore alongside the outside fence so they could steal it later; then the next day, they'd sell it in town to an American engineer.

"How much we gonna make?" asked Juan.

Tomas had to smile. He liked his young friend's greed. "Oh, maybe six dollars each," he said.

"Six dollars!" shouted Juan. He only made a dollar for an eight hour shift as it was. "That's a fortune!" But then he thought again and he became suspicious. "Wait," he said, "just how do you know about this *gringo* engineer, anyway?" Juan was only twelve, but he had forty years' worth of experience.

"Buddy," said the tall, good-looking young man, rolling his eyes to the heavens with great style, "I got my means." And he laughed a good, full, manly laugh, and Juan believed him.

They did it, and it worked beautifully. The next day they sold the ore to the American engineer in town for six dollars each. But, the following night, as they came up alongside the fence to do the same thing again, the lights came on and they were surrounded by sixteen armed men. The American engineer that they'd sold the ore to had set them up. He also worked for the Copper Queen. They were immediately taken to town, tried, found guilty and taken to Tombstone, Arizona.

"But I'm only twelve years old!" screamed Juan. "And my family will starve without me!"

"Shhhhhhh!" said Tomas. "You tell them that and they'll send you to a boys' place, and I won't be able to protect you! I got a plan. You just keep quiet and stick by me!"

So Juan stuck by his friend, saying he was eighteen, and that night in Tombstone, he saw what his friend's plan was. When the other prisoners saw them, and they came on them like wolves to rape the sheep, Tomas turned his ass up at them so they wouldn't beat him.

"Not me! You son-of-a-bitches!" bellowed Juan with all his might. "I'm from Los Altos de Jalisco! I'll castrate the first *puto cabrón* who touches me!"

That night, shooting broke out in front of the jailhouse, and a terrible explosion blew out the back wall. A Mexican on horseback yelled "*Vámonos, Aguilar!*" Prisoners ran every which way as a dozen horsemen continued shooting. They had their brother on a horse, and they took off. Everyone else was left standing there, naked as plucked turkeys under the cold, night sky.

Instantly Juan took off on foot after the horsemen through the *arroyo* behind the jail. He ran uphill all night. And daybreak found him at the foot of a great mountain. But in the distance, there came a dozen armed horsemen, cracking leather. He took off as fast as he could through the cactus. It was his birthday, August eighteenth, 1916. He was thirteen years old, but the only presents the *gringos* brought him were well-placed bullets singing by his ears. Finally, they caught him, beat him, tied him to a horse and dragged him back to town.

By the time his mother, two sisters, his nephew and two nieces finally found out what had happened to him, Juan was in the Arizona State Penitentiary at Florence, Arizona.

His mother cried and cried. Luisa screamed and cursed and banged her head. Emilia couldn't stop coughing, and his nephew and nieces wept hysterically.

Then, the rich Mexican from Sonora, who'd driven Juan's family to the penitentiary to visit him, asked to speak to Juan alone.

"Juan," said the tall and thin old man once they were alone, "your mother is a wonderful lady. She's nursed me back to health with herbs and massage. I love her dearly, and I regard you as my own son."

Juan almost laughed at the stooped-over old man. Why, the son-of-a-bitch was an even smoother talker than the big bastard who'd converted Tomas into a woman.

"You see, Juan, I have a very high-spirited son like you. And I love him and I'd do anything for him. But you see, *mi hijito* killed a Texas Ranger." The dignified old man began to cry, leaning on his gold-headed cane. "I've been told that it was an honest battle, but the *americanos* don't see it that way and they're going to execute him."

Juan's heart came to his eyes. "I sympathize with you, *señor*," he said.

"I'm glad to hear that," said the old man, "because, well, I have a proposition to make you. I'll give your mother, God bless her soul, two hundred dollars in American money if you confess to the crime my son committed."

Juan couldn't believe his ears. He felt like spitting in the old man's face. Hell, he only had six years to serve for stealing the six dollars worth of ore. But for murder, shit, man, son-of-a-gringo-bitch, he'd be executed or be in for life.

"Calm down," said the old man, "please, and listen to my whole proposition. After all, they already have you locked up, so how much more can happen to you?"

Juan calmed down and looked into the eyes of the old man who, it was said, owned more cattle in the State of Sonora than the rails had ties.

"Your mother, look at her," he continued, "see how desperate she is. This is a terrible time for us *mejicanos*." He went on and on, and Juan didn't curse him and send him packing—as the *gringos* said—but, instead, he listened and looked at his mother and sisters and nephew and nieces over there by the far wall. Finally, Juan pulled down into his gut with all the power of his balls, his *tanates*, and spoke.

"Make it five hundred in gold!"

And so the deal was made, and a new trial was set for the murderer of the famous Mexican-killing Texas Ranger of Douglas, Arizona. Juan Salvador Villaseñor—known as Juan Cruz—was found guilty and was sentenced to life imprisonment.

The big, fat Mexican cook from Guadalajara was the best man with a knife in the penitentiary at Florence, Arizona. He took Juan under his wing because they were both from Jalisco.

Two years before, the Mexican cook had won a lot of money in a poker game in Bisbee, Arizona. But then he'd been walking home when the three *gringos* that he had won the money from jumped him outside of town.

He was fat, so they'd made the very bad mistake of thinking that he was slow. Two died instantly, and the big Mexican had the third one down on the ground, ready to cut his throat, but the *gringo* kept crying for his life so much that the big Mexican finally decided to let him live on the promise that he'd admit to the authorities the following day that it had been a fair fight. But the next day, the third *gringo* went back on his word, saying that a dozen armed Mexicans had cut him and killed his two unarmed friends.

"So you see, Juan," said the fat cook, "I got life because I was soft in the head. If I'd killed him, no one would've fingered me."

The fat cook found out that Juan didn't know how to read, and he explained to Juan the power of the written word. "Look," he said, "the Mexican Revolution didn't start with Villa or Zapata, as so many people think. No, it started with the power of the words written by my friend, Ricardo Flores Magon. I heard from Flores Magon that if a man can't read and write, he's nothing but a little *puto* weakling!"

And so, there in the penitentiary, Juan's education began. He didn't want to be a *puto* weakling, so he worked hard at learning to read. His earthly body was locked up, but his mind was set free as a young eagle soaring through the heavens. The fat cook became his teacher, and Juan loved it. Juan ate better than he'd eaten in years, and life was wonderful except for the days when his mother came to visit him. Then Juan wanted out. He couldn't stand to see his mother's tears.

A year later, a new road camp was started outside of Safford, Arizona, near Turkey Flat, and prisoners got to volunteer. The big, fat cook warned Juan not to go because there'd be no guards with them at night and other prisoners would be sure to gang up on him and rape him like a female dog.

"Don't worry," said Juan, "I can take care of myself."

"But your reputation of having killed that Ranger won't protect you there," said the big cook. "Believe me, it's been my wing that's kept you from the fate that got your friend Tomas."

Tomas was now being bought and sold like a woman all over the prison to anyone who had the makings for half a dozen cigarettes. They'd knocked his teeth out and painted his ass for better service, it was said.

Juan looked at the big cook for a long time without speaking. "I'm going," he said. "It's my only chance to escape and stop my mother's tears."

"All right," said the big cook, "then good luck to you. And always remember, *un hombre aprevenido* is a man alive. A guarded man is a man who's wary, cautious, and lives life as if he's lived it many times before."

"I'll remember," said Juan, "*aprevenido*."

"Yes," said the big cook, and they shook hands, taking each other in a big *abrazo* like men do, and said farewell.

Five days later, Juan Salvador was in a Ford truck along with four other men chained by their feet to the bars of the iron cage. Two of the other prisoners were black-skinned, full-blooded Yaqui Indians with eyes as sharp as knives. Immediately, Juan liked them and he found out that they'd been put in prison for ten years for eating an army mule.

Getting to Turkey Flat, it turned out just as the big, fat cook had said it would. During the day they had armed guards on horseback all around them as they worked on the road over the mountain; but during the night, when they were locked up behind the barbed-wire fence, there were no guards with them.

The things Juan learned in the first three nights were so awful—so completely inhuman—they would haunt him for the rest of his life. Here, men were worse than mad dogs. When he wouldn't let them rape him, they beat him, with clubs; then they courted him with flowers as if he were a woman. When that didn't work, either, the big German pit boss and the black snake came at Juan in the night. But Juan was *aprevenido*, and he got the pit boss in the eyes with boiling coffee, but not before his big, black friend cut Juan's stomach open with a knife.

The last thing Juan remembered was the smell of his own intestines coming out of his stomach, between his fingers, as he desperately tried pushing the whole slippery mess back inside himself.

When Juan came to, he was in the tent hospital, and the big German and his friend were tied down to the beds next to him. They were screaming, foaming at the mouth, and straining against their ropes with all their might. The guards had castrated them, and blood covered their thighs. Juan pretended he was still unconscious and lay there quietly.

Later that same day, they brought in the two Yaqui Indians who'd been poisoned with canned food. For two weeks, Juan drifted in and out of death. The German raved and screamed. The big black died. The Indians never made a sound. Then one day, just at dusk, Juan heard the two Indians whispering, and they slipped away. Quickly, Juan got up and crawled after them.

"Turn to stone," one Indian said to him as they got out the door. He did as they told him, squatting down, and they were stones.

The guards walked right by, searching for them, but they didn't see them. Then the armed men saddled horses and took off after them. But they never moved. They just sat there, squatted to the earth like stone, moving a little and then a little more as they went down the mountainside and, finally, took to the creek.

For seven days and nights they walked and hid and ran. Juan never knew how they did it, but they'd turn into stone anytime anyone came near them.

Near Douglas, Arizona, Juan left the two Yaquis and went to church, waiting all day until his mother showed up for her daily prayers. They hugged and kissed, then she told him the news that his blind sister Emilia had died. They wept and prayed for Emilia to regain her sight in heaven. Then his mother got him a change of clothes and Juan took the name of his grandfather, Pio Castro. He immediately signed up with fifty other Mexicans to go north to work at the Copper Queen in Montana.

In Montana, Juan and his Mexican companions were put in with thousands of Greeks and Turks. The Greeks had never seen any Mexicans before and so, when they heard the other Mexicans call Juan "Chino" because of his curly hair, they thought he was Chinese, so they named him Sam Lee.

Sam Lee became Juan's official name. He lived among the Greeks and Turks for two years, working for the Cooper Queen Mining Company in the winter, the railroad during the spring, and in the sugar beet fields during the harvest.

Then one day, a huge, brutally handsome Turk came to their camp. That night he stopped a fight between two men just by staring them down.

Immediately, Juan took a liking to this formidable-looking man of granite. He watched him set up a poker game that weekend and take everyone's money fair and square. The big man noticed Juan watching him and hired him to clean up the tables for him. They became fast friends. The big man's name was Duel. He told Juan that his mother had been Greek and his father a Turk.

"Here, inside the heart," he told Juan when they went out for dinner, "are the greatest battles a real man can fight. Blood to blood, a war is going on inside me that's ten thousand years old! The Greeks and Turks are mortal enemies! And I'm half and half, just like you with your Indian and European blood!"

Hungrily, he talked to Juan all night long, telling him of Greece and Turkey and the history of that part of the world. It was the first time in all his life that Juan had ever come close to a man who not only wasn't a Catholic, but readily admitted that he didn't believe in God.

Hearing this, Juan opened up his heart, too, and he sadly told the Greek-Turk how he, too, had left God at the Rio Grande.

"I knew it," said Duel, "the first moment I laid eyes on you. I said to myself, 'That boy, he's been to hell and back.' For no real man like us can believe in the puppet-God of the churches. The devil, yes, of course, but not God!"

And so that winter, Duel set up a gambling room in the basement of the best whorehouse in Butte, which was owned by a famous English woman named Katherine. Duel made Juan his protege, teaching him the art of taking money from the greedy workmen who drank too much.

For the first time in his life, Juan saw cards as a solid business. He now realized that he and Epitacio had never had a chance in the world to double their paychecks back in Douglas. Why, he and Duel took money hand over fist every night, giving free liquor to the big losers and maybe even a girl.

And the famous lady Katherine took her share, too. Over and over again, Duel explained to Juan that all of life was a gamble and so, "At gambling," he said, "a real man must be king!"

But there were problems. Especially with the local cowboys who didn't like foreigners taking their money. One night there was a bad knife fight. A big, powerful, raw-boned cowboy was going to cut up a girl that he blamed for losing all his money when, to everyone's surprise, Juan just stepped in, disarming the big cowboy with a number twenty-two cue stick, and knocked him unconscious.

Katherine quickly gave the cowboy's two friends each a free girl and the tension broke. That night, after closing up, Katherine called Juan to her private room and thanked him for his quick action. The next day, she had her hair dresser cut Juan's wild-looking curly hair, then sent him to her private tailor.

Coming out of the tailor's shop wearing a new suit, Juan would never forget, as long as he lived, what happened when he saw his reflection in the window in downtown Butte, Montana. Why, he didn't even recognize himself, he looked so handsome and civilized.

That night back at the house, he was taken aside by Katherine once again, who presented him to the young girl whom he had saved. Her name was Lily, and she was beautiful. She was so grateful that he had saved her life that all night she purred to him like a kitten in love, teaching him things of the human body that he had never dreamed.

The next morning, he was taken in hand by the English woman again. They had tea together on fine china, and she spent the whole morning explaining to Juan the mysteries of life, love, women and good manners.

In the next year, Juan and Katherine became very close, and Juan came to respect her as the smartest and toughest woman he had ever known—except, of course, for his own mother—and she wasn't even Catholic.

But then Duel began to grow jealous of their friendship and one dark night, Duel got drunk and accused Juan and Katherine of cheating him out of some money. Juan denied it. But still, Duel drew his gun. The next thing Juan Salvador Villaseñor did was something he'd never stop regretting for the rest of his life. He had loved Duel, he really had, like his own father.

A few months later, Juan got a telegram from his sister Luisa in California, saying that if he wished to see his mother alive again, he'd better come home immediately.

The day that Juan left Montana by train, all the land was white. Only the tallest trees poked up through the blanket of snow.

Both Katherine and Lily stood at the depot, seeing him off. The year was 1922, and Juan Salvador was nineteen years old, but he looked more like twenty-five. He was well dressed, had a moustache, and the aura of a very cautious man, a man who'd lived many lifetimes.

"I'll be waiting!" called Lily.

"I'll be back!" said Juan.

Katherine only watched him go, following him carefully with her eyes.

14

*And so he thought he'd died and gone to heaven,
smelling the orange blossoms and seeing the sky so blue
and warm and beautiful.*

It was a long, cold, miserable train ride, coming down from Montana. It was Christmas day the morning that Juan Salvador came into the Los Angeles train depot.

Juan was wearing a hat and fur-lined gloves and the great overcoat that Katherine had specially made for him. Glancing around, Juan couldn't believe his eyes. Why, it was the dead of winter and, yet, it was as warm as summertime in California.

Taking off his overcoat, Juan breathed in the warmth, feeling it go all the way to his bones. He hailed a taxi, giving the driver his mother's address in Corona. For the next hour, Juan sat back in the cab and looked at the luscious orchards of oranges and lemons on both sides of the road and the great, rich fields of produce.

He lit up a long cigar and breathed in the fragrance of the land. This was, indeed, the most beautiful country that he'd seen since he and his family had been forced to leave their beloved mountains of Los Altos de Jalisco.

"Tell me," said Juan in good English to the cab driver, "is it usually this warm or is this an unusual day?"

"Where you from?" asked the small, dark-skinned Anglo.

"Montana," said Juan Salvador.

"Well, then for you, mister," said the man, "it's always this warm! Montana, man, that's cold up there! Myself, I'm from New Jersey! Came out here last year to visit my brother, and stayed! To hell with those cold winters, I say!"

"You bet," said Juan Salvador, smoking his cigar.

The small, dark driver continued talking in a fast-sounding strange English, but Juan quit paying attention. He looked out the window and thought of Katherine and Lily and Duel and all that he'd learned up there. Montana had been the greatest teacher that he'd ever had. Montana had gotten him away from his own *gente* and showed him a whole new way of looking at *la vida*.

Getting to Corona, Juan noticed the well-paved streets of the American side of town, and then he saw the rutted dirt road as they entered the Mexican side of town. Coming into the *barrio* was like entering a different country. The houses were tiny, run-down, and there were chickens and pigs and goats running loose in the street. The driver had to honk at a mother pig and her five little piglets to get by.

Juan laughed. It never failed to amaze him how different his people were from the Anglos. *Los mejicanos* never wasted anything. Instead of green grass in front of their homes, they had vegetable gardens. And they didn't fence in their livestock, but let them roam free so they could eat anything they could find. Instead, they fenced in their crops.

Juan had never understood the Anglos' reasoning of fencing in their animals that could roam, and leaving the crops, that could not move, free.

Looking out his window, Juan saw that *la gente* were staring at him. He wondered if his mother and Luisa would recognize him. He had been nothing but a kid when he'd escaped from prison. He hadn't even started to shave yet. And now he had a big moustache, fine clothes, and had to shave twice a day if he wanted to keep a smooth face.

He suddenly remembered Luisa's telegram, and he wondered if his mother was even alive. Oh, how he'd loved that worn-out, old sack of Indian bones; his mother had been his everything!

Goats ran everywhere as the cab driver came up to the last two little houses at the end of the block. There were four half-naked children playing in the mud between the two houses. Juan smiled, remembering how much he'd always enjoyed playing in the wet corn fields back home when he'd been a child, feeling the itchy-good soil between his toes. He wondered if any of these children were Luisa's. He knew she'd had another child after he'd gone to prison.

Putting out his cigar, Juan stepped out of the cab into the warm sunshine. Across the street, two old Mexicans with machetes at their sides watched him from under their big hats. But Juan felt no worries; he was armed, too. Ever since he'd started working for Duel, he'd been carrying a .38 snub-nose under his belt.

He reached into the front pocket of his well-tailored pants, bringing out a wad of money. All the children stopped playing and stared at him.

"Well," said the taxi driver, coming around with Juan's luggage, "this is the address you gave me, but maybe you better check and make sure before I go." He seemed a little nervous.

"That's not necessary," said Juan.

"You sure?" asked the man.

"Yeah, I'm Mexican, too," said Juan.

The man's eyes widened.

Juan laughed. "How much?"

"Fifteen dollars," said the man.

Juan peeled off a twenty. "Keep the change," he said.

"Thanks!" said the cab driver. "Any time you need me, just call!"

Juan watched him drive off, then turned around. All the children were still staring at him.

A large goat rounded the corner, racing fast, with a young boy holding onto the rope tied around the goat's neck. The goat had horns and he turned and charged the boy, hitting him in the gut. But the boy was tough and only laughed, wrestling the goat to the ground. Seeing the boy's face as he looked up, Juan instantly recognized him. It was Luisa's oldest son, Jose. He was the spitting image of his father, Jose-Luis, a man whom Juan had loved very much.

"*Buenos días, José*," said Juan to the boy, feeling a strangeness come to his tongue as he formed the Spanish words, "*¿Dónde está Doña Margarita o tu mamá Luisa?*" Juan had to lick his lips to speak. His tongue just didn't seem to remember how to speak Spanish. It took more movement of the entire mouth than to speak English.

The boy said nothing. He just held his ground, regarding Juan suspiciously.

Picking up his luggage, Juan came closer. "*¿Qué tal?*" he said to the boy. "I'm your *tío* Juan. I used to take care of a hundred goats back in Los Altos when I was your age."

Suddenly, the rear door of the front house opened with a bang and a powerful-looking woman with a knife in her hand came out. "You leave my children alone!" she bellowed.

Juan started to laugh. She'd aged and gained weight, but he still recognized her. "Luisa," he said, "I haven't seen you in six years, and you come at me with a machete?"

Luisa closed her mouth, staring at him, then she let out a blood-curdling scream and came racing off the steps.

"Oh, Juan!" she cried, knife still in hand. "Juan!" And she grabbed him in her arms, yanking him off the ground. "You've grown so much, just look at you! These clothes, and that taxi, what did you do—rob a bank? I couldn't believe my eyes when I saw that taxi come up to our house. I thought it was the sheriff!"

She had tears in her eyes—she was so excited. "Come," she said, wiping her eyes, "Mama's been praying all week that you'd get here by Christmas."

"Is she going to live?" he asked.

"To live?" screamed Luisa. "Hell, she's going to see us all to our grave!"

"But in the telegram you said to hurry home if I wished to see her alive."

"Oh, that!" said Luisa excitedly. "I didn't mean to scare you, but Mama insisted, saying it was the only way to get you home for Christmas! And she was right! Here you are!"

They walked past the larger house to the little shack in back. "Mama lives in back," said Luisa. "She talks too much. That's why we turned the goat shed into a house for her."

Juan laughed. "And you, you hardly talk, eh?"

Luisa stopped dead in her tracks, whirling about with the big knife. "You trying to start trouble?"

Juan didn't know what to say. Here he was, only back for two minutes, and his sister was already threatening him with a knife. "Oh, no," he said, laughing. "I'm not trying to start trouble, Luisa."

"Good," she said, relaxing her grip on the knife, "so now wait here while I go in and warn Mama. I don't want her dropping dead now that you've come back from the dead."

Luisa opened the door of the goat shed. And in the long, thin spears of light coming in through the cracks between the thick, wooden planks of the shack, Juan could see that there was a little wood-burning stove by the far wall, and a small mattress on a bed of box springs to the side of the stove. The whole place smelled of dust and smoke and decay.

Juan watched his sister cross the room, passing through the spears of light with floating particles of glistening dust to the bed of box springs. Then, to his surprise, she bent over, talking to a tiny bundle of dark, flat blankets.

The blankets moved and Juan saw two little cat eyes peer toward him from under the covers. Instantly, he knew that the tiny bundle was none other than his beloved mother! Tears came bursting to Juan's eyes, and he rushed across the shack, taking his old mother in his arms.

"Mama!" he yelled.

"¡Mi hijito!" she said.

They hugged and kissed, and their eyes filled with tears. The children came to the doorway and watched.

"The only thing that's kept me alive, mi hijito," said the old woman, trembling, "is the promise that I made you in the desert, that I'd live to see you grow big and married."

"Yes, I remember, Mama," he said, tears streaming down his face. "And you did it!"

"Yes, you're big now," she said, "but I still have to see you married, and I don't have much time. ¡Júrame! Promise me that you'll never leave me again!"

"But, Mama, I have a business in Montana. I can't just—"

"Don't you dare speak to me about business!" she said. "You are my son, my last-born child, and you were robbed from me when you had to flee and I didn't get to see you grow into manhood before my very eyes!

"Look at you, a fully-grown man! A giant compared to me, and I didn't have the joy to see it happen. Oh, you must never, never, never leave me again! ¡Júrame! ¡Júrame! Promise me that you'll never do anything to have to leave me again!"

"All right, Mama," he said, tears pouring down his face. "¡Te lo juro! ¡Te lo juro! With all my heart! I'll never leave you again!"

And so they hugged in a big *abrazo*, mother and son, heart-to-heart, and all of Juan's years in prison and in Montana suddenly vanished. He was home at last, back in his mother's arms—his most perfect love in all the world. But still, a big part of him knew that he should return to the north where he had a fine business waiting for him, playing cards in the back room of the best house with the finest women in all of Montana.

That afternoon, Jose killed the big goat and they dug a hole in the ground for the *barbacoa*, and all the people from the barrio came to celebrate. It was a time of wet eyes and big *abrazos*. They, too, had been separated from many of their loved ones because of the Revolution.

The celebration lasted long into the night—people crying, laughing, rejoicing—and then they all left, going home. Juan, Luisa, and his old mother sat down together in the kitchen, still talking, still eating, still drinking terrible bootleg whiskey.

"And little Inocenta?" asked Juan. "What became of her?"

"She married," said their mother, getting up to go to the outhouse. "Oh, this whiskey is awful! It kills!"

"Married? But she's only a child!" said Juan.

"Oh, no!" said Luisa. "She's a woman! Taller than me! And she and her kids live with her parents, Lucha and Tomas."

"Lucha?" yelled Juan. "You mean that you've seen those bastards? They abandoned us like dogs in Mexico!"

Lucha was the sister who'd left them back in Mexico with the soldiers who'd raped Emilia.

"Quiet down," said Luisa, glancing at the door where their mother had gone. "We found them in Bisbee, starving to death after you went to prison. And Mama, well, she didn't want you to know."

"Why?"

"Well, because," said Luisa, "you know the money that you got for us when you sold yourself? Well, she gave some of it to Lucha and Tomas."

Juan rammed his fist into his mouth. "But I did that to help you and Mama; not those bastards!"

Lusia nodded. "Yes, I know, Juan," she said. "But what can you do? A mother's love sees no wrong when it comes to helping her children."

"And the money that I've been sending you from Montana?" he asked.

"It's gone, too," she said. "We used some to live on, and Mama gave the rest to Lucha and Tomas."

Juan's whole chest came up. "I'm going to kill them," he said, getting to his feet. "Right now. Where are they?"

"Don't even think that," said Luisa. "Killing them won't help anyone."

"Yes, it will," he said. "It will help me!"

Juan was up so high, flying with such rage, that it frightened Luisa. But

then their mother came back inside and Juan tried to calm down. He asked
about the rest of their family. But it was very difficult.

"And Domingo?" asked Juan. Domingo was the brother that Juan had
grown up with, and he missed him dearly.

Doña Margarita sat down. "Only the Lord God knows," she said. "Every
new *mejicano* we meet, we ask them about Domingo and they ask us for their
lost ones, too."

"But," said Luisa, "we have heard about our cousins."

"Which ones?" asked Juan anxiously. Half of their cousins had been
raised in their home and were more like brothers and sisters than cousins.

"Everardo and two of his younger brothers," said Luisa. "And supposedly Everardo lives here in California, too."

"And how did you find this out?" asked Juan.

Luisa glanced at their mother.

"Well, go ahead," said the old lady. "You started it, you finish it."

Luisa really didn't want to, but she could see no other way. "Well," she
said, "right after you went to prison, just before we got that money, we ran
across Everardo's younger brother, Agustin. And he saw how desperate we
were so he took off his coat, putting it over Emilia and her child who were
sick from hunger. He cried and cried, telling us that he was on his way to see
Everardo who lived in California, but that he'd first stay and get a job to help
us." She strained to not cry. "But, well, Juan, he only ate the last of our food
and . . ." She couldn't go on.

"Don't tell me!" yelled Juan. "He ate your food and never came back!"

Luisa nodded, tears running down her face. Her two sons came to her
side, giving her comfort.

"And you weren't going to tell me, were you?" bellowed Juan, leaping to
his feet once again and the muscles of his neck coming up like ropes.

Luisa shook her head and her boys hugged her, feeling frightened of their
uncle.

"That son-of-a-bitch!" continued Juan. "After eating our food all those
years, sleeping with us, being our brother, then he stole our sister Lucha,
abusing her, and now he sees you starving and he eats your food and runs.
My God, is there no justice? I swear it, only Everardo was any good from all
that family!"

"*Mi hijito*," said their mother, "they were good people, too. Agustin just
got scared because he saw our situation so desperate."

"Mama!" screamed Juan. "Don't say that! I sold myself for murder so
you could eat!"

"But," she said, "was I able to eat that food? No, it was food stained with
the blood of your soul."

Juan was stunned. He stared at his old mother, hating her words, filled
with rage and frustration.

"Oh, *mi hijito*," said the old lady, seeing his insane anger, "I love you so
much. And I'm so happy to have you back. But please, let's stop all this and

rejoice. You are my love. And you must promise me never to do such a thing again. Money comes and goes, but the blood of our soul is eternal. You had no right to sell yourself. God would've shown us another way."

And so they hugged and kissed and wept together, but still Juan felt betrayed. He'd sacrificed so much and his mother made light of it. A part of him felt like spitting on God; if He was going to show them another way, then why the hell hadn't He?

The sun was coming up behind the hills in the east, and they ate breakfast, still talking, still drinking, still ironing out their differences.

"*Corazón de mi vida*," said the old lady, reaching for Juan's huge, thick hand, "look at me, look into my eyes, and give me your hand."

Juan did as he was told, taking his mother's two tiny hands in his huge one.

"I didn't send you that telegram to cause you grief because of our past. I sent it to you because you are now a man and it's time for you to look at the future and fulfill the promise I gave to you in the desert—that I'd see you married."

"Oh, Mama," said Juan, thinking of Lily and Katherine.

"Don't 'oh, Mama' me!" she snapped angrily. "I'm old! I don't have much time! And I'm going to finish my earthly task and see my last-born child married and on his own and that's that!"

"But I am on my own. I've been on my own for years, Mama."

She laughed, showing her red, swollen gums. "That's not on your own. That's alone! Now you must marry and start your own *casa de la vida*. And remember, the woman you marry isn't just another woman; no, she is the sacred mother of your offspring, and so you must prepare yourself—and now. Not tomorrow. Now!"

"Oh, Mama, don't you ever change?"

"Does God? Do the birds in the sky? The rivers in the mountains? No, of course not! I'm perfect as I am. Now you hold my hand and understand, you are a fully grown man and no man is worth his salt if he doesn't marry and have children." And she closed her eyes, still talking. "Blood of his blood, flesh of his flesh, and now you must prepare yourself by getting pure inside your heart and soul so that you can open yourself to the love *del corazón*. Remember, we are not of the bull, nor of the stallion, but of God, the Creator Himself. And just as the Almighty spoke to Don Pio and gave him a dream, you must now open your ears and eyes and find your own dream. For no man or woman is anything without a dream."

And Juan didn't want to, he really didn't; but there it began again, and he was once more under the spell of his mother, the greatest force that he'd ever known.

Juan had been home a few days before he realized how truly poor his family was and how run-down their two little houses were. He bought hammers and nails and got some roofing paper and fixed their roofs.

Then he bought some shovels and hoes and went to work with Luisa's children, Jose and little Pedro, cleaning the outhouse and turning the soil under the big avocado tree. They fixed the hen-house and put new siding on the goat shed so that the boys' grandmother wouldn't get so cold in the night.

Jose was an excellent worker, and Juan and his two nephews talked as they worked. Jose wanted to know about Mexico and especially about his real father, Jose-Luis, whom he'd never met.

"Was he a good *hombre*?" asked the boy.

"The best," said Juan, "a real *macho a las todas*! Big and strong and slow-moving, and he never lost his temper or got impatient when things went wrong. I was just about your age when he and Luisa got married, and he showed me a lot of love. I'd stay with them and he'd put me on his lap, calling me his *amo*. I loved him. He never abused me like my own father did."

"You mean that your own father was bad to you?" asked the boy.

Juan had to laugh. "Hell, my father treated the dogs better than me. He only had eyes for my brother Domingo, who was blue-eyed like himself."

"You mean our papagrande wouldn't have liked us either," said Jose, turning to his brother Pedro, "because we both got dark eyes?"

Juan was sorry that he had started the whole thing, but he wasn't going to lie to his nephews now. "Maybe not," he said. "There's a lot of prejudice in Mexico, too, you know."

Jose flinched and he didn't ask any more questions, and they continued working together. Juan thought about the good men of his life—his brother Jose, the great protector of their mountain, and his grandfather, Don Pio, and the two big giants, Basilio and Mateo—and all the manly examples that he'd had of what a real *hombre* could be.

Luisa brought them some tacos and the three of them sat down to eat in the shade of the big avocado tree. Juan couldn't believe it—Jose actually ate like his father whom he'd never known. He chewed with his mouth open, showing his big teeth, and rolled his mouth to his left side.

Juan glanced at Pedro and he was again amazed. Why, he, too, ate like his father, Epitacio.

Juan shook his head in wonderment. Why, his mother was absolutely right—blood was blood. So a man really did have to be very careful who he married if he wanted to have good offspring.

"Tell me," said Jose, chewing his food in the big, mouth-rolling, lazy dog action his father had always done, "is it true that we were once a big, powerful *familia* back in Mexico, *tío*?"

"Yes," said Juan.

"But not rich, eh?" said Pedro.

"Why do you say that?" asked Juan.

"Because Mexicans are always poor, right?" said Pedro.

Juan reached out, scratching the younger boy's head of sandy brown hair.

He, also, looked a lot like his father Epitacio—small, quick, cute, with eyes that danced full of happy mischief.

"No, not necessarily," said Juan. "Mexicans sometimes have money, too, Pedro. But we didn't. We had land and livestock and fields of corn."

"See, I told you," said Pedro, laughing at his brother. "Mexicans can't be rich! That's all bull what Mama has been telling us."

"What?" said Juan.

"Nothing," said Jose, giving his seven-year-old brother the mean eye. "It's just that, well, when Mamagrande and Mama tell us of the past, Pedro and I sometimes . . . well, can't really believe them."

"Oh, I see," said Juan. "So you don't believe your own blood, eh? But you do believe the *gringos*, eh, that only *gringos* can be rich, eh?"

"Well, that's all we've ever seen," said Pedro. "Not one Mexican in all the barrio has even a good car."

Juan took a big breath. "Oh, I see. So when your mamagrande and your mother tell you of Don Pio, who fought alongside Benito Juarez, and Jose the great, who defended us from the Revolution for over four years, you doubt them?"

The two boys could see that their uncle was getting angry.

"Well, do you? Answer me!"

The two boys nodded. And tears came to Pedro's eyes.

Juan looked from one nephew to the other. He didn't know what to do. Never in a thousand years would he have believed that the flesh and blood of the great Don Pio would come to doubt the worth of their own *familia*.

He got to his feet and walked away before he strangled his two nephews. Oh, he was crazy, *loco*, raging mad. He and his mother and sister had suffered so much; and for what? To come to this? Your own not having faith in themselves anymore? Oh, he felt like killing the whole damn world!

Later that day, Juan was smoking a cigar out back, watching his two nephews play baseball with the neighbors across the street. The sun was setting behind the luscious orchard of orange trees, and Juan was thinking about Lily and Katherine and Montana and how good he had it up there.

But, he'd promised his mother that he would never leave her again, so he couldn't just take off like a thief in the night. Oh, a part of him wished that he hadn't come back.

"Don't do it, Juan," said Luisa, coming up behind him.

"Don't do what?" he said, glancing up at his sister.

"Leave us," she said, sitting down beside him. "Remember, I could have left you all behind at the border, too. But I didn't. I forced Epitacio to return for you."

Juan looked at her, taking a deep breath. "But I can make big money running those poker tables back in Montana," he said. "And I could send you and Mama money regularly."

"Money isn't everything," said Luisa. "Our family, our blood, our dreams—these are the reasons that we've been struggling all these years; not money."

Juan picked up a stick, poking the ground in front of him.

"Juan," she said, "I can't do it alone, I'm a woman and unfortunately a woman alone can't do it. Look at them, playing baseball like little *gringos*, and every time I try to tell them about our once great *familia*, they laugh. Not in my face, of course, but inside their souls which is far worse." She stopped and looked at him. "Juan, we need you. You're the only one left."

Juan stopped poking the ground with the stick and looked at his sister, at her eyes, her mouth, her wide strong cheekbones, and he felt trapped. Yet, he fully knew that what she said was true. Their own mother, if she had been a man, would've ruled Mexico with the greatness of Benito Juarez. And Luisa, with her power and cunning, would be an *hombre* to be reckoned with.

"But we can't force you, Juan," said Luisa. "It's got to come from you. Just as it came from Don Pio when he spoke to God and started our settlement. Just as it came from Jose, our great brother, who defended us from war. It's got to come from you, Juan, come from your *corazón*," she said, tears coming to her eyes.

Juan saw her tears and breathed deeply. He thought of Don Pio and the night that he'd camped on that knoll with his two brothers and how all their lives had been changed because of that. He thought of Jose, the great, and how he'd almost spared them of the war. Two great *hombres* who'd taken up ground and reached for the stars and brought miracle after miracle down here to earth. His eyes filled with tears. It was true, it really was true—he'd been alone up in Montana, not on his own. For a man, a real *macho* to be on his own was to be rooted to the earth with his balls, his *tanates*, with the blood and flesh of his *familia*.

"All right," he said. "I'll stay, Luisa. I'll stay."

"Good," she said. "I knew you'd do it."

And she took him in her arms and it was good, brother and sister holding, heart-to-heart.

The next afternoon, Juan decided to go to town to see if he could find a poker game. After all, since he was going to stay, he would have to find a way to make a living.

It was a long walk to town, past acres and acres of raw, unused land and a few orchards and fields of well-fed cattle.

"Man, oh, man," said Juan to himself, "if one day I could just buy a nice little piece of land and build a house on a knoll like Don Pio. Then get a car—a good one—and prove to the boys that a Mexican can be somebody. That would be beautiful."

He smiled, thinking that maybe the Almighty had sent him to California, just as He'd sent their grandfather to Los Altos de Jalisco.

He began to whistle, feeling good, realizing that something had been missing down deep inside himself when he'd been all alone up in Montana. He'd just been thinking of himself—which, of course, was easy for any good, healthy, strong young man.

Getting into town, Juan quickly found out that they played poker at the poolhall across the street from the park in the center of town. Walking through the little park, Juan glanced inside the poolhall and saw that it was still too early. There was no real action going on except for a few young boys playing pool and some old men passing the time with cards. He decided to go and get something to eat before he got ready for a long night of poker.

A professional never entered a game for just a few hours. A professional always went into the game fully prepared to play until the early hours of the morning when everyone was tired and drunk and loose with their money. A professional was a very well organized *hombre aprevenido*, watchful, fore-warned.

Up the street, Juan found a little café and he went inside and sat down by the far wall. He was hungry, and the waitress was a nice-looking young American girl. He ordered a cup of coffee, and ham and eggs, even though it was almost dinner time.

This was another trick that he'd learned from Duel: when you are getting ready to play all night, treat the early evening like daybreak, treat the middle of the night like high noon, and play your cards like a job—never a sport of passing the time.

Eating the eggs and juicy, thick ham, Juan sipped his coffee, and he began thinking about Montana and all the years that he'd spent up there. His mother was right; he really had become a loner, always going from here to there by himself, following the railroad and mines and the sugar beets until he'd met Duel. He wondered how difficult it was going to be for him to fit back into a family after all those years of being alone. He just wasn't used to being with people day in, day out. And he did miss Montana. Especially Katherine. My God, that woman had been a fine lady. She'd taught him so much.

Finishing his breakfast, Juan lit up a long cigar and quit thinking of the past. With slow deliberation, he began to think about the poker game that lay ahead. He pulled down into his guts, as Duel had shown him how to do, and he concentrated on the possibilities of the cards, the men, their faces, their weaknesses. Poker, after all, wasn't a game of chance or luck or cheating. Only fools thought that. Poker was a game of power, of one man's personal strength over another man's weaknesses. A professional had to concentrate, prepare himself inside.

And so Juan was smoking, thinking, remembering all that Duel had taught him when he suddenly got the feeling that someone was staring at him. He turned around and, sure enough, there was the cook, a short heavy-set man with a dirty white apron, staring at him.

"Excuse me," said the man, "but you see, my waitress, she's new and so she didn't know that we can't serve Mexicans."

At first, Juan didn't quite understand.

"Look, I don't want no problems," said the cook with a heavy Greek accent, "but I'm only trying to make a living, so you got to get out."

Now Juan understood. "But who says I'm Mexican?" said Juan in Greek, smiling as he glanced around and realized for the first time that all the other people in the place were looking at him. "I could maybe be Greek, you know," he continued speaking in fluent Greek.

The cook's eyebrows knitted together. He apologized and quickly started speaking in Greek, too, asking Juan his name and where he came from. Juan grinned and answered him rapidly in Greek.

"That's pretty good," laughed the Greek, "but still, your accent's a little bit off, *amigo*." He came close to Juan. "Look," he said softly, "I live just around back with my family and, to my home, you're welcome any time. But here, you know how it is; I have to stay in business, so I'm still going to have to ask you to leave."

Juan's whole face turned red. Never in his life had he been asked to leave a place just because he was Mexican. He stared at the man in the eyes and he could see that it was truly hurting the Greek to ask him to go, but he was still doing it.

"All right," said Juan, getting to his feet, towering over the man and feeling the .38 under his coat, his heart pounding with rage. "How much do I owe you?"

"Ham and eggs, fifteen cents," said the cook. "And five cents for the coffee."

Juan peeled off a dollar. "Keep the change!" he yelled, tossing the money to the floor. He turned around, staring at all the people who were looking at him. They quickly glanced away. Oh, he was flying so high that he was ready to kill.

Now he suddenly knew why those two old Mexican men had stared at him with hate in their eyes the first day that he'd come into the barrio in the taxi. He also knew why his own two nephews had so much doubt. Mexicans were nothing but dog shit down here, along the border, and he'd forgotten.

He walked out of the restaurant, head high, straining not to draw his gun and kill every son-of-a-bitch in the place.

Still trembling with rage, Juan walked into the poolhall and breathed in the full smell of the cigarette smoke and the sweat of the men. He saw that half of them were Mexicans and realized that, here, no one cared what you were as long as you had money so they could take it from you.

Dropping his cigar into the brass spittoon, Juan walked across the room, surveying the three poker tables beyond the pool tables. The overhead fans were blowing good, and Juan's trained eyes immediately told him that they were playing for peanuts at two of the tables. He knew this, not so much by the amount of money that was on the tables, but by the lack of intensity in the men's eyes. The third table, on the other hand, was of a whole different caliber.

At this table, the men weren't just there to pass the time of day and lose a little money for the fun of it. No, at this table, the men were deadly serious. There were two tough-looking Mexicans at the table, two big, raw-boned Anglos, a small-boned, quick-eyed Filipino, and a formidable-looking dark-skinned man of, maybe, Italian blood.

Suddenly, the hair came up on Juan's neck. His instincts told him that the Filipino and the Italian were in together. There was just something too perfect as they sat directly across the table from each other.

Juan went to the long bar, ordered a Coke, and watched the action for a while. He decided not to play at the main table, this being his first night. After all, it was always very dangerous to come into another professional's setup without having someone protecting your back.

Sitting down at one of the lesser tables, Juan was only able to win two dollars in a couple of hours. He knew that he'd never get ahead playing like this. If he wanted to make a living at cards here in California and buy a car to show his nephews, he was going to have to kick caution to the wind and move to the big table.

Besides, he'd also been trained by the best, so he figured that he could pull in a couple of big pots and not upset the action that the Filipino and Italian had going. And a couple of twenty-dollar pots would put him in a good place. Five dollars alone would pay the rent for his family's two little houses for a month. And within the week he could maybe win enough to get himself a good car.

Sitting down at the big game, Juan acted awkward and not too confident when it was his time to deal. He was the youngest player, after all, and so he figured that he'd go easy at first and let these older men bluff him out of a few hands, pretending that he was a reckless fool to loosen them up.

It was approaching midnight and everything was going well. Juan had lost a few small hands as he had planned. Someone brought in a bottle of bootleg whiskey from the back alley. They passed the bottle around, each man taking a good drink, and then it came to Juan. He took a small swig. It was the worst damn rot-gut whiskey that he'd ever drunk. He spat it out.

"That's shit!" he said.

They all laughed.

"Where you from?" asked one Anglo.

"Montana," said Juan.

"Whadda you drink up there?" asked the other Anglo.

"Canadian whiskey!" said Juan.

"You lucky son-of-a-bitch!" said the first Anglo. "Since Prohibition, all we got down here is this rot-gut shit. A man could make a fortune if he could bring down that good Canadian stuff."

Juan marked these words down inside his head, realizing that the man was right. He pretended to drink a little of the terrible whiskey every time it came his way. After all, drinking men didn't like to play with a man who was sober, and it was getting close to the time for Juan to make his move.

It was after midnight, and Juan figured that he'd set them up well. They were sure he was just a kid, and so they were beginning to drop their guard, becoming a little loose with their money. Greed, good old greed, was blinding these men, getting them to think that they could bet heavy and take all his money. Greed was a professional's best friend; Duel had taught him this, too.

A couple of the men were pretty drunk and tiring fast, so Juan figured it was time for him to push. After all, he'd taken a nap that afternoon and the coffee, ham and eggs were holding him.

He hit the next pot hard and won over twenty dollars. That's when he first saw the big Italian glance at the quick-eyed Filipino. But Juan didn't think too much of it. What could they do? He'd won the pot fair and square. And besides, he was still mad. He didn't like getting run out of two-bit little restaurants.

Two hands later, Juan pushed again, having faked at first that he didn't have anything, and he won a huge pot of nearly thirty dollars.

He was just raking in his money, feeling good and indestructible, when the Filipino got up to leave, saying that he had to go to the bathroom.

At that moment, Juan should have realized that he'd gone too far. But he was flying so high, so drunk on ego, thinking about the fine car he was going to buy to show his nephews, that he didn't see it coming.

He was piling up his winnings when he saw the big raw-boned *gringo* across the table jerk his head up. The *gringo*'s eyes went wide with terror as he looked over Juan's left shoulder.

And in that hundredth of a second, Juan knew that he was a dead man. But still, with lightning-quick reflexes, he turned to look over his left shoulder just as the Filipino's hooked blade came under his chin to take his head off his neck.

His razor-sharp knife—the kind they used in the fields for the grapes— didn't get Juan's open neck because he'd turned in time. Instead, it caught the right side of his chin, cutting along his jawbone all the way to his left earlobe.

A spurt of blood came shooting off Juan's jawline, and everyone leaped back, thinking that he'd had his throat cut.

And in that moment of confusion, the Italian grabbed all the money from the table and ran for the back door.

But Juan was young and strong. He still managed to lunge to his feet, drawing his .38, as he spun about to shoot the two men.

He had to get his money back for his family. He couldn't die now. But the world turned black before he could fire, and he fell face-first into his pool of blood, holding his jaw together.

People were shouting, yelling. And far away, like in a dream, Juan could still make out the overhead fan blowing on him, making little waves in the pond of blood about his face as footsteps shook the hardwood floor under him.

15

And so the stars above them smiled, and the angels of destiny brought her through his barrio *in a caravan of trucks.*

After crossing the border, Lupe and her family contracted to work the cotton fields of Scottsdale, Arizona. Then, during the winter, they went to the town of Miami, just east of Scottsdale, where Victoriano and Esabel got work in the mines. Lupe and Carlota helped their father gather firewood in the surrounding hills to sell in town, and their mother and Maria took in laundry for extra money.

One Sunday, during their second winter in Miami, Lupe and her family were coming home from church when Lupe saw a beautiful dress in a store window. It was pale orange, almost the color of peaches, and it had tiny white polka dots all over it and delicate white lace about the neck and arms. It was the most beautiful dress that Lupe had ever seen. But the price tag said ten dollars, so Lupe realized it was completely beyond her family's means. Even with all of them working, they made less than seven dollars in a week.

Two days later, Lupe got the shock of her life when she came home from gathering wood and found the very same dress lying on her bed.

"Oh, Mama!" she said. "Is it for me? Oh, you shouldn't have! We can't afford it!"

"You damned right, we can't!" yelled her father, putting down the load of firewood. "Jesus Christ, a man makes less than a dollar a day at the mines and that dress was marked for ten dollars!"

"They gave it to me for six," said the grey-haired old lady, "and it didn't cost you a cent. I used the last of our gold," she added proudly.

"The last of our gold?" screamed Don Victor. "Oh, my God! How could you, woman?"

"Easy," said Doña Guadalupe, refusing to be intimidated. "And I'd do it again. All our lives we work and work, and for what . . . if we can't have a little joy now and then? Now don't you dare spoil this for Lupe, or I'll brain you!"

"All right, all right!" said Don Victor. "Do as you wish! You've done it all your life anyway." And he got his hat, took the fifty cents that they'd gotten for selling the firewood, and went out. "Kids, I swear, we should've had pigs! At least you can eat them when they grow too big!"

"Oh, Mama," said Lupe, picking up the dress once her father was gone. "Really, you shouldn't have done this. Papa's right, and we should take this dress back."

"*Mi hijita*," said her old mother, "last year I bought a beautiful dress for Carlota, so why shouldn't I buy a dress for you now?"

"But, Mama," she said, "when you bought Carlota her dress, it was so she could go to the dances and we had lots of gold. Now we have no gold, and I don't even like to dance."

"Look, Victoriano and Esabel both have good jobs," said the old woman. "And who knows? I might die tomorrow, and no one, but no one, is going to rob me of the pleasure of buying each of my daughters at least one store-bought dress before I die." She laughed. "Isn't it gorgeous?"

"Oh, yes!" said Lupe. "It's the most beautiful dress I've ever seen in all my life." Lupe just couldn't stop caressing the dress. The pale orange material was so smooth and lovely, and the lace was so white and truly delicate.

"Well, try it on," said her mother.

"Oh, no," said Lupe. "I have to bathe and fix my hair first."

The following Sunday, Lupe put on her new dress and they all went to church. After mass, they lit a candle for Sophia, and they were walking home when Carlota came running up with three young girls.

"Mama," she said, "I just met these girls from Sinaloa, and they want me to go to the movies with them! Everyone is going! It's a brand new movie!"

Doña Guadalupe could see Carlota's excitement. "All right," she said. "But Lupe and Victoriano will have to go with you, and you must obey your brother and sit together and then come straight home afterwards."

"Oh, thank you!" said Carlota. And she kissed her mother in a big hurry, then took off with her new friends.

Carlota always made friends wherever they went. But Lupe and Victoriano were still too shy to talk to strangers.

Lupe and her brother went up the rocky, dirt street behind Carlota and her girlfriends. Miami was a company-controlled mining town, which supplied various forms of entertainment for the workers. The movie was called "The Silver Automobile." All the young people in town were excited about it. It was a series, and this was the third part. "The Silver Automobile" was always full of beautiful cars and rich, gorgeous people.

After the movie, Carlota and the other girls went giggling into the bathroom. Lupe and her brother stayed behind in the lobby. Then some young men that Victoriano knew from the mine came over and started talking to him as they gave Lupe the eye.

Lupe grew self-conscious, excused herself, and went to join the girls in the bathroom. She was walking with her head down, avoiding people's glances, when she entered the bathroom and looked up, only to see the most beautiful young woman that she'd ever seen in all her life coming toward her through a doorway surrounded by shiny little lights.

She stopped. And the beautiful young lady stopped, too. They stood there, looking at each other, and Lupe saw how tall and slender and perfectly made this young lady was with a high, open forehead and large, dark eyes. Why, she took Lupe's breath away.

Then Lupe saw that the young woman was wearing the identical dress that she was wearing. She laughed, realizing that this was why the young woman had stopped to stare at her, too.

Then in that moment, as Lupe saw the young woman laughing, too, she suddenly realized that she wasn't looking through a doorway, but into a large, full-length mirror surrounded by lights. And the shock that Lupe felt in realizing that this marvelous creature was none other than herself was so complete, so stunning, that she would never forget it for the rest of her life.

Why, all these years that Carlota had been teasing her, calling her the beauty queen of the world, she hadn't been ridiculing her. No, she'd been telling her the truth. And all those people who'd been staring at her in every work camp they came to hadn't been ridiculing her, either. No, they'd all been telling her the truth. She really was a beauty. Why, she was even better-looking than all the women that they'd just seen in the American movie.

Lupe blushed, turning this way and that way, looking at herself in the lovely peach dress. It was a whole new discovery, like finding a bright new star in the heavens.

The weeks passed and then one night, Esabel didn't come home with his paycheck from the mine. Lupe watched as her sister Maria grew uneasy. The next day when Esabel still didn't show up for work, it was rumored that he'd lost his check in a poker game the night before and that he'd gone back to Mexico.

All that day, Lupe watched Maria cry and curse the card sharks who followed the poor, defenseless workmen from camp to camp, tempting them with prostitutes and liquor, then cheating them out of their hard-earned money. Once more, Lupe swore that she'd never have anything to do with a man who gambled or drank.

The family got cold and hungry that year in Miami, Arizona. Their father was too old to go back to work inside a mine and women were not allowed to go underground. Victoriano got a second shift, and Lupe and Carlota climbed higher into the surrounding hills to search for firewood with their father, who got sick and almost froze to death when the hills turned white with snow.

Returning to Scottsdale to do the cotton late that summer, the weather was so hot that Lupe got sick from the heat and wasn't able to work. Maria told Lupe to take care of her children, and she went to work with Carlota and

Victoriano. They worked from sunrise to sunset, picking the cotton. Lupe felt terrible, but she just couldn't figure out what was wrong with her. She'd done better in the cold in Miami. All she did was cough all day in the heat and dust. Carlota teased her for being lazy, but it was all Lupe could do to breathe.

This was also the summer that they began to fear that their mother was losing her mind. Doña Guadalupe refused to accept the fact that Sophia was dead and kept going from tent to tent, asking every stranger she encountered if they'd run across Sophia or heard of someone who had.

Then, finishing the cotton, they decided that they didn't want to do another cold winter in Miami, so they decided to work their way west. Besides, if they could make it to California, it was said that there was year-round work and that Don Manuel lived in Santa Ana and maybe he'd heard of Sophia.

Working their way west through the deserts of Yuma, Brawley and Westmoreland, Lupe almost died. Her eyes became inflamed and her throat swelled up so tight that she could hardly breathe. But when they arrived in San Diego and smelled the sea breeze, something magical happened to Lupe. Once again, she was able to breathe. In no time, she grew strong, blossoming like a peach tree in full bloom. They worked their way up the coast, passing Del Mar, Encinitas, Carlsbad and Oceanside. Lupe had so much extra energy that she began to crave books so she could study at night after work. They were doing pretty well by the time they reached Santa Ana, California.

Upon finding Don Manuel, they discovered that he knew nothing of Sophia and that there was year-round work in Santa Ana, but it didn't pay much, especially after Don Manuel—who was a labor contractor—took out his percentage for getting them jobs.

They'd been in Santa Ana for almost a year when Doña Guadalupe insisted that they were doing so well that Lupe could go back to school. After all, education was their only hope of ever really getting ahead.

At school, Lupe was put in the third grade—even though she was going on fourteen—and the other students teased her because she was a head taller than all of them. But she'd been teased at school before and so Lupe ignored them and worked so hard that she was moved up to the seventh grade within three months. Her long hours of studying with Manuelita back in La Lluvia de Oro had given her an enormous amount of self-discipline.

Late one afternoon, Lupe came home from school to start dinner for her family, who were still out working, when there was a knock on the front door. Lupe cleaned her hands on her apron and went to the door.

"*¿Sí?*" she said, opening the door.

"Excuse me," said the small, tired-looking old man, taking off his sweat-stained hat, "but is this the house of the Gomez family?"

"Yes," said Lupe, "it is."

"And you come from La Lluvia de Oro, no?" he asked.

"Why, yes, that's right," said Lupe, taking a better look at the man, wondering if they knew him.

"Oh, thank God!" said the man, his tired eyes taking on new life. "I was so afraid it would come to nothing again."

"But what are you talking about?" asked Lupe. She stood half-a-head taller than the man and she felt as awkward as she always did talking to men who were so much shorter than she.

"Please," said the man, "I don't mean to be a bother, but could I please have a glass of water?" He swallowed. "I've come a long way on foot, you see."

"Why, yes, of course," said Lupe. She closed the door and went through the tiny living room into the kitchen and got him a drink of water in an old chipped cup and came back to the front door.

Lupe was tired. She'd had a hard day at school. Her new teacher was a man and he'd kept her after school to help her, but she had felt very uncomfortable with him.

The old man was sitting down on the steps when Lupe reopened the door. He didn't look well at all. Quickly, she handed him the cup.

"Oh, thank you," said the man, gulping down the water. "That saved my life. Now tell me, is your mother's name Doña Guadalupe?"

"Well, yes," said Lupe, "but really, I don't see what—"

"And your father's name is Don Victor?" he interrupted.

"Yes, that's right," said Lupe. "But I don't think that we know you, señor."

"Oh, no, not me," he said, standing up, and his chest filling with power, "but you do know the love of my life, your sister Sophia. I'm her husband."

"Sophia? My sister?" said Lupe. "But she can't be your wife. She was killed at sea years ago."

"Oh, no," said the man. "Sophia lives!"

Lupe's mind went reeling, pounding at her temples. For the last year their mother had been going crazy, praying every night for them to find their lost sister. Everyone else had given up hope, including Lupe.

"Tell me," said Lupe, still not believing this man, "and what does this Sophia of yours look like?"

"Why, just like you, but shorter," he laughed. "You must be Lupe, no?"

Lupe's legs went weak. "Then, Sophia didn't die," she said, beginning to cry. "She's really alive!"

"Oh, yes!"

"And her little Diego?"

"He's fine, too, and so is Marcos. And we have one more of our own and another one on the way."

"Where?"

"In Anaheim," he pointed, "just up the road six or seven miles." He stood up as tall as he could, then he bowed to Lupe. "Francisco Salazar *a sus órdenes!*"

That same afternoon, when Lupe's family came home from the orchards, she quickly told them the news and introduced them to Sophia's husband, Francisco. Doña Guadalupe gripped her chest, thanking the heavens, and they all got into a neighbor's truck, along with Francisco, and drove to Anaheim.

And Sophia came to them, plump and older, but still very much alive, rushing out of her home with her two boys and another in her arms. "Oh, Mama!" she screamed, grabbing their mother in her arms.

It became a time of miracles, of hugs and kisses. Sophia took Lupe into her arms, then Victoriano, Carlota, Maria and their father. She just couldn't stop hugging them and kissing them. It was one of the most exhilarating moments of Lupe's entire life. A dream come true, a gift given to their family by God Himself.

Then they all went inside, and Francisco put on an apron, just like a woman, and went to work. "You people talk, and I'll make dinner for all of us!" he said. He began making tortillas as if he'd made them all his life, cooking the meat and vegetables at the same time.

"And all these years," cried Don Victor, "I've been blaming myself for your death, *mi hijita*, thinking that you'd died in that ship I put you on."

"Oh, no, Papa," said Sophia. "I never even realized that you people thought I was dead. You see, when you put me on that boat, Papa, I didn't have any food, expecting that they sold it on board. But I was wrong; they didn't have anything. Not even fresh water to drink. So I had to get off the boat just before they sailed. And it wasn't until two days later, after I'd bought provisions, that I boarded the next ship."

"But didn't you know that the other boat capsized?" asked her father.

Sophia shook her head. "No, I never heard about that until months later because, well, I was out at sea at that time and I had enough problems of my own."

Sophia stopped and started to laugh, and Lupe saw a strange mixture of anger, yet joy come into her eyes. "Oh, those wretches," she said, laughing lightly as she smoothed out the apron on her lap the way their mother always did. "Do you realize that they robbed me the first night I was on that boat while I slept with my baby? It was terrible," she said, still laughing. "Why, they had us all stacked up like cattle, and by the time we got to land, the whole ship smelled of human waste."

She laughed, shaking her head, and Lupe realized that this was something that her family always seemed to do when they spoke of the terrible misfortunes that they'd suffered. They didn't get angry or upset, like so many other Mexicans did; no, they smiled and laughed as if even these bad fates had been handed to them by a mischievous but good-hearted God.

"Oh, it was difficult for me," she continued. "I'd come with all that gold from La Lluvia but, by the time I got to Mexicali, I had nothing. But, well, what could I do? I was a woman alone."

"So what did you do?" asked Maria, no doubt thinking about herself now that she was without a husband, too.

"Well, getting to Mexicali I sold my earrings and wedding ring, wanting to get American dollars so I could get across the border. But the money changer tricked me, by giving me useless currency from the Revolution. Oh, I argued with him, Mama, as hard as you would have, to give me back my earrings and wedding ring. But he told me to get out of his place or he'd call the police." Sophia's eyes danced with fire. "But not before I knocked over one of his elegant vases," she said, laughing. "And then that night my fortune changed. I met some people who were going across the border, and I became friends with a woman and her husband. I told them my story, and they took me in as part of their family, and I had Marcos in the camp where they worked. Then I got contracted along with them to work in the cotton fields on the American side of the border."

"Where?" asked Victoriano. "We worked in the cotton fields when we first got across, too."

"Oh, I don't know," said Sophia. "I was lost."

Sophia continued her story, and she told them how they'd been transported out of the town of Calexico in big trucks, going across tracts of flatland for hours. Then that night, they came to a ranch and she was given a little house to share with the family that she'd come with. The next day, they were at work before daybreak. Sophia left Diego and her infant with the woman who had befriended her, and she worked with the woman's husband in the cotton fields all day long. Within a few days, Sophia and the woman's husband became the two best cotton pickers in all the fields.

"I did, too!" cut in Carlota. "Victoriano and I were the best in all Scottsdale, Arizona! We even beat the big Negroes from Alabama," she said.

"You, too?" laughed Sophia. "Well, I'll be. It must be because we've always been quick of hand."

"And we're quick because we're short!" said Carlota.

"All right, go on," said Doña Guadalupe. She knew why Carlota had said that. Ever since Lupe had gotten so tall, Carlota picked on her.

"Oh, yes, where was I?"

"Picking cotton," said Lupe, "with that woman's husband."

"Oh, yes, well, there we were, and I thought we were becoming rich because we were doing so well, until at the end when we went to get paid."

Sophia stopped and, for the first time since she'd been talking, Lupe saw her sister get angry with rage. But then her husband, who'd finished with the tortillas and was now feeding the children dinner, came over and took her hand. Lupe saw her sister's eyes go soft with love. It moved Lupe's heart to see such tenderness between a man and a woman.

"You see," said Sophia, "I was in line to get paid along with the other people, but when it came for my turn to get my money, the foreman gave me only half my wages. Oh, it still makes me so mad, I could scream," she said.

"Calm down, *querida*," said Francisco. "It's done now, it's done."

"Thank you," said Sophia, holding her husband's hand. "Well, anyway, then I said to the foreman—his name was Johnny—'But why do you do this? I made more money than this.'

" 'Move aside,' he told me, 'I have other people to pay.'

"Seeing all the people behind me, I moved aside, but I didn't leave. No, I just stood there, waiting until the last man was paid.

" 'Well, I see you waited,' Johnny said to me.

" 'Well, of course,' I said, 'you still owe me half my wages.'

" 'Are you married?' he asked me.

" 'No,' I said, 'but I don't see what that has to do with this.'

"He stood up. He was a big *pocho* who could speak both English and Spanish and liked to brag that he'd been born on this side of the border. 'If you had a husband, I'd give him your money for you,' he said, 'but since you haven't got a husband, I can't give you any more money than I've already given you.'

" 'But why not?' I asked.

" 'Because you made too much money, and the other men will get angry at me if I give you as much as you made.'

" 'But I earned it!' I yelled at him. 'I worked hard for it!'

" 'Yes,' he said, 'I know you did, but these men have families to feed.'

" 'But so do I! I have two children!'

" 'Yes,' he said, 'but you should be married. It's not right for a beautiful woman to be alone.' Then I'll never forget, he came around the table and smiled at me and said, 'Look, I'm a good man and I make good money, so marry me, and I'll take care of you and your children.'

"I couldn't believe what I'd heard. I was so outraged that I began to cry. But the fool didn't know who he was dealing with. So he took my tears to be weakness and drew close to me, saying in a very nice voice what a decent man he was and how much he'd been loving me since the first day that he'd seen me.

"Oh, Mama, I tell you," said Sophia, turning to their mother, "that man had absolutely no idea how we'd been raised by you. 'You're no decent man!' I screamed at him so loudly that all the camp could hear me. 'You're a bully, and a coward, and you have no idea of how to treat a lady!' And saying this, I turned and walked away.

"But then that same afternoon, the trucks came and loaded the people up to take them to the next ranch. You see, the cotton was done where we were, so it was time for us to go. But, when I tried to board the truck, the driver said I couldn't go on his truck. I went to the next truck and was told the same thing. The man I'd been working with said it was an outrage, and he tried to get me aboard the truck that he and his family were on, but the driver only threatened to take him off his truck, too. So he had to think of his family and keep quiet.

"After the trucks were gone, I was all alone on that ranch with the foreman and this old lady who kept the main house. Oh, I tell you, I thought it was the end of the world for me.

"Then that night, to make matters worse, the old lady came to my house and said, '*Mi hijita*, I don't know why you're so upset. It's a very good offer Johnny has proposed to you. He's rich. He works all year round for these big farmers on both sides of the border. I say, give your thanks to God that you're so attractive that such a man came forward and made you an offer like a gentleman. It could be worse, you know. He could have just grabbed you and used you like it's happened to me so many times.'

"Oh, I became so enraged! No human was going to break my will. I'm your daughter, Mama! So I grabbed the old lady, pushing her out of my house, but then she began to cry. Can you believe that? And she told me that she'd get in trouble if she went back without having talked me into marrying Johnny. Poor woman. So I let her stay, and we talked some more and I proposed to her that we run away together."

" 'But where will we run to, child?' she asked me.

" 'Down the road!' I told her.

" 'But which road?' she asked me.

" 'That one,' I told her, pointing to the road in front of the ranch.

" 'But that road goes nowhere, child,' she said. 'There are hundreds of roads crisscrossing all over these flat fields. I've come out to this ranch three seasons already, and I still don't know where I am.'

"And suddenly, I realized that she was right. I had no idea where I was and, in the heat of the day out in those treeless fields, a person could easily die of thirst. Also, I had a child to carry, and the land was perfectly flat in all directions. There were no hills or high ground to show you where you were. It was like being lost in the middle of the ocean, I swear.

"That night Johnny came by again and said, 'Listen, honey, be reasonable and accept my offer. I'm rich, and I ain't so bad to look at, either.' "

Carlota laughed. "He really called you 'hoe-ney,' just like an *americano*?" she asked, laughing all the more.

"Well, yes."

Carlota went into hysterics, yelling. "Hoe-ney! Oh, oh, oh, hoe-ney!" And she continued laughing until her eyes watered.

Everyone just looked at her, wondering why she thought this was so funny. But then they, too, started to laugh, breaking the tension of this awful story.

"Anyway, to go on," said Sophia after Carlota calmed down, "Johnny went on and told me, 'Look, be reasonable; you got nothing, and I promise you that I'll take care of you and your two sons for the rest of your lives.' Then he gave some candy to Diego and played with Marcos, trying to show me what a good man he was.

" 'Look, yourself,' I told him, 'if you were really a good man, like you say you are, then you'd pay me my money and take me to town in your truck so I could clean up and buy a dress and look really pretty for you. Then, there in town, where I'm free to decide, you can ask me if I wish to marry you. But not here, where you have me trapped like a prisoner. Because, believe me, no matter how much you try to impress me here—even by playing with my two sons—I know it's all false!'

"And I got up, screaming at him and telling him that he was a bad man, trying to take advantage of a woman alone. And I pushed him out of my house, hitting him with my fists, but he only laughed, telling me that I was the prettiest woman he'd ever seen, especially when I got mad.

"The week passed, and every day he'd come by and propose to me, and every day I'd throw him out. But then, the second week, he closed the doors to the little ranch market so I couldn't get any food to eat. By the third day Diego was so hungry that he was crying all the time. That's when I knew that he was the devil, and a woman has absolutely no chance in this world without a strong man.

"Late that same afternoon, I was holding my children, praying to God for a miracle, like you always taught us, Mama, when I saw this—excuse me, Francisco, but this is what I thought when I first saw you—an old man coming up the road, and he looked like he could barely walk.

"Getting to the buildings, he glanced around, saw no one, and began to search around. He found the water trough where the livestock drank but, instead of taking a drink, he just laughed and jumped into the trough, with his clothes and all. He looked so funny splashing around, that I began to laugh like I hadn't laughed in months. But hearing my laughter, he jumped out of the trough and began to run.

" 'No,' I yelled after him, 'don't run! I need your help.'

" 'My help?' he asked, pointing to himself.

" 'Yes. Please, come back here.' But he wouldn't come. So finally I had to go out and get him."

"But why should I have come back to her?" said Francisco, laughing goodheartedly as he stood by the stove, cooking. "I'd been bitten by the dogs on the last ranch, so no one was going to catch me this time."

"But I got hold of him," said Sophia, "and brought him back to my little house and fed him the last of our meager soup that we had."

"I was starving," said Francisco. "I'd walked all day and hadn't eaten; it was a great feast for me."

"Then I told him my story and he became so red-faced with what I thought was anger," said Sophia, "that I was sure that he was going to go up to the main house and massacre Johnny when he got home."

"But she was wrong," laughed Francisco uproariously. "I was so scared that I was just trying to keep the food down that I'd eaten so it wouldn't come up on me." He laughed again. "So getting my food back down, I said to her, 'Well, then, I better get out of here quick! Because if he finds me with you, he's sure to beat me up.' "

" 'Beat you up?' I said to him. 'But it's me he's mad at, not you!' "

"I finished my bread and got up to go," said Francisco. " 'I'm going,' I told her. Oh, I was scared."

"I didn't know what to do," said Sophia. "Here was my miraculous prince sent to me by God, and he wanted to run away. So I looked at him and his balding head and his big scared eyes; I remembered how he'd jumped into the water trough with his clothes on, and my heart went out to him. 'Okay,' I said, 'let's go then, I'll go with you.' So he helped me get my things, and we left immediately.

"We followed a cattle trail across the fields, and he carried Marcos most of the way—he was much stronger than I'd expected. We traveled for three days, and every night we found plenty of water. Francisco trapped rabbits, and we ate well. By the time we came to town, I knew I loved this man, Francisco Salazar, very much. He was a good man. And he respected me, and he was so funny. He reminded me of you, Papa, especially with his thinning hair."

Everyone else laughed, including Francisco, but Don Victor didn't think it was funny. He mumbled something under his breath, turning uneasily in his chair.

"So in the town of Brawley, we got work at a ranch together, and we worked side by side for several months and made good money; then I decided to marry him."

"Just like your very own mother!" said Don Victor, jumping to his feet. "There I was, free as a bird, a finish carpenter making good money, when she came into my life with two children and married me, just like that, too!" He laughed and laughed and went across the room and gave Francisco a big *abrazo*. "Welcome to our family, Francisco; may God help you! Because I can't! These women are tyrants! All of them!"

And so they ate the food that Sophia's husband had prepared, and it was delicious. The tortillas were round and perfectly cooked. Maria got so excited about Francisco's cooking that she couldn't stop complimenting him.

"I swear it, you're the lucky one, Sophia," said Maria. "You lose everything and still come up with a prince! Oh, if only I could be so lucky."

"Francisco has a friend, Andres, that he works with," said Sophia.

"Can he cook?" asked Maria.

"He taught me," said Francisco.

"Then it's settled, I'll marry Andres," said Maria. "He's mine!"

They all howled with laughter.

The following afternoon, they all gathered together by the orchard behind their rented house in Santa Ana. Lupe helped Victoriano dig a hole so that they could plant the lily bulbs they'd brought from La Lluvia.

"Let us pray," said Doña Guadalupe, "for I promised God that I'd plant my beloved flowers the day that we found Sophia. And we've found her."

The sun was going down as Lupe and her family knelt down on the rich, dark soil and gave their thanks to God. They were far from home and they'd been fearful that God hadn't come with them. But they had been wrong. God lived here, too. This land, this country, was filled with God's grace as surely as their beloved canyon had been full of miracles.

They bowed their heads in prayer, and the right eye of God turned to liquid flame, disappearing behind the orange trees in colors of red and yellow, as round and golden as the fruit hanging in the dark-green trees.

Several months later, Lupe and her family were in a caravan of old trucks, going to Hemet to pick the apricots. They'd found out that they couldn't make ends meet staying in Santa Ana. They'd have to follow the crops part of the year to support themselves.

As they were passing through Corona, one of the rusty old trucks overheated and they had to pull over. They also had to get fresh milk and provisions.

Lupe was riding in the back of the third truck. She was wearing loose-fitting work clothes and a big straw hat. Lupe was holding Maria's daughter, who had curly black hair and huge dark eyes. She was absolutely beautiful. Maria was holding her other child, a boy, and she was sitting across the truck bed from Lupe, next to her new husband Andres, whom Sophia's husband Francisco had introduced to her.

Andres wasn't big and handsome like Esabel, but he was kind, steady, hardworking, and he did love to cook.

Sophia hadn't come on this trip with them. She'd decided to stay home with her newborn infant and see if she and her family couldn't make a living without following the crops. After all, it was time for her oldest to start school, and she did want them to be educated.

Pulling into the *barrio* of Corona, Lupe looked out at the rutted dirt road and the tiny, run-down houses as they drove up the street. They were hoping to find a place with chickens and goats so they could buy some milk and eggs. Maria's children couldn't drink cow's milk, so they were constantly looking for fresh goat's milk.

At the far end of the street, Lupe spotted a bunch of chickens and a nice big milk goat tied in back of a house under a large avocado tree.

She knocked on the back window of the truck. "Over there!" she said.

Victoriano, who was riding up front in the cab, got out of the vehicle before the driver had even brought the truck to a stop. Victoriano was six feet tall now and going on nineteen, but he looked much older. He went up to the larger house in front and knocked on the door.

Inside, Juan Salvador was lying on a bed in the front room of Luisa's house. His face was all bandaged up. He was still recovering from his wound.

Hearing the knocking, he started to get up, but thought better of it and lay back down, making sure that his .38 was by his side. It had only been two weeks since he'd almost had his throat cut, and he was still very wary.

"I'll get it," said Luisa, coming out of the kitchen. She went to the door and opened it. "Yes?" she said, seeing a tall, handsome young man.

Victoriano took off his hat. "We saw your chickens and the milk goat in back," he said, "and we wondered if you couldn't please sell us some eggs and milk for the children."

"All right," she said, looking at the caravan of worn-out old trucks behind him, "how much?"

"Well, we don't have any money, but we do have stringbeans and squash from the last place we worked," he said.

"All right," she said, "give me a box of them and you can look around for the eggs in the henhouse, but you'll have to milk the goat yourself."

Victoriano looked at her and he suspected that this crafty-looking woman had already collected the eggs that morning and milked the goat, too. But they needed whatever they could get so they could keep going.

"All right," said Victoriano, "a box it is."

He hurried back to the truck to get the box of produce and told Lupe to milk the goat and the kids to search for eggs.

"Eh, Luisa," said Juan, still lying down, "why are you so hard on those poor people? You know you already collected the eggs today."

"Don't you tell me nothing!" snapped Luisa. "For days you've been saying how you're going to kill those two bastards for your money. And these eggs and goat's milk are my money!"

"All right, all right," said Juan. "Don't bite me."

He lay back down, being very careful not to touch the side of his face that had been cut open like a watermelon. Oh, it was true. He really was going to get that damned Filipino and his friend. He'd been playing honest poker and those two cheating bastards had tried to kill him.

Outside, Lupe was walking across the yard with Maria's child in her arms. The big she-goat had horns, and she was eyeing Lupe as she approached with the child and a clay pot.

Doña Margarita was at the back door of Luisa's house, watching Lupe through the window as she approached their goat. Luisa had been the devil to tell the poor, unsuspecting people to milk the goat themselves. No one could milk that goat except for Luisa. She was a big, mean she-goat. She knocked down everything, including grown men.

"Oh, Luisa," said Doña Margarita to herself as she watched Lupe go near the goat, "you should have been born a man, you're so heartless sometimes."

But then, to the old lady's surprise, Lupe did something that she hadn't expected. She simply quit advancing on the animal and she squatted down, took some stringbeans out of her pants pocket, and reached out with her hand, offering the beans to the big goat.

The big she-goat lowered her horns, looking as if she might charge, but the young woman held her ground, squatting there, and the big goat finally came over, little by little, and started eating out of her hand.

Doña Margarita smiled. "Luisa, you better come and see. It didn't work this time," she said, laughing.

"What didn't work?" asked Luisa. "Hasn't the goat run them off already?"

"No," laughed the old lady. "Whoever this girl is, she's smart."

"What do you mean, 'smart'?" said Luisa, coming to the window.

And seeing that the big she-goat was allowing herself to be milked, Luisa let out a scream. "Hell, if I'd known they'd get any milk, I'd have charged them two boxes!"

Luisa went back to the stove, and Doña Margarita laughed and laughed, truly enjoying herself, until she saw Lupe finish the milking and stand up, taking off her big straw hat and tossing back her long, dark hair. Doña Margarita's old toothless mouth dropped open.

"Why, she's an angel," she said to herself. "An absolute angel!" Immediately, she thought of her son. She rushed across the house to get him. "Juan!" she called. "Juan! You have to see this girl! She isn't just smart, she's an . . ."

But coming into the front room, Doña Margarita saw the empty bed and, glancing about, she saw that Juan was out in front, watching the men work on their overheated truck.

And there was the young woman that she'd just seen do the milking, coming up behind Juan with the pot of milk and the child at her side, but Juan didn't see her because that side of his face was bandaged up.

Doña Margarita noticed that Lupe did see Juan. And she saw that the young woman stared at the handle of Juan's shiny black pistol sticking out of his back pocket. She saw the young woman's face wince with revulsion, put on her hat, pick up her niece, and hurry to the back of the truck.

Doña Margarita quit smiling. It saddened her, but she could see that the girl had done the right thing to get away from him. Her son wasn't ready for marriage. No, his stance, the gun, everything about him radiated a brutish toughness, not an image of a young man ready to open his heart and settle down.

The weeks passed and Doña Margarita prayed to God, asking him to heal her son's wounds. God heard her prayers and the bandages came off. Juan could see in the broken bathroom mirror that he had a long, swollen scar, thick as a worm, across his chin and all the way to his left ear. Turning his head side to side, he discovered that if he lowered his chin and kept his head slightly turned to the left, the scar wasn't quite as noticeable.

He decided to grow a beard and keep it until the red ridge of swollen flesh went down. In some ways he'd been very lucky. It had been such a clean, razor-sharp knife, the wound would eventually disappear.

A couple of days later, Juan went to town to look for work. He was broke. The two bastards had stolen all of his money. He had to get some tortillas on the table before he went searching for those two sons-of-bitches to kill them.

In town, Juan found out that they were hiring at a local rock quarry, so he walked out to the quarry while the sun was still low. Getting there, Juan could see that there were at least fifty other Mexicans waiting to be hired ahead of him. The tall, lanky Anglo who was doing the hiring dropped the clipboard to his side. "Well, that's it for today," he said. "But you guys just all come on out tomorrow and maybe you'll get lucky."

Hearing the word "lucky," Juan became suspicious. As a professional gambler, he never liked to leave anything to chance. He glanced around at his fellow countrymen, wondering what they were going to do about this. But he could see that they weren't going to do anything.

Juan took up ground. "Excuse me," he said. "But I'm new in town, so I'd like to know how you do your hiring. Should I give you my name for tomorrow, or do you only hire the same men every day?"

The tall Anglo smiled at him as if he'd said something ridiculous. "What's your name?" asked the Anglo.

"Juan Villaseñor," said Juan, pronouncing the double "l's" of his name like a "y" and giving his name a dignified, natural sound.

"Well, Juan Vilee-senoreee," said the foreman, twisting his name into something ugly, "you just come on out here tomorrow if you want a job. That's all you gotta do. You ain't got to know no more. Catch my lingo, *amigo*?" And saying this, the man rocked back and forth on his feet and spat on the ground. Juan could see that the man was so mad that his jaw was twitching. But Juan said nothing. He simply lowered his eyes and turned to go. His heart was pounding. Why, this bastard had twisted his name into a piece of dog shit.

The other workmen moved aside, letting Juan pass by. Juan could feel the foreman's eyes burning into his back. But he already knew that he was never going to return. This bastard could take his job and stick it up his ass, as far as Juan was concerned.

But Juan had gone no more than a few yards when another Anglo came out of the office. "Doug!" he yelled at the man with the clipboard. "We need another powder man! Ask them if any of 'em has a license!"

"Hell, Jim, they ain't nothing but Mexicans," he said.

"Ask 'em," repeated the big, beefy man named Jim.

"¡Oyen! ¡Espérense!" called Doug in perfectly good Spanish. "Do any of you have a powder license?"

Juan had a license to handle dynamite from the Copper Queen in Montana, but he glanced around to see if anyone had priority over him. No one raised his hand.

"I got one," said Juan.

"Where'd you get your license?" asked Doug.

"From the Copper Queen Mining Company," said Juan.

"Oh, in Arizona," said Jim.

"No, from Montana," said Juan.

The two Anglos glanced at each other. They were a long way from Montana.

"Let's see your license," said Doug.

Calmly, deliberately, Juan walked back to the two Anglos. They both towered over him. But Juan's mammoth neck and thick shoulders were wider than either of theirs.

He brought out his wallet and carefully took the paper out of his billfold that said he was licensed to do dynamite work. He handed it to Doug, who unfolded it, glanced it over, then handed it to Jim.

Reading it, Jim said, "Looks good to me," and he handed the paper back to Doug. "Hire him."

"All right, Juan Villaseñor-eee," said Doug, pronouncing Juan's last name with less of a mean twist this time, "you got a job for the day. But just one little screw-up and you're out! Now go over to that shed and ask for Kenny. Show him your license and he'll fix you up."

"Sure," said Juan, taking back his license and going across the yard.

Everywhere were Mexicans bent over shovels and picks. It was a huge rock quarry. They looked like ants crawling about the great slab of rock that had been cut away from the mountain. Teams of horses and mules were moving the loads of rock, and the Mexicans drove these teams, too.

At the toolshed, Juan asked for Kenny. An old Anglo came up. He was chewing tobacco. He was short and thick and his eyes sparkled with humor. Juan liked him immediately. He didn't have that dried-out, sour-mean look of Doug's. He handed him his license.

"So how long you been a powder man, eh?" asked Kenny, looking over the license.

"Oh, three or four years," said Juan.

"All in Montana?" asked Kenny, walking over to the sledge hammers and bars.

Juan froze, but only for a moment. He'd originally learned his trade in prison at Turkey Flat, but he saw no reason for this man to know that. So he lied. "Yes," he said, "all in Montana."

"I see," said Kenny, coming forward with a sledge and a fistful of bars. He looked into Juan's eyes, but Juan didn't shy away. "Well," said the old man, handing Juan the tools, "where or how a man learned his trade ain't my concern." He spat a long stream of brown juice. "What interests me is the result," he added.

Walking around the shed, they headed for the cliff of cut rock in the distance. Climbing halfway up the face of the cliff, Kenny showed Juan where he wanted him to drill his holes to set the charges. Juan set his tools down and slipped off his jacket. The other dynamite men were already hard at work, drilling their holes. They were all Anglos.

Juan glanced up at the sun and saw that it was already beginning to get hot. He slipped his shirt out of his pants so it would hang loose and the sweat could drip off him freely. He'd learned this trick from an old Greek when he'd worked in Montana. A big, loose shirt could work like an air conditioner. Once the sweat started coming fast, the garment would hold it and let the sun evaporate the sweat like a cooling unit.

Juan could feel the other powder men watching him. A couple of them had already stripped down to their waists and they were bare-chested to the sun. They were all huge, well-muscled men and towered over Juan. But Juan felt no need to hurry or show off. He'd worked with the best of them up in Montana before he'd gone to work for Duel. He knew his trade.

Spitting into the palms of his thick hands, Juan set his feet and picked up his short bar with his left hand and his sledge hammer with his right. He centered the point of the bar on the rock in front of him and he raised the sledge over his head, coming down real soft and easy on the head of the bar. He did this again and again, turning the bar each time with his left hand. He knew that Kenny and the other powder men were watching him, but he never let on. He just kept up a soft, steady, easy pace. He wasn't about to push the sledge. He would let the weight of the big hammer do the work for him all day long. Only a stupid, young fool pushed the iron. An experienced man let the iron do the work for him.

Kenny brought out his chew, cut off a piece, put it in his mouth and continued watching, but Juan still felt no nervousness. He'd worked at his trade for three months at Turkey Flat, and in Montana he'd done it for nearly three years, so he knew that he was good at his job. He wasn't one of these men who rushed in the morning to show off to the boss and then had nothing left to give in the afternoon. No, he could work all day long, from sunup until sundown, without ever slowing down. In fact, he was so steady and sure at his job that he'd won many a bet in Montana by placing a dime on the head of the bar and hitting it so smoothly that the dime wouldn't fall off, even after a hundred hits. An old Greek had also taught him this trick. Why, he could make the sledge and the bar sing, once he got going.

It was noon, and the sunlight was blinding hot on the great slab of rock. Juan had gone past all the Anglo powder men except one. This Anglo was huge. His name was Jack, and he wasn't just big, he was extremely well-muscled. But Juan wasn't impressed by this. He'd seen many big, strong men collapse under the hot noon sun. And Jack had been one of the first to strip to the waist to show off his muscles, so he was now sweating fast and Juan knew that he wouldn't be able to keep up his pace all afternoon.

Juan decided to slow down and not push the man. He'd already proven himself. All he had to do now was give an honest day's work.

Then the horn blew, and it was time to eat lunch. The powder men all took their tools and put them in the shade so they wouldn't get too hot to handle when they came back to work.

Jack, the big man, came walking up close to Juan. It looked like he was going to say hello to him and shake his hand; but he didn't. He just laughed and turned away, joking with the other powder men. Juan didn't take offense, figuring that he was just having fun. He walked alongside Jack, hoping that maybe he and the big man could quit the competition that had started up between them and they could become friends. After all, he'd become friends with many Greeks and Anglos in Montana. But walking across the yard, the powder men acted as if Juan didn't exist.

Then, when they got in line to wash up before they ate, and it was Juan's turn to wash, the man in front of Juan didn't hand him the tin cup. No, he dropped it, instead. At first, Juan thought it was an accident, but then, when he bent over to pick up the cup, the man kicked it away.

Juan stood up and saw that all the powder men were sneering at him, especially Jack, who was grinning ear-to-ear. Quickly, Juan lowered his eyes so none of them would see what he was thinking. And he turned and walked away, tall and slow and with all the dignity he could muster. These smart-ass *gringos* had just made up his mind for him. This afternoon they were going to see a Greek-trained drilling machine.

He never once turned to glance back at them. No, he just kept going across the yard as slowly and proudly as he could. Getting to the Mexicans under the shade of a tree, he was given a cup when it was his turn to drink and wash up. But he had no lunch to eat, so he just sat down to rest.

Oh, it was a good thing that he hadn't brought his gun to work, or he would have been tempted to kill Jack and the seven other powder men. No one ridiculed him. Not even in prison when he'd been a child and they'd tried to rape him. He was his father's son when it came to having a terrible temper. He was truly of the crazy Villa*señors*. Why, he'd once seen his father grab a mule's leg that had kicked him and yank it up to bite it, dislocating the mule's hip. Then his father had beaten the mule to death with his bare fists.

Juan was sitting there, seething with rage, when a thick-necked Mexican named Julio called him over.

"*Amigo*," he said, "come and eat with us."

Julio and several other Mexican men were sitting under a tree, heating their tacos on a shovel that they'd washed.

"No, *gracias*," said Juan, "you go ahead and eat . . . to your health, my blessings." And saying this, Juan moved his hand, palm up, welcoming the man to fulfill himself. It was a very Mexican gesture, one especially common in the mountainous area of Jalisco.

"So you're from Jalisco, eh?" said Julio, turning over the bean tacos with a stick on the shovel.

"Why, yes, how did you know?" asked Juan.

Julio laughed. "Oh, I'm just a visionary from Guanajuato," he said, "who's seen that gesture of the hand too many times not to know a *tapatío*." A *tapatío* was what the people from Jalisco were called.

"Come on, don't be so proud," said another Mexican named Rodolfo. "You got nothing to eat and you got to be strong for this afternoon." Rodolfo was tall and slender and had pockmarks all over his face, but he wasn't hard to look at. His eyes had a twinkle of mischief, and he had that confident air of a man who'd seen many battles. "We all saw that little movement of the cup across the yard. Those powder men, they're all *cabrones!*"

"You saw it, eh?" said Juan, glancing across the yard to the powder men who were all sitting together and eating.

"Of course," said Rodolfo, "and we knew it was coming the moment we learned that one of our people had gotten a job so elevated."

"Go ahead," said Julio to Juan, taking the shovel off the little fire, "take a taco before this son-of-a-bitch schoolteacher from Monterrey eats all our lunches again." Saying this, Julio picked up one of the tacos with his fingertips from the hot shovel and tossed it to Juan, who reflexively caught it. "Eat, *hombre*," he said to Juan good-naturedly, "so you can fart like a burro and screw those *gringo* sons-of-bitches this afternoon!"

"Which leads us to a very important question," said Rodolfo, the tall schoolteacher from Monterrey, "just how'd you ever get up there, anyway?"

"I have a powder license," said Juan, starting to eat.

"Oh, and how did you manage that miracle?" asked Rodolfo. "Hell, we got men here who know how to drill and set dynamite with the best of them, but none of them has been able to get a license." He ate his taco in two huge bites, working his big, lean jaws like a wolf.

"In Montana," said Juan, eating in small, courteous bites to show that he wasn't starving—but he was. "The Greeks up there, they'd never seen a Mexican, and so they'd thought I was Chinese and they made me a driller, thinking all Chinese know powder."

The Mexicans burst out laughing. But Rodolfo laughed the hardest of all.

"So that's how it's done, eh?" said Rodolfo. "We *mejicanos* got to be Chinese!"

"It worked for me," said Juan, laughing, too.

"I'll be damned," said the teacher, reaching for another taco. "Next you'll tell me that we'd be better off if we were Negroes, too."

"Shit, yes!" said Julio, who was very dark-skinned. "The blacker the better!"

They all laughed and ate together and Juan felt good to be back among his people. The jokes, the gestures, and the way they laughed with their heads thrown back and their mouths open, it was all so familiar.

Then the horn blew, and it was time to get back to work. The pock-faced man came close to Juan. "Be careful, my friend," he said. "That scar you wear may only be a small token compared to what awaits you this afternoon."

Juan nodded, having thought that no one could see his scar with his five-day-old beard. "*Gracias*," he said, "but I haven't gotten this far in life without being as wary as the chick with the coyote."

The tall man laughed, offering Juan his hand. "Rodolfo Rochin."

Juan took the schoolteacher's hand. "Juan Villaseñor," he said.

"He's right," said Julio, coming up. "They're going to try and kill you. Hell, if they don't, soon we'll have all their jobs."

Juan nodded. "I'll be careful," he said.

"Good," said the thick man. "Julio Sanchez."

"Juan Villa*señor*," said Juan once again.

Then Juan turned and started across the open yard, and all the Mexicans watched after him. Not one of their people had ever worked up on the cliff before.

Picking up his tools, Juan walked by the powder men and climbed up the cliff. Jack came up and took his place alongside Juan, grinning at him. But Juan paid him no attention and went to work, iron singing at a good, steady pace.

Jack picked up his sledge and tore at the rock. He was still half a hole ahead of Juan and wanted to keep it like that. The big man pounded at the rock, arms pumping, iron pounding, and he tried to pull further ahead of Juan. But Juan only smiled, glancing up at the hot sun, his ally.

The sun was going down, and it was the last hour of the day when Juan came up even with Jack. The other powder men stopped their work and watched. Jack grinned, still feeling confident, and began his new hole. He was huge and rippling with muscle, but Juan could see that he was all used up because he just didn't have the rhythm of the hammer down to a steady song.

Juan grinned back at Jack, spat into his hands, and began his new hole, too. But at a much slower pace. And the big man pulled ahead of him and the other powder men laughed, truly enjoying it. But Rodolfo and Julio and the other Mexicans down below knew what was coming. So they stopped their work and looked up at the two men pounding the iron up on the tall cliff.

The muscles were standing on the big man's back, and his forearms were corded up into huge ropes. But still, Juan kept going at a slow, steady, easy pace, fully realizing that the boiling white sun was on his side and the *gringo* wouldn't be able to keep up his reckless pace for long.

Kenny saw what was going on, and he started for the cliff to bring the senseless competition to a stop when Doug came up behind him.

"Don't, Shorty," he said to Kenny. "Let that little bastard kill himself, trying to keep up with Big Jack."

Kenny never even smiled. Juan was his own size, so he just spat out a stream of tobacco, already knowing who was going to win. "Whatever you say, Doug," he said.

And Kenny and Doug took up watch, too.

Jack was pounding on, tearing into his bar with his big sledge, but he could see that Juan was keeping up with him at a much slower rhythm. It seemed like magic. Juan was going so easy and, yet, his iron was still drilling into the stone at a good pace.

Jack began to tire but he was tough, so he just forced his body to go harder. His lungs screamed for air, his huge muscles began to cramp, but he'd die before he gave up and let a Mexican beat him.

But then here came Juan, coming in for the kill, and he now picked up the pace, too. Juan was catching up to Jack, closing fast, and then going past him with good, steady power when, suddenly, a bunch of bars came sliding down the face of the cliff from above them.

"Watch out!" yelled Kenny.

Juan just managed to leap out of the way before the bars struck him.

Kenny turned to Doug and saw that he was grinning ear-to-ear. "All right!" barked Kenny. "No more of this horseshit! Now all of you, get back to work! You got thirty minutes to quitting time, damn it!"

Turning in their tools that afternoon, Kenny took Juan aside. "*Amigo*," he said, "you and me, we're short, so we don't got to always go around being the big man. Jack, he's not so bad, believe me. I know him. It's just that a lot is expected of him." He cut a new chew with his pocket knife, offering Juan some, but Juan refused. "I like your work," he added, putting the new cut in his mouth, "you ease off *mañana* and I promise you that you got a job here as long as I'm powder foreman."

Juan looked into the old man's bright blue eyes, blue like his own father's. "You got a deal," he said.

"Good," said Kenny, and he put his knife away and stuck out his hand and Juan took it.

This was the first time that Juan had ever met a man who had even bigger, thicker hands than his own. Why, Kenny's hands were monstrous, just like his own father's.

That day, Juan Salvador was paid two dollars, twice as much as the regular laborers. Walking back to town that afternoon with his people, Juan was a hero. He was the Mexican who screwed the *cabrón gringo*!

Getting home that night, Juan announced to his family that he was rich. He took his mother to the grocery store. Jose, his nephew, went with them, having already heard all over the *barrio* of his uncle's great feat.

In the store, Doña Margarita took hold of Juan by the arm. "Listen to me," she said, going up the aisle, "when we go up to the counter to pay, you let me do the talking. These *gringos* are tricky, always trying to cheat us and charge us too much. But I've learned how to deal with them. All I do is smile like this," she said, opening her mouth and showing her one good, brown-stained tooth, "and nod and say, 'yes, yes,' acting very agreeable. Because *gringos* are polite people above all else, smiling and saying, 'yes, yes,' all the time. I know, believe me. And, also, I guess because we don't speak English, they think we can't add. So you just keep quiet when we go to the counter to pay."

Juan winked at his nephew. "Whatever you say, Mama."

"Look at this," said Doña Margarita, picking up a can of condensed milk with a carnation on the label. "These *gringos* are so treacherous. Why, look at this can. Here, they try to make us believe that these cans with the flower are cans of milk but they're not, *mi hijito*. I've tasted this milk and it's so sweet that, of course, the truth is that it comes from these flowers."

Juan had to laugh. His mother's mind just had no end to it. Seeing Juan laugh, the old woman laughed, too. They continued shopping, buying a mountain of food, and Jose put everything into the basket that he carried.

"All right," said the old woman, coming up the last aisle, "now all we need is a little coffee and a pack of Luckys for me—if you got enough money—then we can go home."

"Don't worry," said Juan, "I got plenty of money, and I'm going to be doing good every day from now on. The powder foreman, he told me as long as he's foreman, I got a job."

"Then let's pray that he continues being the boss," said his mother, and she gripped his arm, drawing him close. She was very excited. "I'm so happy to see you settling down, *mi hijito*. Remember that angel that I told you of who milked our goat? It frightened her when she saw that gun in your pocket."

Juan took a big breath. They'd already gone over this story a dozen times. But he was just sure that anyone who his mother thought was an angel would be far from his idea of beauty.

"All right, Mama," he said. "I'm not carrying it now, but please don't expect too much. I'll be carrying it again when I see fit."

"Yes, I know," she said, "but at least you're settling down." And she patted his hand as they got in line for the cash register. "Oh, I love my Luckys, *mi hijito*," she said. "They are the best *cigarritos* in all this country. The others are terrible. Especially those with the picture of the camel. They say they're a blend of Turkish tobacco, but smoking them, I knew they were made from the *caca* of that ugly animal. Oh, these *gringos*, you have to watch them constantly."

On this one, Juan drew his mother close, laughing wildly, and he kissed her. Then he got hold of his nephew and drew him close to him, too.

"Jose," he said, "no matter how old you get or how far you go in life, remember this: if it hadn't been for this old woman's power, none of us would be here today. She is our life, our strength, our proof of God here on earth." And saying this, tears came to his eyes, but he didn't care who might see, he was so proud to be with his mother, his greatest love in all the world.

"And don't think he's exaggerating," said Doña Margarita; "I'm every bit what Juan says, and don't you forget it.

"And now, you, Juan," she said, laughing happily, "give me your money and remember, I'll do the talking and say, 'yes, yes,' or 'excuse me,' every few minutes, and the *gringos* will think I speak perfect English!"

The following morning at the rock quarry Juan was just starting to cross the yard over to the other powder men when Doug called out.

"Hey, you, Vil-as-enor-eeee!" he said, twisting Juan's name worse than ever, "we ain't got no work for you today . . . unless you all want to work with the other Mexeee-cans," he added.

Juan glanced across the yard to where Kenny was talking to the other powder men. "I need to work," he said.

"Good," said Doug, "I figured as much." And he smiled, truly enjoying it.

"You showed them up!" said Julio, as Juan went into the yard with the other Mexicans. "That's why you don't got that job today! You outdrilled 'em bad, *mano!*"

"I shouldn't have pushed so much," said Juan, thinking that this was also why he'd gotten his throat slashed. If only he hadn't won both big pots, he might not have been cut.

"No," said Rodolfo. "There's nothing you could've done. They would've fired you, no matter what."

Juan figured the teacher was probably right. But still, he had to learn to hold back in life. He got a pick and shovel and went to work with his own people as the sun climbed up into the flat, smooth sky.

Then it was noon, but the horn didn't blow. They had to be told by one of the foremen that it was time to quit for lunch. This day, Juan had plenty of food to eat, so he shared his good fortune with Julio and the others.

It was late afternoon when the charge went off and the whole cliff blew out in one sudden explosion. Juan dove for cover. So did Julio and Rodolfo. Rock came down all around them—a million flying pieces. Then, when the noise of the deafening explosion subsided, Juan could hear men screaming in pain. He stood up. As the dust cleared, he could see that some men had been caught in the rock by the base of the cliff.

Juan raced across the yard to help the injured men. Julio and the teacher were right behind him.

Legs and arms were sticking out of the debris every which way. One man's whole face was twisted around with his eyes bulging out. Before they were through digging, they'd uncovered three dead Mexicans and five others were critically injured.

That night in town, Juan and the other workmen got drunk. It was that same rot-gut whiskey that Juan had been drinking since he'd come to California, but this time he didn't care. He was outraged. It had been such a stupid accident. If the horn was broken, then they should have called off the dynamite job or sent a man around to warn everyone.

"But this isn't the first accident we've had," said Julio. "And it's always only the *mejicanos* who get injured."

"And you stand for that?" asked Juan.

"What do you suggest?" asked Rodolfo. "That we quit?"

"We're not dogs!" said Juan angrily. "In Montana, I saw the Greeks sit down when one workman got hurt."

"But this isn't Montana," said Julio.

"It's the same country!" yelled Juan.

"Keep talking," smiled the schoolteacher. "This is what I've been saying all along. But these *cabrones* don't want to strike. They're willing to accept whatever bones are thrown to them!

"Oh, my General Villa, he could stir men's hearts! He'd get men up in arms and ready to fight with nothing but their bare hands. So you're right, my young friend," he said to Juan, "it's time we stopped just getting drunk and unite like one fist and demand our rights!"

They were pretty well drunk by now.

"So do it, *mi coronel*!" said Julio. "Unite us!"

"All right," said the tall pock-faced man, and he stood up. "*¡Compañeros!*" he yelled. There were over twenty men from the rock quarry in the alley behind the poolhall. "Are we men or dogs? Are we *mejicanos* or oxen to let men treat us like this?"

And Juan saw half of the men get to their feet and yell, "*¡Vivan los mejicanos!*"

They were drunk and ready to take on the bosses at the quarry. The teacher-colonel from Monterrey drew up a paper listing all their complaints, plus a demand of money for the families of the dead and injured men. The meeting lasted long into the night.

Juan went home singing, feeling proud of his fellow countrymen. They were good people, men of the Revolution, and they knew how to stand up and be accounted for. In the morning Juan had such a terrible hangover, he could barely move. But still, he was there with Julio and the teacher-colonel at the quarry before sunup. They were surrounded by eighty-some men, and any man who hadn't been at the meeting the night before had been told about it, so they all stood united.

When Doug came out of the office with his clipboard, Juan could see it in Doug's eyes—he sensed something. Juan smiled. This son-of-a-bitch, dried-out *gringo* was going to get what he deserved.

"Go ahead," whispered Julio to the teacher-colonel, "now's the time, *mi coronel*!"

The man with the pocked face stepped forward. "Doug," he said, "we had a meeting last night." He was nervous, but still his voice sounded strong. "And concerning that accident of yesterday, we came up with a list of complaints that we wish to voice!"

"Well, I'll be go to hell," laughed Doug, chewing his jaw, "so you monkeys all had a meeting. Don't that beat all? Well, then, Rodolf-eee, you all hold on here. I think I best get ahold of Jim and the others before you go on with your list, eh?" He laughed, truly enjoying himself, and it made

Juan's skin crawl. So this was a regular thing that this tall, lanky man did with their names. He mispronounced their names on purpose, telling them in no uncertain terms that they were nothing to him but dog shit and, if they didn't like it, it was just too bad.

Juan took a deep breath, heart pounding, as he watched Doug go up on the porch and go inside the office, closing the door.

Juan, Rodolfo, Julio and all the men waited. They waited ten minutes, then twenty minutes more. The workmen began to talk among themselves, saying that maybe the bosses weren't going to come out and, if they didn't get back to work, they might be fired.

"Calm down," said the teacher, "they're just trying to scare us. Believe me, everything is going to be fine. These complaints we have here are more than fair. Isn't that right, eh, Chino?" he said to Juan.

Juan looked at the teacher and wondered why he'd asked him. He was just a kid, after all, and this man was in his late thirties and had been a colonel with Villa. He didn't need to ask anyone on earth for their approval. But still, Juan found himself saying, "Why, yes, of course, they're more than fair, *mi coronel.*"

The sun climbed higher and the day grew hotter. Juan's head was still exploding with pain from the whiskey that he'd drunk the night before.

Juan took off his jacket and pulled his shirt out of his pants. He looked across the yard to Jack and the other powder men who were over in the shade of a tree, drinking water and taking it easy. Once, Juan's and Jack's eyes met, and the big man lifted his tin cup of water to Juan. Juan nodded back to him. Jack just grinned.

Then, suddenly, a car drove up behind Juan and the other *mejicanos*, and four big men with shotguns got out. Juan hadn't expected this. He glanced around and saw that the other workmen hadn't expected this, either.

"Don't no one move," said Rodolfo. He took up ground, and the schoolteacher truly did look like a colonel in Villa's army at this moment. "We're *mejicanos!*" he shouted proudly.

"That's right," said Julio. "Keep calm. And everything will be asshole okay!"

The four men raised up their weapons like professional soldiers, and they came toward them. At this same moment, Jack and the other Anglo workmen got to their feet and picked up bars and shovels and came marching on them, too, from behind. But seeing the situation, Rodolfo still didn't panic. He shouted, "Let the armed men pass! Don't do anything! Remember, this isn't the Revolution! Just step back and let them pass. They're scared of us! That's why they called in these *pistoleros!*"

The workmen did as told, and the four armed men passed through them without incident. The powder men quit their march, stopping in mid-yard, and the armed men went up to the office. One went inside. The other three stationed themselves by the door. Juan's heart pounded. He was so proud of his countrymen. They'd held themselves well. Just as good as he'd seen the Greeks do up in Montana.

He glanced over at the powder men, and his and Jack's eyes met once more. The big Anglo raised up his right hand, pointing his index finger like a pistol at Juan. But Juan only grinned. They were going to break these Anglos' backs, after all. No one was taking them for granted anymore. But then Juan heard his people start talking. They were saying that they really hadn't expected all this trouble and maybe they weren't going to gain anything.

"And why did they bring those men with guns?" asked one man.

"To bring us tacos for lunch," said Julio, laughing.

Everyone burst out laughing. But Juan could feel that something was happening. They were losing it. Then the office door opened and Doug and the other armed man came out.

"All right," said Doug, "we have everything settled. Jim just bought us a brand new horn. It will get here tomorrow, so today we don't do any dynamite work." He opened his clipboard. "Now line up! And let's see who gets to work today."

A dozen men stepped forward, just like that, wanting to be the first ones to be called back to work. Juan was flabbergasted. He turned to Rodolfo. The colonel saw the rage in his young friend's eyes.

"No, wait!" yelled the teacher. "How about the families of the men who died? And the list of points that we drew up last night?"

Just then the front door of the office opened wide, and the big, beefy man named Jim came out along with Kenny and all the other foremen. They quickly lined up on the porch in front of the office door, facing Juan and the other men below them. Juan and Kenny's eyes met, but then Kenny looked away.

Juan felt his heart wanting to hide, he felt so embarrassed. He'd just seen a good man lose all honor. But that's the way it went, and this was the moment of truth. It had all been a little testing game up until now. Now was when things were really going to happen, and his countrymen were truly going to show these *gringos* what they were made of.

Juan took a big breath, trying to keep himself calm. He'd learned with the Greeks that it was much easier for a man to fight a war, compared to the guts it took to hold a line and do nothing. To grab up a machete and attack with your heart pounding was natural. But to hold still and think when your heart was going so fast your head felt like it was going to spin off, was more difficult.

"All right, Rochin," said Jim, "so I understand you have a list you want me to see. Well, that's fine. You just turn in that little list to my office, after these men get back to work, and I'll read it and see what can be done. But the main thing here, Rocheee, is that I've ordered a new horn and you'll all get plenty of warning in the future."

Juan almost burst out laughing. Why, this *gringo* son-of-a-bitch thought they were just children. The issue wasn't the horn. The issue was that good men had been killed three different times this year. The issue was the dead men's families and the injured men's hospital bills. And the issue was all the damned conditions of the quarry. Places had to be built for the men to go during an explosion. And water needed to be put near where they worked. Men needed to be given time to put their tools away in the evenings. And also, simply, they needed toilet facilities. There was a whole list of things that needed to be attended to. Hearing what they had just offered, the Greeks would have laughed in their face and sat down, not moving, until the bosses were ready to talk seriously and get down to business.

But, what happened next took Juan totally by surprise.

As Rochin began to talk and make their point, one man said something and walked past the teacher toward the men on the porch. At first, Juan hadn't understood what the man had said. But he figured that he'd cursed at the men standing in front of the office and now he was threatening them with their lives because one of his friends had been killed yesterday.

But then another man went forward and said something. This time Juan heard what he had said. He said, "Okay!" Just like that, and then he'd walked past the teacher and past the office, going back into the yard.

"NOOOO!" screamed Juan, rushing up to the schoolteacher. "Not that way! Don't you see? They'll have us by the *tanates* from now on if you give in!"

Everyone looked at Juan, except for the two men who'd just crossed the line. And then there went a third, and a fourth. They were all going past Juan, back to the quarry as fast as they could, when Juan screamed. For no Greek would have ever done this. The other Greeks would have killed him.

"All right, Rocheee," said Jim, "turn in your list and get back to work before all the jobs are taken."

Juan turned to the schoolteacher and their eyes locked. But only for a moment. For what Juan saw happen next, told him everything. The ex-colonel was just too tired and old to fight anymore. And so he stepped across the line, turned in his list, and continued across the yard to go to work, too.

Juan went wild. Rodolfo Rochin had been their best. Screaming and bellowing, Juan ripped the shirt off his back and threw it on the ground, stomping it with his boots. Julio tried to calm him down, but Juan knocked him away like a paper doll. The men on the porch watched, and Juan continued screaming. He was crazy. Totally *loco*. All these years that he'd been away from his people—up in Montana among the Greeks and Turks— he'd missed them so much, but now he hated his people from the bottom of his soul.

"*¡Cabrones pendejos!*" he screamed at his fellow countrymen, who were filing into the quarry. "You don't deserve the shit a dog leaves in the streets! These *gringos* tricked you worse than children! They have no more respect for you than pieces of dried-out horse shit!" He grabbed his crotch, pulling

up on it. "I piss on you! DO YOU HEAR ME? I piss on you for all eternity!
¡Mejicanos pendejos!"

And Juan's bellowing screams echoed across the entire quarry. He was
that mad, that crazy, that wild. And then he began to bite himself.

The men on the porch couldn't believe what they were seeing. They'd
always heard that Mexicans had to let blood. But they didn't know that they'd
eat the flesh off their very own bones, too.

Blood was coming off Juan's arms and shoulders with each bite. And he
spat the blood at the Anglos on the porch. "Shoot!" he screamed at the
Anglos. "Shoot, you sons-of-a-bitch!"

And he pulled at his crotch again, showing them his *tanates*, and the
muscles on his body rippled like fish in fast water.

Julio and the two other men who hadn't crossed the line tried grabbing
Juan to turn him around before the armed men shot him. But Juan threw
them like children. He was at that human place from which a man could go
through a wall of bullets and kill five men with a machete before he died. He
was at that human place where a mother could grab a car and throw it off her
dying child. He was crazy, insane, hating the Mexican flesh he had on his
bones.

Giving witness, Kenny signalled the men with shotguns to go on inside
and leave the rabid man alone.

Juan and Julio ran most of the way back to town
together. They were just too excited to walk. Juan couldn't calm down. He
was flying, reeling, a million thoughts were flashing through his mind. He
was going crazy. His body was exploding with power. They bought a bottle
of that terrible bootleg whiskey, and they drank all morning long.

"Shit," said Juan, "let's go across the border and get some real tequila!
This *gringo* crap is killing me!"

"You've got it!" said Julio.

So they found a guy with an old truck, gave him a few drinks, borrowed
his truck on a handshake, and they took off. But neither Juan nor Julio knew
how to drive, and so they almost went off the road several times.

They got to Mexicali the next morning and got drunk on good tequila
and ate tacos and chased women. Then Juan got an idea, and they bought
fifteen gallons of excellent tequila for three dollars. They drove around in the
desert until they found a dirt road going around the Border Inspection
Station, back into the United States.

Back in Corona, they sold the liquor for a dollar a quart, making a huge
profit. They paid the man for the use of his truck, and split the remaining
money. Juan now had money in his pocket once again and felt much better.
He'd never work for another son-of-a-bitch *gringo* bastard again.

In the following year, Juan grew a full beard and he followed the crops, setting up poker games wherever his people were. He made good money and bought an old car, keeping a constant eye out for the two men who'd stolen his money and left him for dead.

And many times, when Juan got into a new town, he'd find out that the Filipino and his formidable friend had just left. Juan bought a .45 automatic and two extra clips and he practiced shooting until he could hit the center of a fifty-cent piece at twenty yards. His reputation grew and spread until, finally, he came to be known as the man who couldn't die.

16

*It was springtime, and Saint Peter closed the floodgates
of heaven and the fields of cutting-flowers blossomed
into a wondrous rainbow of color, dazzling even the
birds and the bees.*

Lupe awoke, all wet with perspiration. She'd had that
awful dream again. She got up and rearranged the layers of newspaper on the
bed of box springs and lay back down, looking out the flap of their rented
tent. The moon was out. She breathed deeply, trying to relax and go back to
sleep.

But finally, not able to stand it anymore, she got up and went outside.
She sat down on the cool earth. It was a clear night, except for a few white
clouds. The mosquitoes were out by the hundreds. Lupe slapped her legs
and naked arms, trying to keep them away.

Looking at the blue-wrinkled moon, Lupe fully knew what was troubling
her. The day before, they'd come into the north county of San Diego—from
having worked the fields down in the Imperial Valley—and, in a few weeks,
they'd be going back up the coast to Santa Ana, and she still hadn't told
anyone why she'd quit school.

"What is it, *mi hijita*?" said her mother from inside the tent.

"Oh, *nada*, Mama," said Lupe, quickly wiping her eyes and straightening
up. "Please, go back to sleep. I'm fine, Mama."

"Yes," hissed Carlota from inside the tent, too, "she's fine, so please keep
still so we can all sleep!"

"Shhhhhh!" said her mother, getting up and going out into the star-filled
night. "It's a beautiful night, eh?" she said.

Lupe tried to smile. "Yes, Mama."

"We have so much to be grateful for but . . . ooh, these mosquitoes!"
said her mother, slapping her arm.

Lupe laughed. Her mother laughed, too, sitting down alongside her.
Neither one of them said anything for a while. They just sat there, brushing
off the mosquitoes and giving warmth to each other.

"You know," said Doña Guadalupe, watching the moon slide behind a
softlaced cloud, "my father Leonides always told me how the moon gave him
a pathway of light on those nights that he rode from the authorities, saving

my life. He said that the moon came down from the heavens and sat down on his right shoulder like the eye of God, guiding him through the terrible *arroyos* as we rode night and day like the wind." The old woman breathed deeply. "The full moon has always been my special friend, *mi hijita*, giving me hope even in my darkest moments. And now look, here above us, we have the very same moon smiling down upon us that we had back in Mexico. The full moon is Our Lady of the Universe, *mi hijita*, giving God the Father a steady hand as He reigns the heavens."

Then she said it, right there, as she spoke to Lupe of the moon. "*Mi hijita*, why is it that every time we get ready to return to Santa Ana you become troubled?"

Lupe was stunned. She hadn't realized that it was so obvious. She glanced around at the lines of tents sitting like upside-down paper bags in the moonlight.

"Is it," continued her mother, "that you want to return to school, *mi hijita*?"

"Oh, no," lied Lupe quickly, "it's not that at all!"

"*Mi hijita*," said her mother, "are you telling me the truth?" she asked gently.

"Oh, Mama," said Lupe, and she didn't want to, but she began to cry. "Even if we could afford for me to go back to school, I'm too old!" she said.

Suddenly, Lupe realized what it was that the teacher had yelled at her: "You dirty little Mexican prick-tease! Who do you think you're kidding? You're too old to be in school!" Oh, the horror, the shame that she'd felt.

Breathing deeply, Doña Guadalupe reached out, touching her daughter's cheek which was glowing with wetness in the moonlight.

"*Mi amor*," said the old woman, "but what's gotten into you? You're not too old to reach up for the stars. Don't you remember the night you helped us give birth to the twins? The power that we women felt, sitting under the light of the full moon . . . the strength, the feeling of life being so strong that it made us feel immortal!

"Well, *querida*, we've come too far and suffered too much to lose hope now, especially of our dreams. But you must open your heart and be strong! And then the full moon will always be your special friend."

"But that's not it, Mama," said Lupe, shaking her head. "The teacher . . . he told me that I was too old."

"What teacher?" asked her mother. "I thought that that woman, Mrs. . . ."

"Mrs. Sullivan."

"Yes, Mrs. Sullivan, was your teacher."

"She was, Mama," said Lupe, her eyes double-crossing her and filling with tears. "And she was wonderful. She helped me after school and I learned so fast that I was able to skip three grades."

She stopped, not able to continue.

"Yes, but go on," said her mother, "what about this other teacher?"

Lupe shook her head.

"Lupe," said the old woman, "tell me. I'm your mother, I want to know."

"Well, I was in the seventh grade and Mr. Horn, my new teacher, was real nice to me, too, helping me after school; but then one day he, he, he grabbed me from behind while I was writing on the blackboard."

Doña Guadalupe looked up at the blue-wrinkled moon playing hide-and-seek among the clouds. "Did he hurt you?" asked the old lady, her hands clawed into fists.

Lupe shook her head. "No, not really. I screamed so loud that I scared him away. But he called me names, Mama, the way he'd looked at me, oh, it was awful!"

"But you're okay now?"

Lupe nodded. "Yes, except when I think of school and how much I'd wanted to learn bookkeeping so I could get a job in an office. I could scratch his eyes out, I get so mad."

Seeing her daughter's anger, Doña Guadalupe felt better, safer, and she held Lupe in her arms, watching the moon skipping from cloud to cloud.

"But you know," said Doña Guadalupe, "who says that you can't go back to visit . . . what's your first teacher's name again?"

"Mrs. Sullivan."

"Yes, her, and ask her if you can't borrow books and study as we travel? Eh, you tell me!"

Lupe's whole mind went spinning. She'd never thought of that. Why, yes, maybe she really could go and visit Mrs. Sullivan and do as she'd done when Señora Muñoz had left their canyon and she'd left Manuelita and her an outline of what to study for the next five years!

"Oh, Mama, I'd love to do that!" she said excitedly.

"Good!" said Carlota from inside the tent. "So now keep quiet and let us all go back to sleep."

"You keep quiet, too, Carlota!" snapped Victoriano.

"What's the racket?" said their father, waking up.

They all laughed. Their old father was getting so deaf lately, he must not have heard anything until now.

And so for the rest of the night Lupe lay in bed, thinking of how she could complete her studies and one day work in an office and do figures, as Don Manuel had done back in La Lluvia de Oro, and she'd be able to help support her parents in their old age.

It was mid-morning and Juan was at the poolhall in the barrio of Carlsbad in the north part of San Diego County. Several cardsharks were in town, following the crops, and he wanted to make a deal with the owner of the poolhall, a big half-breed American Indian named Archie

Freeman, so that he could control the poker games while the people were in town.

"There's no need to cheat these workmen," Juan explained to Archie. "All we do is charge 'em five percent of every pot and, hell, and the end of the evening we got most of everybody's money—winners and losers alike."

"Sounds good," said Archie. "But then what do I need you for?"

Archie was also the deputy sheriff, and so Juan had to go very easy with him.

"Because cards aren't your specialty," said Juan. "And you got enough problems with that dance you're putting on. Plus, I'm a professional, so I can guarantee you a solid profit and no problems."

Towering over Juan, Archie pulled at his lower lip like a big sad-faced cow, thinking, figuring, then he said, "Okay, I'll try it your way one night."

"Oh, no," said Juan, grinning. "Three nights, minimum."

Both men laughed, continuing their negotiations.

Just south of town in a place called La Costa, Lupe and her family were picking tomatoes. It was almost noon and the sun was high overhead, and Lupe could see that her mother and father were exhausted.

"Mama," said Lupe, "why don't you and Papa go ahead and set up lunch? Victoriano and I will finish up your boxes.

"Lupe's right," said Don Victor, "I'm tired."

"Well, okay," said their mother, "I do need time to set up a place for us to eat."

So the old lady took off her wide-brimmed hat and wiped the perspiration from her face with her handkerchief. Then she and her husband started down between the rows of tomatoes.

Doña Guadalupe and Don Victor were two of the oldest pickers. And working out in the treeless fields was a job only for young people, not for people who'd already had all the juices sucked out of them with years of working in the sun.

Lupe and her brother watched their parents go down between the rows. They looked so old and tired, yet beautiful, walking together; two old people who'd seen so much life.

At noon Lupe and Victoriano left the field, too. Lupe breathed deeply and she could smell the ocean in the distance and the fragrance from the fields of cut flowers down below them.

At the edge of the tomato field, Carlota came rushing up to them. She was working with another group of workers down below in the fields of flowers.

"Lupe," she said excitedly, "there's going to be a dance in Carlsbad tonight and Jaime and his friends want us to go with them."

Jaime and some other young men were several yards away, talking among themselves but glancing over toward the girls. Lupe couldn't understand why

Jaime and his friends always kept getting Carlota to ask her to go to the dances with them when they knew perfectly well that she didn't dance.

"Oh, come on, please say yes," said Carlota, glancing nervously toward Jaime and his friends.

Seeing how anxious her sister was, Lupe nodded. "All right," she said, "but we'll have to ask Mama."

"Oh, thank you!" said Carlota, waving at the boys.

Then Lupe and her sister and brother continued down the dirt road that circled the field to where the people were setting up places to eat under the trees and brush.

From here, the whole lagoon was visible, and the flat horizon of the sea could be seen, too. White seagulls circled overhead and the sky was blue and wide and clear. The fields of cutting-flowers were in full bloom and they looked like a great rainbow covering the soft, rolling hills all the way down to the sea. Next to their box canyon, this was, indeed, one of the most beautiful sights that Lupe had ever seen.

Coming up to the brushline, Lupe saw that her father was asleep in the shade of a small tree and her mother had cleared away the brush and spread a blanket out on the ground for them to eat on. It never failed to amaze Lupe how her mother always managed to make a little home for them no matter where they were.

Sitting cross-legged, looking plump and regal, Doña Guadalupe sliced a big juicy tomato and put the luscious red-orange wheels next to the slices of the rich, green avocado that she'd already cut. Lupe's family was one of the poorest in all the fields, but still, they always ate very well, getting food from the different ranches where they worked.

"Mama, there's going to be a dance in Carlos Malo tonight," said Carlota, "and Lupe and I have been invited!"

Carlos Malo was what the Mexicans called the town of Carlsbad.

"Well, you can only go if your brother agrees to take you," said their mother, putting a couple more tortillas on the little open fire.

"Will you take us?" Carlota asked her brother.

"Well, I don't know," said Victoriano, getting a tortilla off the fire to nibble on. "I'm a busy man. I have a lot of very important business to attend to tonight."

"Lupe!" yelled Carlota. "You tell our brother to stop teasing me!"

Lupe only laughed, turning over the tortillas on the little fire. They were going to have *quesadillas* with tomato slices and avocado. "I agreed to go with you," she said. "I can't do more, Carlota."

"Oh, you and Victoriano are just old goats!" said Carlota. "Never wanting to do anything! This is the Stringbean Festival! The most important dance of the year!"

"I thought the most important was the apricot dance of Hemet," laughed Victoriano.

"Well, that one's important, too," said Carlota.

"And the orange blossom dance in Santa Ana," continued Victoriano. "We'd be going to dances every weekend if it was up to you!"

"Yes," said Carlota. "Exactly! And some day I want to own my own dancehall and put on dances every night!"

They all laughed and Lupe wondered deep inside herself why it was that she didn't like to go to the dances like her sister Carlota did.

But then, thinking further, Lupe knew why it was that she didn't like to go. Dancing wasn't really that important to her. What was more important for her was to have a special person to dance with. Why, if her Colonel were alive, she'd go dancing with him every night. She breathed deeply, realizing that she hadn't thought of him in a long time.

"*Buenas tardes*," said Jaime, suddenly coming up to them.

Lupe turned and saw Jaime and his two friends. They were as lean as jackrabbits and they wore brightly-colored bandannas about their heads and tight-fitting, sleeveless undershirts and loose pants. They were what the people called showoffs because they didn't wear hats or long-sleeved shirts to protect themselves from the sun.

Seeing that Lupe had turned to look at him, Jaime gave her his best smile, showing her his beautiful white teeth. The muscles on his arms raced up and down like rabbits. All the girls were crazy about Jaime, and the men respected him, too, because he was a semi-pro boxer. But Lupe didn't really care for him.

"*Buenas tardes*," said their mother. "Would you care to join us?"

"Oh, no, thank you, *señora*. We have our own lunches waiting for us," he said respectfully. "I just came by to see if Carlota has told you about the dance," he added, looking directly at Lupe.

"Yes, she has," said Doña Guadalupe, "but we won't have an answer until my husband awakens and we talk."

"Very well," he said, giving a polite nod. "Then with your permission, enjoy your lunches. And I hope that you'll be able to join us, too, Lupe," he said. He gave Lupe another smile, nodding goodbye to her.

After they were gone, Carlota turned to Lupe. "I just don't know what's wrong with you!" she said. "Every girl is just dying for him to ask her out, and for months you've ignored him like he has lice!"

"Well, maybe he does," said Victoriano, laughing, mouth open.

Lupe joined her brother, laughing, too. But inside her soul, she felt very nervous.

After shaking hands on a deal, Archie and Juan decided to go up the street to eat lunch at the Montana Cafe. The people who ran the Montana Cafe were a big German named Hans and his wife Helen. They'd moved out to California from New Jersey a couple of years before.

"Hello, Hans!" said Archie as he sauntered into the cafe in a big, loose-rolling gait.

"Good to see you, Archie," said Hans. "But you better eat all you order this time," he added.

Archie only laughed, pulling up his gunbelt as he sat down with his back against the wall. "That Kraut son-of-a-bitch," he said laughing, "you got to be careful you don't order more than you can eat or he'll force you to eat it, crazy son-of-a-bitch."

Helen came up with two cups of coffee. "Hans says the roast beef is best today, Archie," she said, smiling. "And then my special homemade hot apple pie for dessert, I say."

"Sounds good, Helen," said the lawman, tipping his hat. "I'd like you to meet my friend, Juan."

"Oh, 'John' in English. Same as my Hans," said Helen. "Glad to meet you, Juan."

"Very glad to meet you, Helen," said Juan, also tipping his Stetson.

The café filled up with local businessmen, and Archie and Juan were eating their roast beef, truly enjoying the good, cheap food, when three loud-mouthed boys entered.

They were in their late teens, large, muscular. They were the sons of local ranchers who'd been away to college, and they thought that they were pretty hot stuff.

Archie only grinned, picking up his cup of coffee. "Oh, this is going to be good," he said.

"What?" asked Juan, not quite understanding.

"You just watch," said Archie, sipping his coffee in big, air-sucking sips. "Them boys are in for a rude awakening." And he winked at Juan, truly enjoying it.

Still, Juan had no idea what was going on.

He and Archie had just been served their big juicy slices of hot apple pie when the three boys got a little too loud. Hans came from behind the counter with a big butcher knife in his hand.

"Boys," he said, chewing his words in his big square jaws, "this is no place to fool around! I work hard to cook good food, and I got good, cheap, honest prices! So now you three boys settle down and eat, and everything will be just fine!"

But the biggest boy wasn't about to be told what to do, and he pushed his plate away. "Hell, we don't have to eat this shit if we don't want to, grandpa," he said.

Suddenly, the big, blond German's face exploded, and his eyes rolled over like a bloodshot bull's. Bellowing with rage, he hit the boy in the back with the big wooden handle of the butcher knife, stunning him.

"You eat!" he bellowed. "All of you! And you enjoy that food you ordered, now!"

The three boys saw his bloodshot eyes and the huge knife. Terror-stricken, they began to eat.

"But aren't you going to do something?" asked Juan. "You're the law."

"Not me," said Archie. "I ain't no fool. I'm eating my pie. Hell, last month he hit me on the head with a coffee cup when I came in half-tanked up and refused to finish my steak."

"He hit you? A deputy?" asked Juan incredulously.

"Hell, he's a German," said Archie, pulling back his hat and showing Juan a red scar across his skull. "I was lucky he didn't scalp my ass!" And he laughed and laughed, truly enjoying himself. Archie was half California Indian, and he didn't have a mean or revengeful bone in all his body.

It was almost dark, and Lupe and Carlota were standing in line with Victoriano across the street from the poolhall, waiting to get into the dance. The music had already started, and it could be heard halfway up the barrio. Lupe was wearing her polka-dot dress and some beautiful earrings that her mother had gotten for her in Arizona.

Across the street Juan was overseeing the card tables. He was all dressed up in a white shirt and dark suit, and his beard was neatly trimmed.

"Well," said Archie, seeing that Juan had control of the situation, "I think I'll mosey on over and see how things are going at the dance. I don't want no young studs getting in for free."

"Go ahead," said Juan, "everything is fine here."

"It better be, for the price I'm paying you," said Archie.

The big lawman went out the open door of the well-lit poolroom and across the rutted dirt road to the church that he'd rented to put on the dance. Approaching the line of young people, Archie immediately spotted Lupe in her pale peach dress, but he paid no attention to her. The one he liked was Carlota. She was dressed in red, and she couldn't stop moving. Her feet were dancing back and forth on the hard-packed ground that the people used as a sidewalk, as she whirled about in her full-skirted dress.

"Hey, you!" called Archie to Carlota. "Come over here to the front of the line," he said, grinning ear-to-ear.

"Me?" asked Carlota, pointing at herself.

Everyone in town knew that Archie was the local law and a big shot in the barrio.

"Yes, you, and that whirling red dress! Come on up here with your friends, baby!"

Carlota screeched. Archie had said "baby" to her just like a *gringo*. "Come on," she said, quickly going up to the head of the line with Lupe, Victoriano, and Jaime and his two friends who'd just joined them.

"Here are the tickets," said Archie to Carlota, towering over her and Jaime and everyone else. "You sell 'em for me, but don't let no one in who ain't paid." He winked. "I'll be right back. Just gotta go inside and lift my leg to a fire hydrant."

He laughed good-heartedly, pulled up his gunbelt, and went inside. Carlota was ecstatic.

"Line right up!" she shouted.

"Give me the tickets," said Jaime. "This is a job for a man!"

"Oh, no!" yelled Carlota, jerking the tickets close. "I'm the boss! He gave them to me!"

"Oh, 'the boss'?" laughed Jaime.

"You damned right," said Carlota, laughing excitedly as she began to take people's money.

Lupe smiled, realizing that her sister's dream of having her own dance room had come true. She looked across the street, and through the open doors of the poolhall, she saw a well-dressed man with a lion head of hair. Her heart stopped. There was something strangely familiar about his back, his posture, his stance.

The dance had been going on for some time when Archie came back into the poolhall and asked Juan how it was going.

"Pretty good," said Juan, "but you didn't tell me that you'd be selling whiskey in the alley, you bastard. Liquored-up men are harder to handle."

Laughing, Archie slapped Juan on the back. "Shit, does the coyote tell the fox where the chickens are?"

"You sneaky bastard!" said Juan.

"Whatever," said Archie. "But I'll tell you this, you get hold of some good whiskey for me, instead of this rot-gut shit, and I'll make us both rich!"

"How about some good tequila?" asked Juan.

"Nope," said Archie, "*gringos* like whiskey."

"I see," said Juan.

They were talking, going over the different possibilities of doing business together, when suddenly there was a commotion outside and everyone rushed to the open doors of the poolhall.

Archie and Juan went to the doors, too, and they could see that a fight had broken out in front of the dance hall across the street. It looked like the same three boys that they'd seen at the Montana Cafe, fighting with four Mexicans.

But one tall, slender Mexican wasn't really fighting. He was just trying to get the short woman in the red dress, Carlota, away from the fight. She looked tough, as if she wanted to get into the middle of the fight and scratch people's eyes out.

Someone came running up to Archie. "They're killing each other!" yelled the man. "You got to stop them!"

But Archie only grinned and brought out a stick of gum. "It's all right," he said. "Just let them soften up each other a little for me." And he put the stick of gum in his mouth and began chewing calmly, watching the fight.

That's when Juan saw Lupe. She was standing under the outside light of the dance hall, looking so fresh and tall and slender—a flower in full bloom.

Juan felt his mouth go dry and his heart come pounding up into his throat. He didn't know what was happening to him. It felt as if far away, in another lifetime, he'd known this fantastic creature—her posture, her simple dress, just holding there with such regal grace under the glow of the light.

Juan forgot all about his responsibilities and started across the street. He needed to find out who this woman was, right now, before the magic passed.

But then Archie grabbed Juan from behind. "Hey, just hold on there," said Archie, turning him around. "You get back in there and watch 'em tables. I'll handle this."

Juan had to concentrate down to the marrow of his bones in order not to go crazy and hit the big lawman. Oh, she was so beautiful, it made him all weak and dizzy inside. Sobering up, Juan went back to the poolhall to watch the tables.

Archie sauntered on over to the fight, nice and easy, sizing up the situation. He could see that two of the Anglos were already pretty well used up, but the third one—the biggest one—was still going at it toe-to-toe with a very fast Mexican who knew a lot about boxing.

Carlota was screaming at the top of her lungs, "Get him, Jaime! Get him!"

Pulling out another piece of gum, Archie moved up close to Carlota. "How'd it get started, baby?" he asked, bending down so he could hear her over the ruckus.

"Those three!" she yelled, pointing at the Anglos. "They didn't pay and were forcing their way inside!"

"Oh, I see," said Archie, popping the gum into his mouth. "Should've figured as much."

He straightened up to his huge six-foot-five frame and walked into the fight with his rolling gait. Grabbing the two Anglos from behind, who were well-done-in already, he popped them together with his huge hands. Their heads slapped up against each other, and they sank to the ground as nicely as wet paper dolls.

"You two are deputized," he bellowed at Jaime's two friends who'd been fighting the Anglos. "Now just drag these gents across the street and tell my barkeep to tie 'em up."

The two young men jumped to it and began dragging the two Anglos across the street.

But the big Anglo and the Mexican named Jaime continued fighting. They worked their way up and down the street. The big Anglo tried to grab Jaime and wrestle him to the ground, but Jaime was fast and he just kept moving and hitting.

Having checked the tables, Juan went back to the front door. "I need to calm down," he said to himself. "Hell, I don't even know her and I'm going crazy."

Stepping outside, he saw the woman in the pale orange dress again, and he was flying once more. He could see that she wasn't really enjoying the fight, either. No, she was holding back, cringing. Juan was glad to know that

Doña Guadalupe (Lupe's mother)

Lupe, age 15

Maria and Don Victor in California (Lupe's sister and father)

Victoriano and Doña Guadalupe (Lupe's brother and mother)

Juan Salvador Villaseñor in Montana, age 20

Luisa (Salvador's older sister)

Deputy Sheriff Archie Freeman (Salvador's partner)

Juan Salvador and Lupe's wedding, 1929

she wasn't one of these crazy women who enjoyed violence, like that little one in the red dress who was jumping up and down alongside Archie.

Then Lupe turned, and their eyes met. He stared at her, eyes burning, eyes talking, singing, taking her into his heart and soul forever and ever. And she stared at him, eyes talking, too. He saw her look and smiled. Seeing his smile, she quickly averted her eyes and drew close to the tall, slender young man who was beside her, taking his arm. Juan grinned, fully realizing that she'd felt for him as much as he'd felt for her.

Juan brought out a cigar, lit up and continued watching her. He thought about his mother and how she always told him about the first time she'd seen his father riding into town with his brother on two matching sorrel stallions: tall, handsome strangers with hair as red as the setting sun. She and her sister had instantly known that these were the two men that they'd marry and build their lives with.

Juan blew out a cloud of smoke. It filtered up into the overhead light. He'd never really believed his mother's story until now. But, looking at this woman across the street, he was beginning to think that his mother had, indeed, told him the truth. For something was truly happening to him that was so powerful, so incredible, he had no words to describe it. His whole body felt like it was coming off the ground. And he didn't even know this woman in the pale orange dress. So how could all this be happening to him?

Then he remembered the Mexican story that said the true horseman could always pick the right horse, even from a great distance, just by seeing the silhouette of the horse in the light of the full moon. A true horseman knew so much about horses that just the posture, the movement, the tilt of the horse's head told him everything that he needed to know.

Juan glanced up and saw that yes, indeed, the moon was full. And he looked at Lupe—at her head, her posture, the silhouette of her body holding there with such a fine, regal beauty. He just knew all that he needed to know about her.

She was proud, she was strong, she was intelligent, she didn't like violence and respected life. She was a woman that a man could build a home with to last ten generations! She was the woman that he'd been searching for ever since he could remember.

It looked like the fight was almost over. The big Anglo was ready to go down when Archie stepped in and gave him a little rabbit chop to the left ear, knocking him to the ground like a gun-shot pig.

"Good fight," he said to Jaime who was blowing hard, "you and your friends now go into the dance, free, on me!"

"And you," he said, winking at Carlota, "I'm deputizing you! Me and you, we got to do some quick-stepping as soon as I clean up this little mess."

And saying this, he got hold of the left foot of the big Anglo kid and dragged him across the street, his head bouncing in the ruts of the dirt road.

Juan saw all the girls flock around the man who'd been fighting the big Anglo, but the boxer ignored them and walked over to Lupe. The boxer looked at Lupe, and she looked at him, and then they all turned to go into the dance hall—the boxer, Lupe, Victoriano and Carlota. But not before Lupe turned to see if Juan was still watching her.

And when she saw that he was, their eyes met and held once again. But only for a moment. Then she followed her group into the dance.

Juan snapped his cigar in two. Oh, he was flying! He'd never be the same again. The floodgates of love had opened. He was gone, lost, never to be without this woman in his dreams again.

"Juan," said a man, "you better come quick! Someone says that his money was stolen!"

Juan went into the poolhall and found a little short, dark-skinned Mexican shouting that he'd lost his money.

"How much?" asked Juan, trying to stop thinking about the girl.

"Everything I had!" yelled the man.

Juan glanced around at the five other men who were at the same table with him. They all looked pretty nervous. But still, Juan didn't want to just start accusing anyone.

"Look," said Juan, "how much did you start with?"

"All my pay!" said the small, dark-skinned Mexican.

Everyone in the poolhall was tense. The fight had gotten their blood boiling, and now the idea of having a thief in their midst was all they needed to go crazy.

"Please, do me a favor," said Juan as calmly as he could to the others at the table, "check your chips and make sure no accident happened."

The men all checked their chips, then each one said that they had what they were supposed to have.

"Well, I'm sorry," said Juan to the man who'd lost his money, "but unless you can tell me exactly how much you started with and how much you had when you left the table, I can't help you."

"Oh, that?" said the man. "Hell, I know exactly how much I started with."

"How much?"

"My whole week's earnings! Eighty cents!"

"Eighty cents!" said Juan, having expected something more like five or ten dollars.

"Sure, I got fired."

"Fired?" said Juan. "But nobody gets fired from the fields. Not even a wino."

"Well, I did. That's why I only had eighty cents."

"All right," said Juan, "and what did you have left of your eighty cents when you left that table?" he asked.

"Oh, that? Nothing."

"Nothing?" said Juan, now getting really confused.

"Sure, I'd already lost all my money before I left the table," said the man.

"Well, then, what the hell you complaining about?" said Juan, getting angry.

The dark-skinned Mexican burst out laughing. "Well, you asked if our money's okay and mine isn't. It's gone."

"But you lost yours!" said Juan.

"So?" said the man. "It's still gone."

"Why, you lousy little shit!" said Juan, coming after the little man. "Here you almost got me calling these innocent men thieves because of you!"

But the small man was quick and he dodged away from Juan, laughing the whole while, and everyone joined him. His name was Pepino, meaning cucumber. He was a local jokester.

It was near closing time at the poolhall, and the dance was winding down. Juan asked Pepino to watch the tables for him while he went to the dance for a few minutes.

But stepping outside, Juan found himself too nervous. He glanced up at the full moon. He thought of his mother and how she'd been insisting all year that it was time for him to choose his partner for life.

He decided to go up the alley and arm himself with a few good pulls of whiskey before going to the dance.

Oh, he was nervous. Having drunk a few shots of the rot-gut whiskey, he brought out a piece of gum to cover the smell of it before he went inside the dancehall.

The music was loud. The whole place was lit up and people were still dancing. He took a big breath, chewing his gum, and glanced around, but he didn't see her. He did see the small woman in the red dress. She was dancing up a storm with Archie. He looked like a great big Saint Bernard dog dancing with a little Mexican Chihuahua, and they both were having fun.

Juan was just about to forget about the girl, thinking it had all just been a dream, when she came out of the restroom. And in the bright lights of the dance hall, he got his first full look at Lupe, and his knees went weak.

Why, she was so young. She saw him and once more their eyes met, but this time he didn't stare at her. He could see the fear in her eyes.

He suddenly felt like a dirty old man, a monster, and he quickly turned and walked out of the dance hall. Who was he kidding? He didn't have a chance with a young, innocent thing like her. He was the reincarnation of the devil. He could have whipped that big Anglo and the pretty little boxer at the same time. He was the man who couldn't die! Not even in prison when he'd been a child and they'd cut his guts out and left him for dead.

He was trembling, he was so shaken by the time he crossed the street and went back into the poolhall. He decided to close up for the night and get stinking drunk.

Still in the next few days, Juan Salvador found out all he could about this girl. He learned her name was Lupe Gomez Camargo, and, yes, the tall slender man that had been with her was her brother Victoriano. The other guy, the boxer, did have romantic intentions, but they weren't engaged. The shorter girl in the red dress was her sister Carlota. Their permanent home was in Santa Ana, but they followed the crops for part of the year.

Juan also found out that her family was very religious. They didn't drink or gamble. He'd have to lie a lot about his life, if he ever wanted to get near her. Oh, the stars above were having fun in the heavens!

Then life took a dangerous twist.

A few days later, Juan was in Corona. He stopped by the poolhall after seeing his family and ran into Julio and Rodolfo Rochin.

"Why, hello, *mi general*!" said Rodolfo, greeting Juan.

But Juan walked right past the pock-faced man without saying a thing. "How goes it?" he said to Julio.

"Just passing it here," said Julio, sipping a Coke.

"Hey, you, goddammit!" said the tall schoolteacher, getting to his feet as he came zigzagging across the room to Juan and Julio. It was obvious that he had been drinking. "I'm talking to you!"

"Julio," said Juan calmly, "do you hear something? It must be the wind. Because I don't believe in ghosts."

"Look, *cabrón*!" yelled the teacher. "I got family to feed! I'm not just some snot-nosed kid like you! I had to keep my job that day, goddammit!"

"I'll be damned," said Juan, still talking calmly, "the wind sure gets noisy around here. Because I can't hear dead men, especially not *gringo*-shit-covered turn-coats!"

"All right," said the teacher, "you son-of-a-bitch! Don't talk to me! But then I'm not telling you where the two men are who cut your throat!"

Instantly, without hesitation, Juan drew his .45 and rammed it into Rodolfo's face. Everyone froze. But the teacher only laughed.

"It will cost you a drink, *mi general*, man-to-man, out back," he said.

"You got it," yelled Juan, chest heaving with rage.

And so they went out back and they had a drink together of the terrible bootleg whiskey.

"The word is that they've left the area," said the teacher. "They know that you're looking for them and so they've gone north up toward Fresno."

"How long ago?" asked Juan.

"A few weeks," said the teacher.

"All right," said Juan, reaching into his pants pocket. "Here is a twenty for you," he said, ripping the bill in half. "But you don't get the other half until I come back with their balls!"

The teacher burst out laughing. "Your reputation doesn't do you justice!" he said, tossing the half bill away.

Julio dove after it like a cat on a mouse.

"You're a real *cabrón*!" continued the teacher and, straightening up, he gave Juan a military salute. "Keep your fire, my young general. But they're going to kill you. We *mejicanos* don't got a chance here."

He turned and went up the alley into the night. Julio showed Juan that he'd picked up the half of the twenty.

"Hey, *mano*" said Julio, "I'm holding on to this! I know you'll be coming back. Shit, back in Mexico after they killed my father, a poor man, I hunted them down for months and I finally killed that big handsome captain with my own bare hands. A man intent on killing cannot be stopped! You'll get them!"

"Yes," said Juan, still looking at where the teacher had disappeared.

"Hey," said Julio, "why don't you and me make a run down to Mexicali for old times' sake and pick up some tequila and sell it?"

"Next time," said Juan, starting to go. "Right now I'm heading north."

"All right, *compa*, but be careful; they're waiting for you."

Juan only smiled.

The weeks passed and Juan went from town to town playing poker. He thought a lot about Lupe as he searched for the two men. But he was losing it. He was beginning to believe that he had been an ignorant fool. A man in his profession couldn't allow a woman to affect him like this. It was wrong, it was dangerous, it made a man weak. Only women and children could afford the luxury of love. He began to drink and go with many women, trying to forget Lupe.

Late one afternoon, after work, Lupe and her family packed their belongings and headed north up the coast to their home in Santa Ana. Lupe rode in the back of the truck next to her mother. She watched the moon come up and follow behind them, slipping in and out of the clouds. She thought of the talk that she and her mother had about school. She thought of Mrs. Sullivan and how she could visit the teacher and explain to her that she needed to borrow books to study to be a bookkeeper.

Lupe smelled the sea as they went up the coast, and she thought of her future—of getting a job in an office some day. She watched Carlota sleeping against her father's side and she felt so close and good with her family and, yet, a little bit apart and lonely.

It felt as if this life that she now had with her parents would one day be as far away as the life that they'd known up in their beloved canyon—a dream, a memory from another lifetime.

Lupe watched the moon, the same moon that had gone past their cathedral rocks each night back home, and she felt strangely foreign to her family for the first time. Then she suddenly thought of that well-dressed bearded man who'd looked at her from the poolhall and how frightened she'd become when she'd seen him at the dance.

Oh, it still made her whole body shiver, remembering how he'd stared at her with his dark, penetrating eyes. And, yet, she'd had dangerously good feelings for him, too, as if she somehow knew him or was destined to know him.

She looked up at the stars and the blue-wrinkled moon and realized that maybe a whole new life was opening up for her.

Two days later, Lupe was in the library in Santa Ana, selecting the books that Mrs. Sullivan had suggested. She was dressed in a homemade white dress. She was nervous and was having trouble concentrating. All around her were real students—educated people—and they all seemed to know what they were doing.

Then, when she went to reach up on the high shelf for another book, she bumped the shelf and dropped the books she was carrying. They struck the hardwood floor with a terrible clatter. Instantly, Lupe bent over, trying to pick up the books before she got in trouble for making so much noise. But she was so upset that she kept dropping them all the more.

Then, Lupe saw two black shoes standing beside her. The shoes were huge and shiny. Lupe was sure she was going to be asked to leave. But when she glanced up, she saw that a handsome young Anglo was smiling down at her.

"Hello," said the young man, bending down beside her. "Do you need some help?"

"Thank you," said Lupe.

Helping her gather her books, they both stood up. Lupe nodded her thanks to him and was just starting to leave when she saw his eyes—eyes so blue and kind—and her heart went out of her.

"My name is Mark," he said. "What's your name?"

"Lupe," she said, shivering.

"Lupe. I like that," he said. "Do you speak English, Lupe?" he asked.

She nodded yes, feeling a nervous excitement go all through her body.

"Do you live around here?" he asked.

She nodded again, feeling so self-conscious that she couldn't speak.

"Good," he said, "I do, too, so if you don't mind . . ." He became embarrassed, putting his hands in his pockets. ". . . I'd like to walk you home."

Seeing his embarrassment, Lupe realized that he wasn't as old as she'd thought. He was perhaps only a few years older than she was. She went over the words, "if you don't mind," inside her head and now understood why it was that she always felt so uncomfortable with Jaime and other Mexican men.

All the Mexican men that she'd ever known never would've asked her permission for anything. No, they would've just picked up her books for her, given her a flowery compliment, then assumed that she now belonged to them and they could walk her home without asking for her consent.

Oh, it felt so good to be respected that she found herself nodding yes once again.

"Good," he said, looking relieved.

Mark helped Lupe check out her books and then they hurried out of the library and into the bright sunlight. The whole day was alive—the trees, the grass, the birds, everything! Colors so bright, they sang out, "Look at me!" Everyone seemed to know Mark, but he never left Lupe's side. He just nodded hello to the different young men and women who greeted him and they continued up the street, as excited as the springtime.

In the months that followed, Juan never did find the Filipino and his friend. They always seemed to be just ahead of him. One night outside Fresno, Juan came up with a plan. He'd set up his own casino and reel the two men in so he could kill them.

Driving over to Hanford, Juan got an old Chinese friend of his to put on a game in the back of his restaurant. The night of the game, Juan dressed in his best suit and stood behind the front door with both of his weapons. He was watching the different customers come in to play when the cops arrived.

Instantly, Juan took out his guns and buried them in the sacks of rice. He had no fight with the cops. They were just men doing their job. Juan was arrested along with the others and taken away.

At the trial, Juan saw the Filipino and the Italian. They'd turned stool pigeons and set him up. The chicken-shit bastards had gone to the law when they'd found out that he was trying to get their asses. They weren't *hombres*! They were *cabrones*!

The men who'd come to play cards were released. But Juan and the Chinaman—who'd set up the gambling place—were given two years, until Juan slipped the judge a hundred dollars under the table. Then the white-haired old man reread the law and gave Juan and his Chinese friend sixty days in the local jail in Tulare, California.

In the tank in Tulare, Juan saw that he and his friend were in for problems. There were over twenty men in the fish hole, and they were fighting amongst themselves like mad dogs.

Realizing that they'd be spending the next two months in the hell hole, Juan immediately decided to buy a carton of cigarettes and bring peace to the tank as quickly as he could.

Going to the far corner of the tank with his cigarettes, Juan sat down by himself and watched things, planning his strategy. He listened to the men arguing among themselves and quickly came to the conclusion that the two main troublemakers were a big, blond-headed farmboy and a small, short-nosed, bulldog Anglo. There were five other whites in the tank, but they didn't matter. The rest were all *mejicanos*, except for four blacks and Juan's friend, the old Chinaman. The blacks were of no consequence to Juan. Inside a prison, the main battles were always between the *gringos* and the *mejicanos*; blood and guts were the main issues, not the size or muscle.

Sitting in the corner alone, Juan saw that the *mejicanos* were keeping watch over him. But he'd deliberately stayed away from them. After a few minutes, the tall farmboy came over toward Juan, acting abusive as he came. He was a big, raw-boned kid, about nineteen years old. Juan acted frightened. The big, unsuspecting boy loved it, closing in.

"Hey, you son-of-a-bitch chili-belly," he roared. "You give me 'em cigarettes or I'll fry your greaser-ass!"

Saying this, the tough boy made the mistake of taking his eyes off Juan so he could look around and make sure all his friends had heard his threat. That was the poor boy's mistake. Instantly, Juan sprang to his feet and hit the big boy under the chin with the top of his head as he slugged him in the balls, then spun him around and rammed his head into the concrete wall. Blood splattered, his teeth coming through his lower lip, and the boy collapsed. And when Juan whirled about to go after the other troublemaker, the man with the short nose backed away as fast as he could.

The *mejicanos*, seeing Juan's worth, shouted, *"¡Viva Méjico!"* And they came over to meet their fellow countryman. But Juan didn't join them. He'd quit trusting his people since the rock quarry. No, instead, he organized them as Duel would've done. He gave out cigarettes and promised everyone that he'd buy them more. Then he had them elect a judge and three advisors, and Juan made sure that the Chinaman got to be an advisor, too.

By nightfall, Juan had the tank running as smoothly as a cardroom, and he told them that he'd tolerate no more bullying. They were men, after all, not dogs. And so they would get along with each other like civilized people or they'd answer to the judge and would be severely punished.

That night, Al, a huge old Italian who'd been sitting quietly all this time in his own corner, came over to Juan.

"I been watching you," said Al. "And I've been here two weeks and we been fighting each other like so many fools, but you been here only half a day and you make the peace." He smiled, showing a fine gold tooth. "You going to go far, young man," said the huge, dignified old man. "You have real talent. It's an honor for me to meet a man of peace. The name is Al Cappola."

Juan took the old man's hand, which was every bit as large as his own. "Juan Villaseñor," said Juan. "The honor is mine, *señor*. It's not every day that I have the pleasure of meeting a man who respects the peace."

The old Italian smiled even more and invited Juan to his corner. They sat down together and talked quietly all night. Al Cappola told Juan that he was a professional liquormaker who'd been brought over from the old country by a group of Italians for the sole purpose of making fine liquor for a big operation in Fresno.

His friends were all Italians, and they supplied ninety percent of all the liquor in the San Joaquin Valley, from Sacramento to Bakersfield. They even took care of parts of San Francisco. But the distillery where Al worked, outside of Fresno, had been raided last month.

"But still, I got no worries," said the handsome old man, "I'm *paisano* with the bosses, and so I'm getting paid five dollars a day for every day I spend in jail."

Juan was very impressed. He'd never heard of such a group of people—outside of his own family back in Mexico—being this close and responsible for one another. And five dollars per day was a great fortune. The old man had to be first-rate to be paid such an amount.

"My hat is off to you," said Juan. "I respect your organization and this term you use of *paisano*. And, also, I wish you to know that we have the same word where I come from in Mexico. *Paisano*, meaning countryman, is also what we call the long-legged bird that runs along the roads. Because that bird, you keep him near your house, and he'll kill all the rattlesnakes in the area and make it safe for you and your children."

Al smiled. "Small world," he said. "*Paisano* means exactly the same thing back in my hometown, too. A friend who keeps away the evil snakes of life."

And so they continued talking, quickly becoming friends as men do in jail, showing their true worth to each other, and it was good.

The following night, Juan licked his lips, measuring his words very carefully, for he knew that the knowledge of making fine liquor was worth millions right now. That was why they'd brought this magician all the way from the old country: just for this purpose. "Look, *señor*," he said, "we've talked and become friends, so I hope you don't take offense at what I'm going to ask, but, well, I'm a gambling man, you see, and I've got a little money put away, and . . . well, I've tried making liquor before, but believe me, it's a talent far beyond my humble abilities. So, well, I was thinking," continued Juan carefully, cautiously, "if it wouldn't put you in badly with your *paisano*s, that I'd like to pay you a few dollars per day to teach me how to make liquor while we're here."

The old man looked at Juan a long time before he spoke. "You know," he said, "if anyone else asked me this, I'd spit in their face, but," he said, smiling, "I like your style. So, yes, for a few extra dollars per day, I'll teach you the art of fine liquor-making as only they know in Italy or France! But, remember, you no sell in my *paisano*s' area or they'll kill you four times before you die, and I'll help them!" he whispered under his breath, staring at Juan.

But Juan didn't shy away, fully realizing that he was no lightweight, either. And he pulled down into his guts and stuck out his hand. "Agreed," he said, "man to man, *a lo macho!*"

"Good," said the old man, "then it's a deal!"

For the next two weeks, Juan listened to the detailed lectures that the old man gave him, asking questions when he didn't understand. And, little by little, Juan began to comprehend just how fine liquor was made. It wasn't that complicated once you got the basic concept. In fact, it was quite easy once you knew how. It all made perfect sense, just like a magician's trick.

Two weeks before Al was to be released from jail, Juan paid a guard twenty dollars for him to smuggle in the supplies they needed to make a batch of liquor. They made several gallons of whiskey right there in the county jail. By the time the Italian was released, Juan was a quality liquor maker, and all the guards and prisoners were happy, they got so drunk.

The day Al left, Juan felt as sad is if his own father was leaving, they'd become so close, talking day and night for five weeks.

There had been only one time in all their talking that Juan had ever seen the gracious old man's eyebrows come up. And that had been when Juan had told him that he'd been searching for a quick-eyed Filipino and his big Italian partner when he'd gotten arrested.

"And what will you do to these two men when you catch them? Ah, cut their throats like they did you and draw the law to yourself?" The old man had shaken his huge, lion-headed face sadly. "I'd thought you were a man of peace. Too many good young men have I seen die in senseless vengeance. Forget them; get rich and find a wife," he'd advised. "Enjoy your life."

"Thank you," said Juan. "I think you're right."

And Juan had said nothing more. He wondered if maybe the formidable Italian was Al's relative. Maybe even his son.

But getting out of jail, Juan Salvador immediately went looking for the Filipino and his friend. He hunted them for several weeks but could find no trace of them. Juan decided to quit his hunt for the time being and looked up Al Cappola in Fresno. He was tired of being poor and wanted to make some real money.

Juan and the old Italian broke bread and drank together, truly enjoying themselves. Al gave him the address of a place owned by some *paisanos* in Los Angeles that sold everything that a quality bootlegger needed to get started.

"Also when you're down that way," said Al, "stop by and visit my younger brother Mario. He makes a little whiskey, too," he said, handing Juan his brother's address. "Who knows? Maybe you two can help each other keep the snakes away, like true *paisanos*."

Juan thanked Al and took off. Getting to the big warehouse in downtown Los Angeles, Juan was shocked. Why, Al hadn't been joking. They really did sell everything that a bootlegger needed, short of the actual liquor itself.

Juan bought a kettle, a stove, a needle for aging the whiskey, and half a dozen oak barrels. Now he was on his way.

He rented a big house in the barrio just east of downtown Los Angeles, put the barrels to ferment, and went home to visit his family and tell them how he was doing. Then he stopped by and saw Al's brother, Mario. The man was friendly and treated him well, but Juan just didn't trust him the way he'd trusted his older brother.

Juan returned to Los Angeles and finished making his first batch of liquor, and it was excellent! The best he'd tasted since he'd left Montana. He took it to Santa Ana, where Archie Freeman had a second home, and sold it all to him.

He hired Julio, his old friend from the rock quarry, and brought him up to Los Angeles to help him make up a bigger batch. He was able to sell half of this one to Archie, too. Juan made so much profit that he decided to buy himself some new clothes and the finest car that money could buy.

What the hell! Having money to burn in your pocket made the whole world look so good that it was hard to keep murder in your heart. Maybe Al was right; he should forget about the Filipino and his friend and enjoy his life.

Juan parked in front of a big luxurious car lot in downtown Los Angeles, and got out of his beatup old car, feeling great. Oh, walking down the street with a roll of money in your pocket so thick that you couldn't fold it in half made a man feel ten feet tall!

"Which one do you like?" asked a young blond salesman, walking up behind Juan.

"Don't know," said Juan, walking around a big, dark-green Dodge convertible. He was dressed in a navy blue pin-striped suit and had a pair of tan calfskin gloves and a full-length, ivory-white car coat. "But this one with the brown seats goes well with my gloves and coat."

The salesman laughed. "That's a good one, my friend," he said, sticking out his hand.

But Juan didn't take it. "How much?" he said, wanting to cut through the bullshit.

The salesman lowered his hand. "Fifty bucks down and you can drive it home today."

"No," said Juan, "how much cash for the whole thing?"

"You mean all seven hundred and ninety-five dollars?" asked the salesman. He was in his early twenties, and he'd never sold a car for cash before.

"Sure," said Juan, "unless you got something against cash."

"Oh, no," said the salesman, becoming extremely courteous, "believe me, I have nothing against cash. Come right this way; we'll go into our office and write you right up, sir!"

The salesman walked Juan across the lot and opened the office door for him, smiling and talking politely the whole time, and Juan loved it. It felt good being treated like a king by a *gringo*.

Pulling out his wad of money, Juan paid the man in fifties and twenties. The salesman got so nervous, he had to call someone else in to recount the money. Juan loved this, too. Cash, he'd found out in the last couple of months, made grown men squirm like anxious virgins.

Lupe didn't know what was happening to her, but she thought she was falling in love. Still, the first two times that Mark walked her home from the library, she'd deliberately told him goodbye when they had reached the barrio. But this afternoon, Mark insisted that he walk her all the way home.

"Well, yes, of course," said Lupe, trying to sound calm. But inside, she was going crazy. She really didn't want him to walk her home. Lupe wasn't ashamed of her family's poor, run-down house or anything like that; no, it was just that she knew that people would give them the eye and start talking badly about her, saying she thought she was too good to go out with her own kind.

But what could she say? Mark was wonderful, always so kind, and polite and respectful. They talked about books and school, and it was so much fun.

Walking up the tree-lined street, Lupe prayed to God that no one was back from the fields yet and they wouldn't be seen. But turning the corner, Lupe saw her next door neighbor digging the weeds out of her roses.

"*Buenas tardes*, Lupita!" said the old lady, seeing Lupe with the tall Anglo.

"*Buenas tardes*," said Lupe. It would be all over the barrio within an hour. This old woman was the biggest gossip in all of Santa Ana.

"Are you all right?" asked Mark, seeing how nervous Lupe was.

"Oh, yes, I'm fine," she lied. "It's just that I have to hurry inside and start dinner."

"Well, goodbye, then," said Mark, "see you tomorrow. And I've talked to my dad, so I can borrow the car and drive you home sometime," he added.

Lupe felt her skin crawl. She just wished the old woman hadn't overheard him.

Then, to make matters worse, Mark was just going back up the street when Lupe's family drove up in the truck. Lupe hurried inside their house. But Carlota was right behind her.

"Oh, Lupe!" she said. "He's gorgeous! Can I have Jaime all to myself now?"

Lupe didn't know what to say. She put on her apron and started rolling the dough for the tortillas.

Her mother, brother and father came in, all grinning. No doubt the old lady next door had already told them everything.

"Why didn't you ask him to stay, *mi hijita*?" asked her mother, taking off her sweat-stained straw hat.

"She's ashamed of us," said her father, sitting down, dirt-tired.

"That's not true!" said Lupe. "I've never been ashamed of us!"

"All right, enough," said her mother. "We're all just tired."

But all through dinner Lupe was so tense, she couldn't eat. When they were getting ready for bed, Doña Guadalupe called Lupe aside.

"Where did you meet him, *mi hijita*?" asked her mother.

"In the library," said Lupe.

"Is he a student?"

"No, not at the school where I go, but at a university in San Francisco." She felt very nervous. "He's studying to be an architect. He was returning some books for his younger sister when I met him."

"Oh, I see," said Doña Guadalupe, "and his parents, has he introduced you to them?

"No, of course not," said Lupe, feeling annoyed. "We just met, Mama!"

"I see," said her mother, smoothing out the apron on her lap. "Let me be perfectly frank, *mi hijita*. Your father and I have been talking about you for some time now."

"But why, Mama? I've done nothing wrong!"

"No, of course not, *querida*. But, well, ever since you were a child, perfect strangers have been coming up and touching your hair, caressing you."

Lupe shivered. "And I hated it! They had no right!" she said.

"No, they didn't," said her mother. "But your beauty has always been so special and, now that you've developed into a full woman at such a tender age, the temptation will be even greater for men to want to possess you. Even your teacher, if you'd looked different, I'm sure that he never would have . . ."

"But, Mama, I told you, I did nothing to provoke him!" said Lupe, her face filled with anger.

Doña Guadalupe took in a big breath. "Please," she said, "please, give me your hand."

Reluctantly, Lupe gave her mother her hand.

"I don't want to upset you, but I need to talk to you. Tell me, this Anglo, how does he treat you?"

"Oh, Mama," said Lupe, her eyes bubbling with excitement, "we talk about school and books and, and, it's so much fun! Just like it used to be with Señora Muñoz and then with Manuelita and the two little Indian girls."

"Well," said her mother, seeing her daughter's happiness, "I'm very glad to hear that. So why don't you bring him home sometime so we can meet him."

Lupe got tense once again. "But, Mama, the way the old woman looked at us made me feel so, so ugly, and if he comes to our home, she'll tell everyone!"

Doña Guadalupe took another big breath. "*Querida*," she said, "what other people say is not of our concern. Remember, ever since that shooting star kissed the earth, you've been specially blessed."

"But I don't want to be specially blessed!" snapped Lupe.

Doña Guadalupe laughed. "And the sun, does he want to be the sun? And the moon, the moon? And God, God?" She shrugged. "No, you are not to complain or question who you are, but instead, grow, reaching for the light that's inside you. But remember," added her mother, "when you think of this Anglo, and not so well of the men of our own people, think of all those young girls who married American engineers back in La Lluvia, only to be left behind with children.''

"Mama!"

"Don't 'mama' me," said the old woman. "Just think and be careful. You're not a child anymore."

And saying this, Doña Guadalupe stared into her daughter's eyes, wondering how she could possibly pass on to Lupe all that she knew about life. Her youngest was leaving the nest; she could see it in Lupe's eyes.

The old woman took a big breath, fully realizing that no one could pass on to anyone the experiences of life. Each had to find their own way. This was, indeed, the frustration and yet the challenge of every parent. She drew Lupe close, giving her all her love. After all, wasn't it love, and only love, that a parent could pass on?

The people all stared at Juan as he drove into the barrio of Corona in his big new green Dodge convertible. He looked like a king, the mayor of Corona, as he nodded hello to them and went slowly down the street.

At the end of the road, Juan saw Jose and Pedro playing baseball in the open field with a bunch of other kids, and he honked at them. Seeing his great new car, they came screaming!

They were barefoot and half naked and they ran up to the big Dodge, and touched it all over, wanting to be a part of such grand luxury. The Dodge was the car of the day. Only a Cadillac or the grand Packard was more luxurious.

"*¡Tío!*" screamed Jose. "Is it ours? My God, it's beautiful!" He was twelve years old now, a big kid, just half a head shorter than Juan.

"No," said Juan, laughing happily. "It's the mayor's!"

"Oh, then he loaned it to you?" asked the big, husky kid.

"Sure," said Pedro, laughing at his older brother. Pedro was only going on nine but already was quicker than his brother in many ways. "The mayor always loans us *mejicanos* his cars, stupid!"

Jose turned and started after his younger brother. But Pedro only laughed and dodged away.

"Give us a ride, Uncle!" begged Pedro.

"Why should I?" said Juan. "I thought you told me only *gringos* could have good cars."

"I was wrong!" yelled Pedro. "All wrong! Please, let us ride with you!"

"But you're all dirty!" said Juan, enjoying it.

"We'll jump in the canal and wash off!" cried Pedro.

"No, then we'll be all muddy," said Jose realistically.

"Oh, please, *Tío!*" begged Pedro. "Give us a ride and we'll even go to church and pray ten rosaries so the law don't get you!"

On this one, Juan spoke hard. "What did you say?"

Pedro knew he'd gone too far. Very clearly they'd been told never to mention to anyone what it was that their *tío* had gotten into. "I mean we'll pray for you so you'll be sure to go to heaven," he said, correcting himself.

Juan had to laugh. His nephew Pedro had a mouth as big as his sister Luisa's, but he also was smart enough to catch on as quickly as she did.

"Look, Pedro," said Jose, "saying ten rosaries might help our uncle get into heaven, but it isn't going to stop us from getting his car all dirty. I think what we should do is promise to wash his car inside and out if he'll take us for a drive."

"All right!" yelled Pedro, turning to the others. "My big brother is right! And I'm personally going to make sure you guys all do a good job washing my *tío*'s car or you can never have another ride in our family's car again!"

Juan laughed again, seeing how Pedro was going to make sure he didn't do any of the work. He just loved his two nephews. They were so completely different from each other. Blood really was blood; there was just no getting around it.

"All right," said Juan. "Get in. All of you."

The seven other boys made a mad rush at the car, grabbing the doors. Jose had to knock down two of the boys with his fists to get them to calm down.

"You will get in quietly!" shouted Jose. "If one of you so much as scratches my *tío*'s car, you'll have to answer to me!"

The boys calmed down and got in quietly. Juan was amazed. When Jose talked, he sounded just like the father that he'd never met.

Once they were all in the Dodge, Juan put the big car in gear and they drove off. The dirt street was full of pot holes and chickens. At the end of the street Juan drove into the orchard, almost getting hit in the face by the low-hanging limbs.

He raced up and down the rows of orange trees, honking his horn and whirling around a lone tree. The boys crowed with glee. When he'd had enough, Juan stopped the car in front of their two houses and got out.

"Go on, Jose," he said, "you drive now."

"Me?" said the big boy with absolute terror and yet an on-rush of wonder.

"Sure," said Juan, "you drove my old car for me before. So go ahead!"

"But this one's new," said Jose nervously.

"Do it!" yelled Pedro. "Or move over and I'll do it!"

"Oh, no, not you, Pedro," said Juan. "You put your hands on that steering wheel, and I'll skin you alive!"

Pedro was like his father, quick-witted and cute; he wasn't responsible like Jose.

"You heard our *tío*!" shouted Jose, and he shoved his younger brother aside and took hold of the wheel.

All the boys stared at Jose with anticipation. He started the motor, put the big car in gear, and popped the clutch. They were off through the orchard in a series of quick-lunging leaps, screeching wildly. Hitting a low-hanging branch, oranges showered into the convertible and Juan stood there laughing so hard that he had to grip his stomach.

Hearing the commotion, Luisa and Doña Margarita came rushing out of the front house.

"Stop them!" screamed Luisa. "They're going to get killed!"

"No, they're fine," said Juan.

"They'll ruin your car!" she continued screaming.

"So what?" he said.

"You're teaching them disrespect!" said his sister.

"Good," said Juan, "too much damned respect kills people."

The Dodge jerked and lunged, weaving dangerously close to the trees, and Pedro was screeching the loudest of all.

"Oh, Juan," said Luisa, coming up close and hugging her brother, "you get them so excited every time you come, they don't obey me for weeks."

"Good," said Juan, hugging his sister close. "You're too damned bossy, anyway."

"Oh, no, *mi hijito*," said his mother, smiling as she watched the big car full of children go racing in and out of the trees, "they've even quit going to school."

"What?" said Juan.

"Yes," said his mother. "Luisa tells them to go but they say, 'Why go? The way to make money is with a gun, like *tío* Juan; not books.' "

"I see," said Juan, watching the boys race up and down between rows. "I'll have a talk with them."

"But don't hit them," said Luisa. "They must be made to understand. They never saw all the death we saw, and so they know nothing of the terrible chances that you take."

Juan nodded. "You're right. I hadn't thought of that."

He took a big breath. These nephews of his were in for a surprise. Bootlegging and guns weren't the answer. They were only to help him get started.

It was late that same night when Juan was with his mother in the little shack in back. They just couldn't stop talking. In the last six months, Juan hadn't seen too much of his old mother.

"Come here to the light," she said, taking hold of his heavily-bearded face, "and let me see how the cut has healed."

After Juan had his chin cut, his mother had continued soaking his face with herbs and oil. She was one of the best healers in the whole barrio.

"It looks pretty good, *mi hijito*," said the old woman, glancing between each hair. "I think it's now time for you to shave your face and start looking in earnest for a wife." She fixed herself a cup of coffee with some of Juan's good, smooth whiskey. "You tell me, what good does it do a man to inherit the earth if he doesn't get married and have children?"

Juan laughed. His mother just wasn't going to stop until she saw him married and settled down.

"It's been two years since you arrived from Montana," she continued, "and I still don't see you with a wife!"

"All right, all right," said Juan, thinking of Lupe. It had been weeks since he'd thought of her.

And they would've gone right on talking, truly enjoying themselves, had they not been abruptly interrupted by a strong, hard knock on the front door. It was dark and no one ever came to his mother's house at night, much less knocked. Quickly, Juan signaled his mother with his eyes to go to the rear of the little one-room house, and he went to the front door with his snub-nose .38 in his hand. His .45 was under the seat of his big Dodge.

Doña Margarita got down as small as a rabbit and made the sign of the cross over herself. But no, the old lady wasn't really frightened. She was still stouthearted in her belief that God was on their side.

The knocking sounded again, hard and forceful.

"Yes?" shouted Juan, moving to the side of the door, making sure that his mother was out of the line of fire.

"Villa!" called a foreign-sounding voice. "Is that you?"

"Maybe," said Juan. No one called him Villa, short for Villaseñor, except for some of the Italians whom he'd become friends with in the last few months.

"Damn it, Villa, open up! It's Mario, I got to talk to you!"

"Oh, Mario," said Juan, feeling relieved. He turned to his mother, nodding that everything was okay, but still he picked up his coat, which was hanging over a nail on the wall, and draped it over his shoulder so he could hide his snub-nose .38. "He's a friend," he said to his mother, and he went to open the door.

"But be careful, *mi hijito*," said the old woman in Spanish. "Even Judas was our Lord Savior's friend at one time, too."

"Yes," said Juan, "I remember." Opening the door, he stepped outside, saw that Mario was alone, and closed the door.

"*¿Cómo estás*, Mario?" said Juan. Getting to know the Italians, Juan found out that their languages were very similar. They could actually understand Spanish with very little trouble.

"Good," said Mario.

"How's my *paisano* Al?" asked Juan.

"He's fine," said Mario. "In fact, yesterday he asked about you. He was in the hospital, you know."

"Oh, no, I didn't," said Juan, genuinely moved. "How is he?"

"Well, considering his age, he's fine," said Mario, glancing toward his car which was parked alongside Juan's Dodge. "But that's not what I came to talk to you about, Villa," he said, licking his lips. "Could we go for a little drive?" he asked.

Juan glanced behind Mario. It looked like there was someone sitting in Mario's car. Suddenly, Juan didn't like the smell of the whole thing.

"No," he said. "I can't now."

"Villa," said Mario, "but this is important. It could mean a lot of money for you."

Juan almost laughed. Who was Mario trying to kid? Hell, if there was any money in a deal for him, then there was a lot more money in it for Mario.

"Well," said Juan, pretending not to be too smart, "why don't we just talk here? My mother, she's old, you know how it is, and we were just visiting."

Mario's face hardened. "Villa, I said this is important!"

Juan didn't meet Mario's stare. He simply stepped back, tightening the grip around his .38. If things turned to violence, he hoped that his nephews wouldn't come out. His mother, he knew was good. She had the intelligence to stay put.

"Okay, Villa," said Mario, realizing that getting tough just wasn't going to help. "I'll tell you the truth. I want to buy all the liquor from you that you can make in the next month. Fifty barrels, sixty barrels, whatever you can make, but, well . . ."

Juan's eyes widened. So far he had only made a total of less than thirty barrels in all his life.

Mario laughed. "Smells good, eh?" he said. "You see, there's a new hotel opening up in San Bernardino next month that needs all the liquor it can get. It's a great big place. First class, bigger and better than anything in Los Angeles. People will be coming from everywhere for the grand opening. Hell, they've already spent over a million dollars on construction alone."

And saying this, Mario rocked back on his feet, giving Juan the time to get properly impressed. After all, a million dollars was a lot of money.

"And they want only the finest liquor they can get for the grand opening," said Mario, bringing out a pack of Chesterfields. "You got a match?" he asked.

"No," lied Juan. He didn't want to release his grip on the .38.

A twinkle of merriment came to Mario's eyes. "Jesus Christ, Villa, I'm your friend, remember? Al's brother. You don't have to have that gun on me."

Juan's face caved in. He hadn't realized he'd been so obvious.

Seeing Juan's face twist with embarrassment, Mario burst out laughing. "You damned Indian! Did you really think you could hide a gun from an Italian? Hell, it can't be done! We were hiding guns while you guys were still living in caves and carrying bows and arrows!"

Juan lowered his jacket. What else could he do? He'd been caught cold. He put the .38 in his pants under his belt.

"Anyway," continued Mario, "the hotel man found out about me and Al and he tasted our liquor and liked it. He called it the best Canadian Whiskey he'd tasted since Prohibition."

He brought out a lighter and lit his cigarette. "So he's put me in charge of finding good liquor. But only the best. None of this cheap bathtub gin that can blind a man. And he'll be paying seventy dollars a barrel on delivery."

"Seventy dollars?" said Juan, louder than he'd meant to. Hell, he'd only been getting forty dollars per barrel from Archie. He couldn't believe it. It just sounded too good. Long ago Juan had learned to be very suspicious of any deal that sounded too good.

"That sounds good," said Juan, "very good; but tell me, Mario, why are you coming to me? Why don't you and Al—now that he's moved down here—just handle it yourselves or go to that big organization of your *paisanos* in Fresno?"

Mario was taken aback. He hadn't expected this. "Look," he said, "I didn't come here for advice, Villa. Hell, I've already presented this deal to five other guys, and they've all jumped on it! I don't understand you, Villa. I just told you that Al barely got out of the hospital, and he's sick. So we can't do a big job like this. And our *paisanos* from Fresno, hell, they got more action than they can handle. So what is it with you? Hell, I thought I was doing you a favor to cut you into the big times."

Juan grinned. "But, Mario," he said, "I'm not turning you down. No, not at all. I appreciate the offer. It's just that, well, I'll have to think on it and see how much I can deliver." He licked his lips. "After all, I don't want to say 'yes' and then not be able to deliver and end up looking bad or making you look bad, either."

"Juan," said Mario impatiently, using his first name for the first time, "you don't seem to understand. I need to know now. This deal is big and . . ."

"Did you give this hotel man my name?" Juan asked.

"Did I what?" said Mario, coming up to his full height, towering over Juan as he stared at him in disbelief. "Just what kind of two-bit fool do you take me for? You think because you're my brother's friend you can talk to me like this? Well, you can't! I'm a man! You hear? I'm no little two-bit fool that goes around giving names in our business! I'd die first, do you hear me? I got honor!"

Instantly, Juan acted cowed. "I didn't mean that," he said. "I'm sorry. Calm down, please. I'm not trying to insult you. I'm just trying to understand this deal. Remember, it's not every day that you hear about a million-dollar hotel." And he laughed, reaching out to pat Mario on the shoulder gently. "All this talk of millions just confused me. I thought maybe . . . being so big a deal and wanting a guarantee of the quality . . . you know, the hotel man demanded the names of these quality manufacturers that you know."

Mario came back down to his normal size, and Juan took a deep breath. He'd known Mario would get mad at him if he suggested he'd given any names. Secrecy between bootleggers was all-important. But he'd never expected Mario to get this angry. He wondered why.

"Please, accept my apologies," continued Juan. "Yes, of course, I know you're a man of respect and I know that you'd never give out names. But, well, like I said, I just got confused. Now, please, go on, tell me the rest of the deal. Like how do we deliver or do they pick it up?"

The huge rage that had taken hold of Mario's big body left him, and he now said, "We deliver."

"I see," said Juan. "And how do we do this? Do I deliver to you and then you take it from there? Or do I follow behind your truck and deliver on my own?"

Mario's face flushed red again. "Listen," he said, "are you in or not?"

"Mario," said Juan, "please be patient with me. I'm not as experienced as you and Al. So explain these things to me so I can understand. After all, you and your brother and me, we get along, we're *paisanos*; we help each other keep the snakes away."

Speaking like this, Juan realized that he sounded as smooth as his mother. It had been his mother, after all, who'd taught him the art of acting weak and soft in order to get what he wanted. And people fell for it. Especially big, tough men.

Mario relaxed and he explained everything he knew about the deal while Juan leaned back on the door and listened carefully. And they parted on good terms, shaking hands and giving each other a big *abrazo*.

Back inside the little shack, Juan served himself a good-sized drink of his own whiskey and laid out the whole thing to his mother.

"It sounds good, Mama, and it would put me on my feet for a long time," he said, sipping the whiskey. "I'd be able to buy these two houses for you and Luisa and that big open lot, too. But," he added, "I've never done such a big deal. I don't know if I even got the right equipment to do it. And, also, it smells fishy to me somehow."

"I agree," said Doña Margarita, sipping her own whiskey with relish. She loved the whiskey that her son made. It reminded her of the excellent tequila that they'd made back in their settlement. "Even for an Italian, he became too angry when you simply asked him to clarify the matter. Remember, *mi hijito*, your own father got this way with me, too, but only when he was hiding something and I accidentally got too close for his comfort."

And saying this, she picked up her little pint bottle of whiskey and went across the room to go to bed, smoking her homemade cigarette from the good weed that she grew in back.

"Let me sleep on the matter and we'll talk again in the morning," she said.

"All right, in the morning, Mama," said Juan, starting to undress.

"But wait," said his mother, sitting down on her bed, "tell me more about this equipment and why is it that you can't do bigger, eh?"

Juan smiled. There was just no problem that his mother didn't think that she could solve.

"Well," he said, "I guess it's not really the equipment that gives me the biggest problem, now that I think more about it. The problem is, that, well, all the neighbors keep coming over to be friendly with me and take up too much of my time. And, also, I don't want them to get wind of what it is that I really do," he added.

"Oh, I see," said his mother. "And this house that you rent is in the barrio of Los Angeles, no?"

"Yes," he said.

"I see," she said. "And the neighbors come over too much, wanting to be friendly, eh?"

"Yes," he said, smiling, watching the wheels turn inside his mother's head, "that's right."

"Well, then," she said, opening the pint bottle of whiskey and taking a small pull, "the way I see it, you need to find a place where no people will want to befriend you, *mi hijito*,"

He grinned. "Yeah, that would do it, Mama, moving to the moon. And, also, while you're at it, you might as well figure out a way for me to cover up the smell of the liquor."

"All right," she said. "I'll do that, too. But you should've come to me sooner." She took another small sip. "Now let me see, first a place where no one will want to be your friend. Let me see," she said, closing her wrinkled-up old eyes, concentrating with all her might.

Juan almost laughed. What could this old dried-up bag of bones possibly come up with to help him? Hell, she didn't know how things worked in this country. But then, suddenly, her old eyes opened up wide.

"I got it!" she said excitedly. "Oh, why didn't I see it before? It's so obvious," she added, laughing. "Why, *mi hijito*, all you do is rent a big house in the *gringo* part of town! A big house! And, oh, I'm sure that no *gringo* will ever try to befriend you. Why, they'll be mad that you're even there. They'll be sure to keep away from you!"

Juan was flabbergasted. Why, his mother was absolutely right. This would work; it really would.

"But also," she said, eyes still large with excitement, "this Julio that works for you, you'll have to get him to move into the house with his family or else the *gringos* will see you two men alone and get fearful for their women and maybe even call the police for no reason."

"Jesus!" said Juan. "How'd you get so smart, Mama?"

"I had no other choice," she said. "It was that or perish." She took another sip of the whiskey, capping the bottle. "But I'm not done," she said, "smart ideas are a dime a dozen, unless you figure out all the thousands of little details that give life to an idea so that the idea can survive."

Juan came over and sat down on the bed with his mother. "Oh, I love you so much, Mama," he said, taking her in his thick arms.

"No, none of that!" she snapped. "I'm thinking!" She pushed him away. "Now, how will you be able to rent that house—you a *mejicano* with supposedly no real means of support? This is the question. And once you do rent the house, then what can you do to cover that smell and all suspicion of how you make your living?"

She closed her eyes, concentrating, thinking, figuring, trying to decipher the problem. And Juan watched her as another man might watch a great mountain, or a great river, or a great volcano just before it sprouted fire. Oh, she looked so old and all dried up and useless, but underneath she was a universe of mystery, still a force to be reckoned with.

"Well, to solve the problem of smell next, because it's easier, you could get Julio's wife . . . what's her name?"

"Geneva."

"Yes, Geneva, to cook plenty of spicy food with lots of garlic. The garlic alone will keep the *gringos* away. They just can't stand strong smells." Her eyes lit up once again. "Yes, that's it! *Gringos* don't like strong smells, so you also put some chicken shit in that old truck of yours and let everyone know that you move manure for a living. Oh, I can just see it now! No one will ever want to get close enough to you to question you!"

And she laughed and laughed, truly enjoying herself, and then got under the covers.

"All right," she said. "That's enough for tonight. I'm going to sleep. And in the morning we'll talk some more and see what to do about the Italian's offer with the hotel. Then, after that, we'll talk about this girl. I saw her again. She came by to milk our goat once more while you were gone."

"That angel?"

"Yes. And she's not just beautiful, *mi hijito*, she's smart, too. And to make a home a woman must be very, very smart, remember. But now let me go to sleep so I can chew things over like the cow with its cud. In the morning I'll know everything."

Juan laughed. "Sleep with the angels," he said, kissing her. And she kissed him, too, holding him tenderly.

Juan dumped everything out of the pockets and took off his pants, then lifted the mattress up off his bed. There were two wide boards on the box springs. Picking up the top board, Juan put his pants down on the lower one, making sure all the wrinkles were out of his pants before he lowered the top board again.

Feeling satisfied that his pants would get ironed out as he slept, he put the mattress back down over the two boards and then took off his vest and shirt and shook them out. These he hung carefully alongside his suit coat on the other two nails on the wall. He only had two suits, and he liked to take good care of them.

Turning off the big lantern, Juan took off his red silk underwear and put on his red silk pajamas. Juan had first learned about silk from Katherine up in Montana. Then again from a Chinese doctor that he'd smuggled in from Mexicali to Chinatown in Hanford. Ever since then, Juan had been wearing nothing but silk against his private parts. He was protecting his investments à la Chinese so he could sire a dozen healthy children—children who'd come with the finest of blood.

Lupe hadn't seen Mark for several days. But then, coming out of the library late one afternoon, there he was in white slacks and a dark blue sweater, leaning back on a long black car.

Upon seeing him, Lupe's whole face lit up. He grinned with pleasure.

"Hi," he said, "where've you been?"

"Me?" she said. "I've been back for three days. We were in Hemet, working."

"Oh, I see," he said.

Two well-dressed Anglo girls walked by and said hello to Mark. But he never took his eyes off Lupe.

"Come on," he said. "Get in and I'll drive you home."

Lupe had never been in a fine car before, much less all alone with a man.

"No," she said. "I can't."

"Why not?" he asked.

"Well, because . . ." She didn't want to say it, but she didn't have her mother's permission.

"Lupe," he said, "we've been seeing each other for months now. I'm not going to bite you. Look, I don't even have fangs," he added, showing his white, even teeth.

Lupe laughed and she knew that she shouldn't, but still, she got in his car and he closed her door.

Another couple of young, well-dressed Anglo girls passed and said hello to Mark. He waved to them, then he came around and got in and started the motor, and they were off. But then at the corner, he didn't turn toward the barrio. No, he turned in the opposite direction.

"Where are you taking me?" asked Lupe anxiously.

He laughed. "You'll find out."

"Stop!" she screamed. "Or I'll jump out!"

"You're kidding," he said.

Lupe opened the door and started to jump. But he grabbed her by the arm, bringing the car to the curb.

"Jesus Christ! What's wrong with you?" he said. "You really were going to jump!"

"Yes!" she said, chest heaving with emotion.

"But why? I don't understand. I was just taking you to meet my parents, for God's sake."

"Let go of me," she said. "I'm getting out."

"Why?"

"You didn't tell me the truth," she said, prying his fingers off her arm. "You tricked me!"

He stared at her. "But, Lupe," he said, "I didn't trick you. I was teasing you."

But she said nothing and got out. "Bye," she said, starting up the street, back toward the library.

"Come on, get back in," he said. "No more teasing."

She just kept walking on the sidewalk under the tall, green trees.

"I'll follow you and I'll honk my horn," he said, giving the horn a small tap.

She got embarrassed. He loved it.

"Come on, Scout's honor, no more tricks," he said.

Finally she quit walking and came over. "Straight to my house?" she asked.

"Straight," he said.

"All right," she said.

He reached across the wide smooth seat and opened the door for her, and she slipped in once again.

The next morning Juan shaved off his beard and saw that with a few days of sun, the scar would hardly be noticeable. He decided to drive over to San Bernardino to take a look at the hotel that was being built.

Once there, he saw that there were dozens of Mexican laborers moving dirt by hand. Asking around, he found out that he knew a few of the laborers. In fact, one of them, named Don Manuel, was the timekeeper. A few months back Juan had sold him a barrel of whiskey.

Don Manuel was the type of proper-looking little man who always managed to get himself a good, soft job. He'd told Juan that he was putting his youngest daughter through an expensive Catholic finishing school with profits from the liquor he sold.

"Hello, Don Manuel," said Juan.

"Oh, good morning," said Don Manuel, glancing around. "But what are you doing here?" he whispered.

"Hey, relax, *mano*, I'm just looking around," said Juan. "Maybe I can get the contract to do the fertilizer for your trees and plants."

"Look," whispered the elderly man who'd aged tremendously since he'd been the mayor in La Lluvia de Oro. "I don't want no one here knowing about our business dealings."

"Of course not," said Juan, speaking loudly. "I don't, either. So why don't you just show me around? It's a very impressive place you have here."

"Yes, isn't it?" said the old man, chest swelling up as if the place truly belonged to him. "And my job is to check the men and make sure it remains a fine place."

"And I bet you do," said Juan, looking at the three pens in Don Manuel's breast pocket.

Don Manuel was the worst kind of Mexican, in Juan's opinion. He wore pens in his pocket to show the whole world that he knew how to read and write. And, in matters of value, he would always side with the *gringos*, thinking he was one of them, and look down his nose at his own people.

Quickly, Don Manuel showed Juan around the hotel, and Juan was very impressed. He was just beginning to relax and think that maybe everything was on the up-and-up until Don Manuel took Juan to the basement. It was made of concrete and had no windows.

"And this is where they'll park the cars," said Don Manuel.

"You mean," said Juan, feeling his heart pounding, "this is where the deliveries will be made?"

"Oh, no," said Manuel. "The deliveries will be on top, around the back. This basement is only for the customers, so that they won't get caught in the rain or cold and they can go up to the lobby in the elevators."

"Oh, I see," said Juan.

Don Manuel was seeing Juan to the door and Juan was just beginning to relax again when a big Anglo came walking up behind them.

"What's going on, Manuel?" asked the big, hairy-armed Anglo.

Juan looked the man over carefully. He was a big, powerful brute in his early thirties. He reminded Juan a lot of Tom Mix, the Mexican-hating western star who, in his no-good movies, knocked down five Mexicans with every punch.

"Oh, nothing, Bill," said Don Manuel respectfully. "This man is in the fertilizer business. He just came by to see when we'll be putting in our shrubbery so he can bid on the job."

"I see," said the big Anglo, looking at Juan's good suit and white shirt. "So you move manure, do you?"

"Horseshit," said Juan, "and a little cow, too. But no chicken. It's too hot and it burns the roots."

"I'll be damned, so you know a lot about shit, eh?"

"Yeah," said Juan, staring straight into the man's eyes, "I see a lot of it."

"I bet you do," said the big man, not quite knowing how to take Juan's last remark. Juan didn't look like your typical bow-down-to-the-Anglo-boss Mexican.

"Well, so long," said Juan, turning to Don Manuel. "I'll check back in a few weeks."

"Hey, just a minute," said the Anglo. "What's your name, *amigo*?"

Juan's heart leaped, but still, he held as quiet as a desert reptile in the noontime heat. "Juan Raza," he lied. He was glad that he'd lied and he was, also, very glad that he'd parked his car a few blocks away.

"Well, Juan Raza," said the big Anglo, "glad to meet you. Bill Wesseley's the handle." He stuck out his hand. "I'm from Texas. Where you from?"

Juan took his hand. "My mother," he said.

The big Anglo's eyes filled with fire. But then, he burst out laughing, squeezing Juan's hand with all his might.

But Juan didn't squeeze back. He only held his hand firmly, being careful not to show his own strength. Long ago he'd learned that it was best for your enemy to underestimate you.

Getting to his Dodge, Juan was trembling. That whole damned hotel had smelled of cops and prison. But, on the other hand, seventy dollars a barrel was hard to pass up. And also, he had to remember that a man just couldn't be too cautious or he'd never get ahead.

Driving down the road, Juan lit up a cigar and decided to go over to Santa Ana and see Archie. The oranges were in and Archie was putting on another dance. Juan figured that he'd sell him a few barrels and ask him if he knew anything about this new hotel.

And, while he was in Santa Ana, Juan also figured that he'd drive through the barrio and see if he couldn't maybe get another look at Lupe. It had been nearly seven months since he'd last seen her.

Juan breathed deeply, thinking of the tender feelings that came up inside him every time he thought of Lupe. But then he also remembered the fear that he'd seen in Lupe's eyes when she'd seen him at the dance hall. He thought of his grandfather, Don Pio, and how the white-haired old man had waited each morning on the terrace to have the day's first cup of hot chocolate with his wife Silveria. Don Pio had been a man's man, and yet he'd still been able to have soft, tender feelings.

Juan was just driving into the Santa Ana barrio, daydreaming as he went along, when suddenly there she was: his Lupe. And he couldn't believe it; she was with an Anglo. She didn't see Juan; she and the Anglo were talking together in the automobile.

Passing by them, Juan parked up the street, watching them in his rearview mirror. He was trembling. Lupe and the handsome Anglo were parked in front of a little house at the edge of the barrio. The tall Anglo got out of his car and came around and opened Lupe's door for her like the most gentlemanly *cabrón* that Juan had ever seen.

Juan mimicked him, making a face of pure repulsion. Hell, he felt like getting his .45 and going down the street and shooting the son-of-a-bitch *gringo* and his shiny black Ford—he was so angry.

But when Lupe stepped out of the car, her figure filled out her dress so well that Juan forgot everything. Why, this girl had blossomed! She had the most dangerous curves Juan had ever seen on a woman! She wasn't young and innocent anymore. No, she was a luscious peach just waiting to be picked. Oh, he'd been a fool to have gone away. She was the most ready-looking woman that he'd ever seen!

Juan watched them walk up to the little white picket fence. At the door, the Anglo took her hand and it looked like they might kiss, but the door suddenly opened and out came Carlota to call Lupe inside.

Juan grinned, truly enjoying it. The Anglo went back down the steps, mumbling disappointedly to himself.

Putting his big Dodge in gear, Juan drove off. Oh, he was shaking like a leaf, he was so excited. Lupe wasn't just a dream. No, she was truly real. He had to get the pint bottle from under his seat and take a few good belts to calm down.

He thought of going home and telling his mother of this woman, this girl, this angel that made him feel so alive inside. But, no, a part of him just wanted to keep it to himself.

Oh, he was going crazy inside. And he knew that he'd be better off forgetting about this woman and just whoring around and keeping his mind on business, but down deep inside, something so powerful was happening to him that he couldn't think straight. It was as if all these years of running around and fighting and wanting to be a man like Duel were suddenly evaporating before his very eyes. It was as if he knew that at the very center of his being something had been missing all these years but he'd been unable to see it until now.

He breathed deeply, feeling, thinking, remembering the boy inside himself before he'd gone to prison and had been forced to live with monsters. He felt so sad and lonely. His mother was right; he'd been alone, not on his own.

Oh, the stars above were truly enjoying themselves. It really was like his mother had said: "One look at your father sitting so proudly on his horse, and I just knew this was the man I'd been born to love and marry."

Juan decided not to stop by and see Archie on this trip. No, he drank down the pint and decided to drive directly to Los Angeles and go to work. His mind was made up. This was it; this was the woman that he'd court and marry and build his family with for ten generations!

But to do this, he'd need money, big money, so he could buy a good-sized piece of land and never have to kiss any *gringo*'s ass again. He would have to go through with the hotel deal, whether he liked it or not.

By God, he'd lose Lupe if he didn't move quickly. She was a full, hot-blooded woman and had to be caught, and given rein before she got away. He began to sing, feeling wonderful—in love with love itself.

17

Love was in the air, choking the very atmosphere. The birds and the butterflies began their seasonal courtship.

Not wanting to waste any time, the next day Juan decided to look in the Anglo part of town for a house in which to get his distillery going. He washed the Dodge and dressed in his best clothes. Then he braced himself with a few good shots and took off. But no matter how much he tried, he couldn't get any Anglo to rent him their house. And, of course, they never came out and said that it was because he was a Mexican, but Juan could guess the truth.

He began to feel helpless. No matter how much money he had in his pocket or how well dressed, he was still a nobody. He was glad that he and Lupe weren't married and looking for a home, she witnessing how truly useless he was.

One day, driving back toward the *barrio*, Juan saw a large real estate office, so he went inside. After giving them a Greek name, Juan was able to get a big, beautiful house the following day.

On the day that Juan moved Julio, his wife and daughters into the house, he deliberately got dressed in his dirtiest work clothes. His truck was loaded down with old pipes and mattresses and big barrels. If anyone asked them anything, Juan was prepared to say that they were in the plumbing business. But no one came near them. They just watched them from behind their parted draperies.

Juan was carrying in the big metal stove when a little white dog came running up, barking, and bit him.

"Don't, Tiny!" shouted the elderly lady from across the street. "They're dirty!"

Juan couldn't believe it. The old *gringa* came rushing across the street and got her dog, but never apologized.

"That old bitch!" said Julio, helping Juan inside with the stove. "I'll make a taco out of her dog!"

"I wish we could," said Juan. "But, remember, we're only here to do our business."

Julio's wife, Geneva, fixed the kitchen with her three little girls while Juan and Julio set up the stove in the back room. They had already set up the big fifty-gallon drums for the fermentation. It would be ten to twelve days before they could start the distilling.

Al had explained to Juan that the secret to the fermentation process was to use plenty of sugar and yeast with the water, then to let it sit for approximately ten days, until you got the exact kind of sour mash that you needed for the liquor you were making. And the sweet could be sugar, raisins, cane, beets, or even potatoes. The formula Juan had used for the first two batches had been fifty pounds of sugar cane and one pound of yeast for each fifty-gallon drum of water. Each drum had then distilled out to approximately six gallons of alcohol, which, then, Juan had put in the charcoal-burnt barrels to age.

But now, to get enough sugar to try to make fifty barrels of whiskey was going to be a big job. Hell, all the grocery stores that they'd gone to the last time only carried five-pound sacks of sugar. They were going to need half a ton of sugar to do this big job.

While taking a bath, Juan thought about Lupe and the hotel deal. He truly wondered if he'd be able to pull off the whole thing. After changing his clothes, he told Julio and Geneva goodbye and got into his big Dodge. He was going to drive around and think about the sugar problem and then maybe, possibly, drive by the *barrio* and see if he might see Lupe again. Oh, he couldn't get her out of his mind. Especially her sitting in the car with that damned Anglo.

Juan was just getting to Santa Ana when he saw a big delivery truck pulling away from a large grocery store. The truck was delivering bread and cakes. Juan drove around the block, thinking, figuring. Obviously, a bakery used tons of sugar and a bakery couldn't just run down to its local grocery store every few minutes to get a five-pound bag.

He continued around the block. He'd have to go inside the store and ask them where a bakery got its sugar.

By the time Juan came back around the block to the large deluxe-looking store, his hands were sweating. He wondered why it was that he wasn't afraid to face down two armed men, but it scared the hell out of him to approach a *gringo*'s place of business. He'd never felt like this up in Montana. Something very bad had happened to him since he'd moved down here and seen his people treated like dogs.

Parking in front of the store, Juan was glad that he was dressed up, but still, he needed to reach under his seat and pull out a pint bottle and take a long pull. No wonder his nephews thought that the only way for them to get ahead in this country was with a gun. Hell, he was an adult and he felt frightened.

Juan put a stick of gum in his mouth, remembering how Al had always told him that the proof of good whiskey was when you gave a drink to a mouse and the mouse pounded his chest, saying, "Bring on the cat!" Smiling,

Juan said, "Bring on the *gringo!*" He got out of his Dodge and approached the store, whistling as if he didn't have a problem in the world. But inside, he was trembling.

Entering the store, Juan picked up a newspaper so he'd have something in his hands. There weren't many people inside, and there was an Anglo at the cash register.

"Good afternoon," said Juan to the man at the register.

"Hi," said the man. "Can I help you?"

"Well, I'd like to see the boss," said Juan.

The Anglo looked Juan over. "Why?" he asked.

Juan was completely taken aback. He hadn't expected this response. But pulling himself together, he said, "Well, why not?"

"Why not?" repeated the man. "Well, I guess you got me there, friend." He laughed. "All right," he said, "so talk. I sign the checks."

"Then you're the boss?" asked Juan.

The man nodded. "Yep, me and the bank."

"You and the bank?" said Juan, not understanding.

"Sure, I don't own this thing outright, friend. I got a loan on the place like everyone else. Hell, I'm not rich."

"Then, you mean, the bank loaned you money so you could start this business?" asked Juan. He'd never realized that banks loaned money for businesses. He'd assumed banks were only places where the rich put their money for safekeeping.

"Absolutely," said the man. "Hell, no one has the money to build a place and buy the merchandise. I had a little money and the bank loaned me the rest."

"Eh, I like that," said Juan, excited with the idea of a bank helping a hardworking, honest businessman like himself some day.

The man looked Juan over, truly amazed by his good clothes, and yet his complete ignorance of business. "Where you from, friend?" he asked.

Juan could see he'd become suspicious. "From Pomona," he lied.

"Tom Smith," said the man, extending his hand.

"Juan Castro," said Juan, using his mother's maiden name as he took the Anglo's hand.

"What do you do in Pomona? Those are pretty fancy clothes."

"Oh, thank you. I . . . ah, haul manure."

"Good business, eh?"

"If you got enough shit," said Juan.

The man burst out laughing. "I guess the same thing could be said about my business. Well, anyway, what did you have in mind, *amigo?*"

"I want to know where I can buy lots of sugar," said Juan. "You see, I plan on opening up, well, a little Mexican bakery and make sweetbreads, Mexican-style."

"Oh, I see," said the man. "Here, I'll give you the names of two of the largest wholesalers in Los Angeles. Tell them I sent you." He wrote down the names and addresses. "And when you get the bakery going, bring me some. Maybe I can move some of your goods for you."

"Great," said Juan, "thank you very much. I'll be sure to stop by and see you."

"Good luck to you, *amigo*," said the man.

Driving off in his Dodge, Juan brought out the pint bottle of whiskey and took another long pull. It was crazy, but that man had treated him so well, and still, it had scared him.

He breathed deeply, thinking about the rock quarry and how his fellow countrymen had broken down like stupid babies. He thought of his two nephews and how they'd quit school and were losing all respect for anything Mexican. He thought of Lupe and what they would do when they had children. Raising children among the *gringos* was very different from raising kids in Mexico.

Then he remembered how he'd seen Lupe that first time, standing so tall and proud and regal under the outside light of the dancehall. His nostrils grew long and thin. He decided to drive by the *barrio* and see if he couldn't get another look at her.

By the time Juan got to the *barrio*, it was dusk and the people were inside their homes. Driving down the street, Juan saw that each little house was lit up with a soft yellow glow and looked so warm and good. He breathed deeply and thought of Don Pio's house and realized that he'd never had another real home since then.

He parked his car across from Lupe's home and sat there looking at her well-lit little place. He could see the figures of her family through the worn curtains. They were sitting down to eat. He glanced up at the stars, feeling so lonely. His mother was right; it was time for him to settle down and build a home of his own.

Then, suddenly, he felt that someone was watching him. He gripped his .38 and turned around slowly. There was an old woman standing in her garden, looking at him. He tipped his hat to her, put the Dodge in gear, and drove off. By tomorrow, everyone in the *barrio* would know that a stranger had been looking at Lupe's house. He thought of going back and buying the woman off, but decided against it. Instead, he brought out his pint bottle and finished it off. By the time Juan got to their two houses in Corona, he was drunk. The lights were out and everyone was asleep.

In the morning Juan was sound asleep when his mother jerked the covers off his head and handed him a cup of coffee.

"All right," said the old woman, "you've been gone for days and you left me in the middle of a conversation! Now get up, drink this coffee, and let's talk. Luisa told me that you went over to see the hotel. Good thinking; that's what I was going to recommend. Because we don't have much time if this Italian is serious about needing that liquor in thirty days."

His mother went on talking and talking and Juan sat up, gripping his buzzing head. It was still dark outside, and he had a terrible hangover. "Mama, please," he said, "I got to go outside and water the tree."

"All right," she said, "but hurry. I've got it all figured out."

He rolled his eyes to the heavens.

"Did you get the house in the *gringo* part of town, like I told you?" she asked.

"Yes, Mama," he said, trying to get away from her.

"And you moved in Julio and his family, like I told you?"

"Yes," he said, opening the door.

"And you put plenty of chicken shit on your truck?"

"No," he said.

"Why not?" she yelled after him.

"Because I decided that we're plumbers instead," he shouted back at her.

"Plumbers," she repeated, considering the idea. "Good thinking. Not bad."

After relieving himself, Juan turned on the faucet and ran the water over his head, trying to get rid of his hangover. He'd put away four pint bottles after he'd left Lupe's house. Oh, this woman was driving him crazy. He thought of telling his mother about Lupe and how he felt about her, but a part of him just didn't want to. He still felt too unsure about his feelings for Lupe to put it into words yet, much less share with someone else.

"All right," she said, seeing him come back inside, dripping wet with water, "you tell me about the hotel first, then I'll tell you about Luisa's boys."

"What about Luisa's boys?" he asked.

"No, first you tell me what you found out at the hotel," she demanded, putting more wood in the little stove so he could dry off.

"All right," he said, remembering the basement and the big hairy-armed man. "The hotel looks good, Mama. All on the up and up—first class, just like Mario said."

"I see," she said, looking at him in the eyes. "And there was nothing that you saw wrong?" she asked.

He took a big breath, feeling like his mother could see right through him but, still, he lied. "No," he said, "nothing."

He didn't want to tell his mother about the basement and get her worried. Especially since he'd decided to go through with the deal one way or another.

"Okay," she said, "very good. Then I'll tell you about Luisa's boys. She got them to go back to school. But these no-good skunks took the pants off their teacher and threw him out the window."

"They what?" said Juan. "He must've done something."

"*Mi hijito*, if he did something or not, that's not the point," said his mother. "The point is that we live in this country, and they must have respect."

Juan could see that his mother was absolutely right. No matter how badly he was treated, he never lost his respect for the law. No, he didn't fight the cops; he hid his guns instead.

He got dressed. "I'll talk to them," he said, going out the door.

Outside, the day was just beginning to paint the eastern sky yellow and rose and lavender. Juan took a deep breath and walked into his sister's house.

"Get up," he said, kicking his two nephews, who slept on the floor in the front room. "We're going to work. You two don't want to go to school, okay? You come with me and earn your keep. Move! Move! We're going! Right now!"

"But we haven't ate breakfast," said Pedro, rubbing his eyes. "Mama's still asleep."

"Breakfast?" said Juan. "You want to eat? Come on, I'll feed you like a real man!" He hurried the two boys out of the house and into the hen coop, and handed them each two eggs.

"Now, pick a lemon off the tree," he said to them as they walked to his old Model-T truck, "and do just like me." And saying this, Juan tapped the big, rounded end of his egg, breaking the shell, and picked the broken pieces off until he had a nice, clean little round hole about the size of a dime.

"All right," he said, "now put the hole to your mouth, go on, do it, and suck hard. Then chew and swallow and bite the lemon in half, eating it, too."

Pedro made a face of revulsion, but still, he put the egg to his lips, sucked hard, then swallowed and bit the lemon—peel and all—like his uncle, and chewed vigorously.

"Good, eh?" said Juan. "Now eat the other egg, too."

"Oh, my god, do I have to?" asked Pedro.

"That's all you're going to get to eat," said Juan. "And we're going to work all day."

Jose didn't hesitate. He quickly put the second egg to his lips, sucked hard, and then bit into the lemon again.

"There, see!" said Juan. "Jose did it and it's good! The lemon cooks the egg in your stomach. Now you, too, Pedro, hurry up!"

Pedro did it once again, but he gagged and yellow yolk and white slime ran down his chin.

"All right," said Juan, "grab those shovels and get in my truck! We're going!"

"Where?" asked Jose, getting the shovels.

"You'll see," said Juan.

The first bright fingers of daylight were just climbing up into the eastern sky when they got on the main highway heading out of town. The highway was made of dirt and gravel and had a high center so the rains would run off.

Up ahead, Juan turned off his headlights and pulled off the road into a big chicken ranch.

"Shhhhh," said Juan.

"Are we going to get in trouble?" asked Pedro.

"Not if you obey me."

"Okay," said the young boy, looking worried.

"All right," whispered Juan, backing up to a huge pile of manure, "now both of you get out and load up the truck with chicken shit as quick and quiet as you can."

"But, Uncle," said Pedro, "why are we . . ."

But the boy never got to finish his words. Juan grabbed the frightened boy by the throat and yanked him close. "Damn it, *muchacho*, not one more question," he said under his breath. "You just work!"

He threw the boy back against the seat, staring hard. Both boys did as they were told. Two dogs started barking at the ranch house in the distance.

"Faster!" said Juan. "That old bastard has a shotgun!"

"Oh, my God!" said Pedro, and both boys shoveled as fast as they could.

When the truck was full and they got back on the gravel highway, Juan could see both boys were looking pretty worried, but they weren't questioning him anymore.

"Good boys," said Juan, "good boys. This is going to be a long, long day. We probably won't be back home until way after dinner. So pay close attention, like the cat on the mouse, and maybe we'll have a good, safe day and no one will get killed."

The two boys' eyes got so big that Juan saw the whites of their eyes, but they said nothing as he continued down the road. Then, just this side of Lake Elsinore, Juan slowed down.

"All right," said Juan, "up ahead we're going to turn into some oak trees and go up the creek on foot. And we got to do it quick. The sun's up and in a few minutes people will start driving by on their way to work. Do you understand me?" he asked.

Both boys nodded, saying nothing.

"Answer me when I talk to you," said Juan. "With words, not just nods."

"Yes," said both boys loudly.

"Yes, what?" said Juan.

Pedro glanced at Jose. He was scared.

"Yes, that you understand?" said Juan.

"Yes, we understand," said both boys.

"Good," said Juan. He turned off the highway into some oak trees and quickly drove into the brush.

There was a light blue mist over the mostly dried-out creekbed, and Lake Elsinore could be seen in the distance. This was still a very desolate place. Not one farmhouse was in sight.

"Quick, each of you grab a shovel and follow me!" said Juan.

The two boys had to run to keep up with their uncle as he went through the underbrush down into the sandy river bottom.

"Here," he said. "Start digging by this boulder."

"But why?" asked Pedro. "Is it a dead man?"

"Damn it, Pedro!" said Juan. "No more questions! Now dig!"

The two boys went to work and Juan kept watch on the road. Then, two feet under the sand, the two boys hit something hard.

"Be careful," said Juan. "That's the first barrel. Let me get it and you keep digging, Jose. And Pedro, you bring your shovel and come with me."

"Yes," said both boys obediently.

Grabbing one end of the barrel, Juan yanked the ten-gallon oak barrel out of the sand, put it on his shoulder and started up the embankment through the brush to the truck.

"Get on the truck, Pedro," said Juan, "and dig a hole in the shit so I can put this barrel in it."

Pedro climbed up on the truck, sinking knee-deep in fresh chicken shit. He began to dig without question or hesitation.

"Good boy," said Juan. "Now help me put this barrel up there. And then make room for three more barrels! And hurry! I'll be right back!"

"Yes, Uncle!" said Pedro, going to work with power. He was only nine years old, but he was tough and strong.

Ten minutes later they were back on the main road, headed south toward Temecula.

"All right," said Juan as they approached the little cow town, "if we're stopped by the law for any reason, I want you two to do just like me and act stupid, okay? You pretend like you don't understand much English and twist your face to one side like this and let some spit drool out of your mouth."

The boys saw their uncle stick his tongue out, letting spit run down his face, and they started to laugh. With his dirty old work clothes and twisted face, he looked worse than any tramp.

"Eh, don't laugh," said Juan. "I'm not joking. I'm very serious. Now you try it; come on, act stupid and drool some spit. Stupid, dirty Mexicans make the *gringos* nervous, and they'll keep away from us."

But both boys kept laughing. They just couldn't take him seriously.

"Okay, then," he said, leaving the block-long town and crossing the river, "we won't act stupid. If they stop us, we'll just kill them." And he pulled out his .38, handing it to Jose. "You use this," he said, "and I'll use my .45. And you, Pedro, keep down so you don't get killed."

Jose held the .38 as if it were a rattlesnake as they started up the winding mountain road south of town.

"What's wrong?" said Juan. "You've fired that .38 before."

"Yes," said Jose, his eyes filling with tears. "But I don't want to kill no one, Uncle."

"Good," said Juan, "because killing people isn't any good."

And he was just going to explain to both boys that their job for the day was getting the delivery of liquor to the marketplace—not to play cops and robbers with the law—but Pedro grabbed the .38 from his older brother before Juan could speak.

"Give me the gun!" said Pedro with a wild gleam in his eyes. "I'll help our *tío*! I'm no chicken-shit! I'm the one who always has to lead! Jose wasn't even going to help me with the teacher until I got in trouble."

"Oh, tell me about it," said Juan, looking at his little nephew who, only a couple of hours before, had practically been wetting his pants at the chicken ranch.

"Well, we pantsed our old teacher," said Pedro proudly, gun in hand, "and threw him out a window!"

"Oh, you two pantsed a teacher, eh?" said Juan, acting very impressed. "And threw him out a window."

"Yeah," said Pedro, pointing the gun at the windshield. "But it was only the first story, so he didn't get killed or nothing."

"Oh, I see," said Juan, acting disappointed.

But he could see that Jose wasn't falling for it. He was getting nervous, feeling sure that they were going to get in trouble. Pedro, on the other hand, was in heaven, handling the gun.

"And why did you do this?" asked Juan.

"He called us names," said Pedro.

"What names?"

"You know, Mexican this and that."

"Oh, I see, and so you got him?"

"Yeah," said Pedro.

"And now you're ready to help me shoot it out with the cops, eh?" said Juan.

"Sure," said Pedro, smiling. "I'm ready!"

"You'll kill 'em, eh, if I tell you, eh?"

"Like a *macho*!" said Pedro, using both hands to point the .38 at the windshield.

"You'll pull the trigger when I say, 'kill that cop,' eh?"

"You tell me, and I'll do it!"

"All right," said Juan, "then pull the trigger."

"Right now?"

"Yeah, go ahead!"

"Where at?"

"In front of you. Do it."

The snubnose exploded, and the glass from the windshield splattered, engulfing them in an echoing roar. The early morning sunlight hit the pieces of splintered windshield, blinding Juan, and he hit the brakes and went into a skid. The weight of the whiskey barrels and wet chicken shit swung the rear of the truck around.

"No!" screamed Jose, "we're going over the cliff!"

"Oh, my God!" yelled Pedro, dropping the gun and grabbing the dashboard.

But the truck didn't go over. It came to a stop just at the edge of the deep slope. Seeing that they might go over, Juan turned the steering wheel toward the middle of the road and gave it all the gas, but the tires only dug in, shooting a spray of loose gravel into the deep canyon below.

"Get out!" yelled Juan, as the truck teeter-tottered on the cliff's edge. "Quick! And you, Jose, put some rocks under the rear tires! And you, Pedro get on the hood in front!"

Both boys got out and they saw that it looked like the truck was going to go over at any second. The barranca was deep, five or six hundred feet straight down into jagged rocks and boulders and trees and a little running brook.

"Uncle!" screamed Jose. "You better get out, too! It's going over!"

"NO!" bellowed Juan. "It's not going over!" And he sat there, gripping the steering wheel with white knuckles. "Do as I say! Put rocks under the back tires and you, Pedro, get on the hood."

"But it's going over!" said Pedro.

"Damn it!" roared Juan, his neck muscles coming up like cords. "Get on that hood before I kill you myself, you little shit!"

Trembling, Pedro went around to the front of the truck while Jose began putting rocks under the rear tires with outstretched arms so he wouldn't get caught under the vehicle if it suddenly went over. But Pedro still wouldn't get on the hood. He just stood there, looking terrified.

"Damn it! Get on that hood!" bellowed Juan.

"In front, right here?" asked Pedro, watching the truck teeter-tottering on the edge.

"Yes, right there!" yelled Juan.

Seeing the rage in his uncle's face through the broken windshield, Pedro finally got on the bumper, leaned on the hood and, to his surprise, the vehicle didn't go toppling over the edge of the cliff but, instead, came down on the road, holding solid.

"Good," said Juan. "Now don't move. Don't even fart, Pedro. And when you finish with the rocks, Jose, you, too, get on the hood."

Finishing with the rocks, Jose did as told, and got on the hood; now the truck was good.

"All right," said Juan, "now I'm going to get out and get the barrels off the truck, but you two just hold there. Don't move!"

Opening his door carefully, Juan began to get out of the truck, but he felt the vehicle starting to go over so he held on to the door, giving it weight as he got out. He could see that Pedro was praying.

"Don't move, just hold there," he said calmly. "I'm going to take two barrels off and then everything will be fine."

The two boys were trembling, beginning to sweat.

"Hold still!" snapped Juan as he got a shovel and moved the manure aside, then reached for the first barrel.

He was so strong that he was able to lift the barrel with his outstretched arms, pulling it toward himself across the bed without once touching the truck with it. Then, when he'd unloaded the barrels, he turned to his nephews.

"All right," he said, "you two can get down now."

But when they went to move, both boys found that their legs were missing. They'd gone numb, they'd been holding on so tightly. Smiling, Juan Salvador came around the truck and lifted Pedro off the hood and then Jose. They both had tears in their eyes.

"All right," he said, "now come on, we're alive, so move it! We got to hide these barrels before somebody comes by here and catches us with our pants down."

Quickly, the two boys did as told. Then, having hidden the last barrel, Juan called Pedro aside. "Come on," he said to Pedro, "you and I got a little unfinished business. You stay here, Jose, and watch the truck. We'll be right back."

Juan and Pedro walked back down the road about half a mile, then Juan cut off into the brush. Pedro was right behind him.

"Well," said Juan, "that was quite a shot, eh?"

"You told me to," said the boy quickly.

"I'm not complaining," said Juan. "You did just what I said, and that's good. But, also, a man has to learn how to think for himself, too.

"And that reminds me," continued Juan, coming to a small opening in the brush, "you haven't had a chance to drive my new Dodge, have you?"

"Oh, no," said the boy, "but I'm ready!"

"Good," said Juan. "I'm glad to hear that. Because being ready is half of the battle in life." He brought out his pocket-knife and cut a long, thin new branch off a tree. "But also, there's responsibility that comes with everything we do. You ride a horse, then you have to feed him, brush him, cool him off, clean his stall, and care for your saddle and bridle. You kill a pig, you have to sharpen your knives, know what you're doing and not make the animal suffer, then clean up everything and be prepared to cook the meat or to cut it up and put it away. There's a lot of work and preparation; you just don't shoot the pig for the fun of it, you understand?" said Juan, peeling the bark off the branch.

"Yes, I understand," said the boy excitedly. "But what's that stick for? To help me to reach the pedals of the Dodge?"

"No, not exactly," said Juan Salvador calmly, deliberately. "But just like some branches are used for finding water, others are used for finding human wisdom."

"No, really?" said Pedro, laughing happily. "But how can you find wisdom with a branch?"

"I'll show you," said Juan Salvador. "But first I want you to know and respect this word 'responsibility' above all else. And realize that to do anything in life—drive a car, rob a bank, or kill a pig—you must be a man of responsibilities. For instance, if you decide to rob a bank, you just don't go shooting into a bank like a savage. No, you plan, you organize, you think, you figure the odds and then, maybe, you decide to not even do it."

"Why not? Have you robbed banks, too, Uncle?" he asked excitedly.

"No, I never have and I never will," said Juan Salvador. "And I'll tell you why; because I'm an honest man and I think out everything I do. So I'd never put myself in the position of needing to kill people just for money. Do you understand? I don't want to kill anybody. And I don't steal, either. That chicken shit we got this morning, I got a deal with that man. We weren't stealing. And I got no fight with the cops, either; that's why I act stupid and drool spit, so I don't have to kill no one, you understand?"

"Well, yes, but you always carry a gun, Uncle."

"Yes, and I carry my balls, too, but I don't go around leaving kids like stray dogs all over the place, either," he said. "Do you understand? I have respect!"

And saying this, Juan Salvador suddenly leaped forward like an enraged bull and he grabbed his nephew by the arm and began to switch him with the long, green limb. The boy screamed out in surprised terror. But Juan had a good hold on him, and he never let up. He just switched him all the harder on the legs and butt.

"I work for my living!" yelled Juan. "I don't go around shooting people! And I wouldn't shoot a gun inside a house or car no matter if God Himself tells me to! I think, I use my head, and I work hard! I make my own liquor! I don't steal from no man! I'm a businessman! I'm not a stupid gang of little two-bit, ass-turning punks, ganging up on an old teacher and pantsing him! I got balls, you understand? I got respect! I sweat! I work! Now, repeat! After me! I work! I got respect!"

"I work! I got respect!" screamed the boy, leaping like a fish on a lure as Juan held him and whipped him.

"I'm a businessman!" yelled Juan. "And I steal from no man! And I respect the law!"

"I'm a businessman! And I steal from no man! I respect the law!" bellowed the boy at the top of his lungs as he leaped with each swishing, hitting, cutting strike.

"I don't do nothing without thinking and planning!" yelled Juan, giving the boy three quick hits. "And when I kill the pig to eat, or deliver liquor for money, I take the responsibility to do it quickly and cleanly and with RESPECT!" And he swatted Pedro five more times. "Repeat!"

Pedro screamed at the top of his lungs. "When I kill the pig to eat or deliver liquor for money, I take the responsibility to do it quick and with respect!"

"Repeat! All of it! AGAIN! I work! I have respect!"

"I work! I have respect!"

"I have honor! And I don't abuse no one, not even a pig when I kill him to eat, much less a human being . . . because I'm responsible!"

"I have honor! And I don't abuse no one, not even a pig when I kill him to eat, much less a human being . . . because I'm responsible!"

"Killing is no fun!"

"Killing is no fun!"

"I respect life!"

"I respect life!"

"And I'll never shoot no gun in no truck, no matter who tells me, because I think first!"

And he swatted the boy three more quick ones.

"I won't! I won't! Oh, please, no more, Uncle!" begged Pedro.

"And I'll never think killing is fun again! And in the future, I'll act stupid and drool spit to avoid a fight."

"I will! I will! Honest!"

"And if you ever think that killing or pantsing a teacher is fun again, you just remember this whipping!" said Juan. And he whacked the boy three more good ones. "Is pain fun? Eh, tell me!"

"NOOOO!" screamed the boy. "It hurts!"

"Good," said Juan, releasing the boy.

Pedro ran down the hillside and jumped into the little river, rubbing his ass and legs and crying desperately.

Trying to calm down, Juan Salvador brought out a cigar and went back up on the road. Next, he'd have a talk with Jose. But he wasn't going to have to whip Jose. He'd been more respectful from the start.

Juan breathed deeply. Oh, raising kids in this country was going to be much more difficult than he'd ever imagined.

"Did you hear the screams?" he asked Jose, walking up to him, cigar in hand.

The big, husky boy nodded. "Yes," he said.

"Well, don't worry," Juan said to his nephew, bringing out a match, "I'm not going to whip you. You had the good sense not to want to kill someone in the first place." He struck the match. "And, also, you're too big for a whipping, Jose. You're not a boy. You're twelve years old; you're a man."

Still, the boy looked very wary.

"Now tell me, how did all that business with the teacher get started?"

"Well, you see, Uncle, he's one of these *gringos* who doesn't like *mejicanos*, and he's always saying little things."

"Oh," said Juan, sitting on the hood of the truck and smoking his cigar. "He's like that Tom Mix *cabrón* we see in the movies, eh? That son-of-a-bitch! I've seen people get in fights inside the theaters because of his movies and good men die. William Hart, on the other hand, fights against Mexicans, too, but he always does it with respect."

"This teacher is like Tom Mix," said Jose, "but not that brave. More like an old-woman Tom Mix."

Juan laughed. "So go on, what happened?"

"Well, Pedro and some of his friends had had enough, so they put some dog shit under his desk and he got it all over his shoes. He was so mad that he got Pedro by the neck and was going to whip him, but I told him to put Pedro down." Jose stopped.

"Well, go on."

The big, husky boy was embarrassed. "Well, he called our mother a name, Uncle, saying that our race came from whores, so I dropped him."

"You what?"

"I hit him," said the boy, looking ashamed.

"One hit?"

The husky boy nodded. "Yeah. And that's when the peewees pantsed him and threw him out the window."

"Peewees?"

"Yeah, Pedro and his little friends."

"I see, I see, but is he a good teacher?" asked Juan. "Did you learn anything from him?"

"Well, yes, he was all right in that way. He taught us a lot. But you don't understand, Uncle. He was always saying little things."

"And you're not man enough to put up with some little things to learn your lessons?" asked Juan.

Pedro was coming up the road. He was all wet and still rubbing his behind.

"Well, yes, Uncle, but day after day?"

"And you don't think I get the same thing out here? Hell, just to find out where to get the sugar, I sweated blood!"

"But, Uncle, you got respect. No man even dreams of stepping on your shadow."

Juan took a big breath, watching Pedro come up. "That's true," he said, "in the *barrio*. But not with the Anglos. Hell, to rent the new house, I had to say I was a Greek. Jose, I was a boy—no bigger than you—when I went to prison and grown men tried to abuse me, but I fought 'em. Look!" he said, ripping his shirt open. "They cut my stomach open, left me for dead, but I never gave in! Because I'm a man, goddammit! I don't care what an old-fart teacher tells you; you pay attention and learn! Reading, education, that's what's going to get us ahead in the long run. Not this bootlegging. Think! Look around you! Use your head!"

And Juan would've gone on talking, but they heard the sound of a vehicle coming up the grade behind them.

"Quick," said Juan, rushing to get his .38 out of the truck, "we got to get that car to stop and help us!"

Opening the cylinder, Juan ejected the spent cartridge and slipped in a new one, then put the snubnose under his shirt in his pants.

"You're the lightest, Pedro. Quick, get up on the pile of manure and make sure that barrel I left on the truck is well hidden. And Jose, you put your weight on the hood."

Both boys did as they were told.

"All right," said Juan, "I'll do the talking. You two just stay by the truck and act hurt. Remember, we just had an accident and you boys are hurt and scared, got it?"

"Yes," said both boys.

"And remember, if I spit and drool and act not too smart, you just keep still. This could get very dangerous if we're not careful. Last week a car full of no-good bastards tried to rob me because they're too lazy to make their own liquor, and I had to deal with them," he said, getting his .45 from under the seat. "But we got no fight with the law. We just act stupid like this if it's the law," said Juan, twisting his face and drooling spit.

Seeing his uncle twist his face and drool, Jose began to laugh. He just couldn't help it. But this time, Juan said nothing. He just stepped in and hit Jose in the mouth with his fist. The boy went spilling backward into the truck. Blood burst from his lips.

"Don't wipe the blood!" shouted Juan. "Just stay down! Remember, you broke the windshield with your face!"

Jose did as told, and Pedro didn't need to be told anything. He dropped to the ground, terrified.

"Very good," said Juan, winking at both of them. "Now, not a word, remember."

Juan walked out into the middle of the road with a rope in his hands as a big black Buick came racing around the last curve. Quickly, Juan started waving his arms, pointing at the two boys. The man driving the Buick braked hard. Juan ran up to him.

"We had an accident!" Juan yelled.

The man stepped out of his Buick. He was a great big, tall Anglo with a long nose and bright blue eyes. He was wearing a full-length car coat and fine gloves. He looked educated and well-to-do.

"How badly are the boys hurt?" he asked.

"Oh, I don't know," said Juan. "They bumped their faces hard. So we need a pull so I can get them to the doctor."

Juan was nervous. He'd never gotten help from a rich-looking *gringo* before, and he needed this pull. He was losing money every minute that he waited, plus he was taking an awful chance of the sheriff or some thieves coming by.

The tall, well-dressed man looked Juan over and walked around him, going over to where the boys were lying alongside the Model-T. He saw the blood on Jose's face and the fear in Pedro's eyes.

"Are you okay?" he asked Jose.

But Jose didn't answer him. He glanced at his uncle.

"He's not too bad," said Juan, cutting in. "But still, I want to get him to this doctor I know on the coast. So tell me, mister, can you give us a pull?"

"Maybe," said the man, "I don't know why not, if we can get rid of some of the manure to lighten the load."

The blood left Juan's face. If they removed the shit, they'd expose the barrel. Oh, he should've thought of that. He'd been a fool not to think of that ahead of time.

"Oh, no," said Juan, shaking his head. "I need to get the manure in, too. No thanks. We'll just wait, then."

The tall Anglo looked at Juan, his blue eyes blazing like a hawk's. Then he turned away from Juan and walked to the Model-T, inspecting the situation. He saw that both boys looked very frightened. But then, getting around behind the truck and glancing over the ledge down into the steep canyon, he decided that these poor bastards had almost gone over the cliff's edge and were still in shock.

His furious blue eyes turned gentle, and he smiled. "All right," he said, taking off his right glove. "Fred Noon, attorney-at-law," he said, extending his hand to Juan.

Hearing the words, "attorney-at-law," Juan froze. But then he put his hand out, too.

"Juan Villaseñor," he said, "respect the law!"

"Respect the law?" repeated Fred Noon, not understanding.

"Well, yes, you say, 'attorney-at-law,' " said Juan.

"Oh, I see," said Noon, laughing. Then he helped Juan tie the big Buick to the Model-T and dig out in front of the truck's tires. They got the truck back on the road, and they were off.

By the time they got to Carlsbad, twenty-some miles toward the west, Juan and Fred Noon were pretty good friends. Fred Noon spoke Spanish fluently. He practiced law in San Diego. He also knew Archie Freeman and had worked with him a few times.

Getting into Carlsbad, Juan had Noon pull him to the old woman's house who sold liquor for him. Her name was Consuelo and she was a tough old woman who moved a lot of liquor for Juan when the crops were in.

"Thank you," said Juan to Fred Noon. "How much do I owe you?" he asked.

"Nothing, Juan," said Noon. "You just take good care of the boys."

"All right," said Juan, "but, well, are you a drinking man?" he asked.

Juan knew that he was taking an awfully big chance by asking this question if, indeed, Noon didn't drink. But he looked rugged enough to be a drinker, and he did know Archie, who was always drinking like a fish.

"Well, just exactly what do you mean by 'drinking'?" asked Noon, getting a twinkle in his eyes as he took another look at the pile of chicken manure on the truck.

Seeing him glance at the Model-T, Juan was sorry he'd brought up the question. But he couldn't back off now.

"Whiskey," said Juan. "Do you like good Canadian whiskey?"

"Canadian whiskey!" said the tall, hawk-eyed man, licking his lips. "Hell, I don't know a lawyer who doesn't! Do you have some?" he asked anxiously.

Juan was glad he'd asked. The man was biting at the bit, he was so excited. "Well, not exactly," said Juan. "But I got a friend who might have some. So why don't you drive on up to the Montana Cafe, just across the street from the Twin Inns, and I'll meet you up there in fifteen minutes. But don't order more than you can eat."

"All right," said Noon. He got in his Buick and drove off.

Juan took Pedro and Jose inside Consuelo's house to have their cuts and bruises attended to.

Lupe was outside saying goodbye to Mark when Carlota and two of her girlfriends came rushing out of the house.

"I hate you!" said Carlota to Lupe, going down the street with her friends. "You didn't even enter, and he comes to the house for you!"

Lupe had no idea what her sister was talking about. But after Mark was gone, she went inside and she saw that her mother and father were in the tiny front room with an elderly man dressed in a dark suit. Lupe felt her heart leap, thinking that it had something to do with Mark walking her home.

"Lupe," her mother said, "this is Señor Gonzales, and he's come to see you."

Lupe said nothing.

"Please sit down, my dear," said Señor Gonzales.

Lupe sat down. But she didn't like it.

"Well," said the polite-looking man, smiling at her, "you see, my dear, I'm one of the officials for the Cinco de Mayo. And this year, for the first time, we want to have a big celebration with a parade and extend it past the *barrio* into the *americano* part of town so we can include the *gringos* in our celebration.

"You see, many of our people who came here during the Revolution, as did your own family, are beginning to think that maybe this country is going to be our permanent home. So that's why we want to include the *gringos* and teach them of our Mexican traditions so we don't lose our culture."

He coughed, clearing his throat. Lupe could see that he was getting nervous, but she still had no idea what any of this had to do with her.

"The point," he said, "is that we want to put our best foot forward, as the *americanos* say, and even though we realize that you didn't enter our beauty contest, we all still know that you're the most beautiful young lady in all the *barrio*, so we'd like you to please give us the honor of being the queen of our festivities."

Lupe was stunned. She glanced at her parents. Now she knew why her sister and her friends were so mad at her. They'd made dresses and worked on their hair for weeks, preparing for the contest. She hadn't even entered. Oh, there was just no way she could do this.

"Lupe," said her mother, seeing her daughter's hesitation, "we explained to Señor Gonzales that you're not the type of girl who even likes to go to dances. But, well, he's assured us that you won't have to do anything that will embarrass you."

"Yes," added the man. "all you'll have to do is sit in the open car with your princesses. We'll take care of the rest," he said, smiling.

Still, Lupe said nothing. She was just too shocked.

Señor Gonzales glanced at her parents. "Also," he said to Lupe, "if you like, we can let you pick your own princesses so that way you can choose your sister and your friends so that there won't be any hard feelings."

"Thank you," said Doña Guadalupe, "I'm sure that will make it easier for Lupe."

But they could all see that Lupe was still not responding.

"Well, at least think about it," said Señor Gonzales. "And I'll stop by for your answer in a few days. But we don't have much time. We want to invite the mayor of Santa Ana and the City Council."

He got up and got his hat. "One more thing," he said, "if it's the money for the dress that you're worried about, well, then, I think we can supply the material for your mother to make you your dress so that it wouldn't burden your family."

"Thank you," said Lupe. "I was thinking of that, *señor*."

He took her hand, kissing it. "I thought so," he said. "My, they are right, you are beautiful. Please, talk things over with your mother and father, and do accept. We really do want to make the best possible showing we can for this Cinco de Mayo."

Lupe saw him to the door.

That night, when Carlota found out that Lupe had the power to pick her own princesses if she accepted, she went crazy.

"Oh, you've got to say yes, Lupe," she begged. "You've got to! Or I'll hate you, I swear! You didn't even enter the contest and they came to you!"

After taking care of business in Carlsbad, Juan drove three hours up the coast to Los Angeles with his two nephews. He thought of Lupe and of the hotel deal and of that big, hairy-armed man who'd smelled of a Mexican-hating Tom Mixcop. He fully realized that he would have to go very carefully and not let himself get caught. The more he found out about Lupe and her family, the more he could see that they were God-fearing, law-abiding people. It would kill his courtship with her if they ever found out about his business.

By the time they got to the warehouse in Los Angeles, Juan was feeling very cautious. His nephews were fast asleep. Juan woke the two boys up and put them to work, loading the truck with sugar and yeast.

It was dark by the time they got to their big house south of Los Angeles. Jose and Pedro were so tired, they were ready to cry. They'd been at it for over fourteen hours. But Juan was determined to show them that bootlegging was no game. He yanked them out of the truck and had them wash their faces with cold water and get to work unloading the supplies. He and Julio went to work, preparing the metal drums in the backroom.

"We're going to need more drums," said Juan to Julio, scraping out a drum, "so once we start the distilling, we can work around the clock."

"Ah, come on, Juan," said Julio, washing out another drum, "we'll never get fifty ten-gallon barrels of whiskey made in time. Hell, it took us almost a month to just make up those fifteen barrels last time."

"Yes, but we got more experience and we'll work day and night, taking naps and never stop," said Juan, putting saliva on Pedro's eyelids as he came walking by with a sack. "Wake up," he said to the boy, "and keep working."

"But, Juan, my wife and I can't be locked up here for a straight month," said Julio.

"Why not?" asked Juan. "In a month, we'll be rich!"

"Well, yes, that's true," said Julio. "But Juan, we need time off to visit our friends in the *barrio*."

Hearing this, Juan couldn't believe his ears. "Goddammit, what's wrong with you?" he bellowed. "You were broke when I took you in, Julio! Now you got your own truck! A big house! All the food you want! What the hell is thirty days? I could do them hanging by my thumbs! Has a little money made you soft in the head, *hombre*?"

"Hey, you can't talk to me like this!" said Julio, seeing his kids crouching down in the corner in fear.

Jose and Pedro were finally wide awake. Their uncle looked ready to fight, he was so mad.

"Damn it, Julio!" shouted Juan. "Then how the hell am I supposed to talk to you? When you talk such ridiculousness!"

"With respect, Juan!" he yelled, glancing at his family. "With respect, goddammit!"

"All right, then with respect," said Juan, trying to calm down, "pull yourself together and realize that this is a chance of a lifetime!"

Juan Salvador tried to back off. But he couldn't. He was boiling inside his chest. He felt like ripping the clothes off his body just so he could breathe. He felt he was exploding like a volcano, as if all his ancestry was raging up inside him, wanting to breathe, wanting to live.

"Julio, goddammit!" he said. "I respect you! I do! But damn it, my mother begged so we could eat! I went to prison to get money so we could live! This is nothing!" he bellowed, the cords of his neck coming up. "Do you hear me? *¡Nada! ¡Nada!* I'd work ten years, twenty-four hours a day, to never kiss no man's ass again!"

"All right, all right!" said Julio. "But still, it's hard on my family, Juan! They got no one to visit here, with all these *gringos* hating us!"

"That's why we moved here!" yelled Juan. "So people won't visit!"

"Yes, I know, I know, but, well, damn it, we were doing so well already, Juan. Why do we need to get bigger?"

Hearing this, Juan just knew that he'd kill Julio if he kept talking. So he went out of the room, raging, crazy inside, wild-eyed, insane, furious; there was just nothing he could say to this man.

It wasn't just the money; it was the way people had looked at him when he'd tried to rent a house. It was how the *gringos* looked at his old mother when she crossed the American side of town to go to church. Tears came to his eyes. Why, they looked at his beloved mother as if she were dog shit. He had to get big. Big! Rich! So he could court Lupe and build a house on a hill with a red-tile roof, and he'd never have people look at his family with disgust again.

It was three o'clock the next morning when Juan pulled up to their two houses in Corona with his nephews. And it was five that same morning when he woke them up. "Come on!" he said. "We got to get those barrels we hid by Temecula right now!"

"But I just got to sleep," said Pedro, tears coming to his eyes.

"Bull shit!" said Juan. "You don't go to school, you work!" He got both boys out of the house and into the chicken coop for breakfast once again.

For the next three days, Juan worked his nephews fifteen to sixteen hours a day, scrubbing floors, washing out drums and moving fertilizer. By the fourth day, Pedro was begging to go back to school.

"Please, Uncle," he said, "we want to go back to school."

"You, too, Jose?" asked Juan.

Jose nodded. "Yes."

"All right," said Juan, "you two can go back to school. But understand, you're going to have to face that teacher you pantsed. You did it, you pay. I gamble, I pay. Look at my throat; see that scar? And remember the scar across my belly? We all pay, believe me. Your mother, my mother—those great women—they paid in blood more than once to get us here alive, and so you two are going to work and get educated or you answer to me! Understand?"

They both nodded, taking their uncle very seriously.

"No nodding to me," said Juan. "You answer in words! *Mejicanos* are tough roosters! Every prison I been to, they run the place! Not the Negroes or *blancos*! But us, *la raza*!"

"Yes, Uncle," they both said.

"Yes, what?"

They glanced at each other nervously.

"Yes, we're good *mejicanos*," said Pedro.

"And?" said Juan.

"And killing isn't fun," added Pedro, "because we're responsible when we kill the pig. We think, we plan, we sweat and work."

"Very good," said Juan, "very good. And you, Jose?"

"Well, we figure the odds," said Jose, "so maybe we don't even kill the pig or rob the bank because we're *prevenidos* in everything we do and don't want to put ourselves in a position to kill just for money."

"Excellent," said Juan. "Excellent!" He hugged both of them, kissing them. "Good boys; I'm proud of you. Now I'm giving you each five dollars for the work you did. But, of course, you'll give three dollars each to your mother because . . . tell me."

"Because we're *machos* with big *tanates*!" said Pedro.

Juan burst out laughing. "Exactly," he said, "exactly!"

"Hey, now we can get a real baseball bat," said Jose.

For two weeks Juan and Julio worked around the clock, doing the distilling day and night. But it was a very dangerous process. The sour mash boiled inside the big kettle and if they didn't keep alert and watch it constantly, it could blow up like a bomb. By the eighteenth day, they were both so tired that they were beginning to make mistakes. Once, the kettle almost blew.

"Okay," said Juan, "I think we both need a break. Let's count out how much liquor we've made and take a few days off. I'll take the first two days off, then you and your family take off the next two days. But, while I'm gone, don't leave the house for nothing—not even for ten minutes."

"Yes, *mi general*!" said Julio. "Hell, we already got thirty barrels!"

Juan gave Julio a big *abrazo*. "We've done good, *amigo*. And I'm only going to have to sell five of these barrels so we got the money to get the rest of the supplies to finish the job. We're on our way!"

Juan fixed them each a good-sized drink and they toasted. Then he showered and put on his best suit, whistling as he dressed.

It was the Cinco de Mayo, and Archie had a dance going on in Santa Ana. Juan figured that he'd deliver two barrels of whiskey to Archie for the dance, then he'd begin his official courtship of Lupe. Hell, it had been nearly a year since he'd first seen her, and he was ready.

He got his .38, checked to see if it was loaded, put it under his vest inside his pants, and he had Julio help him load the two barrels of whiskey in the trunk of his big Dodge convertible.

Pulling up to Archie's house, Juan saw that the front door was open. He glanced around, wondering if everything was okay.

Archie kept a house in Santa Ana and his wife and kids in another house just south of Oceanside. He'd once told Juan that the secret to a successful marriage was never to live with your wife, except on Sundays when you took your kids to church.

"Hello?" called Juan, walking up cautiously to the open door. "Are you in, Archie?"

"Yeah, come right in," said the huge lawman, coming down the hallway with shaving cream all over his face. "The door ain't locked. Just get your ass in here and get the whiskey and a couple glasses from the kitchen," he said. "And hurry up! We ain't got much time! I'm leading the parade!"

"What parade?" asked Juan, going into the kitchen and finding a sink full of dirty dishes.

"Don't you know?" said Archie, shaving himself with a straight razor. "The *barrio* is putting on a big shebang and I'm officiating it for the sheriff's department."

"But I thought you were a deputy for San Diego County, not up here in Orange County," said Juan, rinsing the dead flies out of a couple of glasses.

"I'm a deputy in both counties," said Archie, finishing his shave.

"How the hell did you do that?"

"Same as I'm a registered Republican and Democrat," he said, looking at himself in the mirror as he washed his face. "Man, I sure wish I would've been born rich instead of so damned good-looking!" he said, pouring some whiskey into his hand and slapping it on his face.

Juan laughed. He just couldn't believe that Archie really thought he was good-looking. Hell, Juan couldn't remember when he'd seen a more homely-looking man. Why, Archie was damn-right ugly with his ears sticking out and his long, cow face with thick, liver-colored, loose-flapping lips.

They tipped their glasses together and drank, then went out the door. They had to get the two barrels of liquor to the big place that Archie had rented for the dance before going to the parade.

"Did you find out anything on that hotel in San Bernardino?" asked Juan, getting in his car.

"Nope," said Archie, "ever since those two FBI agents got killed over in San Bernardino, nobody is talking too much."

Juan felt his heart leap, but he showed nothing, holding as calm as a reptile in the noon-day sun. The word in the *barrio* had it that Juan was the one who'd killed the two agents, and Juan had done nothing to contradict the rumors. Hell, it was helping his business. Men gave him a wider berth.

"Oh, I see," said Juan, "nobody talking, eh?"

"Nope," said Archie, searching Juan's eyes.

But Juan still showed him nothing. He could well see that Archie was fishing.

They both got in their cars and drove off. Juan breathed deeply, feeling very wary. Archie had been one hundred percent lawman when he'd stared at him.

After unloading the barrels, Juan drove over to see the parade. The people were lined up five feet on both sides of the tree-shaded street. Killing the motor, Juan stood up on the driver's seat of his Dodge convertible so he could look from above the crowd. He spotted Archie in his black Hudson, coming real slowly down the street. There were half a dozen horsemen dressed in complete *charro* outfits right behind him.

Juan thought of his grandfather's great sorrel stallion and he remembered the day that he'd seen Don Pio go down the mountain with his old *compadres* to see Don Porfirio in Mexico City.

A dozen *mariachis* followed on foot behind the horseman, playing loudly. Juan listened to their music and his eyes turned toward the finely-dressed horsemen in their Mexican attire and felt his heart swell with pride. Oh, how he wished that he'd known about this parade so he could've brought his mother and sister and, especially, his two nephews. This was Mexico to him: dancing horses, glittering conchos on the riders' clothes, loud music, and happy laughter.

One rider, on a dappled white horse, stopped his mount in the middle of the intersection and stood up on his saddle, doing a series of rope tricks. Everyone cheered. The young horseman brought out his long rawhide rope and made a large loop. He was going to attempt to do the devil's cut by trying to get his horse to jump through the loop as he whirled the lariat from on top of the saddle.

Juan grinned. The last time he'd seen this trick successfully done had been by his brother, Jose, the great, way back before the Revolution. Oh, there had been a horseman!

Whirling the lariat around and around, the circle got bigger and bigger, and the young horseman jumped through it on foot on top of his saddle and then took the rope over his head, making the loop larger and larger so he could pass his horse through it, too. The crowd fell silent. The young man had an enormous loop going horizontally around him, large enough to encircle both him and his horse. Then came the moment of truth, the exact moment for him to throw out the whirling loop, then bring it in vertically so both could pass through. But the horse just stepped in too quickly, and the whirling loop collapsed.

Everyone sighed with disappointment, but applauded the effort anyway. The young horseman laughed, showing a mouthful of beautiful white teeth, and he pushed back his big *sombrero*, exposing a lock of shocking red hair.

Seeing his reddish hair, Juan immediately thought of his father's side of the family and wondered if this boy was from Los Altos de Jalisco. He could even be a distant relative.

The six horsemen and the band of loud *mariachis* passed by, followed by a flatbed truck decorated with a mountain of flowers. There were four beautifully-dressed young ladies sitting on the flatbed nestled among the flowers. One was dressed in a long, pink dress, another in green, another in orange, and the last one in red. Their large, full dresses blended into the white-capped mountain of flowers. The girls smiled and waved to the people enthusiastically.

Then, Juan was just going to get back down in his car and drive off, when he saw Lupe. There she was, sitting motionlessly in the middle of the flatbed truck, on the floral mountain's peak. She was dressed in white and surrounded by a sea of snow-white lilies.

Juan's heart exploded. "My God, she's the queen of the parade," he said swallowing, going dizzy, fully realizing that the stars above were smiling down on them. This was, indeed, the perfect day for them to start their courtship.

Then she saw him, too. Their eyes met. He smiled to her, raking back the brim of his white panama with his right hand. Lupe saw his smile, his eyes, the hat, his clean-shaven face, and the flashy convertible. She admired his suit—a navy blue pin-stripe—white shirt, and polka-dot die. Realizing she was staring, she blushed and quickly glanced away.

Juan took a big breath and watched the flatbed truck continue up the street. Then came the mayor in a grand car. But Juan paid no attention to him and got back down in his Dodge.

Oh, he was flying so high that he could hardly breathe. The sight of the queen of his life had sent him soaring to the heavens. He was in love. There was no doubt about it. He started the motor, backed up, and drove off.

That same afternoon, Juan drove over to the Anglo part of town where Archie was having the dance. There was already a long line of Mexicans and a few Anglos waiting to get in. Over to one side was a little stand where tamales and tacos were sold. The four princesses were at the front door selling the tickets.

Juan parked across the street and brought out a piece of gum. He was sure that Lupe was already inside. He chewed his gum, trying to decide how to best start his courtship. Then he spotted Lupe's tall, thin brother in the crowd, and he got an idea.

Juan started up the motor of his big Dodge and made a U-turn, pulling up next to the crowd. He honked his horn, waving at Victoriano.

"Me?" said Victoriano, pointing at himself as he looked at the big beautiful car.

"Yeah, you," said Juan.

Quickly, Victoriano came over to the sleek convertible.

"Look," said Juan, "I don't know much about cars but someone told me you do, so I was wondering if you'd drive with me and listen to this noise I got."

"Sure," said Victoriano, smoothing the door of the grand automobile.

"Good," said Juan, feeling good that his scheme was working so far.

Victoriano started around the car to the passenger's side.

"No, you drive," said Juan.

"Me drive?" repeated Victoriano.

"Sure," said Juan. "So you can feel the car."

"All right!" said Victoriano, rushing to the driver's side. "My God, it's beautiful," he said, getting in and taking the wheel. He'd never been in such a car. He put it in gear, let out the clutch, and they were off. Everyone watched after them. No one knew who Juan was. They assumed he was some rich friend of Victoriano's.

Driving up the street, Victoriano said, "It sounds fine to me."

"Give it the gas," said Juan. "Sometimes it doesn't make the noise until I gas it hard!"

Victoriano stomped down on the gas pedal, and they flew up the street in a blur of speed. Victoriano was in ecstasy, grinning ear-to-ear. By the time they got back to the dance, Victoriano was talking to Juan like an old friend. Juan knew he'd won the first round. Not only had he managed to slip past one of the guards of Lupe's castle, he'd made friends with the man who could help him win her over.

Oh, it was war! Juan was determined to use every trick he could to get the woman of his dreams!

"Well," said Victoriano, parking the Dodge and handing Juan his keys, "I'm sorry I wasn't able to help you, but I never heard any noise."

"It's okay," said Juan, putting the keys in his pocket, "maybe after the dance I can drive you home and you can listen to it again."

"Oh, I'd like that," said Victoriano, "but I'd have to take my sisters, too."

Juan only smiled. "Sure," he said, "why not? How many sisters you got?"

"Two still at home," said Victoriano, walking across the street with Juan, "the others are all married."

"Oh, I see," said Juan.

And they would've continued making small talk and getting to know each other better, but at that very moment, Juan spotted the Filipino. He was with the crowd that was going into the dance.

Juan started to go for his .38, but he stopped himself. Was he crazy? He couldn't very well just gun down the son-of-a-bitch right here in front of Lupe's brother. He took his hand off his .38 and breathed deeply, trying to calm down as he got in line with Victoriano to go into the dance. But, oh, he was raging mad. Those two bastards had stolen his money and cut his throat. They had to pay.

At the door, Carlota wasn't selling tickets anymore. Archie had replaced the princesses with some other girls. Juan paid for both of their tickets, a dollar each. Inside the huge hall, Juan glanced around and saw Lupe sitting across the room. She was with Carlota and the other princesses. They were surrounded by a crowd of anxious-looking young men. The Anglo that Juan had seen Lupe driving with was by her side.

"Those are my sisters," said Victoriano, pointing across the room.

"Hey, wasn't the one in white the queen of the parade?" asked Juan.

"Yes, that's Lupe, my youngest sister," said Victoriano proudly. "She didn't even enter the contest, but they came to the house to ask her to be the queen."

"Oh, really?"

"Yeah, she doesn't like dances or parties or anything."

"She doesn't?"

"No. Carlota, my other sister, in red, she's the one who loves the dances. Come on, I'll introduce you and tell them that you'll drive us home."

Juan grinned. It was working out just perfectly. "Sounds good; let's go."

They were just starting across the room when Juan saw the Italian. Their eyes locked and the big man smiled, lifting his glass to Juan. Juan felt the rage burst inside him. He went for his gun, wanting to rush across the room and kill the bastard. But then he stopped himself, again.

"Wait," he said to Victoriano, lowering his face so his future brother-in-law wouldn't see the murder in his eyes, "I can't right now. I have some business to take care of. But I'll see you after the dance."

"All right, then see you later," said Victoriano, continuing across the room.

Juan watched after him, his heart was filled with envy. There was Lupe, the woman of his dreams, only a few feet away but, in truth, it was more like ten million miles. She would run in fear if she saw his eyes right now. He turned back around to where he had last seen the Italian, but the man was gone. Instantly, Juan felt the hair come up on the back of his neck. He whirled about to see the quick-eyed Filipino no more than ten feet away. There were five people between them. Without hesitation, Juan marched straight for him but the man ducked and cut through the crowd, disappearing before Juan could get to him.

Glancing around, not knowing where either man was now, Juan decided that this just wasn't the day for him to begin his official courtship of Lupe. Hell, he couldn't keep his mind on Lupe and these two bastards at the same time.

He went out the front door and crossed the street, looked around to make sure that no one was behind him before he approached his car. He didn't want any son-of-a-bitch jumping out from behind a parked car to cut his throat once he got behind the wheel.

But then, opening the door of his Dodge, Juan leaped back in terror as the headless body of a big rooster rolled out on his feet. He kicked the bloody carcass with his boot, his heart pounding with rage. There was a trail of blood across the entire length of his front seat, leading to the rooster's head which was jammed down on the gear shift. Then he saw both men across the street by the entrance of the dancehall. They were grinning as contentedly as fat cats. And the Italian even had the audacity to once more raise up his glass to Juan, mocking him with another silent toast.

Juan stared at them, holding his ground. Oh, he'd been a fool, thinking that a man in his profession could be in love. Why, he'd almost gotten killed. He got in his car and started to drive off, but then stopped.

"No," he said to himself, "I won't run. I won't!"

He got out of his Dodge, prepared to face the two men. He was in love and he wasn't about to quit. A man, a real *macho*, had to learn to be soft and tender, hard and tough, all at the same time.

But after going back inside, Juan never found the two men. And while he searched for them, Lupe left with her brother.

For the next two weeks, Juan worked at the distillery day and night, like a man possessed. He hoped to make so much money from this hotel deal that he'd be able to take time off and devote himself completely to his courtship of Lupe and still have enough time left over so he could hunt down the Filipino and his friend and kill them both.

With only twenty-four hours to go before the appointed time of the delivery, Juan and Julio had managed to make enough whiskey to fill the fifty ten-gallon barrels. At seventy dollars a barrel, Juan stood to make about two thousand dollars after expenses—enough to buy a house for his mother and sister and a little ranch for himself.

But still, it truly upset him when he realized how he'd missed the perfect opportunity to meet Lupe. It had been set up so beautifully. Her own brother was going to introduce him and tell her that they'd be riding home with him in his grand car. Oh, he would've loved to see the look on Lupe's face when she'd slipped into the big luxurious seats of his Dodge, a car much better looking than her Anglo's car.

Juan took a big breath and tried to get Lupe out of his mind and get back to the business at hand. He'd have plenty of time to think of her once he was done with this deal.

"Well," he said to Julio, "in the morning I think I should go in front with my little Ford truck. I'll carry five barrels. But I won't cover them with chicken shit. Too much weight."

"If we use a tarp and forget the chicken shit," said Julio, "my big Dodge truck can handle ten barrels."

"Yes, I'm sure it can," said Juan, "but I think five each is enough. I don't want us taking too much on our first load in case things don't turn out like we expect and we got to move fast."

"But I thought you said you already checked the hotel," said Julio.

"I have," said Juan Salvador, "but it pays to be prepared. Remember what my mother always says, 'It's not the bravest nor the strongest chick who survives the hawks in life, but the most cautious, who's always got his eyes peeled to the heavens.'"

"Well, maybe so," said Julio, "but my Dodge is powerful. I can take a lot more on our first haul than you."

"Okay, maybe," said Juan, and they went over everything, step by step, getting it all out on the table, so that they could look at it from every angle. And Juan once more remembered Duel's words, that a professional never left anything up to chance. No, before a poker game, a professional took a bath, shaved, took a nap, opened up his mind and prepared himself for a night of poker like a priest preparing for the mass.

For gambling wasn't gambling; it was life, and life was made up of a million little decisions that a professional prepared for ahead of time. Dreaming, thinking, a man could see the game of life as if from another lifetime. Look for the unlooked, suspect the unsuspected.

Then it hit Juan, and he knew that it was time for him to go and see his mother, the smartest human being that he knew on earth. But he realized that he couldn't. He'd lied to her about the hotel, not telling her about the basement and the big, cop-smelling man, and he didn't want to give her unnecessary worries now.

He got up and went outside, looking up at the sky, thinking of all that he and his mother had been through. He thought of Lupe and what Victoriano had told him—she hadn't even wanted to be the queen. He smiled, loving Lupe all the more. She wasn't a show-off and, since she didn't like dancing, that meant that men hadn't been putting their greedy hands all over her luscious body.

Suddenly, Juan heard something and he whirled about, going for his gun. But then he saw that it was his nephew Jose coming up the alley.

"What is it?" asked Juan. "Is Mama all right?"

"Yes, everyone is fine," said Jose. "It's just that, well, you haven't been by for over two weeks and Mamagrande had a bad dream last night and is very worried for you."

"What dream?"

"That you drove into a prison made of concrete with no windows."

"My God," said Juan, wondering how his mother always knew. "And how'd you get here?"

"Rodolfo, you know, the schoolteacher, drove us over."

Juan's face exploded.

"No, Uncle, please," said the boy quickly, "I didn't bring him here. I left him at the park downtown with Pedro, more than a mile away."

Juan came back down, the anger leaving his body as quickly as it had come. "Good thinking, Jose, good thinking. Well, let me drive you back so you can go home and tell everyone that everything is fine."

"Uncle, Pedro and I want to stay," he said. "We can send Rodolfo back to tell our mothers that everything is fine."

Juan reached out, gently putting his hand on the boy's shoulder. "How's school?" he asked.

He shrugged. "Good."

"You straightened it out with that *gringo* teacher?"

Jose nodded. "Yeah. And Pedro got an A."

"What's that?"

"A good grade; the best, Uncle."

"And you?"

"I'm doing a little better."

"Good, I'm glad to hear that. Okay, you and your brother can stay. But you don't go on the deliveries. You stay at the house and help us load."

Jose's whole face lit up. "Thank you. I was hoping you weren't still mad at us. We been trying in school; we have, really."

Giving his nephew a big *abrazo*, Juan held him close, giving him comfort. Then they both got in the Ford truck and drove to the park in town.

The schoolteacher from Monterrey was glad to see Juan, and Juan gave him ten dollars for helping them out.

Driving his nephews back to the big house, Juan was feeling pretty good until they went inside and found Julio so upset that he could hardly speak.

"Quick, shut the door!" said Julio, getting Juan and the two boys inside. "We're not going to be able to make the delivery tomorrow. That *pinche* old lady across the street is spying on us!"

Juan went to the window and, sure enough, there was that old *gringa* with her little white dog looking at them with a pair of binoculars through her front window.

"How long has this been going on?" asked Juan.

"I don't know," said Julio. "I just noticed it."

"Well," said Juan, taking a deep breath, "you're right, this could be trouble."

"Could be? It is!" yelled Geneva. "Why do you think we're going crazy? I don't want my daughters and me going to prison!"

"Calm down," said Juan. "No one's going to prison."

"Sure, you can say that!" she yelled. "You got no kids!"

It took all of Juan's power not to slap the woman. Were his nephews not his own family? Hadn't he been doing all he could to keep them safe?

"Hey, Uncle!" said Pedro excitedly. "Why don't you just do your mouth drooling and scare her away?"

Juan glanced at his nephew. "Eh, maybe that could work," he said. "Sure, I'll get my plumber's tools and go over there, asking her if she needs some help."

"No!" yelled Geneva. "She'll call the cops for sure!"

"Julio, calm your wife down," said Juan.

"No one's calming me down!" screamed Geneva so loud that Juan was sure they could hear her two houses away. "We worked so hard, living here like prisoners, and now everything will come to ruin because of you wanting to get bigger and move in with the *gringos*."

"Damn it," said Juan, turning to Julio. "I'm not putting up with this, Julio! You two are out after this job, if you can't handle your wife!"

Juan went into the kitchen. He was trembling. He had enough troubles without a hysterical woman. His mother would never act like this. She had nerves of iron!

Juan decided he'd have to get his nephew Jose to help him tomorrow with the delivery. Things were really getting out of hand. Also, he was glad that he hadn't mentioned anything to Julio about his problems with the Italian and the Filipino. A married man just wasn't a man who could live on the edge gracefully. This, also, Duel had explained to him. "Make your money before you marry," he had said to Juan. "Make it big and then marry a young, innocent thing and retire."

But he knew that Lupe wasn't going to wait for him to make it big. She was ready now. He had to get this hotel deal behind him and do his courtship.

Ten minutes later, Juan was ready to go out the front door. He was dressed in his dirtiest old overalls and a twisted, funny-looking little round hat.

"All right," he said to Jose and Pedro, "you guys come out the front door with me and start doing some yard work. Then, when I see her come to her window, I'll go over by myself. Understand?"

They both said that they did.

"Good," said Juan, lighting up a half-burnt, three-day-old cigar. They went out the door.

Julio was with Geneva in the next room. Geneva was still screaming, and Julio was promising her money and a car if she'd stop crying.

Juan and the boys hadn't been outside more than a minute when the woman came to her window. Juan winked at them as he picked up his plumbing tools. Seeing Juan coming toward her home, the woman closed her drapes. But still Juan continued across the street and up her walkway, puffing on his cigar.

At the door, Juan put his box of tools down and knocked politely. But the old woman didn't come to the door. He knocked again, a little harder, and got some spit to drool out the side of his mouth. He turned back around and winked at his nephews who were cleaning up the front yard. Finally, she came to her door.

"Yes?" she said, barely opening the door. She had her small white dog in her arms.

"Excuse me, lady," said Juan, taking the chewed-up cigar out of his mouth, "but you see I'm a plumber-rrr," he said, blowing out so hard on the word "plumber" that he sprayed spit and cigar smoke on her and her dog. "And I see you looking at us, so I say to myself, 'Juan, I bet that fine lady over there, she wants a little plumbing work done for her, but she's too shy to ask.' " And saying this, Juan leaned in close to her, smiling an awful smile with his two front teeth blackened out by pieces of tobacco, and he let some spit drool out of his mouth. "So let me come inside and see what you need fixed," he said, pushing the door open and stepping forward.

"No!" screamed the woman, and her little dog leaped out of her arms, barking furiously at Juan.

"But I no charge," said Juan, blowing so much cigar smoke on the dog that he stopped barking and gagged, rolling on the floor.

"No, get out! Get out! I have nothing wrong with my plumbing!" Still Juan walked in. "No, please, you're dirtying my carpet!"

"But I see you looking at us, so I . . ."

"Oh, my God!" she yelled, pushing him out the door. "Go away! Please, I don't want your help!"

Across the street, Jose and Pedro couldn't stop laughing. Their uncle was the best show in town.

It was midnight, and Juan, Jose, and Julio were in back of the big house, loading the barrels of whiskey into the two trucks. Juan had decided that they'd take the first load early so that they could keep watch on the hotel before they delivered.

"But what's the time we supposed to deliver the first load?" asked Julio.

"Like I've told you, Mario wants us to deliver our first load at nine sharp," said Juan. "But we're going to go earlier so we can watch like a hawk."

"Oh, I just can't wait!" said Julio. "Imagine all that money waiting for us! And our second load," asked Julio, "when do we deliver that?"

Juan straightened up. Why, Mario had never mentioned a second load. Suddenly, Juan just knew down deep in his soul that his mother's dream was right and this whole "hotel thing" really was a trap.

"What is it?" asked Julio, seeing Juan's face go pale. "Hell, we got no more worries, *compadre*. That old lady hasn't shown her face again!"

"Nothing," lied Juan. "I'm just tired." And he went to bed but he wasn't able to sleep. He could hear Julio and Geneva making love. He tossed and turned, and it wasn't just the hotel that was on his mind; it was everything— Lupe and his mother, the Filipino and the Italian, and his need to get money so he could get beyond the shame of the day he'd seen his beloved mother begging in the streets.

It was four in the morning when Juan awoke with a start. His father had come to him, riding a big black stallion across the heavens like a shooting star. Juan sat up, breathing deeply. He'd never dreamed of his father before. Calming down, Juan got up, relieved himself, dressed, and got Jose and Julio.

"Come on, we're going!" he said. "Now!"

"But it's still dark," said Julio. Geneva was right behind him.

"Julio, listen to me closely," said Juan. "The day I went to check on the hotel, I saw something I haven't told no one. They have a basement with no windows."

"So what has that to do with us?" asked Julio.

"Nothing, I hope," said Juan. "But today is a very big day for us. So I want you to pay attention, and do as I say."

"Oh, yes, the lord and master," said Geneva, scratching her armpit, "keeping us locked up here like prisoners, doing all the work!"

"That's enough!" said Julio to his wife.

"Oh, no, it isn't!" yelled Geneva. "I'm sick and tired of this whole thing! Who does he think he is, God?"

And she would've gone on speaking if Julio hadn't slapped her. But she was a tough woman. She didn't go down. No, she was on him like a wild cat, scratching and biting.

Juan and the boys went outside and Julio and Geneva continued fighting and screaming.

"When he comes out," said Juan to Jose, "I want you riding with him. Here, take my gun and make sure he follows me."

The boy didn't want to take the gun.

"Take it," snapped Juan. "It's not going to bite."

The boy took it.

"Good," said Juan, "and remember, we don't kill. We just get the job done. You'll be okay, believe me, you're a good man."

Coming out the door, Julio was smiling but his face was covered with blood. He saw Jose put the .38 in his jacket. "What's that?" he shouted, putting on his hat.

"He's going with you," said Juan.

"Hey, you don't give a gun to a boy to get me to do what you want. I follow you because you're *mi general!*" said Julio, turning with dignity and going to his truck.

Jose looked at his uncle.

"Keep the gun anyway," said Juan. "Things don't look so good. And you, Pedro, stay here and calm that woman down. Tell her jokes . . . do something."

"Yes," said Pedro.

"Remember," said Juan to Jose as they went to the trucks, "guns are part of life, so a real man must know how to use them. Relax. It's okay to be scared. Boys your age were men back in Mexico during the Revolution."

The first signs of daylight were just beginning to paint the sky above the huge towering mountain when they got to San Bernardino. Up ahead, on a hilltop, they pulled off the road into the trees. Juan killed his engine and got out, walking back to Julio and Jose.

"Cut your motor," he said to Julio. "We're going to wait here until it's our turn to deliver."

Julio did as told, getting out of his truck to stretch his legs. It was cold up here in the mountains.

"And, Julio," said Juan, "believe me, I want to make this delivery as much as you do, but we got to be careful."

"We got to do it," said Julio sheepishly. "Hell, I promised Geneva a new car and a trip to Mexico. You just can't imagine how difficult it's been," he added.

Juan put his hand on Julio's shoulder. "You're a good man, Julio," he said, "you're a good man; just hold on a little longer and this will all be over."

Julio nodded. "Okay, but I'm going to take a little nap." He laughed, rubbing his belly. "Hell, Geneva loves playing my violin. She gets that way after a good fight."

Juan laughed. "Go on, we'll call you."

So Julio got back in his truck to nap, and Juan and Jose walked through the trees until they could see the hotel down below them. The light of day was just beginning to color the jagged horizon above San Bernardino. Juan and his nephew sat down on the ground, chewing a blade of grass. It wasn't until seven that the first truck showed up.

Mario had told Juan that he'd have bootleggers arriving all day. The truck below had a huge load in the back covered with a tarp, just like Juan's. Juan watched as it circled the building—the driver trying to find where to unload—when the huge double doors of the basement slid open and two men stepped out, waving him inside.

Juan's heart pounded wildly as he watched the poor, unsuspecting man drive through the big doors, and the two men closed the doors behind the vehicle.

"Well, what do you think?" said Juan, trying to sound calm.

"I don't know," said Jose. "I guess it depends if he comes back out or not."

Juan loved it. It made sense. He reached out, rubbing his nephew's head of hair. "Good thinking," he said, "so that's what we'll do, wait and see. Just like Mama said: chicks with our eyes peeled." He had to smile; his old mother had been right once again.

After that, trucks began arriving every thirty minutes, but they never came back out. By nine o'clock, Juan was ready to burst. They had eight trucks trapped inside that concrete prison.

"Come on!" said Juan. "Let's go!"

Julio was still asleep inside the truck. Juan kicked him.

"Wake up!" yelled Juan. "We got to get out of here!"

"To the hotel?" said Julio, sitting up.

"No, to hide these barrels in the hills before they realize that we're not delivering," said Juan. "Then we got to get back to the house and get all those other barrels out of there, too!"

"Are you crazy? I can't go home with no money! She'll kill me!" yelled Julio.

"Julio, damn it! Don't be stupid! No truck has ever come out!"

"Well, maybe they just needed time to count their money," he said.

"Damn it," said Juan, pulling out his .45, "two FBI agents were killed in San Bernardino a few months back! This is no joke! It's a setup!"

Hearing this and seeing the .45, Julio sobered up and they took off. They drove back down toward Lake Elsinore and hid the first load of barrels. Then they went back to the rented house and got a second load. They worked all day and long into the night. When they returned late that night, Geneva was fit to be tied, she was so mad. And nothing Julio or Juan could say would calm her down.

"You're all just a bunch of no-good cowards!" she screamed. "I told you, Julio, I told you, that he was crazy and didn't know what he was doing!"

"Shut up!" said Julio.

"Why? I don't care!"

And she would've gone on screaming but Julio jumped up and knocked her across the room. But still, Geneva wouldn't shut up. She just jumped to her feet and leaped on Julio's face like an enraged jaguar, biting and scratching and kicking as she'd done before.

Juan and his two nephews went out. "Never in his worst days did my father hit my mother," said Juan to his nephews. "A man who hits a woman is no man."

They got in the truck and went to have breakfast together. As they went into a little restaurant, Jose saw the newspapers on the counter. There it was on the front page.

Quickly, Jose poked Juan.

"What is it?" asked Juan.

"The cops," said Pedro, staring at the headlines.

"Shut up!" said Jose.

Juan now caught on, but still, he didn't know what it was all about. He didn't read any English, nor too much Spanish, either.

"Here," he said, handing Jose a nickel, "buy the paper and tell me while we eat."

They got the newspaper and went to the far corner of the little café.

"Read it to me," said Juan, sitting down, "and don't worry about nothing. We're just three Mexican plumbers out for breakfast."

Nervously, Jose glanced around and then began to read. The FBI had set up the biggest bootlegging bust in Southern California history. Fifteen trucks of illegal liquor had been confiscated. Twenty-two people had been arrested.

By the time they were back to the big house, Juan knew that they were in serious trouble. "All right," he said to Julio and Geneva, showing them the newspaper, "no more fighting between you two; we got to get smart or we're dead!"

"But you told us that we'd be safe here!" yelled Geneva, holding her two little daughters close.

"And we were," said Juan, "that's why we didn't get arrested like the others. And now we got to disappear for a few months. Believe me, when that hairy-armed gorilla starts pounding on Mario, and Mario sees that I wasn't caught along with him and all his friends, he's going to turn on me and they'll come looking for me and you, too, Julio!"

"Oh, my God!" yelled Geneva, "I knew we should never have gotten into this, Julio! I told you so!"

Juan looked at the big-mouthed woman, realizing that he could never do business with Julio again because of her. She was one of these simple-minded people who thought they could get whatever they wanted in life without paying the price.

"Look," said Juan, pulling out the keys to his big Dodge, "I'm going to give you the use of my car."

Instantly, Geneva stopped whining and looked at the shiny keys with lustful greed.

"But, on the condition," said Juan, dangling the keys, "that you two go back to Mexico now, today, this very morning, as you wanted to do, and not come back for two months. And I'll give you fifty dollars to hold you over. But don't, I repeat, don't go near those barrels that we hid, Julio, until you see me and we talk. Because they'll be looking for bootleg whiskey. Believe me, cops aren't stupid!"

"Of course, *mi general*," said Julio, reaching for the keys to the grand car.

"No!" yelled Geneva, grabbing the keys first. "I'll take the keys!" she shouted.

"But you don't know how to drive," said Julio.

"So?" yelled Geneva.

Ten minutes later, Geneva and Julio were on the road. Juan and the two boys loaded the last three barrels on Juan's truck and took off with the two trucks, Jose driving one and Juan driving the other.

A couple of miles outside Corona, Juan pulled off the road into some thick brush and Jose pulled in behind him in Julio's big Dodge truck.

"You drove good," said Juan, walking into the bushes to take a leak. "You handled that big truck just fine."

Jose and Pedro quickly unbuttoned their pants, too.

Juan laughed. "You know," he said, "I always wondered why it is that animals on the run have to piss and shit so much. Hell, a coyote outruns the dogs until he can't shit no more and then falls apart." He smiled, milking the last drops of urine from his thick cock. "When I was on the run from prison with those two Yaquis, I pissed and shit all the way. Nothing like being on the run à la Gregorio Cortez with the rangers after you to clean a man out," he said with *gusto*.

"Yes, I've never pissed so much," said Pedro, laughing.

"All right," said Juan, buttoning back up, "now you two go home without me."

"Without you?" said the boys.

"Yes," said Juan, "and park away from our place and then go home on foot."

Juan took a big breath. "And from now on you two must learn to think like the mouse—scared, careful, and eyes all ready for the big cat. But not too scared, you understand. Just quiet-scared inside, so no one knows you're scared but you." He smiled. "You're both good little men. And you, Jose, the truck you drove is clean, so you got no worries. But still, you park the truck down the street and then walk home like you're coming from work."

He could see that both boys were getting nervous. "It's okay," he said, patting them on the shoulders, "everything is fine. You two must go home and tell Luisa and my mother what's happened and that I'm going to Mexico for a while."

Tears came to Jose's eyes. Pedro hugged his uncle with all his might. Juan was the closest thing that either boy had ever had to a real father.

"Look, don't worry," said Juan, hugging them both. "Hell, I'm not going to get killed, I promise you. Shit, I'll be back in a few months and we'll laugh about all this. But, don't tell that to no one. As far as everyone is concerned, I've returned to Los Altos for good. Do you understand? I'm gone. Never coming back, as far as anyone is to know."

"Yes," said both boys, "we understand."

"Good," said Juan, "good. But, on the other hand, if for some misfortune, I don't come back in a few months, then you two are the men of the house. You are the *machos*, the life, the future of our families. You are all that's left, so you must protect our mothers and grow and do good and have families of your own. I love you. I do. I do."

They were all three crying, tears running down their faces. "And remember, we think, we work, we have respect and honor above all else. And those barrels we hid, they're almost all ours. Only eight belong to Julio. And you get Archie to help you sell them at fifty dollars each, but don't trust the son-of-a-bitch. Be tough. Listen to Luisa. She's made of iron! Don't let nobody cheat you!"

"But, Uncle," said Pedro, a flood of tears bursting from his eyes, "you'll be back! You got to!"

"Of course, I will," said Juan, "but just in case, you be ready and you remember, we're *mejicanos* and . . . and . . . and you never kill even a pig to eat without respect and unless you do it quick so he don't suffer."

"Oh, Uncle, please, don't go!" said Jose. "We can hide you in the hills!"

Juan's eyes narrowed. "Jose, don't be stupid," he said. "Think, pay attention; this is no joke. This is the FBI and many people think that I'm the one who killed those two agents last year."

"Didn't you?" asked Pedro.

Juan stared at his nephew. "*Mi hijito*," he said, "if I did or didn't, isn't the point. The point is that a *mejicano* can't stay around to see if the *gringos* will believe him or not. I'm running just like the coyote, as far as I got the shit to take me!"

Saying this, he hugged his two nephews close once again, holding them, squeezing them in a big *abrazo* between *hombres*; then he kissed them on one cheek and then on the other.

"Tell my mama that I love her," said Juan, more tears coming to his own eyes, "and tell her that I'm sorry that I couldn't come and tell her goodbye. But I will return! I swear it! I'll be back some night with the full moon!" he said, squeezing his nephews. "Oh, God! I love you boys so much! Bye. Take care of our *familia*. You're the men of the house!"

Juan turned and got in his truck and took off, heart pounding, head throbbing, lips dry, and mouth choking with emotion as he drove off.

His eyes cried desperately and he thought of his mother and wondered how she'd take the news of yet another son of hers disappearing. Would this be the last straw to finally kill the grand old woman? Oh, how he hated himself for having put her through this.

He dried his eyes and concentrated on the road. Strangely enough, he began to feel better. He was free at last. Free to run, to hide, to fight for survival. Oh, to be on the run felt almost wonderful in a crazy kind of way. Life was so simple. There were no complications. But then his thoughts drifted to Lupe.

"No, I can't think of her now," he said to himself. And he began to whistle and then sing the ballad of Gregorio Cortez, who, like his own brother Jose, had been chased by hounds and hundreds of armed men.

He breathed deeply, trying to keep calm, but inside he was going crazy, thinking of what could have been: a life of love, a life with the woman of his dreams.

Jose and Pedro had been home no more than fifteen minutes, telling their family of the situation, when Rodolfo came rushing in the back door.

"They're coming!" yelled the schoolteacher with the pocked face. "Five cars full of *gringo* lawmen!"

Everyone leaped with fear, except Doña Margarita.

"Thank God that they've arrived," she said, making the sign of the cross. "Waiting is what makes fear; not the devil's entrance." And saying this, she took up her rosary with the greatest of calm and began to pray as she'd done a thousand times before. The five cars came rushing up to the front yard, scattering the chickens and pigs alike.

"Open the door, Luisa," said the old lady, "so they don't break it down. Show them we have nothing to hide. Also, go feed the chickens with Pedro, but give them no attention. Just do your chores as if everything is fine. Remember, we speak no English and we know nothing, so what can they do to us if we stay calm? Nothing, absolutely nothing, if we don't provoke them."

Outside, the lawmen were surrounding the house.

"And don't move, *mi hijito*," said the old, wrinkled-up lady to her oldest grandson. "You just sit still, because you're big and they would like to provoke you so they can unleash their anger, the anger of trained dogs."

Jose obeyed his grandmother, keeping still, trembling, his mind going crazy with fear. Outside, he could see that they were questioning his mother and brother. Then they came, rushing at the open door, bursting in with guns drawn as other armed men broke the glass out of the windows in the back of the house. Finally, he couldn't stand it anymore and he started to get up.

"Don't move!" snapped his grandmother in Spanish, watching the men search the house. "Let them destroy everything! Houses, furniture can all be replaced; but not you, my love."

Jose sat back down, his whole body vibrating with such emotion that he was sick. Oh, he was so frightened and yet outraged at the same time.

For over an hour, the lawmen tore things apart, looking for evidence of a distillery, but they found nothing. Bill Wesseley, the big man that Juan had seen at the hotel, led the lawmen. Mario was handcuffed inside one of their cars. When the lawmen finally left, the two houses were in a shambles, and one of their little pigs had been kicked to death by two over-zealous young lawmen.

Late that afternoon, Doña Margarita and her family went to church along with several other people from the *barrio*. It was just like the Revolution for them all over again, and so they prayed as they hadn't prayed in years.

18

*And so here they were, two human hearts, struggling
for survival as they searched for the miracle of love—a
dream come true.*

Two days before, Lupe and her family passed through
the barrio of Corona on their way down to the Imperial Valley. They were
following the crops once more. They stopped at the two houses at the end of
the street, traded for some eggs and goat's milk, and continued over the
mountains. The following day they found work down in the valley near
Brawley. That night they set up camp under some big trees outside of town,
behind a little gas station. There were five families, and in the morning they
would go back to work across the highway in the fields.

But they had a hard time sleeping again. The mosquitoes were out by the
millions. Finally, Doña Guadalupe made a mixture of fresh garlic and oil to
put on their exposed skin so they could get a few hours of sleep before they
had to go to work.

Down in the Imperial Valley, Juan sold two barrels of
whiskey for twenty dollars each, telling each buyer that he was headed for
Mexico. Then he headed for Mexicali, wanting to get there before midnight,
but the headlights of his truck began to grow dimmer and dimmer.

Finally, he pulled over at a little gas station just the other side of Brawley.
Smiling, the owner of the gas station, a little short Anglo, got a rag and a
bucket of water and washed the dead insects off each blackened headlight.

"Happens all the time," said the Anglo good-naturedly. "People come
through here just after dark, thinking their headlights are going out, but it's
only the bugs. Hell, last Spring we had up to ten million mosquitoes per
square foot. A man could get rich if he could figure a way to flatten 'em and
sell them for meat!" he said, laughing.

Juan could see that he was an old, wrinkled-up desert rat and that he had
a wild side to him.

"So you wanna get rich, eh?" said Juan.

The man stopped and looked at Juan. "Sure," he said, grinning. "Who don't?"

"But I mean right now," said Juan.

The man started laughing. "Sounds good. What we gonna do, *amigo*, rob a bank?"

"No, nothing that illegal," said Juan.

The man laughed all the more. "Well, then, shoot! I'm rough and ready!"

"You buy this truck off me for cash right now and I'll throw in a ten-gallon barrel of the finest Canadian whiskey you ever drank," said Juan, grinning.

"Canadian, really?" said the man, looking like a starving fish ready to bite the hook.

"Sure," said Juan. "But you got to close down and drive me across the border right now."

"Shit, why not?" said the man. "Who are you, some famous bootlegger on the run?"

"You guessed it!" said Juan Salvador, laughing.

"I'll be damned!" said the old man, licking his lips, thrilled at the thought of getting involved in something exciting for a change.

So, they made a deal and Juan sold him his truck for two hundred dollars cash, and they unloaded the barrel, hiding it behind his barn.

There was a group of migrant workers camped under some trees behind the station. Juan took a long, hard look at them, thinking that Lupe and her family were probably down here right now, following the crops. Then he saw the tall, regal silhouette of a woman walking by a tent and his heart exploded. Could that be Lupe? He wanted to walk over and see, but he couldn't. He was on the run. Then the strangest thing happened. The woman stopped and looked his way, too. My God, he thought, it's either her or an angel from God put down on earth to drive men insane—she's so beautiful.

"Well, let's crack leather!" said the gas station owner, coming up behind Juan.

"Oh, yes, sure," said Juan. He got in the truck with the old man and they took off. They got to the border station at midnight. Crossing into Mexicali, Mexico, Juan felt a lot better. They went into an all-night bar and had a few legal drinks together. Then Juan told the man goodbye.

"Thanks for your help," said Juan. "Maybe I'll see you some day if you come down to Los Altos de Jalisco."

"So, you're not coming back, eh?" said the man.

"Nope, never," said Juan.

"Well, so long," said the man, and he headed back across the border.

Juan took a big breath. He was good now. He'd made a big enough impression on that old desert rat so that he'd be telling the story to every person that came into his station. The law would finally get wind of the story and check it out. He'd be so excited that he'd probably even show them the barrel of whiskey, proving to them that his story was true.

Turning up the street, Juan headed for Chinatown. He'd made quite a few good Chinese friends when he'd smuggled Chinese across the border a couple of years back.

In the morning, Lupe and her family went across the highway to the ranch and got jobs. The day grew so hot, that Lupe and her father became sick. The wind picked up right after lunch, and the dust hit them with blinding speed. Lupe and her father began to cough. They just weren't able to put up with the heat and dust like everyone else.

That evening, when the people that Lupe's family was traveling with gassed up their truck, the attendant offered to sell them whiskey in quart jars. Don Victor bought a quart and said that it was the best whiskey that he'd ever tasted. The other men bought several jars, too. That night, Lupe watched her father and the other men get drunk and sing and make fools of themselves.

A few days later, Lupe came in early from the field and she found Doña Manza and her family at their camp. Lupe and Manuelita were so happy to see each other that they couldn't stop talking. But then Carlota and the others came in from the fields and Lupe was never able to get in another word.

Manuelita had recently become engaged, and Carlota just couldn't stop asking her questions. Lupe said nothing more. She was going to wait until she and Manuelita were alone so that she could talk to her privately. Lupe had something very important to ask her friend about engagements.

Two days later, it was decided that they'd go to the coast along with several other families. Leaving the great, flat valley, they headed for the towering mountains to the west. Lupe rode in the back of an open-bed pickup along with Manuelita and her sisters, Cuca and Uva, and Carlota. Don Victor and Victoriano rode in front with the man who owned the truck.

Looking out behind, Lupe could see her mother and Doña Manza sitting in the back of the third vehicle as they climbed up the winding road. It made her heart swell with happiness to see her mother and her best old friend together once again. In the distance, Lupe could see the heat waves dancing in the huge valley below and the glistening mirages of flat shimmering lakes beyond the heat waves.

It never failed to amaze Lupe how much the country of Southern California changed once they started up over the mountains. The Imperial Valley lay hot and flat and wide behind them, stretching grey and white for hundreds of miles. The farming communities of Brawley and Westmoreland sat like little green-checkered islands in the white-flatness of the infinite desert.

It began to cool as they climbed the towering, jagged mountains filled with brown cliffs and huge orange boulders, and shelves of red rock with naked batches of glistening granite so white that it hurt the eyes. It was a land so colorful and yet forbidding. It seemed impossible to Lupe that anything could grow here. And yet, it did. It grew in the forms of cactus, short and wide, tall and graceful, round and thick. And at this time of year, the cactus plants had flowers of such bright, dazzling colors of pink and yellow and red that the flowers seemed to pop off the mountainsides, hitting you in the eyes. The colors were so bright that one just knew they reflected the brightness of the burning sun, the right eye of God. Just then a huge raven swooped down, landing by a huge yellow cactus flower. Lupe watched him, thinking that there was something strangely familiar about this big black bird.

Two of their trucks overheated, and Lupe and the young girls had to get out and walk ahead while the men cooled off the engines. Walking up the steep road, Lupe got close to Manuelita.

"Manuelita," she whispered, "I need to talk to you, alone."

"All right," said the older girl, falling behind with Lupe so that their sisters would get ahead. "What is it?"

"Well, you know," said Lupe, "Mark that I wrote to you about?"

"Yes," said Manuelita.

"Well, he asked me for my hand before we left."

"He did?" yelled Manuelita.

"Shhhhhh," said Lupe, pulling Manuelita in close. "Not so loud. I haven't told anyone."

"Then you didn't say 'yes'?"

Lupe shook her head. "No. But I did promise him an answer when we get back."

"Oh, my God!" said Manuelita excitedly. "Maybe our children will grow up together, too!"

"That would be heaven," said Lupe, "but, well, I just didn't know if he's the one."

"Well, tell me about him!"

Just then they were all called back to the trucks.

"I'll tell you later," said Lupe as they headed back, "when we have more time."

Topping the mountain crest, Lupe breathed deeply, smelling the cool freshness of the sea, which was still more than fifty miles away. And here, on top of the mountains, the rocks and granite stopped and the high country began. The mountaintops were clothed with tall brush and pine trees, looking like green woolly sheep in the distance.

Lupe held her friend's hand and thought of Mark. Some day he'd have an office of his own and she could work for him. They'd have two boys and two girls, and their children would grow up with Manuelita's children and they would all go to school together and become fine, educated people.

Lupe breathed in the cooling air, holding Manuelita's hand, and she glanced around and saw that the country was changing again. They were coming off the rugged mountains and now there were oak trees and small, rolling hills with fat cattle. Here, the wildflowers were of softer colors than they'd been in the desert. They were lilac and rose and gold and white. Lupe's heart went soaring to the heavens. Every time they came closer to the coast, she just felt so much better. Then in the distance, Lupe saw the sea and was filled with a wonderful feeling; a much kinder God lived there.

In Carlsbad that night, Lupe slept well for the first time in weeks. In the morning, her eyes didn't burn, her throat wasn't raw, and she was able to work with power in the fields of cutting-flowers south of town.

Juan stayed in Mexicali for several days, drinking and sleeping and getting his nerves to calm down. Then he headed west on the Mexican side of the border to Tijuana.

In Tijuana, Juan bought all the American newspapers he could find to see if there was anything more about the setup in San Bernardino. But he had such a hard time trying to read the paper that he swore to himself he was going to take the time to teach himself how to read well in English, too. Especially before he had children and proved to be an embarrassment to them.

Not finding anything in any of the papers, Juan decided to take the bull by the horns. He sneaked across the border to San Diego and paid a man ten dollars to drive him up the coast. Walking into the barrio of Carlsbad, Juan spotted a man who looked about his size. He stopped him and offered him a crisp twenty-dollar bill for his dirty work clothes. The man stripped his clothes off right on the spot.

After changing into the dirty clothes, Juan decided to go to the poolhall, hoping to see Archie. A couple of trucks loaded with workmen came down the road. But Juan paid no attention to the trucks. He was too preoccupied. After all, Archie was the local law, so if things had truly gotten bad in San Bernardino, there was a good chance that Archie was out to get him, too. Selling a little whiskey on the side for a lawman wasn't too bad, but helping an accused killer was no good at all.

With his heart pounding, Juan mounted the steps of the poolhall. There were a dozen men inside. Juan spotted Archie behind the bar, talking to the tall, one-armed man who ran the poolhall for him. Juan had his .45 under his pants, feeling big and flat. He changed his mind, deciding that there was just too much at risk. He turned and was going back down the street, when he saw Lupe and Victoriano in the back of a truck.

Juan stopped, rooted to the earth, and he watched Lupe and her brother get down from the tall flatbed truck full of workmen. Oh, he just wanted to rush up and grab Lupe and tell her that they were destined to be together, that ever since he could remember, he'd been searching for her so that they could marry and have children and a wonderful life together like his grandfather Don Pio had had with his wife, Silveria. But he was on the run. So he couldn't just go up and pour his heart out to her.

Juan pulled down the brim of his dirty little hat and went down the alley behind the poolhall before Lupe or her brother saw him. Behind the poolhall, he leaned back on the wall, trying to calm down. Oh, just the sight of Lupe drove him crazy-*loco*. He gripped his forehead, trying to gather his thoughts. "Calm down," he said to himself, "first things first."

He decided to go over to Consuelo's house and have her go to Archie in order to feel him out about the San Bernardino situation. But then, getting to Consuelo's place, the world exploded.

"Juan!" said the old lady, "where the hell have you been? There's no liquor in all Southern California! Everybody is going crazy! I need five barrels right now!"

"How much?" he asked, suddenly feeling rich.

"Price is no problem!" said Consuelo. "Give me credit, and I'll pay ten dollars extra a barrel!"

"On credit, I need seventy a barrel," he said.

"*Cabrón!*" she laughed. "That's twenty extra! But all right! I need it tonight."

"Tomorrow," he said.

The old woman stopped her words. "By the way," she said, "Archie, he's been looking for you."

Juan felt his balls move up into his body, but still he held, showing nothing. "Alone?" he asked.

"No," said Consuelo, "he had a man with him."

Suddenly, Juan wanted to run, to escape, just like the coyote. But no, he couldn't abandon Lupe and everything he had going here and return to the safety of Mexico.

"Well, are you going to get the liquor for me or not?" asked Consuelo.

Taking a breath, Juan pulled down into his guts. "Yes," he said, "but right now I'm hungry and I need to rest and figure things out."

"I'll fix the bed for you in back," she said, "but don't take too long. We're losing money!"

After having rested a couple of hours, Juan told Consuelo that he'd need a truck. She told him that a friend of hers had just opened up a garage across town and had several trucks.

"He was married to one of my cousins," said the old lady, clearing the table where they'd eaten together. "But she died at childbirth. He's a good *gringo*. You can trust him."

"He drinks, eh?"

"What man doesn't?"

Outside, there was still plenty of daylight. Juan pulled down his hat and started up the street, following the directions that Consuelo had given him. Finding the garage, Juan stepped inside, and, to his surprise, there sat Kenny, the tough old Anglo from the rock quarry in Corona.

"I'll be damned," said the old, white-haired man, grinning ear-to-ear. "Ain't you a sorry sight!"

"What are you doing here?" asked Juan.

"I own this place," said Kenny.

"No, really?"

"Hell, yes! I gave you my word, so hell, when I saw all that trouble wasn't gonna stop, I quit," he said.

"You're kidding," said Juan.

"Nope, my word's my bond. Tried to find you after that, Juan, but I was told you'd left town."

"I'll be damned," said Juan, shaking the old man's huge, ham-like hand. "I'll be a son-of-a-bitch!" He'd never known a *gringo* who'd kept his word to a Mexican before.

"Me, too," said Kenny, "I've been a son-of-a-bitch lots of times," looking at Juan in the eyes, feeling proud that he'd finally come to see, face-to-face, the man whom he'd given his word to. "So what can I do for you?"

Juan laughed. He hadn't felt so at-home in days. "Well, I'm a good friend of Consuelo's and she . . ."

"Yeah, I know," said Kenny. "Archie and I went looking over there for you."

"You know Archie, too?"

"Hell, everyone in the southland knows that old Indian son-of-a-bitch!"

"Then wait, hey, you couldn't be the same man who came looking for me with Archie at Consuelo's the other day?"

"Yep," said Kenny, "one in the same. Archie can't find any whiskey, and he's powerful thirsty."

"You mean Archie's looking for me to buy whiskey?" asked Juan, feeling the blood coming back into his heart.

"Yeah, that's what he said. I don't think he was out to arrest your ass." He grinned. "But you can't tell about Archie. Hell, if that bastard had his way, he'd arrest every son-of-a-bitch in the state and give the whole country back to the Indians!"

"Yeah, I guess you're right about that," said Juan, still feeling a little cautious. "By the way, Kenny, I'm not going by 'Juan' anymore. From now on my name is Salvador. Juan, he's gone back to Mexico and he died. I never knew him."

"I see," said the old man, asking no questions. After all, California was mostly uninhabited and a lot of people changed their names and started new lives. "So, Salvador," said Kenny, "tell me what you need."

"Well," said Salvador, eyeing the old Anglo, wondering if he was making a mistake to trust him, "I need a truck and, also, I'm going to need a little help," he added, fully realizing that he couldn't just drive up to Corona by himself, even if Archie wasn't out to get him. That big hairy-armed gorilla might still be after him.

"Shoot! I owe you one, *amigo!*"

"All right," said Salvador, watching his eyes closely, especially the left one, "but this one could get dangerous."

"Just how I like my women!" yelled the old man, his bright blue eyes dancing with merriment.

"Okay, then," said Salvador, "you meet me tomorrow at daybreak with a truck, but dressed in your Sunday best."

Kenny laughed. "You got it, *amigo*."

All night, Salvador tossed and turned, thinking about Kenny and if he'd been a fool to bring a *gringo* into his confidence. Hell, every man in the barrio would laugh at him if his plan backfired.

Then in the early morning hours, Juan had a dream of Lupe coming to him on a cloud of white flowers like an angel. He opened his arms and they were just going to embrace when Tom Mix suddenly grabbed her. Salvador awoke in a sweat. Oh, he could just feel it; he was going to lose Lupe and everything if he wasn't careful.

The sun was just beginning to paint the sky when Kenny drove up in his truck to Consuelo's house. He was dressed in a dark brown suit and his hair was slicked back. Going up to her door, Kenny noticed there was a red-eyed drunk sleeping on her steps.

"Is she open already?" asked the drunk.

"No, not yet, *amigo*," said Kenny.

The old drunk sat there, looking Kenny up and down, sniffing at his shaving lotion. Finally, the front door opened and out came a woman wearing a black dress with a red shawl over her head. Kenny had to fight hard not to laugh. Why, it was Juan Salvador! He was wearing lipstick and powder and eye-coloring.

"*Buenos días*," said Kenny to Salvador, "how about a kiss, *querida*?"

"Knock it off," said Salvador under his breath, pulling the shawl closer around his face. He could see that the old drunk was giving him the eye.

"Well, of course, my dear," said Kenny, taking Salvador's arm.

"*¡Oye, mamacita!*" said the old drunk, getting to his feet. "So you don't think *mejicanos* are good enough for you, *puta!*"

"Hey, this is my wife, *amigo!*" snapped Kenny, hugging Salvador closely.

"Oh, excuse me!" said the old drunk, slapping his hand over his mouth and taking off his hat. "I didn't know!"

Mass was just letting out when Salvador and Kenny arrived in Corona. But Salvador knew that his mother would stay inside, praying alone for a while.

Helping Salvador out of the truck, Kenny walked him up the steps of the church, arm-in-arm. Several people glanced at them. Kenny pulled Juan in closer, kissing him on the cheek.

"You son-of-a-bitch!" whispered Salvador, jerking loose.

But Kenny only laughed. "Such language, my dear," he said, "and at church!"

Inside, Salvador immediately spotted his mother in one of the rear pews, praying with her rosary. Salvador dipped his fingers into the holy water and made the sign of the cross, then genuflected as he stared down the side aisle.

He went up to the pew that his mother was in and slipped in beside her and knelt. At first his mother just moved over, giving him room, and continued her prayers. But then, when the woman moved closer again, his mother looked at her, wondering why this heavy-set lady was being such a nuisance when the church was empty and she could have taken any pew she wished. But then Doña Margarita saw that the woman beside her was none other than her own son. She gasped, gripping her heart.

"*¡Dios mío!*" she said. "I was just praying for a miracle, and here you are!"

She made the sign of the cross, thanking God, and drew Salvador into her arms. Hugging him, kissing him, she began to cry. All this time Kenny kept watch over them from the rear of the church where he stood with his hat in his hand. Kenny's family had never been one for hugging or showing much emotion. The sight of this reunion moved his heart.

Then Kenny saw the priest coming down the aisle toward them. Quickly, he walked over to Salvador and his mother and told them that they had best be going.

Driving out of town, Kenny pulled off the road into some trees in a river bottom and parked.

"Well, if you don't mind," said Kenny, "I'll stretch my legs while you folks talk."

"Thank you," said Salvador.

Kenny got out of the truck, cut a chew, and walked over to a place where he could see in all directions.

"Oh, I'd thought I'd lost you like all the others," said Doña Margarita, running her fingertips over his face, trying to memorize his every curve. "I was asking God to take me to my rest if I couldn't have you back. You are my inspiration, *mi hijito*! My gift in old age!"

"Oh, Mama," said Juan Salvador, "you'll never lose me!"

"With God's help, I hope it's true," she said. "Because I don't want to live without you."

"Me, too," he said. "I love you so much."

"Then stop all this nonsense and get married," she said, pushing her son away. "Now tell me what's going on. They came looking for you right after Jose and Pedro came home."

"The police?"

"Yes, five cars, full of armed men."

He took a big breath. "Did they hurt any of you?"

"No, we kept calm, but still, they keep two policemen hidden in the orchard, watching our house night and day. We sent the children to give them tacos and they saw their guns and badges." She laughed. "They'd thought no one knew about them! But, of course, everyone knew."

Once more, Salvador thought of the big, hairy-armed Tom Mix-bastard back at the hotel. He now knew for sure that he'd gotten Mario to talk. This was every bit as bad as he'd figured. So maybe Archie was just pretending to want to buy liquor and was really after him, too. He tried to keep calm and not show any fear in front of his mother.

"Also," continued the old lady, "I think you should know, *mi hijito*, that it is said that Julio and his wife arrived in town last week and they're driving your car all around and spending money like fools."

"What?" screamed Salvador. "Why, they're supposed to be in Mexico! I bet those son-of-a-bitches are stealing my liquor!"

His mother made the sign of the cross over herself. "Thank God you have the liquor for them to steal, *mi hijito*."

"Don't be ridiculous, Mama. That's my money!"

"I'm not being ridiculous," she said calmly. "Who do you think the cops will follow?"

Salvador stared at his mother. Why, she was right. So, all he had to do was keep away from Julio and Geneva, pick up whatever liquor was left, and let the cops chase them like dogs after a rabbit. Oh, his mother was brilliant!

They visited a while longer and then Salvador finally decided to tell his mother about Lupe.

"Mama," he said, "I've found the woman of my dreams."

"Oh, *mi hijito*! You just don't know how happy this makes me! This is the day I've prayed for! What's her name?"

"Lupe," he said.

"Lupe," repeated the old woman. "Oh, Lupe is a beautiful name. And is she beautiful, too?"

"Oh, yes! She's an angel!" he said, tears coming to his eyes, seeing how happy the news made his mother.

"Good," said Doña Margarita. "And have you met her mother?"

"No, not yet," he said.

"Well, then do, *mi hijito*. Because until you do, we know nothing. Remember, the seed never falls far from the plant. And when you see the old woman, you search her eyes, you talk to her, you learn all you can about her mind and soul. Because no matter how much you don't want to believe it, that young beautiful woman that you see now will one day be much more like that old plant than you can ever imagine."

"I will, Mama. I'll meet her mother."

"Good, then you come and tell me about her. We must be very careful. Choosing the woman you marry is the most important decision of your life. Oh, I've waited so long to hear these words, *mi hijito*. I'll pray day and night for you from now on. This is my dream: to have lived long enough to see my last-born child in love and married!" And her eyes filled with tears and they hugged and kissed, heart-to-heart.

"Well," said Salvador, "I better be going, Mama."

"And don't worry about the police," she said. "One day we'll feed them tacos with so much old chile that they'll get diarrhea and their assholes will burn for weeks!"

She laughed and laughed, and they hugged again. He was glad that he had told his mother about Lupe. Her heart was soaring, her eyes were dancing in anticipation of meeting her son's beloved.

After dropping his mother back off at the church, Salvador and Kenny drove up into the mountains. Salvador washed the makeup off his face in the creek and put on his dirty work clothes. They hiked up the dry side of the riverbed. After finding the place where he and Julio had buried the barrels, they began to dig. But the barrels weren't there. They dug up the whole area and found a few remaining barrels.

Juan went crazy with rage. Julio and Geneva had, indeed, stolen his liquor. He and Kenny loaded up what was left, sweating like animals as they ran up and down the creek. They finally took off.

Stopping by the second riverbed, they found that all those barrels were still there. They spent the next two hours muscling them a quarter of a mile farther up the creek, where they hid them in the brush behind a fallen tree.

Driving back to Carlsbad, Salvador added up the barrels they had left. He figured that Julio had stolen sixteen of his barrels, nearly a thousand dollars worth. Salvador was sure that Geneva had put him up to it. By himself, Julio would never have double-crossed him. Oh, Salvador felt ready to kill. Marrying the wrong woman could destroy a man. He thought of his mother. He thought of Lupe. He thought of Katherine up in Montana, who'd taught him so much about life and love and women. His mother was right; he'd have to meet Lupe's mother and be very, very careful.

The fields of cutting-flowers were in bloom as far as the eye could see: rows of pink, red, yellow and blue. Coming down between the rows, Lupe saw that her father was sweating profusely. It was only eleven in the morning, but already the sun had drained Don Victor and he needed water.

Quickly, Lupe took his arm and started to the water truck. But, approaching the truck at the end of the field, Lupe saw the foreman sitting inside the cab. She stopped; they weren't supposed to come in for water until noon, but Don Victor was coughing so badly that Lupe didn't care what the foreman might say.

Her father was ice-cold by the time Lupe got him to the vehicle. On the back of the truck was a barrel of water and hanging on hooks was a row of tin cans with wire handles twisted around them. Lupe sat her father down in the shade of the truck and reached for one of the cans.

"Hey, you!" said the big, heavy-set foreman, getting out of the cab with the comic book he'd been reading. "It ain't noon. You get your asses back out there!"

"But my father," said Lupe, "he needs water."

"Water, hell!" said the Anglo. He was a huge, fat man, six-feet-four and well over two hundred and fifty pounds. Lupe could smell him as he approached. "He looks more like an old wino to me," he said.

Lupe turned red with anger, but still, she refused to be intimidated. She took one of the tin cans, holding her head high with dignity.

"Eh, girlie, I thought I told you no water 'til noon," he said.

But Lupe ignored him, filling the can with water and handing it to her father, who was now panting dangerously fast, like a tongue-swollen dog.

"Hey, stop that!" yelled the huge man, rushing up and knocking the can out of Don Victor's hand. "You're fired!" he yelled at the old man. "And you," he said to Lupe, "get back to work or I'll fire you, too!"

But Lupe didn't move. Her father was gasping. He could die if she didn't get him cooled down. "We're not dogs," she said, holding back her tears. "We've been working hard since before five! You have no right to abuse us like this!"

"No right?" yelled the big Anglo. "Well, you got another think coming, moo-cha-cha-girl!"

And just then, as the big, red-faced Anglo began shouting insults at Lupe, he was grabbed by a blur of motion, spun about and hit in the stomach with such power that his feet came off the ground.

"No!" yelled Lupe.

But it was too late. It was Salvador, dressed in the dirty work clothes, who hit the foreman two more times in the face with his huge, iron-driving fists. The big, soft-bellied Anglo went crashing into the side of the truck.

Still moving, still feeling his whole heart pounding with rage, Juan reached down and got the can that the Anglo knocked away from Lupe's father, rinsed it off, filled it with water and handed it to Lupe.

"Here," he said, smiling, "for your father."

"Thank you," she said, "but you didn't have to hit him so hard."

"What?" said Salvador.

"So hard," said Lupe. Her heart was pounding. Oh, how she hated violence. She turned back around to help her father drink the water down.

Salvador stood there, adrenaline pumping wildly, feeling confused, not understanding why Lupe hadn't enjoyed how he'd hit the foreman, especially after how he'd treated them.

He watched Lupe help her father drink. Other people came off the field to drink water, too. They congratulated Salvador, telling him that this big Anglo was one of the most abusive foremen that they'd ever had. Several young women started flirting with Salvador. But then they heard the roar of the boss's truck come rushing up the field and the workers tossed their cans and started back into the fields.

"Hold your ground!" yelled Salvador. "You've done nothing wrong! Drinking water is your right! Don't move! We're human beings! Not dogs! Damn it!"

His blood was boiling, just as it did back at the rock quarry. But still, most of the people ran back into the field, not wanting to be fired.

Seeing his people flee, Salvador got so mad at how little they thought of themselves that he reached down and grabbed the fat Anglo by the feet and dragged him around to the other side of the truck. Glancing around to make sure that no one was looking, he pulled out a pint bottle of whiskey and savagely rammed it into the fat man's mouth, forcing him to drink it. The big man came to, coughing and choking. He jerked his head and tried to yell. His eyes bubbled up as if he were drowning, but Salvador only kneed him in the gut, forcing him to drink all the more. Don Victor, who was lying on the ground, saw the whole thing from underneath the truck.

When the boss's truck came roaring up in a cloud of dust, Salvador dropped the bottle and started talking sweetly to the gasping Anglo, pretending that he was trying to stop him from choking.

"What the hell's going on?" yelled the boss, leaping out of his truck. He was dressed in a western hat and cowboy boots and was as wide as a bull, but he wasn't fat.

"I don't know," said Salvador, acting all scared and nervous. "He just went crazy."

The boss grabbed the fallen foreman, smelled the whiskey all over him and said, "All right, Chris, this is the last time! You're fired!"

Chris tried to talk, pointing at Juan Salvador, but still, he couldn't make himself understood, he was gasping so much. The boss got him in his truck, yelling at everyone to take their noon break, and drove off.

Don Victor just couldn't stop laughing. "Eh, you showed him," he said excitedly to Salvador. "I saw everything! *¡Lo chingaste!*"

"Shhhhhhh!" said Salvador. "I did nothing. He just went crazy himself."

"Oh, yeah, sure," said Don Victor, patting Juan on the back. "He just went crazy by himself!"

A very good-looking young lady came up and handed Salvador a tin can of water. "For our King David," she said, rolling her eyes at him suggestively.

Two other girls came up to Salvador and several men, too. Then one young man asked him if he wasn't the same man who'd paid a workman a fortune for his dirty old clothes a few days back.

Salvador only grinned, saying nothing. And looking over the heads of the fieldworkers, he saw that Lupe was eyeing him in a most intriguing way. He smiled, feeling godly, and she smiled back.

When Victoriano and Carlota came out of the field, Victoriano immediately recognized Juan Salvador.

"Hey, Juan!" he said. "Where have you been? You never came back that day."

"Salvador," said Juan Salvador, taking Victoriano's hand. "My full name is Juan Salvador Villaseñor, but I only go by 'Salvador' now."

"Oh, I see," said Victoriano, asking no questions. He knew that many of their people had several names for one reason or another.

"You know him?" asked Lupe, looking surprised.

"Sure," said Victoriano, turning to Lupe, "Salvador is the one who had me drive his convertible around the block in Santa Ana for him." He turned back around to Salvador. "By the way, did you ever find that noise?" he asked.

"No, never did," said Salvador. "I think it just stopped."

"Glad to hear that," said Victoriano. "Why don't you join us for lunch?"

"Well, I'd like to, but . . ."

"Oh, no, please do," said Don Victor. "I haven't had so much fun in years! Victor Gomez at your service!" he added with a flair, tipping his hat.

"Salvador Villaseñor."

"Glad to meet you," said Don Victor, taking Salvador's thick hand. "What a beautiful name, Villaseñor; the mister of the village," he said, giving Salvador's last name a rolling, dignified sound. "Here, I'd like you to meet my two daughters, Lupe and Carlota."

Taming his pounding heart, Salvador turned and reached out to take Lupe's hand—this woman, this lady, this queen whom he'd been worshiping from afar. But Carlota stepped in front of Lupe, taking his outstretched hand.

"I'm Carlota," she said.

"Glad to meet you," said Salvador.

Then he let go of Carlota's hand and he reached for Lupe's. Their eyes met and Lupe took his hand. And something happened, something wonderful happened as their two hands touched, pulsating palm-to-palm—a power of life, of warmth, of enchantment.

"*Mucho gusto*, Lupe," said Salvador, watching her watching him.

"The pleasure is all mine," said Lupe, giving him a slight curtsy, but still holding his hand.

"Weren't you the queen at Cinco de Mayo in Santa Ana?" he asked, pressing his fingers about her hand.

"Yes," she nodded. "And weren't you standing in a car, watching the parade?" She squeezed his hand, giving him warmth.

"Oh, yes," he said, feeling her fingertips tightening about his hand.

She blushed, feeling embarrassed with all the thoughts that were racing through her mind. Seeing her blush, Salvador became self-conscious, too, and let go of her hand.

"I've seen you before, too," said Carlota, not liking how her sister was behaving.

"I don't think so," said Salvador.

"Oh, I think so," said Carlota. "I remember, I saw you with Archie at the string bean dance last year."

"Could be," said Salvador. "I do know Archie."

Suddenly, Lupe remembered the man who'd stared at her from the poolhall across the street from the dance. But no, that man had had a full beard and his eyes had looked so dark and penetrating—completely different. This man's eyes were large and kind and surrounded by the longest eyelashes that she'd ever seen on a man.

"Well, come on, let's go eat," said Don Victor, still laughing, still thinking about that big, fat foreman and how Salvador had gotten him fired.

They walked along the edge of the field, going toward the brush that grew in a little *arroyo* beyond the field of flowers. The rows of cutting-flowers stretched out behind them, going over the rolling hills for miles in beautiful color—pink, yellow, gold, red, blue and lavender—all rolling down the hillsides in a dazzling rainbow of brightness, all the way down to the green lagoon and the blue sea in the distance.

Lupe could feel Salvador's eyes on her as she walked ahead of him, and she couldn't help but wonder about him and what he was doing here since he owned a big, luxurious car. She could still feel the touch of his thick hand in hers. It had fit her large hand so well.

"My wife isn't feeling well, so she stayed home today," said Don Victor as they walked along. "But the girls here, they'll feed us."

"I'm sorry to hear about your wife," said Salvador. "I'd like to meet her. My own mother, she's been a little tired lately, too. I think maybe it's the weather."

"Weather, hell," laughed Don Victor as they went into the tall brush. "It's old age! And it gets us all!"

Salvador laughed, too, and stole another glance at Lupe as they continued down the trail through the foliage.

Oh, he was flying inside. Everything was going so beautifully. Here he was, where he'd always wanted to be. He was no longer over there, staring from the distance, hoping, dreaming of being alongside this angel. No, he was here, in the center of the storm, walking alongside his truelove, feeling wonderful, feeling hot flashes exploding inside him. Heaven was here on earth with him now.

They came out at the other end of the tall brush to a place where the undergrowth had been cut away. The rocks and leaves were cleared off, and they had a view of the glistening flat lagoon and the sea in the distance.

"This is our little place," said Don Victor, taking off his hat. His eyes were sunken and he looked very tired once again. "My wife, she fixed this place for us. Please make yourself at home."

But, of course, Salvador didn't just sit down first. No, he waited courteously for them all to sit down so he could see how they managed their little noonday home in the brush. Each family made a little place for themselves to eat and rest in the heat of the mid-day sun. There were no bathrooms or eating facilities provided for the migrant workers. Everyone had to make do for himself. And here, on the coast, they were lucky. There were trees and tall brush for them to make a place with shade to eat and for the women to hide and relieve themselves in privacy.

Breathing deeply, Salvador watched Lupe and Carlota squat down and make a little fire so that they could prepare lunch. Victoriano helped their father lie down on the ground to rest.

The other *campesinos* were also in the thicket, fixing their own mid-day meals. Blue smoke filtered up through the brush from their little fires. There was laughter and there were children running about and playing. But Salvador paid no attention to this. He only had eyes for Lupe, watching her roll up the long sleeves of her white shirt and take off her hat to fan the tiny fire.

Oh, the nearness of her drove him crazy. Why, just being beside her felt more deeply satisfying than he'd felt in all his years of being with other women.

Don Victor began to snore. Victoriano went down to the lagoon to get water.

"So, what do you do for a living?" asked Carlota. "Certainly you don't work in the fields," she added, laughing. "You work too slow."

"Ah, well, I have a couple of trucks," said Salvador, trying to figure out what to say.

"Carlota," said Lupe, "where are your manners? You know it's not proper to be so intrusive."

"Talking about manners, what do you call how you're behaving?" snapped Carlota.

Lupe said nothing more. Salvador just sat and watched.

The food was ready when Victoriano came back with water from a spring by the lagoon. Carlota woke their father and they all began to eat. But they did not talk, they just ate the fire-warmed tortillas with hard-cured cheese and avocado and round wheels of tomato with plenty of salt and *salsa*.

Salvador could feel Lupe's closeness and hear her breathing as they continued eating in silence, listening to the birds in the branches above them and watching the small white clouds high overhead. All around them were the other fieldworkers, who made up the hidden village in the brush.

The afternoon breeze came off the lagoon, cooling the air. Lupe chewed her food, feeling more conscious of Salvador's presence than she'd ever felt of any man except her Colonel. She chewed her food and sipped her water, sitting on the smooth, hard earth, regaining her strength from the long, hard morning. She thought of Mark and how much she enjoyed talking to him about school and books and how he respected her intelligence and her ambition of some day working in an office.

Oh, she felt so confused inside. She had so much with Mark. So, why was she feeling like this towards a perfect stranger? Then, like a sign from the Almighty, Lupe heard a buzzing sound above her. Looking up, she saw an enormous swarm of golden bees, humming with such fury as they came over the tall brush. Lupe just knew that God was speaking to her.

Magic was in the air; the flowers, the bees, the birds—all a proof of God's miraculous love—transported her back home to their beloved box canyon.

"Look, God is with us!" said Lupe, eyes dancing with excitement as she pointed at the glittering swarm.

They all looked. And Salvador saw the white underside of Lupe's arm as she raised her hand, pointing to the sky, exposing the unsunburned part of her body.

Oh, the sight of her private flesh sent Salvador spinning! He was in heaven, surrounded by golden honey bees, magnificent blue sky, rich green growth, glistening white water, and his truelove at his side. He thought of his mother and how happy she'd be to see him here in the brush with this family that passed its noonday meal with such dignity.

The rest of the day, Salvador was hardly able to work. Every time he and Lupe glanced at each other, they'd blush with embarrassment.

Getting back to the barrio that afternoon, Lupe knew she was in trouble. Carlota hated Salvador.

"I'm telling Mama," said Carlota as soon as they got off the flatbed truck.

"But what are you going to tell her?" asked Lupe. "That we gave lunch to a stranger who helped Papa and me?"

"Don't play the fool with me!" snapped Carlota. "You were disgusting! And he's no good, I tell you. You should be thinking of Mark and your future; not this man!"

"All right, Carlota," said Lupe, stopping outside their tent, "think what you want. You always do!"

"Ho, ho, ho," said Carlota, "look who's getting mad. And when he comes over to see you tonight, I'm telling Mama to get rid of him!"

"You know," said Lupe, "maybe you're upset because it's you who's really interested in him."

"Me?" screamed Carlota. "Don't be ridiculous! He's too short and his ears stick out!"

"Well, you sure noticed a lot for not being interested," said Lupe, laughing.

"Oh, you're in trouble now, Lupe!" yelled Carlota, rushing into the tent.

Inside, their mother was lying down on a mat, resting. The years had truly come down on her in the last few months.

"Mama," said Carlota, "Lupe made a fool of herself!"

"Where's your father?" asked the old lady.

"He went with the other men to buy liquor," said Lupe, coming in behind her sister.

"I see," said their mother, sitting up. "Well, at least it will relax him and he'll sleep tonight."

"But, Mama," said Carlota, "Papa shouldn't be drinking! And we met this man today and he's no good and Lupe was flirting with him!"

"No, I wasn't," said Lupe, taking off her hat. "I was simply grateful to him because he helped Papa and me."

"Ha!" said Carlota. "You were being more than just grateful, giving him the biggest tortilla and then being all goo-goo-eyed over the bees with him!"

"All right, all right," said the old lady, "enough! Both of you! Now, Carlota, you start your bath and, Lupe, you sit down here and tell me about this man."

"A no-good, Mama!" called Carlota, going to the wash basin at the back of their rented tent. "Ask Victoriano, he'll tell you. And I'm going to ask Archie, too; you'll see!"

Lupe clenched her hands. Her sister was going too far. Victoriano had only spoken well of Salvador.

"Well, who is he?" asked her mother.

Lupe shrugged. "Who knows, Mama? We just met him. His name is Salvador and he knocked down that big foreman who's always bullying us when I went to get water for Papa."

"I see, and did he also go with the men to that lady's house to buy liquor?" asked the old woman.

"No, Mama, he went the opposite way, to the American part of town," said Lupe. "To do some business, he said."

"I see," said her mother, smoothing out the apron on her lap. "So, maybe he doesn't drink, eh?"

Lupe shrugged once more. "Who knows? We don't know him, Mama. He was nothing but considerate, so I don't know why Carlota degrades him so."

Doña Guadalupe studied her daughter for a long time, searching her eyes. "Do you like him?" she asked.

Lupe shrugged, avoiding the question. "Mama," she said, "I don't think I'm ready to like any man."

Her heart was pounding. Lupe fully realized that she'd lied, because she was interested in Salvador, plus she'd promised Mark to have an answer for him when they returned.

But the crafty old lady wasn't about to be fooled. She'd seen that her daughter had glanced off toward the left before she'd answered her. The left eye never lied. When it did lie, it always said that it was lying by glancing off to the left.

"**K**enny!" said Salvador, bursting into the old man's garage. "I need to buy a new car! Right now!"

"All right," said Kenny, calmly chewing his tobacco. "Sit down and let's talk. I know a gent in Oceanside named Harvey Swartz. He sells good used cars."

"I can't sit down," said Salvador. "Let's go!"

"What you got up your ass?" asked Kenny, laughing. "Did you fall in love or something?"

"Better!"

"Better?"

"Yeah, I found my dream! My miracle of life! My, my, everything!"

"Jesus Christ!" said Kenny, laughing. "Sounds good!"

There was still plenty of daylight when Kenny and Salvador got to the car lot in Oceanside. Then, Salvador saw it, parked over in the far side of the lot. It was the most beautiful roadster that he'd ever seen, looking as long and sleek in the dimming sunlight as a desert jaguar crouched down low, ready to leap into action.

"That white one!" yelled Salvador to Kenny.

"A Moon, eh?" said the old man, approaching the grand-looking roadster. "Good car, Sal, but it's gonna cost a fortune."

"Hell, just one?" laughed Salvador excitedly. He could already see Lupe sitting beside him, looking like his queen, his wife, the mother of his children.

Kenny grinned. "Let me do the talking, Sal," he said. "You just keep still. I know Harvey, he's a drinking man, so maybe we can work out something."

"Sounds good!" said Salvador. "But hurry! We got to move! I need to be there before sundown!"

The sun was going down when Salvador cruised down the long line of tents in his Moon. He'd shaven and showered and he was wearing his navy blue pin-striped suit and his white panama. He drove his ivory-white roadster real slow, snaking along, truly enjoying all the stares he was getting from field hands.

He thought of the first time that his mother had seen his father come riding into their village on a great sorrel stallion, the sunlight turning his reddish-brown hair to gold under his great *sombrero* and the *conchos* of his riding pants to eyes of dazzling silver. Oh, Salvador just wished that he could push a magic button and make his Moon rear up on its back wheels, like a stallion taking a bow.

This was wonderful! In Santa Ana she'd been the queen of the parade, and now here in Carlsbad he was the king of the barrio!

In the back of their rented tent, Lupe was finishing up her bath. Drying off, she threw her bath water out the rear flap of the long tent. She'd just put on her dress when Manuelita came rushing in.

"Lupe!" said her best friend, "he's coming in a beautiful car!"

Spotting Victoriano in front of one of the tents, Salvador pulled up. Lupe was nowhere in sight. Carlota was cutting her father's hair. The old man waved at Salvador, but Carlota gave him a dirty look.

"My God," said Victoriano, coming up to the grand automobile, "you have more than one car?"

"Well, not exactly," said Salvador. "I'm selling the Dodge." He got out of the Moon. "You like it?" he said to Victoriano. "Take it."

"You mean around the block?"

"Sure," said Salvador. "Check it out for me and see what you think."

"My God," said Victoriano, "come on, Papa! And you, too, Carlota!"

"No, you two go on," said the old man, carefully removing the towel from his shoulders and brushing the hair off his pants.

"All right," said Carlota. And even though she didn't like Salvador or want him around her sister, she couldn't resist the temptation of going around the block in such a fantastic automobile, and showing off to everyone.

She handed her comb and scissors to her father and rushed to the car. Salvador and Don Victor watched them drive down the long line of lit-up tents, with everyone watching.

"So," said the old man, getting a twinkle in his bloodshot eyes, "you came by to see me, no doubt."

"Of course," said Salvador.

"And that foreman, he just went crazy by himself, eh?" he said, laughing. "Oh, you are a first-class wonder, aren't you?" he added, truly enjoying the memory. "The way you rammed that bottle into his mouth, almost killing him, then lying so beautifully to the boss. Hell, a man like you is used to getting anything he wants, isn't he?"

Salvador glanced around. He didn't want anyone to overhear Don Victor. But it was too late.

Looking through the crack of the flap, Doña Guadalupe saw how well her liquored-up husband and the young man in the fine clothes were getting along. She rushed about like a she-boar getting ready to do battle.

"Lupe, you go to the back and do the dishes. And you, Manuelita, go get your mother. Tell her I need her right now!"

"Yes," said Manuelita, shrugging to Lupe and going out the rear flap.

"But, Mama," said Lupe, "I already did the dishes."

"Well, then, do them again!" snapped her mother, fixing her dress. "And don't come up front until I call you."

"Oh," said Lupe sarcastically, "and should I hide behind the boulder, too?"

"That's enough," said her mother.

"Yes," said Lupe, and she went out the rear flap to do as she'd been told. But she couldn't figure out what was going on. Other boys had been coming over to see her and Carlota for years, and her mother had never behaved like this.

"*Querida*," said Don Victor, opening the front flap of the tent, "come outside. I'd like you to meet our champion, Salvador Villaseñor!"

"*A sus órdenes*," said Salvador, taking off his hat and bowing with a flair.

"*Con mucho gusto*," said Doña Guadalupe, coming outside. "Guadalupe Gomez."

Salvador took her hand.

"Well, sit down, make yourself at home," she said, making room for Salvador to sit on one of the crates that they'd gotten from the orchard across the road. "Or would you prefer to go inside?" she asked.

"Whatever you wish, *señora*," said Salvador, looking at the short, plump old lady very carefully. She had beautiful white hair and large, wonderful hazel-green eyes that sparkled with mischief and contrasted with her dark, serious Indian features.

"Well, then, come in," she said, deciding that she could best handle this innocent-girl-stealing coyote inside.

On going into the long tent, Salvador felt like he'd entered the web of a spider, the old woman was eyeing him so deliberately.

"So, where are you from?" she asked, sitting down on the crate that Don Victor had brought in for her.

"Los Altos de Jalisco," said Salvador, sitting on a crate.

"I see, and are your parents living?"

"Thank God, my mother is," he said, smiling grandly. "She's the love of my life!"

The old lady raised up her left eyebrow, smoothing out the apron on her lap. Either this man was too good to be true or he was the worst kind of coyote, a man capable of stealing a woman's heart and soul.

"And where does your mother live?" she asked.

"In Corona, just north of here."

"I see. And may I ask, how do you manage to do so well here in this country?" she said, eyeing his fine clothes.

Salvador was taken by surprise. He hadn't expected such direct questioning. Especially before he'd even made his intentions known regarding Lupe. He looked at the old lady, choosing his words carefully, staring straight back at her as she studied his eyes. After all, he wasn't a professional gambler for nothing.

"I move fertilizer," he said, lying to her, staring at her, eye-to-eye, giving absolutely nothing away. "I have trucks and contracts with several ranches."

"Oh," she said, noticing that neither of his eyes had moved. "And this pays well, eh?" she added.

He laughed. She'd accepted his words. Duel had, indeed, taught him well. "Yes, very well, if you got enough manure," he said.

Watching the whole exchange, Don Victor burst out laughing, thinking of all the times that his wife had outwitted him. Doña Guadalupe gave him a dirty look. Getting to his feet, Don Victor returned his wife's dirty look and went outside to smoke. He could see that his crafty old wife had her hands full.

For the next ten minutes, Doña Guadalupe pounded Salvador with question after question, but Salvador only smiled, answering whatever she asked.

The sun was going down and it was getting late. Salvador still hadn't seen or heard Lupe. He began to feel trapped. Yes, of course, he remembered that his mother had told him that he had to get to know Lupe's mother, but this was ridiculous.

Then Doña Manza came through the front flap. She, too, had fixed her hair and changed her dress.

"You've come just in time, Doña Manza," said Doña Guadalupe to her old friend. "I'd like you to meet Salvador Villaseñor."

Standing up, Salvador pulled at his collar nervously. He'd seen this before, back home when the she-boars got together, going after the lion that had gotten into their den.

"Glad to meet you, *señora*," said Salvador, taking Doña Manza's hand. Salvador could hear Don Victor laughing outside, truly enjoying his predicament.

O ut back, Lupe was done re-washing the dishes. She was watching the little children play in the sewage water that ran down the line between the tents. She couldn't figure out what was going on. Her mother was behaving as badly as Carlota.

Manuelita came running up. She'd changed clothes and fixed her hair, too.

"But what is going on?" asked Lupe. "First, Carlota doesn't like Salvador and then my mother fixes herself up to meet him, and now you come all dressed up like we're going to a dance."

"Oh, Lupe, don't you really know what's going on?"

"No, I guess not," said Lupe.

"Well, remember back in La Lluvia when the Colonel decided to stay at your house above all other houses in the village?"

"Well, yes, but that was only because he didn't want his wife near the plaza where the soldiers stayed."

"But then why didn't he stay at someone else's house?" she asked, watching Lupe's eyes. "Oh, Lupe, you really don't see it, do you? This is why Rose-Mary hated you so much and still does. No matter how many private finishing schools Don Manuel sends his daughters to, they will never have the dignity that you acquired from your own home.

"Lupe, that's why our mothers are best friends. They have a sense of values that cannot be taught. They are *el eje* of their *casas*, the inspiration of our lives. And now this man who slayed the dragon out in the fields has come to court you with the force of the heavens! Every girl in the camp is excited with envy!"

"Of me?"

"Yes, of you!" said Manuelita.

Lupe looked her friend in the eyes and she knew deep down inside that Manuelita spoke the truth. This man, Salvador, did cause excitement, just as her Colonel had done.

Doña Guadalupe was just beginning to continue her questioning when Victoriano and Carlota drove up in Salvador's grand automobile.

"Mama!" said Carlota, rushing inside the tent, "come outside and see his car; it's beautiful!"

"Here," said Victoriano, giving the keys back to Salvador, "that's the most powerful car I've ever driven! It's even more powerful than your Dodge!"

"Yes," said Salvador, taking the keys. "It is nice, isn't it?" he added, hoping that the interrogation had ended. But he was wrong.

"All right," said Doña Guadalupe, "enough about cars."

"But don't you want to see it?" asked Victoriano.

"No," said the old woman, "I know nothing about them. Now, please, keep still while Doña Manza and I continue talking with Salvador. And you, Carlota, go to the back and help your sister make some tea for us."

"Maybe I can help," said Salvador, jumping to his feet, hoping he might get away from this old lady and see Lupe before it became too late.

"Certainly not," said Doña Guadalupe, "you sit down. They'll bring us the tea."

Salvador sat back down.

"Well," said Victoriano, giving Salvador a look of sympathy, "you three talk; I'm going outside to look at the car some more."

Salvador tossed him the keys. Victoriano caught them.

"Well," said the old woman, smoothing out her apron once more, "as we were saying, Doña Manza and I saw the Revolution ruin many *familias*. But, still, we both think that the greatest threat to a marriage is alcohol and cards. Don't you agree?"

"Well, yes, in a way," said Salvador.

"Good, I'm glad you agree with us," said Doña Guadalupe, "because speaking quite frankly, I want you to know that we will never permit one of our daughters to marry a man who drinks alcohol. In fact, we've both instructed our daughters since they were small of the terrible vices of liquor and cards.

"I worked hard, Salvador," said the old woman, tears suddenly coming to her eyes, "to keep my family together through the war, and I will protect my flesh until my last breath! Do you hear me?"

"Well, yes, I do," said Salvador, taken aback by her sudden outburst. Hell, he hadn't even asked for the hand of any of their daughters. So why were these two old ladies saying all these things to him? Was his love for Lupe so obvious that everyone already knew his true intentions?

He glanced away, trying to gather his thoughts. This old woman was incredible. But, on the other hand, maybe his own mother would have done the same thing if she'd had the chance.

Finding Lupe and Manuelita in the back, Carlota picked up a carrot and started munching.

"Mama wants you to make tea for them," she said.

"But what is she doing to him?" asked Lupe.

"Just showing him up for what he really is," said Carlota, chewing her carrot.

"Carlota," said Lupe, "you don't even know him, so how can you talk like this?"

"You'll see," said Carlota. "I'm going over to Archie's and ask about him while you two make the tea."

"That's not right!" said Lupe.

"Let her go," said Manuelita, getting the pot to heat water. "If you stop her, it will only be worse."

Looking inside through the open doorway, Carlota could see that Archie was behind the bar. She knew that women weren't allowed inside the poolhall, so she waved at him from the doorway, trying to get his attention. Seeing her, Archie wiped his mouth with his wide tie, excused himself from the two men he was speaking with and came around the bar.

"Hi, baby!" he said, grinning as he came up to the doorway. "What can I do to you that hasn't been done before, you sweet little dumpling?"

"Archie, I need to ask you something," said Carlota.

"Sure, ask away, but that don't mean you get. Not here in public, anyway."

"Do you know a man named Salvador?"

"No, can't say I do."

"He said his full name is Juan Salvador Villaseñor."

Archie's whole face flushed with anger. "You seen him?"

"Yeah, sure. He was in the fields today, working with us. Then tonight he came by in a big car to see my . . ."

"That son-of-a-bitch!" said Archie.

"Then he's no good, right?" asked Carlota excitedly.

"For you, no way, baby. You stay away from him," he said, putting his huge hand on top of Carlota's head, stroking her like a man would a lap dog.

"But for someone else, he's A-1 okay. The best damned deputy I've ever had."

"He's your deputy?" she asked, completely taken aback.

"Yeah," he said, still stroking the top of her head. "Man, you got lovely hair, baby."

And he bent down to kiss the top of her head but Carlota whirled away, running back up the dirt street.

L upe and Manuelita were just getting ready to take the tea inside when Carlota came rushing up.

"Well, what did you find out?" asked Manuelita.

"Nothing," said Carlota.

"Nothing?" said Manuelita, laughing. "Then it must've been good or you'd be talking a mile a minute."

"No, smartie, it wasn't good!" snapped Carlota. "The rumors all over the barrio are that he's a bootlegger on the run; that's why he bought those work clothes—to hide in the fields."

"But Archie, what did he have to say?"

"Nothing; he said that he hardly knows him."

Not believing her, Manuelita turned to Lupe. "Come, let's take in the tea. Rumors mean nothing, Lupe. My mother always says that no home can survive if a woman listens to rumors."

"N o, *señora*, I don't drink or gamble; I'm a businessman," said Salvador.

"Well, we're very glad to hear that," said Doña Guadalupe as the girls came in with the tea.

Seeing Lupe, Salvador leaped to his feet. But he hit the hanging lantern with his head, almost knocking himself back down.

Putting down the teapot, Lupe rushed to his side. "Are you all right?" she asked.

"I don't know," he said. He then got an idea and gripped Lupe's arm. "I'm pretty dizzy. Maybe you better get me a wet towel. Here, I'll go with you."

Salvador quickly started toward the rear of the tent with Lupe before anyone could say anything. Doña Guadalupe and Doña Manza glanced at each other.

"Well, he is quick," said Doña Manza.

"Yes, I noticed," said Doña Guadalupe. "And don't take too long!" she shouted after Lupe and Salvador.

"My God," said Salvador, once they were outside, "I thought I'd never get to see you."

Lupe laughed. "I just don't know why my mother is behaving like this." She took a clean rag, wringing it out. "Does it hurt?"

"Yes," he said, "but standing here with you, I can never feel pain again."

Their eyes met, the world stopped again—just as it had out in the fields—and it was paradise. Lupe blushed, becoming self-conscious, and put the wet rag to Salvador's head.

"There," she said, "I hope it will help."

"How can it not," he said, "coming from you?"

And he wanted to say more, much more, all he had locked up inside his heart and soul, but he couldn't. It was just too much. He now knew why it felt so good being with this woman. It was as if he'd known her from another lifetime; as if every move, every expression she made, reminded him of another great love that he'd had before. Oh, he was swimming with good feelings, bursting with love!

"Well," said Lupe, "I think we better go back inside before the tea gets cold."

"Of course," he said.

It was almost midnight when Salvador got back to Kenny's garage. He cut the motor and was just getting out of the Moon when suddenly a huge man leaped out of the darkness, shoving a pistol against his temple.

"Don't even think of it," said the huge man. "One move and you're a dead son-of-a-bitch!" He reached in and took the gun out of Salvador's coat. "Now get inside."

Salvador did as told. He'd been caught cold. His mind had been a million miles away, thinking about Lupe and how much he'd have to tell his own mother when he saw her.

Inside the garage, Kenny was waiting for them. He was also armed. He had a 30/30 in his hands. Salvador turned and saw that the huge man was none other than Archie Freeman, himself. Instantly, he knew that it had been a setup from the start. Why, he'd been a fool to trust the old *gringo*. Now they knew where his liquor was and everything.

"Sit down," said Archie, pointing to the chair that had been placed in the middle of the empty garage. "And shut up! Not one word!"

Salvador didn't move. Not one muscle. He'd never seen Archie like this. The guy was absolutely crazy.

"Did you kill 'em?" asked Archie, staring at Salvador in the eyes.

"Kill who?" asked Salvador, his heart ready to explode, remembering the two federal agents.

"Damn it!" screamed Archie, grabbing Salvador by the neck and yanking him out of the chair, his feet dangling in space. "Don't fuck with me!" he roared. "Or you'll see why old Archie is called the king of four counties! Nobody fucks with me!"

But still, Salvador gave him nothing.

"Talk! Did you kill 'em?" bellow'ed Archie, slamming him back into the chair so hard that it shattered, dropping Salvador in the oily dirt of the garage.

"Look, Archie," said Salvador, staying down so he didn't rile up the lawman any more than he already was, "I've been beat by the best, I've seen my brothers killed left and right; this won't work with me. So tell me what's going on."

Archie stared at Salvador a long time. "All right," he said, "I've been notified that your partner and his wife were murdered."

"What?" said Salvador. "Julio's dead?"

"Yeah," nodded Archie, studying Salvador's eyes.

"When?"

"Yesterday."

"Jesus Christ!" said Salvador. "How did it happen?"

"They were in your car when it blew up like a bomb."

"My Dodge?"

"Yeah," said Archie, the whole time watching Salvador's eyes like a hawk.

"Jesus Christ!" said Salvador again.

"And," said Archie, "the word is out that they were stealing your liquor and you wanted 'em dead."

Salvador stared at Archie. "Yeah, they were, and I did want them dead, but I didn't do it. My God, Julio was a good man. And my friend."

"Man," said Archie, "you're either innocent or the best actor I ever seen."

"You mean, you thought I did it?" asked Salvador.

"Why not? Kill 'em, take all the whiskey and let people think it was you in the Dodge so you can start a whole new life."

"But I've been here all this time," said Salvador. "Ask Kenny, he'll tell you."

"He already did," said Archie. "Defended you 'til I thought maybe he was in cahoots with you, too."

Salvador turned to Kenny, feeling badly that he'd misjudged the old man a second time.

"You looked damned suspicious," said Archie, "changing your name and giving a man twenty dollars for his dirty clothes so you can hide in the fields.

"Give me a drink," said Archie, turning to Kenny. "Shit, ever since that big bust-up in San Bernardino, they've been pushing Big John up in Orange County and Whitey down here in San Diego to clean up their counties, too, and I ain't been able to get a decent drink of whiskey.

"Hell, I don't trust those Fed bastards any farther than I can throw 'em. They don't live here. They just come in quick-like and make a big name for themselves, then mosey on back home and drink whiskey with their own local bad boys in Washington, D.C." He downed the whiskey Kenny gave him. "Hell, I wouldn't be surprised if they ain't the ones who killed Julio and his wife."

"The Feds?" asked Salvador.

"Sure, why not? They gave disease-infested blankets to my people, push an honest live-and-let-live lawman like Big John to the edge. But you tell me this: Why'd you come into town, sneaking around old Archie and change your name if you're innocent?"

"Well, I almost did come to see you as soon as I got here, Archie," said Salvador, "but then I got scared, not knowing what was going on."

"Don't you ever do that again unless you want trouble, goddammit! Especially if there ain't no whiskey to be had!"

"I won't!" said Salvador. "I promise. But with the FBI involved, well, naturally, I thought they'd put pressure on you and you'd be after me, too."

"Because of the Feds?" bellowed Archie. "Shit, no one puts pressure on Archie Freeman! I'm a free man! Do you hear me? Free, goddammit!"

Salvador said nothing. The huge lawman was ready to kill once again.

"That goddammed bust was nothing but publicity! You don't see the Feds going after the real big boys, do you? Of course not, 'cause they'd come out looking bad and they don't want that! Take Bill Wesseley who ran that sting; hell, I've locked horns with him several times and he's an A-1 asshole! Same kind who's always sold out my people!"

"Then you're really after me only because of Julio and Geneva?" asked Salvador.

Archie nodded. "Damned right, I can't stand a son-of-a-bitch who'd kill his own," he added.

"Well, I didn't do it," said Salvador.

"And I'm half inclined to believe you," said Archie, "but the Feds ain't buying it, so you and me gotta work out a little deal."

Saying this, Archie put his huge right arm around Salvador's shoulders and walked him over to a corner.

"You want to start a whole new life, Salvador?" asked Archie, using Juan Salvador's new name for the first time. "You wanna be in love and start a family, eh?"

Salvador took a good look at the lawman.

"Well, do you?" asked Archie. "I hear you're in love and I can understand that, 'cause that's happened to the best of us, sorry to say."

Salvador took a deep breath. "Yeah," he said. "I'd like that. A lot."

"Good," said Archie, "and I think I can arrange it. But it will cost you and you got to lay low 'til I pull it off. No more buying men's clothes off their back and leaving them half naked in the street. No more dressing up like a woman and going up to Wesseley's territory. You catcheee my lingo?"

"Yeah," said Salvador, truly liking the idea, "but how much will it cost me?"

"Ten barrels for starters."

"For starters?"

"Sure, why not? Every man's gotta pay his taxes!"

"Five barrels," said Salvador.

"All right, five now and five every month after that."

"Five every month?"

Archie laughed. "Look, you dumb bastard, you're wanted for murder; you can't argue with me!"

Salvador took a big breath, thinking, figuring. This was a deal with the devil; this was like half admitting that he'd committed the murders. But what else could he do? He couldn't keep running all his life.

"All right, you got it," he said. "But you're going to have to give me protection."

"Now you're talking," said Archie.

And so the deal was made and Salvador would get to start a whole new life, but first he'd have to lay low for a while and not leave town. Except, of course, to go up and get some whiskey so he could pay Archie his first five barrels.

The following morning, Salvador didn't go to work in the fields with Lupe and her family. No, instead he borrowed Kenny's truck and headed north to get the barrels of whiskey that he'd promised Archie.

In Corona, Salvador decided to stop by the church to see if he could find his mother. He was dying to tell her about Lupe, and especially about her mother. But, driving up to the church and going inside, he didn't find the grand lady.

His heart fell. Oh, he'd truly wanted to see his mother and tell her about his truelove's mother and how the old woman had torn into him. Why, he could just hear his mother laughing, telling him to be prepared for a tough marriage because the seed didn't fall far from the plant.

He got back in Kenny's truck and took off, not noticing that the priest had seen him, the very same priest who'd seen him with his mother when he'd come to the church dressed as a woman.

Driving out of the Anglo part of town, Salvador thought of going by the barrio to see his mother, but then he remembered that car full of cops hiding in the orchard. He realized he couldn't go anywhere near his home. And he also remembered how his brother, Jose the great, had been ambushed and killed.

His heart began to pound. Quickly, he headed for the mountains to dig up the whiskey and get back to Carlsbad. He wasn't going to take any more chances, especially now that he had so much going for him.

He began to pray, talking to God, realizing that this was the first time that he'd asked anything of the Almighty since he'd left God at the Rio Grande.

"Oh, please, dear God," he said, "help me to not get caught or die. I want to live now, I really do, and have a *casa* of my own. And, maybe, even reach the age of thirty-five so I can see my children grow."

He fully realized that not one of his brothers had ever lived past the age of twenty-five. For him, to hope to reach the age of thirty-five was an incredible thing to ask, even of God. Then he remembered his grandfather, Don Pio, who'd lived to an old age along with his wife, Silveria, and he wondered if that long of a life was possible for his people here in this country.

He breathed deeply, and he realized that something was happening inside himself; he'd spoken to God and he wanted a long life. Being in love was changing his whole outlook.

Hell, ever since crossing the Rio Grande, he'd been dealing only with the devil. As Duel had said, "Men like us can't believe in the puppet God of the churches, but in the devil, of course." And Salvador had agreed.

But now, it felt different. Being in love truly made the idea of God not just seem possible, but most probable.

Salvador pulled off the road and parked. He got out of the truck and started up the sandy creek bed to where he and Kenny had hidden the barrels. He thought of Julio and he felt badly that his friend and his wife had died. But he also realized that their tragedy had become his salvation.

After pulling the brush off the barrels, he went to work, feeling strong. He grabbed up a barrel as if it weighed nothing and rushed up the creek bed with power. It felt good to talk to his old Friend, God, and have love in his heart once again.

The break of day was just beginning to paint the sky to the east as Lupe and her family walked down between the rows of flowers with their short-handled hoes.

"Is that her?" Lupe heard one girl ask another.

"Yes," whispered the other girl, "she's the one."

Lupe could feel both girls staring at her.

By noon, Lupe was so aware of the fieldworkers' attention that she felt awkward. It was as if they thought that she'd suddenly become special, and good things could happen to them, too, if they just got near her.

"Excuse me," said one girl to Lupe as they went into the brush to eat, "but, well, my friends and I were wondering if we couldn't come to your tent tonight," she said, turning to the two girls who were with her, "and get a ride with you and Salvador in his car?"

Lupe stared at the girl, not knowing what to say.

The girl took Lupe's silence to mean "no," and she became angry. "Well, then, forget it!" she snapped. "I didn't really want a ride in his car anyway! My uncle in Mexico was a general, and he had a good car, too!" Saying this, she turned and walked away.

"But, wait," said Lupe, "I didn't mean that you can't come by. It's just that, well, I hardly know Salvador."

"You're engaged to him, aren't you?"

"Engaged?" asked Lupe. "No, I'm not."

"Well, that's what everyone is saying!"

"Look," said Lupe, "come by if you want, but the truth is I don't even know if he'll be by again."

"Well, then, excuse me!" said the girl, and she left, not believing Lupe, figuring that she just thought they weren't good enough to meet her fiancé.

Going back to her family, Lupe realized that she'd made an enemy. But there was nothing she could do about it. She sat back down to help with lunch.

"Don't pay attention to her," said her mother. "She's just excited. It's not every day that people see the possibility of a girl getting out of the fields."

"Oh, Mama, please," said Lupe.

"Please what?" said her mother. "To not admit to myself that you've grown? That only yesterday you were running up and down the hillsides with your pet deer? And now you have two very serious suitors, *mi hijita*."

"Two? But, Mama," said Lupe, "I don't even know Salvador. And the way he looks at me, and his walk . . . sometimes he reminds me of a strutting rooster," she laughed.

Doña Guadalupe laughed, too. "Like I said, *mi hijita*, you have two very serious suitors, and we have much to talk about. But, of course, we don't really know anything about either one until you meet the parents."

"Yes, I know. You've told me a thousand times, Mama."

"Only a thousand? Well, then, I still have more telling to do. For remember, *querida*, in choosing the right man it's sometimes very difficult to tell the difference between the eagle and the hawk. Especially when the raven appears, dazzling us with his noisy commotion and bag full of trickery."

"The raven?"

"Well, yes, the raven, *mi hijita*. Don't you remember, I've also told you this a thousand times. He'll come to you when you least expect it. Like out of a gorgeous flower or chasing a hawk across the heaven, pretending to be so brave and capable when in fact he isn't, unless he loots and robs."

"I see," said Lupe. "I'm glad you reminded me, Mama."

The right eye of God was just going down into the great, rippling sea when Salvador drove up between the lines of tents in his ivory-white Moon. He snaked along real easy, tipping his panama to the watching people, and he pulled up to Lupe's castle. Don Victor and Victoriano were playing checkers on a crate over to one side, and Doña Guadalupe and her friend Doña Manza were sitting at the entrance of his queen's home like grand old lionesses ready to do battle. But Salvador didn't panic. He only smiled, getting out of his car with a bouquet of roses in his hand. This evening he was ready to do battle, too. He wasn't about to get caught with his pants down as he'd been caught the first evening.

"*Buenas tardes*," he said to Don Victor and Victoriano as he came around the long, sleek roadster.

"*Buenas tardes,*" they both answered him as he approached the two old women with the roses.

"Oh, he's brought flowers for us," said Doña Manza, feeling full of the devil.

"*Buenas tardes,*" said Doña Guadalupe.

"These are for you," said Salvador, taking off his hat and handing the flowers to Lupe's mother.

"Thank you, they smell wonderful," said Doña Guadalupe. "You remember my friend Doña Manza?"

"How could I forget?" said Salvador, bowing.

"The pleasure is all mine," said Doña Manza.

"Why don't you sit down and join us?" said Lupe's mother.

Salvador grinned. "I'd love to," he said, glancing at the men. "But you see," he added, bringing some tickets out of his breast pocket, "there's an excellent new movie in town and I took the liberty of buying tickets for your son and two daughters and myself."

"Oh, I see," said Doña Guadalupe.

"I'm deeply sorry," continued Salvador, "but with your permission, I'd like us to postpone our conversation for some other time."

Don Victor burst out laughing. Doña Guadalupe gave him a dirty look, seeing that she'd been outmaneuvered.

"Well," she said, "since you already went to the expense of buying the tickets, I guess it's all right this time. Wouldn't you say so?" she asked, turning to her husband.

Don Victor only grinned. "Whatever you decide, my dear," he said, truly enjoying the whole thing.

"All right," said the crafty, old she-fox, "you can go this time, but only with the understanding that you'll come early enough next time so we can continue our conversation."

"Of course," said Salvador, "and the pleasure will be entirely mine. I truly enjoyed out last talk. It reminded me a great deal of the wonderful conversations that I have with my beloved mother."

Both old women couldn't help but smile. This young man was being very smooth in the keeping with their customs.

"I'll go get my sisters," said Victoriano, getting to his feet.

"Good, and please hurry," said Salvador. "We don't want to be late. It's a William Hart movie."

"My favorite!" said Victoriano, hurrying inside.

Nervously, Salvador put on his hat. He was hoping that they'd get away before the two old women got started in on him.

Carlota and Victoriano came out. Salvador could see that they were both very good looking young people, having inherited the best from each of their parents. But then Lupe stepped out of the tent and his heart exploded. Why, she had to be the most beautiful woman in the whole world, standing there in a simple, cream-colored dress with her long, dark hair flowing down to her shoulders in rich, full curls.

"Good evening," said Salvador to Lupe, taking off his panama again.

"Good evening," said Lupe, giving a slight curtsy.

He came forward and reached out to take her hand and when their two hands touched, there it was again. Something truly magical happened every time they touched—a warmth, a mysterious power, passed between them.

"Well," he said, "we best be going so we can make the movie."

He put his hat back on, tipping it to Lupe's mother and Doña Manza and he took Lupe's arm, walking her to his car. But, before he could put his truelove in the front seat, Victoriano—who'd been checking out the Moon—climbed into the front passenger seat.

"Let them ride in back," he said to Salvador, acting just like a brother. "I want to talk to you about the car."

Salvador smiled. "Certainly," he said.

Helping Lupe into the rumble seat in back with Carlota, Salvador felt her squeeze his hand, giving him reassurance. He felt such a wonderful rush of emotion shoot through him that he almost grabbed her.

The movie was good. But, what was far better was the soft darkness of the theater and Lupe and Salvador sitting together, feeling the magic of their closeness. Lupe had never been to the movies like this before. Sure, she'd gone with her brother, sister, Jaime and his friends, but she'd never been driven in a grand automobile to the theater with a man for whom she felt so many different feelings.

She breathed deeply and wondered what was expected of her. Her sister was sitting on her left and Victoriano on the other side of Carlota. If Salvador tried to take her hand and caress it, was she supposed to let him do it?

She began to giggle, remembering how girls back home in La Lluvia had thought that they could get pregnant by just holding an *americano's* hand. She watched the movie, eating popcorn, reaching into the bag and bumping his hand now and then. Oh, to be this close to a man. How far away that world of her childhood now seemed.

And there they were, two human beings, holding, feeling, breathing, staring at the screen, watching William Hart and his fine horse. Then the screen went dark, going into a nighttime scene, and Salvador reached for her hand, taking it.

Lupe gasped, and she didn't really want to, but her hand took on a life of its own, and she gripped Salvador's hand with such power that it frightened her.

Oh, Lupe was ready to scream, she was so excited! Oh, to touch, to feel, to truly come to know the warmth of another human being was so profound a sensation—why, she was trembling.

And Salvador was feeling the same intensity. Wonderful, hot feelings, palms growing damp and sweating, but still not being able to let go of her hand until the screen was bright again. Then, they quickly let go of each other, not wanting anyone to realize what was going on between them. They were reeling, shooting to the stars, two human beings knowing down deep inside themselves without a shadow of a doubt that this love that they were feeling came from God, and only from God.

The movie continued, dark and then bright, and they continued feeling magical—man and woman, finally touching, finally beginning the courtship of love after so many years of searching, yearning, and sometimes thinking that they'd die without fulfillment.

Dropping Lupe and her brother and sister off, Salvador drove over to see Archie to tell him that he couldn't stay in hiding. He had to go and see his mother and tell her about this miracle that he'd found.

But walking into the well-lit, almost empty poolhall, Salvador didn't find Archie. The smell of the hard night of smoking and drinking and sweating almost knocked Salvador off his feet.

The poolhall was the center of the barrio for the young men. It was the place where single men got their mail and came to drink bootleg whiskey in the alley and hang out with other men. It was as much the heart of life in the barrio for the men as the church was the lifeline for the women.

In the back, Salvador found Archie untying a couple of men that he'd arrested earlier. It also made good sense for the local law to own and run the poolhall, since that's where all the fights got started anyway.

"All right, guys," Archie was telling the two men, "now you two go home and sleep it off. I don't want to see either of you out again tonight or I'll take you out of town and make you walk home to cool off. Get me?"

Both men nodded and Archie told Don Viviano, the one-armed man who worked for him, to escort them out.

"So, it's been a good night, eh?" said Salvador once they were alone.

"Not bad," said Archie, grinning. "So how does it go with you, lover boy?"

"The best!" said Salvador.

"Well, that's great; I'm glad to hear that, but be careful. A man in love can be a very stupid *hombre*."

"That's what I got to talk to you about," said Salvador.

"Shoot," said Archie, closing the door.

"Well, you see," said Salvador, "my mother, she'd old, Archie, real old, and all my life we been close. So I got to go see her and tell her about Lupe," he said, breathing deeply, holding back an avalanche of emotion.

"Well, well," said the big lawman, pouring himself a drink. "I was close to my mother, too, Sal. But I just can't let you go up there right now. It could jeopardize everything I'm doing. You see, I told Wesseley that I got first-hand information that you're back in Jalisco and ain't never coming back, so he better just round out his report so he don't look bad and say that you were killed along with Julio and his wife in that wreck."

"You what?" said Salvador. "But don't that mean you need a third body?"

"Hell, getting dead bodies ain't no problem," said Archie. "Especially Mexicans. Hell, that's the easy part. The big problem is that I gotta convince Wesseley that it won't backfire on him later. Catcheee my lingo? Hell, these Fed bastards don't give a shit about justice, Sal. They just wanna look good in black and white so they can get their suck-points."

"All right," said Salvador, "then what you're saying is I got to stay put here in Carlsbad until you give me the word."

"Exactly," said Archie. "I can cover your ass here in the barrio, but I can't do shit for you if you leave."

Salvador didn't say anything. He was thinking, figuring how else he could get word to his mother.

"Don't even think it," said Archie. "Like I've told you, old Archie here ain't half dumb! Fuck up and I'll come down on you myself!"

Salvador started laughing. Archie knew him too well.

All that night, Salvador tossed and turned on the mattress on the floor in the back room of Kenny's garage. He dreamed he was a child once again and the soldiers were coming through their mountains, raping and plundering.

He jerked awake, sitting up in a bath of sweat. The dream had been so vivid, so real, he was still shaking. He thought of his mother, of all that they'd been through together, and he just knew he couldn't live another day without telling her about Lupe. What if his old mother died before she ever got to know that her struggle hadn't been in vain, that he'd truly met the woman of his highest dreams?

He got up. Archie or no Archie, he was going to take the bull by the horns and go up to Corona and see his old mother. But he had to be careful, very, very careful.

Borrowing Kenny's truck, Salvador took off before daybreak. He was just coming into the Anglo part of Corona when he saw his mother and Luisa walking up the street to the church. His mother looked so dark and tiny, all bent over with age, talking constantly as she went shuffling along. Luisa, on the other hand, was wide and fair-skinned, walking with power.

Salvador's whole heart came bursting into his eyes. Why, he'd just found a treasure worth a million dollars. His sister and mother—the two great women of his life—coming to the church so he could tell them both about his truelove.

Watching them climb the steps of the church along with the other people, Salvador saw something happen that twisted his heart. The well-dressed Anglos looked at his beloved mother and sister as if they were the plague. They moved away from his family with disgust.

Salvador pulled over and leaped out of the truck, wanting to kill the bastards. But he knew he couldn't afford to bring attention to himself. He calmed down and ran up the steps to his sister and mother.

"Luisa!" he called.

Seeing her brother, Luisa let out a shriek, startling the people about them. She grabbed her brother in her powerful arms, tears bursting from her eyes, she was so happy.

"Where have you been? she yelled. "We found Epitacio! You'll never believe it! He didn't desert us in Douglas! He was tricked and shipped north to Cheea-cago or some place like that." She continued speaking rapidly in Spanish. The people coming up the steps moved farther away from them. "And he found someone! Guess who!"

"Who?" asked Salvador, turning to his mother, releasing himself from his sister's bone-crushing *abrazo*.

"Domingo!" said his old mother, wiping the tears of joy from her old eyes.

"No!" cried Salvador.

"Yes," said the toothless old lady. "Epitacio says that he found a man named Domingo Villaseñor in Cheea-caco! So we hired Rodolfo to write a letter for us to that address! The teacher has beautiful penmanship. It will be a letter to respect when it arrives there." she added, eyes dancing with happiness.

"Oh, Mama! That's wonderful!" said Salvador.

"And that's not all," said Luisa, lowering her voice. "The police have left, so you can come home now."

"The ones in the orchard?" asked Salvador.

"Yes," said his mother.

"Oh, my God," said Salvador. "Someone really is watching out for us in heaven!"

"But of course," said his old mother, taking him in her skinny old arms. "Did you ever have doubt? Now come, let us go inside and give out thanks to the Almighty."

"Domingo, my God!" yelled Salvador. He just couldn't believe it; here he was, crazy in love, and they might have found one of his lost brothers, too.

Taking his mother by the arm, they went up the stairs and into the dark coolness of the high-ceilinged church.

The priest came out in his long robe, the same one who'd been watching Salvador, and the services began. Luisa and her mother fingered their rosaries, then went up to the altar to receive holy communion, the sacred body and blood of Christ. But Salvador didn't. Ever since he'd crossed the Rio Grande he'd avoided Our Savior.

After the services, their mother asked Salvador for five dollars to put in the poor box and she lit a candle for the American Postal Service so that God, in his Almighty wisdom, would help their letter get safely to Chicago.

They could hardly wait to get outside so they could continue talking.

"Is Epitacio at home right now?" asked Salvador.

They were outside on the steps of the church, and the sun was just beginning to get warm.

"No, he went to find work," said Luisa, "and I know what you're thinking, so stop it. He didn't desert us, he really didn't, so it's not his fault that you went to prison."

"Oh, so it's not his fault, eh?" said Salvador.

"Mama," said Luisa, "you tell Juan that he better be nice to Epitacio when he sees him or I'll brain him!"

"*Mi hijito*," said Doña Margarita, "your sister is right. We can't just go around blaming people about the past, because there are no 'ifs' in life. Remember the saying, 'If my aunt had balls she'd be my uncle.' Bygones have to be bygones or we'll go crazy. And not only because you went to prison, but everything! What if Don Pio had been able to speak to Don Porfirio? Then maybe there wouldn't have even been a Revolution and I'd still have my entire family," she said, tears coming to her eyes. "Or what if your father hadn't come into town and I'd never married and never had kids, eh? It's endless."

Salvador nodded. "All right, I'll keep all that in mind, Mama," he said. "But now, no more about this. I want to hear about Domingo, so then I can tell you my good news." But inside, his heart was pounding. He truly did blame Epitacio for all the misery that he'd endured.

"What good news?" asked his mother.

As they spoke, the tall priest came up behind them in the darkness. His eyes looked like he was up to no good.

"Well, one," said Salvador, trying to calm down, "it looks like a friend of mine is going to be able to fix it up so the cops will stop looking for me. You see," he continued, "Julio and his wife got killed in my car, so he's going to fix it so they think I'm dead, too."

"What?" said his mother, making the cross over herself. "Julio and his wife are dead? That's awful. I prayed for the cops to go after them, but I never meant for God to go this far."

"Oh, Mama," said Luisa, "do you really think you have that much power?"

"Of course," she said, making the sign of the cross again. "We're going to have to pray for their souls," she added.

"Thank you, Mama," said Salvador. "Julio was a good man. And also, from now on, call me 'Salvador,' " he said. "Juan, he's gone; he went back to Los Altos."

"I see," said his mother, "so my prayers have indeed been answered, and you can quit what you do and start a whole new life."

Salvador nodded. "Yes, I can."

"Good," said his mother, wiping the tears from her eyes, "and what else do you have to tell us? Did you meet Lupe's mother?"

Salvador's whole face lit up. He couldn't help himself. "Yes," he said, "I did."

Tears streamed like rivers from Doña Margarita's wrinkled-up old alligator eyes. "Oh, it gives me such joy to have lived to see this day!" she said. "The baby of my family in love, and one of my lost sons resurrecting from the dead. So tell us, don't waste time," said the old lady, kissing her rosary.

"Well," said Salvador, grinning ear-to-ear, "her mother is an old conniving she-fox. The first time I went over to see Lupe, she kept me at her side the entire evening, drawing blood with question after question, telling me that no daughter of hers will ever marry a drinking man. Then she explained to me all the vices of gambling!"

"Oh, that's wonderful!" said Doña Margarita. "A mother of any worth should protect her daughters."

"But not like this! My God, Mama, I never even got a chance to see Lupe that first night, except when she brought in the tea."

His mother and Luisa both laughed, enjoying Salvador's predicament.

"Why, I had to trick her mother the second night. I showed up with tickets for the movies so that I could get to see Lupe!" he said, half laughing, half angry.

"Good, I like what I hear so far," said Doña Margarita. "But I want to warn you, *mi hijito,* that these sound like very good, honest, God-fearing people and so we're going to have to put our heads together and figure out a campaign so you'll be able to win this girl's hand in marriage. You can't just go around tricking honest people with movie tickets, *mi hijito.* You got to give honest people what it is that they want."

"How?" asked Salvador, getting defensive. "By telling her mother the truth: that I'm a gambling man and I don't just drink liquor, I manufacture it, too?"

"Of course not, *mi hijito,*" said his mother calmly. "Honest, God-fearing people don't want to hear the truth. They want you to lie to them."

"Mama!" snapped Luisa, glancing up at the towering church. "Please, watch what you say! We're on the steps of the holy house of God!"

"So," said their mother, full of mischief, "do you really think that if we weren't on these steps the Almighty couldn't hear us?"

"Oh, Mama, please," said Luisa, getting more nervous by the moment, "don't talk like this," she pleaded, making the sign of the cross over herself, hoping that they wouldn't be struck down by lightning.

"Oh, *mi hijita,* you woman of such little faith! God respects my honesty that I admit that I lie. He's a hundred thousand years tired of people preaching the truth in His home, but then lying to all the world once they get away from the shadow of His domain!"

"Mama, stop it!" said Luisa. "I'm begging you, you're right, I know! But couldn't we just get off the steps and talk across the street?"

She looked so genuinely frightened, staring wide-eyed at the church, that Doña Margarita began to laugh.

"All right, if that will please you, Luisa," said their mother, "but keep in mind that lying and tricking are the very foundation of love and courtship! Like you, what did you do, *mi hijita,* when you went after Epitacio to marry you and you were big with child? You lied, you used every form of trickery that we've learned since Eve tempted Adam, and Maria told Joseph that God had visited her."

"Dear God, please don't listen to her!" shouted Luisa. "She doesn't know what she says, dear God! I didn't really lie! No, I just kind of, well, didn't tell the whole truth."

"Exactly!" said Doña Margarita. "And those are the best kind of lies! Always keep close to the truth, *mi hijito,* so in case you're caught ankle-deep in your own *caca,* you can crawl out."

"Oh, Mama!" screamed Luisa, rushing off the church steps as fast as she could go. "You're just awful!"

Seeing his sister flee, Salvador burst out laughing. Taking his mother's arm, they went across the street.

"So, I shouldn't trick her mother anymore, eh?" said Salvador, truly enjoying his mother. "I should just lie straight out."

"Precisely," said the old lady. "That's what honest, God-fearing people really want. They don't want the truth."

Salvador laughed again. "And you, what do you want, Mama?" he asked with a twinkle in his eye.

"Me? Well, I want the truth, of course," she said without hesitation. "My world isn't based on right and wrong, *mi hijito.* It's based on love and doing whatever a mother needs to get done to survive. Just like God in the heavens and His responsibilities of the universe, I'd lie ten thousand times a day to help my family."

"Then God doesn't hate us if we lie or cheat or swear?" asked Salvador, thinking back to that day when he'd cursed God at the Rio Grande.

"Ha!" said his mother. "And who's the biggest liar of all the universe? Giving us a mind that knows all the questions but none of the answers!" She laughed. "Why, God is the biggest lying jokester of all! Remember, He even created the devil just to amuse Himself with our predicament! No, of course, He won't hate you for lying or cheating or swearing if it helps you to survive. But, of course, you don't injure others."

"Oh, Mama," said Salvador, "I love you!"

"Of course you do," she said. "You had no other tit to suck the first year of your life. But now, no more of this; tell me more about her mother. And her father, too."

So Salvador told his mother and sister all he knew about Lupe's parents and brother and sister. And all this time, the priest was spying on them.

"Well," said his mother, kissing him goodbye, "you be careful and don't be tricky like the sneaky old raven with these people. You be stouthearted like the eagle and, also, pray for our letter to reach your brother."

"I will, Mama," said Salvador, hugging them both, feeling so good to have shared his good news with his mother and sister, and to hear about his brother Domingo.

"But remember," said his mother, "you don't just follow the crotch of your pants and promise her anything until I meet her. Men lie to women and women lie to men, but it is a very different matter between two people of the same sex. You mark my words; I must meet her. And I don't have much time. So move!"

"Yes, Mama," he said, kissing her again.

Back in Carlsbad, Lupe was growing anxious. The sun was starting down and Salvador hadn't come by to see her. Last night at the movie house, they had held hands and been so close. Oh, it angered her to realize that she'd allowed herself to get so touched by a man that she hardly knew.

It was getting late and Lupe decided to join Manuelita and the others who were going to the seashore. If Salvador came by and missed her, she didn't care. In fact, she'd feel relieved. It just wasn't proper for a lady to care so much for any man. No, she'd seen what it had done to her sister Maria with Esabel. Maria was now much better off with Andres, who was a good man, although she didn't love him very much. Besides, Salvador didn't know much about her, so there was no real reason for him to respect her or admire her the way Mark did. She quit thinking of Salvador and began to think of Mark and of all the wonderful walks that they'd had coming home from the library.

It was low tide and the rocks and tidepools were visible down below the bluffs. Taking off their shoes, Lupe and the girls climbed down to the wet, cool sand. Lupe walked alongside Manuelita; Carlota and Cuca and Uva went up ahead of them.

"I just don't know what to do," said Lupe to Manuelita. "Before, I only had thoughts for Mark, but now I'm not so sure. And Mama keeps insisting that I tell her everything but, well, a part of me just doesn't want to tell her everything."

"Then don't," said Manuelita.

"But if I don't, then she worries so much and, yet, if I do, then she'll . . . oh, I just don't know what to do, Manuelita! I still haven't even told her about Mark's proposal!"

"Don't torture yourself," said Manuelita, taking Lupe's hand. "We have to admit that we both have mothers that are, well, to put it mildly, so strong-willed that if we don't keep quiet about part of our lives, we'd never have any privacy!"

Lupe laughed. "Yes, that is true," she said.

"Of course it is," said Manuelita. "How do you think I ever managed to get engaged? I kept quiet about everything until the last moment!"

"No! Really?"

"Of course," said Manuelita, glancing around to make sure they wouldn't be overheard. She drew in close to Lupe, talking a mile a minute, telling Lupe everything.

Just then, Salvador drove up above them on the bluff in his long, ivory-white automobile. He'd stopped by Kenny's and bathed and changed his clothes. Then he'd gone to the camp and was told that the girls had gone to the beach.

Spotting the five young women below him, Salvador breathed in so deeply that his nostrils narrowed and then went wide and dark. Why, Lupe looked like a living picture, walking along the surf with her girlfriends. She was taller than the others, looking as graceful as a deer moving up the coastline with the glistening sunlight in her hair and her long, muscular arms moving as she spoke. It was a picture that Salvador would take to his grave.

Quickly, he backed up his car and drove farther up the beach. Getting out, he sneaked down the bluff through the brush. He could see Cuca, Uva, Carlota, and right behind them, Lupe and Manuelita. As they approached, Salvador stepped out from behind the brush.

"Good evening!" he said, taking off his hat.

They all turned, giggling with surprise, except for Lupe. She was mad. He'd shown up late, causing her to worry.

Seeing her anger, Salvador put on his panama and, as he came across the sand to them, something very interesting happened. Cuca, who was the closest one to him, gave him the eye and a movement of hips. And Lupe, seeing her friend's flirtatious behavior, forgot her anger; and with fire in her eyes, she walked straight up to him and took his arm very possessively.

Salvador wanted to laugh, but he didn't. He and Lupe walked arm-in-arm up the seashore. Good old jealousy did it every time; as surely as greed did it in the game of cards, jealousy gave you the edge in the game of love.

The girls followed behind them, laughing and talking and, in the distance, they could see the Oceanside pier jutting out into the dark blue sea.

Lupe and Salvador smelled the salt air and watched the right eye of God turn into liquid flame as it slid down into the flat, blue sea. They walked on, touching, talking, brushing up against each other.

Then it was time to turn around. The four other girls ran ahead. It was almost dusk by the time they all got back to the Moon automobile.

They drove back to the migrants' encampment where the tents were lit up like glowing paper bags with candles inside them. And there they were: the two old lionesses guarding the castle's entrance.

"You're late!" snapped Doña Manza to her daughters.

"It's my fault," said Salvador quickly.

"Oh, no it's not!" said Doña Guadalupe. "These girls have minds of their own!"

"I told you so, Lupe!" said Carlota.

"Carlota!" snapped Lupe. "You never said any such thing!"

"Enough! All of you!" said Doña Guadalupe. "Now go inside and make some tea while we talk to Salvador!"

The girls obeyed their mothers. Salvador nodded nervously to Don Victor. "Whatever you say, ladies," he said. "But before you start, well, I'd like to tell you that I drove up to Corona this morning and saw my mother, and she told me the most wonderful news that I've heard in years."

"Oh, and what might that be?" asked Lupe's mother, still pretending to be upset. But she wasn't, really; it was mostly just an act. A mother could never be too careful.

"My brother Domingo," he said, "we'd lost him back in Mexico in the Revolution, and we think we've found him."

"Oh, that's wonderful!" said Doña Guadalupe. "Especially for your mother! The very same thing happened to us. Sophia, one of my older daughters, came ahead of us to the United States and we'd heard that she'd drowned at sea. But then, years later, we found her in Santa Ana. So, please, sit down and tell us all about this."

"Well, of course," said Salvador, feeling good to be in control once again.

Finishing the story, Salvador thought that he'd done a wonderful job and he figured the two old she-boars weren't going to drill him with any questions tonight. But he was wrong.

When Lupe and the girls came out with the tray of tea and sweetbreads, they were told to go back inside. Then, Lupe's mother came after him, wanting blood.

"Well," she said, "now getting back to our conversation of the other night, I want to ask you what you think of the Mexican tradition that says that money should only be handled by men."

Salvador almost spilled his tea. "Well, to tell the truth," he said, putting his cup down, "I've never thought too much of it."

Lupe's mother glanced at Doña Manza. "Well, to be perfectly frank," she continued, "my *comadre* and I have spoken of this topic at great length and we think that this custom of ours that says money should never be put in the hands of women and children isn't just wrong, but actually destructive for the very survival of the family."

"Oh, I see," he said. "I never thought of that."

"Of course not," she said, going right on without hesitation, "because tradition tells you that men are free to do with the money as they please and the church agrees with them, making our tradition sound as if it came straight from God. And so no one ever questions it. But my *comadre* and I, who raised our children alone half of the time, were forced to think of this," she continued, "and so we can't possibly agree with this very Mexican belief that men alone were made superior by God to handle money. In fact, personally, I'll go so far as to say that I believe that some women are more capable of handling money than men."

And saying this, she stopped and stared at Salvador straight in the eyes, daring him to contradict her.

But Salvador gave her nothing, then taking a deep breath he glanced at Don Victor, who must have known what was in store for him this night, because he winked at Salvador.

"Yes, of course, I can see what you mean," said Salvador calmly. But inside his soul, he was raging. He'd never heard such talk in all his life. The first time, this old woman had said that cards and liquor were worse than war for marriage, and now she was saying that women were more capable of handling money than men. This was blasphemy! Why, the Pope, himself, was a man! And Jesus Christ had put him in charge of mankind's destiny on earth!

But before Salvador could say anything, the old lady went right on. "And to go further," she said, "I'll tell you this: I believe that women, with their instincts of a mother protecting her young, have the obligation for the survival of the family to handle the money that their husbands make. And I don't say this lightly or with malice or with ignorance. No, I say this from what I've seen again and again all my life. And if a man is a man, he, too, can open his eyes and see this very important fact. Money must be used for the good of the entire family and not just for a man's arrogant need of cards and liquor!"

Salvador put down his sweetbread. Why, next she'd be saying that a son-in-law's obligation was to turn his paycheck over to his mother-in-law.

"And now, Salvador," she said, sitting back, "what do you think?" she asked, smiling. "And be perfectly frank. Because, after all, what I've just said is far removed from the common ideas of our people. So, of course, it would be unfair of me to not understand a young man being disturbed with these ideas of mine." And there she stopped, smiling such a sweet, innocent little smile that Salvador almost laughed. Why, she was as cunning as his own mother.

He took a deep breath and glanced at Doña Manza. She, too, was smiling sweetly. He glanced down at his shoes, trying to gain time and think of how his own mother would handle this situation. But looking down, he saw that his beautiful black and white shoes were covered with flies. The bacon grease that he'd taken from Kenny's kitchen to shine his shoes with had melted and attracted all these flies. And one big horsefly was stuck on the tip of his right shoe, crawling around in a circle, making desperate sounds as it tried to get free. His mind went blank. He could think of nothing. And yet, he fully realized that this was the most important test of his life, if he ever hoped to marry Lupe.

Glancing up, he saw that both women were also staring at his shoes. He turned crimson with embarrassment and reached down, pinching the fly off his shoe, then brought out his red silk handkerchief, wiping off his hand.

"Well," he said, wishing that he had a pint bottle of whiskey so he could take a good swig. "What can I say?" he continued, brushing the crumbs off his pant legs from the sweetbread he'd eaten. "Except that you're right, *señora*, absolutely right." He figured that he'd lie straight out, but that he wouldn't stray too far from the truth, in case he had to eat his own lies some day. Oh, it was a good thing that his mother had prepared him or he'd be feeling pretty helpless right now.

"And my dear mother would be in complete agreement with you," he added, not quite knowing where he was going, but hoping to wing it. "For I remember my parents' arguments when I was small and, most of the time, they were about money. My father was a hard worker—the hardest—and excellent with horses and cattle, too, but he just wasn't good with money."

He glanced into the well-lit tent and he saw Lupe and the other young women. Carlota was giggling and pointing at his shoes. He breathed deeply, brushing the rest of the crumbs off his pants, and stomped his feet, getting rid of the flies, then coughed, clearing his voice.

"And so, as I was saying," he said, "my father was a big, handsome man with a huge, red two-handled moustache and he had tremendous power for fighting and working. But, still, even as a child, I somehow knew that my mother knew more about money matters than he did. Once, I'll never forget, we were up on the slopes and he got so mad at our goats that he began to yell and scream. A shrewd businessman happened to come by on horseback.

" 'Don Juan,' he said to my father, 'I'll take those troublesome goats off your hands right now. Here's a twenty peso gold piece.' And before my older brother Jose could say a word, my father said, 'All right. Give me the money, you got a deal!'

"And so, angrily, my father took the money, sent my brother and me home, and went to town to drink. When he got home that night, my poor mother—who, in the meantime, had borrowed and scraped together all the money she could from friends and relatives—said to my father, 'Look, Don Juan, you must go back to that man you sold our goats to and buy them back. Here is twenty-five pesos gold. Let him make a five-peso profit, but get our goats back. We need them to live.'

"But my father said, 'I can't do that, woman! I made a deal with that man and my word is my honor!' 'But, Juan,' pleaded my mother, 'those goats are our life. The cattle and horses don't give us the money we need to buy our staples. It's the cheese that we make from the goat milk that buys our supplies in town. Please, I beg of you, take this money and go back to that man. Tell him you were angry this morning and you weren't in your best frame of mind and he'll understand.'

"You would have thought my mother had insulted my father, for he turned on her with such a rage, yelling at her, 'Woman, are you crazy? No Villaseñor has gone back on his word in five hundred years!'

" 'But, Don Juan,' begged my mother, 'that man tricked you. He knows about your famous temper, so he took advantage of you.'

"Well, I'm embarrassed to tell you, *señora*, but my father—a gigantic man, whose family had come from northern Spain—then grabbed my poor little mother and shouted into her face like a wild man, 'No man takes advantage of a Villaseñor and lives!' he bellowed.

"And so he got his gun to go kill the man and my mother had to turn around and plead with him that everything was all right and maybe it hadn't been such a bad deal. But still, since she'd already raised the money, could he please go back to that man and talk reasonably to him and get their goats back."

"And your father?" said Doña Guadalupe, looking very concerned, "was he also one of these men that hit women?"

Instantly, Salvador could see where the old woman was headed with this one. "No," he said, breathing deeply. "My father had many faults, but that wasn't one of them." And he wasn't lying; it was true.

"I'm glad to hear that," said Doña Guadalupe. "Go on." She glanced toward the tent, hoping that the girls were listening. And, of course, they were. Especially Lupe and Manuelita, who were catching every single word.

"And so that night my poor mother begged my father as no wife should ever have to beg," continued Salvador. " 'Querido,' she said, 'please, understand me, I'm not complaining that you spent part of the money. Please, believe me, I'm only saying that we need those goats back.'

"But my father never heard my mother's words. No, he just flew into another rage, saying if she wasn't complaining, then why in the devil was she bringing it all up! And then he shouted that he was a Villaseñor and that he came from kings and no little . . ." But here, Salvador stopped, tears coming to his eyes, remembering how his father had next called his mother *una india pendeja*, a stupid, backward, ignorant Indian. And that night, his brother Jose, the great, left their home never to set foot in it again while his father was there. Oh, Jose's eyes had burned like fire, wanting to kill their father.

"And so, well, to make it short," said Salvador, never having meant to go this far, "I can truly say that I sympathize with you, *señora*. For that shrewd businessman robbed my father, and we went hungry that year." Salvador tried to stop, but he just couldn't. He was hot, wishing that he'd been big enough to knock his own father down!

"So, yes, *señora*, to answer your question, I can honestly say with all my heart that I agree with you one thousand times one thousand! That a man is not necessarily superior to a woman in handling money!" He wanted to stop, he truly did, but he just couldn't. "In fact, it has been my experience to find almost the opposite to be true!" he yelled. "I have found that women—with their instincts of the mother pig protecting her young—are often more capable of handling the family finances than men!

"My mother, I swear it," he said, standing up and pounding the air with his huge fists, "if she'd handled our money, we would have never come to ruin, even in the middle of the Revolution!" His hands were fists and he didn't want to, but he couldn't help himself, and he struck the heavy crate that he'd been sitting on with such force that it shattered into pieces. "We went hungry after my father sold those goats!" he bellowed, the cords of his neck coming up like ropes. "Hungry! And I'd never seen this, *señora*, until now! But that was the beginning of our destruction! And my poor mother, what could she do? Nothing! Even when she turned to Jose, my older brother, and tried to get him to come back home and talk things over, my father was against it, and gave the reins of our family to Alejo, who was blue-eyed like himself!"

When Salvador finally stopped, he could see that everyone was staring at him. He tried to apologize, to say that he was sorry, but he was still so upset that he could do nothing but tremble like a leaf.

Getting to her feet, Doña Guadalupe took each of his big hands in hers. "It's a heart-warming experience to find a young man as strong and capable as you who can also see the predicament of women. Your mother must be a great, great woman to have raised such a son!"

"She is," said Salvador, wiping his eyes, "she really is, thank you."

"The pleasure is all mine," said Doña Guadalupe. "Would you like to come and join us for dinner tomorrow?" she asked.

"Why, yes, I'd like that," he said.

"Good, and please come early so we can continue our conversation."

"I will," he said.

And just then, as they were talking, a cat came up and started licking Salvador's shoes. Salvador didn't move, hoping to God that the cat would go away.

"Well," laughed Lupe's mother, "at least you didn't frighten the animals," she said.

"How could he?" said Carlota, coming out of the tent with the other girls, "wearing shoes that smell like *chicharrones*!" Carlota laughed, and she would've gone on ridiculing Salvador if Don Victor hadn't chased the animal away.

"Enough!" he said to Carlota. "I, too, have put bacon grease on my shoes many times. It preserves the leather and makes it waterproof." He stuck out his hand to Salvador. "I salute you!" he said. "I don't know of any man who could've stood up better than you have under the fire of these women!"

"The pleasure was mine," said Salvador, taking his hand. "And I'm sorry about the crate. I just got so mad, thinking of our goats and the hunger we went through, that, well, I just . . ."

"There's no need to explain yourself. It was a terrible Revolution for all of us," said the old man. "I respect you; you are a real *macho*!"

"Well, thank you, but really I didn't mean to hit that crate," he said again, hoping that this wouldn't be the straw that broke the burro's back in his relationship with Lupe. Oh, this lying business wasn't turning out as simple as his mother had made it seem. He was exposing a lot more of himself than he'd ever expected.

That evening Lupe walked Salvador to his automobile and, when he opened the door to get in, she did something that told him everything. She took his hand, whispering, "Thank you for being so gracious." And she squeezed his hand, eyes dancing.

Driving back to Kenny's place that night, the Moon was still filled with Lupe's smell, and Salvador could still feel her hand in his hand and see her dancing eyes looking like stars in the heavens. Oh, he was so crazy in love that he couldn't come down. He was up in the clouds, sailing through heaven, feeling God's breath.

It was still dark the next morning when Archie came bursting into Kenny's garage, grabbing Salvador where he slept on the floor.

"Wake up!" he said, yanking him to his feet, "and get your ass in gear! I need five more barrels!"

"What the hell you talking about?" said Salvador, still half asleep.

"You're free," said Archie, grinning.

Salvador straightened up. "I'm free?"

"Yep," said Archie. "Wessely's gone!"

"Jesus! That's wonderful!" screamed Salvador, leaping to his feet. "I'm free! I'm free! No more looking over my shoulder all the time! Jesus Christ, I love you Archie!" He grabbed Archie in a bear hug, lifting the huge man off the ground and kissed him.

"Put me down, you crazy son-of-a-bitch!" yelled Archie. "Get me five barrels to show your appreciation! Not this kissing shit!"

Shaking his head at the sight of them, Kenny brought out a quart of whiskey.

"Well, about your barrels," said Salvador, putting Archie down, "I'm gonna need a little time to set up another distillery so I can pay you, Archie."

"You mean you've sold the rest of my liquor out from under me?" asked Archie.

"Well, not exactly, but I only got two or three barrels left," lied Salvador, fully realizing that a month's time wasn't up yet and this was a shakedown. "Everyone and his brother has been begging me for whiskey."

Archie started laughing. "Why, that damned Wesseley made you rich, locking up all 'em other bootleggers!"

Salvador nodded.

"Shit, I want another free barrel per month, or I'm telling Wesseley he made you a rich man!"

"You bastard!"

"Never denied that," said Archie. "But you better start making some whiskey *pronto*! Out by Escondido."

"You'll cover me out there?" asked Salvador.

Archie grinned. "No one searches that close to the border. They figure folks down there just mosey over to old Mexico for their whiskey."

"And I gotta pay you protection for that?"

"You damned right! Ain't nothing free in this life but your mama's tit!"

Kenny came up with some glasses and the quart of whiskey, pouring a round of drinks. They all saluted and drank down. Salvador felt wonderful. There really was a God in the heavens. He was free at last, and in love, too.

Drinking a few shots, the three of them decided to go up to the Montana

Cafe for breakfast. Taking a booth in the cafe, Helen suggested the morning's special of two big juicy pork chops and four eggs.

"Great!" said Salvador. "And I'm buying!" He was floating ten feet off the ground. After all these years of suffering, things finally seemed to be going his way.

That same morning, Salvador asked Kenny to go with him to Oceanside to buy a good used truck from Harvey Swartz. Then Salvador put on his old work clothes and drove north three hours to Los Angeles. He wanted to buy another stove and kettle so he could set up a new distillery.

When he arrived at the big wholesale house in downtown L.A., Salvador got the terrible feeling that something wasn't quite right. He drove around the block and then took off. He'd make his own stove and kettle. And Salvador's instincts were right. Across the street, the FBI had set up a team of agents to watch the building.

Driving back south to Carlsbad, Salvador decided to swing by Corona and see his family and tell them the wonderful news. Also, he wanted to look Epitacio in the eyes and have the son-of-a-bitch tell him that he hadn't deserted them, the lying bastard!

Everyone stared at Salvador as he came down the rutted street of the barrio. Men watched him from behind their fenced-in gardens, whispering to their sons about him. Salvador was the man who had refused to die, *el macho* that even the *gringo* cops couldn't kill. He was a man so fearless that the blood ran backwards from his heart.

And, of course, every man, woman and child in the barrio knew that Salvador was wanted by the law, but not one of them would even dream of saying anything to the Anglo law. For Salvador took care of his family; he was an example of what a *mejicano* could be if only he carried his balls with pride.

Salvador parked and got out of his truck. Jose rushed out the door with Pedro right behind him.

"Uncle, Uncle!" shouted Jose.

Salvador hadn't seen his nephews since that terrible day he had taken off for Mexico, escaping for his life. Jose grabbed his uncle in a big *abrazo*, kissing him. Then, Pedro came.

"Pantsing any more teachers?" asked Salvador.

"Oh, no, Uncle!" said Pedro, hugging Salvador, too.

"I'm glad to hear that," said Salvador. "Because I'm proud of both of you. The other day, when I saw your mother, she told me you two have become men of respect!"

He held both boys closely. His old mother and Luisa came, and behind Luisa was a small, older, chubby man with white hair at his temples. Salvador couldn't believe his eyes. It was Epitacio. He'd aged tremendously.

Seeing her brother stare at her husband, Luisa put her arm around

Epitacio protectively. "Juan," she said, "I mean Salvador," she added, correcting herself, "you got to talk to Mama, she's gone crazy! Now she wants that schoolteacher to start writing a letter every day to Chee-a-caco!"

"Don't listen to her," said their mother, grinning. "I know what I'm doing!" She came up and took Salvador by the arm, leading him away. "You see," she said, "I went to church the other day and I spoke to the Virgin Mary, woman-to-woman, telling her of my grief at having lost so many sons, and then I had this vision."

"A vision?" asked Salvador.

"Yes, and it was so beautiful," she said. "I'd been inside the church, praying for hours—realizing that maybe the letters we sent to Domingo hadn't reached him—when suddenly, Christ came down to me from the cross, as surely as you stand here, and He spoke to me so calmly that I was suddenly filled with this power, this strength, this glowing fire inside me and—"

"Just wait," said Salvador, cutting in. "I thought you said that it was the Virgin Mary you spoke to."

"Oh, it was," she said. "But you know how Her Son is always putting His nose into everything."

"Oh, I didn't know that," said Salvador, glancing at Luisa, wondering if their mother had finally broke. "Then you're saying that Christ and Mary both spoke to you in this vision, eh?"

"Exactly," she said. "and the three of us got together, and we came up with the plan. That's why I need a little money so I can hire Don Rodolfo to write a letter for me every day."

"I see," said Salvador. "But one thing I don't quite get, Mama; if you have Jesus Christ and His Most Holy Mother already helping you, then why do you need money for a schoolteacher?"

His mother burst out laughing. "Because Don Rodolfo won't write the letters for free, since that's how he makes his living, and the American Postal Service still costs money, *mi hijito*."

"But, Mama, hasn't the schoolteacher already sent two or three letters to the address that Epitacio gave you?"

His old mother shouted with *gusto*. "That's the whole point! We sent those letters to the right address! And now I want to send letters to the wrong addresses!"

Straightening up, Salvador stared at his mother. "But why in God's name do you want to send a letter to the wrong address, Mama?" he asked, struggling to keep calm.

"Because the Virgin and her Son told me to," she said, making the sign of the cross. "For we want the neighbors on the left of where Domingo used to live to get a letter and the neighbors on the right, and the neighbors across the street! I want all those people on that street to get letters, for blocks and blocks, until everyone knows about this man named Domingo Villaseñor!

"I want their curiosity to get so strong, *mi hijito*, that they'll start opening the letters and reading them. And seeing Rodolfo's fine penmanship, they'll come to know that a serious mother from California is in search of her lost son. And then these mothers in Cheee-a-caca will start talking amongst themselves and soon they'll all be searching for my son.

"For, I swear to you, the Virgin told me that a mother is a mother, no matter where on earth, and so they'll take my toil to their hearts, and soon all of Cheee-a-caca—no matter how big it is—will join in our search! Mothers and sons, daughters and fathers, and then, soon even the police and the mayor himself! And, in no time, Domingo will be found and sent home to us! I swear to you before God, before His Most Sacred Son and His Most Sacred Holy Mother, that this will come to pass!"

Salvador saw the fire—the glow in his mother's old, wrinkled-up eyes—and he knew that the powers of heaven had, indeed, spoken to her. She was glowing, burning, shooting through the heavens like a timeless star!

"Twenty is all you need, Mama?" he asked.

"Oh, make it thirty! For, remember, even God needs help for making miracles."

"Then, here, take fifty!" he said, taking out his bankroll. His mother wasn't crazy. No, she was riding on God's wings.

He gave her the money and they went inside to eat. Salvador told his mother and sister about his latest adventure with Lupe's mother. He explained to them Doña Guadalupe's idea of money, that it had to be protected by the woman for the survival of the family.

"She's absolutely right!" screamed Luisa, poking at Epitacio in the ribs. "See? I'm not the only one who thinks that way," she said to him.

Epitacio said nothing. He just sat there quietly.

"Oh, I like this woman!" said Doña Margarita. "I think that she and I will get along just fine!"

"But, Mama," said Salvador, "sometimes I don't even think I'm courting Lupe; it's as if it's her mother that I'm really courting."

Doña Margarita burst out laughing. "That's as it should be!" she said.

When they were done eating, Salvador told them about his other wonderful news.

"And so," he said, "because of Julio's and Geneva's death," he swallowed hard, "Archie was able to fix it up, and now I'm free, Mama. I'm free for the first time since I escaped from that road camp in Arizona. I'm not going to have to be looking over my shoulder anymore."

"Oh, *mi hijito*," said Doña Margarita, "this is a moment I've prayed for. I'm so happy for you." She took him in her arms. "I feel terrible about Julio and Geneva, especially with the children they left behind, but God works in mysterious ways."

"The children are with their aunt," said Salvador. "They're okay."

"Good," said the old woman.

"This is wonderful," said Luisa. "And now that you're going to start a new distillery, I'm wondering if Epitacio couldn't work for you?"

"What?" said Salvador.

"There's no work anywhere in the area," continued Luisa, "so I was wondering if Epitacio couldn't . . ."

"But this is the son-of-a-bitch who got me put in jail!" screamed Salvador, leaping to his feet and the cords of his neck coming up like rope. He turned to Epitacio. "All right, you want a job, Epitacio? Then we got to talk, goddammit!"

"No!" screamed Luisa, getting to her feet, too. "You leave him alone!"

"Leave him alone?" yelled Salvador. "It was you who started this whole thing! I was talking about my freedom, and you bring up this piece of dog-shit that put me in jail in the first place!"

"That's not true!" yelled Luisa.

"Luisa, please," said Epitacio. "He's right. He's got to talk to me."

"But he wants to kill you, you fool!" she yelled, getting between them. "He blames you for everything bad that's happened to us!"

"Luisa," said Epitacio as calmly as he could, "it's between Juan, I mean Salvador and me." He got to his feet.

"Come on!" bellowed Salvador, kicking the screen door off its hinges as he went out.

"Don't go!" screamed Luisa. "You'll never come back!"

But Epitacio didn't obey her. He followed Salvador out the door, and they got into his new truck and drove off.

Jose ran down the street, saw which way they were headed, and took off through the orchard. Pedro was right behind him. Luisa stood there, bellowing like a cow who'd lost her young. The neighbors came out of their houses. Luisa continued bellowing. Only Doña Margarita didn't seem affected by the whole thing. She went back inside and brought out a bottle of whiskey and served herself a shot.

"*Que chinga*," she said, laughing. "You chop the head off of one of Satan's snakes, and the devil presents you with two more."

She drank down her drink.

Driving out of the barrio, Salvador circled the orchard until he was out of sight. Parking alongside the fruit trees, he drew his .45 out of his jacket and rammed it into Epitacio's mouth with such force that he split open his brother-in-law's lips, bloodying his face.

"Go on, tell me!" he screamed, "that you didn't desert us, so I can shoot your brains out!"

Blood was dripping off Epitacio's chin. But still, he held himself well. "Juan! Juan!" he said. "Shoot me, go on, shoot me if you must! But realize that I didn't desert you!"

"Then why the hell didn't you come back?"

"Please, the gun, the gun," he said, staring cross-eyed down the barrel of the gun. "I can't talk like this."

Staring at him in the eyes, Salvador uncocked the huge .45 and took it out of Epitacio's face. Beads of sweat were gathering on Salvador's forehead.

And behind them, in the orchard, came Jose and Pedro, sneaking through the trees.

"Well, after we lost our checks . . ." began Epitacio.

"You lost 'em! Not 'we,' you bastard!"

"I mean, after I lost our checks, well, I got so scared of what Luisa would do to me that I took off. And I got all the way back down to Texas before I realized that I had no life except with your family."

"Bullshit!" said Salvador, leveling the .45 between his eyes again. "You're going to die!"

"No, for the love of God!" cried Epitacio. "You are my family! And I wanted to come back to you! But the rangers arrested me, saying that I was drunk, and I hadn't touched a drop. They beat me and put me in jail," he continued, beginning to cry. "Then they shipped me off with over a hundred other *mejicanos* to Cheee-a-cago to work in the slaughterhouses, I swear it!"

"And you want me to believe this bullshit?" asked Salvador, cocking the hammer of the big automatic.

Not being able to stand it anymore, Pedro started around the tree to save his father. But Jose grabbed him. "Keep still," said the older boy. "If he was going to kill him, he'd already done it!"

"I went to jail because of you!" bellowed Salvador. "I was beaten and had my guts cut open!"

"Hit me!" said Epitacio. "Hit me like you hit my son, but don't shoot me!"

"Hit you like I hit your son?" said Salvador, taken aback.

"Yes, beat me! Beat me!" said Epitacio, breaking down in sobbing cries. "I didn't want to leave! Why else would I come back to Douglas looking for you, then search for you, all the way here to California, if it isn't true? I never meant to desert you, Juan! I swear it before God!"

Breathing deeply, Salvador uncocked the .45 and lowered it. He looked at the frightened man for a long time. His story made sense, but still he couldn't really believe him. There was just something about his eyes, his crying little ways, his entire person, that filled him with disgust.

But what could he do? Kill him and draw attention to himself, exactly what Archie had told him not to do? Salvador got out of the truck, still raging, still angry, still unsatisfied after all these years of dreaming of killing this little rat, and he fired the huge .45 into the ground in frustration, emptying the entire seven-shot clip, filling the air with thundering sound. Jose and Pedro came screaming out of the orchard in terror.

"Don't shoot, Uncle! Don't shoot!"

"You crazy kids!" screamed Salvador, now more upset than ever. "Don't ever come sneaking up on an armed man! I could've killed you!"

It was a long, exhausting drive back to their two houses. They were all drained, completely spent.

Salvador hired Epitaco and drove back down to Carls-
bad. He had to see if Kenny could help him build a kettle and reinforce a
white-gas-burning stove. He decided to not go by Lupe's for dinner until
he'd calmed down. He was just too crazy. He'd break crates right and left,
the way he was feeling right now.

For two days, he and Epitacio worked around the clock with Kenny
building the kettle. Epitacio joked and told stories and, little by little,
Salvador began to forget about all the hate that he'd been carrying inside his
soul for this little man. The poor man was probably telling the truth. It
wasn't that he'd really wanted to desert them; he'd just been afraid of Luisa's
wrath. And then he'd been taken by the Texas Rangers in the sea of people
escaping from the Mexican Revolution and was shipped to Chicago.

On the third day, Salvador took a bath and got
dressed so he could go to see Lupe. The sun was going down as he drove up
the line of tents. He had two bouquets of flowers this time: one for Lupe's
mother and the other for Doña Manza. But, on arriving at their tent, he
braked in horror. The tent looked empty.

He jumped out of his Moon and rushed up to the long tent and opened
the front flap. Everything was gone. His stomach turned, and he felt he'd
vomit. He grabbed hold of the tent, steadying himself, not knowing what to
think. It almost felt as if they'd never existed, as if these wonderful people
and his whole courtship had been nothing but a dream.

His mind went reeling. He remembered how he'd broken the crate, and
he guessed that they'd left because they didn't want Lupe seeing him
anymore. Oh, he'd been a fool. A man like him could never end up with a
girl like Lupe. She was an angel, and he was nothing but a dirty, filthy
monster. He wiped his eyes, beginning to tremble.

Down the way, an old woman recognized Salvador's car and came up the
line of tents to him. "Are you looking for *la trensuda* and her family?" she
asked.

Salvador turned and looked at the old woman. "Yes," he said, "I'm
looking for the family who lived here." He figured that the old lady was
referring to Doña Guadalupe's braided hair by calling her *la trensuda*.

"They left yesterday," she said. "They went up the coast to Santa Ana
with the other people, following the crops."

"Oh, the crops!" said Salvador, remembering that the harvest was almost
over here in Carlsbad and so, of course, it was time for the fieldworkers to
move on. It wasn't his fault that they'd left, after all. No, it had nothing to
do with him. He felt much better.

"Thank you very much," he said to the old lady. "And here, I brought
these flowers for you," he added, handing her both bouquets."

"*Muchas gracias*," said the old woman, taking the flowers graciously.

But driving away, Salvador got to thinking and realized it wasn't all that simple, either. Lupe's family had extended a formal invitation to him to come to dinner at their home, and he hadn't even had the decency to come by and say he couldn't make it.

By God, he'd been a fool. They'd probably even prepared a special meal for him. He decided that he should go up and see them as quickly as he could and straighten things out. But, no, he couldn't do that, either. First, he had to rent a house in Escondido and get the fermentation process going. After all, he'd be no good to anybody if he didn't take care of his business first and have money in his pocket.

These were very hard times. Luisa hadn't been exaggerating when she'd said that Epitacio hadn't been able to find work. There were thousands of people out of work. Only the fastest and hardest-working people were finding employment.

He breathed deeply, hoping to God that Lupe and her family weren't too angry with him.

The day Lupe and her family left Carlsbad, heading north for Santa Ana, Lupe, Carlota and their parents rode in the back of the neighbor's truck. Victoriano rode up front so he could learn to drive. Lupe was feeling very quiet. It had truly upset her the evening that Salvador hadn't shown up for dinner and her parents had gotten into a terrible argument.

Her mother had bought a piece of pork, a luxury they rarely afforded, and she'd prepared a wonderful meal for them. Then when they waited and waited and Salvador didn't show up, her father had told her mother off.

"You and your big mouth," Don Victor had said to her mother, "you drove the poor man off with your endless talk!"

Lupe had never seen her father so angry and her mother began to cry. Lupe now watched the sun go down into the flat, smooth water as they drove north. Just south of San Clemente, one of the trucks in their caravan broke down and they all got out to stretch their legs. Lupe and some of the younger people walked down the wide valley, past the fields of produce, to the sea. The moon came up, and the crickets began making noise and the first stars began to shine.

Lupe took off her shoes and wiggled her toes into the cool wet sand and she thought of Salvador and how they'd walked on the seashore together a few evenings before. She thought of Mark and all the hours they'd spent together in the library. Then she remembered that she'd promised Mark to have an answer for him about his proposal when she returned to Santa Ana.

She breathed deeply, looking out at the sea. There was just no way that she was ready to give Mark an answer. Salvador had come into her life and touched her, really touched her, and yet . . . well, she didn't really know Salvador. For all she knew he could be a raven in the disguise of an eagle. She thought of Mark and how tall and handsome and truly gentle he was. Why, he was as different from Salvador as any man could possibly be.

She thought of her Colonel and she thought of Sophia and her first marriage with Don Tiburcio. She thought of Maria and her first marriage with Esabel. She thought of the two fine men that her sisters now had. Oh, love was so complicated. And when she'd been little, love had seemed like the easiest thing in the world.

Getting to the caravan, she found her father and mother all cuddled up together in the back of the truck. They looked like angels with their arms wrapped around each other. She had to smile. Looking at them at this moment, no one would have ever guessed how angry they'd been with each other just the other night.

She took a blanket and covered her parents, feeling a pleasant strangeness. It was almost as if she were now the adult and her two old parents had become the children. She decided that she definitely wasn't ready to say yes or no to any man about marriage. Love, after all, her mother had always told her, was just so special that you had to be more careful with it than anything else in life.

FIVE

A TIME OF MIRACLES

It was payday. Lupe was in line with her sisters and their families to get paid when it happened again. The paymaster wasn't going to pay the women as much as he paid the men.

"Why not?" said Sophia softly. "We work as much as the men. Or more."

"I'm sorry, but I can't do it," said the paymaster. "It would be an insult to the men."

"An insult to the men?" screamed Maria, coming up from behind Sophia. "Why, you fish-colored *cabrón*! I can outwork you, outfuck you, outfight you!" she said, grabbing the table to hit him with it.

Lupe and Victoriano had to drag Maria away. But she kept screaming, wanting to beat the frightened paymaster.

That night, Sophia called for a meeting at home. The whole family showed up, plus many of the neighbors. Lupe watched her oldest sister calmly lay out a plan.

"This country is our home now," began Sophia, "so we can't allow people to treat us like dirt. We can't just keep saying to ourselves that it's okay because we're going back to Mexico someday."

Don Victor and several of the other men began to protest, saying that they were going back to Mexico, so she was wrong.

"Papa, please!" said Sophia, beginning to anger. "Those are dreams! We must face up to the fact that we're here now and we must take a stand!"

The women rose up in Sophia's defense and shouted at the men, "Sophia is right! We have children to feed! There is no other way!"

Sophia continued, laying out her plan on how to cut the balls off the paymaster. She was a tiger. Lupe had never seen her sister Sophia like this before. It filled Lupe's heart with great pride, but it also frightened her to see how Sophia had stood up to their father with such total lack of respect or fear.

The following day, they picked tomatoes, but then when the tomatoes got to the packing sheds, the women in the packing sheds quit their labor. And the people in the fields came in and joined them. At first, the paymaster and the labor contractor just humored them a little. But when it continued all afternoon, they began to get worried. They were going to lose the whole day's picking if they couldn't get people to pack.

That night, the paymaster and the labor contractor went around to find new people from other barrios so that they could get rid of Sophia and her troublesome lot. But, to their surprise, Victoriano and the other men had already passed the word along to all the neighboring barrios. Most of the people were not going to go against Sophia's strike, especially when they were told that Sophia and her children would be physically sitting at the entrances of the ranch, stopping all traffic.

The strike went on for three days and nights. It reminded Lupe of the time when the villagers had gathered in the town square back in La Lluvia and they'd stopped the soldiers from hanging Don Manuel and their mother. The people were a power when they united in force.

The women cooked big pots of soup, and every day Lupe watched her sister Maria threaten physical violence on anyone who attempted to cross the picket line. Sophia, on the other hand, talked softly and reasonably and people listened to her.

"This country is our home now," Sophia would tell each person who came to cross the line. "We must realize the truth, we're not going back to Mexico, so we have to stand up to these bosses and not let them treat us like lost slaves. We must stick together and show them that we're people of value, and we won't be cheated out of our wages. And I'm not saying that they should pay the children as much as a man; but for us women who work as hard and as well as any man, they should pay us equally."

Then Sophia would send the people over to be fed, and she'd make them feel at home so that they'd join the strike in spirit, if not in body and mind.

Every day Lupe went into the hills with the women and children to help gather cactus and other wild plants and roots to eat. They continued making the large pots of soup, and Sophia's strike took flame and spread to the neighboring ranches, too. Within a week, the rancher came to terms and they agreed to pay the women as much as they paid the men.

Lupe and her family rejoiced, seeing what could be done if only they united and held their ground. But it didn't go so well in other areas outside of Santa Ana and Tustin. The times were bad, and a lot of people were out of work.

Then, when things were just going well again for Lupe and her family, Maria's first husband, Esabel, returned from out of nowhere. He was as big and as handsome as ever. Maria slapped him and told him off. But then she threw herself at him and they were like two sex-crazed burros in heat. Her new husband, Andres, became so embarrassed for the children that he took them out and stayed with them in the garage in back. The following day Esabel and Maria were still at it, so Andres brought the children over to Lupe's parents' home. No one knew what to say to Andres. He just sat there, being such a good father to his children and Esabel's children, too.

Two days later Maria and Esabel came to the house, searching for the children and looking as happy as newlyweds, Doña Guadalupe took Maria aside and tried to talk some sense into her, but she'd hear nothing of it. Maria took her children home and set them up in the garage with Andres so that she could continue her lovemaking with Esabel. Everyone felt so confused and ashamed for Maria. But she didn't feel confused or ashamed at all. No, she blossomed like a rosebush in rich manure, looking younger and better than she had in years and announced to the world that she was now a woman with two husbands and that was that.

Carlota blamed everything on Esabel and swore that all men were pigs and she'd never get married. Lupe, on the other hand, began to pray for Maria with all her heart and soul. For she now knew deep down inside herself that it was easy for a woman to be in love with two men at the same time. But still, she couldn't forgive Maria for what it was doing to her children. Especially when she'd seen how strong and confident Maria had been all through the strike. Why, she'd been a mountain of power, but now she became a wild, mindless, sex-crazy woman every time this man Esabel came near her.

Lupe truly wondered about this world of sex. Was it really so powerful that it could destroy a woman as strong and good-hearted as her sister Maria?

19

And so the gates of heaven opened and Saint Peter smiled down upon the earth, giving la gente *a whole new season in life, the dream called love—a miracle born only of God.*

That week in Santa Ana, Lupe, Carlota and Victoriano had their first family meeting without their parents, and it was decided that the three of them should now start supporting their parents so that they wouldn't have to work in the fields anymore.

At first, when their mother learned of her children's decision, she protested; but not for long. Especially when she and Don Victor saw what a joy the prospect brought to their children.

Lupe and her brother and sister began going to work alone, working sun up to sun down, and they were so proud to come home and see their parents playing checkers on the front porch, looking more rested than they had in years.

Victoriano learned to drive, and he drove one of the trucks for the labor contractors who took them to the fields. Lupe began to go to the library on weekends once more. She was more determined than ever to get educated so that she could one day get a year-round office job to help support her family.

It was on the second weekend that Lupe ran into Mark. He'd just come home from the university, and he'd immediately come looking for her. He only had one year left of college, and this summer he'd be working for his uncle's architectural office in town.

"That's wonderful!" said Lupe.

"So how have you been?" asked Mark. "With everything proceeding so well, I think we can get engaged sooner than I'd thought."

"But, Mark," said Lupe, "I haven't said yes. I told you when we left that . . ."

"That you'd tell me when you got back. And you're back," he added, smiling grandly.

Seeing him smile, Lupe marveled at his good looks once again. He had such beautiful white teeth and sparkling blue eyes. She realized that he was almost as tall and handsome as her Colonel. A part of her wanted to say "yes," a thousand times, and yet another part of her remembered Salvador and how angry she was with him because he hadn't shown up for dinner.

"Look, Mark," she said finally, "my brother and sister and I have just made a deal among ourselves to support our parents. They're too old to be working in the fields anymore. I'm working every day and then I'm studying bookkeeping on weekends so that I can get an office job some day. I can't be thinking of marriage right now."

"Lupe . . ."

"No, please, let me finish," said Lupe. "You must understand what I've seen happen with my own sisters. Once they marry, they have so many of their own problems that it's impossible for them to think of our parents anymore."

He laughed, "But, Lupe, I'm not arguing. I'm agreeing with you. I've thought about this, too, and, well, I spoke to my uncle about you working part time for him, helping him with his bookkeeping."

"You did that?"

"Yes."

"What did he say?"

"He said sure, when we're ready."

"When we're ready," she said, feeling her heart pounding. What did this mean? That if she said yes to his proposal, then she'd have a job? Oh, she felt she was being deceived. Life was getting crazier by the moment. Especially when it came to love.

The following day, Lupe and all the women and children were inside the house waiting for the men. Don Victor, Andres, Francisco and Victoriano had gone with the neighbor across town to the Anglo part of Santa Ana to look at trucks. Ever since the strike, the labor contractors in town didn't want much to do with Sophia and her extended family. Even Don Manuel didn't want to help them to get work anymore. Buying their own truck was an important decision. A family with their own truck could follow the crops with ease and didn't have to pay Don Manuel or any other labor contractor to take them to and from the fields.

Now Lupe and her mother and sisters waited nervously for the men to return from having looked at trucks once more. They heard the sound of the neighbor's truck pulling up to their house. Every night for the past month, Sophia and Doña Guadalupe had been getting everyone in the family to pool their monies together so they could buy a truck. The men had been out looking at trucks all month. They didn't want to get cheated by the *gringos*, as so often happened to their people.

"Oh, I hope it's beautiful!" said Carlota.

"I hope it runs," said Sophia.

Victoriano came rushing into the house. "We finally found a good truck! Come on, Mama! And bring the money!"

"But, *mi hijito*," said Doña Guadalupe, seeing her son's excitement, "maybe you young people should go on without me. I don't really know anything about trucks anyway."

"Oh, Mama," said the tall, lanky boy, "you've got to come. This is the most important step in all our lives. It just wouldn't be any good without you!"

"Victoriano is absolutely right," said Sophia. "We can't go without you. And I won't take no for an answer," she added, crossing the room and taking her mother by the hand.

"Oh, all right," said Doña Guadalupe, accepting Sophia's hand. "If it pleases you, then I'll go."

So, they all piled into the neighbor's truck—Victoriano and his father in front with the driver, and the rest of the eight adults, plus the six grandchildren, in back.

At the car lot, the three Anglo salesmen saw them drive up and they were ready for them, realizing that this was payday, now that they were coming in with the women and children. For no matter how often the men came in, kicking the tires and looking the trucks over, the salesmen knew that the Mexican people never bought anything until they showed up with all their children and women, and their old mama standing over to one side, clutching her purse full of wrinkled bills. Mexicans always paid in cash, no matter how poor they were. The bills were damaged from all the years of hoarding.

The men, women and children came swarming into the car lot looking with hungry eyes but holding back cautiously, timidly. The Anglo salesmen moved in for the kill, beginning the dance of car lot negotiations, quickly positioning themselves with a gleam in their eyes as they tried to steer everyone away from the better buys over toward the older, cheaper trucks that they'd been trying to dump for months.

But it didn't work this time. Victoriano and the men had done their homework well.

"No," said Victoriano loudly and clearly, "we already know which truck we want. And it's way over there!" he added, slipping out of the entanglement of salesmen and taking his people with him over toward the better trucks.

But, still, the owner of the lot—a thick-necked, bulldog of a man—wasn't about to be outdone. He just figured that it would take him a little longer to move these simple, ignorant people back to where they belonged.

It was Sunday and Lupe came home early from the library to tell her family the wonderful news. She'd seen Mark and he'd told her that his uncle had said yes, he'd teach her how to do the bookkeeping for his office now, and that it didn't matter if she and Mark were engaged or not.

"Mama! Papa!" yelled Lupe, rushing in the front door, "I'm going to get a job in an office!"

But no one was home. She went out the backdoor to see if they were in the backyard. They weren't. She went down the driveway alongside the house, passing their new truck, to go and see if they were visiting Doña Manza's family down the street.

But then she got a gleam in her eyes and turned around and stared at the parked vehicle. She glanced around and saw that no one was home. Lately, she'd become sick and tired of how her brother and all the men were acting so superior just because they knew how to drive.

She headed back to the shiny black truck. She would teach herself how to drive right now, while no one was home.

Just then, Salvador came around the corner in his Moon automobile. He caught a glimpse of Lupe going down the side of her house. He could tell that she was up to no good by the way she'd glanced around.

He started laughing. Why, his angel wasn't such an angel, after all. She had some devil in her, too.

He parked across the street and took his .38 out of his coat pocket, slipping it under his seat. He got out of his Moon and started across the street.

Lupe was in the truck. She'd started the motor, and now she was trying to figure out how to get it going when, suddenly, the vehicle leaped forward but died.

Salvador laughed. This was so ridiculous. Women didn't know how to drive. He started towards her, figuring that he'd better stop her before she hurt herself. But before he could get to her, she started the motor again, put the truck in reverse, and came roaring backwards, right at him. Salvador leaped out of the way. Lupe went flying by him out into the street.

Quickly, he ran after her, wanting to stop her before she killed herself.

Lupe saw Salvador for the first time, coming towards her, waving his arms for her to stop. But she wasn't about to be stopped once she'd made up her mind. Especially not by this awful man who'd sneaked into her heart and then hadn't come to see her in nearly a month. She put the truck in first and it went jumping forward in a series of leaps, knocking down the fence in front of their house, running over her mother's flowers. Lupe screamed the whole while, trying to brake, but instead gave it more gas. The Model-T hit the steps of the front porch and charged up the stairs like a wild stallion, shattering her father's rocker.

The neighbors came out of their houses. Seeing what she'd done, they laughed hysterically. Lupe put the truck into reverse, trying to get off the porch, but the tires just spun. Angrily, she turned to see Salvador and all the neighbors laughing at her. With great indignation, she opened the door and got out of the truck.

"Salvador," she said holding herself as proudly as she could, "will you please put the truck away? I'm through driving for the day."

She turned around, not saying another word, and went inside the house. Everyone stopped laughing and stared at her with admiration. She truly was the queen of their barrio.

Salvador asked a couple of men to help him. They physically lifted the Model-T off the porch. Then, Salvador started the motor and drove it around to the side of the house. He thanked the men for helping him and came back around to the front, picking up the fence and straightening the flowers.

Going inside, he found Lupe pacing back and forth in the front room like a great, caged jaguar. She was furious. Looking at her carefully, Salvador came to the realization that in some strange way this beautiful creature reminded him of his own mother. She was a woman to be reckoned with.

"Oh, I made such a fool of myself!" said Lupe, gesturing with her large hands and long, well-muscled arms. "And my mother's flowers . . . and the fence! Oh, my God! What will they say when they come home? But, well, I'm glad I did it, anyway. My brother and all the men were making me ill, the way they kept bragging about driving the truck as if only men were meant to be free and come and go as they please."

She stopped, giving a nervous little laugh. "It was fun, though, I tell you. And I think I was actually getting the feel of it before I hit the porch."

Salvador laughed. "The feel of it! My God, you're lucky you didn't kill yourself!"

"Oh," she said, squaring off, "then you think a woman can't learn to drive, too?"

He saw her stance, her eyes, and quickly backed off. "No," he said, "I never said that. Hell, if you want to learn to drive, I'll teach you."

"Really? You'd do that?" she asked, recalling the way her brother had just laughed at her when she'd told him she wanted to learn.

"Sure, why not?"

She stared at him. She just didn't know if she could really believe him.

"What is it?" he asked.

"Well, most men, especially *mejicanos*, don't want women to know how to read, much less drive."

"Well, not me," he said, smiling, not really needing to lie this time, "I think a woman should be able to read. And driving is fine with me, too. Hey, whose truck is it, anyway?" he asked.

"Ours," she said.

"Really?" he said.

"Yes, and Victoriano is so proud of it. I hope I didn't break anything. Oh, he's going to kill me!"

"Just a headlight and a little dent," said Salvador. "But don't worry, I can get a new headlight for it from my mechanic and the dent fixed, too, if you want."

Lupe rubbed her arms, feeling a chill come over her. She hadn't realized that she'd broken a headlight. And this man was being so good. Oh, it just confused her. She'd been getting along so well with Mark. Why did Salvador have to come back into her life now?

Seeing how pensive she was, Salvador glanced around. "Where is everyone?" he asked.

"I don't know," she said. "I just came from the library and, well, no one was home." Her heart began to pound. "Maybe they're down the street visiting our friends—you know, you met them in Carlsbad—Doña Manza and her family from Brawley."

"Oh, yes, I know your mother's friend and I met her daughters at the beach."

Lupe turned red. "Yes, the one you flirted with on the beach," she said.

"Hey, I didn't flirt with anyone, Lupe," he said. "I only have eyes for you."

"Ha!" she said. "If you only have eyes for me, then why didn't you come for dinner that next night?"

His heart exploded. "Oh, Lupe, I'm sorry. I really am, but some unexpected business came up and then one thing led to another. I've been working day and night."

"You could've written or sent a message."

"Well, yes," he said, "I could have, I guess. But, well, you see, I . . . I don't know how to read or write very well," he said, feeling like the lowest creature on the face of the earth to admit this.

She stared at him. "And not being able to read or write very well, you still believe that women should be educated?" she asked.

His face turned red. But still, he forced himself beyond his embarrassment, pulling himself together, and said, "My own mother went to school in Mexico City during the time of the French occupation. And she's always told me that to make a home, a woman must be not just smart, but educated."

"Your mother said that?" asked Lupe incredulously.

"Yes, of course," he said. "In fact, she's always told me that men who seek out a dumb woman, thinking that they can manipulate her and make a better home in this way, are only stupid fools looking for trouble. To make a home takes great cunning and strength and, above all else, intelligence. Just as the mother deer has to teach her fawn how to survive, so does the human mother have to teach her children the art of survival. Any man whose true interest is in his offspring has the responsibility to find the smartest, most educated women he can find, because the mother is, after all, a child's first and most important teacher."

Lupe stood there mesmerized, listening to Salvador's words, just as Salvador had always stood in awe of his mother's. And as Salvador went on talking, telling Lupe of all that his mother had taught him, something magical began to happen between them once again. Sitting together on the old couch in the tiny living room below the picture of the Virgin Mary and a crucifix of Jesus, The Savior, the two of them—the babies of their families—touched, truly touched and began slipping, sliding into each other's world.

It was a truly wonderful time for Lupe. Much like the time she first met her Colonel, only it was better now, for she was no longer a child. And when Salvador stopped talking, the words came pouring out of her, words that Lupe had never thought she'd share with anyone outside of her own immediate family.

She told Salvador of how she'd been raised in a box canyon full of God and miracles. She told him how she'd learned to read and write and she'd loved to study about faraway places. Then she told him of how she'd gone to school here in the United States and she'd felt so out of place.

"So, you see," she concluded, "I now know that I can never become a schoolteacher, as I'd once hoped to be, but maybe I can still learn bookkeeping and become a secretary so I can make good money all year round and help my parents. My brother, sister and I don't want our parents working in the fields anymore."

"I know just what you mean. The times are hard right now. But, fortunately, I do well enough so my sister Luisa and my mother don't have to work under the sun anymore. And soon, Luisa's boys will be big enough to help her. At present, they're in school, and I tell them that school is work, too, and they must take it seriously or they'll have to answer to me."

Lupe gazed at Salvador. She just couldn't get over the fact that a Mexican could think like this.

"Then you want your family to get out of the fields, too?" she asked.

Salvador laughed. "Of course. The only fields I want my family to slave in is the land we own ourselves. I hate to be pouring sweat for another man's profit."

Lupe laughed, too. "I can certainly agree with that. Why, in the Imperial Valley we work under such a hot sun that I get headaches. Oh, I like the coast so much, especially around Carlsbad with those long, beautiful beaches and the air so cool and clear."

"Oh, me, too!" said Salvador. "I love it around Carlsbad and Oceanside!"

"You, too?"

"Oh, yes! The sea always gives me such a feeling of peace inside, just like I always felt back home in our mountains."

"Why, that's what the sea does for me, too!" she said excitedly. "The canyon we lived in in Mexico was so high in the mountains, you could see forever. And I'd been feeling so lonely, so homesick ever since we left, until I met the sea."

"I'll be," he said, "that's the same for me!"

"No, really?"

"Oh, yes!"

They looked at each other, truly seeing each other for the first time, and their eyes shone, scared and nervous, and yet full of hope.

"Tell me more about your mother," said Lupe.

"Gladly," he said. "She was born in Mexico City, and she went to school all the way to fifteen years old, studying French as well as Spanish."

"My God!" said Lupe, feeling very impressed.

"But then she and my grandparents moved to the mountains of Jalisco," continued Salvador. "That's where I was born—four days ride by horse to Guadalajara, our nearest city."

"But why did your grandparents decide to move to such a desolate place?" asked Lupe. "Especially after going to the trouble of having their daughter educated."

"Those were difficult times, my mother tells me. Mexico was as torn apart by the war with the French as it is now by the Revolution. People were hungry. Families were scattered to the winds, trying to find new lands, new hopes, a place to call home. But my grandfather on my mother's side, the great Don Pio Castro, was a man of vision," said Salvador.

Lupe smiled. "Go on, please."

"Well, my grandfather was poor, uneducated, from the most humble of Indian peasants," said Salvador, "but he had this dream, this vision to establish a town high in the mountains away from all the rich *hacendados*—a place where men could raise their families in peace. He was uneducated but determined that his children would all go to school and be free men!"

Salvador continued and told Lupe the story of Don Pio and his two brothers riding north from Mexico City after the French wars. Lupe was spellbound. Why, this was one of the most beautiful stories that she'd ever heard.

But then Salvador's eyes filled with tears, and he couldn't go on.

"What is it?" she asked.

"It's all gone," he said.

"You mean the town Don Pio built and everything?" she asked.

"Yes," he said. "Everything. The cattle and horses and goatherds, all the orchards of peaches and apples and pears. Everything. The buildings and barns and corrals—the whole community!"

"Oh, I'm so sorry to hear that," said Lupe, tears coming to her own eyes. "The very same thing happened to our town, La Lluvia de Oro. The gold mine closed down and the whole settlement returned to the jungles."

"Exactly," said Salvador, "the last time I climbed back up the mountain to look for my father—who'd abandoned us—it looked almost as if no settlement had ever been there."

"Oh, my God," she said, gripping her chest. "Why, I saw that very same thing from our cathedral rocks the last time I climbed up to say goodbye to my Colonel."

"Your Colonel?" he said.

Lupe froze. She'd never mentioned her Colonel to any human being outside her own immediate family. And, here, she'd just blurted it out to an almost complete stranger.

"Yes," she said, wiping the tears from her eyes, "a fine, wonderful soldier who came to stay at our home with his wife when I was very small."

"And you cared a lot for him?" asked Salvador.

Lupe searched his eyes, trying to guess what was going on inside his mind. But then she just nodded. "Yes, very much," she said, hiding nothing.

"I see," he said, breathing deeply. "Love is very powerful. It stays with us all the days of our lives. But myself, my only love has been my mother. Until now."

"Until now?"

"Why, yes," he said. "Don't you know, Lupita, you're the one." His whole chest came up. "Ever since the first day I saw you . . . I've known . . . completely . . . without a doubt . . . that you're the one that I've been searching for all my life."

Lupe felt herself going faint. Why, there were just no higher words that she'd ever dreamed of hearing from a man in all her life. She was suddenly filled with terror. What if he was real—her truelove come true? A part of her felt like running away, not wanting to hear another word. But no, she didn't run. She stood still, ready to see this through.

He looked at her and she returned his gaze. They sat there silently. The moment was so fragile, so delicate; they were almost afraid to breathe.

Then Salvador said, "Give me your hand, *querida*."

Without hesitation, Lupe gave him her hand.

"Lupe," he said, trembling, "tell me, what are your dreams? My mother has always told me that we never know another human being until we know their dreams. So, please, tell me yours."

"My dreams?" she asked, feeling her mind go reeling. What a beautiful thing to be asked. Oh, she was flying.

"Yes, your dreams," he said. "Mine are easy. I'm going to be rich. I don't know how, but I am. And I don't care if I have to work for twenty hours every day, seven days a week, but I'm not going to work for nobody but myself ever again. And I'm going to buy a ranch. A big one! And, in the middle of it, on a hill, I'm going to build my home like my grandfather built, and my children will go to school and they'll never suffer like I suffered, I swear to God!"

And saying this, Salvador's whole chest came up and his eyes filled with tears. Lupe felt his power, his strength, his conviction of mind, and she believed in him. She was overwhelmed by his presence.

"And now, tell me, what are your dreams, *querida?*" he asked.

How he'd said the word, "*querida*"—so softly, so gently—sent shivers up and down Lupe's spine. She—the quietest of all her family—began to speak as she'd never spoken before. She was suddenly a flood of words, telling him of all the hidden feelings she'd never known existed inside herself.

And as she spoke, she knew that she was ready to follow this man to the ends of the earth. Why, he was her Colonel all over again. And no, he wasn't tall and handsome this time; he was short and wide—the most beautiful man Lupe had ever seen on earth.

Lupe continued talking, telling him about everything and anything that came into her mind. And as she spoke, she couldn't help but wonder about this man's mother and if she'd know how to behave in front of such a grand, educated, fine lady.

"So to conclude," she said, "my dream is no longer for me to be educated or be a fine lady myself, but . . . for my children to be," she said, tears coming to her eyes. "And like you, I also want my children not to have to suffer what I suffered."

Her eyes overflowed with tears, but she wasn't crying; no, she was just that happy. Salvador had touched her very soul.

Salvador brought out his red silk handkerchief and handed it to her. "I'd like you to meet my mother," he said.

"Thank you," she said, taking the handkerchief. "The honor would be mine."

"Oh, no, mine," he said, bringing her hand up to his lips, kissing her fingertips gently, softly, as tenderly as butterflies kissing the breeze. And they would have drawn close and truly kissed, if Carlota hadn't come bursting into the room at that moment.

Seeing Salvador, Carlota yelled to everyone coming in behind her. "Mama, the one that you thought you'd chased away has returned! And he's with Lupe on the couch!"

Lupe could've died. And Salvador could've shot Carlota a thousand times. But then they both started laughing. Salvador remembered that every rose has its thorns and Lupe's was this big-mouthed sister of hers. He was going to have to learn how to put up with her, if he and Lupe were going to make a life together.

Then, Lupe's mother, father and brother came in. Don Victor came straight up to Salvador with open arms. "I'm glad to see you back!" he said. "I was getting worried! Because I have a business proposition for you."

The old man took Salvador and led him away. Salvador glanced over his shoulder, shrugging to Lupe. Lupe smiled, watching her father take Salvador out the door to the back.

"Look," said the old man once they were alone, "how about you and me getting rich, eh? Just the two of us."

"Sounds good to me," said Salvador.

"Good," said Don Victor, "then you get some money together and you and me, we'll go back to Mexico and reopen the gold mine that the Americans abandoned. Eh, how's that? Oh, I tell you, I'd like to be so rich once in my life that I can go out gambling and have money to burn so I'm not afraid of every little pair of deuces on the table! And I'd love to tell my old wife just once, 'Here's the money, choke on it, you old so-and-so!' That would be heaven!" he added.

"Well," said Salvador, "let's do it."

"Really, you mean it? I told my *vieja* that you're the kind of man who'd jump on it but, no, she kept saying that I'd scare you away! So when do we go? Mexico is still in ruins, so American businessmen haven't returned yet. I know. I've been asking around and listening to the news. So right now is the perfect time for us to go back and do it, and we'll be rich! Kings of our own lives!"

"Good," said Salvador, starting to truly consider the idea. "But it will take me, oh, maybe a few months to get the money together. How much do you think we'll need?"

Don Victor's eyes narrowed. "I hadn't thought that far ahead. I'll have to discuss it with my son, Victoriano. I'll get back to you. But please, in the meantime, say nothing to the women. It frightens them."

"All right," said Salvador, truly liking the old man's spark. Salvador was sure that if this old man had had a little success in life, he would have been a man to reckon with in a game of cards. Being dirt poor all life long ruined a lot of good men.

Coming back inside, Salvador could hear the women in the kitchen. Don Victor asked Salvador to stay for dinner. He introduced him to Francisco and Andres. The men were talking about work, labor contractors, and trucks. Then the conversation changed to Mexico, their homeland, and the men all told Salvador wonderful stories of opportunities that they'd left behind but as soon as they got on their feet financially, they'd go back and start where they'd left off.

Salvador said nothing. He just listened to Don Victor and Andres and Francisco and their neighbor from across the street, knowing that they'd never go through with these grand plans. But romanticizing Mexico now that they weren't there, and talking about their great plans did make their daily existence here in the United States easier.

Twice he caught a glimpse of Lupe in the kitchen as he listened to the men talking, and he truly felt like he was at home. Why, these people were all so happy to see him, treating him so well. They weren't mad at him for having busted that crate; no, in fact maybe it had impressed them, reminding them of how he'd dropped the big foreman.

At last it was dinner time, and they all sat down at the table made of boards. Victoriano told Salvador about their immediate situation. Victoriano was the only one who never spoke of the past. He told Salvador that he and his two brothers-in-law now had a truck, but they were still low on work.

"You see," he said, "ever since we pulled that strike here, we've been having trouble finding work. So I was wondering," Victoriano added, "if you have anything for us to do in your feritilizer-moving business for the next few weeks."

"What fertilizer business?" said Salvador, having forgotten that that's what he'd told them he did for a living.

"Your contracts with the big ranches," said Victoriano, slightly taken aback.

"Oh, those!" said Salvador, suddenly remembering. "Oh, yeah, sure!" he added, his heart pounding, realizing he made a bad liar when he wasn't on his toes.

"Well," continued Victoriano, "do you have work for us?"

Salvador's mind went reeling. Everyone was staring at him. Even Lupe and all the women. "Sure," he said, smiling at Lupe. "Lots of work. I'll stop by here for you at daybreak tomorrow, if you like."

"Good," said Don Victor. "I'll come, too!"

"Great," said Salvador, not having the slightest idea what to do, but fully realizing that he'd have to come up with something, and fast.

Driving home that night, Salvador couldn't stop singing; he was flying, sailing through the heavens, feeling God's breath. Oh, he was an eagle soaring through the star-filled night! And his Moon automobile was flying down the road at the neck-breaking speed of thirty miles an hour, gliding over the ruts with its fantastic suspension!

By the time he arrived at their two little rundown houses in Corona, everyone was asleep, and so he wasn't able to tell his mother the wonderful news. Lupe's family liked him, they really did, and tomorrow he'd be going to work with the men of Lupe's household like a real future son-in-law. But, still, he had absolutely no idea what he'd do when he picked up Don Victor and the other men at daybreak.

Finally, Salvador went to sleep, but he was so restless that he awoke a few hours later. He had to figure out what he was going to do to find work for them.

He went out and relieved himself, washed up, got dressed in his work clothes, and started a little fire in his mother's wood-burning stove. Watching the flames, he concentrated, realizing how vital it was for him to show Lupe and her family that he did, in fact, make his living moving fertilizer. Oh, he'd lose them all for sure if they ever found out that he was a bootlegger.

He made the sign of the cross over himself. "Oh, please, dear God," he said, "I know I've hardly spoken to You ever since we crossed the Rio Grande, and I haven't been to church, either, but I'm in love for the first time in my life, and I need Your help. So, please, help me; don't let me down now."

The light of the fire brightened, and he felt a warmth come into him, traveling to the center of his being. Then the warmth grew and grew, until he felt he was on fire. He stared at the glowing coals, feeling mesmerized, then it hit him like a cannonball between the eyes, and he saw everything.

He glanced at his old mother sleeping on her mattress across the room and he knew that God had spoken to him. Why, one second he'd absolutely had no idea what to do, and the next he'd seen the answer so clearly inside his mind's eye. It was like a miracle sent to him by heaven.

He breathed deeply and watched the flames dancing inside the little stove, feeling better than he'd felt in years. He wondered if this was how it had been for his grandfather, Don Pio, when he'd spoken to God on that knoll. He thought of Lupe and wondered if she was the woman that he'd finally be able to tell his most secret thoughts to. To tell her about Duel, about the two FBI agents—tell her everything, especially about his bootlegging. But he couldn't do that now. Not while she still thought that gambling and liquor were destructive to the survival of a family. Oh, he longed for the day that Lupe and he were married and she got to see how well he did at cards and liquor, so that he could then tell her the truth about everything.

It was time to go. Salvador finished his coffee, kissed his sleeping mother goodbye, went outside and got in his truck. He was in Santa Ana just before daybreak. Don Victor and the others were waiting for him.

"*Buenos días*," he said. "We have to hurry. One of you come with me, and the rest of you go in your own truck."

"I'll ride with you," said Don Victor. "I need to talk to you."

"Good," said Salvador.

They took off.

"I asked Victoriano," said the old man, "and he thinks we'll need about five hundred dollars just to get started."

"For what?"

"For the gold mine."

"Oh, yes, the mine," said Salvador. "Five hundred, eh? That's a lot of money."

"Then we're not going to do it?"

"No, I didn't say that," said Salvador. "It's just going to take a little more time."

"Good!" said Don Victor. "I knew you wouldn't back out! You're a real *macho*! A man who steps in when other men run!"

Salvador grinned. He really liked this worn-out old man.

Getting to the Irvine Ranch office, Salvador went inside alone. He slipped the foreman, Mr. Whitehead, a pint bottle and told him that he'd give him a gallon of his finest whiskey if he hired him and his men to move fertilizer for a week.

Being a drinking man, Mr. Whitehead said, "You got it, Sal." Archie had introduced them, so he knew that Salvador was a good man.

Coming out of the office, Salvador had a big smile. It had gone just like he'd seen it inside his mind's eye this morning. Talking to God was damned good business.

They went to work just as the sun was coming up over the distant hills. Andres and Francisco worked on one truck while Victoriano, Don Victor and Salvador worked on the other. It was hard, back-breaking work and Salvador was out of shape, so he had to grunt and put his whole body into it so he wouldn't look bad in front of Lupe's family. After all, he had to show these men that he was a good worker so they'd know that he'd be able to provide for Lupe when they got married.

The sun was two fists off the horizon and Salvador was pouring with sweat when he suddenly felt a huge fart coming. Quickly, he tried getting away from Don Victor, but it was too late. And Don Victor, who was bent down behind Salvador scooping up a pitchfork of manure, took Salvador's huge, roaring fart right in the ear.

Don Victor jerked up and saw a little burro standing alongside Salvador. "My God, Salvador!" he yelled. "Why, this little burro just farted on us!"

He poked the poor innocent animal in the ass with his pitchfork. The startled burro leaped five feet in the air, farting an enormous fart, and took off running.

"That filthy little beast!" screamed Don Victor, spitting on the ground. "Why, I can actually taste that fart, it was so foul!" he said, wiping his mouth.

Salvador rushed with his pitchfork full of manure to the truck. He could hardly keep from falling down with laughter. That poor little burro was racing wildly around the corral, kicking and bucking, and Lupe's poor old father was still spitting in disgust.

That night after work, Salvador was once again invited to stay for dinner. And during dinner, Don Victor told everyone about the burro's terrible fart. Salvador had a hard time keeping a straight face.

After dinner, Salvador offered to do the dishes so that he could be close to Lupe, but Doña Guadalupe didn't let him. No, she sat him down right after they'd finished eating and started in on him again.

Sipping from his cup, Salvador got an idea. He spilled his tea on his lap and jumped to his feet, excusing himself, and rushed into the kitchen to clean himself off. And there was Lupe, with a rag in hand. They both started laughing. Carlota looked at them, wondering how her sister could like such a clumsy man.

For the rest of the week, Salvador worked with Lupe's father and brother and two brothers-in-law. They had a fine time talking and laughing and sweating together, moving tons and tons of manure. Each night Salvador was asked to stay for dinner, and after dinner Doña Guadalupe would corner him, asking him about cards and liquor and all the other vices that endangered a good marriage. But each evening, Salvador would spill tea on himself and excuse himself, rushing into the kitchen.

Finally, by the third evening, Carlota became so indignant that she left the kitchen to go and tell her parents.

"Mama!" she said, "he's doing it on purpose! You got to stop him!"

"Quiet!" said her mother under her breath.

"But, Mama!" continued Carlota, still not realizing that her parents already knew, "don't you see? He's spilling his tea on himself on purpose so he can be with Lupe!"

Doña Guadalupe rolled her eyes to the heavens and Don Victor went out the front door, shaking his head.

In the kitchen, Salvador and Lupe covered their mouths, trying to hold back their laughter.

The following week, Mr. Whitehead checked their progress and he liked what he saw. Taking Salvador aside, he asked him for another gallon of whiskey and gave them two more weeks of work. But Salvador told Victoriano that they'd have to go on without him because he had to go down to Carlsbad to work on some avocado trees.

"Oh, you put manure in avocado orchards, too?" asked Victoriano.

"Sure, all the time," said Salvador, lying. But he planned to talk to the Germans who owned the Montana Cafe so that they could back him up. Hans and Helen owned several orchards, and he didn't want to be caught in another lie with his future-in-laws.

"Well, so long, Salvador," said Victoriano. "I'll tell Lupe you'll be gone a few days."

"Please do," said Salvador, and he took off.

At their distillery in Escondido, Salvador found that Epitacio had done an excellent job. The second fermentation was done, and it was time to start the distilling again.

For five days they worked day and night; then they had a batch of liquor ready. Salvador and Epitacio put the barrels of whiskey in the truck to take them to a hiding place behind Lake Hodges over by the San Pasqual Valley. They were going leisurely up a dirt road when suddenly a sheriff's car came rushing at them from between two big boulders in a burst of speed.

Epitacio screamed and Salvador smashed down on the gas pedal, racing up the old dirt road as fast as he could. But the cop car was right behind them, gaining quickly.

Salvador didn't know what to do. Glancing around, he saw an open field and he turned off the road, busting through a barbed wire fence. Crossing the rocky field, Salvador held on to the steering wheel while the old pickup leaped and jerked, bucking wildly. The steering wheel came off in Salvador's hands.

Epitacio screamed hysterically. "Oh, my God! Now I'm going to get killed, after all those years of dodging bullets!"

Using his huge hand like a wrecking iron, Salvador rammed the steering wheel back on. But the truck was just too loaded down with whiskey for them to get away. The sheriff's car was gaining on them again.

There was a herd of cattle up ahead by a watering hole. Salvador headed straight for the herd. But it was too late. The lawman's vehicle caught up with them, coming around on their left, just as they came into the cattle. Epitacio shouted in terror, and Salvador turned and saw the killing end of a double-barreled shotgun poking out the window at them from the sheriff's car.

Salvador slammed on his brakes. Epitacio flew forward, shattering the windshield with his face. Salvador dropped the truck into reverse and spun backwards, and the sheriff's car went flying into the muddy water hole, scattering the herd.

"Ha!" said Salvador. "The bastard's stuck now!" He was in ecstasy. Blood was running down Epitacio's face, and he was crying in pain. But Salvador paid no attention to his brother-in-law as he maneuvered through the cattle and up the grassy fields of the long valley, leaving the sheriff's car far behind.

"Well," said Salvador, getting to the foothills, "whadda you think, pretty good, eh?" he said. "We lost their ass!"

"My God, I hope so," said Epitacio, still picking glass out of his hands and face. "Look at me; I got half my face cut off!"

"Better than going to jail," grinned Salvador, bringing out a cigar.

But coming around a huge outcropping of boulders, there sat the sheriff's mud-covered car, parked squarely in front of them. Ten Mexican cowboys stood alongside the vehicle, aiming their rifles at Salvador and Epitacio.

Salvador braked and raised his hands. What else could he do? They'd been caught cold. Then, stepping out of the sheriff's car, lifting up his Stetson, was Archie Freeman.

Salvador's whole face exploded. "You goddamn bastard!" he screamed, getting out of his truck, too. "You son-of-a-bitch, you almost got us killed!"

"Don't get your ass in an uproar," said Archie calmly, swaggering up to Salvador good-naturedly, "we got to talk."

They went off to a private distance and Archie got down on his haunches Indian-style and pulled up a blade of grass and chewed on it.

"You see," he said to Salvador as he glanced off at the distant cattle, "they're pushing on Big John pretty hard again."

"So?" said Salvador, still angry.

"Well, I need to give him a little something so we ain't caught empty-handed," said Archie. "So how about a few of 'em barrels and that guy in your truck."

Salvador smiled like he hadn't smiled in years. Oh, this was beautiful! "You mean you want me to give you Epitacio so you can put him in jail?"

Archie nodded. "Yep, that's it."

"And he'll do time—real time—in prison?"

Archie nodded. "Yep, you got it."

Salvador grinned. Epitacio would now get to know what it had been like to go to jail. This was wonderful!

"And how many barrels?" asked Salvador.

"How many you got?" countered Archie.

"Ten," said Salvador.

"That sounds about right," said Archie.

"Why, you bastard!" screamed Salvador.

"Oh, all right," said Archie, "then I'll only take five."

"But how many of 'em are for Big John?" asked Salvador, "and how many are for you?"

Archie only grinned. "You guess," he said.

"You double-dealing son-of-a-bitch!" said Salvador.

"I'll shake on that," said Archie. "So, then, we got a deal, eh?"

Picking up a rock, Salvador tossed it up and down, then stole another quick glance at Epitacio. The frightened little man was standing alongside their truck, surrounded by armed cowboys. "How much time will he do?" asked Salvador.

"Two or three years," said Archie.

"Oh, that's beautiful!" said Salvador, laughing, truly enjoying it. But then he threw the rock as far as he could. "Nope, can't do it. He belongs to my sister, and I'd never hear the end of it."

Archie glanced at Epitacio, too. "Tough woman, your sister, eh?"

"The toughest," said Salvador.

"Well, all right then," said Archie, standing up. And he whipped out his .44 revolver, firing five shots into the air before Salvador could even move. "They got away, boys!" he yelled. "So we'll just take their truck and everything!"

"Jesus Christ!" said Salvador, taking off his hat and throwing it on the ground. "I didn't mean that! Not my truck, too, goddammit!"

"Too late!" said Archie. "A deal ain't offered twice!"

He drove off in his car with one of the *vaqueros* driving Salvador's truck close behind.

Salvador and Epitacio were left there in the middle of nowhere. "Epitacio, you son-of-a-bitch!" yelled Salvador, jumping up and down on his hat, "you cost me over a thousand dollars! I should've just let them take you to jail!"

Hearing this, Epitacio passed out. He'd lost a lot of blood, and this was just too much.

It was almost nightfall when the Mexican cowboys came back with a horse and wagon, singing in a happy, liquored stupor, compliments of one of Archie's barrels of whiskey.

The cowboys attended to Epitacio's wounds with some horse medicine. They brought out the side of beef that Archie had sent out, then they built a fire and Salvador and Epitacio ate: *barbacoa*, tortillas, *frijoles*, chile, tomatoes, onions and lots of *nopalitos* with them. They washed it down with plenty of whiskey.

The coyotes began to howl, and Salvador and Epitacio joined the cowboys, singing Mexican songs under the stars. Salvador slept that night as he hadn't slept in years, dreaming that he was back home on their rancho in Los Altos, smelling the cattle and horses and green grass. Oh, he was in love, and his woman was wonderful. She was a miracle of creation made especially for him by God.

T hat week, while her brother Victoriano and the other men worked at the corrals moving fertilizer without Salvador, Lupe went to the library and studied. She saw Mark almost every day, and they spoke of books. Once, they drove to his uncle's cool and spacious office; it was much more than she'd ever imagined.

Lupe felt so confused inside. She loved books and education, and especially the idea of working in the office for Mark's uncle. And yet, deep down inside, she felt closer to Salvador, especially now that he'd helped her family.

Late the next day, Salvador got into Carlsbad and told Kenny what Archie had done to him.

Kenny laughed so hard that he fell down on the garage floor, rolling around, holding his stomach. "Oh, that Archie! That Archie! Ain't that son-of-a-bitch the best!"

But Salvador didn't join him. His feet still hurt, and he was pissed. He wasn't used to walking all day, as he used to do back in Mexico when he'd been a child.

He told Kenny that he'd need another used truck.

"You got it," said Kenny, still grinning.

For the next week, Salvador and Epitacio busted ass making whiskey. They made back the ten barrels that they'd lost, then they hid the barrels behind Carlsbad, west of San Marcos. Salvador decided that he could now visit Lupe. He drove Epitacio to Corona and dropped him off so he could go to see his truelove by himself. But before Salvador could drive off, Luisa came screaming out of the front house, bellowing like a cow.

"Salvador! Salvador! Don't go! We need you! Mama's gone crazy, and she's gonna get lost and fall off the end of the world!"

"But what are you talking about?"

"Go to the church and see for yourself!" yelled Luisa. "She wants to go to Chee-a-caca, and everyone knows that that's the end of the world!"

Salvador got out of his new used truck and approached his sister. He really wanted to see Lupe before it became too late, but he couldn't drive off with his sister going on like this about their mother.

"Luisa," he said, taking her in his arms, "calm down and tell me what's going on."

"Don't you understand? Our mother is going to get killed! Domingo hasn't come home to her, so she's mad at the Virgin Mary and she's at the church right now, telling God off or she's going to go to Cheee-a-caca to get Domingo!"

"All right, Luisa, I'll talk to her," said Salvador, "but get hold of yourself. Mama has always been very capable."

"Yes, in Mexico, where people understood her and she was younger!" yelled Luisa. "But not here! And Cheee-a-caca is on the other side of the world. Ask Epitacio, he was there! He even saw the ocean and was told that he was near New England!"

"England?" said Salvador. "But isn't England near China?"

"Exactly," said Luisa. "And everyone knows that China is on the edge of the world!"

"All right," said Salvador, "I'll drive over to the church and see Mama right now."

"Good. The boys are with her. I'll go with you and you got to make her understand!"

"I will," said Salvador, helping his sister into his truck. He sighed, thinking that he was going to miss Lupe once again.

In front of the church, the two boys were coming down the steps with their grandmother.

"Mama," said Salvador, going up to her, "Luisa says that you're going to Cheee-a-cago alone."

"But I'm not going alone," said the old woman, "I'm going with Our Lord God Almighty!" And she bowed, making the sign of the cross over herself.

"Mama, be reasonable," said Salvador. "Luisa is right, Cheee-a-cago is so big that even with our Lord God at your side, you could still get lost."

"That's blasphemy!" said the old lady harshly. "Our Lord God owns the universe, so what's Cheee-a-caca to Him? And besides, I ask you, what more do I need, than to take another letter with me like the ones we've already sent? Why, the streets of Cheee-a-caca are going to be filled with my friends, waiting to help me!"

"But you don't speak English, Mama," said Salvador.

"And, you tell me, what can possibly be foreign in any language in the world that a mother looking for her own flesh and blood cannot say to another mother with her eyes alone?"

"But how, Mama?" asked Luisa, getting out of the truck. "None of us even knows where Cheee-a-caca is."

"Did I know where Guadalajara was when I went there to save Jose from his execution? Did we know where the United States was when we left our mountains? No, a person never needs to know where to go. What is needed is the conviction, here inside your soul, that you will overcome whatever it takes to get there!"

"All right, sounds good to me," said Salvador, seeing his mother's strength and throwing up his arms. "I didn't know where California was when I left Montana. All I did was buy a ticket and get on the train and they did the rest."

"Now stop it!" screamed Luisa. "Don't encourage her, Salvador!"

"Mama's right," said Pedro, speaking for the first time. "Don't encourage her, Uncle. Because grandmother really can't go alone. Look at her. She's so old and ugly that no one will even talk to her."

"What do you mean, 'old and ugly,' you stupid kid!" screamed his mother, grabbing her son by the hair. "She's our sacred mother! How dare you speak about your grandmother like that! I'll thrash you!"

Hearing the commotion, the priest came out of the church.

"No, Luisa!" pleaded Doña Margarita, grabbing Luisa by the arm. "Leave the child alone! He's the only one who's said anything that makes sense to me. Just look at me; these are rags! I truly do look so old and ugly that people might not talk to me, much less let me inside their homes and help me.

"Salvador," she continued, turning to her son, "I'll need some money for new clothes and a little *whiskito* to take to Cheee-ooo-caca with me." She winked, putting her arms around Pedro affectionately. "You'd be surprised how handsome you get, *mi hijito*, after people have a few drinks."

"All right, you got it, Mama," said Salvador, feeling relieved that she wouldn't be going immediately. "But it will be a few weeks."

Just then the priest came down the steps. They all turned and saw him. Instantly, Salvador was on guard. He didn't trust priests.

"Excuse me," said the priest, "but I couldn't help but overhear you, and I think that I could be of assistance to you. Could you, Doña Margarita," he added in perfect Spanish, "come inside with your son so we can discuss this privately?"

"Sure," said the old lady. "Salvador, this is Father Ryan, the good priest that's helped me so much."

"Glad to meet you," said Salvador, looking over the tall, elegant man carefully.

"The pleasure is mine," said the man of the cloth, extending his hand. Salvador took his hand.

The priest led them down the side of the church, through an enclosed private garden and into the backdoor of the church. It was dark inside, and the floors were made of hardwood and their steps echoed as they went. But Salvador felt no immediate threat until, at the end of the long hallway, they entered an office lined with bookcases, and the priest closed the door behind them. Suddenly, Salvador felt like this could be a trap.

"Well, well," said the priest, sitting at his desk and putting his hands together like a tent on top of the desk, "I couldn't help but overhear that you might be going to Chicago, *señora*. Well, I happen to know a priest there who might be of service to you. So you just tell me when you decide to go, and I'll send a letter ahead for you."

"See?" said Doña Margarita, turning to her son. "Ask and you will receive! Now I have even another friend waiting for me in Cheee-a-caca!"

"Yes, you do, *señora*," said the priest, shifting his weight in his chair. "But, now, the reason that I asked you inside," he continued, working his two hands together, "is that I understand that you people are from Los Altos de Jalisco and I know that the finest tequila of all Mexico is made in that state. And, well, being perfectly frank, people talk, you see, and so I know what you do, Salvador. So I was wondering if you couldn't get me some of your . . . ah, merchandise for me."

Salvador was stunned. He couldn't believe what he was hearing. So he just sat there, saying nothing, and the silence grew until it screamed.

"Well, all right," said the priest, turning to Doña Margarita, "I should have realized that a man in your son's business wouldn't exactly be open, even to a priest. But you see, *señora*, we priests are also men, and there are three of us here in the diocese who used to get together several times a month to enjoy ourselves, playing cards and drinking in the evenings. And, well, with circumstances being what they are in this country, we can't do that anymore."

Salvador looked at his mother. Up to this point, she hadn't shown anything to the man of God, either. But now hearing the priest speak directly to her, she nodded for Salvador to go ahead. Still, Salvador decided to go slowly. His mother had always warned all of them to be cautious even of priests, for they were men, after all, with the weaknesses of the flesh, like all other mortal men.

"Well, Father," said Salvador, "you've heard wrong from these people who talk. Because I don't handle any liquor myself, you see. But I do know a man who might have some."

The priest smiled. "All right," he said, "could you talk to this man?"

Salvador nodded. "Okay, I can pass on your message to him. And, well, maybe not tonight or tomorrow night, but some night this week you'll find a couple of bottles of the finest whiskey by your back door. And when you want some more, you just tell my mother that you'd like to see me, and I'll understand and pass on the word, and you'll get a couple more bottles, free of charge.

"But understand this, Father, I haul fertilizer for a living. I don't know anything about this bootlegging business. So you please tell these people who talk about me that I'm an honest, law-abiding man, Father."

"Of course," said the priest, looking at Salvador with new respect. "And I salute you, *señora*; you raised a very cautious man. He would have gone far in our Church. Maybe even a Cardinal!" he laughed.

Driving his family back home to the barrio, Salvador had his mother sit up front with him, and they got a chance to talk together. He told his mother of how he'd worked with Lupe's family for nearly a week before he'd gone to Escondido to work with Epitacio. He told her how they'd treated him so well.

"That's wonderful, *mi hijito*," said Doña Margarita. "But what happens now? From what you say, this girl sounds ready for marriage, and I've seen many young men lose the woman of their dreams because they didn't move fast enough. When a girl is ready, she is ready!"

"Oh, Mama!"

"Don't 'oh, Mama' me until I see you married and settled in your own home. But, oh, how I wish you would've met that angel that I've told you about that came to milk our goat."

"Mama, not again," said Salvador, having heard about this angel many times. "Lupe is the one for me. I feel it here, inside my heart and soul, as I've never felt anything before in all my life."

"That's how it was for me with your father. But I didn't waste time, I tell you. I had him in my wedding bed within two months after I met him."

Salvador blushed; he couldn't help it. This was his own mother, after all. But then he started laughing. His mother was just never one lost for words. She got to the heart of the matter immediately.

"I'm going over to see her now," he said.

"Good," said his mother. "And I'll start preparing for my trip to Chee-a-caca. Oh, I gave the Virgin a warning; I can't be waiting for Her anymore. Sometimes one has to take even the heavens by the horns, I tell you!"

The sun was going down behind the orange groves when Salvador drove into Santa Ana. He found that no one was at Lupe's house. The woman from across the street came up to him and handed him a letter.

"They were waiting for you," she said, "but they had to go to Hemet to do the apricots. Lupe told me to give you this letter. They said that they'll be back in a couple of weeks or so."

"*Gracias*," he said, taking the letter. The envelope bulged out, and Salvador could feel that it had something other than just paper inside it.

He went up to the porch and sat down on the new rocker that they'd bought for Don Victor. Opening the letter, Salvador found dried mountain lilies inside. He smiled, putting the dried flowers to his lips, kissing them, smelling them. He was overwhelmed with emotion.

Lupe was so different from any woman that he'd ever met. And her family was so different from his, too. No one in his family would ever have thought of putting crushed flowers inside a letter. He glanced around and saw how nice and clean their home was. Lupe's people were village people who'd always lived with neighbors close by and were used to keeping things neat and orderly. On the other hand, his were ranch people, six miles from their closest neighbor, and used to riding horses up to the front door and coming inside with guns on their hips and cowshit on their boots.

Oh, part of him just wondered if Lupe and he would ever be able to make a home together, they were so different. Why, even the holy pictures and crucifixes that hung in Lupe's home were different than his people's, who had tortured-looking saints and crucifixes with huge, gory thorns and lots of blood. Lupe's holy pictures and crucifixes looked kind, unbloody, and their faces weren't tormented.

He sat there, rocking in Don Victor's rocker. He hugged Lupe's letter close to his heart, and he thought back on his life before he'd met his truelove. He'd done so much and he'd been with so many women. But now all his past life seemed like it had only been a lesson, a preparation for what he was going to undertake in making a home.

Tears came to his eyes, and he squeezed Lupe's letter against his face, not needing to try and read it, but feeling it, breathing it, holding it to his heart. He realized that his father and mother had not had a good marriage, but his grandparents had had a wonderful life together. He remembered how his grandfather, Don Pio, had always gone down to the corrals to see the men off to work when he first awoke, but then he'd return to have his first cup of hot chocolate with his beloved wife, Silveria. Oh, their love, their admiration and respect for each other had been legendary! And this was the kind of marriage that he wanted for himself and Lupe.

He sat there, rocking, holding Lupe's letter and, yes, he fully realized that Lupe and he were as different as two people could be, but still, he was sure that they could make a home together.

He brought the letter to his lips and kissed it, smelled it, and he trembled with desire. Oh, just the thought of her sent him shooting, flying, sailing across the heavens like a timeless star and yet, he also was so afraid.

And all this time, the woman across the street watched out her window, and she was moved. Love was in the air, reeking off him. He was a young buck deer in heat; he was a human being made in God's own image of pure love, and he was burning, going crazy with life's juices.

Going over the tall, green-grey mountains to Hemet, their truck overheated and Victoriano had to pull off the road into a grove of oak trees. There was water in the canyon behind the oaks, with tall ferns and large boulders. Lupe took off her shoes and walked up the creek to cool off. Her father and mother had come along on this trip, but with the strict understanding that they wouldn't do any work.

Doña Guadalupe followed her daughter up the creek. Lately, she'd noticed how quiet Lupe was. Finding her daughter by a small pond surrounded by tall ferns, the old lady took off her own shoes, sat down on a boulder beside Lupe, and put her feet in the cool water.

"Look, *mi hijita*," she said, glancing up at the mighty oak tree overhead, "why this tree is almost as big as my crying tree back home. See those broken branches? This tree has seen lightning, too."

Lupe looked up at the great oak tree and saw the large, broken branches, and it was true. This tree did, in fact, look a lot like her mother's crying tree back in La Lluvia.

"We women need our trees," said the old woman, "and our flowers, too. They listen to us as no man ever can, no matter how much we love him or he loves us." She breathed deeply. "What is it, *mi hijita?*"

Lupe looked down into the pond, watching two oak leaves caught in the current go down between the boulders. She really didn't want to get into it with her mother. She was now seventeen years old, after all, and it was time for her to start solving her own problems.

"Lupita," said her mother, reading her mind, "I might be too old to work in the fields anymore, but, believe me, I still know a lot more about life than you. And, besides, you either talk to me or you're still not so big that I can't grab you by the ear and discipline you," she said, laughing.

Lupe smiled. Her mother was still the same. She had to know what was going on with everyone in the family at all times or she'd go crazy. The oak leaves now went rushing around the last large boulder and went cascading down the creek, out of sight. Lupe breathed deeply.

"Come on, *mi hijita*," said her mother, taking her hand, "I'd like to be your friend. Please, tell me, is it that Salvador didn't return like he told Victoriano he would?"

Lupe nodded, but then shrugged. "No, it's only partly that," she said. "It's more like—oh, I just don't know how to say it!" she added in frustration, grabbing a rock. "Salvador makes a game of things. Like leading Papa on with the gold mine and then leading me on, too. Oh, Mama, I truly think that I hate him sometimes!" she said, throwing the rock into the pond.

Her mother smoothed out her dress on her lap. "About the gold mine and your father, don't worry, *mi hijita*. Men need their entertainment. It's either that, or cards and liquor. But, now, about leading you on, you hate him, eh?"

"Oh, yes! I do!"

"But Mark you don't hate?"

"No!" said Lupe. "That's what's so confusing to me! I love being with Mark. He's so wonderful, and we talk about books and the future and I feel so happy when I'm with him."

"And you never hate him?"

"No, of course not."

"But Salvador you do hate sometimes?"

"Oh, yes! I hate him good sometimes, Mama!"

Doña Guadalupe only smiled. "Well, then, it's settled. It's Salvador that you really love."

"No!" said Lupe, staring at her mother. "Didn't you hear me? I hate him!"

"Yes, I heard you, *mi hijita*," said the old woman calmly. "But, sadly, the things of the heart are seldom what they seem." She wiped her own eyes. "Believe me, I know. I, too, was once in the same place that you are in now."

"You, Mama?"

"Well, yes, *mi hijita*. I wasn't always married to your father, even though it may seem that way to you. I, too, once had to make a choice between two very different men."

"You did?" said Lupe, looking shocked.

The old woman laughed again. "Yes, and I chose your father with his hat and that little flare of his. Little did I know that he wore the hat because he was losing his hair, even back then."

Lupe tried to picture her father as a young man with thinning hair, and she started laughing. Her mother joined her, and it was good.

"I almost envy you, *mi hijita*," said the old lady, reaching out and stroking Lupe's dark, rich hair. "You have so far to go. A whole new world is just beginning to open up for you."

"But I feel miserable, Mama!"

"Oh, if only I could hurt with such misery once again, to feel the powers of love here inside my heart, the joys of heaven and the pains of hell!"

Lupe stared at her mother. "But what shall I do?" she asked.

"When the time comes, you'll know, *mi hijita*; believe me, you'll know."

Lupe looked at her mother for a long time—at her eyes, her face, her wrinkled old neck—and she went over her words once more inside her mind, "When the time comes, you'll know," and she wondered if she'd ever be as smart and as strong and as beautiful as her mother.

Then, the men started calling, saying that the trucks were ready and it was time to go. Lupe and her mother got up and started back down through the creek, going around the boulders, past the tall ferns. Lupe listened to the breeze blowing overhead through the treetops, and she heard quail calling in the distance. Oh, she felt so close to her mother. Life truly hadn't changed much since their days in La Lluvia when she'd awaken each morning and reach across the warm-smelling covers, searching for her mother's warmth. A life of dreams, a life of sleepy thoughts and feelings, a life of mystery and wonderment; they continued down the creek, hand-in-hand—mother and daughter.

20

The angel of love came down from the heavens,
whispering to the butterflies and the bees and the birds,
"Be careful of love; you might just receive your heart's
desire."

Entering the church, Doña Margarita went straight up
the aisle to the statue of the Blessed Virgin Mary and knelt down and brought
out her rosary, making the sign of the cross over herself.

"I've come to talk to You, woman-to-woman, one last time, before I go to
Chee-a-caca to get my son," she said in a firm, strong voice. "So, I don't
want Your Most Holy Son coming in this time and interrupting us.

"Besides," she added with a twinkle of mischief in her eyes, "I just heard
a good one, and I think You might like this one.

"So, anyway, there was this old married couple who'd been married for
over fifty years," said Doña Margarita to the statue, "and one day they were
sitting on the porch, passing the time, when the old man turned to his wife
and said, 'Tell me, *vieja*, have you ever been unfaithful to me? Come on, you
can tell me if you have. We're old, so what does it matter now?'

"But the old woman just shook her head, saying nothing. The old man
got closer to her. 'Come on, *querida*, it's all right,' he said, 'let's be open
with each other and entertain ourselves with our little adventures. Look, I'll
go first, if it will make it easier for you,' he said, becoming excited with
memory.

" 'Remember your cousin that came to stay with us one summer about
forty years ago when we lived on the ranch by the river?' he asked. 'Well, to
tell the truth,' he laughed, 'she and I, we got it good, right down there by
the river when she did the wash. Oh, that was good. And remember the
neighbor we had when we lived in town? Well, I got her good, too—she and
her sister, both of them—real good.' "

And he was all smiles, remembering the past. "Now you tell me, come
on, let's be open,' he said. 'We're old, so what could it possibly matter now?'

"But still, the old lady wouldn't say anything. She just sat there quietly
while her old husband went on and on, telling her of his different adventures.
But, finally, the old lady couldn't stand it anymore and she dried the tears
from her eyes and spoke up.

" 'Well, to tell you the truth, dear husband,' she said, 'I've never been as adventurous as you. But you know the wrangler we've had all these years, the one who still lives here behind us? Well, I've only been with him. And still am.'

"The old man heard the words, 'still am,' and he leaped from his chair. 'Why you lousy, dirty old lady! Don't you have any shame?' he yelled."

Doña Margarita laughed and laughed and she saw the statue of the Virgin Mary start laughing, too. "Oh, My Dear Lady," she said, "isn't that the truth of men! Bragging all the time until they get a little bit back, then they go wild! Oh, I can just see that old man's face; he must've gone mad with rage."

She continued laughing, looking at the statue of the Virgin Mary. Her eyes overflowed and her sides began to hurt, but still, she couldn't stop laughing. Laughter was the greatest healing power of all.

But then she wiped her eyes, stopped her laughter, and looked up at the statue of the Virgin Mary and said, "All right, My Lady, enough of this. Now let's You and me get down to business!"

And saying this, she stood up. "What I came to ask You for today—I do not ask! I demand as one mother to another! Do you hear me, Maria? I demand that You send my son home to me before the end of the next full moon, and I don't care if Domingo has been killed or drowned or fell off the end of the world and gone to hell! I want him here before the end of the next full moon, which is in two weeks, or I'm going to Cheee-ooo-caca myself and cause more problems than You can ever imagine!"

A young priest came in through the backdoor to see what the commotion was. He was stunned. He'd never heard such outrageous blasphemy.

"I'll go to every church in Cheee-ooo-caca and even to the Protestant churches, too, if I have to! But I will not rest until I get my son back! DO YOU HEAR ME?" she yelled, standing up to her full height of four-foot-ten. "I'm speaking to You! Woman-to-woman, so You pay attention good!"

The young priest was aghast, and he turned to go to get Father Ryan.

"And I will accept no excuses from You or Your Son or Your two husbands! Do You hear me? I want my son here at my side before the end of this next full moon, and I want him well and strong and all his bones and flesh intact, or You're in for trouble! After all, we're good friends, You and I. You lost one son and so You know how I feel. I lost seven!

"Seven!" she repeated, tears streaming down her face, "that came here from my loins and I had baptized in Your Most Holy Family's name." She wiped her eyes. "So, please, grant me this, and then I'll gladly turn over my soul to You for all eternity.

"But don't You dare say to me that You can't do this, for You and I both know that Your powers are infinite when it comes to ruling the universe. Two husbands, You have, and they still call You a virgin! So You use those persuasive powers of Yours and talk to Your Son and Your Heavenly Husband, Our Lord God, and get them to bring my son Domingo back to me."

Just then, the young priest came rushing back into the church with the older man of the cloth. Father Ryan was still chewing his food and wiping his mouth. The young, terrified-looking priest pointed at Doña Margarita.

"And so to conclude," said Doña Margarita, kneeling back down, "I remain Your most humble servant, but not a docile one, believe me. You do Your part up in heaven or I'll do more than my part here on earth, and there'll be trouble!"

Doña Margarita bowed her head and kissed her rosary, the very same one that her father had used to pray for guidance up on the knoll half a century before.

Seeing this, the old priest turned to the younger priest, questioning him with his eyes. The young priest tried to explain what he'd heard, but Father Ryan cut him off.

Doña Margarita got up and went out of the pew, genuflected in the aisle, and started for the door.

Father Ryan hurried after her. The young priest followed.

"Excuse me, Doña Margarita," he said to her in Spanish as she went out the door, "but I'd like to introduce you to Father Anthony. He's my new assistant."

"Oh, it's a pleasure," said Doña Margarita, taking the young priest's hand.

"The pleasure is mine," said Father Anthony. "Do you come here often, *señora?*"

"Almost every day," she said.

"But I don't believe I've seen you at our daily mass."

"Of course not," she said. "I only go to services on Sundays. It's enough that I have to listen to you priests once a week when I can talk to God directly myself every day."

The young priest was stunned once again. He'd never heard such disrespect. The older priest only smiled.

"Doña Margarita," said Father Ryan, going down the steps of the church with her, "I'd like you to please thank your son for me. His friend's gift was most appreciated."

"And you'd like some more, eh?" said Doña Margarita, glancing at him with a knowing eye.

"Well, if it wouldn't be too much trouble," he said.

"Trouble or not, I'll tell my son. And he'll see what he can do."

"Oh, thank you. The Lord be with you."

"Yes, He better be with me," she said, "or, like I told the Virgin, there's going to be trouble!"

He laughed. She ignored him.

At the bottom of the steps, the priest shook Doña Margarita's hand and told her goodbye. Father Anthony watched them from the top of the stairs. He still didn't feel comfortable with what was going on.

When they got to Hemet, Lupe and her family found that the canneries had closed down. They weren't going to be canning the apricots this year.

The year was 1928, and this year the farms were going to dry the apricots. They were only going to need half of the women to work for them in the long-roofed packing sheds.

Lupe and her sisters managed to get work in the sheds because they had a reputation for having extraordinarily fast hands. But many of the other women were turned down and put to work with the men in the orchards, picking the apricots.

All day long, Lupe worked alongside Carlota, Maria and Sophia, splitting the golden fruit in two with a small knife. Then they'd take out the pit and put the halved fruit in large, long trays. The trays were then passed through an oven and put to dry-bake in the bright, hot sunlight.

For the first five days, Lupe had no problems, and she worked from sun up to sun down with her sisters. But then, in the middle of the second week, she began to suffocate in the constant fragrance of the ripe fruit and the terrible heat of the open sheds. Lupe began to sneeze, and her skin started to itch with such a vengeance that finally, one afternoon, she tore the hat off her head, threw it down and stomped on it with her feet in rage. She began to scratch her skin, wanting to tear it off. Carlota shrieked with joy, laughing at Lupe.

"You better get married quick," she said. "You're too lazy to work!"

"Shut up!" yelled Lupe.

"I will not!" said Carlota. "You're just spoiled!"

"Spoiled?" yelled Lupe, and she threw her tray of apricots at her sister, hitting her in the face.

Carlota screamed and threw her tray at Lupe.

"That's enough!" said Sophia, coming between them.

Lupe began to gasp, not being able to breathe. Sophia helped Lupe walk out of the suffocating shed.

"Go home and help Mama with the children," said Sophia once they were outside.

"But I have to keep working!" said Lupe, wiping her allergy-swollen eyes.

"Don't worry; Maria and I will do your share. You help Mama take care of our children for us."

"Oh, I feel like such a failure!" said Lupe, beginning to cry.

"It's all right," said Sophia. "Your day will come, *mi hijita.*"

"You really think so?" asked Lupe.

"Of course," said Sophia, getting the hair out of Lupe's face. "Remember, you are our sister of the meteorite; you have always been very special, and don't you forget it."

"Oh, thank you," said Lupe. "I feel like such a failure at times."

Sophia laughed. "Believe me, we all do at times, *querida.*"

Sophia went back inside the shed with all the women who were gossiping about the fight. Lupe walked home by herself. Her eyes became so swollen that she could hardly see. By the time she got to the little shack that they rented on the edge of town, Lupe had lost all strength, and her vision was so blurred that she could only see a mass of glistening white sky. She passed out. The dull, hot earth came up with power, hitting her in the face.

"Aunt Lupe! Aunt Lupe!" shouted the little four-year-old girl playing in front of their shack. Her name was Isabel; she was Maria's last child from her first husband.

By the time Doña Guadalupe came out of their rented shack, Lupe was gagging and choking to death.

All that afternoon, Doña Guadalupe sat by her daughter's side, putting cold compacts to her forehead, trying to get the swelling to go down. It had become very scary for a little while. Lupe had come that close to death. She was just beginning to rest peacefully when everyone came in from the fields.

"What's this?" said Carlota, seeing her sister lying down. "Are you still pretending to be sick, Lupe?"

"Quiet," said their mother.

"Oh, yes, that's right! Stick up for her when it's us who do all the work!" yelled Carlota, going out back to shower with the hose.

"Don't listen to her," said Doña Guadalupe to Lupe. "She's never been sick in her life, so she has no idea what you're going through." The old lady breathed deeply, massaging Lupe's forehead. "And also, remember, *mi hijita*, it was you that was able to help deliver the twins that night, not Carlota. People are strong in different ways."

Lupe was far away in a dream, but she could still hear her mother's words, "People are strong in different ways." Then she heard Sophia's words, "Your day will come." And far away in a deep, dark tunnel, Lupe went down and down, and then she came out to bright sunlight and green meadows, but it wasn't hot and dusty; no, it was cool and wonderful, just like after a wonderful summer storm, and all the people were dancing, singing, having a wonderful time—dressed in costumes of the deer, the rabbit, the bear. Lupe slept, feeling her mother's hand on her forehead and hearing her wonderful words, "People are strong in different ways."

After showering, Carlota got dressed, ate dinner, and went to the dance in town with her father and brother. Lupe could stay sick for all she cared, she got to go to the dance.

That night, while everyone was at the dance, Lupe awoke often, and for the first time in her life, she began to understand why so many of the young women in the fields thought that the only way to get out of their drudgery was to marry a rich man. Lupe also understood now why, back in La Lluvia de Oro, Lydia had entertained the idea of marrying old man Benito when he'd promised her shoes of gold so her feet would never touch the dirt of the earth again. She thought of Salvador's dream of being rich one day, and she liked it.

Lupe was sound asleep when the first dark clouds came over, dropping down a few delicious drops of moisture. Then it began storming hard, and the lightning split open the skies. Lupe awoke, smelling the fresh, clean air; her nose opened up and she was able to breathe. Oh, it was heaven! It was almost like being back in La Lluvia de Oro!

It rained the rest of the night and Lupe and her family got soaking wet inside the little shack, it had so many leaks. But, still, it felt so good to smell the fresh rain, especially after all the dust and heat of the week before.

In the morning, Lupe felt strong and she decided to go to work with the men in the orchard instead of with the women in the sheds. Among the wet trees, there wouldn't be any dust. Going with the men, Lupe was able to work well. Breathing in the rain-washed air, she finished out the day, working with strength and power.

It was quitting time, and Lupe was coming down between the trees with her sack full of apricots and her little niece Isabel in tow when she suddenly glanced up, and there was Salvador. She stopped. Her heart pounded wildly. He was no more than fifteen feet away from her, dressed in a beautiful white suit, with the sunlight coming down behind him in colors of gold and silver. She thought of her Colonel, of that first day that she'd seen him down by the creek, and she felt the skin grow tight across her chest, she was breathing so quickly.

Without a word, Salvador smiled and came forward, step by step like a game cock. Lupe laughed, he looked so ridiculous. Then, coming up to her, he whipped out a bouquet of flowers that he'd been hiding behind his back like a matador fighting the bull.

"For you, my queen!" he said.

"Why, thank you," she said genuflecting like Cinderella to her Prince Charming.

"The pleasure is all mine," he said. "And I would've brought diamonds," he shouted, "but they didn't have any good enough for you!"

Lupe laughed all the more. This was wonderful. He took the sack from her shoulder, and they walked down the line of trees. People looked at them and, when Victoriano saw them, he came over and said hello to Salvador, like an old friend.

They dumped their apricots at the nearest dropping station, and Victoriano excused himself and went over to visit with some of the other men so Lupe and Salvador could be alone as they all went out of the orchard. And there, beyond the last line of apricot trees, stood Salvador's Moon in the open field, glowing in the late day sunlight.

"Your car, my queen," said Salvador. "I parked it in the middle of the field so you can finish your driving lesson without hitting anything."

"You what?"

"Get in and take it," he said.

"Right now? In front of all the men?"

He nodded. "Sure. Why not?"

"But what if I wreck it?" she asked.

"So what?" he said, taking her by the arm. He put her in the Moon, started the motor, put it in gear and stood back. "Gas it!" he yelled.

She gave it the gas, and the Moon leaped forward. Victoriano and the other men looked on in complete horror. They'd thought Salvador was joking. Women didn't drive.

The Moon was racing wildly across the open field, and Lupe was screaming in fear, trying to maneuver the steering wheel.

Salvador slapped his legs and shouted, "Ride 'em, Lupe! Ride 'em!"

Filled with fear, Victoriano tore off his hat and raced across the field, shouting at the top of his lungs. Lupe saw her brother coming towards her, waving his arms for her to stop, and she turned the car on him—he who had laughed at her when she'd asked him to teach her to drive.

Victoriano saw his sister coming at him and he turned and raced for his life. Now everyone was laughing hysterically along with Salvador. Lupe had the time of her life, racing the car around the grassy field, chasing her brother. Finally, Victoriano managed to jump aboard with her and he brought the Moon back to Salvador and the rest of the waiting people.

Lupe was in ecstasy. She got down and went to Salvador. And in that moment of sun and joy, Lupe knew why she loved and also hated Salvador. He gave her wings. He didn't try to lock her in, as had Jaime and the other boys she'd known. No, she could dream her wildest dreams with him and so she loved him for this; but she also hated him because it made her fearful. No one in her family was like this. They were always very cautious.

"Great, eh?" he said.

"Oh, I don't know, I was so frightened and all you'd do is laugh when I asked you what to do!"

Seeing her anger, Salvador just laughed some more.

"Aunt Lupe!" said little Isabel excitedly. "Aunt Lupe! Are you and Salvador going to get married?"

Lupe blushed. "But why do you ask, child?"

"Because she can see it in your eyes," said Salvador. "Because she can smell it in the air! It's springtime! and the bees are gathering, the butterflies are migrating, so, of course, it's in God's great plan for us to marry!"

Everyone applauded.

"Oh, Salvador," said Lupe, feeling so embarrassed with all the people standing around.

"Well, are you?" insisted the little girl again.

"That's enough," said Lupe, wanting to pinch Isabel to silence her.

"Will you be our ring bearer?" Salvador asked the little girl.

"Salvador!" snapped Lupe. "Don't mislead her! The girl carries the bride's train, not the ring!"

The people laughed, and Salvador laughed the hardest of all.

"You're absolutely right, Lupe," he said. "Then you'll carry the tail of the wedding dress, *mi hijita*," he said to Isabel, "not the ring."

"Oh, good!" shouted the little girl. And she began to shout to everyone that Lupe and Salvador were getting married and she'd get to carry the tail of the wedding dress.

That night, Salvador stayed for dinner. He ate with Lupe and her family outside their little rented shack under a tree. And it wouldn've been paradise, if it hadn't been for all the mosquitoes. The children started crying, and Doña Guadalupe had to prepare oil and fresh ground garlic to put on their naked limbs.

Lupe and Salvador came to realize that the mosquitoes were God-sent because Doña Guadalupe was kept so busy with the children that she didn't have time to corner Salvador. He was left free to visit with Lupe while she finished her chores.

It was late, and Lupe walked Salvador up the line of shacks to his car. Passing the last large tree, Salvador suddenly grabbed Lupe and pulled her behind the tree. He kissed her full on the lips. It took Lupe by surprise. She hadn't expected this. It angered her, too, and she was just going to say so, but then, to her own dismay, she gripped Salvador by the face, instead, kissing him back.

"Ah," said Salvador, laughing, "you make the kiss, too!"

"Oh, no, I don't," she said, "you made it first? So I was only getting even!"

Hearing her explanation, he burst out laughing. She began to laugh, too. That was the first time that they'd kissed. In fact, it was the first time Lupe had ever really kissed any man outside of her own immediate family.

They stopped laughing and gazed at each other. Then, without a word, they drew close again and started kissing, truly kissing, and holding each other closely.

Lupe began to tremble, feeling a strange, hot, aching sensation come up into the center of her stomach. She'd never felt anything like this before. She felt as if she'd burst, erupt like a volcano from down deep inside the center of her being. She pulled away to catch her breath, feeling so hot all over. She smiled, brushed back her hair, and she was just going to start kissing Salvador again when little Isabel came running up to them.

"Aunt Lupe! Aunt Lupe! They sent me to get you!"

Salvador grinned. "I best go, I think."

"Not yet," said Lupe.

"Yes, go!" said Isabel, taking Lupe's hand and tugging at her to come home. "It's late!"

Lupe shrugged. "Well, *buenas noches*," she said. "Drive carefully."

"I will," he said, "and when you get back to Santa Ana, I think that maybe I'll have a little present for you."

"Really?" she said.

"Yes, really," he said, drawing close to her once again.

But Isabel squeezed in between them. "No more!" she said. "You aren't married!"

And her tone of voice was so authoritative, so full of scolding, just like an adult, that Lupe and Salvador began to laugh once again.

"Good night," he said.

"Good night," she said, too.

He got in his Moon and drove off. Oh, he was flying. He was the happiest man in all the world. He wanted to drive over immediately and tell his mother the wonderful news. She'd been right once again; Lupe was ready for marriage, as ready as a ripe peach for eating. He shouldn't lose any time.

But he decided that by the time he got to Corona, it would be too late and his mother would be asleep. He decided to drive down to Escondido and check on the distillery. He was flying too high to sleep. He drove down the road, whistling as he went. Oh, he was in love, and his truelove loved him, too!

Walking back to the little shack, hand-in-hand with Isabel, Lupe couldn't believe what she'd done. Why, she'd kissed him right back. She just didn't know what had gotten into her. But it had angered her when he'd grabbed her and kissed her like that, so she'd just done it right back to him before she'd realized what she was doing. Oh, the look on his face! He'd been even more shocked than her!

She laughed, racing down the way with her little niece. Kissing was fun. No one had ever told her this.

The sun was only one fist off the horizon when Salvador pulled into the barrio of Corona, having checked the distillery in Escondido. He hadn't been able to sleep all night. He just couldn't believe how Lupe had gripped him by the face with her two hands and kissed him right back. He'd never forget the look on her face for as long as he lived when she realized what she'd done. Oh, she had a wild side to her. She wasn't just an angel. She had quite a bit of the devil in her, too.

His mother wasn't inside the house, and no one was up at Luisa's place yet. Then he saw cigarette smoke coming from the outhouse.

He sneaked up on the outhouse under the avocado tree. He could hear his old mother singing quietly. The early morning sunlight was coming down through the tree branches in sheets of gold and silver, illuminating the slender building like a tall, upright altar.

"Mama," he said, "hurry! I have to talk to you."

"But, why should I hurry?" she asked. "This is one of my most enjoyable moments of my entire day."

"But, Mama, I talked to Lupe about marriage last night."

"So," she said, "come back when you have something a little more definite, like grandkids or something."

She laughed, truly enjoying herself, and she pushed the door open. There she sat covered with her serape so the morning breeze wouldn't chill her. She had the Bible open on her lap, a cigarette hanging from her lips and a glass of whiskey in her left hand. She took the cigarette out of her mouth, sipped her whiskey and then handed Salvador her empty glass.

"Go and get me a little more *whiskito*," she said, putting the Lucky back to her lips, "while the Virgin and I finish our visit."

"But, Mama," said Salvador, "all my life I've waited to come to tell you this news, and now you just sit there, preferring to do *caca*?"

"Of course," she said, "to start off each morning praying for God, smoking and drinking for myself and crapping for the devil is one of my greatest pleasures. Now go on, please, and get me a little more *whiskito* and then start the fire and put on the coffee and heat me a sweet roll. Then, when I'm all done here and feeling good and clean inside, I'll come into the house and listen. But, now, go on, the Virgin and I are in the middle of some very juicy gossip!"

Shaking his head, Salvador did as told, leaving his mother to talk to the Virgin Mary. He went inside and got her a whiskey and then started a fire in the wood-burning stove and put on the coffee.

His mother came in, carrying her Bible, just as he was heating up her sweetbread.

"You know," she said, "this toilet paper that Luisa got me is extraordinary. It's far better than the avocado leaves. The leaves slip too much when they're green and break up too easy when they're dry."

"Mama!" said Salvador, cutting her off. "Enough about all that! Didn't you hear me? I talked to Lupe about marriage! And, well, she sort of said yes."

"Sort of?"

"Well, it wasn't really an official proposal, Mama," he said. "You see, Lupe was driving the Moon around the open field and then her little niece asked if we were going to get married."

"Her niece?"

"Yes," said Salvador, and he told his mother the whole story as they drank their coffee and ate their sweetbreads. It was wonderful, sitting there, talking with his mother. There was no one in all the world that Salvador loved to talk to more than his own mother. She truly listened and made him feel so special.

"Oh, *mi hijito*," said his mother once he was done with his story, "come and kneel here beside my chair so I can hug you to my heart. I've waited for this day all my life, for my youngest to join in holy matrimony. Remember how desperate we were at the Rio Grande, but I swore to you before God that we'd survive and I'd live to see the day that you marry?

"Well, I did; I survived, and I'll tell you why: because marriage is the greatest journey any man and woman can ever undertake—two strangers, not knowing each other, but yet still willing to join together in heart and soul—hoping, guessing on which star that might land as they cross the heavens, hand-in-hand like two clouds gliding on the winds of God's breath. Oh, I'm so proud of you. Give me your hand; let me kiss you." They kissed and held each other close, feeling, thinking, dreaming, then she pushed him away, holding him at arm's length. "All right, no more of this, for I want you to realize that now is no time to sit back and enjoy the fruits of your labor.

"No," she said, closing her eyes and raising her bony index finger, "as I told you the other day, I've seen many a young lover lose the one that they love because they hesitated. This is war! Do you hear me, *mi hijito*? Time to do battle! Now you must move forward relentlessly and make your proposal formal so that the whole world can recognize your commitment.

"Your own father and I were talking of marriage with our eyes and caresses but, I'll tell you, it meant nothing to the other single girls of my village until we announced our formal proposal so that the whole world could see that we were serious."

"Oh, Mama! Do you always have to . . ."

"Don't 'Oh, Mama' me anymore!" she snapped. "I'm old! I don't have much time! So stop this nonsense and let's put our heads together! Some people think that the things of the heart are so delicate that they must be handled with great care. But I'm not one of these people. I say that the heart is tough and vigorous, overflowing with life's juices, so I say that we must be equally tough and decisive, too, and get to the heart of the matter or we'll lose everything!

"Do you really think for a minute that I got your father to propose to me because I was so kind-hearted?" she said, making a face. "He was gorgeous! I had to wrestle him away from every girl in our village to get him in my bridal bed!"

"Oh, Mama," said Salvador.

"I said don't 'Oh, Mama' me!" She took a deep breath. "Now, to get you married and settled down, let me see, we'll need a ring. And not just any ring. But a ring worthy of this occasion. For you must realize," she added, tears coming to her eyes, "that this will be the first marriage of one of my children that I'm having the pleasure of witnessing during peacetime. Oh, war is terrible! It robs a mother of all her joys in life."

"I'll be," said Salvador, taking his old mother in his arms as he knelt on the floor beside her. "I'd never thought of that. I'll make this wedding the biggest *fiesta* the barrio has ever seen!"

"Good," she said, "I'd like that. You see, you haven't had children yet. So you're not even half grown. You have no idea how important this is to me." She drew herself up, drying her eyes. "And we must do everything by tradition. We're going to need someone to ask for her hand for you." She breathed deeply. "Maybe Domingo will get here in time to do it. He'll be the oldest male in our family when he gets here. Oh, that Virgin better do Her part, or I swear the heavens are going to be in deep trouble, I tell you."

Back in Hemet, the people were still talking about Salvador and how he'd let Lupe drive his grand automobile around the open field without her even knowing how to drive. The men loved it, Salvador was a real *macho* and the rumors started once again that Salvador had to be a bootlegger to have such utter disregard for a valuable car.

Hearing the talk, Victoriano angered and told the men off.

"Those are lies!" he said. "We worked with Salvador moving fertilizer. He has trucks; that's how he makes his money!"

The men just shrugged, realizing that liquor was looked down upon in Victoriano's family, but they'd meant no harm. Hell, *la bootlegada* was a good business as far as they were concerned, and they admired Salvador if, in fact, he was a bootlegger.

Lupe heard the rumor, too, but she paid no attention to the men talking. She, like her brother, didn't want to believe that Salvador could possibly have anything to do with that awful business of bootlegging.

For the next few days, Salvador asked around about wedding rings, but he found nothing that he thought was special enough. He decided to go up to Pasadena to see the madam of the whorehouse that sold liquor for him and ask her. Some of her girls were sometimes given expensive jewelry by rich customers and so, maybe, she'd be able to make a deal with one of them. And, also, Salvador was missing Lupe so much that his whole body was exploding; he had to release the tension from his loins or he'd rip apart.

Salvador arrived at the whorehouse just before midnight. The place was hopping. This was one of the finest houses of pleasure in all the Southland. The girls were absolutely beautiful. Many of them were aspiring actresses waiting to break into the movies.

Salvador was in the backroom waiting to speak to the madam, Liza, when he overheard a couple of well-dressed young men talking about a ship full of Canadian whiskey that had caught on fire off the coast of Santa Monica.

"But some of the stuff was salvaged and is going for over a hundred dollars a case!" said one of the men.

"Man, I'd give anything to get hold of some Canadian whiskey," said the other young man.

Instantly, Salvador got an idea, and he left without waiting to speak to anyone.

He drove over to the big warehouse in downtown Los Angeles and waited for it to open its doors. He bought all the empty cases of Canadian whiskey that they had and then drove over to Corona and picked up Epitacio and Jose.

"We got to work fast," he said. "This won't last for long."

They drove into the hills to where they'd hidden the barrels. All day long and into the night, they filled the empty Canadian whiskey bottles with their bootleg whiskey. They added a little brown sugar to each bottle and sealed it. Then they took the cases down to a riverbed and burned them and tossed sand on them.

That night, Salvador drove back up to Pasadena to the fancy whorehouse and offered a deal to the madam.

"Listen, Liza," he said, "I found a few cases of that shipwrecked whiskey. Taste it. It's good. And I'll give you twenty dollars for every case I sell here at your place."

Liza only grinned. "I don't need to taste it, Sal," she said.

"Then we got a deal?"

"That's right, honey," she said.

"Good," said Salvador.

That night alone he managed to sell every case that he had for one hundred dollars each. Salvador made better money that night than he'd made in all his life. Selling retail instead of wholesale was damned good business, especially if you happened to be the manufacturer.

He was so excited and was so much in love that he went with five different women that night. Oh, he was burning with desire. He now understood why it was traditional for the bridegroom to have a bachelor's party at a whorehouse the night before he got married. The way he felt, it would be dangerous for him to go to bed with a virgin. He needed a very experienced woman to calm him down and make him civilized.

It was late afternoon the next day when Salvador left Liza's place and headed back to Corona. He was going to pick up Epitacio and make up one last batch of Canadian whiskey to bring back to the whorehouse. People had actually started fighting over the chance to buy some of his shipwrecked whiskey. Oh, life was wonderful here in this country. Liquor making was illegal, and yet there was a big warehouse in Los Angeles legally selling everything a bootlegger needed.

When he got to Corona, there was a *fiesta* going on. Their neighbor, Rodolfo the schoolteacher, had killed a pig and everyone was eating and drinking. Doña Margarita was packed and ready to leave for Chicago the following day. The Virgin Mary hadn't come through for her, and she was saying goodbye to everyone in the barrio.

"Oh, Salvador!" yelled Luisa, having had a few too many, "you got to stop Mama!"

"But how?" asked Salvador. "Tie her up? That would break her spirit,

Luisa. I'd rather see her dead than kill her by stopping her from following her dreams!"

Lunging forward, Luisa slapped Salvador across the face with all her power. Salvador went flying backwards. He couldn't remember ever being struck harder by a man in all his life.

"Don't you dare talk like that!" she screamed, going to hit him again. "She has to live; do you hear me? Live!"

Salvador grabbed her hand in mid-air. "You're drunk, Luisa! Stop it!"

"Stop it yourself! You just don't care if Mama lives or dies!"

Doña Margarita saw them fighting and came rushing up. "Have you two no shame? What's wrong with both of you?"

"But, Mama, I love you so much that I don't want you going to Cheee-a-caca," said Luisa. "You'll never come back! Salvador is wrong to say you can go."

"Luisa, where is your faith?" her mother said. "Don't you see that it's peacetime here in this country? It was a thousand times worse for me when I went to Guadalajara to get your brother Jose released from prison!"

"But, Mama, you don't speak English! This is all different! And I love you too much!"

"And Salvador loves me less?" she snapped. "No, Luisa! This has nothing to do with love! You've just lost your faith in the Almighty and are trying to impose your will on everyone, like a priest gone bad! Now sit down and listen to me and see if you can't recapture your senses and see that what I'm about to undertake is nothing more than another trial given to me by Almighty God!"

The old lady made the sign of the cross over herself and sat Luisa and Salvador down so she could talk to them. She began to tell them the story of how she'd gone to get their brother Jose released from prison back in Mexico during the Revolution. All the people at the *fiesta* gathered around the old lady to listen, too.

"Remember, we had nothing left and we were alone," she said. "All the men of our family were gone or dead, only God knew which. And the authorities had arrested Jose because he'd embarrassed our local marshal by protecting a widow's honor.

"Remember, Salvador," she said, turning to her son, "you were about seven or eight, and you and Domingo still had that black bull, Chivo, that you'd raised from a calf?"

Salvador nodded. "How could I ever forget, Mama? I'd never been without you and I broke away from Luisa, and ran after you. But you paid me no attention. So I just followed behind you up the road, crying my head off, and Chivo stayed right beside me like a big black dog."

"It was the end of the world for us, Mama," said Luisa. "Papa was gone to the United States to look for work and we didn't know if he'd ever return. And Alejo, Jesus, Mateo—all my big brothers—were dead, having been killed in the war, and Domingo had also disappeared; and here you were, going off, leaving me to take care of my little brother and my two sisters." Luisa wiped her eyes. "We almost died of fear, Mama. That's why I don't want you to do it again."

"But the point is that you didn't die," said Doña Margarita, "and you're big now. So quiet; no more of this, and let me finish my story." She sipped her whiskey.

"I went down our mountain and past the lakes to the road," said Doña Margarita, "and you followed me, Salvador, crying the whole way. Finally, just this side of Josephine's place, I stopped, thinking that you'd cried enough, and I sat you down on a rock underneath an oak. You were breaking my heart with all your crying, but I still explained to you that I had to go alone.

" 'But why can't I go with you, Mama?' you asked me. And I said, 'Because a person alone is an army, *mi hijito*. They're frightened, they have no distractions, so they keep their eyes as alert as the newborn chick. And I need this, *mi hijito*,' I said to you, 'for I have nothing else except my wits and the backing of God Almighty!'

"And so I kissed you goodbye on your tear-covered cheeks one more time and then I left, leaving you there with your pet bull, barefoot and with your little pot belly hanging out over your pants," she said, laughing.

"And so when I got to Arandas, I was so tired that I immediately went to the church to pray. I needed to regain my strength and figure out what to do. For, remember, even God needs help in making miracles here on earth."

A murmur went through the crowd.

"Then, I don't know, but I must've fallen asleep, for the next thing I knew I heard a voice speaking to me like in a vision. And I was told that I did, indeed, know someone very powerful in Arandas who could help me: the enemy of my husband.

"A great peace came over me and I wanted to go back to sleep, but you know how God is once He starts talking to you. He just wouldn't shut up."

She laughed and everyone laughed, too, not thinking that it was strange or uncommon for one of their people to be spoken to by God. After all, they all had relatives who told stories just like these. And they cherished them.

"So, not being able to sleep, I went out of the church armed with God, and I went across town to my husband's enemy, the very same man who'd tricked him out of our goats years before. I went into his store of business and I waited my turn to introduce myself. When I did, he got very angry. But, of course, I didn't shy away, having the Lord God on my side, and I simply told him that I'd come for his help. He was shocked.

" 'But don't you realize that I have bad blood with your husband?' he said to me. 'Señora, I want nothing to do with you or any of your family for as long as I live,' he yelled.

" 'Sometimes I feel the same way,' I said, refusing to take insult. 'Now, as I was saying, my son Jose is in prison and I need your help.'

"The man sat back. 'Señora,' he said, 'a revolution is going on! We all have our problems! Now, no more of this; I have work to do! Get out! I have no time!'

" 'But I do,' I said. 'All the time in the world. Look, I brought food and water so I'll just settle down in this corner until you have time for me.'

"He stared at me as if I were crazy. 'Lady,' he said, 'either you don't understand Spanish or something is very wrong with you! I hate your husband and all his offspring for all eternity! I would do nothing to help you and your son, even if I could!' And he turned his back on me, returning to his customers, but I had God on my side so I had no doubt; I just sat down on the floor and began to eat my tortillas and sip my water."

Doña Margarita smiled and took up her glass of whiskey, but it was empty. Quickly, someone served her a little more. Everyone was enthralled with her story, marveling at her tenacity. She was their pillar of life, a woman who couldn't be thwarted.

"The poor man," she continued, sipping her whiskey, "he had no idea what to do with me. But I knew what to do. I just sat there for hours until I disappeared, becoming part of the furnishings, and people could no longer see me.

"And so that's when the miracle began to happen. People forgot about me, and my husband's enemy began to speak as if I wasn't there, and he told someone about what had happened between him and Don Juan. I suddenly understood everything. God had opened the door of this man's heart for me. So, I made the sign of the cross over myself and stood up, fully armed with God's words; and in one swift terrible attack, I gave that businessman what it was that he'd been wanting all these years. I gave him honor! I said to him, 'Don Ernesto, I fully realize that what happened between my husband and you was terrible. And I further agree with you that my dear husband was a fool and you are a man of honor!'

"Everyone in the place stopped their work and turned to stare at me. Especially the men. For no woman, I'm sure, had ever spoken of her husband like this and lived. But I'd never been a woman who was impressed with men's habits, not even of the Pope, himself, so I had no such scuples and I wasn't about to be silenced. So I closed my eyes in concentration and continued.

" 'I've been here for nearly three fists of the sun, Don Ernesto, and I've seen you handle situation after situation like a man of high intelligence,' I said. 'And, sadly to say, I know my good husband only too well, and I realize how he always prides himself on being able to settle business matters with his fists or guns. And I further realize that he should never have sold you those goats that day, but, also, he had no right to later rope you off your horse and beat you with his fists like a fool!

" 'For, I swear to you, as my father the great Don Pio always told me, fists and guns are only the tools of children and fools! The real battles of life are won by planning, thinking and hard work; having the confidence not to panic into violence but, instead, to hold steady as a rock and keep working as you yourself have done here in your business, Don Ernesto!'

"And then I opened my eyes, looking at the businessman, and I saw that I had him. I'd given him what he'd wanted with conviction. But now I needed more, much more. I needed his love. So I closed my eyes again, drawing up from my deepest powers of what God had given me, and said, 'And, furthermore, I'd like to apologize for my husband's foolish behavior and salute you, Don Ernesto, who's done so well! For yes, I fully know that your father left you money and I know that fools talk and they say that that's how you got to where you are today in this fine office, but they are wrong! " 'Give a fool money, and he'll lose it by sunset, especially with this war going on all around us. The truth is that it takes greater cunning to keep what's been given to you than to build up from nothing. For when you have nothing, you have nothing to lose, and so you can afford to be brave. But you were brave even when you had much to lose, and so I salute you! You have done wonders with what your father left you. You are a man to respect! And I do!' "

The people applauded, and Doña Margarita grinned, showing her one good tooth. "Oh, I had him good by then, I tell you! He just sat there, staring at me, seeing me for the first time, seeing my bare feet and rags; and I guess that he thought of his own mother because tears came welling up in his eyes.

" 'Señora,' he said, standing up and coming around his desk to take my hand, 'you can have whatever you want within my capacity! You are an inspiration! You are a living tribute to your father, the great Don Pio, who, of course, I remember well, even though I was very young when he came to this region and drove the bands of bandits out of our mountains. I bow my head in respect to you and his great memory.' "

" 'Thank you,' I said, 'thank you. And all I need from you is train fare to Guadalajara. God will provide me with the rest.'

" 'I'm sure He will,' he said to me, and he gave me the money I needed, plus some extra cash, and then had one of his best men drive me to the train depot over the mountains, two towns away.

"And that was just the beginning, Luisa," said their mother, turning to her doubting daughter, "the beginning of my God-given days of miracles!"

"Oh, Mama, I'm sorry I doubted you," said Luisa. "But I'm just so frightened for you. Especially since you insist on going alone again."

"Your lack of faith tires me," said the old lady. "And, besides, the point is that Cheee-a-caca will be easy. Nothing compared to what I had to do to get your brother Jose released. Domingo isn't in jail, as far as we know."

"Please, Mama, go on with the story," said Salvador. "Tell us what happened on the train. That's my favorite part."

"Yes, please go on, *señora*," said several of the people.

"Well, all right, but give me a little more *whiskito*, and then I'll go on if you insist."

She loved all the attention she was getting. Pedro rushed inside to get another bottle of whiskey.

"You know," she said, confessing, "in my dreams lately I've been dreaming that I'm the Pope and Cheee-a-caca is the whole world."

"And you are the Pope!" said Rodolfo, "of my heart and soul!"

Everyone laughed. Don Rodolfo and Doña Margarita had become very close with all their letter writing.

"Well," she said, sipping the whiskey that she was served, "getting on the train, I decided to find the richest, most powerful-looking man I could. For you can't squeeze water out of the poor any more than you can out of the rocks. So, I finally found a well-dressed man in a private car, reading. I sat down next to him and told him that was a fine book, that I'd read it many times myself.

"He glanced at my ragged clothes and he didn't know what to think, so he got up and moved away from me. But I stuck to him like a tick on a dog's ass, saying to him 'Don't you realize you can't get away from me? You're on this train, *señor*, because you were sent to me by God.' "

"You really said that?" asked Salvador.

"Of course," she said. "And I'll tell you," she continued, "he tried to get away from me again, but I grabbed him this time. 'Sit down,' I said, 'I can't keep chasing you up and down the train. I'm too old for that. And, besides, I'm no prostitute making an advance at you!' "

Everyone roared with laughter. Especially Salvador. He loved this outrageous part of his mother's story. He could just picture the rich man shitting in his pants.

" 'I'm a mother that's here before you because my son is in prison and doesn't deserve to be! And the story I'm about to tell you makes that book you're reading pale in comparison! Because what I'm about to tell you is absolutely true and it comes from here, inside a mother's burning soul!'

"And at that moment, the train jerked in its tracks, as if by the mighty hand of God, and the man was thrown back into his seat; and I knew that I had him now."

And so, closing her eyes, Doña Margarita continued speaking, telling everyone of how she'd given this man what he wanted, too: a spellbinding story of her son, Jose, the great, the protector of their mountains, and how he and only a handful of youths had kept the Revolution away from their mountains for years.

"And I explained to him that Jose was short and dark like myself," said the old lady, "but that such a man isn't measured in height from his feet to his head, but from his head to heaven above! For a man like Jose gives proof to the living world that God lives here on earth! And each new generation needs to do this for themselves, if God's name is to remain a living force!

"Then I explained to him how my son had gotten arrested, not because he'd destroyed army after army, but because he had put to shame the local federal marshal who'd tried to force himself on a beautiful young widow.

And now he was sentenced to be executed in Guadalajara for such an act of chivalry!

"And, oh, I tell you, I kept that rich man on the edge of his seat with Jose's great feats and daring examples of greatness until we reached Guadalajara. Getting there, the rich man took me to his home, gave me money, and introduced me to all the important people that he knew. Armed with the names of these rich, influential people, I went to their homes and I petitioned them day and night until I got a dozen of them to go with me to the prison to get my son released to me in my custody.

"The officer in charge of the prison was outraged, saying that no one, but no one, had ever been set free from his prison before. He told me that I was either the devil himself or I was the most cunning, determined woman he'd ever had the misfortune of encountering.

" 'If my soldiers had half of your balls, *señora*,' he said, 'there'd be no Revolution!'

" 'No, you're wrong,' I told him, 'for my *tanates* are the breasts that give milk to every child in every village in all of Mexico—no matter how poor— and that's why you will LOSE! Now! And for all eternity!'

"He got so mad that he threw me out, along with my son Jose, but only on the condition that Jose promise never to fight against them again. And he did—he kept his word—God rest his soul. But for what? Only to be shot down by the Rangers in Albuquerque when they mistook him for another *mejicano*!"

Tears came to her old, wrinkled-up eyes and she got to her feet. "I will not lose another of my sons!" she shouted. "I will not! So help me God! And so that's why I'm going to Chee-a-caca and I'm going alone! Alone, but with God! And the devil be warned, for I'm armed to do battle with the entire populace of the earth!"

And hearing this, Luisa fell to her knees, begging for forgiveness, and there wasn't a dry eye in all of the yard.

"But, it is not for me to forgive you!" said her mother. "It is for you to make amends with your brother!"

The people saw that it was time to move away, so they all went back to the *barbacoa*. Luisa took Salvador aside and apologized to him for having slapped him.

"I'm sorry, Salvador," she said, "but I keep forgetting how incredible our mother is. You're right, we shouldn't try to stop her. Doing the impossible gives her life!"

Some of the people had gone home and things were calming down. The moon was bright and the stars were plentiful. Luisa and Salvador were visiting together when Pedro came running up to them.

"Grandmother!" shouted the boy. "She fell down dead!"

"No!" screamed Salvador, rushing across the yard, thinking that his beloved mother had had a heart attack.

But getting there, Salvador saw that his mother was already coming to, and a tall, redheaded man was beside her. At first, Salvador couldn't figure out who the stranger was. But then he almost dropped dead in his tracks, too. Why, it was their father, Don Juan, standing before his beloved mother. But he was so much younger than the last time Salvador had seen him.

"Is that you, Juan?" asked the tall, handsome man, grinning with outstretched arms toward Salvador. "I don't know what happened. I came up to Mama and she just . . ."

And in that split instant, Salvador suddenly realized that he wasn't looking at his father after all, but he was, indeed, seeing his long-lost brother Domingo. Why, this truly was a miracle sent to them by God. Domingo was the reincarnation of their dead father all over again: tall and handsome and eyes as blue as the sea.

Salvador rushed up and hugged Domingo in a big *abrazo*. Luisa came, too, and she was shouting at the top of her lungs:

"Domingo! Domingo!"

It became a joyous time of wet eyes and big *abrazos*. Two neighbors slaughtered a goat, and Salvador brought out another barrel of whiskey. It became the biggest celebration that the barrio had seen in years. Every one of them had lost a brother or sister, and so they knew what the family of the Villaseñors was feeling. The winds of war and the turmoil of poverty had separated many a loved one.

"Oh, *Dios mío!*" said their mother, reaching for Domingo for the umpteenth time. "Why, you're your father all over again!"

And she drew him close once more, running her fingertips over Domingo's face, inch by inch, curve by curve, memorizing them. Then she drew him to her heart, closing her eyes, holding him in rapture.

Salvador had tears in his eyes as he watched his old mother holding his brother in her arms with such adoration. Oh, he loved his brother, too; he really did. They'd grown up together, being so close in age. Domingo was only five years older than Salvador, and they'd been constant companions until Domingo had suddenly disappeared at the age of thirteen, just before Jose, the great, had been arrested.

"Oh, I loved your father so much," Doña Margarita was saying to Domingo, "so very, very much! And now here you are, his living image! For the first fifteen years of our marriage, I don't think that there ever lived a happier woman. Why, we were so strong," she said, "and every eighteen months I'd pop us out another child, and we'd just hurry back to making more!"

Her eyes filled with tears. "But then came that terrible winter when the mountaintops turned white and the wolves came down in packs, and we went hungry and the livestock died. Then the Revolution came upon us, too, and oh, *mis hijitos*, you youngest ones just never got to see Don Juan when he was young and strong! He was wonderful! But, when you last children saw him, he was a broken, tired old man."

And so she continued talking, and they stayed up all night: Luisa,

Epitacio, Jose, Pedro, Salvador, Domingo and the American woman named Nellie that Domingo had brought with him from Chicago, and a couple of the neighbors.

Nellie was a big, tall redheaded woman with a complexion as beautiful as Domingo's. She smiled constantly, had on a lot of makeup and had a very shapely body.

In the early morning hours of the night, a neighbor brought out a pot of *menudo*. Luisa chopped some fresh cilantro and green onions, then started making tortillas. Everyone laughed themselves silly when Nellie went up to the counter and started making tortillas with Luisa.

"I've taught her well, eh?" said Domingo proudly, wolfing down his *menudo* and asking his woman to fix him another bowl.

Nellie came over and got Domingo's bowl, and she didn't seem to mind when he patted her on the ass in front of everyone. But Salvador noticed that his mother wasn't comfortable with it at all.

"Are you Catholic?" their mother asked Nellie in Spanish.

"Yes," said Nellie, also in Spanish. "I'm Irish Catholic."

"And you two are married then?" continued the old lady.

Good-naturedly, Nellie began to answer Doña Margarita's question, but Domingo cut her off with a look, then turned to his mother.

"No, not yet, Mama," he said, "but we do plan on getting married."

"Well, I hope that it's soon," said the old woman. "What are you, Nellie, four or five months?"

Salvador was stunned. Nellie absolutely didn't look pregnant to him.

"Four and a half," said Nellie.

"Is this your first?" asked their mother, already knowing the answer, but wanting to see if the girl would lie to her.

"No," said Nellie, glancing at Domingo nervously, who was getting more upset by the moment.

"How many have you had?"

"Mama!" said Domingo, getting to his feet. "Please, we just arrived. There's more to talk about than just Nellie's condition. I still don't know what happened to Papa. Is he here or is he still back in Mexico?" he asked.

"All right," said his mother, "we won't talk about Nellie right now, if that pleases you, Domingo. But, before I tell you about your father, answer me this: Why didn't you answer our first letters that we sent you?"

"All right," said Domingo, putting his arm around his woman, "I'll tell you. When the first few letters came, I thought nothing of it. But then, when all the neighborhood began receiving letters and could talk of nothing else, I began to believe it really was you, Mama! 'Who else,' I said to myself, 'would have the faith to just keep writing?' " He laughed, squeezing Nellie close. "Oh, for so long I'd thought you were all dead! Epitacio, here, I remember him trying to tell me about some Villaseñors when I met him, and I almost killed him, I got so mad."

He laughed again, sitting there, and Salvador still couldn't get over it.

Why, he was the living picture of their father: the blue eyes, the reddish-brown hair, the fair skin with freckles, the beautiful white teeth and large, well-carved masculine features, plus the way he laughed. Domingo was a man among men who didn't just turn women's heads when he entered a room, but men's, too.

"You see," continued Domingo, "when I went back to our mountains, I found no one . . . and . . . and . . . everything was destroyed—the orchards, the barns, the corrals, the whole settlement—everything."

"You mean you returned to our mountains after we'd all left?" asked Salvador.

"Why, of course," said Domingo. "I'd never intended to stay away. Hell, I'd been trying to get back for years." Tears came to his eyes. "But I was in debt-labor to an American company in Chicago, and they told me I'd be put in prison if I tried to leave. I was only thirteen, so how was I to argue? Oh, I was lost, I tell you!" he screamed in agony.

Nellie hugged him, giving him comfort, and he wiped his eyes. "You must realize that when I left home, I came to the United States with two other boys," he continued. "I'd thought I'd surprise Papa in Del Mar, California, and work out the season with him and return home with him. But I was such a fool! I had no idea of how the *gringos* thought of us."

"Then you knew where Papa was?" asked Luisa.

"Sure," said Domingo. "He'd come to work with our cousin Everardo, driving mules to build the new highway up the coast from San Diego to Los Angeles. I figured I'd find him easily. But the Texas Rangers didn't contract me to California, like they promised; those sons-of-bitches . . ." he screamed, "lied to me and sent me to Chicago!"

"Exactly!" yelled Epitacio. "Laughing at us all the way, those damned Rangers, they give their word of honor as men and then they send you wherever they damned please instead!" He was furious. "Excuse my language, ladies, but it's just . . . oh, they've ruined so many families, those tricky Texan bastards! They don't consider us *mejicanos* people! Just mules! Dogs! Worse than slaves!"

"Exactly!" said Domingo. "Slaves they have to pay money for, so they have value and treat 'em better."

"Yes, that's true!" said Epitacio.

"All right," said Doña Margarita, "enough! Now go on."

"So, well, anyway, I was in Chicago for years, looking for Del Mar," said Domingo. "I spoke no English and so they just kept lying to me, until I finally paid off my debt, which took me four years! Then I immediately returned to our mountains, expecting to find you there."

He began to cry so hard, he couldn't speak. Nellie began to cry, too. She really loved Domingo.

"But you were all gone and everyone kept saying that you'd been killed," he continued. "Oh, I felt like an orphan! And the ranch was destroyed! Nothing existed that I'd known."

Salvador handed Nellie his handkerchief.

"Finally, beaten and crazy with grief, I returned to Chicago, and that's when I met you, Epitacio," said Domingo.

"But my letters," said Doña Margarita to Domingo, "didn't you read them?"

Domingo looked at his mother full in the face. His eyes were bloodshot. "You want to know the truth, eh, Mama?" he asked with a vicious look in his eyes.

"Yes," she said, unflinchingly. "I do."

"Well, the truth is," he said, "that I didn't believe those letters, and . . . I wished you all DEAD!" He jumped from his chair, falling on his knees. "Forgive me, Mama," he screamed, "forgive me! But I'd suffered so much that I didn't want any more pain."

He hugged his mother around the legs and buried his face in her lap, crying freely now. His mother hugged him and patted him on his head and glanced at the others, but no one was embarrassed. For they all well knew what it was like to lose faith.

"It's all right, *mi hijito*," said Doña Margarita, holding his huge head on her tiny lap, "God will understand and forgive you. Faith, after all, is very difficult. I know, believe me, for I've lost mine time and again."

Salvador stared at his mother. How could she speak like this? She was always the power, the light, even in their darkest hours.

"Sit up, Domingo," said his mother. "Believe me, I understand; I've wished you and my other lost children dead many, many times so I could just quit my vigil." Her eyes overflowed, too. "War, it's no fun for a mother or a child." She said no more.

Salvador was stunned; he'd never realized that his mother's faith also faltered.

They finished breakfast, and Salvador brought out a bottle of his best twelve-year-old whiskey.

"Here, taste it, Domingo," said Salvador. "This is my best."

"Not bad," said Domingo, rolling the whiskey about inside his mouth. "But you should taste the whiskey I've made. Oh, yes, I was in the big time," he added, smiling handsomely, "with Al Capone's people."

"With Al Capone?" said Salvador. "But I thought you said you worked in the slaughterhouses and then in high-rise construction."

"That, too!" said Domingo quickly. "I'm a man who's done a lot of different things!"

And he would've gone on bragging about himself, but Doña Margarita cut him off.

"Domingo," said his mother, "your father . . . your father, he's dead. He died up on the ranch."

Domingo stared at her. "But how?" he asked. "Oh, my God, Mama! How? In your arms?"

She looked straight into her son's eyes. Salvador and Luisa looked, too. This was going to be bad.

"No, Domingo," said the old woman. "I wish it would have been that way, but it wasn't. He died alone up on the mountain."

Domingo glanced around the room. "But what do you mean, 'alone up on the mountain?' Are you keeping something from me?" he asked. "I demand to know what happened!" He leaped to his feet, eyes bloodshot, with sudden, unexpected rage.

"Your father," continued Doña Margarita calmly, "when he came back from the United States and found the ranch destroyed and you gone, Domingo, he started drinking like he'd never done before."

"Oh, no! NO!" screamed Domingo.

"Yes; he wouldn't eat, and he'd go yelling from mountaintop to mountaintop, searching for his sons. Then one day, some neighbors found him dead in the barn, clutching the remains of his horse." Her eyes drew inward. "The poor man must have shot his horse when he felt his hour coming, so that he'd have a mount to ride across the heavens."

"And you weren't there when it happened?" yelled Domingo, pounding the table, shattering the dishes. "BUT WHY DID YOU PEOPLE DESERT HIM!" he screamed. His eyes were as bloodshot as a bull's in battle. The vein across his forehead pulsated. He was wild, crazy, insane, staring at them with vengeance.

But no one said anything. They were too shocked. Domingo was Don Juan Salvador all over again, screaming at them as Don Juan had always done, too.

Luisa was the first to speak. "But we didn't desert him," she said calmly. "He left us, Domingo."

"Lies!" roared Domingo. "You left him on the mountain!"

"No, we didn't!" yelled Salvador, leaping to his feet, too. "He left us, just like you left us, you fool! And we starved!"

"Oh, so now I and my good father are to blame for our family's misfortune, eh?" said Domingo, smiling viciously.

"Yes!" screamed Salvador. "A thousand times, yes!"

Domingo went to hit Salvador, but quick as a cat Salvador hit Domingo first full in the face, knocking him over backwards, crashing into the tall cabinet full of cups and dishes.

Salvador continued crying. "And when I went up to get our father, begging him to come down and be with us because Luisa's husband had gotten killed and we needed him, he just bellowed to the heavens to leave him alone to die in peace because all his sons were dead. I told him that I was his son, too, Domingo. But he just kicked me away like a dog because I wasn't blue-eyed and tall like you and Alejo."

"Oh, this is getting good," said Domingo, turning to Nellie and wiping the blood off his lips as he got to his feet. "I told you that there'd be hell to pay, coming to see my family."

Doña Margarita just shook her head.

"I'm going to whip you, Juan," said Domingo calmly. "I'm going to whip you as you've never been whipped before!"

"Come on, you piece of shit!" yelled Salvador. "I'm not your little punching bag anymore, like when you used to bully me all the time. I spit on you, you coward! Running away and leaving us! You big, stupid, ignorant *pendejo*! We went hungry!"

Domingo just smiled, moving in for the fight.

"No, Domingo!" said Luisa, rushing between her two brothers. "It's true, Domingo! No one loved Papa more than me! But he left us! We never left him!"

"Oh, no, Luisa," said Domingo, still grinning, "my little brother here is saying much more than that. And what he needs is a whipping, just like I used to give him when we were kids because he'd run out on a fight and leave me holding off two or three boys alone!"

Then Domingo screamed. He was a huge giant of a man, bellowing to the heavens, just as their father had always done. "I never ran from a fight in all my life! And Papa never did, either! You people left him, and that's the God-awful truth!"

Saying this, Domingo charged on his younger brother, but Luisa and Nellie got between them. Seeing his brother's insane rage, Salvador suddenly remembered all the terrible things that his brother had done to him when they'd been small, and he knew that he was capable of going for his gun and killing his brother without mercy.

"Don't hold them!" yelled Doña Margarita. "Let them kill each other if they're such dogs that they have no respect for their mother!"

She downed her whiskey, got to her feet and turned on Salvador. "You had no right to strike your brother! Are you a savage that can't see he was just shocked to learn of his father's death and he knows nothing of our suffering or starvation!

"Salvador, you did wrong! Wrong! Wrong!" She grabbed him by the ear and twisted him down to the floor until he was kneeling.

"No, Mama, please!" yelled Salvador. "I'm not a child anymore!"

"Oh, yes you are, behaving like this! Now kneel there and apologize to your brother!"

"No!"

"Yes! Now!"

"No!"

"Yes! Yes! Yes!"

"All right, all right, but let go!"

"No!" she yelled, twisting all the more. "You do it now and with all your heart and soul! And you promise that you'll never strike him again as long as you live!"

"Okay, okay," said Salvador. "I apologize, Domingo. Mama's right! I had no right to strike you!"

"And you'll never hit him again as long as you live!" said his mother. "Swear it!"

"I swear it!" added Salvador.

"Good!" said Doña Margarita, letting go of Salvador's ear and then turning to Domingo.

"And now you, Domingo, understand this," she said to him, "you had no right to provoke us like that! No right, do you hear me?" she said, her eyes filling with tears. "We didn't desert your father any more than he deserted us, either!

"We were all lost! Do you hear me? Lost! Trapped by the war just as much as you were trapped in slavery in Chee-a-caca! Lost so far inside our minds and souls that your father went crazy with grief, bellowing to the heavens like a madman, searching for his sons.

" 'Alejo! Jose! Agustin! Teodoro! Jesus! Mateo! Vicente!' And you, 'Domingo!' And all his daughters, too, and all your twenty-two cousins who'd been raised under our same roof like our own children! Oh, he was a lost, broken man!

"And so now you kneel down here, too, right now, and kiss your brother; right now, take him in your arms and kiss him and ask for his forgiveness, too!"

Domingo didn't want to; he still had the devil in his eyes, but nevertheless, he did as his mother said, and it was beautiful; two big, strong men, kneeling down before their tiny old mother and taking each other in their arms, kissing and holding, giving love and warmth in a big *abrazo*. Heart to heart.

Nellie was weeping, and so was Luisa, Pedro, Jose and Epitacio; they were all so happy. For they all knew that this was the beginning of a whole new *familia* for them here in the United States. If only they could forget the past and forgive each other and go forward with open hearts.

And their beloved old mother, that great woman of God, had made it possible by making yet another miracle here on earth!

21

And so they'd found it inside themselves—the angel's head, the true love of life—a return to the Garden of Eden, the seed of their ancestry.

"Look," said Domingo to Salvador, "back in Chicago I got connections and I own a house, but I came out here so quick that, well, I'm low on cash. So, you loan me fifty dollars and I'll pay you back when the house sells, eh?"

"Sure," said Salvador, taking out his wad of money. But seeing how his brother gaped at the wad, Salvador realized that he'd made a big mistake to show it to him. After all, this wasn't money that Salvador could spend. It was his working capital, his stake, the cash he used for gambling and bootlegging.

"*Gracias*," said Domingo, putting the fifty in his pocket. "And can I borrow your truck, too?"

"Of course," said Salvador. "We're brothers. And I'm really sorry I hit you. I was wrong."

"Forget it," said Domingo. "I've been hit harder by women!"

They laughed and Domingo hung around the house, drinking whiskey and visiting with Luisa and their mother for the next few days. Epitacio and Salvador left to go back to work.

Coming back from delivering the second batch of Canadian whiskey to the whorehouse in Pasadena, Salvador figured out how he could buy a ring for Lupe and not get cheated. He was going to do as the old Mexican saying advised: "For the wild bulls of the *barrancas*, the horses of there, too," which meant that if you wanted to round up cattle in the hill country, then you had to use a horse that had grown up in that same terrain.

Over and over in his life, Salvador had found that this saying was absolutely true. A flatland horse, no matter how agile and strong, was no match whatsoever for a horse raised in the mountains. Or, as the *gringos* said, never play another man's game.

So just as Salvador had used Kenny, a good friend and a fine mechanic, to go with him to buy a car, he'd now use the smartest, coolest businessman that he knew to help him buy Lupe a fabulous ring without being robbed.

He drove over to see his tailor. Salvador was pretty nervous by the time he pulled up to the little tailor shop in Santa Ana where he had his suits and shirts made. He'd never forget how he'd managed to find this little store in the first place. A couple of years back, he'd been shopping for a place that made quality suits like the ones that Lady Katherine in Montana had taught him to wear. But every good place he came to was so big and deluxe-looking that he felt too intimidated to go inside.

Then one afternoon, he was driving through Santa Ana after delivering some whiskey to Don Manuel when he saw this little tailor's shop on the edge of town. He drove around the block three times before he got up the nerve to park his old truck in front. These were the days before he'd purchased his first fine automobile, the big green Dodge convertible. He'd learned a big lesson the day he'd been thrown out of that little two-bit restaurant in Corona. A Mexican couldn't go very far in California dressed like an honest workman. Oh, that big Dodge had really given him a lot of confidence.

And so now, driving his gorgeous Moon gave Salvador even more confidence as he pulled up to the little tailor shop. He had a good car, was well-dressed, and had money in his pocket. He asked for Harry, the owner of the place whom he'd become friends with over the past few years.

"Do you know Harry?" asked a handsome young Anglo, giving Salvador the once-over.

Instantly, Salvador felt threatened. He didn't know this salesman. He thought about leaving without even answering the question, but out of the back came Harry.

"Oh, Salvador, *amigo mío!*" said the owner in perfect Spanish.

Salvador had taught Harry and his wife Bernice a few words in Spanish, and they, in turn, had taught him a few in Yiddish.

"*Muy bien*, Harry," said Salvador. "*¿Y usted? ¿Cómo está?*"

"*Muy bien*, also," said Harry. "So what can I do for you today, Señor Villaseñor?"

"Well, could we speak alone?" asked Salvador, glancing at the salesman.

"But of course," said Harry, motioning for his helper to leave the room. The salesman did so, but he didn't like it. "Let's sit down over here in this corner and have a cup of coffee while we talk."

"Okay," said Salvador. "You see, Harry," he said, once they had their coffee, "I'm planning to get married."

"Wonderful! Marvelous!"

"But I need help to get her engagement ring," he added, looking at Harry in the eyes carefully.

"Oh, and why did you come to me?" asked Harry. "You know I'm only in the clothing business."

"Yes," said Salvador, liking that Harry hadn't jumped at the chance like a hungry wolf. "But, also, I know that business is business and you're a very smart businessman, Harry. And so, I've come to you, the man who knows how to dance the dance of fine business matters because, well, if I go to buy the rings alone, I'm afraid that, well, I'd be just a sitting duck." Having said all this, Salvador said nothing more. He was studying Harry's eyes. This was a poker game of the highest stakes.

And Harry was good; he never even grinned. No, he came through with respect. "You don't have to say another word," he said, looking at Salvador straight in the eye like a real man. "A diamond is what you want, and I know just the man to help us."

"A diamond would be fabulous," agreed Salvador. "But how does a man go about getting such a stone, Harry, without ending up with glass? I'm not a rich man; I can't afford a mistake."

Harry loved it. "*Amigo mío*," he said, taking one of Salvador's huge, calloused hands into both of his, "you don't have to be a rich man to buy a real diamond," he said. "Diamonds come in all prices and in all different qualities of perfection. But even a bad diamond isn't good enough for you, my dear, good friend!"

Salvador still felt cautious, but the man's eyes were holding good. He didn't have a wild, greedy look. "Yes, but what are all these prices?" asked Salvador.

Harry laughed. "How much money you got, Salvador?"

Suddenly, Salvador was very wary once again. But, still, he answered Harry's question. "Well, maybe if I'm lucky, two hundred dollars."

"Make it four hundred," said Harry, "and she'll be the queen of California!"

Salvador's heart missed a beat. "Okay, four hundred, but not a penny more," he said, feeling his palms beginning to sweat. Oh, he just didn't know if he was doing the right thing to trust this man.

"Great," said Harry, "that's enough if we go to this wholesale place I know in Los Angeles. But then, of course, you'll be buying all the wedding clothes here from me."

"Naturally," said Salvador.

"Perfect," said Harry, "then we go up there first thing tomorrow morning."

"Tomorrow morning?" said Salvador. He hadn't expected to move this fast. But his mother had told him not to waste any time.

"Sure," said Harry, "my friend, he's very superstitious. You see, he's Jewish and thinks that his first customer of the day brings him good luck all day long."

Salvador looked at the store owner with great suspicion for the first time. This sounded like a hustle.

"But," asked Salvador, "aren't you Jewish, too?"

"Well, of course; aren't we all?" said Harry.

"No, not all," said Salvador, "some are *mejicanos*."

"Small technicality," said Harry. "Essentially we're all lost tribes."

They both laughed.

The next morning Salvador was back at Harry's store at seven sharp. Harry's beautiful young wife Bernice saw them to Salvador's Moon, and they were off.

"You got the money?" asked Harry, once they were on their way.

"Yes," said Salvador.

"Well, give it to me," said Harry. "Because this is going to have to go fast or it isn't going to work."

Salvador didn't like it, but still, he reached into his pocket and brought out the money, handing all four hundred to Harry. Harry counted it and put it in his pocket.

"Don't worry, Salvador," said Harry. "This man we're seeing is the best wholesaler on the West Coast. I've known him since New York. He deals in only the very best of jewels."

"Yeah," said Salvador. But to himself he thought, "I just hope this whole thing doesn't backfire and they find out in the barrio that I handed all my money over to a Christ-killer. Jesus, I'd be the laughingstock of every Catholic!"

"You drive very good," said Harry to Salvador as they were getting into Los Angeles. "Myself, I can't drive. But my wife, she's ambitious, so she's learned."

"I bet she did," said Salvador.

Salvador was so anxious that he was just ready to ask for his money back so he could get away from this race of people that he knew so very little about, when they arrived at the store.

"Park right in front," said Harry. "You see, we beat him. He hasn't opened his doors yet. And when he opens, you just follow me quickly, and I'll do all the talking. You just agree with whatever I say. Understood?"

"Okay," said Salvador.

They waited twenty minutes for the store to open its doors at nine sharp, and then they got out of the car.

"You see, Salvador," whispered Harry, going to the door, "we're the first customers. Very, very important."

"Hello, Harry!" said an old man from behind the counter as they walked in. "What brings you out of the woodwork?"

"Diamonds!" said Harry.

"Good, you came to the right place. Just come this way and see what we have," said the older man.

"No," said Harry. "I want your best, Sam. The ones you keep in back."

Sam stopped cold. "You got thousands, Harry?" he shouted angrily.

"Of course," said Harry, winking at Salvador.

"All right," said Sam, turning to his young assistant, "you heard the man! Open the vault!"

Quickly, the young man hurried to the back. Harry and the older man,

Sam, made small talk. Salvador glanced around at the fine, highly-polished store. Never in a thousand years would he have dreamed of coming into a store like this. It was a place beyond any poor *mejicano's* wildest dreams.

Finally, the young man came back in with a chest of the finest polished wood that Salvador had ever seen. Salvador remembered the treasure chest in the book El Conde de Monte Cristo. The fat cook in Arizona, who'd tried to teach him how to read, had read that book to him in prison. Oh, his heart was soaring to the heavens. Then, Sam opened the small chest, and it was full of diamonds.

"Let me see that tray of rings," said Harry.

With great care, Sam pulled out the tray and placed it on the counter.

Harry looked the rings over carefully and chose two, showing them to Salvador. Then he brought out his eye-glass, put the rings to his eye, and started studying the diamonds themselves.

"How much for one of these?" asked Harry.

"You still got a good eye, Harry," smiled Sam. "We could have got rich if we'd stayed together." He put back the tray and closed the chest, just leaving out the two diamond rings. "One thousand for this one, two thousand for this other one."

"Fine," said Harry, glancing at the larger of the two rings again, then he handed it to Salvador.

Salvador took it with even more care than he'd used in handling dynamite. Why, he couldn't believe it; here he was, handling a diamond ring five times as large as any he'd ever seen, even in the movies. And he was nothing but a little backward, ignorant *mejicano* from Los Altos de Jalisco.

"You like it?" asked Harry.

"Well, yes, of course, but the price . . ."

"No buts," said Harry, cutting Salvador off sharply.

"We'll take it, Sam," said Harry, "right now, at this very moment of seven minutes past nine, for four hundred dollars."

And saying this, Harry put the roll of money on the tabletop, spreading out the twenties and fifties. The smile that had been on Sam's face left; he stared at Harry with utter hate.

Suddenly, Salvador knew that they were going to be killed.

"HARRY, YOU SON-OF-A-BITCH!" roared Sam. "I brought out these diamonds in good faith!"

"And here are four hundred dollars in good faith," said Harry.

"This is a two thousand-dollar ring, wholesale!" screamed the man.

"I know, and it's seven and a half minutes past nine right now," said Harry, showing Sam his watch. "Customers are going to be lining up to come in here all day long because of this!"

Sam heard Harry's words, and he glanced at the money, then he screamed, "All right, you cheating bastard! But don't you ever come back! Now get out of here! Before I kill you!"

Harry picked up the diamond, and they went out the door. Salvador jumped in the Moon and started the motor, expecting to see a shotgun coming at them any moment.

"Slow down, slow down; don't worry," said Harry, once they were pulling away from the curb, "he's not going to really kill us. He's my brother."

"Your brother?" gasped Salvador.

"Sure," laughed Harry, slapping Salvador on the leg as they sped away. "Oh, we got us a deal, I tell you! You're going to have to buy a lot of clothes from me, Salvador!"

"You got it," said Salvador.

But Salvador still didn't know what to think. Either these two brothers were crazy and this whole thing was all on the up and up and he'd gotten a diamond ring worth five times his money, or these two old Jews were the greatest actors in all the world and he'd been robbed. But one thing was for sure; he could never tell this story to anyone in the barrio for a thousand years! It was too incredible!

Driving back to Santa Ana, Salvador opened a bottle of his best, and they passed it back and forth. Harry told Salvador the story of his life. He and his brother had come to America from Russia with their parents and settled in New York. And the more Harry spoke, the more Salvador began to realize just how similar their stories were—full of war and bloodshed, but lots of love and respect for family.

"But then how could you do that to your own brother?" asked Salvador.

"You mean the ring?" he asked. Salvador nodded. "Hell, he's brought lots of his friends to my place and gotten clothes off me below cost, the bastard!"

"Then there's no real hate between you?" asked Salvador.

"No, not at all," said Harry. "Money isn't important."

"No, not if you got it," said Salvador.

"True, and business is just a game. Money comes and money goes. But my brother is my brother, no matter how we might disagree."

Salvador thought of his situation with Domingo and he saw a lot of wisdom in these words.

They were both pretty drunk by the time they got back to the shop in Santa Ana. They were hugging in big *abrazos* when Bernice came out of the store to take her husband inside.

Salvador thanked Harry a dozen times, then took off to Corona to show his mother and Luisa the fabulous diamond ring.

"**N**o!" screamed Luisa, taking the ring in her hand, showing it to her two boys. "A diamond! *Un diamante!* This big! And it's real! Oh, *Dios mío!* Lupe and her family are going to be so proud of you, Salvador! But, wait, who will ask for her hand for you?" she added.

"Why, Domingo, of course," said Salvador.

Their mother shook her head. "No," she said. "He won't be able to do it."

"Why not?" asked Salvador.

Domingo was visiting up the street with Nellie at a neighbor's house.

"Because, well, I didn't want to have to tell you this," said the old woman, tears coming to her wrinkled-up eyes, "but, well, when I took Nellie to church to pray with me the other day, I found out that . . . that . . ."

She couldn't go on. Luisa and Salvador glanced at each other. Pedro and Jose couldn't figure out what was going on, either. Nothing ever upset their grandmother. She was their anchor in life.

"Go on, Mama," said Salvador, taking her hand.

"*Mi hijito*, your brother is living in mortal sin!" she said with power.

"You mean because he and Nellie aren't married?" asked Salvador. "But, Mama, ever since the Revolution, people have been forced together by circumstances and then they get married later when they have the chance."

"Oh, I only wish it was that," she said. "I'm speaking of Nellie; she is already married."

"You mean to another man?"

"Yes," said their mother, "and she left her three small children, one not even a year old, to come with your brother!"

"No!" said Luisa. "She, a mother, left her children? What is this world coming to?" she added, making the sign of the cross over herself.

"Luisa," said her mother, "it's not her that I'm worried about. But what kind of man is he, my son, I ask you, to encourage a woman to abandon her child while she's still nursing from her breasts?"

Salvador was stunned. He hadn't thought of it that way. He'd been ready to put all the blame on Nellie, too. But his mother was absolutely right. What kind of man would do that?

"Oh, I didn't want to have to tell you," continued their mother. "I was hoping, praying that Nellie and Domingo would straighten out this awful mess somehow. But the more I see of them touching each other in front of us, with no regard for us or Luisa's children whatsoever, I realize that they're unconcerned with this monstrosity that they've created.

"So, no, *mi hijito*, one thousand times no; Domingo can't represent our household to ask for Lupe's hand in marriage."

Their mother took a big breath and tears began streaming down her face. Salvador and Luisa glanced at each other. It felt as if a death had just occurred within their family. After all these years of praying and hoping and agonizing for Domingo to return, it wasn't turning out to be the wonderful situation that they'd envisioned.

"I just don't know what became of this boy who came from my loins," said their mother. "Or, was he always like this and I was just the blind mother, seeing only what I wished? Or was his captivity in Chee-a-caca so long and so terrible that he lost all memory of what is moral? These are the questions that have been haunting me ever since Nellie and I prayed together before the Blessed Mother of God."

She stopped and wiped the tears from her eyes. She looked old and beaten—older and more tired than Salvador had ever seen her before. His hands became fists. He could kill his brother for what he was doing to their mother. All through their hunger and hardships, he'd never seen his mother looking destroyed like this before.

"Oh, Mama," said Luisa, "you should've told us immediately. I'll tell Domingo that he has to get out. They have to get a place of their own so they don't continue being so disrespectful with each other in front of you and the children!"

"But, Luisa, we can't do that," said the old lady. "How can I possibly allow you to tell one of my children that they aren't welcome in our home? We are a family, for better or worse. A family!"

"Mama," said Salvador, cutting in, "it's not that he won't be welcome to come by any time he wants, it's just that Luisa is right and these two houses are too little."

"Yes, that's what I meant, Mama," said Luisa. "Of course Domingo will always be part of our family."

Doña Margarita wiped her eyes and turned to see her two grandchildren. Neither boy had said a single word.

"Well, what do you two boys think of what's happened, eh?" asked the old woman. "What do you think of your fine Uncle Domingo, sucking the milk from the breasts of this woman—milk that belongs to the children that she abandoned?"

"Mama," said Luisa, "you don't have to be so . . ."

"Quiet!" said the old woman. "How else do you expect them to learn, if not now with strong words before their balls swell up and they think they're too big to listen anymore!"

Luisa didn't like it, but still, she shut up. Doña Margarita turned to her grandchildren.

"You're good boys, the two of you," she said, "so I want you to listen closely and remember this for as long as you live: a man doesn't have the choice of how or where he is born, nor does he have the complete choice of how he must die. But, to bring the miracle of life into this world, he has the absolute complete choice every time!

"DO YOU HEAR ME?" she screamed, leaping forward and grabbing Jose between the legs by his balls. "These *tanates* of yours," she said, yanking the startled boy by his balls, "are your responsibility!"

She twisted them, and Jose cringed in pain, rolling to the floor. Then she went after Pedro. But he dodged to get away. "Don't you dare run!" she yelled, tripping him. "You hold still!"

She grabbed hold of him, too, like a rangy, old she-cat in mortal battle. The boy screamed out. But she didn't let go of his balls.

"These little things you carry between your legs can impregnate a whole nation! So you got to be responsible or you'll leave children scattered to the winds like a dog in heat, and that's not right! Do you hear me?"

"Yes, yes, yes!" screamed Pedro, crying in pain.

"Good," she said, "because you're both good boys and you will grow into good men, too, or else!"

"I will!" yelped the boy. "I promise! I will!"

"Good," laughed the old lady, letting go of Pedro and smiling. "I should have put more fear into Domingo when he was little, too," she laughed, truly enjoying herself.

Pedro lay on the floor alongside Jose, rubbing himself in pain. Jose was as white as a sheet. The old lady had truly put the fear of God into him, too.

Salvador found himself readjusting his pants. He could still remember getting this same treatment from his mother when he'd been small. His mother was a terror. It was really strange that Domingo had turned out to be like this. But, then, on the other hand, he'd always been closer to their father than to their mother.

Salvador took a deep breath. He was sure glad that Lupe was strong. A good, strong woman made all the difference in making a home and raising the children. Especially the boys.

Returning to Santa Ana from Hemet, Lupe was surprised to find Mark sitting on the porch waiting for them.

"*Buenos días,*" said Mark respectfully to Lupe's family as they got down from their truck.

"*Buenos días,* Marcos," they said to him.

Then Mark looked at Lupe, and she could see it in his eyes; he'd been crying. Lupe excused herself, and she and Mark went down the street together under the tall, dark green trees. Her heart was pounding. She felt very nervous. Something was very wrong with Mark. High overhead, a huge flock of red-shouldered blackbirds came swooping in unison through the sky. The great flocks of birds were making their way back from the fields to the tall tules in the irrigation ditches to roost for the night. Lupe and Mark walked to the corner without a single word.

Turning the corner, Mark suddenly took Lupe in his arms and drew her close to kiss her as Salvador had also done, but she pushed him away. He grabbed her harder.

"No!" she yelled.

"But, my God, Lupe!" he said in frustration. "What is it? I thought you liked me!"

"I do!" she said.

"Well, then, what is it?" he asked. "Am I just being too respectful? Is that it? All my friends keep telling me that I've been a fool and you people don't understand anything unless the man's aggressive!"

He started to grab her again, to force her to kiss him. Lupe was filled with such anger, with such rage at hearing the words, "You people," that she grabbed him by the hair and yanked him away from herself. And she would have hit him if she hadn't seen the hurt look in his eyes.

"Your friends are wrong!" she said, chest heaving. "I loved it that you were gentle, Mark," she added, tears coming to her eyes.

"Then what went wrong?" he asked, wiping his own eyes.

She shook her head. She wanted to tell him about the American engineers back home marrying local girls and then leaving them. She wanted to tell him about Salvador, about how he'd looked so ridiculous when he'd come strutting towards her in Hemet and then he'd flashed out those flowers that he'd been hiding behind his back. She wanted to tell him so many things, about how she'd already been kissed by someone, and so she wasn't free to kiss anyone else anymore. But she just didn't know how to say any of this and have it come out right.

"Oh, Mark," she finally said, "it's just so complicated."

"Is it someone else?"

She thought of Maria, of her two husbands. She wanted to say no, that she loved him, too. But she couldn't. Life was difficult enough. She nodded. "Yes," she said.

He stared at her, and he was angry. It looked like he might hit her. But then he turned and started down the street away from her.

She began to cry. She loved him, she really did love him. But simply, Salvador had kissed her first. Her mother was right. When the time came, she'd know what to do. There was no question in her mind.

She turned and started for home alone. No one had ever asked her about her dreams. Salvador had, and so she was ready to follow him to the world's end.

Suddenly, she heard footsteps behind her. She turned and Mark raced up to her, grabbed her in his arms and gave her a big kiss.

"I'll be back," he said. "Believe me, I'll be back."

And he turned and sprinted off.

She stood there, feeling the touch of his lips on her lips. Oh, she would've started kissing him back, if he'd kissed her one more time. Now, she knew exactly what Maria was going through. Oh, the things of the heart truly weren't what they seemed.

She watched him disappear down the block, and she headed for home once more. Oh, Salvador and Mark just baffled her mind. She remembered the day that Salvador had caught her trying to learn how to drive. She smiled, feeling all warm.

I t was mid-afternoon when Salvador got to the distillery in Escondido to pick up the barrels of whiskey that he had to take to Archie for the Ortega Chile Dance in Santa Ana. After parking his car, Salvador was just getting ready to go inside when Epitacio came racing out of their rented house, glancing over his shoulder.

"Salvador," he whispered as he came up to him, "I don't know what to do. The last two barrels got ruined. Your brother Domingo, he . . . he . . . and I told him not to do it like that. You showed me the way to do it, but he gets so mad, telling me that he knows what he's doing, because he was bigtime in Chee-a-cago and he knows best."

The front door of the house opened, and Domingo stood leaning on the door jamb, stripped to the waist, tall and handsome and well-muscled, with a pint bottle in his hand and loud Mexican music blasting from the radio inside.

Salvador glanced around to make sure that none of the neighbors were watching. Quickly, he headed for the door to get his brother back inside. He caught a glimpse of Nellie covering her nakedness with a blanket inside the house as he came up to his brother.

"Get back inside with that bottle!" snapped Salvador angrily. "What the hell are you trying to do, get us all arrested? This is no little game, goddammit!"

"Relax, little brother," smiled Domingo, not moving, just standing there grandly. "I got everything under control."

"I bet you do," said Salvador, trying to control his rage. He walked past his brother into the house, turned off the music and glanced around. The place was a mess. He faced his brother, seeing his bloodshot eyes.

"Domingo," he said, "I don't know what's going on inside your head, but this is a distillery. And we're in the *gringo* part of town. You're lucky they haven't already had your ass arrested!"

"I thought you said you had the law in your pocket," said Domingo. "Hell, back in Chee-a-cago we'd do whatever we damned pleased."

"Domingo!" shouted Salvador, cutting him off. "I've told you a dozen times, we're not in Chee-a-cago! We're in Escondido, California. And, yes, I have the law's help, but they can only look the other way so far. We got to be careful and smart!"

"Shit, you just don't know how to handle the law," said Domingo, taking a big drink. "That's your whole trouble. Hell, Al Capone and me, we used to . . ."

"Damn it!" exploded Salvador. "I don't give a shit about your Al Capone! I'm me, Salvador! Here! Right now! And I'm not going to be put in jail because of your stupidity! Now stop your drinking! You and Nellie, get dressed! We got to get out of here quick! This place is no good anymore!"

"Oh, come on, Salvador," said Domingo, still refusing to get excited, "your whole problem is you just don't know how to live."

Salvador could see it was useless. He'd have to shoot his brother between the eyes to get him to understand. For the first time in his life, Salvador thought that maybe the whole problem with their father all those years hadn't been his terrible temper, but that he'd been just plain stupid. He decided to lie to his brother to get him out of there.

"Domingo," he said, "I got word that the sheriff's coming. Now let's move! Now!"

"But why didn't you say so in the first place?" said Domingo. "Hell, protection was my business in Chee-a-cago! You know me, little brother! I'll kill the fucking sheriff; you just give me the word!"

"All right," he said, "if I need somebody killed, Domingo, I'll give you the word. But right now, let's just go," he said, fully realizing that the dumbest little cop could make mincemeat out of this big handsome brother of his. He was a bullshitter, nothing more.

They went to work, loading the barrels of whiskey that they already had made up and took them into the hills and hid them. After getting back to the rented house, Salvador took Epitacio aside.

"We're going to have to close down this place and move," Salvador told Epitacio. "I don't want to take any chances. The neighbors might have seen something."

"I kept telling him to stay inside when he was drinking, Salvador," said Epitacio, looking like a frightened mouse, "but he just wouldn't listen to me."

"It's all right," said Salvador, putting his hand on Epitacio's shoulder. "You did the best you could. I respect you."

"You do?" he asked anxiously.

"Yes, I do."

It was like he'd given Epitacio a million dollars. The man stood up taller than Salvador had ever seen him do.

"Thank you!" he said, looking at Salvador right in the eyes. "Very much."

"You're welcome," said Salvador, and he took his brother-in-law in a big *abrazo*.

Life was really crazy, thought Salvador. Who on earth would've ever predicted that he'd be embracing Epitacio, whom he'd been hating for so long, and that he'd end up wanting to kill his brother when he'd been longing with such love to see Domingo for years? Oh, his mother was absolutely right; life was twisted with surprises. And good ones, too, if we only lived long enough to see them through.

He laughed, and he and Epitacio went to the front part of the house, looking for Domingo and Nellie.

"All right, you two," said Salvador to Domingo and Nellie, "I'm going over to Santa Ana with these first barrels, then I'll be right back. You two get ready to go. Epitacio will help you pack up your things. I want us out of this place by nightfall. We got to move fast. Remember, the slow always get killed."

"You got it!" said Domingo. "But wouldn't it be easier just to kill the sheriff?" he added, putting his arm around Nellie, wanting to impress her.

Salvador just looked at Domingo. His brother made him want to puke. He couldn't believe that they were even brothers. He was as different from him as Carlota was from Lupe. Blood just wasn't always blood.

"No," said Salvador, "it wouldn't. You get ready. I'll be back as soon as I can."

"All right, if running is how you like to live," said Domingo.

Salvador didn't even bother to answer him. To give him any more attention would just go to his head. He was a fool, no doubt about it; he was an idiot trying to impress his redheaded girlfriend.

Arriving at the well-lit place where Archie was putting on the Ortega Chile Dance, Salvador thought of Lupe, and he wondered if she was already back from Hemet. If she was, then she'd probably be coming to the dance with her sister Carlota. But, he also realized that he didn't have the time to go by and find out. He had a lot to do before sundown. His big, handsome brother was really going to put them in jail if he wasn't careful.

"Well," said Archie, coming to the backdoor when he saw Salvador drive up, "you got the liquor?"

"Yeah," said Salvador, "the first three barrels."

"Well, hurry up, then," said Archie, "let's unload 'em and get 'em inside so you can go and get the rest."

"Just hold a minute," said Salvador. "We got to talk, Archie. You and me, we've been doing business for over two years now, and well, I need a little favor."

"Sure, you name it," said Archie enthusiastically. He was in a good mood. He was sure he was going to make a killing on this dance.

"I got this brother of mine, Domingo, and, well . . ."

"It will cost you fifty dollars," said Archie.

"Fifty dollars!" said Salvador. "But what the hell are you talking about? I haven't even told you what I want yet!"

"Sure, you have," said Archie. "A man mentions his relative with a long face, and I know his relative ain't worth a shit, and he's trying to pawn him off on me for a job!"

Salvador had to grin. "But, Archie," said Salvador, "he plays the guitar good, and he has a beautiful voice."

"Sixty-five dollars," said Archie.

"Sixty-five!" shouted Salvador.

"Sure, you just told me he's lazy, not dependable and chases women and drinks!"

"You son-of-a-bitch!" said Salvador.

"You damn right!" said Archie. "But not a stupid one! I got a lot of worthless relatives, too!"

Archie laughed and laughed, slapping Salvador on the back, and they unloaded the three barrels of whiskey, while having a good time. Then Archie told Salvador to bring Domingo by this evening and that maybe he'd hire him to sing with the band.

Leaving Santa Ana, Salvador drove by Lupe's house and he saw that no one was home. He assumed that they were still gone. He took the diamond ring out of his pocket and looked at it, then gazed at Lupe's home. Ever since he could remember, he'd always known that one day he'd fall in love and marry. But he'd never really realized what falling in love truly meant until now. It meant that he wasn't lost and searching anymore. He now had a face, a person, a human being to dream about. Not lots of women, as he'd always had, but one specific woman—one face, one body, one mind, one certain kind of smile and twinkle in the eyes—on whom he could focus all his secret thoughts and feelings. Oh, it was such a joy, beyond all understanding. A person to dream of, a person to hold, here, inside your heart and mind, with such all-consuming power that it took your breath away; this was love!

He kissed the diamond ring and decided to drive by Harry's and order another suit, then go by and see his mother. But he wouldn't tell her what had happened in Escondido with Domingo. The main thing was to keep Domingo and Nellie out of his mother's home, so she didn't see how they behaved. They were people with very little shame. Love was lust to them and nothing more. They just didn't know the difference.

Harry was happy to see Salvador and they had a fine visit. Bernice was friendly with him for the first time, too.

"I can't wait to meet your fiancée," she said. "She must be very beautiful!"

"Oh, she is!" said Salvador. "The most beautiful woman in all the world!"

"I'm so glad to hear that," said Bernice. "I'll tell you what, I'll create a special wedding dress just for her!"

"Thank you," said Salvador, leaving the store.

When Salvador arrived at his mother's home, he was feeling ten feet tall. He had money in his pocket, a woman that he loved, a Jewish tailor and his wife who couldn't do enough for him, and a deputy sheriff at his side. Walking into the little shack in back, Salvador felt like a hero and he found his beloved mother in a grand mood, too.

"*Mi hijito*," she said, "I've been in church praying every day, trying to solve our problem of who should ask for Lupe's hand, and then there it was, before my very eyes."

"Another vision?" he asked excitedly.

"No, the priest," she said. "He came to tell me that he enjoyed your last gift very much."

"Yeah, I'm sure he did," said Salvador, feeling disappointed. "Man, that priest can drink! He's costing me a fortune. But what does this have to do with our problem?"

"Salvador," said the old woman, "think, don't make me have to show you how to eat at the table of miracles, too."

He still didn't get it.

"The priest," she said. "He's our answer; he's the one who should ask for Lupe's hand for us."

"Oh!" said Salvador, the light coming on inside his mind's eye. "I'll be damned! You're absolutely right. Lupe's family is very religious. Why didn't I think of that?"

"Because you're not as smart as me, *mi hijito*," she said, grinning good-naturedly. "And, also, I'm a woman, so I've had to figure things out all my life. Men can just go out and get things done without thinking. They have all of history and the good church behind them. Poor things."

"You're right," said Salvador, thinking of his brother and how he'd just stood at the doorway with the pint bottle in his hand, as if he were daring the whole world to try and do anything to him. His mother was absolutely right; so many men were so cocksure, that they never even learned how to think.

"You know, Mama," he said, "that's what Duel taught me, too. Oh, I wish you could've met that man."

"What ever became of him?" she asked. "You never said."

Salvador's whole stomach came up into his throat. "I don't know, Mama," he lied. "We just kind of went our different ways." He stood up. "Well, I got to be going. I have another delivery to make."

"When will you see the priest? We mustn't lose time."

He laughed. "Tomorrow, Mama."

"Good. I want you married soon!"

"Yes, I know," he said. Salvador kissed his mother and thanked her, and then took off to get Domingo and Nellie. He didn't have much time. Oh, how he'd wished that Lupe were back from Hemet and coming to the dance so he could propose to her. The diamond was burning a hole in his pocket.

"Now remember," said Salvador to Domingo as they came into Santa Ana that evening, "Archie is a deputy sheriff and he seems friendly and easygoing at first, but he's not. He's as cagey as a fox, so you be respectful. No playing around, understand? He's very important to me."

"Hey, stop worrying," said Domingo, patting Nellie on the thigh. "I know how to handle lawmen. Like I told you, protection was my specialty in Chee-a-cago."

Salvador just couldn't stand it anymore. He pulled the Moon over to the side of the road. "Come on, Domingo, we got to talk alone," he said, getting out of the car.

"Okay," said Domingo. "Now you're talking." And he got out of the Moon, thinking that he and his brother were finally going to have it out, man-to-man, without the women around.

He followed Salvador into a a grove of trees. There, Salvador whirled around. "Look," he said, "I don't know what the hell is wrong with you, but first you tell me that you know how to make liquor and then ruin five barrels for me, costing me a fortune. And now you bullshit me again, saying that your specialty was protection!"

Domingo only grinned. "So how are we going to settle this?" he asked. "With fists or what?"

Salvador stared at him. Why, the stupid fool thought that he'd called him out to have a fight with him. He had no concept of what it was to work out a problem.

"Jesus Christ in heaven!" yelled Salvador. "I'm talking about you lying all the time! About you not being able to tell the truth! Not about fighting, don't you understand?"

"Sure, I do," said Domingo, taking off his jacket and rolling up his sleeves. "You're trying to make a fool of me, and I'm not going to let you do it."

Salvador stared at him, at his bright blue eyes and fine, handsome features, which were so different from his own.

"Domingo, I didn't come out here to fight you or make you look like a fool. I came out here to get you to understand that I got my whole life riding on this bootlegging, and I need for us to be careful and truthful with each other or we're going to go to jail.

"Bullshit! You just want to insult me!"

"Insult you? My God, don't you understand? I want to get married. I want to buy a big ranch. I'd like for you to be my partner so we can work together as brothers should—from sun up to sun down, as Don Pio and his men did when they settled those mountains of Los Altos de Jalisco. And I'm sure that we can do this here, too. You and me, we can buy half of Oceanside and Carlsbad, from the sea to the mountains, and build us a great ranch, just like our grandfather. But we got to be careful. And no more bullshitting me. You be straight with me. I got to be able to depend on you *a lo macho*!"

"You mean it, Salvador?" said Domingo

"Of course, I mean it," said Salvador.

Domingo threw down his coat and raised his arms to the heavens, swaying back and forth like a giant under the shade of the tall oak trees. Tears came to his eyes. "Oh, Salvador!" he screamed. "I will never lie to you again! I swear it! You are my brother! My flesh and blood! All these years that I've been moving from Texas to Chicago I've dreamed of a man saying these words to me. A ranch—a big one—so we can work from sun to sun like free men, like our grandfather Don Pio and his men did! Free to breathe, to dream, to raise our families!"

Tears were streaming down his face. He lunged forward and grabbed Salvador in a huge *abrazo*, lifting him over his head. Holding him up to the sky with outstretched arms, he bellowed, "I love you! I adore you! I'll do whatever you say! You are my king!"

And they hugged and kissed, and it was wonderful.

"Oh, I've been so lost!" said Domingo, putting Salvador down. "So all alone. I left children everywhere I went, like a dog! I wanted to rebuild our family, but I didn't know how."

He talked and talked and Salvador listened, and it all started making sense now. His brother was a good man, but he just didn't know how to behave.

"Yes, I've been lying to you about everything, Salvador," he said. "I saw you doing so well, and I just wanted you and Mama to be proud of me, too. No, I never met Al Capone. That's all bullshit. And I don't own a house, and I never made any liquor, but I drank a lot of it."

"And this protection business?" asked Salvador.

"Well, that I did do for some people for a while," he said.

"I see," said Salvador, not knowing if he could believe this, either. But he let it go.

They went back to the Moon and drove off. Nellie wanted to know what had happened, but Domingo simply patted his hand on her thigh very affectionately and told her that it was between brothers, winking at Salvador. Nellie asked nothing more, enjoying the affection she was getting. Salvador was amazed. His brother just had no end to his charm. He wondered if their father had been like this, too.

By the time they arrived at the dance hall, there was already a crowd of young Mexican people walking around the block in front of the building. They were courting, Mexican-style. The girls were walking arm-in-arm in one direction in groups of four or five, and the boys were walking in the other direction in small groups, also.

Back in Mexico, this was how the young people conducted their ritual of courtship on Sundays around the plaza. But this wasn't Mexico, and there was no village plaza, so now the young people from Mexico did their Sunday courtship around the block of the movie houses or at the dance halls.

"Look," said Domingo, seeing the procession of young people, "Mexico is gone, but they still carry our traditions in their hearts."

"What do you mean?" asked Nellie, seeing how happy the sight made Domingo.

"Back home, Nellie," he said, "you'd be with your girlfriends like that, walking around the plaza, and I'd walk around in the opposite direction with my brother and friends. And when I saw you, I'd smile and say hello. Like this. Very shy, but coquettish." Nellie laughed, loving it. "Then, if you liked me, you'd smile back." She did so. "And then I'd separate myself from my friends and buy an egg full of confetti and I'd wait for you to come by again and then I'd walk up and hit you on the head with the egg," he said, laughing. "And if you gave me the eye and giggled, then I'd invite you to walk with me. But if you didn't give me the eye when I hit you with the confetti, then I'd know I'd made a mistake and I'd take off running before you hit me with a rock!

"Oh, I tell you, Nellie," he said, "I can still feel the scar I have here on my head where a girl hit me with a rock. Remember, Salvador, you were just a boy, but I was oh, maybe, a man of twelve already?"

"Yes, I remember," said Salvador, laughing. "You pinched the girl on the rumble seat, that's why she hit you with a rock."

"That's right! I'd forgotten that!" said Domingo. "Oh, I was a terror with women, even back then, Nellie!"

"Then I'm glad she hit you," said Nellie. "You deserved it!"

"Oh yeah?" said Domingo, and he grabbed Nellie, hugging her close, kissing her.

Salvador turned away, giving them privacy. "I'll go inside and see where Archie is," he said.

But then, just as Salvador was walking up to the back, the backdoors flew open and Archie came out with two men, each in a headlock under one of his huge arms. Archie's face was terrible with rage. He threw the two men head-first into the dirt.

Instantly, Domingo was out of the Moon and ready to fight, figuring that the big man was Archie and it was his job to help him.

"No!" screamed Archie, as Domingo started kicking the fallen men. "They work for me! I was just showing them a few tricks in case they have to throw somebody out!"

"Oh, so you're pretty tough, eh?" said Domingo to the huge lawman, sizing him up.

"I can take care of myself," said Archie, glancing Domingo over, too.

"All right," said Salvador, stepping between the two big men. "Archie, I'd like you to meet my brother Domingo and his fiancée, Nellie."

Nellie came up. She was dressed to kill. No one would've dreamed she was pregnant.

Seeing her, Archie took off his hat. "Glad to meet you, Nellie," he said, taking her hand and kissing her fingertips. "Salvador told me about his brother Domingo, but he failed to mention his brother's fine taste in beautiful women."

"Oh, my!" said Nellie, blushing innocently.

Fixing his tie and coat, Domingo came up and put his arm around Nellie. Domingo was only half a head shorter than Archie.

"Glad to meet you, Domingo," said Archie. "Sal has told me a lot about you. He says you play the guitar and can sing, too."

"We both sing," said Domingo, pulling Nellie in close.

Archie glanced at Salvador. "Hey, Sal, you never said anything about her needing a job, too."

"Don't worry," said Domingo. "As you can see, she has more than enough looks, and I'm real good with the guitar. So what do you pay?"

"You willing to help behind the bar, too?" asked Archie.

"Look, I'll tell you what," said Domingo, taking his arm off Nellie and grinning like a cat that had found a mouse, "in Chicago, I was in the protection business, so I'm willing to make a bet with you."

Salvador rolled his eyes to the heavens.

"I'm listening," said Archie.

"Well, you're a pretty big, strong man yourself, and you handled those two men with ease; but I'm willing to bet you can't throw me through that door like you did those two men. And if you do, then my woman and I are yours free for the whole night. But if you can't, then you pay us good. Twenty-five dollars each!"

"Twenty-five each!" yelled Archie. "Why, that's five times more than I pay anyone!"

"Yes, but you're way bigger than me; so hell, why not?" said Domingo.

Salvador was mad. He'd told Domingo not to clown around. "That's enough," he said, stepping in. "I'm sorry, Archie. I didn't know anything about this hustle. Let's just forget everything. You don't have to give my brother a job."

"No, hold on," said Archie. "This ain't no bet. Hell, I haven't been beaten in a wrestling match since I turned fifteen!"

"So then fifty it is?" asked Domingo, winking at Nellie.

"Right," said Archie, "fifty it is." And saying this, he made a mad rush at Domingo, arms stretched out and hands open like claws, so he could ram him through the two huge, open doors.

But, when he went to grab Domingo in his famous bear hug, something happened. And it happened so quickly, so suddenly, that no one saw what it was. Archie went sailing through the air, ass-end pointed to the sky, and he landed so hard on the ground that he shook the building.

Salvador didn't know what to think. He'd never seen such a thing. Only Nellie didn't seem surprised. In fact, she was in ecstasy, she was so excited.

"All right, Archie," said Domingo, offering him a hand up, "we better stop. I'll show you sometime how that's done. It's just a trick I learned with Al Capone's people. I hope I didn't hurt you."

Salvador glanced toward the heavens.

"Hurt me, hell!" yelled Archie. 'You just woke me up! That bet is still on!" And he leaped to his feet like a great cat, pulling up his suspenders.

"All right," said Domingo, "but you better put up those fifty dollars before we go any further. Collecting money from dead men is a tough job."

"Don't worry about me, little pigeon," said Archie, "it ain't me who's going to fall this time, *amigo!*" And Archie spat in his hands, rubbed them together, and made another mad rush at Domingo.

But, once more, Domingo just took three quick steps back and one to the side, ducked in close and grabbed Archie's outstretched arm, then dropped, flipping Archie through the air. This time, Archie landed against the building itself, hitting so hard that it rattled his teeth. His two bartenders came rushing out.

"Son-of-a-bitch!" screamed Archie.

"Oh, yes!" screeched Nellie with joy.

Salvador stepped in. "All right, no more," he said. He'd seen this type of setup before. Nellie was the type of woman who loved violence, and Domingo was the type of man who loved to do it for her. It was a stupid game and had absolutely no place in business.

"No more?" yelled Archie. "Hell, I'm just getting warmed up!"

"Archie," said Salvador, "this is no good. You got a dance going on inside."

"Out of my way!" bellowed Archie, seeing that Nellie was sucking her fingers. She was a she-goat in heat. "I'm gonna kill the son-of-a-bitch!"

"Domingo," said Salvador, "you tell him, this has gone far enough!"

"It's up to him," said Domingo, running his right hand up and down his woman's waist.

"Damn it, Domingo!" said Salvador.

"Out of our way!" yelled Archie to Salvador, and this time Archie didn't just attack; no, he picked up a two-by-four that was lying alongside the building and came charging with rage.

But Domingo only ducked and dodged and whirled around, stepping in and hitting Archie in the stomach. The big man dropped the two-by-four, gasping for air and grabbing his stomach, falling to his knees.

Nellie jumped up and down, kissing Domingo all over in a frenzy. Domingo was in ecstasy. Salvador felt like shooting his brother. He was a fool. And he now knew very clearly why he'd never backed up his brother in rock fights when they'd been kids. Salvador hadn't believed in fighting just for fun. But Domingo did. He was strictly a Villaseñor. He had no Pio Castro blood in his veins at all.

Going over to Archie, Salvador offered him a hand up, but Archie knocked his hand away.

"That son-of-a-bitch!" said Archie between gasps. "That son-of-a-bitch!" He started puking.

"You're right," said Salvador. "He tricked you. You should have got him with that two-by-four."

"Damned right," said Archie. "I've never lost a fight. But I just ate twelve tacos! Chrissake!"

Then, to Salvador's surprise, Archie wiped the puke off his face with his wide, colorful tie, and he started laughing. "You're okay," he said to Domingo, calling him over. "Next to me, you're the strongest man I've ever met!" And he laughed again, not looking mad or revengeful in the least. He pulled out his money. "Here," he said to Domingo, "ten for you and ten for your woman."

"Hey, we agreed on twenty-five each," said Domingo.

Archie jerked the two ten-dollar bills back. "Yeah, we did," he said, "but I never agreed on getting a beating, too! Come on, let's go have a drink inside together," added Archie, and he put his arm around Domingo, "and we'll talk things over."

"All right," said Domingo, going along with him.

And just then Archie got hold of Domingo by the back of the neck, and sent him flying through the doors, kicking him in the ass as he went sailing across the dance floor.

"There! I got you through the doors!" screamed Archie. "Now I don't owe you NOTHING! You son-of-a-bitch! And you and your woman work free all night!"

Domingo leaped off the floor, dusting off his pants. "*¡Cabrón indio!*" he screamed. "You tricked me!"

"I outsmarted you, you *cabrón indio*-greaser yourself!" said Archie.

Archie laughed and laughed, and Domingo didn't like it, but then he started laughing, too. They went up to the bar and Archie ordered drinks for everyone.

"Well, Sal," said Archie, downing his whiskey, "you got any more relatives you need straightened out, you just bring 'em to old Archie!"

The band started to play, and people were entering. Domingo and Nellie went up to the stage to go to work, and Salvador helped Archie unload the rest of the barrels, putting them in the backroom. Salvador was just coming back inside the dance hall when he saw Lupe and Carlota walking in the front door.

His heart exploded, and his mind went reeling. Oh, the sight of her just sent him spinning. She was truly the most beautiful woman in all the world. No wonder he hadn't felt like going with any more of Liza's women up in Pasadena—he was consumed by his love for Lupe. She was his angel, his life, his everything! And, seeing his truelove come walking into the huge open ballroom with such a regal posture, Salvador just knew that he'd done the right thing in buying her the biggest, most beautiful diamond that money could buy.

Why, this young lady from La Lluvia de Oro was the queen of California, dressed in her simple pale rose dress. She wore no makeup, except for a little red coloring on her lips; but with her tall, strong posture and her smooth, clear skin, she looked as fresh and pure and beautiful as the newborn day. Her poor sister Carlota, who stood alongside her wearing lots of makeup and a flashy red dress, looked pale in comparison; and she was good-looking, too.

Then, Lupe turned and saw him, and her whole face came to life. Salvador felt his heart wanting to burst. He could see it in her eyes—she loved him, too. She really did. He went striding across the room to meet his queen.

But then Carlota came like a shot, cutting in between Salvador and Lupe. She was in Archie's huge arms, and they went dancing across the room in a wild, happy storm.

Salvador laughed, and Lupe did, too; then they just stood there, eyeing each other.

"Will you do me the honor of dancing with me?" asked Salvador.

Lupe blushed. "I don't know how," she said.

"Truly, you don't?" he asked.

"No, I don't," she said.

Suddenly, Salvador loved his truelove all the more, for he now realized that men hadn't been putting their greedy hands all over her beautiful body, as men did to women when they danced with them and, therefore, she was even more pure than he'd ever imagined.

"Oh, Lupe," he said, "come, and I'll show you how."

"Oh, no, please, don't," she said, feeling embarrassed.

And, yet, she opened up her arms to this man who'd asked her about her dreams, and they went gliding across the shiny hardwood floor, and she loved it, feeling so secure and all warm and good in his thick, hard arms.

They danced and danced, and when the music stopped, they went outside to cool off in the evening breeze along with everyone else.

"Lupe," said Salvador, feeling so nervous inside himself that he was beginning to tremble now that they weren't dancing, "well, I managed to get the little present for you that I spoke to you about in Hemet. And, well," he added, putting his hands in his pockets and kicking the ground with his right foot as he glanced up at the sky, "I was wondering if, you know, your dreams and my dreams, if maybe they can't accompany each other and make a life together."

"Our dreams?" she said, loving it.

"Yes," he said, "our dreams, our wants, our . . . oh, I've missed you so much," he said.

"And I've missed you, too," she said.

"Really?"

"Oh, yes!"

She reached out, taking his huge hand in hers as she'd reached out so many times across the warm-smelling bed to take hold of her mother. She felt so very happy. He hadn't asked her if she loved him or if she'd accept his hand in marriage; no, he'd simply asked her if their dreams—their most private secret parts of all their lives—could accompany each other.

Oh, she felt so free inside herself. She was soaring over the towering cathedral rocks of her youth.

"Lupe," he said, trembling close, "well, I'd like to know when it would be appropriate for me and, you know, my spokesman, to come by and see you and your parents to, well, ask for your hand officially."

"Oh, my God!" she said, looking up at him and seeing his long, dark, thick eyelashes fluttering like frightened birds, he was so nervous. She was glad that it was the man who had to do the proposing. Oh, she'd go crazy if she'd had to do it.

"Well," she said, soothing his hand, "my family and I will be home all this week, working the peppers, so any evening is fine."

"Then you've said yes," he said.

She smiled. "Yes, I'd love for my dreams to accompany yours."

"You would? Really?"

She nodded. And, yes, he could see it in her eyes. She was really saying yes to him, yes to his dreams, yes to their having a life together, yes forever and ever.

"Oh, good," he said, realizing that he'd just taken the most important step of his life. "Then this week I'll be by. Oh, Lupe, this is the happiest day of my life. And, well, I'd like you to know," he went on, not being able to keep quiet, "that I've also been looking around for a place for us, and, well, I found a little ranch for rent in Carlsbad, overlooking the sea, that has avocados and two little houses so that your parents will also have a place to stay."

Tears came to Lupe's eyes. She drew Salvador's hand to her lips, kissing it. "Oh, thank you, Salvador," she said, eyes dancing. "This is the day I've dreamed of, too."

"You, too?"

"Oh, yes!" she said.

"My God, I love you," he said trembling.

And Lupe wanted to say those same words, too, "I love you," but they just wouldn't come out of her. "Salvador," she said instead, "I've been thinking about nothing else but us since I saw you in Hemet and, well, I've decided that I think that the first few years of our marriage we shouldn't be living near any of our relatives."

He stared at her. He couldn't believe his ears. He was stunned. Why, she'd always been the one who'd spoken of needing a place big enough so that she could bring her parents to live with them. But she'd changed her mind. She wanted to be alone with him. She truly did love him! Oh, his mind went reeling.

Seeing how he looked at her, Lupe laughed. "Salvador," she said, "don't tell me that this disappoints you. Especially after being cornered by my mother so much."

It was his turn to laugh. "Oh, no," he said, "I'm not disappointed, *querida*. I'm thrilled. It's just that, well, it surprised me. You and your mother always seemed so close."

"And we are," said Lupe, "but, lately, I've been thinking about my sisters and how they've done with their own marriages . . . and, well, I just think that the first few years of any marriage should be lived alone."

"I agree," said Salvador. "Why, my own mother and I were speaking of this very same thing."

"You were?"

"Yes."

"And what did she say?"

"Strangely, it surprised me, but my mother said that maybe her own marriage would've turned out better if she and my father hadn't settled on my grandfather's ranch. That the proverb that says that the son-in-law who moves in with his in-laws must either be a simple fool or a very brave and capable man."

"You know, I'd always heard that same thing all my life, too," said Lupe, feeling so free to talk with him. "But not until recently did it really start to make sense to me. In fact, growing up I always swore that I'd never leave my mother's side, and if my husband didn't want to live with the two of us, then he could get out!" she said, laughing.

"Me, too!" said Salvador. "That's exactly what I always used to say!"

"You, too?"

"Yes!"

"I'll be!"

Lupe and Salvador laughed, and they continued talking, having a grand time, until Nellie and Domingo came walking up to them, blowing out cigarette smoke through their noses like dragons. After introducing Lupe to Nellie and Domingo, the two young women went off to the bathroom together.

Salvador couldn't believe his ears when Domingo drew in close to him and whispered, "Eh, little brother, what are you doing, making eyes at a virgin? Hell, haven't you learned that the best ones are like my Nellie, women who've been around and know how to play the *coo-coo*?"

Salvador almost slugged his brother. But then he saw the sincerity in Domingo's eyes, and he simply laughed, truly understanding how very little he had in common with this man who happened to be his brother and had come back from the dead.

22

The heavens smiled upon the earth, and the child of the meteorite found herself in love with the nineteenth child—a gift from God, his mother had also been told.

ell, seeing how happy you are," said Domingo, "how about giving me another little loan?"

"How much?" said Salvador, whistling happily.

The dance was over, and they were on their way to Corona. Salvador wanted to tell their mother the good news.

"Oh, make it an even five hundred," said Domingo, winking at Nellie.

"Five hundred!" yelled Salvador, almost going off the road. "That's a fortune, Domingo!"

"Yes, but I've seen that wad you carry," he said, smiling. "It's big enough to choke a horse!"

Salvador decided to pull over to the side of the road. His brother had absolutely no comprehension of what money was.

"Oh, are we going to get out together again?" said Domingo.

"No," said Salvador. "I think it's best that maybe I say this in front of both of you so there won't be any misunderstanding."

Salvador took a big breath. "Look, Domingo, Nellie," he said, "what I'm about to say is very important, maybe the most important thing I've ever learned. Money for us *mejicanos* is something to spend, to throw away on liquor and cards . . . to enjoy."

"Of course," said Domingo, smiling, "that's what it's for!"

"And that's what I always thought. And the rich and the priest in every village wants you to believe that," said Salvador. "So you'll give to the church what you don't throw away, and the rich can keep you poor and slaving for them for all eternity."

Nellie became uncomfortable. She was a Catholic, too, after all. She hated it when people spoke badly about the Church. Salvador saw her reaction, but he wasn't about to be stopped. This was truly one of the most important things that he'd learned in all his life.

"But if you're smart, then money isn't to be thrown away," he said. "It's to be respected. Because it gives a man power and freedom. It allows a man to prepare himself by taking a nap in the afternoon before a night of poker. It makes a man a professional, giving him the time to think, to organize, and it gives him the strength to take the money away from the other men like candy from babies."

"Well, then, make it a thousand," said Domingo, really liking his brother's words.

"And what for? To have you just throw it away?" said Salvador. "No, you listen to me carefully, Domingo; respect, respect of money is the first thing a man must learn if he's going to get ahead. The Greeks, up in Montana, they'd make a dollar from the railroad and they'd put half away every day. Then they'd try to save a little of the fifty cents that they used for living. They were tough, I tell you. Money wasn't money to them; no, it was something that you saved, accumulated until you finally had enough to open a restaurant or the power to do what you really wanted to do. So this wad of money that I carry isn't for me to spend. No, it's my capital, the tool I use to make my living. Just like a truck driver has his truck, I got my money to buy supplies, to carry me as a businessman. Do you understand?"

Salvador stopped, feeling proud that he'd been able to put into words this complicated concept that he'd been taught by his mother and then refined by the Greeks and Duel. But then, to his surprise, Domingo only grinned.

"This is all bullshit, little brother," said Domingo, "I've seen you use your wad to buy things all the time." He winked at Nellie, showing her that he hadn't been taken in by any of Salvador's fancy words.

"Oh," said Salvador, "then, if this is bullshit, how come I've got money and you don't?"

Domingo's face flushed. "I've had bad luck, that's all!" he snapped.

"You call it bad luck; I don't. I call it planning."

Domingo had had enough. "Look," he said, "are you going to loan me the money or not?"

Salvador stopped. He could see that his brother hadn't understood one single word. "Not five hundred," he said.

"Well, then, how about only two hundred?" said Domingo. "We need to get a car and a house of our own, Salvador. The child will be coming soon."

"A house costs five dollars a month," said Salvador. "And you can get a good truck for fifty dollars. I'll loan you a hundred. But no more. And you got to pay me back."

"Sure, when we set up the new distillery, I'll pay you back," said Domingo.

"Hold on," said Salvador, taking a big breath, "before you ever work for me again, we're going to have to come to an understanding. I can't have you doing like you did back in Escondido."

Domingo's eyes flashed. He was ready to spring into a rage, but he caught himself and laughed, instead. "All right, make it a hundred and fifty," he said, "and we'll do things your way from now on, *hermanito*."

"I said a hundred," said Salvador.

Domingo's eyebrows narrowed and he stared at Salvador, giving him the mean eye, just like their father had always liked to do. Salvador almost laughed in his face. Hell, he'd been in too many poker games to be taken in by this cheap trick. It was a game only for fools. After a moment, Domingo folded.

"All right, make it the hundred," he said, seeing that he wasn't going to be able to intimidate his brother.

"Okay," said Salvador. He pulled out his roll and counted out the bills for his brother. He'd won. He'd beaten his older brother two times in one day, but it didn't feel good.

Oh, how he wished that his brother had returned to them as a real man, able to take control of the reins of their family, as an older brother should.

When they arrived at Corona, Domingo and Nellie went to Luisa's house. Domingo was still fuming. He hadn't liked to be put in his place, especially not in front of Nellie.

Salvador immediately went to his mother's place in back to tell her about Lupe. "Mama," he said, rushing inside, "wake up! Wake up!"

"What is it?" she asked.

"I'm the happiest man in all the world!" he said. "Lupe said yes!"

"Oh, that's wonderful, *mi hijito!*" said the old lady, groping for him in the dark. The only light in the shack was the long spears of moonlight coming in through the cracks in the walls. "This is the day I've lived for."

"That's what you always say!"

"Well, it's true. At my age, every day is the day I've lived for."

They laughed together, hugging close.

"And, also, she said something so spectacular that I couldn't believe it, Mama," he said.

"Well, tell me!"

"I told her of the little house that I asked Hans and Helen about, you know, the Germans that I've told you about down in Carlsbad."

"The ones who own the restaurant and the avocado ranch?"

"Exactly," he said. "I told Lupe about the house that we can rent on their ranch with the little house in back for her parents; but, Mama, she told me that she'd thought more about it and she doesn't want any of our relatives living near us for the first few years of our marriage."

"She said that?" said Doña Margarita.

"Yes," he said excitedly.

"Oh, *mi hijito*, this Lupe is a jewel! To be so young and so close to her parents and still have the intelligence to say this to you. Oh, she is made of iron. This is a woman you can never lie to. Do you understand me? I only wish I'd had her intelligence when I'd gotten married."

"But, Mama, I already lied to her. She doesn't know that I gamble or make liquor."

"Oh, that's right," she said, shaking her head. "Well, that's going to have to be straightened out as soon as you marry. Lupe is a woman to respect. But, still, I wish you . . ."

"I know, that I'd met that girl who came to milk the goats."

"Exactly. She was an angel, I tell you. So beautiful and yet capable."

"Mama, you just wait until you see Lupe. No woman on earth could be more beautiful!"

The old lady smiled. "I'm glad to hear you say that, *mi hijito*. For this is how it should be. Every man who takes a wife should feel that his is the most beautiful in all the world. And then she will be; for she'll blossom like a flower with the love that man gives her. I know; our first years of marriage were wonderful and, maybe, if I'd had the intelligence of Lupe, we could have continued in bliss. But we lived under my parents' roof and, year by year, I could see that Don Juan just wasn't the man that my father, Don Pio was. Worse, he could see it, too."

She took a big breath. "You must understand, *mi hijito*, that when a man marries . . . he doesn't just marry any woman. No," she said, lifting her index finger and closing her eyes in concentration, "he marries the mother of his children!"

"Yes, I know. You've told me this a thousand times."

"Good, so then maybe you can begin to understand the miracle of what I'm about to say. Because, I tell you, this is the most important step you'll ever take in all your life, and so you must have your two eyes wide open."

"But, Mama, you talk like I'm never going to see you again."

"You aren't," she said. "Your life with me is over."

"Oh, that's not true, Mama. Lupe and I will come to see you often."

"To visit, of course, but not to be with me anymore."

"Mama," he said, "I love you. I'll always be with you."

"No, you will not," she said, "or you will fail in your marriage."

He was stunned by her awful words.

"Listen to me carefully," she continued. "Lupe is right; the first few years of any marriage should be lived alone. Your *familia* will still be your family, of course, but it can no longer be your first family. This is the miracle of marriage. Each new marriage is like a whole new beginning—a return to the Garden of Eden—and each new couple is Adam and Eve, the first two people on earth."

"I swear, Mama," said Salvador, laughing, "don't you think that you're being just a little too . . ."

"Too romantic? Too dramatic?" she snapped. "No! A thousand times no! You open your eyes and see what I'm saying or your marriage will not work. This life that you and Lupe are about to begin has only the value you place on it, not the value that the Church gives it, or what we, the parents, give it, or even society. Its value is what you two agree upon giving it. And given full value, marriage is then, indeed, a return to Eden, and you two are, indeed, the first man and woman on earth. Marriage isn't sex, *mi hijito*, and it isn't even having children. Sex and children can be had all life long without marriage."

He breathed deeply. His mother always had to make things so complicated. But then, on the other hand, that was probably how all his talk about money had sounded like to Domingo.

The old woman saw his confusion. "Give me your hand," she said. "Look, I'm not saying that you're going to stop loving me or that I'm going to stop loving you. No, I'm not only saying that our family will no longer be your first love. Both you and Lupe have to understand this or you won't be able to make a home. This is the very reason why Adam and Eve are considered the first two people on earth. They were the first to make a promise between themselves to join body and mind and give honor to the glory of God."

"You mean, they weren't the actual first two people on the earth?"

"No, or course not, but for their tribe, they were the first two people who made this most profound of agreements between themselves, relinquishing the devil and giving honor to the greater glory of God."

"Oh, Mama, this is incredible. Where did you learn this?"

"Why, in the outhouse, of course. What in God's name do you think The Virgin and I talk about all these mornings that I spend with her? We speak about the word of God, *mi hijito*, and not as if it all happened years ago, but as it is happening now, here, today, with us."

Salvador's mind was reeling, exploding. "You mean all these years you've really been speaking to the Virgin? And Christ really came off the cross that other day and spoke to you?"

"Of course," she said. "Did you really think that God quit speaking to us here on earth when he finished with the Jews? Oh, no, *mi hijito*, it is for each people to find their own way. This is exactly why I'm telling you that what Lupe said to you is so profound. Being so young, she still instinctively knew that you two must be alone for the first few years of your life, so that you can grow together, so you can make mistakes together without your relatives watching over your shoulders. So you can . . ." Tears came to her eyes, and she drew Salvador close, holding him. "Oh, *mi hijito*, I'm so proud of you. You picked a very, very, very good woman. My job is over. I can now rest in peace."

"Oh, no, Mama," he said. "I still need you! Please, don't die!"

"Who said anything about dying?" she laughed. "I just mean that I can now drink my *whiskito* and smoke my *cigarritos* in peace."

"Oh, good," he said. "I'll make us a whiskey right now."

He got up and fixed them each a drink and they talked late into the night; they were two people so happy just to be with each other.

The next thing Salvador knew it was daybreak. He absolutely had no idea where the night had gone. He put his mother to bed and went outside to relieve himself. His mother's words still rang inside his mind, "Marriage has only the value that a man and a woman put on it".

He brought out the diamond ring from his pocket and looked at it there in the early morning light. Oh, he was happy that he had had the confidence in human nature to entrust his money to Harry. He was a good friend. Just like Kenny and Hans and Helen.

He decided to change clothes so he could go and see the priest. Then, he'd have to talk to Epitacio about setting up a new distillery. He had to make a lot of liquor so he'd be able to throw the biggest wedding feast that the barrio had ever seen.

It was Thursday and Lupe was sitting outside on the porch. It was the evening that Salvador was supposed to come by with his sponsor, and he still hadn't arrived.

Lupe had asked her parents to dress up; they'd done so and were playing cards inside the house, pretending not to be nervous, but Lupe could tell that they were as nervous as she was.

On arriving at the church to pick up the priest that evening, Salvador was shocked to find that the man of God was drunk. He'd finished off one of the bottles of whiskey that Salvador had dropped off earlier that week.

"I'm fine," said Father Ryan. "I'll just have a little coffee, and then we'll be on our way."

The Father's hands were shaking so much that Salvador had to help him put the pot of coffee on the stove.

"By the way, Father," said Salvador, "I think you should know that they don't drink."

"Well, then, it's a good thing I had a couple of sips before we left," he said, smiling.

But Salvador didn't smile. He was having all these terrible visions of the priest ruining everything. He was beginning to think that he'd been a fool to get involved with an alcoholic priest.

"Calm down, my son. Everything will be all right," said Father Ryan. "Here, I think you better have a little drink yourself," added the priest.

"What the hell," said Salvador to himself, and he took a good belt.

They were both singing Irish songs by the time they got to Santa Ana. Driving down the street to Lupe's house, the priest winked at Salvador, popping a piece of candy in his mouth.

"Here," he said to Salvador, "for your breath."

"Thank you," said Salvador, taking the candy.

"Everything is going to be fine," said the man of God as they pulled up to Lupe's home.

Victoriano was on the front porch. He was all dressed up. Salvador had never seen him with a tie and coat before.

"Hello!" called Salvador.

"Good evening," said Victoriano, coming down the steps.

Just then, Father Ryan tried to get out of the car. He almost fell. Victoriano rushed forward to help the man. Salvador could've died.

"These new cars," said the priest, regaining his balance with Victoriano's help, "they're too fancy for me."

As they went up the steps and in the front door, Salvador prayed to God that no one would smell their breath. The place looked immaculate inside. There were fresh flowers on the table. Doña Guadalupe and Don Victor were well-dressed, too; but neither Lupe nor Carlota were anywhere in sight.

Salvador was filled with fear. Maybe Lupe had been sent away and his proposal of marriage was going to be turned down.

But then the priest went up to Doña Guadalupe, and took her hand, and he introduced himself, speaking like an angel. Then he took Don Victor's hand and also spoke to him very well. Salvador began to relax.

They all sat down. Carlota and Lupe came in with a tray of tea and sweetbreads. Lupe looked fantastic. It was hard for Salvador to not stare at her. She served the tea, and Carlota gave them each a sweetbread on a small plate. Then, Lupe and Carlota sat down alongside their parents. No one said anything. The priest drank his tea and ate his bread. Everyone watched him. Salvador began to fear that the priest had forgotten the purpose of their visit.

"Well," said the priest, having finished his bread, "this is a great honor for me, *señor y señora*. So many young people come to me nowadays seeking marriage, but they do not understand the seriousness of this bond between a man and woman. But this young man does."

He brought out his handkerchief, dusting the crumbs of the sweetbread off his lap. He began to use the handkerchief like a magic wand as he spoke. "I know Salvador's mother very well. She comes to church every day, rain or shine. And she raised this young man that you see before you to understand the fundamentals of life. And, most especially, the sacrament of holy matrimony!"

The priest went on, and he had them all eating out of the palm of his hand.

"And from what I've seen," he said, turning to Carlota, "I see that your daughter is also ready for this most holy of sacraments, so I don't think there should be further . . ."

Salvador's hands began to shake. Lupe turned crimson with embarrassment. But Carlota loved it, smiling at the priest.

Father Ryan wasn't to be distracted. "Of course, I know that life has not been easy for you, *señor y señora*," he continued. "I know that you suffered those great tragedies of the terrible war in Mexico as so many other families who've come to the United States. But I will now say that a moment like this makes the tragedies of life worthwhile."

He opened his voice in a grand manner. "For this is a moment to treasure! Two young people in love, coming to their parents in the most respectful and dignified of ways to ask their permission to enter into the sacrament of holy matrimony!"

He glanced at Carlota once again. Salvador almost screamed. He couldn't stand it.

"So now, on behalf of Juan Salvador Villaseñor, who I know is a wonderful young man with honorable upbringing, I ask for the hand of your daughter, Guadalupe Maria Gomez."

And he began to extend his hand toward Carlota, but Salvador leaped, hitting the light fixture above him with his head, and he fell backwards into his chair, breaking it.

Quickly, Victoriano came to Salvador's aid.

But it was Doña Guadalupe who saved the day. She simply stood up and took the priest's hand and led him toward Lupe.

"Oh, yes," said Father Ryan, "thank you."

"You're quite welcome," said Doña Guadalupe. "And you're entirely right; this is a moment to treasure. Guadalupe," she said to Lupe, "come and take the Father's hand, *querida*."

Lupe stood up. She was so embarrassed, but she took the priest's hand anyway and made a small curtsy.

Salvador was on his feet now, blood running down the side of his face. He waved Victoriano away, assuring him that he was fine.

Don Victor was dying to laugh. He could smell the liquor on these two drunk men. "Well," he said, coming up, "my wife and I will consider your proposal very carefully, and we'll let you know within a week what it is that we decide."

"Thank you," said the priest, "then we'll say goodnight."

Salvador and the priest went out the door. Once they were in the Moon and driving up the street, Salvador let out a scream of pain.

"Damn, that hurt!" he yelled, grabbing his head.

"Here, have another drink," said the priest.

"Good thinking," said Salvador.

And so the priest and Salvador drank all the way back to Corona, singing Irish songs once again.

That same evening, Don Victor sat on the porch of his house, smoking a cigarette and thinking very seriously about this proposal. He'd run into Don Manuel a few days before, and Don Manuel had told him a fantastic story about a notorious bootlegger from Corona who drove a Moon automobile.

Don Victor wondered if, indeed, this bootlegger could possibly be Salvador. He decided to do some checking. After all, his daughter's happiness was at stake.

It was the longest week of Salvador's life. And he couldn't very well go to visit Lupe, so he kept away from Santa Ana altogether. He went to work and rented a big house just south of Los Angeles in Watts to set up the distillery. He used up the last of his capital to buy all the materials that they'd need. Epitacio agreed to be in charge of the distillery plant and Domingo agreed to work strictly under Epitacio's orders. No visitors would be allowed. No heavy drinking or fooling around. If the law came down on the house for any reason, it would be Epitacio's and Domingo's responsibility. And if the law came down on Salvador, as he did the distribution and sales, it would be his responsibility. For the first time in his life, Salvador had time on his hands. His capital was working for him. He had a distilling plant going and he didn't have to be slaving day and night.

He decided to spend time with his mother. After all, if she was right and they weren't going to be so close anymore, then there was nothing more in all of life that he'd rather do than be with her.

"So tell me about the days before your own marriage, Mama," he said.

"Oh, those were difficult times for me, *mi hijito*," said Doña Margarita. "You see, back in those days there weren't any telephones or other means of communication, so many times the father of the bride went out to investigate into the life of the prospective groom."

"You mean that Lupe's father could be here, right now, in Corona, investigating me?" he asked.

"Of course," she said.

"Oh, my God!" said Salvador. "I always figured that it was Lupe's mother that I had to watch out for. I never considered her father."

Doña Margarita laughed. "Don't worry," she said. "I've already sent word throughout the barrio. They'll know what to expect. Now, getting back to my story," she said, sipping her coffee laced with whiskey, "about ten days before my wedding, your grandfather went to Guadalajara to find out about your father. It was the longest week of my life. I feared that Don Pio would discover something horrible. Then, I'll never forget as long as I live how your grandfather came riding in on his great stallion with such a look in his eyes the night before my wedding. He took me aside and told me this incredible story about Don Juan and his first cousin, a tall redheaded woman like himself whom he'd grown up with. Don Juan and his cousin had been in love since childhood. But they were first cousins, so of course, they couldn't marry. And the night before she was to marry a local dignitary, Don Juan picked a fight with the man, challenging him to a duel, and he killed the man. The relatives of the dignitary chased Don Juan into the hills and he killed two more men before escaping; that's how he ended up in our mountains."

"No!" said Salvador. "But why hadn't you ever told us this story before?"

"*Mi hijito*, there are many stories between a husband and wife that they never share with their children."

"There are?"

She smiled. "Of course. Remember, you're only half grown. You haven't married, or had children, so there's much you can't comprehend."

He breathed deeply. "What happened to my father's cousin?" he asked.

Tears came to Doña Margarita's eyes. "The poor woman was put in a convent in Mexico City by her relatives for the rest of her life!" she said. "And your grandfather was furious. He said to me, 'You can't marry him. For he still loves his cousin who is tall and blue-eyed like himself, and you're short and dark like me, and this blue-eyed man will throw this into your face every time you two quarrel.' "

" 'No, Papa!' I said.

" 'Oh, yes,' he told me. 'And if you have dark children, he won't love them equally, either.' Oh, I was torn to the depths of my soul, *mi hijito*, but what could I do? I was in love. And so I said, 'Enough, Papa, not another word; I'm marrying him.' "

"And so he didn't say another word, but I can tell you that I went to my wedding with a very heavy heart the next day."

"My God!" said Salvador. He was stunned. He hadn't known anything about this and, yet, it explained so much. "Then you mean that this is the same woman that you used to write to in that convent in Mexico City?"

"Yes," said his mother, wiping her eyes. "The only sin she ever committed was being young and in love, and yet her whole family abandoned her." She breathed deeply. "You know, I've often wondered, *mi hijito*, if Don Pío hadn't gone to Guadalajara and found out all that, maybe our marriage would've turned out differently. Knowing all that about your father caused me to see every argument that we had as a fight of jealousy, of me fighting against this gorgeous lost cousin of his."

"Did you ever discuss his cousin with him?"

"Was your father a man someone could discuss anything with? Especially if it gave him pain? No, we never spoke about her. But I did write to her, as I told you, and she wrote back, and we became great friends."

"Oh, Mama," said Salvador, "but how could you be friends with her?"

"And why not? Her only sin was to be in love with your father; and so was I."

Salvador sat there looking at his mother, realizing that it was true; he was, indeed, only half grown and knew very little about love and women and marriage and many of the great mysteries of the heart. It seemed to him as if he'd been a child all these years, thinking only about survival and his own amusement. He took a big breath, wondering if he was really ready for this big new step in life called marriage. He decided yes, definitely, if he was ever going to be ready it was now.

That afternoon, Salvador went out into the barrio to see if Don Victor was checking up on him. He found out that he was; Don Victor had spent a lot of time with Don Rodolfo. Salvador went over to see the schoolteacher.

"Hello, Rodolfo," said Salvador, walking into his *ramada*.

"Hello to you, too," said the schoolteacher, realizing that Salvador had never been under his roof before.

"I hear that Don Victor came by," said Salvador.

"Yes, he did," said Rodolfo.

"And?" said Salvador.

"And he asked about you, of course," said the teacher. "So I told him the truth."

"You what!" said Salvador, exploding.

"Yes," said Rodolfo. "I told him that you are a man among men. A Francisco Villa and that I'm proud to call you my friend."

Salvador came back down. "*Gracias,*" he said to Rodolfo. "I owe you one. I'll give you a gallon of whiskey so you can sell a few pints on the side and make a little extra money."

"That's not necessary," said Rodolfo, clicking his heels together and saluting Salvador. "I spoke from the heart."

Trying on one of his suits that week, Salvador found out that he'd gained a little weight. He decided to do some hard manual work and lose some pounds. It always seemed to him that he got a small pot belly every time he wasn't doing hard time in prison, or working sun up to sun down.

He quit eating fruit and vegetables, thinking that these were what made you fat, because cattle and pigs ate these and got fat. He ate nothing but beans and meat with lots of chile and tortillas and then washed it all down with plenty of whiskey, which he thought stimulated digestion, because drunks were always so skinny.

He began to run every morning as he'd seen boxers do to get in shape, but still he couldn't lose an ounce. He ate more tortillas and beans and cut back on the meat, figuring that maybe it was the meat that made him fat.

Then one day he got an innertube from a tire and cut it to fit around his waist, and he ran with Jose out of town and past the farthest orchards. He was pouring with sweat; he started to gasp. Jose had to cut the innertube off Salvador before he passed out.

That night, Salvador had terrible dreams. He just knew that Don Victor had found out about him, and now Lupe wasn't going to marry him. He thought of going to the church and confessing all his sins to the priest; but, no, he couldn't bring himself to tell any mortal man of the nightmares he carried inside his heart. Especially not about Duel, whom he'd loved more than his own father.

Then, it was late Thursday afternoon, the day that Salvador and the priest were supposed to go to Lupe's house for her answer. Picking up the priest, Salvador was so nervous he couldn't think.

"Get hold of yourself," said the priest.

"But what if her parents say no?" he said. "Remember, they're not a drinking family, and maybe they've found out that I'm a bootlegger . . . I mean my friend is a bootlegger?"

The priest only smiled. "But bootlegging isn't against the laws of God, my son," he said. "Only in this country is liquor-making illegal. Calm down. Here, have a drink. Remember, the first miracle of our Lord Jesus was turning water into wine."

Salvador laughed. "Then every time I make liquor, I mean my friend makes liquor, then he's close to the Lord?"

"If he makes good whiskey," said the priest with a twinkle in his eyes.

Salvador laughed, loving it, and they drank down their whiskeys and then took off.

"You know," said Salvador as they came into the outskirts of Santa Ana, "I had some bad dreams the other night, and I thought of maybe coming to confession; but you see, Father, it's been a long time since I made my last confession."

The priest turned and looked at Salvador. He was sober today and he looked very pious. "Well, we can do it right now if you want," he said.

"You mean my confession?"

"Of course," said the priest. "We can pull over and do it right here."

"Really?"

"Yes."

Salvador took a big breath. He hadn't expected this. He dug deep down inside himself. But no, no matter how much a part of him wanted to, he still wasn't ready to confess yet. He still had a lot of hate inside himself. "Could we maybe do that some other time and just pray together right now, Father?" he asked. It was the first time that he'd used the term "Father" with this priest.

"Of course," said the man of God, making the sign of the cross over himself. He began to pray, and Salvador followed him, but it was very difficult for him. He glanced up at the sky and the clouds overhead. He saw that there was a large raven flying by alongside them. The big black bird turned his head and looked at Salvador. Quickly Salvador glanced at the priest to see if he'd seen the bird's look. But the priest hadn't. His eyes were closed as he prayed. Salvador was glad that he had this man of the cloth here at his side as a good friend; but oh, he was still far away from confessing to anyone. Not even to God Himself.

After putting his rosary away, the priest took Salvador's arm. "Everything's going to be all right," he said. "You come from good people. Your mother is the finest."

Salvador took a deep breath. "Thank you, Father."

Arriving at Lupe's home, they went up to the door and Carlota answered it. She was so happy, a regular chatterbox. Salvador immediately figured that this wasn't good. Carlota had never liked him, and so for her to be so happy could only mean that his proposal had been turned down.

Inside, Don Victor was waiting for them. He looked at Salvador with a certain kind of mischievousness. Salvador felt his legs go weak. The old man had found out everything about him. Oh, he had been a fool to ever think that a monster like himself could possibly marry an innocent girl like Lupe. He'd lost. And he was never going to be able to find another woman like Lupe, even if he searched to the ends of the earth.

But then, to his surprise, Don Victor came walking across the room and took the priest's hand.

"Come right this way, Father," he said. "Everyone is in the back." He turned to Salvador. "*Buenas tardes*," he said with that same little grin.

"*Buenas tardes*," said Salvador, feeling very cautious.

They went out to the back. Lupe was under the large walnut tree with her brother, talking to the little girl, Isabel. Lupe was wearing a simple white dress with a red ribbon in her rich, dark hair. The going sunlight was coming down through the tree branches, surrounding her in a pond of pale golden light. Salvador's heart stopped.

Lupe truly looked like an angel. "Oh, God," he said to himself, "please help me. I don't want to lose her."

Then she turned, just as he thought these words. Her large, dark almond-shaped eyes were so happy to see him that he just knew God had heard him and her parents had said yes. They really had. He could see it in her eyes. His heart went soaring to the heavens.

Doña Guadalupe walked over to the priest and showed him a pot of beautiful lilies. They laughed and talked, but Salvador couldn't hear a word. He only had eyes for his angel. This was the most miraculous moment of his life.

"Excuse us," said Don Victor, taking Salvador by the arm, "but you and I need to speak alone for a minute."

Don Victor turned Salvador about and led him away. "I've spoken to Don Manuel," said the old man under his breath, still holding Salvador by the arm.

Salvador froze.

"Calm down," said Don Victor, feeling the muscles of Salvador's arm go rigid, "I also spoke to Archie and to lots of other men about you."

Salvador breathed deeply.

"Relax," said the old man, winking at Salvador. "I, too, drank and gambled all my life so, between men I know how these things work. Archie spoke highly of you and so did most of the other men. You are a *macho*, they say, a man of his word. And, also, I realize that drinking and gambling aren't necessarily evil. It's just that I hurt my dear wife time and again, and that's why she fears them. I don't want the same thing to happen to my daughter."

Salvador took another deep breath, looking at Don Victor. "So, then, you haven't told them?"

"No, of course not," said Don Victor. "And I never will. But you got to promise me that you'll never hurt my Lupe."

Salvador could taste the bile coming up from his stomach. He was sure Don Manuel, being the proper little chicken-shit bastard that he was, had told Don Victor every rotten thing he could about him. This old man was all right. He was showing a lot of guts to still allow his daughter to marry him. "I swear," said Salvador, "with all my heart, man to man, that I will never hurt your daughter. She is my queen!"

"Good," said Don Victor. "Excellent."

Then they embraced in a big *abrazo*, heart-to-heart, and it was done *a lo macho*.

The priest and Doña Guadalupe came up to them. She was holding a small potted plant with white flowers.

"Lupe," called the old woman to her daughter, "come. It is time."

Salvador would never forget as long as he lived the ring of these three magic words, "It is time." He saw Lupe get up with her brother on one side and the child, Isabel, on the other. They came walking up, surrounded by golden light. It was a magic moment.

"And so, Salvador," said Doña Guadalupe with Lupe at her side, "I want you to know that the good Father and I have just spoken this matter over at great length and . . . yes, my husband and I do accept your proposal of marriage on behalf of our daughter, Guadalupe. But, only on the condition that you will accept the responsibility of these potted lilies that I dug up with my own two hands in La Lluvia de Oro. And that you promise me that you will attend to them and to Lupe from now until your death with patient, loving hands.

"For I tell you," she said, tears coming to her eyes, "a woman is like a flower, Salvador. And I raised this fine daughter of mine with all the love I have. Lupe isn't just beautiful, Salvador, she's intelligent, hard-working, obedient and thoughtful.

"And I'm not saying this to sound like a bragger, but as a person who's lived and loved and knows life. Lupe is an extraordinary young lady. But like the delicate rose that grows and blossoms with the tender, patient hands of love, if she is mistreated, Salvador, then this delicate rose will grow thorns to protect herself as you've never seen!" she shouted.

"I know, believe me," she continued, tears streaming down her face, "for I was once a delicate flower, too, that would have followed my man to the ends of the earth. But then life became difficult and my husband was impatient and hard with me and our children, so I grew claws that would terrify any mortal man. And those thorns, once grown, cannot be hidden, for they come straight from the heart."

Saying this, the old lady stared at Salvador with such open, naked power that he was stunned. And he wanted to glance at Don Victor and see how he was taking all of this, too, but he didn't dare.

"And so," she said, wiping her eyes, "do you now accept these flowers and promise to nourish them with patient, loving hands for the rest of your life?"

Salvador looked at the old lady and the beautiful potted flowers. He glanced at his angel, standing there beside her mother, and he had to squeeze his eyes so he wouldn't cry, too. His whole chest came up and he reached across that fearful abyss of doubt and took hold of the potted plant. "I will," he said, "with all of my heart."

"To water with love and watch your seed grow? And to trust and always be understanding?" continued Doña Guadalupe, still holding onto the clay pot.

"Absolutely," he said, holding the pot, also. "With patience and trust and understanding."

Then, and only then, as the old lady stared into Salvador's eyes, did she release the pot of flowers and Salvador took them into his own two hands.

He gazed at the old lady, then gazed at Lupe, feeling so intoxicated with the miracle of the moment that he almost forgot about the diamond ring, until the priest, coughing hard, pointed at his own finger.

"Oh, yes," said Salvador, "I have something, too."

He reached into his pocket for the diamond ring, but he almost dropped the flowers.

"Here, I'll hold them," laughed Victoriano. "My mother wants them to last at least until the wedding."

"Thank you," said Salvador. He brought out the little dark blue velvet box that Harry had gotten for him and opened it with trembling hands. Everyone watched in silence.

"A diamond," he said, showing them the ring.

Everyone just stood there, staring at the diamond in the little velvet box. It was just too much for Carlota, and she started laughing.

"Oh, Salvador, it's glass!" she said. "What do you think you are, a millionaire?"

"Well, no, of course not," he said, "but it's not glass. It is real. Honestly. I've worked so hard for this . . . this . . ."

But he couldn't go on. He felt too humiliated. His hands began to shake. Lupe stepped forward.

"Thank you, Salvador," she said, taking both of his hands in hers. "It's beautiful and I feel honored," she added, looking at him straight in the eyes.

He forgot about Carlota, losing himself in Lupe's eyes.

"But, Lupe," continued Carlota, "it can't possibly be a real diamond! What do you think Salvador is? A king?" she said, laughing. "And you, a queen?"

"Carlota!" snapped Doña Guadalupe, grabbing her by the ear, "that's enough!" And she yanked her daughter about with such power that Carlota screeched as her mother led her off in a rush.

Don Victor laughed. "Pigs, like I've always said, it's easier to raise pigs than kids!" he said, coming forward. "Please, accept my apology, Salvador," he added. "It's beautiful! And we all feel honored."

"Thank you, Don Victor," said Salvador.

Then he reached out for Lupe's hand and slipped the ring on her finger. Lupe's eyes overflowed with tears. This was a dream come true for her, too. A miracle of God, as high and great as the majestic feeling of their towering cathedral peaks back home.

The sun was going down behind the groves of orange trees in the distance, and Lupe and Salvador—the two babies of their families—stood, looking down at the large, beautiful stone.

This new land of theirs was filled with magic, too. The sun, the fragrance of the orange trees, the beautiful potted mountain lilies and this fabled diamond. It was paradise, as Doña Margarita had said.

A marriage had the value that a man and woman gave it and a marriage of true love was, indeed, the return to Eden, the birth of man living in God's own image—pure love.

23

*Paradise was now within their reach when the devil
came out of hiding, dancing with his huge serpent's
head, tempting them down into his depths.*

After dropping the priest off, Salvador drove home
that night to his mother's house, honking his horn and howling to the moon.
It was half past midnight when he came into the barrio. The goats and pigs
awoke, calling out to him. But he didn't care how much noise he caused, and
he just kept honking all the more, shouting up to the blue-wrinkled moon.

"Mama! Mama!" he yelled, getting out of the Moon and coming into her
little house. "Lupe and I are getting married! Look, her mother gave me
these flowers for us to take care of for the rest of our lives!"

Doña Margarita sat up, rubbing her eyes. "Oh, *mi hijito*," she said, "turn
on the lamp, let me see. Oh, what beautiful white flowers."

"Lupe's mother explained to me that they grew wild where they came
from, cascading down the slopes. And she wants me to care for them with
love's tender feelings for all my life."

"That's wonderful," said the old lady, looking at the tall, delicate flowers
and then at her son's glowing face. "I'm so proud of you, *mi hijito*, that you
had the strength of mind and the fortitude of heart to go through with all of
our traditions of courtship, even as demanding as her mother was . . . for,
remember, as I've been telling you over and over these last few days," she
added, raising up her index finger, "life only has the value that we place on
it, and you've placed a value of the highest order on your marriage by
remaining faithful to our customs, no matter how far we've come from home.

"I congratulate you with all my heart, *mi hijito*," she said. "All our
sufferings have not been in vain. You've restored dignity to our *casa*. At this
very moment, your father and your grandparents are smiling down on you
from the heavens."

"Oh, thank you, Mama," said Salvador.

"The thanks are mine," she said. "For, believe me, it's not often that a
mother gets to reap the benefits of her labor."

He was so happy. He put the flowers down and took his mother in his
arms and cried like a baby. He was so terribly, terribly happy after all the

years of suffering. It was as if all his suffering had just been washed away with the incredible love that he felt inside his heart.

Then, Luisa and Pedro and Jose came from next door, and they hugged Salvador, too. It became a wonderful time of wet eyes and big *abrazos*, until Luisa asked about the diamond.

"Were they excited?" she asked proudly.

"Oh, yes," said Salvador. "Except for her sister, Carlota. She started laughing at me, saying it was only glass."

"She what?" screamed Luisa. "I'll kill her! The big-mouthed bitch! Where is she? I'll strangle her 'til her eyes pop out!"

"No, Luisa, please, it's all right now," said Salvador, laughing. "Her mother took her away by the ear, and her father apologized for her."

"But, still, how could she? After you went to so much trouble! My God, I'd hoped that Lupe's family would honor you, but this Carlota gets me so mad—oh, I want to get her by the throat!"

Salvador tried to calm Luisa down but he couldn't. She went on and on—raging, screaming—swearing to do Carlota in when she met her.

For the first time in weeks, Salvador was able to sleep. He slept like a baby that night and his heart was at peace. Then, Jose came in and woke him up.

"It's noon, Uncle," he said. "Epitacio came by earlier. He said that it's time to start the next batch of fermentation."

Salvador thanked Jose and got up. "I'm going to be married!" he sang. "Married! Married!" He bathed, changed clothes, and had a cup of hot chocolate with his mother. He just couldn't stop singing.

"Oh, Mama," he said, "I'm so happy!"

"And you argued with me that the holy sacrament of marriage isn't paradise," said the crafty old woman, showing her one good canine. "Oh, I tell you, heaven is here on earth and it's called marriage. That's our true gift from God! I know, I had it once, too, and now I'm having it again, through you, my son."

"Oh, Mama," said Salvador, taking her in his arms. "I love you so much." They hugged and kissed, loving each other.

It was getting late and Salvador took off for Los Angeles. He bought the sugar and yeast and headed for their rented house in Watts.

He was just driving up the alley behind their large rented house, singing to the sky, when he suddenly caught a flicker of movement out of the corner of his left eye.

He braked, feeling every cell of his body talking to him. He put the truck in reverse and backed up. Four men came leaping over the hedges with guns in their hands.

Salvador braked and put up his hands. One man shoved his pistol in Salvador's face. Two others grabbed him and jerked him out of the truck.

They slammed him up against a fence and searched him thoroughly. Luckily, he was in his old work clothes and wasn't armed.

They took him up to the rented house. Inside was Wesseley, the big Tom Mix-gorilla from the hotel bust in San Bernardino. Domingo was over by the corner, handcuffed to a chair. His face was a bloody mess.

Yet, seeing Salvador, Domingo still screamed out, "My partner is a *gringo*, you stupid fools!"

Quickly, smoothly, Salvador watched the big, hairy-armed Tom Mix-gorilla cross the room and hit Domingo in the face with his gloved hand wrapped in barbed wire.

Domingo's face exploded with blood, splattering across the lime-colored wall.

Salvador was filled with horror. He'd heard of this little Texan trick of branding Indians and Mexicans, but he'd never seen it done. Not even in prison. Why, this big Tom Mix son-of-a-bitch had enjoyed it to the root of his being.

Then, the hairy-armed gorilla came, walking toward Salvador, step by step, smiling as he adjusted the wrapped wire about his blood-covered glove.

"Hey, don't I know you?" asked the big man.

"Sure, you know him!" shouted Domingo from across the room. He was wobbling on the floor with the chair on his back. "He fucked your mother!"

Grinning, the man forgot all about Salvador and returned to work on Domingo once again.

By the time they got to jail, Domingo had been beaten beyond recognition. Yet when they asked him his name, he still challenged them.

"I'm Johnny *La Tuya*," he bellowed at the lawman defiantly, meaning Johnny-Up-Your-Own-Mother.

Salvador couldn't believe it. Domingo was a tiger. And the more they abused him, the stronger he became.

Salvador and Domingo were put in separate rooms. Salvador sat down on the floor of his room. He sat and waited for them to come. He sat there and prepared himself inside his mind for the terrible beating he was sure that they were going to give him. But then, to his surprise, when the Tom Mix-gorilla finally came, he was friendly.

"Well, *amigo*," he said in perfect Spanish, "we're not going to have to work you over after all. Your partner broke down and told us everything. So, you're the boss, eh? You been bootlegging ever since I met you in San Bernardino."

Salvador stared at him. His Spanish was so good and his style was so relaxed that if Salvador hadn't been a man of experience, he would've completely believed him and told him everything.

But having gone to prison at thirteen years of age and having been "worked over" physically and mentally by the best, Salvador knew what was going on.

Salvador thought of asking the man where he'd learned his Spanish and why he was so mad at Mexicans, since he'd obviously spent a lot of time with them. But he knew the son-of-a-bitch would only ridicule him all the more, thinking he was weak. Salvador dug down deep inside himself and said, "You're full of shit! No one told you nothing! You're just a tricky Texan coward-bastard like all Texan son-of-a-bitches!"

The big man quit smiling and lunged at Salvador. Instantly, Salvador knew that he'd guessed right; they might kill Domingo, but they'd never break him.

And as the big man hit him, Salvador thought of Lupe and how he'd last seen her under the walnut tree, playing with that beautiful little girl named Isabel, and he forgot about the pain, ignored the beating he was getting, and he disappeared, going far away, beyond all bodily feelings, and it was good. He'd won again, and he was with Lupe, his truelove.

M oonlight was coming in the small barred windows when they finally threw Salvador into the big tank along with all the other prisoners. Domingo was over to one side. He looked far worse than Salvador. Wesseley hadn't used the barbed wire on Salvador. Here, in the jail, someone might have seen. Salvador lay down, face-first, and went to sleep. The concrete floor was cold and stank of piss and sweat and human shit.

Domingo waited until the guards were gone. Then, glancing around and making sure that none of the other prisoners were awake, he crawled over to his fallen brother.

"Salvador," he whispered. "It's me, Domingo."

But Salvador was too groggy. He could only hear his brother as if far away, in a dream.

"Oh, *hermanito*," said Domingo, drawing his younger brother close. "I'm sorry, I really am. It's all my fault." He put Salvador's head on his lap and rocked him back and forth.

Salvador tried to comprehend what Domingo was saying, but he couldn't. His ears, his whole head, was still ringing from the blows that Wesseley had given him. He prayed for the day that he might meet this Wesseley, just the two of them, *mano a mano*. Oh, he'd kill the son-of-a-bitch just like he'd . . . He stopped the words inside his head. Not even inside his own mind could he ever admit to himself what had happened between him and Duel.

Salvador fell back asleep and Domingo held him close, crying all the while. When Salvador awoke next, sunlight was coming in the small barred windows. The other prisoners were eating breakfast. Salvador found himself lying on his brother's lap. Domingo was leaning back against the concrete wall with his mouth wide open and his eyes closed as if he were dead.

Suddenly, Salvador remembered everything.

"Domingo!" he said. "Wake up! Wake up!"

Domingo couldn't even open his eyes, they were so swollen and caked over with dried blood. Salvador got some water and used coffee grounds. The coffee grounds reduced the pain and lessened the swelling. For the next hour, Salvador tried to think and get things straight inside his head as he attended to his brother's wounds. He could think of absolutely no reason why they should've gotten a beating like they had. They weren't suspected of murder. The worst thing they were suspected of was making whiskey. He couldn't understand why this man Wesseley, with his heavy Texan drawl, was so insanely hateful of Mexicans. Salvador decided to get ahold of Fred Noon as quickly as he could. And Archie, too. This wasn't right. No, not at all. He had to get out of here, and quick.

Domingo finally started coming around.

"Did Nellie and Epitacio get away?" whispered Salvador, quietly. For all he knew, the tank could be full of stool pigeons.

"Yes," said Domingo. "When we saw them coming, I went out the front door like a bull, giving them time to run out the back."

"How'd it happen?" asked Salvador.

"Oh, little brother," said Domingo, looking as if he might cry, "we'd been locked up all week. So, Nellie and me went out one day for a few hours while Epitacio attended to things. We met this guy at the poolhall . . . he and I shot a few games of pool together and he asked me if I knew where he could get a drink. I said sure, and we had a drink together from my pint in the alley."

Salvador stared at his brother. "And then he became your friend, right? Telling you anything you wanted to hear . . . agreeing with you on everything, until you finally invited him to the house."

"Well, yes," said Domingo. "But don't look at me like that. I tell you, you would've done the same thing. He looked *macho,* a lot like our own father!"

Salvador didn't even bother to say anything more. Hell, this was the oldest trick in the world and his older, stronger brother had fallen for it like a stupid little baby. What did he think? That the cops would send in a man who looked like a nervous, little stool pigeon?

"All right, so I did stupid!" yelled Domingo, "but what was I to do? We were locked up like in a prison."

Salvador blew out, shaking his head, and sat back against the concrete wall. Well now, at least he knew why his brother had been acting so big and brave with the cops. He felt guilty. He felt like a little piece of dog shit . . . so he'd tried to make up for it by showing how tough he could be now that he'd fucked everything up.

"You know," said Salvador calmly, softly, "I never realized until just now how much you and our father's big muscles were nothing but a joke all of our lives."

"Hey, you can't talk to me like that and expect to live!" said Domingo, sitting up.

"Why not?" said Salvador, getting to his knees, "I'm not afraid of dead men. And you're DEAD!"

"Dead, your ass!" shouted Domingo, kneeling, too.

And there they knelt, face to face, bloody and broken, pulsating with vengeance.

The tender, good feelings of the night before were gone, and now they were ready to kill each other as surely as Cain and Abel.

But then Salvador didn't hit his brother; no, he turned and got to his feet, grabbing the bars of the tank, screaming, shaking them, ripping the clothes from his body, wanting to kill not only his brother, but his father, too. All this blood inside him that drove him insane!

The guards came down the line between the tanks and they beat Salvador's fist so he'd let go of the bars. Domingo now leaped to his feet in Salvador's defense, willing to die for his brother, whom he'd been willing to kill only a moment before. The guards only laughed and beat his hands off the bars, too.

Later that day, Salvador paid twenty dollars to one of the same guards who'd beaten them to call Fred Noon for him. Mexicans weren't allowed to make phone calls. The guard finally traced down Fred Noon in Del Mar—just north of San Diego—where important men kept a little beach house for their mistresses.

Fred Noon was at the jail by noon the next day. He had Salvador out on bail by four o'clock.

"Those bigoted bastards!" said Fred, once they were outside in the parking lot. "They had their feet up on their desks, drinking your whiskey in the backroom, laughing about how they'd worked over a couple of chili-bellies!

"Sure, I'll take your case. And don't worry about money right now. Just reimburse me the fifty I put up for your bail and you can pay me for my services when you can."

"But, Fred," said Salvador, "I might not have any money for a long time. Maybe never."

"So what? You just get yourself to a hospital, Sal," said Fred, "and don't worry about this matter anymore. I'm going to make these racist bastards pay with their jobs!"

Fred Noon and Salvador shook hands, then Noon took off in his big Buick. Salvador got into his truck. He was going to drive back to their rented house in Watts before going home.

The sun was going down when Salvador got there. They'd truly worked him over good. He was having a hard time walking and he was pissing blood.

When Salvador opened the front door, a huge black cat came screeching out. Salvador leaped back, almost shitting in his pants. He had to grip the side of the door to catch his breath. All those terrible fears of evil spirits from his childhood came up inside him.

As he walked down the hallway, he could smell an awful odor. In the big backroom he saw that they'd dumped his drums of mash and destroyed his stove and kettle. Rats were all over the place. He hurried to the basement around back and he saw that they'd also taken all his whiskey. His knees went weak. He was broke; he had nothing, absolutely nothing, and next week he and Lupe had a date to order her wedding gown and the dresses for the bridesmaids.

He began to tremble so uncontrollably that he had to grab hold of the building. He pissed and it was all red. He stood there, shaking like a sick old man. Oh, how he wanted to kill his brother. It was all his fault! Buttoning his pants back up, Salvador turned and there was the big black cat, looking at him. And in that hundredth of a second before he passed out, Salvador know that this cat was, indeed, the devil and he had to stop thinking about killing his own brother or he was going to lose his immortal soul as well.

That night, Epitacio and Jose found Salvador behind the rented house. They took him home. For three days and nights, Doña Margarita sat by her son's side with a rosary in her hand, asking God to please spare his young life. Salvador tossed and turned and pissed blood by the bucket. Luisa hand-fed him liquids and put cold herbal compacts to his wounds.

Salvador screamed in delirium. He could never see Lupe again, looking like this. It brought tears to Doña Margarita's eyes. She sent Luisa and Epitacio down to the jail to find out about Domingo. But the authorities only arrested Epitacio and gave him a beating, too.

Luisa returned home and told her mother what the police had done. They immediately went to get the priest. The priest and Rodolfo spoke English, so they went to the jail, and they were able to get in and see Domingo without getting arrested. But they never told Doña Margarita how badly her son looked. His face would never be handsome again. The Texan had disfigured him, branding him for life.

For two more days, Salvador lay in bed, half-conscious. On the sixth day, he began to come around. He ate *menudo* and was gaining strength. He began to realize that not only was he physically broken inside, but he was broke financially as well. Oh, he needed money quickly if he was to get back on his feet. He'd been a fool to give his brother a second chance. But what could he do? It was done, and now he had to concentrate—not on killing his brother— but on how to get some money.

He thought of Lupe and how she'd looked when her mother had said, "Come; it is time." Oh, those words were magic to his ears, especially when he pictured in his mind's eye how Lupe had looked, coming from the walnut tree with Isabel at one side and Victoriano at the other. She'd looked like the sun itself, giving light to a whole world. Thinking of his truelove, Salvador began to mend quickly. After all, his mother always said that good thoughts were the seed of all healing.

O

ne afternoon, Pedro and his gang of pee-wees were playing cops and robbers outside Salvador's window. They'd made up a ballad of Salvador's encounter with the *gringo* rangers. And when the boys saw that Salvador was moving about in bed, they wanted Pedro to ask his uncle what had happened.

"Uncle," said Pedro to Salvador through the open window, "tell us what happened." He and his friends were all looking with admiration at Salvador's cuts and bruises. "You and Domingo, *los chingaron*, huh?"

"We what?" said Salvador, groaning with pain.

"You got 'em good, eh?" said the boy. "You fucked them over, like Pancho Villa!"

"Fucked them?" said Salvador, not being able to figure out what the hell the boy was talking about.

"That's enough," said Epitacio, coming in behind the boys. "Don't you see they almost killed him?"

Epitacio grabbed Pedro by the ear and ran all the other boys off. But once Pedro was out on the street with his friends again, he wasn't about to have his story ruined, so he made up another ballad about his uncle's latest adventures.

I

t was two more days before Salvador was out of bed. His first day walking around the barrio, he saw the men lined up by the dozens waiting to be picked up by the local ranchers to work. He thought of the rock quarry and how a lot of good men had gotten killed just trying to keep their low-paying jobs.

Late that afternoon, he was sitting in the back resting, when he saw Pedro and his bunch of friends shooting each other with sticks. He heard their screams of joy as they killed the *gringo* rangers. He remembered the days when he'd been a boy and they'd gotten word of Jose the great's death. He breathed deeply and watched them carefully. He thought of all the death that he'd seen during the Revolution. He remembered when Luisa's husband, who'd treated him so well, had come into the room spouting blood across the entire dinner table as he fell dead. He watched Pedro and his friends come running toward him with their eyes full of admiration, asking him if he was going to kill some more rangers.

"Kill more rangers? Why, you stupid kids! You think killing is fun?"

But when he lunged at Pedro, trying to grab him, he only fell. Pedro stopped in fear. Neither he nor his friends could believe it. Their hero was so weak that he couldn't even move.

For days on end, Lupe had a terrible feeling that Salvador was dying. She'd be bent over, working in the fields alongside her brother and sisters, and she would get this eerie feeling that Salvador was dying and her heart would race in fear. But she'd tell no one about it. She knew that to put thoughts into words was asking them to become reality.

The days passed and Lupe's fear grew. One evening when they got in from work, Lupe found that Doña Manza and her family had come in from the Imperial Valley. That evening, Lupe poured out her feelings to her friend Manuelita and showed her the ring that Salvador had given her.

"Oh, it's beautiful!" said Manuelita. "I'm so happy for you. But I'm sure he's fine. It's just that you're so nervous."

Lupe hugged her childhood friend close and they gossiped long into the night. Manuelita explained to Lupe how she and her fiancé were going to start a little business as soon as they were married.

"He has a car and he's building a trailer for it so we can carry clothes with us and sell them in the evenings as we follow the crops. You see," she said, eyes dancing with excitement, "in five years, we'll be able to get out of the fields."

"In five years? But how?"

"With our plan of selling clothes and saving our money, we'll eventually open a little store."

"Really, you'll have your own store?"

"Yes, but I'll tell you, at first Vicente just didn't believe that it was possible," said Manuelita, talking about her future husband, "until I put it all down in black and white on paper. Then, boom, he saw it, and started talking like it had been his idea! Oh, men! They're so childish!"

Lupe laughed, loving it, and her mind went reeling, exploding; she'd never heard of such a thing. To put the dreams of your life on paper, in black and white, and actually have the state of mind to formulate a plan for your future. Why, it almost sounded sinful, it was so foreign to everything that Lupe had ever been taught. Especially, about God and destiny and having to accept whatever came to you.

Oh, she could hardly wait to see Salvador so she could tell him about this incredible revelation. A plan—an organized, itemized schedule—of how to handle your income and get ahead.

But then she wondered if Salvador would accept her coming up with such a plan. After all, Manuelita had just said that she'd had trouble with Vicente until he'd thought that it was his own idea.

Lupe and Manuelita stayed up and visited long into the night every day that week and Manuelita explained to Lupe how to speak to Salvador so he'd think it was his own idea, too. Oh, it was so much fun, talking of the future just as they'd done back in La Lluvia de Oro. And sometimes Lupe found her friend Manuelita to be downright awful, she was so wonderfully ambitious.

Feeling stronger, Salvador started thinking, planning, trying to figure out what he was going to do to get some money fast. He couldn't just go out and rob a bank. Don Victor could let his bootlegging go unseen, but he couldn't very well overlook a bank robbery. Besides, he didn't want to be running from the law again. He'd had enough of that.

He began to wish that he hadn't bought Lupe such an expensive diamond ring and that he still had some of that cash so he could buy a new stove and kettle and set up a new distillery. But what could he do now? He couldn't ask Lupe for her ring back.

He continued thinking, figuring, trying to come up with a plan. Finally, he decided to sell his Moon automobile. But then he remembered how he'd promised himself that he and Lupe would go off on their honeymoon in his wonderful ivory car.

He decided to keep his Moon and see about borrowing some money from some of the people who owed him favors. After all, he'd helped a lot of people in their hour of need.

The next day, Salvador drove over to Riverside and approached a man who'd been selling whiskey for him for a couple of years in that area. His name was Febronio and he was a big, six-foot-six Mexican from Zacatecas who did cement work and had nine sons who all worked for him.

"What the hell happened to you?" asked Febronio, seeing Salvador's face, which still looked like it had gone through a windshield.

"Nothing," said Salvador. "I just had a little car accident."

"With the cops, eh?"

Salvador nodded. "Yeah, but nothing to worry about. Look, Febronio," he continued, feeling his heart pounding—he just wasn't used to asking anyone for anything—"I need your help."

"Sure, you just call it," said the dark, virile-looking man, smiling good-naturedly.

"They destroyed my distillery," said Salvador, "and took all my whiskey. I'm going to need a few hundred dollars to get started again."

"Oh, money," said the big man, putting his huge hand to his chin, rolling his lower lip about. "I'd like to help you, but I'm broke. I got a big family and we just added a new section to the house. But, well, if there's any other way I can help you, you just call it."

Salvador stared at him. The man was lying. He had more money stashed away than any other Mexican in all of Riverside.

"Febronio," said Salvador carefully, evenly, "I'm getting married; I need to get back in business quick. And remember, I've helped you many times in the past with credit."

The tall, well-muscled man stepped back, not liking it. "Well, what can I say? I don't got no money right now, Salvador. But if I had any money, you'd be the first one I'd loan it to."

"*If* you had any money?" yelled Salvador. "You lying son-of-a-bitch, you got money! But you're just scared of the rumors about the cops being after me!"

"Hey, watch it, *amigo*, you can't talk to me like this in front of my own home."

"*¡Chingate!*" said Salvador, and he turned, daring the chicken-shit bastard to come after him. He got in his truck and drove off.

And it was the same thing with every Mexican that Salvador went to asking for money. They had always been his best *amigos*, taking his liquor on credit when they didn't have enough cash, but now that he was broke, they couldn't help him. And some of the bastards were even nervous to have him near them, they were so afraid of the law.

Salvador decided to go and see Archie. He was Salvador's last chance. No one else that he knew had any money. Only the men and women who sold liquor for him and the lawmen who were on the take had money.

It was noon the next day when Salvador got to Archie's house. He found Archie playing poker with four men at a big table under a pepper tree in his backyard. They were all wearing ties and had their shirt sleeves rolled up.

Seeing Salvador, Archie immediately excused himself and came forward. He was wearing his shoulder holster and badge.

"Man, let me look at you," he said. "I heard they really worked you guys over, but I hadn't expected this."

"Yeah, and it was your friend Wesseley . . . who worked that deal out with you for me."

"Hey, hold on, I told you to stay in Escondido. What the hell did you go up to Watts for?"

Salvador breathed deeply. "My brother, he ruined Escondido for us."

Archie laughed. "Damned relatives! I swear, I've gotten in more trouble all my life because of my friends and relatives than from any of my enemies! But I warned you: stay local. Those Feds, they ain't human, like Big John and me. They go by the letter of the law, not giving a shit who they fuck up." He turned Salvador's face this way and that way in his huge hands, looking at him carefully.

"Archie," said Salvador, coming right to the point, "I'm broke and I need some money."

"How much?"

"Three, four hundred, so I can get started again," said Salvador, loving it how Archie had simply said, "how much?"

"Well, that's a little steep for me," said Archie, "but I'll tell you what, I can give you fifty."

"No, I need at least three hundred," said Salvador, fully realizing that

Archie and Big John had made a lot of money off him the last couple of years.

"Look," said Archie, "I'd really like to help you, Sal, but I've lost too many good friends by loaning them money and then, well, them hating me when they can't pay me back. So I'll tell you what," he added, pulling out his roll of money, "I'll just give you fifty for old times' sake."

Bringing himself up erect, Salvador screamed out in a bellowing roar, "Archie, you son-of-a-bitch! I didn't come here for charity! I came here to you, man-to-man, like a *macho*! Take your fifty and shove it up your ass!"

"Well, okay," said Archie, putting his money away, "but no need to get angry, Sal."

"No need? Why, you two-bit chicken-shit excuse for a real man; I have honor! I would have dragged my balls across the ends of the earth to pay you back!"

And in that instant, Salvador realized that he was Domingo's brother, after all. For he was now so raging angry inside that he could yank Archie off the ground with one hand and beat him to death without even working up a sweat.

But he didn't. He was also his mother's child and so he had the fortitude of mind to turn and walk away, knowing down deep in the marrow of his bones that he was man, a real *macho*, and this big, tall piece of human pus would never understand this as long as he lived.

Oh, he'd lost friends by loaning them money, and so now he was scared to take a chance on anyone. Archie was the worst of all cowards! He'd lost faith in mankind!

Getting home that night, Salvador was running a fever, he was so shaken. He had nowhere else to go. And what could be do? Sell his Moon or ask Lupe for her ring back? Oh, he would die first!

He went to bed and he became delirious again. He saw all of his life go slipping by his mind's eyes. He was dying, dying, dying, losing all hope. He'd worked so hard and suffered so much, only to get to the crest of the mountain and then go slipping, sliding back down the mountainside before he'd realized his highest of dreams: his own family.

But then, his mother came, dressed all in black like a great eagle, and she scooped him up, just as the devil in the form of a rattlesnake reached down to engulf him.

"No!" screamed his mother. "You will not die! Do you hear me? You will not die! You will live, *mi hijito*! Breathe! Breathe!"

"But I can't," he said. "I'm all broken inside. I've lost everything, Mama! And it hurts every time I try to breathe!"

"Listen to me," she said, grabbing him by the face, "every wino, every broken man and woman has their story of why they broke, but that's not why. They broke because they broke! Nothing more, nothing less! Because other people have lost more—their limbs, their children, everything! But still, they went on!

"Now sit up, and breathe life into yourself! A woman who loves you is waiting for you, *mi hijito*, and you are going to live, so help me God!"

Hearing his mother's words, Salvador tried to breathe, to bring strength to himself. But a big black cat leaped onto his chest, hissing into his face so he couldn't breathe. And he was dying once again, slipping, sliding, going. But then, his mother came once again and she grabbed the cat by the tail.

The huge black cat twisted and clawed, trying to kill his mother. But with the power of ten thousand years of motherhood, his mother sunk her one good canine into the cat's jugular and tore the devil's heart out with one mighty yank.

The whole sky opened up in a dazzling spectacle of dancing color, and beautiful white clouds did somersaults like playing children. Life had won once more and the devil was gone.

L upe couldn't figure out what had happened to Salvador. She hadn't heard from him in nearly two weeks. And last night the coyotes had howled all night and once more she'd had terrible feelings about him.

Oh, Salvador was dying. Lupe just knew it. She asked Victoriano to drive her over to Salvador's in Corona that weekend.

L ooking in the cracked mirror, Salvador could see that most of his face had healed, but he still had quite a few small scars. His mother and sister had done a marvelous job once again. Salvador decided to grow a beard, as he'd done when he'd had his jaw cut. After all, he couldn't just go over to see Lupe looking like this.

But first, Salvador had to drive his Moon down to Carlsbad and have Kenney sell it for him. There was just no other way. He asked Epitacio to follow him in the truck so he'd have a ride home afterwards. Both Pedro and Jose asked if they could come, too.

"Of course," said Salvador.

Getting to Carlsbad, Salvador passed by the house of the old lady who sold whiskey for him and he thought of maybe stopping by and asking her for a loan, but he decided against it. He just didn't want to go through another embarrassment of being turned down again. He laughed at himself. Hell, he was getting as bad as Archie.

"What's so funny?" asked Pedro, who was riding with Salvador. Jose had gone with Epitacio so he could practice driving.

"Oh, nothing," said Salvador, "I just thought that I'm becoming like an ex-friend of mine. Now I'm afraid to even ask anyone for anything because I don't have faith in people anymore, either."

"I don't understand," said the boy.

"Don't worry, you will when you're broke some day and you try to collect debts from chicken-shit bastard *mejicanos!*"

"You're mad at our own people?" asked Pedro. "But it was the *gringos* who beat you and Domingo."

"Yeah, they did. But they never claimed to be my friends. Our own people are the bastards who've doubled-crossed me!"

Pedro didn't know what to think. He'd always thought that only the *gringos* were the bad guys.

Salvador pulled up to Kenny's garage. The wide, powerful-looking old man came out grinning ear-to-ear.

"What the hell you so long-faced about?" he asked. "Did she find out you like wearing dresses to church and called off the wedding?" asked Kenny, doubling over with laughter.

Salvador started laughing, too. He just couldn't help it. Kenny was always in such fine spirits that it was contagious.

"How are you, Kenny?" said Salvador, getting out of the Moon.

"Great! Hell, if I felt any better, I'd get arrested!"

Looking at his sparkling blue eyes and the stance of his thick body cocked forward, ready to go at life, Salvador thought of asking him for a loan instead of having him sell his car for him, but he quickly decided against it. Hell, Kenny was a *gringo*. If his own people had refused him, how could he possibly think that an Anglo might help him.

"Well," said Salvador, walking inside with Kenny so they could speak privately, "what I came down here for, Kenny, is . . . well, that I got in some legal troubles and so . . ." Oh, it was so hard to ask for help. ". . . I'm broke." He put his hands in his pockets. "So I need your help to sell my Moon for me so I can get back on my feet."

"Sell your Moon?" said Kenny. "Bullshit! That's a good car! Hell, you need money? I got money! How much you need?"

Salvador was completely taken aback. These were the very words that he'd expected to hear from his own people—not a goddamn *gringo!*

"But, Kenny," said Salvador, suddenly feeling that the man didn't quite understand, "I don't mean twenty or fifty dollars! I need big money!"

"Good," said Kenny, spitting out a stream of tobacco juice, "the bigger the better! Hell, that's how a man finds out who his friends really are, goddammit! And I don't got many, believe me! So how much?"

Kenny closed up the big front doors and locked them, leaving Epitacio and the boys outside. He took a shovel and began to dig a hole in the middle of the garage ground. Salvador watched Kenny dig down two feet and then reach into the hole and bring out a small metal box. It was full of yellowish-looking paper money.

"Damn it," said Kenny, "look at that color! It's been buried too long. How much you need, Sal?"

Salvador was moved to tears. "Kenny," he said, "you got to understand

. . . I could get killed or end up in jail, then you'll never get your money back."

Kenny only shrugged. "So what? This place could burn down or I could get robbed. You're a man, Sal, and I trust you! And that's that! How much? I got nearly five hundred here!"

Salvador's eyes overflowed. He just couldn't help it. Why, this was the first time that any man had ever offered to help him outside of his immediate family.

"Kenny," said Salvador, choking up, "this is, ah, well . . ."

"None of that," said the old man. "Just tell me how much, goddammit!"

"Well" said Salvador, "two hundred is all that I figure I really need, but, well, to get the big stove and kettle and really get rolling again . . ."

"Well, then, hell!" said Kenny. "Let's make it four hundred to make sure to get you rolling good again!"

"But that won't leave you hardly anything," said Salvador.

"So what?" said Kenny, standing up. "Hell, I'm not the sorry bastard getting married!"

He counted out the money, handing it to Salvador, and Salvador stood there looking at his blue eyes—blue like his own father's—and he was overwhelmed with such a flood of thankfulness that he suddenly lunged at Kenny, grabbing him in a big *abrazo*.

"Christ Almighty!" bellowed the old man. "I told you, none of that! Let go of me! You crazy Mexican!"

But Salvador didn't let go. He kept hugging him and kissing him.

"Shit!" yelled Kenny, breaking loose and wiping his face where Salvador had kissed him. "Good thing the damned doors are closed. See if I ever loan money to another crazy Mexican!"

"You saved my life!" shouted Salvador.

"Bullshit!" said Kenny, slamming the metal box closed and dropping it back into the hole. "You owe me four hundred dollars whenever you got it, and that's that. But don't you ever kiss me again! Shit, my old man and I, we never hugged, even on his deathbed!"

Driving home with Pedro in his Moon, Salvador couldn't stop whistling, he was so happy. Hell, after he'd gotten the loan from Kenny, he'd stopped by to see the old lady who sold liquor for him and he'd told her that he was broke, just to see how she'd behave. She rolled up her dress, pulled out her roll, and lent him another hundred. Shit, he couldn't wait to get home to tell his mother. This was wonderful! When the chips were down, you didn't go to the *machos* of your own people. No; you went to *gringos* and the old Mexican women!

"Well," said Pedro, beaming with happiness, too, "now that you don't have to sell the Moon, I can drive it, right?"

Salvador looked at the boy a long time before answering. "All right," he said, "when we get near Temecula."

"But why Temecula?" asked the boy.

"Because Temecula is a very inspirational place. Don't you remember? That's where I taught you about the stick of human wisdom."

"Yes," said the boy, suddenly getting very frightened. "But I've been doing good in school, I swear it. You can ask Jose. I don't need another whipping!"

"I don't need to ask Jose," said Salvador calmly. "I trust your word. You're a good boy. But the other day when I saw you playing with sticks, pretending that they were guns so you could kill *gringos*, I began to wonder if you'd forgotten my words about respecting life."

"I won't do it again!" yelled the boy. "I promise! Only don't teach me any more wisdom. Please!"

Salvador burst out laughing. "I wasn't planning to hit you again," he said. "Now you know how to listen and pay attention. So this time I was thinking of teaching you how to shoot my gun so you can see for yourself that guns aren't toys to play with, but weapons to respect."

"Oh, good! I get to shoot your gun!"

"Yes, you do," said Salvador, "because I want you to know that I'm beginning to see that yes, of course, there are bad son-of-a-bitch *gringos* like the bastard that worked Domingo and me over, but there are good ones, too. Kenny—that *gringo* in Carlsbad—he just loaned me money and saved my life when no *mejicano* would. And Fred Noon, another *gringo*, he's a lawyer, and he's helping Domingo right now without pay. Do you understand? Both of these *gringos* came through for me when all of our miserable, son-of-a-bitch *mejicanos* ran from me in fear!" he shouted. "*Gringos* saved me! So I don't want you pretending to shoot *gringos* anymore just because they're *gringos*. That's bad, just as bad as the ranger who beat us for no other reason except that we're *mejicanos*."

"But, Uncle—"

"No buts! If I ever see you shooting men again just because they're not of our people, I'll bring out the stick of wisdom again."

"No, Uncle, please, don't make me wiser! I understand! I understand!"

"Good, I'm glad you do."

"I do, I do, believe me, I never meant anything bad," said the boy, tears streaming down his face. "It's just that Domingo and you were beaten and jailed, and I love you so much."

Calming down, Salvador reached out and put his huge, thick hand on his nephew's thigh. "Look," he said softly, "I know you love me and I love you, too, but we got to be smart if we're going to do good in this country. Killing is never going to get us anywhere except into jail. To make money, real money, and have power, you got to go to school and get educated. Become an attorney, then you can fight the bad cops with their own game like Fred

Noon is doing right now for Domingo and me, and you can cut their balls off where it hurts!''

"A lawyer can do that?" asked the boy.

"Yes, and make money, too."

"Oh, boy! Then I want to be a lawyer! And I'll have a suit and tie and a big car and my guys will work for me and I'll . . ."

The boy was off to the races once again. Salvador shook his head, laughing. This little kid Pedro was truly indestructible. Any way you turned him, he always came up smiling as if life was a rain of gold.

It was almost dark when Salvador, Epitacio, and the two boys pulled into Corona in the two vehicles. They could hear screams echoing from inside the house. Hurrying inside, they found that Nellie was in labor and Doña Margarita was assisting her.

Nellie was screaming hysterically about her children back home and that she'd been a fool to come out here with Domingo. Doña Margarita almost seemed happy to hear these screams of retribution, and she helped the poor young woman the best she could.

Luisa wasn't much help. She, too, was big with child and expecting any day. Nellie had a girl that night, and Luisa had another boy a few days later. The house was filled with the crying sound of infants once again.

Salvador and Epitacio set up the new distillery at Lake Elsinore. They rounded up all the drums that they could find and got the fermentation process started. Then, Salvador took off to see Lupe. He found her at home. He said hello to everyone and then Lupe and he went for a walk around the block. Flocks of red-shouldered blackbirds flew by. Two ravens gave chase to a huge hawk. The hawk circled higher and higher, trying to get away from the ravens.

"Where have you been?" asked Lupe.

Salvador took a big breath. "Some problems came up. I just couldn't get away."

Lupe stopped and looked at him straight in the eyes. "But what are these problems that always come up?" she asked in frustration. "I was so worried, Salvador. I had all these bad dreams that you'd been hurt and were dying."

He saw the fear in her eyes and it broke his heart. But what could he do? He couldn't very well tell her that she was, indeed, right and he'd been beaten and had been near death. He had to lie to her. He couldn't afford to tell her the truth about his life until they were married.

"Lupe," he said, "some of my trucks broke down. And I'm sorry, but, well, after we're married, things will get better. I promise, things like this won't happen anymore."

"Good," she said, "because I've been so worried, Salvador."

"Really? You have?"

"Of course," she said.

"Oh, Lupe," he said, and he took her in his arms, holding her close. He could feel her heart pounding against his chest like a frightened bird. He felt like such a liar, such an awful beast, and yet, he couldn't think of how else to handle the situation.

Lupe never asked him about his beard that day. They set the date for their wedding—August 18, 1929—Salvador's twenty-fifth birthday.

The following week, Salvador picked up Lupe and Carlota to drive them across town to Harry's store. He was still feeling pretty shaky. All the money that he'd gotten from Kenny had gone into his business. He didn't have the money for their wedding clothes.

Arriving at Harry's, Salvador parked and walked around the car, opening the door with a big smile for Lupe and her sister. But, oh, he was dying inside. A man without money was a nobody.

"But this is such a little place," said Carlota, looking at the small tailor shop. "I thought we were going to a good place like Sears."

Salvador felt like bashing Carlota in the mouth. According to her, he couldn't do anything right. But Lupe took Salvador's hand, winking at him.

Harry and Bernice met Salvador and the two young women at the door.

"Come right in, *amigo mío!*" said Harry to Salvador. "And this must be Lupe, the lucky girl," he said, seeing the diamond ring on Lupe's finger. "Oh, what a ring! But it's even a thousand times more beautiful on your hand, my dear!"

"It's glass!" said Carlota, glancing around at the small shop which happened to be one of the most exclusive places in all of the southland.

"Glass!" said Harry, astonished. "Why, this is a nearly faultless diamond!" he shouted. "You can't find a more perfect stone in all of California! You just don't know how to appreciate quality, my dear!" he snapped.

Carlota didn't know what to say. She was speechless. Salvador loved it; he couldn't have asked for anything more.

Bernice came over and took the two young women away before her husband destroyed the poor girl. Oh, Harry was as mad as hell.

"I'm sorry," said Harry, once his wife had ushered Lupe and Carlota away. "But for her to have said such a thing," he said, bringing out his handkerchief to wipe the sweat off his forehead, "is unforgivable!"

"It's all right," said Salvador, smiling ear to ear, "believe me, it's all right."

"I hope so," said Harry. "I'm normally a very patient man, but . . ." And then he smiled. "So, anyway, how can I help you today, *amigo mío?*"

Salvador took a deep breath. "Harry," he said, "I got some bad news for you."

Instantly, Salvador saw Harry's face twist with a look of real concern.

"Yes, Sal, I'm listening," he said.

"Well, you see, Harry," continued Salvador, "in the past I've always come into your store with cash in my hand. But, well, this time I'm here—and I'm embarrassed to say—a little short."

"You mean that this is about money?" asked Harry incredulously.

"Yes," said Salvador.

"Not another word," said the white-haired man, looking greatly relieved. "With me, Salvador, you got credit. My God, I'd thought your beloved mother whom you've told me so much about was ill or something important! Money—that's nothing, nothing—it comes and goes with the wind. It's here, inside you, Salvador, *amigo mío*, that I value."

Salvador could say nothing. He was speechless. Why, here it was once again, another miracle. What was this world coming to?

Harry took one of Salvador's huge hands in both of his. "You can pay me next month or whenever you can," he said. "I'll never forget the first day you came to my store. You circled the block three times before you stopped."

"You saw that?" asked Salvador, feeling slightly embarrassed.

"Of course! That's why I took off my coat and I rolled up my sleeves and took out the trash, so I'd look like a workman, too."

"You mean that you did all that on purpose?" asked Salvador, remembering the incident well.

"Sure," said Harry. "I'll tell you, Salvador, I wasn't rich all my life. I know what it feels like to be afraid of being turned out of a store and . . . not necessarily as fancy as this one," he said, squeezing Salvador's thick hand in both of his. "Come, no more. You get fitted for your clothes, too. A wedding is supposed to be a happy time. It's not until after you've been married for twenty years that you start having long faces." And he laughed, truly enjoying himself. "This matter is closed."

"Thank you," said Salvador.

"So, where is the wedding going to be?" asked Harry as they walked across the store to where Lupe and Carlota were selecting material.

"Here, at the church in Santa Ana," said Salvador.

"On what day?" said Harry. "My wife and I want to be sure to leave that date open."

"You mean you'd come?" asked Salvador, never once having thought of inviting them.

"Why, of course," said Harry. "You give the information to Bernice, and we'll be there." He stopped and looked at his wife helping Lupe with a dress. "You're a very lucky man, Salvador," he said. "Lupe is the most beautiful young woman I've seen in all my life, except for my Bernice. Oh, that girl could model clothes in Paris the way she holds herself." He took a big breath. "She truly reminds me of my wife when I first saw her. Just look at my Bernice—the years have been kind to her. No one believes that we're nearly the same age," he laughed.

Salvador looked at Harry, and then at Bernice. It was true; the white-haired man looked far older than his wife.

They were in the shop for nearly three hours before they finished their business. Then, as they were going out the door, Salvador noticed that Lupe stopped to look at a beautiful royal-blue dress that was trimmed with beige lace and had a matching full-length coat with a soft, dark brown fur collar.

"How much for that dress and coat, Harry?" asked Salvador.

"For you, Salvador, fifty percent off as my gift for your wedding."

Salvador was overwhelmed once again. This man had just given him credit, and now he was giving him a break in price, too.

"Harry," said Salvador, grabbing him in a big *abrazo*, "you're a *gallo de estaca*, a prize rooster!"

Harry was only an inch shorter than Salvador, but he was half his size across the back and shoulders. "*Gallo de estaca* you, too!" said Harry, embracing Salvador in return.

Hearing the mispronunciation of the word, Salvador burst out laughing. Harry did, too. They filled the little shop with cheerful sounds.

After selling the first six barrels of whiskey, Salvador returned one hundred dollars to Kenny and bought a train ticket for Nellie back to Chicago. She'd decided to leave her newborn with Luisa and go back home and see if her husband wouldn't take her back. Nellie was truly sorry that she'd ever left her family in the first place for this guitar-strumming man.

Doña Margarita, of course, agreed with her decision to return home to her husband and three children. She told Nellie not to worry about her newborn little girl; this was God's will. She and Luisa would raise her daughter, giving her a good home, as they'd done for Emilia's child who was now a grown woman and living near Fresno with her own husband and children.

It was the day of the trial and Salvador met Fred Noon at the foot of the courthouse steps. Salvador was dressed in his work clothes, as Fred had told him to do.

"If this case was in San Diego, I could get the whole thing dismissed," said Fred to Salvador as they went inside. "But it's going to be a dirty fight up here. This Wesseley fellow, I did some checking on him. He was raised in Texas by a Mexican family; seems like they treated him real well, so he raped their daughter and has hated Mexicans ever since. Also, he was a Texas Ranger before he joined up with the Feds."

Salvador nodded, having thought some such thing. A man with guilt was a very dangerous animal, especially when he started lying to himself and twisting his guilt into vengeance.

Fred Noon was right. It became a dirty fight. Wesseley lied and twisted everything he could. But he was no match for Noon, who stood up tall and dignified, going over the evidence that they had on Salvador again and again, which was that he had sugar and yeast in his truck.

"Does this make Mr. Villaseñor any more a bootlegger than a housewife coming home with groceries from the store?" insisted Noon.

Wesseley and his attorney squirmed and pushed, but Noon remained cool and reasonable. On the third day, the case went to the jury and Salvador was found innocent, but Domingo was found guilty. On Wesseley's recommendation, the judge gave Domingo the maximum sentence of five years. Fred Noon was outraged, saying that Domingo had no prior record and should only be given eighteen months, at the most. The judge told Fred to keep still or he'd find him in contempt.

"Damn it, Salvador," said Fred, once they were outside in the parking lot, "you haven't heard the end of this! I've drank whiskey with that judge. Wesseley must have something on him. You tell Domingo when you see him that I'm going to screw these bums yet!"

Salvador took Fred Noon in his arms. Fred was a good man. The best. He truly cared. He was a man of honor.

It was a dark, overcast day the morning that Salvador went to see Domingo before he was shipped off to San Quentin. Salvador paid the guard ten dollars so that he'd leave them alone. Once he and Domingo were alone, Salvador brought out a pint bottle of whiskey and handed it to his brother. Domingo's whole face came racing away from the dead. He took to the bottle like a newborn, sucking down half of its contents, then he fell back against the bars.

"You saved my life!" said Domingo. "Oh, that's good!"

Salvador was glad that he'd thought of bringing along the whiskey for his brother.

"So, has Nellie gone?" asked Domingo.

"Yes," said Salvador. "I bought her the train ticket and gave her some money."

"But our baby," he said, "she left her here, right?"

"Yes," said Salvador.

"And Mama, what does she say now?" asked Domingo.

"Not much," said Salvador. "Except that it was God's will and Nellie should've never left her family in the first place."

"You know," said Domingo, "I've been doing a lot of thinking here in jail, and I've come to think that whoever I'd brought home, Mama wouldn't have liked her." He drank again. "She just never gave Nellie a chance."

Hearing this, Salvador tried to keep calm, but he just couldn't. "Listen here, Domingo," he said, "let's not play stupid! You know damned well that's not true. You brought home a woman who'd abandoned her children to a mother that's gone to hell and back to keep her family together! What the hell did you expect? That our mother would approve of your choice in this woman?"

Surprisingly, Domingo didn't anger. He looked at his younger brother for a long time. "Yes," he said, "I should have guessed that you'd say that. But that's not the whole truth, and you know it. The whole truth is that our mother never liked me! She always liked YOU!" he added, bellowing with rage now. "So no matter what Nellie would've done—stay here with our child or go back to her other family—Mama would've found fault with her! And that's the God-awful truth!"

"Bullshit!" said Salvador. "Our mother always loved you, too! She didn't find fault in your woman because of her lack of love for you! And as far as maybe showing more affection towards me, that was only because our father hated me!" screamed Salvador, raging angry, too. He grabbed the pint bottle from Domingo and drank it down.

"What, you stupid *cabrón*!" yelled Domingo. "I'm the one going to prison! Not you!"

But it was too late. Salvador had downed it.

"Shit!" said Domingo, grabbing back the bottle, lifting it up to see if there was any left. There was only a drop. He put the bottle to his lips, raised it up in the air and waited patiently for all the droplets to gather inside the bottle and come sliding, gliding down like little rivers to his mouth. He sucked them in, one by one.

"Hell," he said, blowing out. "This is truly some life, eh *hermanito*? Here we are, two grown men, sitting in jail, and we argue about our parents' love." He wiped his mouth. "Remember, Salvador," he continued, "the time that pig ate the chayote plant outside the *ramada*?"

"How could I forget?" said Salvador. "Papa was going to kill me for it."

"But I protected you."

"Yeah, you did, for a change," said Salvador. "Usually, you were always hitting me, instead."

"True," said Domingo, "I did hit you a lot back then, but this time I saw the injustice of our father's anger toward you. So, well, I took the blame."

"And he didn't hit you."

"No, he didn't," said Domingo, "but he would've hit you."

"You damned right!" said Salvador. "He might have killed me. My God, he was crazy with rage. And it wasn't my fault the pig ate the chayote plant. I was a child and I'd fallen asleep." Salvador took a big breath. "I'll tell you one thing, I'm sure as hell never going to favor one of my children over another. I'm going to work hard to be the best father the world has ever seen," he said. "And raise my kids with love and understanding and never hit them!"

"Well, I hope you do it," said Domingo. "Because so far, I haven't done even as well as our parents. I've left children everywhere. Just like the *gringos* have done to our women, I've done to theirs from Chicago to Texas and back again. And . . . I know that this is partly why Mama is mad at me, for leaving my seed all over the land like a dog, but, still, you have to admit that Mama has always preferred you, just as I admit that Papa preferred me." He wiped his eyes. They were beginning to water. "Now, of course, she wasn't as obvious as our father, but, still, it was there. She did little things all the time which showed me just how much more she loved you.

"Like the corncob she always gave you before you went to bed at night. She'd heat it up special for you, telling you to warm your feet with it, and then munch on it if you got hungry during the night." His eyes were pouring with tears.

"Yes, that's true," said Salvador, "but I was little, Domingo, and the Revolution was going on and I was always hungry."

"That's not true," said Domingo, wiping his eyes. "She did that for you even before those hard times came. I remember, and I was always so jealous of that corncob. In fact, I stole it from you many times and put chile on it so you'd burn your tongue when you ate it at night."

"You put chile on it?" asked Salvador, grinning with surprise.

"Yes," laughed Domingo.

Salvador laughed too. "And all these years I thought that hot taste came from rubbing it against my dirty feet."

"No! You thought that?"

"Yes!" said Salvador.

"Oh, no!" said Domingo. "That's FUNNY! I'd get up and steal the corn from you and put chile on it and then wait up, hoping to see you burn your mouth out, but you never did."

"Well, of course not, because I'd just wake up and eat it, thinking it was hot because of the dirt it got off my feet. Oh, that's wonderful!" continued Salvador. "So then you really had jealousy towards me, too, eh?"

"Oh, I hated you with jealousy!"

"Great!" said Salvador. "I only wish I'd known about it so I could've enjoyed it!"

And then they were both laughing—big laughs from the gut—and it was a sight to see: two brothers at last together, heart to heart, but surrounded by iron bars.

"You know," said Domingo, "I wish we could have talked like this the first night I came in from Chicago."

"Me, too," said Salvador. "But you were so full of yourself . . . trying to impress us with everything you'd done. I couldn't say a thing without you saying you'd already done it, except bigger and better."

"I was that awful?"

"Yes."

"I'll be, I never knew I was doing that. Damn, if only a man could live two or three lives back to back, then I think maybe we could get it right." He reached out and gripped his brother. "I love you, *hermanito*," he said.

"I love you, too," said Salvador.

And there they held, looking at each other, eye to eye, and it was good.

"You know," said Salvador, "I've been doing a lot of talking with Mama now that I'm getting married and, well, she's told me about the days just before her own marriage and how she found out about our father and his love for his first cousin. Did you know about that? About Papa killing his cousin's prospective husband in a duel?"

Domingo nodded. "Yes. Papa told me."

"He did? Well, I'll be!"

"Yes, Papa and I talked a lot."

"Well, Domingo, that's when I think that the problems with our parents' love started," said Salvador. "Our father loving a tall blue-eyed woman like himself, he never really let himself love Mama, Jose, or any of us short, dark ones."

"Hey, that's not true," said Domingo. "The problem started when Mama kept throwing Don Pio's greatness in our father's face, making Papa look so bad all the time."

"No, you're wrong," said Salvador.

"Bull, it works both ways," said Domingo. "Our mother was as much in love with her father as our father was with his cousin."

"I'll be; I never thought of it that way," said Salvador.

"Of course not, you only listened to our mother."

"And you only listened to our father," said Salvador.

"True," said Domingo.

"I'll be damned," said Salvador. "Do you realize how long we've been talking and we haven't gotten in a fight?"

Domingo grinned. "Like the Mexican expression says, 'I thought I'd died and gone to heaven until they told me I was in jail.'" They both laughed, truly enjoying themselves. "Hell, for us *mejicanos* being behind bars is like a vacation," added Domingo.

The guard came up, saying that it was time for Salvador to leave. Salvador slipped the guard another ten.

"All right," said the guard, "but only five more minutes."

"Okay," said Salvador.

"Oh, Salvador," said Domingo, shaking his head, "the truth is that everything could've come out fine if the rangers hadn't tricked me and sent me to Chicago. I would've found Papa and come home with him and we would've had money. Then we could've all migrated to Del Mar and waited out the war and you would've never gone to prison and I'd never gotten lost like a dog in the streets for fifteen years!

"Oh, *hermanito!*" he screamed, grabbing Salvador. "If only the cards would've fallen different! We'd be kings right now!"

"Yes, I'm sure you're right," said Salvador. "But what can we do now? It's all gone, Domingo."

"Oh, no!" said Domingo. "It's not gone! I've been thinking that when I get out of San Quentin we can all return to Mexico and reclaim our family's land!

"And, also," he said, drawing in close to Salvador, whispering to him in the ear, "I know of a gold mine in Sonora that this Indio told me about just before he died in Chicago. It's in the bag, Salvador; we'll get the gold and go back and buy up the whole Cerro Grande of Los Altos and be kings, you and I!"

And saying this, Domingo grabbed Salvador with all his might, squeezing him chest-to-chest in a big *abrazo*.

"And I'll find all my sons from Texas to Chicago!" continued the big man who'd once been so handsome that the women just couldn't resist him. "And I'll raise them strong and pure in Los Altos and Mama wouldn't have to look at me with shame in her eyes anymore—I swear before God!" he added, gripping Salvador with love's desperate need.

The guard came up. "It's time," he said.

But Salvador and Domingo still continued hugging each other in a big *abrazo*; two big, strong men, unafraid of showing love and affection.

"All right," said Domingo, releasing Salvador and wiping his eyes, "you better go now. I got to be alone and start preparing myself inside my heart, here, for San Quentin." He laughed. "San Quentin, the prison especially made by the *gringos* for our people!"

Salvador nodded. "Yeah, you're right." He took a big breath. "The *gringos* sure prepare for us." They laughed, looking at each other quietly. "Mama, Luisa, everyone sends you their best."

"Good, and tell 'em not to worry," he said. "I'll be fine. The whole prison is full of our people from Los Altos, I've been told." He kissed Juan Salvador on one cheek and then on the other. "You go now, get married, and have lots of sons. And don't worry, I'll serve this time for both of us, like a man! Hell, Nellie's gone, so I got no one, anyway." He looked at Salvador in the eyes. "I love you, *hermanito*," he added.

"I love you, too, Domingo," said Salvador, bringing out another pint bottle.

"I'll be damned!" said Domingo. "With this, I'll have no problems! Five years, shit! I can do that hanging by my thumbs!"

Going out, Salvador handed the guard another ten so he'd let Domingo keep the bottle, and each step that Salvador took going down the long walkway between the barred cells echoed and re-echoed like a mighty drum . . . step by step away from his brother that he'd truly found at last.

It was the day before Lupe was to come over and meet Salvador's mother, so Salvador hired Pedro and his gang of little pee-wees to clean up the yard and wash down their two houses.

Pedro was in ecstasy, bossing his five friends around with his little pot belly hanging out. Salvador drove over to the distillery to check on Jose and Epitacio. Everything was going well.

"But we might have a problem," said Epitacio. "You tell him, Jose. It was you that he spoke to."

Salvador turned to his nephew.

"Archie came by," said Jose.

"Archie!" yelled Salvador.

"Yes. He asked for you, said for me to tell you to stop avoiding him, that he needs to see you."

"That son-of-a-bitch!" screamed Salvador. "Sure, now that I got money and liquor again. Tell him to kiss my ass if he ever comes by again! The chicken-shit bastard!"

"Just like that, Uncle? 'Kiss my ass?' " said the boy nervously.

Salvador burst out laughing. "No, I didn't mean for you to tell him that. I mean for me to tell him that."

"Oh," said Jose, looking relieved.

Salvador put his arm around his nephew. "You're a good little man," he said to him. "I'm proud of you. And you, too, Epitacio, I was wrong to bring my brother into our business. He's too wild. From now on I only want good, honest, law-abiding people like you two working for me, especially if what we're doing is illegal."

Jose laughed.

"What's so funny?" asked Salvador.

"What you said, wanting only good, honest, law-abiding people to do illegal stuff."

"Well, that's true. You never rob a bank with a bunch of thieves. The temptation will be too great for them to rob you, too. All illegal business, if it is to be done right and succeed, must be done with the most honest of all people. You need complete honesty to be outside of the law, *mi hijito*. That's one of the rules that Duel taught me."

Jose smiled. "That Duel, he was some man, eh?"

"Yes, he was the best, my teacher, my eyes, when it came to money, gambling and all the things of a real *macho*. Just as my mother has been my teacher, my eyes, in the matters of the heart, marriage and love." Salvador breathed deeply. "I loved that man. Duel was more my father than my own father ever was."

"Whatever became of him?" asked Jose, still smiling.

Salvador's whole face exploded, and his eyes went wild. "DON'T!" he barked. "Don't you ever ask me that again for as long as you live!"

Jose swallowed. "Okay, I'm sorry, I didn't know." Instinctively, Jose stepped back. My God, his uncle could be so happy one moment, then as crazy as the devil the next.

Lupe looked at herself in the mirror for the umpteenth time. Salvador was supposed to have come by over an hour ago to get her and Carlota. They were finally going over to Corona to meet his mother, the great woman herself.

But no matter how much Lupe tried to belt in her dress, this way or that way, she just didn't think that she looked good enough.

Finally, she decided that what was really bothering her wasn't the dress at all, but the fact that yesterday Don Manuel and his family had come by to see her diamond ring, which was the talk of the barrio. And after Rose-Mary had looked at it, she'd said, "Oh, Lupe, I just feel so terribly for you that Salvador is a bootlegger."

Lupe had felt her whole face go hot, wanting to explode. But, still, she held herself calmly and said, "Oh, that's all right, Rose-Mary. I, too, heard those rumors when I'd first met Salvador. But we found out that they're not true, so you don't have to feel sorry for me, my dear."

"But they're not rumors," insisted Rose-Mary. "My father is the one who told me. How else do you think that one of our people could manage to buy such a huge diamond? Look at mine, Lupe. My fiancé is an Anglo teacher and he makes very good money, but still, he was only able to buy me this small, proper-looking stone," she said.

Lupe had said nothing more, not wanting to dignify Rose-Mary's words. But now, as she turned this way and that way, looking at herself in the mirror, she realized that Rose-Mary's words had gotten to her. Especially when Carlota had gotten wind of what was going on and she'd begun haunting Lupe with 'I told you so.' Lupe was, indeed, wondering once again if Salvador was a bootlegger and he'd bought her diamond with illegal money. For, if he had, then of course she'd have to give it back to him and call off their wedding.

"Lupe!" called Carlota from the front room, "the no good is here!"

Lupe swallowed, checking herself in the mirror one last time before going into the front room.

"Now, Carlota," said their mother, "you behave yourself. This is Lupe's day, not yours."

"Oh, Mama, stop worrying," snapped Carlota, going across the room to open the door for Salvador, "I know it's Lupe's day."

"No!" said Lupe. "Don't you open the door! Sit down with me, Carlota, and let Papa open the door."

"But why?" asked Carlota. "I don't see what difference it makes."

"It makes a difference to me," said Lupe. "Please, get the door, Papa," added Lupe softly to their father.

"Of course," said the old man, shaking his head. All this fuss for a woman to allow a man to get into her underwear was just beyond him. But women were strange animals, as far as he was concerned.

Carlota sat down next to Lupe as their father went to the door. But then she jumped up.

"Carlota, sit down," said Lupe.

"No, I'm going to the bathroom!" she said, leaving the room.

Lupe took a big breath, trying to keep her composure. Oh, how she wished that her sister wasn't coming with her. She was worried enough as it was about meeting this great lady who'd been educated in Mexico City. She wondered if she and her sister would even know how to behave in front of such a fine lady. And then, of course, there was this thing about the bootlegging that would have to be addressed.

Walking both young ladies to his Moon, Salvador could see that Lupe was upset. He put Carlota in the back and Lupe up front.

Salvador started the motor and released the brake, and they went up the tree-lined street. "Are you all right?" he asked Lupe.

Lupe nodded. "Yes," she said.

"Ha!" said Carlota in the back.

"Carlota!" said Lupe. "You promised!"

Salvador could feel the tension between the two sisters. It was a long, silent drive out of Santa Ana. Then, coming into Corona, into the Anglo part of town, a police car suddenly came up behind them with its siren screeching.

"Oh, my God!" screamed Carlota. "Rose-Mary was right! And we're all going to go to jail!"

"Hey, calm down. Nobody's going to jail," said Salvador, trying to sound reassuring. "Maybe I was just speeding a little. Nothing more."

But inside his soul, Salvador was climbing the walls. He pulled over. He was just opening his door to get out of his car to see what this was all about, when suddenly there was the cop at his side. He was a huge young man with a mammoth lower jaw. He grabbed Salvador and yanked him out of the Moon.

"Hey, easy, friend," said Salvador. "I'm not fighting you."

"Just keep your mouth shut, Me-chee-cain!" said the big cop, throwing Salvador up against the side of the Moon. "You were speeding, you son-of-a-bitch!"

Hearing the policeman's words, Lupe was shocked. Why, if this man was, indeed, treating Salvador like this just for speeding, then he was crazy. She watched the policeman kick Salvador's legs apart and search him thoroughly.

"All right, boy," said the cop, not finding any weapon on Salvador, "whose car is this?"

"Mine," said Salvador.

"Yours, hell!" yelled the policeman.

"Check my registration," said Salvador.

"Don't tell me how to do my job!" shouted the lawman, drawing his gun.

"We're innocent!" screamed Carlota. "We didn't have anything to do with it!"

"With what?" asked the cop.

"Shut up!" said Lupe, turning to her sister.

"You shut up!" shouted the big man. "Let her talk."

"I will not!" commanded Lupe, getting out of the Moon.

"Get back in the car!" yelled Salvador, not wanting Lupe to get involved. "I'll handle this!"

"But he has no right to treat you like this!" said Lupe, coming closer. "Officer!" she said, "I want the name of your superior."

The cop stared at Lupe as if seeing her for the first time. Her English was excellent. Completely without an accent. And she was very well dressed.

"But, ma'am, I'm stopping a speeder," he said.

"Well, then, officer," said Lupe, her face filled with indignation, "if that's what you're doing, then you do it with dignity. Just look at yourself. Those spots and stains on your uniform—that's disgraceful," she said.

"But, ma'am," said the young cop, forgetting all about Salvador, "I got to buy my own gas and uniform. They don't pay me nothing."

"That's no excuse!" said Lupe, heart pounding with rage, remembering the first day she'd seen her Colonel in his immaculate uniform—and that had been in the midst of battle. "A handsome young officer like you, representing the police department, should have more pride!"

"Yes, ma'am," he said, putting his gun away.

All this time, Carlota was looking from Lupe to the policeman and back to her sister in bewilderment. Never in her life had she ever seen any woman handle authority like this.

"Look," said the cop, turning to Salvador, thinking that maybe he'd made a mistake and these weren't Mexicans after all, "let's just say we never met and you take these two ladies out of here."

"Fine with me," said Salvador.

"No!" said Lupe. "I want you to give me the name of your superior, right now!"

"Lupe," said Salvador, "that's enough! Let's just get out of here!"

"But he . . ."

"Lupe," said Salvador, taking her by the arm, "people are waiting for us."

"Well, all right," said Lupe, still not wanting to give in. "But you best behave in the future!" she snapped at the young officer over her shoulder as Salvador put her back inside the Moon.

"Yes, ma'am!" said the huge-jawed cop.

Salvador wanted to double over with laughter, but another part of him was angry that Lupe had come to his rescue. "My God," he said, once they were driving away, "what got into you, Lupe?"

"Me?" she said. "You're the one who looked like you were ready to try and fight him!"

"I could've whipped him," he said. "Don't you ever do that again! My God!"

"He's right," said Carlota. "Oh, I thought we were all going to jail."

"Why jail?" asked Salvador. "And who's Rose-Mary?"

Carlota clammed up.

"Well, who is she?" repeated Salvador. "You said she was right about something."

"I'm not supposed to talk," said Carlota. "If you want to know anything, you'll have to ask Lupe."

Lupe turned, giving her sister a deadly look. Then she turned back around, took a deep breath, and pulled herself together. Oh, she was going to kill Carlota with her bare hands once they were alone.

"Rose-Mary is a friend of ours," said Lupe. "We've known her and her family since La Lluvia."

"Oh, I see."

"And she told Carlota and me that you're a bootlegger."

Salvador almost drove off the road.

"What?" he said.

"Salvador," said Lupe, feeling her heart wanting to burst, "I'm sorry my sister brought this up. But now, since it's out in the open, I'd like you to answer this question once and for all; are you a bootlegger or not?"

Salvador glanced at Lupe and a million thoughts went reeling through his mind. A part of him really did want to tell her the truth and explain to her that he was a bootlegger, but that *la bootlegada* wasn't bad. It was good. It made him king of his own destiny! And what was bad was the way that Mexicans were treated like dogs in this country. But he also knew that if he told her the truth, now, before they were married and especially here in front of her sister, that he'd never get the chance to explain anything to her because she'd leave him instantly.

"No," he said at last, "I'm not a bootlegger. I'm a hard-working businessman. You know that, Lupe. You saw how I worked with your father and brother, moving fertilizer. I'm surprised you'd even ask."

"I didn't," said Lupe, feeling relieved. "It was my sister." She gave Carlota another terrible stare. "I told her that she was wrong, that I'd heard those rumors when I'd first met you, too."

Carlota returned Lupe's evil look. She was so mad, she could scream. She just didn't care what Salvador or anyone else said. Salvador was a no-good bootlegger in her opinion, and she just knew that she was right.

They were all still pretty shaky when they got to the barrio. That big young cop had truly looked crazy with rage. Driving down the rutted dirt street, Lupe realized that this was, indeed, the same street that she'd come down over the years to get eggs and goat's milk on their way to Hemet to do the apricots.

The street was full of potholes and deep ruts and they lifted dust on the homes and clotheslines as they passed by in the long, sleek Moon. The children playing in the street immediately recognized Salvador and came running up alongside the car.

"The kids, I drive them up and down the street in my car," said Salvador, explaining the children's adoration.

Lupe took his arm, remembering how he'd let her drive, too. Then to Lupe's surprise, they pulled up to the last two houses on the street—the very same place where they'd stopped for the goat's milk so many times.

Her mind went reeling. She recalled the thick-chested young man that she'd seen the first time that they'd stopped by. His face had been bandaged, and he'd had a gun in his back pocket. Rose-Mary's words came rushing back to her mind. She turned and looked at Salvador, wondering if he was, indeed, that same man.

But she couldn't tell. He was all dressed up now in a beautiful suit with an elegant white shirt and gold cufflinks and a fine panama hat. Oh, she just wished that she could get Rose-Mary's words out of her mind once and for all!

"Are you all right?" asked Salvador, parking the Moon in front of the two houses. "You look a little pale, Lupe."

"I'm fine," said Lupe. But inside, she was a ball of nerves. The devil of doubt was strangling her.

"It's all right," said Salvador, taking her hand. "The cop is gone; and don't worry, you did wonderful," he added. "I'm not upset with you anymore. I guess I was just frightened for you when you got out of the car."

She saw his eyes and his beautiful smile. Lupe knew that she had to put the evil thoughts that she was having out of her mind or it was going to ruin everything.

"I was frightened for you, too," she said, caressing his hand.

He took her hand in his. "We're going to do good together," he said. "Very good together."

"All right! Enough!" said Carlota. "Let me out!"

Salvador and Lupe both laughed. They'd forgotten all about Carlota. He got out of the Moon and came around to open the door for Lupe and her sister. There were chickens running every which way. The fenced-in garden on the side of the big house was green and lush and beautiful. A mother pig with her litter of seven piglets came rushing by.

"Oooooooh!" said Carlota, making a face of repulsion. "There's chicken *caca* all over the place! Don't you people ever clean it up?"

"Carlota!" said Lupe. "You promised!"

"Yes, but I never promised to ruin my new red shoes!" she said. "Oh, look! They have *caca* on them!"

Salvador didn't know what to say. He felt so embarrassed. He'd asked Jose and Pedro to clean up the place. And, as far as he was concerned, the place looked pretty good. The animals were all fat and healthy and the garden was a paradise of luscious green. Oh, how he wished that they'd brought Victoriano instead of this big-mouthed, face-painted clown of a woman. He truly wondered if Carlota was even Lupe's sister.

"Come this way," he said as graciously as he could. "I think it will be better."

"Ha!" said Carlota. "It's dirty everywhere!"

Lupe grabbed Carlota by the arm and pinched her in the soft underarm. "Stop it!" she whispered under her breath.

But Carlota wasn't about to be silenced. "Don't pinch me!" she screamed. And she would've gone right on talking if, at that moment, Jose and Pedro hadn't come racing around the corner, chasing after the big male pig that they'd had tied up in back. The squealing pig ran between Carlota's legs, lifting up her skirt and almost knocking her to the ground. She let out a screech of terror. Lupe couldn't help but laugh. Salvador laughed, too.

"Don't you dare laugh at me!" cried Carlota. "I came as a favor to you, Lupe, and now I got *caca* smeared all over me!"

Salvador tried to stop laughing. "I'll buy you new shoes," he said. "I'm sorry. Really. And you, Jose! Pedro! I thought I told you two to clean up the place."

"We did!" said Pedro. "We worked all day yesterday with the boys from the neighborhood. That's why everything looks so good!" he added proudly.

Salvador glanced around. "Then, this is clean?"

"Sure! It's beautiful!" said Pedro.

"Excuse me," said Jose, not having said a word so far, "but aren't you the one," he said to Lupe, "that used to . . ."

Lupe nodded. "Yes, milk your goat."

"I thought so," said Jose, grinning. "But I wasn't sure. It's been a while, and I'd never seen you dressed up before."

"And you've grown so much," said Lupe.

"What are you two talking about?" asked Salvador.

"We stop by here, Salvador," said Lupe, "on our way to Hemet, to buy goat's milk for my sister Maria's children."

"No!" said Salvador. "Then you're the one—the one that my mother has been telling me about all these years!"

"I don't think so," said Lupe. "I never met her."

"But she told me of how you went up to our big milk goat the first time and squatted down, giving the animal stringbeans to calm her down."

"Well, I did do that," said Lupe, smiling. "The goat was ready to charge me."

"But we never saw any great lady when we stopped by here," said Carlota. "Just a fat, heavy-set woman and a . . ." But seeing the anger that flashed across the two boys' faces, Carlota stopped her words.

"Well," said Salvador, smiling, "that was probably a neighbor. Come inside and meet my sister, Luisa, and my mother."

Opening the back door for Lupe and Carlota, Salvador shouted, "We're here!"

"Good! About time!" answered a powerful woman's voice. "We're in the livingroom."

"The livingroom? What's that?" asked Salvador, leading Lupe and Carlota through the kitchen.

There were dirty pots and dishes piled high in the tub that they used for washing. Something was cooking on the stove that smelled so strong with chile that Lupe and Carlota almost gagged.

"Where the boys sleep!" answered Luisa.

"Oh," said Salvador, leading them down the hallway.

Walking into the front room behind Salvador, Lupe and Carlota saw Luisa sitting in a chair across the room, nursing a baby. She had her legs wide apart and she was fanning herself with the front of her dress. Her stockings were rolled down and the soft fat of her thighs bulged above her stockings like little brown innertubes.

"My sister Luisa!" said Salvador proudly.

"Not one word," whispered Lupe to Carlota under her breath as they went across the room to meet Salvador's sister.

"*Mucho gusto*," said Lupe, giving Luisa a small curtsy.

But the damage was already done. Luisa was quick and she'd seen Lupe's strained look and Carlota's open smile of ridicule.

"Please, sit down," said Luisa to Lupe. "My mother will be out in a minute. I have to go to the kitchen."

"But, Luisa, the kitchen can wait," said Salvador. "I want you to visit with Lupe and me."

"Salvador!" snapped Luisa, getting to her feet, "I'm going to the kitchen—and now!"

Holding the baby, Benjamin, in one hand, Luisa pushed past Salvador with such determination that Salvador was sure that she would have knocked him down if he'd tried to stop her.

"Well," said Salvador, smiling and feeling very awkward, "please, do sit down. I'll go get my mother."

Lupe sat down. Carlota brushed off her chair before sitting. Salvador went out the door and went to the little shack in back. He'd been gone no more than a second when Carlota started talking in whispers to Lupe.

"Oh, Lupe," she said, "you can't have anything to do with these people! They're peasants! They're ranch people! I bet they don't even know what an outhouse is for, *Dios mío!*"

"Shut up, Carlota!" said Lupe, glancing around, feeling sure that Luisa was overhearing them from the kitchen.

And Luisa was. She had the door ajar, listening to them.

"But, Lupe, you can't be serious! This is awful! Our mother would never approve of such people!"

"And you seeing Archie, who's married? That she'd approve of?" asked Lupe.

"Oh, Lupe, you are vile! You promised to never mention that!"

"Me? Why, Carlota! I swear I'm going to pull your tongue out by its roots if you don't shut up!"

"Do it!" said Luisa to herself in the next room, looking at them through the crack in the door. "Do it right now!"

Just then, Salvador opened the front door. "And now," he said with his whole chest filled with pride, "I'd like you to meet my mother, Doña Margarita, the love of my life!"

Nervously, Lupe stood up, poking her sister to stand, too. And through the door came the smallest, dirtiest, dried-up wrinkled mouse-of-a-woman that Lupe and Carlota had ever seen. She was all dressed in black from head to toe, and when she smiled, both young women saw that she had no teeth.

Carlota let out a screech. Lupe turned and saw that her sister was fainting.

"Carlota!" said Lupe.

"Get her out!" yelled Luisa, rushing in from the kitchen. "She's sick! And I just cleaned the house!"

"Help me!" said Salvador to Jose and Pedro.

The two boys helped their uncle get Carlota out the door just before she began to vomit.

Watching her gagging outside, Luisa smiled, feeling much better. She turned to Lupe. "How about a good, stiff drink?" she said.

"A drink?" asked Lupe.

"Yes, a stiff one!" said Luisa with *gusto*.

"Luisa!" said Salvador, coming back inside. "You mean a drink of lemonade!"

"Lemonade?"

"Yes, Luisa, damn it, come with me to the kitchen!" said Salvador, grabbing his sister by the arm and ushering her out of the room as quickly as he could. "I told you a dozen times," he whispered under his breath, "that Lupe and her family don't drink."

"Ah, bull! Everyone drinks. Next you'll tell me she doesn't fart, either."

"Damn it, Luisa!"

"Damn it, yourself!"

"Well, well," said Doña Margarita to Lupe once they were alone. "So you're Lupe. I've heard so much about you. Come, sit down with me, and don't worry about your sister. The boys will take good care of her," she said, turning Lupe about and leading her to the table where the chairs were. "But you know, I have the strangest feeling, *mi hijita*, that I've seen you before."

"That's what I was just told. Salvador mentioned that you saw me the first day I came to milk your goat."

"That's it!" shouted the old lady with such power that it took Lupe by surprise. "You're the one! You're the angel sent by God! Here, let me look at you. Yes, it's you! It really is. You're the one that I've been praying for night and day that my son would meet!" She put her right hand over her breast, taking a few deep breaths. "Oh, I'll never forget the first day I saw you," continued the old woman, her eyes filling with a burning glow. "I was here, inside the house, looking out through the crack between the boards, and I

watched you approach our mean old goat with such confidence and, yet . . .
respect!

"I said to Juan, I mean Salvador, 'This girl is an angel from God. Not
only is she beautiful, but she has the cunning, the strength, the very
ingredients that it takes to make a home!' And here you are, my prayers
answered!" she said, kissing the crucifix of the rosary that hung about her
neck. "Oh, God Himself, I tell you, watches over my home!

"Now, sit down; you and I must talk. And don't pay attention to what
goes on in the kitchen or outside with your sister. This is between you and
me, two women of great consequence, and we don't have much time! Because
as I told Salvador the other day, now my life with him is coming to a close,
and it is for you two to begin a whole new life together. And I promise you,
I will not be one of these interfering mothers-in-law, *mi hijita*. For believe
me, I know, marriage is difficult enough."

She smiled, looking into Lupe's eyes. "Here, give me your hand and let
me adore you, for you are the future of our *familia*."

Lupe gave the old woman her hand and Doña Margarita took it, gazing at
Lupe with so much love, so much power, such naked admiration, that Lupe
was mesmerized. There was just something magical about this toothless old
woman. It was here in her eyes, her person, her whole being. Lupe felt as if
she were slipping, sliding back in time to a place where all women used to
gaze upon each other with feelings of wonderment . . . a place of power . . .
the understanding of where life truly began.

"*Mi hijita, mi hijita, mi hijita*," said the wrinkled-up old woman, "this is
the day that I've dreamed of, the day I'd get to see with my own two eyes the
fulfillment of all my urging." She kissed Lupe's hand. "Oh, I tell you, life is
so full of gifts given to us by God. The gift of sight, the gift of feelings, of
taste and smell, of joy and sound . . . but I assure you, the greatest gift of all
given to us by the Almighty Himself is the gift of love."

She closed her eyes in concentration. "For God didn't just give love to us
like He gave us our seven other senses, or like He gave us the sun and the
moon and stars above. No, in His infinite wisdom He gave love to us only in
half and then left it up to us to go out into the world and find our other half."
She smiled. "Isn't that wonderful? He had that much faith in us, to allow us
to help him in the completion of this greatest of all miracles, love; and once
found, the ability to unite in the most sacred of human capacities: marriage."
She glowed. "The opportunity for every young couple to join in body and
mind and return complete and whole to God's graces in His most wondrous
Garden of Eden. But," she added, raising up her right index finger and
opening her eyes, "don't you make the mistake that so many young women
make and think that marriage is so perfect or easy that once they marry, they
think it's done, that they've completed it, and now the man will make the
home for them. For this is certain death for any marriage. Men, I tell you,
do not make the home, *querida*; it is the woman who makes it. And I do not
say this because my son is bad or irresponsible, but simply because we,

women, must realize that men are weak, both in body and mind, and cannot be entrusted to nurture the basic roots of life."

She smiled, getting a twinkle in her old eyes. "After all, wasn't it God, in His great wisdom, who chose women over men to carry the child here inside us? Eh, wasn't it? For just as the heavenly bodies of the sky are all female except for the sun, so is it true here on earth; we, *las mujeres,* are the power, *mi hijita*; we are the strength of our species. We are the ones who know how to endure, how to survive, especially in the darkest of times."

The old woman continued speaking, and Lupe listened to her as she'd never listened to anyone in all her life, except, of course, for her own mother. She felt as if she were being lifted up out of her body and transported back in time to those days of her childhood in La Lluvia de Oro when the whole world had been full of magic and mystery, and all of life had been a daily miracle.

Tears of joy came to Lupe's eyes, and she felt down deep inside herself so proud to be a woman and hear all these wondrous secrets of womanhood. She felt as if she were back in that magical night with her mother and sisters and the old midwife delivering the two sons of her first truelove.

She was back in a time of wild lilies cascading down the slopes in a waterfall of fragrance; a time of giants coming through her life in the forms of her mother and sisters and her Colonel; a time of stars and moonlight and the right eye of God—the sun, himself; a time of love, and life, and yes, miracles.

The world fell away, and Salvador's wrinkled-up old mother became the most beautiful human being that Lupe had ever seen.

Salvador came into the room and saw his mother and Lupe talking together, and he was so moved that tears came to his eyes. He was so happy, so very happy. This was, indeed, his highest dream: to have the woman that he loved talking with his mother, to have the woman that he'd searched for all his life seeing his dear old mother as he saw her—perfect.

Lupe saw him watching them and she smiled, feeling all good and warm inside . . . as in a dream, holding the hand of the mother of the one she loved. Yes, she'd done the right thing; Salvador was the one that she'd been searching for all her life. She reached out for him, and he came to her, and the two of them sat together, listening in rapture to Doña Margarita, a woman of substance, as she continued speaking to them, now and then closing her eyes and lifting her right index finger to point to the treasures of her mind that she was giving freely to them with her all heart and soul—for all eternity.

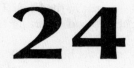

24

Hungrily, the devil watched, hating each step that took them closer to the secret gates of Eden. Then, the devil just couldn't stand it anymore, so he took one last lunge, tearing at their very heart.

The first time that Doña Margarita saw Salvador slip out the back door when Archie came by to see him, she didn't think too much about it. But the second time she saw the same thing happen, she knew that her son was in deep trouble. She waited up for him that night so they could talk, but when he came in, he said that he was too tired to talk. All day he'd been out trading whiskey for pigs and chickens, preparing for the feast that they were going to have at the wedding.

The following morning, Doña Margarita tried to speak to her son again.

"Later, Mama," he said. "Don't you see I'm busy? I have errands to run; then, this afternoon I have to drive over and get Lupe so we can go to Harry's to try on our clothes."

"All right," said his old mother, "we'll let it go for now, but I'm telling you, we have to talk."

"Oh, Mama," he said, sounding like a spoiled boy. "But why?"

"Because I said so, that's why!" she snapped.

"Oh, all right; but not now."

Salvador was going so fast, having so much fun for the first time in his adult life, that he just didn't want his mother giving him another one of her little heart-to-heart talks.

But then, it was two days before the wedding, and Doña Margarita saw something happen so terrible that she knew her son's immortal soul was at stake.

Salvador was in the backyard with his friends, drinking and listening to the *mariachis* that he was going to hire for the wedding, when Don Febronio stopped by with two of his sons.

"Hi, Salvador," said Don Febronio, smiling as he came up to him with his two big sons. All three were taller than Salvador. "I brought by a goat so you can barbecue it. Congratulations on your wedding."

"A goat, eh?"

"Yes, a nice fat one so you and your bride can enjoy it," he said, grinning.

"A goat!" repeated Salvador, beginning to rage as he looked up into their smiling faces. "Well, you can take your goat and shove it up your ass, horns and all! You chicken-shit son-of-a-bitch!"

Salvador drew his .38 and shot the goat in the head. The two boys leaped back in terror. The animal screeched, blood squirting from its mouth and wound.

"Now that I got money, you want to help me! You stupid bastard!" screamed Salvador, rushing at the three of them. "I ought to kill you!"

Febronio's oldest boy, sixteen years old, jumped in front of his father, wanting to protect him from the madman.

Seeing the boy's bravery, Salvador took pity on him and he fired over their heads. "Get out of here!" he bellowed. "Get out!"

Looking at Salvador with murder in his eyes, Febronio grabbed his son, jerking him back. "Okay, we're leaving; but I'm not forgetting this, Salvador," said the big, tall dark man from Zacatecas.

"Good! Don't forget it! Remember it all your life, what a no-good lying piece of shit you are! 'I got no money! I got no money!' When I know you got a box full of money buried under the flooring of your house! And I helped you, time and again!" Salvador fired two more times at their feet, running them out of the yard. "And don't come back, you chicken-shit sons-of-a-bitch!" he screamed at Don Febronio as he and his sons got in their truck and took off.

From inside her house, Doña Margarita watched Salvador's drunken friends congratulate him, telling him that he'd done the right thing, sending Don Febronio packing as Francisco Villa would have done. It disgusted the old woman. That night she cornered Salvador when he came in to go to bed.

"*Mi hijito*," said the old woman, "we need to talk, and now."

"Oh, Mama, can't it wait?" he said, lying down to go to sleep. "I'm too tired."

"No, it can't wait," she said. "Now, sit up!"

Hearing his mother's tone of voice, Salvador sat up. He saw that she was furious . . . absolutely livid with rage.

"But what is it, Mama?" he asked. "Has one of the boys gotten in trouble?"

"Yes, you!"

"Me? But I'm fine," he said. "I'm preparing everything just like you want for a big wedding."

"Everything except yourself!" she snapped. "For over a week you've been going around with your friends, drinking like a fool, getting this and that ready for your wedding, but you forgot the most important thing of all— you, here inside your heart!" she said, poking him in the chest with her index finger.

"My heart? But, Mama, I'm in love with Lupe with all my heart already."

"And how long do you think that love will last?" she said angrily. "Eh, how long? Just because you're young and strong with the urge to make children and she's beautiful, you think you're ready? My God, that shows no virtue, *mi hijito*. Any burro can get excited, too, and have his rope come up hard!

"No, *mi hijito*," she said, "you got to open your eyes and heart and listen to me very carefully, or you are going to ruin your marriage before you even begin."

"Oh, Mama," he said, "everything is fine, I tell you. You've already told me all about love and women and marriage being the return to paradise. I agree with you completely, so, please, no more."

"Oh, no more, eh?" she said, a hard viciousness coming into her voice. "And tell me, have you made your heart clean and prepared your soul so you can enter this Garden of Eden with Lupe? Ah, will you be able to get past the seven temptations that the devil sets in motion against every marriage?"

"Well, yes, I think so. I've talked to the priest and I've—well, I've . . . yes, spent time thinking, preparing myself."

"Bull! I saw how you cursed out Don Febronio today, shaming him in front of his very own sons! I've seen how you slip out the backdoor every time Archie comes looking for you. I say you're a coward to face up to what's really bothering you, and you're ripe for the devil's trickery!"

Salvador's heart began to pound. Hate and anger stampeded inside his skull.

"No, *mi hijito*," she said with tears coming to her eyes, "mark my words, unless you truly make peace inside your immortal soul, and calm all this hateful vengeance that you carry like a cemetery of death inside your heart, then this love you feel for Lupe will not be enough to sustain you even one year."

"Oh, no, Mama, you're wrong. You don't know what happened between me and Archie and Febronio. I got every right to hate 'em."

"That's number one," she said, lifting her right index finger at him, "being right; that's the first temptation the devil always uses."

"What?" he said, not understanding.

"Look, *mi hijito*," she said, "I don't need to know what happened between you and these other men, and I don't care who's right or who's wrong. For, believe me, whatever happened, I can guarantee you that it was old and . . . stupid."

"Well, yes, in some ways, but . . ."

She raised her hand, silencing him, and she looked deeply into his eyes. "Look, I saw it here, with my own two eyes the day you lost your soul when we were crossing the Rio Grande. My child—who I'd raised with so much love—became hard and unforgiving, lost and unsure, then mean and ready to kill the universe, just as I saw you do again this afternoon when Don Febronio came to wish you well."

Salvador couldn't stand it anymore. He came leaping, screaming off his mattress. "But that son-of-a-bitch Febronio spit on me, Mama!" he bellowed. "I was down and I went to him like a good friend, asking him for his help as

I'd helped him so many times, and he lied to me, saying he had no money! And I know he had money! He keeps an iron box full of it under his house. I tell you, I should've killed him today—him and all of his big, strong sons! Killed 'em all, the no-good sons-of-bitch! I hate 'em! Our people don't deserve to live!"

"Oh, I see," she said, seeing her son's insane rage. She'd been right; just touch her son a little bit down deep inside, and the great head of the devil came dancing up, foaming at the mouth. All this love he felt for Lupe was only skin deep. He hadn't learned a thing from her, even after all these years of training.

"Oh, *mi hijito*," said the old woman, "how it hurts me here, in my heart, to see you this way. But, understand me, I do not really care about the poor goat you shot or this man Don Febronio or even his sons. All I care about is you—you, you, my son, my flesh and blood—and this demon of hate you carry inside you here," she said, touching him on the chest.

"But . . . why shouldn't I carry this hate, Mama?" he asked. "Febronio and all the other men of our race turned me down. They're all nothing but a bunch of two-bit bastards! When I was up in Montana with the Greeks, I saw the Greeks organize, Mama, and I saw them stick together like men of honor. But here, I've only seen our people turn into little chicken-shit whores like at the rock quarry!" he yelled, tears coming to his eyes. "Then I started playing poker and went from town to town; and everywhere I went, I'd see our people kissing the ass of the *gringos*, like goddamned dogs! Even when I met Lupe, what did I see? Our people, Mama, they were afraid of a fat-ass foreman that I could kill with one hand tied behind my back!

"Yes, you're right, Mama! I do carry hate inside my heart and soul and it's against our own people, and I'm proud of it! Do you hear me? I'm proud of it! I'm no fool! Our people aren't worth a dog's shit compared to the Greeks or *gringos*!"

And there he stood, dark and short and powerful, looking so very much like the people whom he hated, and the tears streamed down his face in rivers of sorrow.

His old mother saw and took pity on him. She raised up her arms. And, no, he didn't want to, but finally, he came close to her, knelt down on the floor and put his large lion-maned head on her lap, crying like a baby.

"Oh, *mi hijito*, *mi hijito*," she said, soothing his great head with her hands, "what are we going to do? Don't you see that this is the devil's trick, that this is the very same demon that killed Eden for Adam and Eve, the same demon that killed your father . . . the same, the very same demon that's in all of us—myself, included—and that's why we have to keep strong with God's faith." She took a long, big breath, then blew out. "Oh, the devil is upon you, *mi hijito*, surely as we breathe."

"No, Mama, you're wrong. It's not the devil that's upon me; it's truth that's upon me, the God-awful truth of our people that I've witnessed here in this country, and I'm not going to fool myself and deny it. Our *gente* are no good, Mama, and that's that."

"I see, I see," she said. "All right, then, give me your hand, and step back, and look at me."

He did as told. "You see my face, you see my old, dark skin? Eh, you see me—really see me? Well I, too, am one of these *mejicanos* that you hate so much, *mi hijito*."

He shook his head. "Oh, no, Mama, you're not. You're different."

"Oh, and just how am I different? You tell me. I'm dark; I'm short; I'm mostly Indian, and I don't give money to anyone outside of my own family, so I probably would've turned you down, too. So you tell me; how am I different?"

"Well, you're my, well, my mother," he said.

The howl, the screaming howl of laughter that she let out, took Salvador by surprise. "Oh, that's wonderful!" she yelled, howling all the more. "Wonderful! Your mother, eh? Being your mother, that's the only thing that saves me from your damnations, eh?"

"Well, no, I didn't mean that. I meant, well, that I love you, Mama."

"But your mother is Mexican, so how can you love her, *mi hijito*! Eh, look at me—don't look away—and realize down deep inside your soul what it is that you're saying, and know that I'm exactly what it is that you hate."

"No, Mama!" he yelled. "You're not!"

"Yes, I am, *mi hijito*," she said. "I'm the very same woman that your father loved and married and I'm, also, the very same woman that he hated and cursed when he got mad."

Salvador closed his eyes. "No," he whispered, "no."

"Yes," she said, "yes." She could see that she was finally beginning to reach him. He was finally beginning to open his eyes and see what it was that she was really saying.

"*Mi hijito*," she said, taking his hand and stroking it gently, "listen to me closely and I'll tell you a secret, a very special secret that I just learned the other day."

Immediately, Salvador drew close. He just couldn't help himself. Ever since he could remember, he'd always loved his mother's secrets. They were such an adventure.

"You see," she said, "the other day at church, the Virgin Mary came down from her statue and we were gossiping, you know, like we usually do, joking and having a good time, when she suddenly got down to the nitty-gritty. She told me to keep on my toes, for the devil was in the area and he was up to no good; in fact, he was out to destroy a great plan that God had been working on for a long time.

"Well, of course, I quickly looked around at my own household, and at first I thought it had nothing to do with you because you're in love and getting married and so I figured that it was Luisa's soul, or, maybe, even Domingo's. But then today, when I saw you get so mad at a man who'd come to wish you well, and I saw all this hate come exploding out of you like it used to do with your own father, then I knew that it was you that the devil, in his great wickedness, wanted to bring to ruin.

"Oh, I saw it so clearly, *mi hijito*; if the devil could get you to hate your brother *mejicanos,* then one day he could get you to hate this woman that you now love and, eventually, he could even get you to hate your own children, too."

Salvador rocked back, staring at his mother in utter shock. "No," he said. "No, no, no, Mama, you're wrong! I love Lupe, and my children are going to be wonderful! I'll never hate them! Never! Never! I swear it with all my heart!"

"Oh," said his mother, coming in close, "and if one day your children aren't so wonderful, or you're just a little too tired to care, or some of them happen to be dark and short like most *mejicanos,* then what will you do? Will you do like your father did to his? Will you only have patience for the ones who are tall and fair and look more like these *gringos* that you admire so much? Or, will you do the opposite—which is just as bad—and start hating *gringos* and your own fair-skinned children?"

"Mama, stop it!" said Salvador, gripping his head. "You're just playing with me!"

"Oh, and isn't the devil playing with you, too? Well, I'd rather play with you now and have it hurt you a million times more while you are childless, than have you marry and bring children into this world that you are going to hate! And YOU WILL HATE THEM, believe me!" she screamed. "For the seed of the devil is implanted inside your SOUL, right now! And this is the disgrace—you hear me?—the DISGRACE of our people ever since the Spaniard came to our soil: self-hatred! And it must stop, *mi hijito*; it must stop right now! For this is God's great plan: that people rise up beyond their personal hatreds, here, right now, in this new land where so many different people with so many different bloods have come to join together and that we recognize we are all the children of God! Every one of us!

"And you, *mi hijito*, and your wife could lead the way! For you are of the blood of the people who were here since time began! Don't you see, you are the key, the SECRET! And this is your chance of greatness, just like it was for your grandfather, Don Pio, back in Mexico. An opportunity for you to be a man of vision! A man of great spiritual cunning and strength so you can get above your personal disappointments and see the good in your own people and make peace here within yourself and cast out the devil! This was the power of Don Pio. He didn't give up on Mexico or his men who'd turned bad or weak. No, he kept his heart open to them with love and compassion and he took them north with him to build a city high in the mountains where their children could grow strong and free.

"And they, too, were *mejicanos,* people of mixed blood, and their dream was to create a whole new way of life where no man would enslave another for all eternity! This was his dream! His quest! And he was dark! Short!

¡Puro mejicano de las Américas! And wonderful! Do you hear me? Wonderful!"

"But, Mama, please, I didn't mean to insult him," said Salvador.

"Shut up! For you are the seed on the brink of eternal prejudice! You are the messenger of the devil! You are, at this very moment, all the bad things that Don Pio fought so hard to overcome!"

"No, Mama, please! Don't say this to me," he begged.

"Yes, yes, yes! I say it to you! I scream it to you! I slap it to you in the face!" she said, hitting him. "You are evil! Here, inside! Because you're smart and strong and capable of doing the sacred good! But you've chosen to be lazy and to do the blasphemous bad! And you, you were the last one to come from my loins! My miracle from God given to me in my old age! And so I named you Salvador, the savior, in hopes of you becoming, indeed, the savior of our family, where there was already so much hate between father and son, brother and brother; and I raised you special with all the knowledge from the mistakes that I'd made with my other children . . . and now you're willing to take the easy route of hate and prejudice?

"My God, don't you see that here in this land, where we see so much power and accomplishment done by the tall, fair-skinned *gringo*, that we're move vulnerable than ever! I tell you, this hate has got to stop right now! Here! Inside your soul! And you've got to grab hold of your *tanates* and grow bigger than your personal disappointments, or the devil has won before you even begin!"

Tears ran down Salvador's face as he rolled his head from side to side, staring at his dear old mother in awe. Oh, she truly was a terror. She could rise up with such conviction of mind and soul that she could move the heavens themselves. No wonder God sent down the Virgin Mary to speak with her so often—they were all terrified of his old mother up in heaven and had to use a woman to try and talk to her and calm her fury.

Salvador stood up. "Mama," he said, "excuse me, but I got to go and pee real bad."

"Good, I'm glad I scared you this much," she laughed. "Go, and I'll put on the coffee and serve us each a *whiskito*. For I am not done! This is only the beginning!"

Salvador rolled his eyes to the heavens, then kissed her and hurried outside. He went to the avocado tree, unbuttoned his pants, and began to piss, looking up at the stars and moon. Oh, his mother was really something, and yes, he could see that she was right but, yet, well, he still hated Archie and Febronio. Maybe he just wasn't the man that his grandfather had been. Maybe he just had too much "Villaseñor blood" in his veins and he'd never be able to get beyond his personal hatred.

Finishing up, he buttoned his pants and watched the moon go behind some little clouds. He breathed deeply and looked out at the vastness of the star-studded heavens. Oh, he just didn't know what to do. With a heavy heart, he turned and went back inside. He found his mother warming herself by the little wood-burning stove.

"Well, Mama," he said, coming up and accepting the cup of whiskey that she offered him, "you're right . . . absolutely right. I see your point. And I understand it here, inside my head, but, well, you tell me, how am I to deny this hate that I still feel here, inside my heart and soul? Do I lie to myself? Do I hide from the truth?"

She didn't bother to even look at him. She just picked up her *whiskito* and began sipping it. "All right, that's a good question," she said. "A very good question. How do you accomplish this miracle of the heart that your father was never able to do? How do you change this tragedy of vision that kept your father blind to some of the best of his own flesh and blood?

"Oh, I'll never forget how your brother, Jose, when he was little, he'd follow your father around, worshipping the ground he walked on, loving him so much, but then he could never understand why your father was always so impatient with him." Tears came to her eyes. "It was terrible. It made me want to die inside. But what could I do? There was no talking to your father. And so one day in a typical rage your father drove Jose from our home because Jose had accidentally proved that he was a better horseman than your father. And Jose was still a boy, only fifteen years old, and he hadn't meant any disrespect.

"Oh, from that day on, your poor father lived blind—blind, I tell you— with the devil in his soul, and he died a tragic death, thinking that he'd failed—that he had no sons—when, in fact, his seed went on and did well. And you, *mi hijito*, are his seed; you are his second chance. And so, no, you mustn't lie to yourself or hide from the truth; no, you must open your eyes bigger, bigger, and see a larger truth. See further than your personal disappointments with our people. And grow, grow, reaching for the stars like Don Pio did when he first went to Los Altos de Jalisco with his two brothers."

Salvador's heart began to pound, to pound with each word his old mother spoke.

"You must pray for God Almighty's help, gain faith, and realize that the devil is the force that divides mankind with hate, confusion and darkness; and God, on the other hand, is the power—the light—that unites us with love, with the vision of what's the best in all of us. You must gain faith in the basic good of mankind and reach out and take the hand of God. Take it with all your power, like Don Pio did on El Cerro Grande in Los Altos de Jalisco, and realize down deep inside that this was the strength of your grandfather, and this is the strength of any man or woman of vision: to dream, to rise up, and to give honor to God's light!

"Not to fall to the devil's temptation of despair and darkness and these easy thoughts of hate and destruction, but to see beyond these and reach for the stars with the conviction of mind and soul that we, the human species, can only survive in our own house, when we have made peace within ourselves and then with all our fellow human beings on earth! This is God's great plan

that He has been working on for centuries! And now is the time—the hour—
that we, the people, must rise up and go forth, hand in hand, in God's love.
And you must do your part, *mi hijito*, for you are the blood of my blood, the
flesh of my flesh, and I raised you with love . . . you hear me? LOVE!
LOVE! LOVE!"

She stopped, and they looked at each other and Salvador could see that
his mother was glowing, her whole person was on fire. Why, she was
illuminating, and he could see the years strip away from her and, miracu-
lously, she was young once more and very beautiful.

"Oh, Mama," said Salvador, getting to his knees, "I love you so much, I
really do; and, truly, I do want a better life for all of our people here in this
country or back in Mexico but, being completely honest, I'm still mad,
Mama. I'm still mad as hell with Archie and Febronio."

Throwing her head back, Doña Margarita let out a great laugh. "Mad?
Well, no one said you can't be mad, *mi hijito*. Mad is good. Be good and mad
and go talk to Archie and talk to Febronio, too, and work things out with
them, if you can. That's why God gave us the word; the word was our first
step out of darkness. The word is our sword to fight off evil. So go and talk
and be mad, but . . ." she added, raising her right index finger, ". . . what I
don't want, is for you to carry hate. Because hate kills, hate destroys, hate is
the instrument of evil. Do you hear me? Ever since the beginning of time,
it's been hate that's brought ruin to mankind."

"But I can be mad?"

"Sure. Why not? Mad opens doors; mad creates. Look, I was mad at
you; that's why I called you in so we could talk."

"Oh," he said, "I see. I see."

"Good, I'm glad you do. Seeing is a good beginning. But remember, this
hate that came to you so easy against your own people isn't just going to go
away now because you see. No, it will return to you in many forms, *mi hijito*;
sadly, it is the cross that you will carry for the rest of your life."

Salvador took a big breath, then another and another. She took his huge
right hand in both of hers and soothed it tenderly.

"*Mi hijito*," she said, "the fight of good and evil—or God and the devil,
if you will—isn't anything new, and it will never disappear. No, in fact, it is
the blessing—the challenge—of each new generation, so that they can open
their own eyes and learn to see with their own vision. So take heart, *mi hijito*,
and see that this cross that God has asked you to carry is good, just as good
and great as the one that our Lord Jesus carried to Calvary."

She stopped and kissed the cross of her rosary. Salvador looked at her,
and he saw that she was still glowing, like a hot, burning coal—a coal that
had come from an all-hardwood fire—a mesquite coal that had been long in
the making and would now be long in giving warmth after the fire had died
down. Oh, Salvador could now see, really see, that this old woman sitting
before him was, indeed, herself, an inspired human being, one who brought
honor to God's light. Tears of joy came to Salvador's eyes.

"Oh, God, Mama," he said. "I love you, I do, but I'll tell you . . . you're a hard, hard woman."

"Yes, I am," she said, smiling. "And I'm glad you see this, because, I swear to you, even after I'm dead and gone and you're old and half-deaf, I'll still be here. I'll be here inside your heart and soul like a tick up a dog's ass, scratching you, clawing at you, giving you great discomfort. And every time I see you or one of your offspring get lazy and let the devil come near, I swear, you'll hear from me. Do you understand? I'm the tick up your spiritual asshole for all eternity!"

He burst out laughing. What else could he do? "Yes, Mama," he said. "I'm sure you are, and much more."

"Good! We understand each other, so now, let's stop all this and kneel down to pray so we can then have a little more *whiskito* and I can smoke one of my little *cigarritos* while you make us some fresh coffee."

She placed her two hands together in prayer and he did, too, and they began to pray. and this was the first time since they'd crossed the Rio Grande that Juan Salvador prayed to God, asking for forgiveness and a whole new life—within God's great plan for the future.

The next day, Salvador slept in late and got up feeling wonderful, as if a huge stone had been removed from his chest, and he could breathe freely for the first time since they'd left their beloved homeland of Los Altos. He lay in bed breathing deeply and he saw it all so clearly. He was going to go to the priest, confess his sins, and even tell him about Duel— whom he never let himself think of, much less tell any mortal man. Then he'd have to go and find Don Febronio and Archie Freeman and apologize to each of them. For it didn't really matter what they'd done to him. The important thing was what he was doing to himself by carrying all this hate inside his soul.

He got up, shaved, showered, dressed himself in his finest clothes and went to see the priest. The man of God was in the side garden of the church, watering his roses.

"I'm glad to see you, Salvador," said the priest. "I've been waiting for you."

"Waiting for me?" said Salvador. "But how did you know I'd be coming to see you?"

"A few days ago your mother told me that she was concerned for you and that you'd be coming," said the tall man of God, putting his watering bucket away. "Your mother is a great woman, Salvador. I truly treasure the time I spend with her."

"Thank you. I do, too."

"Of course, as she tells me, you are her last carnal gift, given to her by Our Almighty and you have a very special journey."

"Well, ah, speaking of that journey, I've come to make my confession."

"Good," said the priest, and they went inside the church.

Salvador's confession lasted three hours and twenty-two minutes and wrung Salvador out as if he'd been taken to the stream like a bunch of dirty clothes and his heart and soul were pounded with stones and scrubbed hard with soap.

Then Salvador drove over to see Archie. But he wasn't able to locate him. He took a big breath and went over to Don Febronio's house. The big, tall, raw-boned man met Salvador at the door with a 30/30 in his hand. Quickly, Salvador opened his jacket, showing him that he was unarmed. But Febronio wasn't impressed. He levered a shell into the chamber.

"What the hell do you want?" he screamed. "Insulting me in front of my sons wasn't enough?"

He fired a round off by Salvador's feet. "You son-of-a-bitch! I came by to give you a goat in friendship and . . . and—you bastard!"

He rushed down the steps and took a swing at Salvador with the butt of the rifle. But Salvador ducked and dodged and pulled out his .45 that he'd had tucked behind his back.

"Stop it!" yelled Salvador, firing three shots into the ground. "Goddammit, I came to apologize, you stupid bastard!"

"With a gun?"

"How else does a civilized man apologize to a hard-headed mule from Zacatecas?"

Febronio's boys came streaming out of the house, all five of them, weapons in hand. The oldest one raised his machete over his head and charged straight for Salvador, screaming murder.

"No!" yelled Febronio, stepping in front of his wild-eyed boy. "This is between Salvador and me! Don't you see we're talking?"

But the boy wasn't about to back off. He was the one who'd jumped in front of his father the other day, and he wanted to kill Salvador once and for all.

Seeing the boy's raging hate, Salvador lowered his gun. "Look, I owe you an apology, too, *mi hijito*," he said to him. "You're a good, brave man, ready to give your life for your father. I hope I have a son as good as you some day."

The boy spat on the ground. He wasn't going to be bought off with worthless words. No, he was trembling, itching to kill. He wanted blood and now!

"Jesús," said Don Febronio, "calm down. *Cálmate*. Salvador came to us in good faith. Remember your manners, we don't kill people who've come to our home."

"Then," screamed the boy, barely able to talk—he was trembling with so much rage—"you tell him to put that gun away! No! Tell him to hand it to you or be prepared to kill me as I butcher him to pieces, the no-good son-of-a-bitch! We're not dogs! He can't insult us and expect to live!"

Febronio turned to Salvador. "It's your play. I can't stop the boy."

Salvador looked from father to son, then back again, He knew that Febronio was right and the boy was beyond all reason. He'd really have to kill the boy if he didn't hand over the .45 to Febronio.

"All right, you win," said Salvador, "I'm giving my gun to your father, but back off with that machete."

Still, the boy didn't want to, but Febronio pushed him back gently, carefully, respectfully. Then Salvador handed the gun over to the big man. Febronio took the .45 and put it in his belt. "All right, it's over," he said, "now go back inside . . . all of you. Salvador and I have business."

All five boys went back inside the house, but Jesús still stared at Salvador with hate in his eyes. Salvador took a big breath. Oh, that boy had truly meant what he'd said. No matter how many bullets Salvador would've put into his body, Jesús would've lived long enough to do him in. Oh, his mother was definitely right; hate was a powerful force. It truly did have to be conquered with love, or mankind absolutely had no chance on earth of surviving. Man was just too violent a species, too ready to join the devil. The following day Salvador tried to find Archie again, but now it seemed like the big lawman was avoiding him. He decided to let it go until after the wedding.

The morning of the wedding, Lupe lay in bed sleeping, dreaming, hearing the distant sounds of her family laughing, working, talking. She lay in bed under the warm-smelling covers, reliving those wonderful days when they'd lived in their beloved box canyon. She lay there quietly, as she'd always done back in La Lluvia de Oro, enjoying those first few delicious moments of dreamlike reality. She could hear the birds chirping, she could smell the goats behind their huge boulder, she could hear the burros, the dogs—the whole village—coming to life. She stretched and yawned, enjoying the first miracle of the new day—finding herself alive—and she turned, reaching across the warm-smelling bed for her mother, but she wasn't there.

Lupe awoke with a start and her mind went reeling. She remembered that today was the day she was to marry. She heard the sounds of her family in the kitchen, making chicken *mole* with the chickens that Salvador had brought by a few days before. She curled back up under the covers and drifted back to sleep, but she just couldn't sleep anymore. All of these smells and sounds and feelings of her family weren't going to be with her anymore. No, this morning—this moment—was the last one that she'd ever have with her family.

Tears came to her eyes, and Lupe sat up and took a deep breath, trying to keep calm. But she couldn't. Her mind was racing. Maybe, just maybe, she'd made a mistake and she shouldn't marry, after all.

Just then, her mother came walking into the room, humming to herself, happy as a bird. Quickly, Lupe wiped her eyes and got back under the covers. She watched her mother pull open the serape that covered the window, letting in a beam of bright sunlight.

"Wake up, sleepy head," said her mother, "this is the day that we've been dreaming of."

"No, Mama, please. I want to stay in bed a little longer."

"But why? There's so much to do. Now, come on, get up." She began to hum again, doing things about the room. She noticed that Lupe wasn't stirring. "*Mi hijita*," she said, "what is it? Tell me."

"No, it's just silly."

The old lady laughed. "Good. I need something silly, so tell me," she said, sitting on the bed by her daughter's side.

"Well, it's just that I don't want to leave home, Mama. I want to stay. So unless, well . . . he's willing to come and live with us, I don't . . . oh, Mama, he's a stranger!" said Lupe, pursing her lips together like a little girl.

Doña Guadalupe burst out laughing, hugging her daughter, who at the moment looked more like a twelve-year-old than her true age of eighteen. "Of course, he's a stranger, *mi hijita*," said her mother, "and so was your father when I married him. What do you think, that we were always together?"

"Well, no, not in my head, but in my heart, I kind of, well . . ."

Lupe's sisters and brother came in from the kitchen to see what was going on.

"What is it?" asked Sophia, who'd stayed over so she could help.

"Lupe doesn't want to marry unless . . ."

"No! Don't say it, Mama!" yelled Lupe, covering herself up with the blankets. "Don't!"

Smiling with mischief, Sophia, Maria and Carlota completed their mother's sentence without any help. ". . . unless he's willing to come and live with you two, or he can get out!"

"Exactly," said their mother, "just as she always used to say when she was a child. But you're not a child anymore, *mi hijita*; you're a woman, so get out of bed. And thank God that he's a stranger. If he wasn't, you couldn't dream."

"Yes," said Carlota, lunging at Lupe, "come on, you're getting out of this house! All your life you've had more than your share of Mama, and now it's my turn!"

Lupe laughed and fought Carlota, trying to stay in bed, but her other sisters came in to help Carlota, and they overpowered Lupe, throwing her out of bed with tickles and laughter. Don Victor came in to see what the commotion was. Seeing what was going on, he only shook his head.

"Like I've always said," he said, going back out of the room, "it's easier to raise pigs instead of kids."

Hearing their father say this for the millionth time, the girls began to mimic him. "Pigs you can eat, but with kids, what can you do?"

"Listen to that" said their father, acting angry, "now they add to the insult by mimicking me!"

Salvador and his mother were in the Moon, and everyone else was in the big black Packard that Salvador had rented. They were all ready to go to the wedding, but Luisa was still inside the house. Salvador honked his horn a few more times, then, finally, got out of the Moon and hurried back into the house.

"Luisa, come on!" he yelled. "Everyone is ready, and I don't want to be late to my own wedding."

"Well, then go on," said Luisa. She was only half dressed.

"Damn it!" said Salvador. "Don't provoke me! I've been to confession! Now, let's go!"

"No! I'm not going."

"But why not?"

"Because they all think they're too good for us!"

"Luisa, please, stop this, or I swear I'm going to really leave without you."

"Then go!"

"Damn it," said Salvador, losing all patience, "this is the most important day of my life. Please, behave."

"Me behave? It's you who's misbehaved!"

"Me?"

"Yes, you! You never asked me what I thought about her or her no-good family before you proposed to her."

"What? Are you crazy? You never asked me about Epitacio!"

"That's different. I had no choice. It was that or not be able to save our family and escape from the Revolution. Please, Salvador, reconsider and don't marry her. Don't you see? This is the first marriage that our family has had in peacetime, and we can now afford to be choosy."

Salvador's mind went reeling. He just didn't know what to say. He thought he *was* being choosy. In his estimation, Lupe and her mother were wonderful.

Doña Margarita came in to see what was going on. "What is it?" she asked.

"I don't know," said Salvador. "Luisa says that she won't come because I didn't ask for her permission before I proposed to Lupe."

"*Mi hijita*," said Doña Margarita, "what's gotten into you? Now come on, get dressed, and let's go."

"No, Mama," said Luisa. "You should've seen her face when they first saw us. I will not be a part of this! We've come too far and been too close to let someone like this destroy our family!"

"But Lupe isn't destroying us," said the old lady.

"Oh, yes, she is!" said Luisa, tears coming to her eyes.

"Luisa, Luisa, calm down, this is your brother's special day; please, think of him."

"I am; that's why I'm not going!" she yelled.

The old woman shook her head. "All right," she said, "then that's your decision?"

"Yes," said Luisa.

The old lady crossed the room. "Let's go, Salvador," she said.

"But, Mama . . ."

"No buts, *mi hijito*, there is no greater jealousy than a good sister's."

"That's not fair!" Luisa screamed out in agony. "I'm not jealous! I'm mad! You didn't see how they looked at me!"

But Doña Margarita refused to hear any more, and went out the door. Salvador felt torn in two. He didn't know what to do. But finally he, too, went out the door. Luisa was left alone, raging with her anger, cursing and throwing things in a fit of craziness.

Salvador and his mother got back in the Moon and everyone else got in the Packard, except for Epitacio. He said that he'd stay behind and see if he couldn't get Luisa to change her mind.

The pock-faced teacher from Monterrey drove the Packard, and Salvador followed behind him in the Moon. The rest of the barrio went in trucks and old, beat-up cars. It was a caravan of people. Out on the open road, Salvador gave the Moon the gas and got in front of the big Packard.

"Oh, Mama," he said, "I so much wanted Lupe and Luisa to be best friends. I just don't understand what happened. They're two of the most important people in all my world!"

"Don't worry, *mi hijito*," said the old lady. "Luisa is going to come. She only wants to scare you a little so you'll show her how much you love her."

"Scare me? Well, she sure did that."

"Of course, that was her intent; but don't worry, when have you ever seen Luisa give up the chance to eat free of charge? She'll show up."

Salvador laughed, shaking his head, and continued up the road. The big Packard was right behind them, looking so grand and proper and truly luxurious.

Coming into Santa Ana, the street that led up to the church of Nuestra Señora de Guadalupe was blocked off with a big truck full of cattle. Two huge Indians with badges on their shirts came up to Salvador. Each had a 30/30 in his hand.

"Are you Salvador Villaseñor?" asked the smaller of the two giants.

"Yes," said Salvador, "but what's all this about?"

"You're under arrest," said the larger one, putting the talking-end of the 30/30 to Salvador's head.

"Excuse us, *señora*," said the smaller one to Doña Margarita, opening

Salvador's door so he could get him out of the Moon, "but we got strict orders to take this man in."

"But he's getting married," she protested.

"Yes, we know," he said, winking at her when Salvador couldn't see, "but ain't nothing we can do about that; orders are orders."

"Archie, goddamn it," yelled Salvador, getting out of the Moon, "that no-good bastard put you two up to this, didn't he?"

They handcuffed him. "I don't rightly know," said the smaller one, who towered over Salvador. "All I know is that the law's the law, and you broke it, and now you've got to pay."

"But I haven't broke any law, you damned fools! I just refused to invite Archie to my wedding, that's all."

"Well, around these parts that's a crime."

"What's a crime?" asked Salvador.

"Not inviting a friend to your wedding."

"But Archie isn't my friend!"

"Then why did he send this cattle truck full of beef for your wedding? We're taking you in."

They started leading Salvador off at gunpoint towards their car. Salvador yelled his head off.

"Archie, you son-of-a-bitch, where are you? Get these bastards to uncuff me!"

Just then, Archie came out from behind the truck where he'd been hiding. Kenny was with him, too. They were both grinning ear-to-ear. It was obvious that they'd had a few drinks.

"Having a problem, eh, Sal?" asked Archie.

"You son-of-a-bitch!" said Salvador.

"Now, now," said the big lawman, "that ain't the way to talk to a friend."

"Jesus Christ, Kenny!" yelled Salvador, as they put him in the Chevy, "can't you choose better friends? This no-good bastard wouldn't loan me shit, man-to-man, like you did!"

Kenny just laughed, taking a long pull from his pint bottle. "Well, Sal," he said, wiping his mouth with the back of his hand, "I, also, didn't get the hell kicked out of me and my people, either. So, maybe that's why I felt a little more generous."

Kenny took another swig, then passed the bottle to Archie. "You did wrong, Sal. Forgetting and forgiving is what this country is all about. Shit, if we don't, we ain't got a chance in hell. Fuck, every one of us—pardon my French, señora—feels he has the right to kill a dozen times and justifiably, too. But we don't, because, well, if we did, then we'd have nothing."

Salvador could see that this was basically the same thing that his mother had told him; and, also, he really did like Archie. Just seeing the big long-faced bastard made him happy inside.

"So what you going to do, Sal?" said Kenny, spitting out a long squirt of brown tobacco juice. "You gonna invite Archie to your wedding or you going to jail?"

Kenny's eyes filled with a twinkle of mischief. Seeing the twinkle in Kenny's eyes, Salvador turned and saw Archie's big grinning face. He glanced down at his cuffs, giving a big shrug. "Shit, I don't got much choice, do I?"

"Nope, you don't," said Kenny, grinning. "That's the pleasure of doing business with Archie."

Looking back at Archie, Salvador shook his head. "Okay, Archie," he said, "but, damn it, I would've paid you! You should've trusted me, man-to-man! You bastard!"

Sadly, Archie nodded his huge long cow-face. "You're right. I fucked—excuse me, *señora*—screwed up, and I'm sorry."

Salvador took a big breath and glanced around. Everyone was out of their vehicles and watching them.

"All right," said Salvador, "you're invited to my wedding, Archie."

Archie smiled. "Good, I accept. But, just keep him handcuffed 'til we get him to the church, in case he thinks of changing his mind."

"Damn it, Archie!" yelled Salvador. "Uncuff me now!"

"Bullshit!"

"But I can't drive."

"That's okay. I'll drive you."

"You son-of-a-bitch! You son-of-a-bitch!"

"Never denied that," said Archie, getting into the Moon to drive Salvador and his mother, "but at least I'm not a stupid one."

Kenny howled with laughter. Fred Noon drove up in his Buick; he wanted to know what was going on.

"Archie just arrested Salvador," Kenny said, "and he's not going to let him go 'til he has him at the altar."

"Sounds good to me," said Fred, taking the pint bottle from Kenny and giving it a good pull. "Ah, that's good! Hell, sometimes I hope that Prohibition never ends!"

Harry and Bernice came rushing up the side aisle of the church. Hans and Helen, the Germans from Carlsbad, were right behind them. Bernice was wearing a stylish, long, smoke-colored coat that she'd designed. Everyone in the church was already in their places. The music started.

Carlota and Jose—the maid of honor and the best man—came up the aisle in a slow, dignified step. Carlota was wearing a long, beautiful pink gown and carrying a bouquet of gorgeous flowers. Jose was in a navy blue suit, and he looked darkly handsome.

"Oh, no!" whispered Doña Margarita, gripping her stomach. She and Salvador were in the first pew on the righthand side of the church. "I shouldn't have had that *whiskito* on an empty stomach. Oh, I'm going to fart!"

"Mama," said Salvador, "please, not now!"

"Not now with people arresting you and all this confusion!" snapped the old lady. "Cough, quick; cough if you have any decency!"

Salvador started coughing, and here came his mother's explosions. He looked up at the tall ceiling and beautiful stained windows, and he prayed that they were only farts. Pedro started to laugh. Salvador kicked the boy. The explosions continued. Archie began coughing, too; then Fred Noon and Kenny. But still, here came the sounds, and they were good ones—long and strong.

Jose and Carlota were halfway up the aisle when they took notice of all the people coughing at the front of the church. Neither one of them could figure out what was happening, so they just continued up the aisle, step by step, in the most dignified manner they could.

The music continued, and Salvador stared at his mother, wondering when it was going to stop. But it didn't. Just then, Luisa and Epitacio cut into the front pew.

Hearing her mother's explosion, Luisa laughed. "Give it to them, Mama," she said, "give it to them!"

"Shut up, *mi hijita*! Are you crazy?"

In the rear of the church, Doña Guadalupe hugged her daughter one last time, then hurried up the side aisle to the front, where she was supposed to be with her family, across from Salvador's people. She could hear something going on up front, but she didn't think too much of it. All week she'd been cooking and working and sewing so much that she was exhausted. She was so tired that she almost felt like going against all her principles and having herself a good shot of tequila.

Don Victor was dressed in a dark brown suit. When Lupe came out of the little side room full of giggling women, he took her arm, and they started up the long aisle. Lupe was dressed all in white and Maria's little daughter, Isabel, was holding the long white peacock train of her magnificent dress.

The commotion was still going on up at the front of the church, but Lupe ignored it and came up the aisle with her father, taking long, slow, deliberate steps, trying to look as calm and serene as she possibly could.

But, oh, she was going crazy inside. This was, indeed, the most important step of her entire life. This was the man that she was going to marry; this was the man that was going to be the father of her children; this was the person that she was going to share all the dreams and joys and sorrows with for the rest of her life.

The noise at the front of the church subsided. Lupe continued down the aisle on her father's arm, concentrating with all her being, all her heart and soul, trying to keep calm, passing all these people who were smiling at her . . . people she knew but couldn't recognize at the moment because she was so frightened.

It felt like the longest journey of Lupe's life, traveling step by step, towards the distant altar. She breathed deeply and recalled the day they'd come out of their beloved box canyon and that dangerous walk that they'd had along the cliffs called El Diablo. She realized how far they'd come since that day that they'd walked those cliffs and crossed that mighty river. She suddenly saw very clearly that she was once more walking on the cliffs of fate, ready to cross yet another mighty river on her journey of womanhood. She wondered if, indeed, she would ever get to see her beloved canyon again before she died.

Oh, those great towering cathedral rocks, they were the altar at which she'd always thought that she would marry one day. But those great rocks of her youth were gone, gone, just like her Colonel. Then they stopped, and her father drew her close, kissed her on the cheek, and turned her about, giving her arm to . . . to . . . to, oh, my God, Salvador; a total stranger.

"All right," she heard her father say as in a faraway dream, "she's yours now . . . take good care of our angel."

"With all my heart and soul," said Salvador, coming out of the pew and taking her arm.

Lupe felt like adding the words, "you better!" but she didn't. She felt Salvador turn her about, and together they approached the altar, hand in hand, all alone and far, far away from their parents. Oh, she was dreaming, dreaming, gliding over the towering cliffs back home, sweeping over the high country of her youth, and this was beautiful. For this was the sacred dream of all her years of yearning; this was the reality of all her childhood fantasies that she'd had of her Colonel. This was it; this was, indeed, life—*la vida*.

Then, Lupe saw the priest standing before them on the steps of the dark, blood-red carpet. He smiled at them and opened his black book. He began to read, and time stood still. She stood mesmerized, not quite able to comprehend the words that he recited.

But then, she saw the priest turn to Salvador, and she heard him say, "Juan Salvador Villaseñor, do you take Maria de Guadalupe Gomez to be your wife? Do you promise to be true to her in good times and in bad, in sickness and in health, to love and honor her all the days of your life?"

As in a dream, Lupe turned and she saw the moustache on Salvador's upper lip move like a long, fat worm as he said, "Yes, I do."

Then the priest spoke to her. "Maria de Guadalupe Gomez, do you take Juan Salvador Villaseñor to be your husband? Do you promise to be true to him in good times and in bad, in sickness and in health, to love him and honor him all the days of your life?"

Lupe considered the words, especially the ones "in bad times," and wondered if this was wise. Why would any woman in her right mind agree to this?

Leaning in close, the man of God whispered, "Say, 'I do,' my child."

"What?" said Lupe, trying her hardest to stop thinking of all these things that came flashing to her mind. "Oh, yes, I do, of course, Father."

Looking relieved, the priest continued, and the next set of words Salvador repeated, word by word.

Then it was Lupe's turn to repeat the holy words of acceptance. And, when she came to the passage, "To have and to hold from this day forward, for better, for worse, for richer, for poorer, in sickness and in health, until death do us part," tears came to her eyes. For she now understood for the first time in her life what these words truly meant.

The words were, indeed, the secret; these words were the power, these were the words that had given her mother—and her mother's mother—the strength to endure the years. The words "until death do us part" were the foundation of every marriage. They were what gave a woman the vision with which to rise up like a mighty star and join God's graces, just like Doña Margarita had told her.

This, then, was the true secret with which every ordinary woman became extraordinary and gained the power within herself to resurrect her family from the dead, again and again, and give her family the conviction of heart to go on, no matter what.

And these sacred words were now hers, too, "until death do us part."

Tears streamed down her face; and in her mind's eye, Lupe now saw the gates of Eden open, and there lay paradise just beyond her at arm's length— golden, serene, and as beautiful as La Lluvia de Oro right after a summer rain, with all the flowers and plants and trees breathing, breathing, and all the birds and bees and deer and possums playing; and, high above, there were the towering cathedral cliffs, raining down in a waterfall of glistening gold, and an eagle circling overhead, screeching to the heavens.

She'd done it, she really had. Here in her heart of hearts, she'd gotten married in the true spirit of the beloved canyon of her youth.

Salvador saw the tears of joy streaming down Lupe's gorgeous face and he was filled with such joy that he just knew that they'd passed through the gates of Eden. This was his new truelove and yes, one thousand times yes, his mother had been right; only with a clean soul can a man enter into the paradise of marriage.

Lupe and Salvador exchanged their rings and she promised to love, cherish and obey and she noticed that Salvador only had to love and cherish; he hadn't needed to say that he'd obey. They kissed, and the worm on his upper lip tickled her. She tried not to laugh, but giggled anyway.

The bells rang, the people applauded, and then the priest raised up his hands, silencing everyone once again.

"Lupe, Salvador," he said grandly, "from now on, you two are of one body, one soul; and it is your duty to take care of each other, so that your union of marriage will transcend even over death itself, and together you will enter the Kingdom of God for all eternity."

Lupe's whole body was filled with rapture, and her feet never touched the ground as they turned and started back down the aisle, she and her husband—this man, this stranger, her truelove—who was now and forever closer to her than her own brother or sisters, or even her own mother.

She could feel his hand pulsating in her palm, and she could hear his breathing, coming and going in rhythm with her own. These, then, would now be the sounds of her new home. This man's warmth would now be the one that she'd reach across the warm-smelling bed for each morning.

As they came out of the church into the bright sunlight, Salvador hugged Lupe close and two photographers took their photos, and everyone threw rice and confetti at them. The kids set off firecrackers, and everyone cheered.

Salvador then took Lupe's left hand in both of his two huge hands, and he looked down at her diamond ring pensively. The two photographers snapped this picture, too. And it was a lovely moment—Lupe looking at his thick mane of curly black hair as he gazed at her huge diamond, a stone so fantastic that most of the people in the crowd had never even seen one until now.

Oh, they'd done it, they really had. They were so happy, and everyone was so proud of them. Even Luisa. And Carlota, who'd been green with envy of Lupe all these years, was now heard to say, "Yes, that's right, she's my, well, older sister, and, yes, it's a real diamond . . . of the highest quality!"

Salvador walked Lupe to the Moon, opened her door for her and felt so lightheaded, so much in love with love itself, that he gave a shout of *gusto*, feeling wonderful.

25

The secret Gates of Eden opened, and the two children of war passed through—happy, content, and madly in love. For they'd dared to keep faith in the basic goodness of life.

Driving the Moon over to Lupe's parents' home where the reception was, Salvador and Lupe were met by a trio of violins. The violins were Lupe's idea. Feeling like a queen, Lupe stepped down from the Moon, taking Salvador's hand.

The people cheered and threw flowers in front of the feet of the two newlyweds as they walked around the house to the backyard. The aroma of Archie's barbecue filled the air. Archie's two deputies had slaughtered a steer and they'd dug a deep pit in the ground in the field behind the backyard, and they were barbecuing the big slabs of beef à la Archie Freeman, with plenty of *salsa* and hard red oak. There were over fifty chickens cooked in *mole*, mountains of *frijoles* and rice, and a tub full of hot, hand-made tortillas. The whole barrio was going to be able to eat to their fill for three days and nights.

Down the street in another house, Archie had also put up a ten-gallon barrel of whiskey, and he had one of his nephews from the Pala Indian Reservation mind the barrel, which was, of course, like putting a coyote in charge of the chicken coop.

Lupe and Salvador sat down at the main table and the *mariachis* began to play, and everyone started celebrating. Febronio and his family showed up, and they were having a wonderful time until Febronio saw Bernice take her coat off and expose the lowest-cut dress anyone had ever seen. The big man from Zacatecas forgot all about his wife and kids and rushed across the yard and took hold of Bernice, leading her to the dance floor, then put his nose down into her big bosom as he whirled her about. Three other men came up, wanting to dance with her, too. Harry protested.

"Please, no fighting over me," said Bernice, laughing, "just give me a little time to rest, and I'll dance with all of you."

But some of the men were pretty drunk, and couldn't wait and a fight started. Archie drew his gun and fired three shots into the air.

"All right!" he yelled. "Break it up! I'm deputizing her husband here . . . what's your name?"

"Harry," said Harry, looking pretty perplexed.

"Harry is now my special deputy!" yelled Archie. "And from now on, it's against the law for anyone to dance with . . . what's your name, honey?"

"Bernice."

"With Bernice, except for me and Harry!"

Reholstering his gun, Archie took Bernice in his arms before anyone could say anything. He whirled her about, this way, that way, then put his long nose down into her big, full bosom, taking a good long smell of her, too.

Carlota shrieked and came screaming across the yard. She grabbed Archie, yanked him about, and told him, "I got big ones, too! You fool!" Everyone started laughing.

The barbecue was ready and people began to eat and settle down. The *mariachis* stopped their loud music and the violins positioned themselves behind Salvador and Lupe, serenading them with soft sound. People came by and congratulated the newlyweds. The sun turned to liquid gold, going down behind the orchard of orange trees, and Salvador and Lupe could see that their families were finally beginning to get to know each other.

Doña Margarita walked over to Doña Guadalupe, taking her hand, and they sat down together. Luisa and Maria started visiting, and Luisa saw how Maria's two husbands catered to her, hand-and-foot, and they became fast friends. They got themselves a cup full of whiskey and soon felt like they'd known each other all their lives. Luisa began to think that maybe Lupe's family wasn't so bad, after all, since they had a real woman like Maria in their midst. And Maria began to warm towards Salvador's family, too.

"Look," said Salvador, "my sister Luisa, I think she likes your sister Maria's situation very much."

"Yes," said Lupe. "You know, at first everyone was so outraged by Maria's decision to keep both of her husbands, but now with time passing, quite a few women have changed their mind."

"Oh, and what does that mean?" asked Salvador, grinning.

Lupe laughed. "Well, nothing," she said. "At least not right now."

"Oh, you do have the devil sometimes, don't you?" he said, laughing. "I'll never forget how you glanced around, seeing if anyone was watching the day you decided to teach yourself how to drive."

"You saw that?" she asked, smiling.

"Of course," he said. "That's when I saw you weren't just an angel from heaven, but a human being, too."

"That's interesting," she said. "Because that's the same day you asked me about my dreams and I realized you just weren't a big show-off bully, but a wonderful man inside your heart and soul."

"Really? Up to then you thought I was only a show-off bully?"

"Yes. Of course."

And there it began again, and they were talking together with such joy, such happiness that when their two old mothers looked over and saw them, they both knew that they'd done the right thing in raising their two children. Lupe was just talking away, moving her hands like birds in flight, and Salvador listened in rapture.

"It's going to last and with great happiness," said Doña Margarita to Doña Guadalupe, "well past the fires of the bed."

"Yes," said Doña Guadalupe, wiping her eyes. "To talk so freely is to dream!"

"Amen, the lust of marriage is easy. It's the being able to have good times with your clothes still on that's difficult after marriage."

"Oh, yes! I fully agree!"

The two old she-boars looked at each other and started laughing, laughing until they had tears in their eyes.

"Look, I know you and your family don't drink," said Doña Margarita, "which, of course, I rarely do myself, but how about you and me getting ourselves a good stiff one right now. We deserve it!"

Doña Gaudalupe stood up. "By all means. Let's do it!"

"Look," said Lupe to Salvador, "our mothers are going next door where my father hides his liquor."

"You know about that?" asked Salvador.

Lupe just eyed her husband. "Salvador, I might be young and inexperienced, but I'm not blind."

He laughed, and she laughed, too, taking his hand.

Raising his cup for a toast, Don Victor silenced the *mariachis*. "All my life I've said," he announced in a loud, clear voice, "that it's better to raise pigs than kids, because, well, pigs, when they get too big and start to be a nuisance, you can always kill them and eat 'em. But kids, what can you do with them when they grow and start giving you problems?" He stopped and turned to Salvador and Lupe. "I salute you two with all my heart. I was wrong! And I love you both for the joy that you've brought to both of our homes!" He swallowed, standing tall. "Now, Lupe, my child of the night that the star kissed the earth, let us dance, you and I! One last time!"

He downed his drink and went across the yard to take Lupe's hand and *la gente* applauded with tears coming to their eyes. Salvador crossed the yard and took his mother by the arm to dance, too. The sun was dropping down into the orchard of golden fruit and the whole world was smiling upon them. Don Victor held Lupe in his arms, going around and around, feeling the spirit of God come down from the heavens and put wings to his old feet. Nearby Salvador danced with his mother, who'd always been a fine dancer, and he gracefully turned and whirled her about. And Victoriano held his mother about the waist. She kept saying, "No! No!" with her mouth, but her feet were a joy to watch as she glided about the yard under the large walnut tree in her son's great long arms.

The sun was going, going, turning to liquid flame, and Pedro was dancing with Luisa, and Jose was with Carlota. Sophia gripped hold of her husband, dragging him onto the dance floor, and Maria took turns with each of her husbands. Then Don Victor gave Lupe to Salvador and he took Doña Margarita in his arms. The right eye of God began to blink his last goodnights to them and the moon came up smiling, silver and blue.

The song of the violins ended and Lupe and Salvador stopped dancing and went behind their table to watch. Everyone was having such a wonderful time, everyone was so happy and relaxed now that they were feasting.

Taking her hand, Salvador led Lupe away. By the orchard he turned her about. "Oh, *querida*," he said, "I'm so happy, I tell you, it's just so hard for me to realize that we're really married."

"Me, too," she said, feeling a warmth come all over her. "It's still all like a dream to me."

Salvador saw the warmth—the glow—come over Lupe, and he took her hand and kissed her fingertips. "I love you so much, *querida*," he said, "and my hope is that our marriage will always be a wonderful dream."

"Me, too," she said, squeezing his hand and looking into his eyes. "For this marriage is the dream of my life."

"Mine, too," he said. They gazed into each other's eyes, then kissed . . . gently, softly, slowly.

"Haaah, you made the kiss first this time," said Salvador, eyes sparkling.

Lupe pursed her lips together, thinking. "I think we both made it," she said.

"Oh, no," he said. "I think you made it a little bit first."

"Oh, let's see," she said, drawing him close again.

And so they kissed again, in a soft, gentle caressing of lips, of mouth, of prickly moustache.

"I guess you're right," she said. "And I made it first again."

They laughed, feeling so very good and warm inside. They turned and looked again at the fiesta, standing side-to-side, shoulder-to-shoulder, and gave witness to all the festivity that was going on in their honor.

They saw Pedro take little Isabel out on the dance floor and begin to dance. They saw their old mothers talking and laughing together, truly enjoying themselves.

They took each other's hands and just stood there feeling so full of life's riches. They'd won, the two of them, each a child of war, had survived. Not becoming embittered or disillusioned because of the hardships of their childhood, but in fact, they had blossomed, gained a deeper respect for living and joined God's light, bringing honor to the very source of life itself: their mothers.

They stood there at the edge of the luscious orchard of dark, green trees and large, golden fruit, and the sun went down behind them in a miracle of color—of red and orange and silver, a magnificent display of God's magic—and they went slipping, sliding, passing through the needle's eye, and they were now in paradise . . . dreaming, dreaming the dream of living in the greatest gift of all: the union of one man and one woman in the true graces of God. The dream of hope, the dream of joy, from now to all eternity. Amen.

THE BEGINNING

AUTHOR'S NOTES

And so yes, my parents had a long and wonderful marriage, 59 years, and they realized most of their dreams. My mother got her office, and my father was able to work for himself, never needing to kiss any man's ass again. They were both able to help their parents in their old age and their children never suffered what they'd suffered. But, still, I must tell you, that my father's rage didn't stop at my parents' wedding. My grandmother, Doña Margarita, was right when she'd told him that it would be his cross to carry for life. And because of his rage, my parents' married life was hard in many ways; but, also, it was full of enormous triumphs over cultural barriers, wild adventure and great festivity.

I am Victor E. Villaseñor, the middle child of Salvador and Lupe. I was raised the first few years of my life with my older sister and brother in the barrio of Carlsbad, California, right next door to my father's poolhall. I spoke very little English until I started kindergarten and I thought that we lived in Mexico. The *gringos*, the *americanos*, were like foreigners from a strange land to me for the first five years of life.

But getting back to my parents' story—which is, of course, their history in the truest sense of the word, "his story,"—right after they got married, my parents moved to Carlsbad. They rented a little house from Hans and Helen, and they had a wonderful first two years until my father finally admitted to my mother that he'd lied to her and he was, indeed, a bootlegger.

My mother tells me that she felt betrayed and was so ashamed that she would've left my father if she hadn't been pregnant with my older sister, Hortensia. But, also, times were hard—it was the middle of the Depression—so she could see why my father did it.

My father took her to see the priest, and the man of God tried to convince my mother that *la bootlegada* wasn't as bad as she might think. In fact, the priest told my mother (for a case of my father's best whiskey) that bootlegging wasn't against the laws of God and reminded her that, in fact, Jesus Christ Himself had turned water into wine.

But my mother wasn't about to be taken in by my father or the hard-drinking priest. Arriving home, she told my dad that she didn't care what the priest said; she was going to have a child and it would be them, not the priest, who would go to jail. So she made my father promise to get out of his illegal business as soon as he could.

My father promised, but he procrastinated. Then, a few months later, their distillery blew up in Tustin, California, almost killing my father. My mother, big with child, dragged my father's body from the burning house, put him in their truck, and drove off just as the police arrived. She was outraged and she told my father that this was, indeed, God speaking to them—a much higher authority than any priest. My father conceded to her, and this was a major turning point of their life. One, they went legal shortly after that; and two, my mother was never going to allow herself to be taken lightly again. She was twenty-one years old.

Then the following year, Prohibition ended, and my parents bought the poolhall in Carlsbad from Archie, who'd married my Aunt Carlota. A few years later, a man named Jerry Smith came to my father and asked him if he owned the poolhall. My father said, "Yes, I do." Jerry Smith brought out his badge, saying that he was from the Internal Revenue Service and he wanted to know why my father hadn't paid his income tax. My father insisted that he'd already paid his taxes; he'd done it when he'd bought his city business license. Jerry tried to explain to my father that one thing had nothing to do with the other. But my dad just couldn't understand what the man was saying. Finally, my father got mad and told Jerry, "Look, buddy, it sounds to me like you're telling me that the federal government is nothing but a free-loading thief! I got too much respect for this free country to believe this, so, no . . . I can't pay you any yearly taxes!"

Enjoying my dad's independent spirit, Jerry laughed and they had a few drinks together. Then, opening his briefcase and showing my dad the different income tax forms, Jerry came to realize that my father really didn't have any idea what he was talking about, nor could he read the forms. "Tell me, Sal," said the agent, "do you have anyone in your family who can read books and understand numbers?"

"My wife," said my father proudly, "she's educated and reads books easy."

That was the second big turn of events in my parents' married lives. My mother was brought into my father's business, and Jerry Smith taught her how to keep books and explained to her the responsibilities of a business person in the United States. She took over the bookkeeping of my father's poolhall with a power that surprised everyone in the barrio, especially the other women.

Then, the following year when my father couldn't buy an off-sale liquor license because he had a prison record, my mother stepped right in. "I'll buy it," she said, surprising my father and everyone else in the barrio.

In the next five years, my mother blossomed into a full-fledged business-woman . . . even buying a second liquor store in the Anglo part of town in Carlsbad. That's when I was born. And as I grew up, I'd see my mother do the banking, run the books, oversee the payroll, and do most of the hiring and firing of the ten or twelve Anglos and Mexicans alike who worked for them.

I grew up thinking that all women were the money-handlers of every marriage. And I saw that my mother had her own car, and she came and went as she pleased with bags of money and boxes of receipts. My parents became a force to be reckoned with in the area—my dad, the aggressive, imaginative leader, and my mother, the one who'd follow through and make sure that things really got done and weren't just left up in the air, as was my father's style so often. And in the evenings, I'll never forget, I'd curl up at my mother's feet while she did her bookkeeping and I'd nap as if I were in heaven itself until I was put to bed.

Then, one day I remember very clearly, my older cousins came by wearing Army uniforms, and everyone was so excited, saying that the war was going so badly for us that California was now in danger of being invaded. The following week, my parents' friends, Hans and Helen—who spoke with a funny German accent—came by and told my parents that they'd been ordered to move twenty miles inland from the coast or they could have their property repossessed by the government, as was happening to the Japanese. They asked my parents to please buy their liquor store in Oceanside from them immediately. That night, my mother went over the books with Hans, and the next day we all went over to see the store. I remember that it was big and had a huge dark room in back and an attic that smelled bad. The place was booming with business. It was the first time that I recall hearing English being spoken all around me. That week, my parents bought the store and hired Hans as their manager.

Shortly after that, I'll never forget, my father came racing into the house one day all excited, telling us that the owners of the biggest, most beautiful ranch in all the area were moving back to Canada before we were invaded and they were putting their place up for sale.

"This is our chance of a lifetime!" said my father.

"But what if we get invaded?" asked my mother.

"Bullshit!" screamed my father. "We're not getting invaded, and that's that! We got to keep strong in our heads, not panic like fools, and buy this ranch right now! It has orchards and pastures and cattle, horses, chickens, barns, tractors—everything! And, best of all, a dozen hilltops—all overlooking the sea—where we can build our dream home, Lupe, and stand proud for ten generations!"

"But, Salvador," said my mother, "I'm scared; we've been moving so fast."

"It's okay to be scared," said my father, hugging my mother close, "it keeps you alert like the chicks watching out for the hawk. Now, let's do it; pull out your magic books!"

My mother was reluctant, but still, that night my parents went over her books again and again, adding up all the cash they could possibly put together, hoping to see if they could come up with an offer for the ranch before anyone else got wind of it. But trying to do all she could, in the morning my mother had to tell my dad that there was just no way on earth that they could pull it off.

My father raged and raved, making references to Don Pio and how important it was for them to not back down when their dream was so close at hand. I couldn't figure out what was going on. All I knew was that my father and mother were yelling at each other over money once again. Finally, my father said that, well, he'd go and see Archie, but he hated to do it.

Years later, I found out that Archie turned him down again, this time saying it was just too big. My father went to the bank, over my mother's protest, and borrowed $20,000 against everything they owned. He bought the 126 acres overlooking the sea, and I'll never forget how I got to ride in the front of my father's saddle as we rode our horses through the orchards and pastures and fields of produce, going from hilltop to hilltop, trying to decide on which knoll we'd build our dream home.

Six months later, we moved to the ranch in Oceanside, two miles north of where I'd been born in the barrio of Carlsbad. The following year, my grandmother, Doña Guadalupe, died in the master bedroom of the old ranch house under the giant pepper trees. All of my mother's people came in from northern California, Arizona and Mexico. I cried and cried and wouldn't let go of my beloved grandmother, the woman who'd given me tea and sweetbread and told me stories of the past ever since I could remember.

The following year, I started school and was truly shocked when I was told on the playground that I was Mexican and didn't belong in this country. Then to complicate things even further, the new priest came to our home and told my parents that they shouldn't allow us to speak Spanish at home. After he left, my parents looked like they were at a funeral when they told us that from now on, they wanted us to speak only English at home; and at school, I'd get in trouble if my friends and I were heard to say anything in Spanish. Oh, that was a terrible time. School became a nightmare. The only time I was happy was when I was riding my horse or working on the ranch with our workers who were all from Mexico and great with horses and lariats.

I was seven years old when my mother finally decided on which knoll we'd build our dream home. She chose a knoll half a mile away from the sea where the wildflowers grew. "I want plenty of sunlight," she told my father, "so I can plant my mother's lilies and they can flourish; and, also I want roses and night jasmine so they can fill our home with wonderful fragrance, just as I had when I grew up in La Lluvia."

My father agreed, and they hired two architects to work with my mother, who designed the house. There were carpenters, electricians—more than twenty people—who worked on my parents' dream house for the next two years. The foreman was from Detroit and he had false teeth. I'll never forget how frightened I was the first time I saw him take his teeth out and put them in his shirt pocket when he sat down to eat lunch in the shade of a tree.

Finishing the house, my parents had a *fiesta* that lasted a week. The mayor, the chief of police, and over six hundred people came to my parents' housewarming. I remember the celebration well. My mother said that she was dedicating their home to Saint Joseph and Our Lady of Peace. My father said that was fine for Lupe, but he, himself, had built this huge twenty-room mansion in revenge against Tom Mix, a man he hated from the bottom of his heart, because Mix had always knocked down five Mexicans with one punch in his no-good phony movies. "And the best revenge in all the world," my father added, "is to live well! Especially longer and better than the bastard you hate!"

The people applauded and the music began, and I remember stealing a pan of *carnitas* and going out back in the orchard and sharing them with my brother's big coyote-dog named Shep. Also, I remember my father and Archie uncovering the pit full of beef and presenting the mayor and his wife with the head of the big steer, scooping out the brains with a tortilla for the mayor's wife as a special treat. The woman shrieked and passed out, and my mother told my father off and took the poor woman into their master bedroom to lie down. The mayor got drunk on tequila and so did the chief of police. Fred Noon had to drive them both home. My father and Archie and Fred stayed up that whole first night, laughing and drinking and raising hell, remembering the good old days.

Ten days later, I was helping my older brother Jose and a couple of workers clean the place up when a short, little, sleepy-eyed Anglo cowboy came out of the orchard saying, "Where is everybody? Ain't the party still going?" My brother and I burst out laughing, telling him that the party had ended four days ago. He cursed and served himself another mug of whiskey from one of the fifty-gallon drums that was still half full and went back into the orchard to sleep some more.

Of course, I could go on with story after story, but, basically, what I have to say is that my parents had a big adventurous life after they married. And, yes, it was hard—no doubt about that—it was very difficult at times, and yet it was real and good, full of ups and downs, but always a challenge, always a rain of gold with the spirit of God breathing down their necks, giving their hearts wings, hope of a better day. And as my mother recently told me—my father passed away last year—some of the things she hated and resented the most about my dad when he was alive were the very same things that now brought a special joy to her heart. "Unfortunately," she tells me, "this is the way life seems to be. Sometimes we have to lose the person we love before we realize how much we truly loved them. Your father was a wonderful man and I only wish I'd told him that more often."

"But you did, Mama," I told her.

"Not often enough, *mi hijito*. You and your wife remember that. Being loving isn't enough, you must say it, too."

For myself, my biggest personal regret is that I never met my grandmother, Doña Margarita. She died two years before I was born. My father told me that he saw her only days before her death, shuffling down a dirt road in Corona, California, with the sunlight coming down on her through the tree branches. She was almost ninety years old, and he saw her walking along, doing a little quick-footed dance, singing about how happy she was because she'd tricked a little dog and he hadn't been able to bite her again.

My father said that tears came to his eyes, seeing how his mother—a little bundle of dried-out Indian bones—could bring such joy, such happiness, to her life over any little thing. "She was the richest human on earth, I tell you," said my father to me. "She knew the secret to living, and that secret is to be happy . . . happy no matter what, happy as the birds that sing in the treetops, happy as she came shuffling down that lonely dirt road, stopping now and then to do a little dance."

But . . . I did get to meet my mother's mother, Doña Guadalupe, and I was able to sit on her lap and have her rock me back and forth and tell me about the early days of La Lluvia when the gold had rained down the mountainsides and the wild lilies had filled the canyon with "heavenly fragrance." And I was able to speak to my Uncle Victoriano, my Aunts Maria, Sophia and Carlota, and interview them off and on for over a decade, verifying the stories that my mother and grandmother had told me. Also, I was able to interview my godmother, Doña Manuelita, my mother's childhood friend, and, being well-read, she was able to help me tremendously, giving me an added perspective on how life had really been for them in the box canyon. And on my father's side, I was able to interview my Aunt Luisa, who was in her late eighties, but her voice was still strong and her mind lucid.

And I'm proud to say that I was able to finish the book before my father died. He was able to read it and see how I'd portrayed his loved ones, especially his mother. And on the last night of my father's life, I stayed with him, and his last words to me were, "I'm going to see *mi mama*, and I'm so proud of you, *mi hijito*, that you got her right in our book." He took my right hand in both of his, squeezing it, stroking it. "For she was a great woman," he said to me, "the greatest, just like your own mother!" And he hugged and kissed me goodbye.

I put him to bed, and he died in his sleep at the age of 86 or 84, depending on which relative I ask. All his life he'd been so strong and sure and confident and he died the same way. It wasn't that he had lost the will to live; no, he'd gained the will to die. For, I'd asked him, "Papa, aren't you afraid?"

"Of what?" he'd said in his deep, powerful voice. "Of death? Of course not. To fear death is to insult life!"

My God, I'd never heard that. Not from the Greeks or the Jews or the Chinese. No, I'd heard it from my own father, *un puro mejicano de las Américas*! And so after the funeral, we had a big celebration with *mariachis* and *barbacoa* à la Archie Freeman and we sang my father's favorite songs and we cried and danced long into the night. My father had won. He'd completed his life. He'd lived until he'd died, and went to rest in peace, like his mother, Doña Margarita, and his grandfather, Don Pio.

Con gusto,

Victor E. Villaseñor
Rancho Villaseñor
Oceanside, California
The Spring of 1990

P.S. Also, I'd like you to know that my father's sister Luisa died a good death five years earlier outside of Fresno, surrounded by her children and twenty-five grandchildren, most of whom have graduated from college.

Sophia is also gone, and she left a wonderful family, including one of the most highly-decorated soldiers of all of World War II.

And the way Maria, my mother's sister, died is a whole story in itself. She'd been bedridden for nearly three years, but four years ago when she heard that my father was giving a *fiesta* at the big house for my mother and all of the girls from La Lluvia, she bought herself a new pink dress, had her hair fixed and came in her wheelchair. She ate and drank and laughed all evening, looking so pink and beautiful, and then went home and died in her sleep that night—dreaming to awake on the other side of life, a miracle of God's. Amen.

ACKNOWLEDGMENTS

First, I wish to thank my grandmother Doña Guadalupe, who was the first one to speak to me about our past. Then, I wish to thank all of the people I knew in the barrio of Carlsbad, our neighbors, my cousins, aunts, uncles and Don Viviano with the one arm. I wish to thank my uncle Archie Freeman and all of our relatives on the Pala Reservations. I want my *niña* Manuelita to realize how much she truly helped me. And, of course, her brother Jose who showed me which trail to take when I climbed up into La Barranca del Cobre.

I'd like my Uncle Don Victoriano, a fine storyteller with an incredible memory for dates and names, to also realize what a great help he was to me. Without his memory I could never have unraveled the story about Aunt Carlota and my mother, Lupe.

Carlota, I'd like to thank her especially for her perspective of the past—for it was so different from so many other people's—that she caused me to have to check and double-check with other people more times than I want to remember. I wish to say thanks to my Aunt Sophia and her family, the Salazars up in northern California, and tell them all how much I appreciate their help. I want Jose Leon and all of his tribe in Fresno to know that I couldn't have done whole sections of this book without Jose's and Pedro's help. Thank you, Jose, you were great.

Also, I'd like to thank my sisters: Hortensia, who is like a second mother to me; Linda, who was like a little brother tomboy with me growing up; and Teresita, the baby of our family whom we all love to spoil. Thank you, *hermanas*, thank you. And I want to send up love to my brother Joseph, who died so young. And my special thanks to Linda, who typed for me off and on for over ten years, and many times without pay. I wish to thank Dorothy Denny and Myra Westphall, two wonderful women who've helped me with this book for well over ten years. And Gail Grant and Jeannie Obermayer, who've worked long hours into the night year after year. I'd like to say *gracias* to my two old friends Dennis Avery and Bill Cartwright, who have participated in my life and writing for well over twenty-five years. I'd like to take my hat off to Moctezuma Esparza, a good *cabrón,* who went with me to New York City and helped me buy this book back when I was so crazy with rage that I didn't know what I might do if I went alone. My thanks to Alex Haley and his office staff who helped and advised me after my run-in with New York. My thanks to Marc Jaffe, my former editor, who first commissioned

"Rain of Gold" and helped keep me sane while I roamed the streets of New York, learning to love the city's energy.

My many thanks to Helen Nelson and my local Oceanside library, and also the library in El Paso, Texas. Library people are a breed apart—always willing to help and so full of information.

Also, my heartfelt appreciation to my in-laws, Zita and Charles Bloch, and for all their years of keeping the fires of faith burning. They never gave up on Barbara and me, no matter how dark times became. They were always there, like my second parents, in the best sense of the word.

And talking about being there, I'd like to give my best to Gary Cosay, my agent, and Chuck Scott, my lawyer, who've been with me through thin and thinner for over seventeen years. Thanks, guys!

And I'd like to thank Juan Gomez, Alejandro Morales, Galal Kernahan, Jesus Chavarria, David Ochoa, Esperanza Esparza, Stan Margulies, Annette Welles, David Wallechinsky and Flora Chavez, Russell Avery, Hal Larsen, Leslie Hotchkiss, Clare Rorick and Greg Athens, Saram Khalsa, Cynthia Leeder, Bonnie Marsh and Chef Jeff, May and Craig, Barbi B., my nephew Javier Perez, and Victor Vidales, Margaret Bemis, Carl Mueller, Duncan Robertson, Harold, Tony, Robin, and Fernando Flores, my personal philosopher—all these people who've helped me and believed in me so very much.

I'd like to thank and salute Marina, Jorge, My Bao, Cecilia, Victor, all the people at Arte Publico Press—especially Nicolas Kanellos—for helping me to get this first volume of the big book into print after so many setbacks in the Big Mango, New York, New York—another Latino settlement!

I'd also like to thank John Hager, our first sales rep, who got us focused on the big picture. I'd like to thank Blanche Brann, Steve Geison, and especially Elaine Jesmer, for kicking ass and doing a genius job for publicity.

I'd like to give tribute to Nat Sobel, Ed Victor, Phyllis Grann, and Stacy Creamer, my old book publishing friends, who lived my book and believed in me, but then lost faith and forced me to go on without them—causing me to stretch and grow. Thank you; you are my special *amigos*.

I'd like to give tribute to my three brothers-in-law; Steve, who said to me when I first thought of buying my book back from New York, "For anyone else I'd say 'no.' But knowing you, I say 'do it,' because you don't know how to live any other way." Thanks, Steve, thanks. And Joaquin, who simply said, "I hate what Putnam did to our book! Buy it back!" And I'd like to thank Joe, who came late into our family, but learned to love my father as a son and listened to his stories again and again.

Also, I'd like to salute my newfound friends at Dell, Leslie Schnur, Trish Todd, and all the staff. Let's keep the faith, let's produce a rain of gold of books over the next twenty years! We've got the whole world in our hands— yes! And I salute my new agent Margret McBride, who plays with her long red hair like a cat as we plan strategy. Thanks, Margret, and Winifred, and Susan.

Mil gracias, all of you, we did it; we survived!

And last but not least, of course, I'd like to give very special tribute to my wife and best friend Barbara, who has given me unconditional love and support all through these years. And to our sons David and Joseph, two fine boys, who were lucky enough to be raised next door to their grandparents and learned how to plant corn and greet the morning sun with open arms. Thanks. *Con Dios*. It's a good life, no matter what!